ALGORITHM DEVELOPMENT and PROGRAM DESIGN USING C

Gary J. Bronson
Fairleigh Dickingson University

Contributing Editor: R. Kenneth Walter, Weber State University
WEST PUBLISHING COMPANY
Minneapolis/St. Paul   New York   Los Angeles   San Francisco

Text Design: Linda M. Robertson
Copyeditor: Lorreta Palagi
Artwork and Composition: Carlisle Communications
Cover Image: ©Norman McGrath. All Rights Reserved.

WEST'S COMMITMENT TO THE ENVIRONMENT

In 1906, West Publishing Company began recycling materials left over from the production of books. This began a tradition of efficient and responsible use of resources. Today, 100% of our legal bound volumes are printed on acid-free, recycled paper consisting of 50% new paper pulp and 50% paper that has undergone a de-inking process. We also use vegetable-based inks to print all of our books. West recycles nearly 27,700,000 pounds of scrap paper annually—the equivalent of 229,300 trees. Since the 1960s, West has devised ways to capture and recycle waste inks, solvents, oils, and vapors created in the printing process. We also recycle plastics of all kinds, wood, glass, corrugated cardboard, and batteries, and have eliminated the use of polystyrene book packaging. We at West are proud of the longevity and the scope of our commitment to the environment.

West pocket parts and advance sheets are printed on recyclable paper and can be collected and recycled with newspapers. Staples do not have to be removed. Bound volumes can be recycled after removing the cover.

Production, Prepress, Printing and Binding by West Publishing Company.

 TEXT IS PRINTED ON 10% POST CONSUME RECYCLED PAPER

British Library Cataloguing-in-Publication Data. A catalogue record for this book is available from the British Library.

Library of Congress Cataloging-in-Publication Data

Bronson, Gary J.
     Algorithm Development and Program Design Using C/Gary J. Bronson—1st ed.
        p. cm.
     Includes index
     ISBN 0-314-06987-9 (soft: alk. paper)
     1. C (Computer program language) 2. Computer algorithms.
  I. Title.
  QA76.73.C15J64   1996
  005.13'3--dc20

                              95-46503
                              CIP

Preface

This text is designed for a CS1 course, with an introduction to CS2, and follows the guidelines of the Association for Computing Machinery (ACM-IEEE-CS) Joint Curriculum Task Force for this first course. As such, the major objective of this book is to introduce, develop, and reinforce well-organized, structured problem solving skills, and to present the C language as a powerful problem solving tool. The topics recommended by the ACM for a CS1 course form the central content of the text. The basic requirement in presenting this material is that it always be presented in a clear, unambiguous, and accessible manner to beginning students.

C was selected as the support language of choice in recognition of its preeminent position as the systems and applications language of the 1990s. It is both easy to learn as a first structured language, is the language that students are expected to be thoroughly familiar with when they graduate, and has special attributes, such as pointer arithmetic, that provide a firm foundation for more advanced data structures work.

In using this text students should be familiar with fundamental algebra, but no other prerequisites are assumed. A short Chapter 1 briefly presents computer literacy material for those who need that background. Large numbers of examples and exercises are drawn from everyday experience, business, and technical fields. As such, the instructor may choose applications that match students' experience or for a particular course emphasis.

DISTINCTIVE FEATURES OF THIS BOOK

Writing Style.   I firmly believe that introductory texts do not teach students - professors teach students. An introductory textbook, if it is to be useful, must be the primary "supporting actor" to the "leading role" of the professor. Once the professor sets the stage, however, the textbook must encourage, nurture, and assist the student in acquiring and "owning" the material presented in class. To do this the text must be written in a manner that makes sense to the student. My primary concern, and one of the distinctive features of this book is that it has been written for the student. Thus, first and foremost, I feel the writing style used to convey the concepts is the most important aspect of the text.

Modularity.   To produce readable and maintainable code, modularity is essential. C, by its nature, is a modular language. Thus, the connection between C functions and modules is made early in the text, in Section 2.1, and sustained throughout the book. The idea of argument passing into modules is also made early, again in Section 2.1, with the use of the printf() function. In this manner students are introduced to functions and argument passing as a natural technique of programming.

Software Engineering.   Students are introduced to the fundamentals of software engineering right from the start. This introduction begins in Section 1.3 with the introduction of the software development cycle. This is immediately followed by an introduction to algorithms and the various ways that algorithms can be described. The main theme of the text, which is a more formal emphasis on problem solving techniques, is presented in Chapter 2. Here the importance of understanding a problem and selecting and refining an appropriate algorithm is highlighted and the relationship between analysis, design, coding, and testing is introduced. This emphasis on software engineering is supported and maintained as a unifying theme throughout the text.

Focus on Problems Solving.   Starting with Chapter 2, each chapter contains a Focus on Problem Solving section, with at least 2 complete problems. Each application is used to demonstrate effective problem solving, within the context of a complete program solution, using the formal problem solving steps described in Section 2.5. A broad mix of applications has been selected to both heighten the student's interest and reinforce software engineering concepts.

Introduction to Pointers.   One of stumbling blocs to more advanced work is the facility with which students understand and can manipulate pointers. Fortunately, C is an ideal language for introducing pointers because it permits display of the actual memory addresses contained in pointer variables and provides for pointer arithmetic. One of the unique features of this text is the early introduction of pointer concepts. This is done by using the printf() function to display actual memory addresses stored in pointer variables. This approach, which was introduced in *A First Book of C*, is much more logical and intuitive than starting with an indirection description.

Since *A First Book of C* was published, I have been pleased to see that the use of the printf() function to display addresses has become almost the standard way of introducing C pointers. Although this approach, therefore, is no longer a unique feature, I am very proud of its presentation, and have adopted it for this text.

Program Testing.   Every single C program in this text has been successfully compiled and run under Borland's C++ (Version 2.0) Compiler. All programs have been written following the ANSI C standard (Standard X3.159-1989). A source diskette of all programs is provided with the text.

PEDAGOGICAL FEATURES

The text makes use of the following pedagogical features:

Emphasis on Formal Problem-Solving Techniques.   The fundamental software development steps of problem definition, analysis, solution development and refinement, coding, and testing and debugging form the organization around which each complete application is presented. If students are to develop good problem solving habits, they must begin to use these techniques, even with the simplest exercises, and practice them repeatedly.

End of Section Exercises.   Almost every section in the book contains numerous and diverse skill builder and programming exercises. Additionally, solutions to selected exercises are provided in an appendix.

Pseudocode, Structure Charts, and Flowchart Descriptions.   Although pseudocode and structure charts are stressed throughout the text, material on flowchart symbols and the use of flowcharts in visually presenting flow-of-control constructs is also presented.

Common Programming Errors and Chapter Review.   Each Chapter ends with a section on common programming errors and a review of the main topics covered in the chapter.

Closer Looks.   A set of shaded boxes that highlight important abstraction concepts.

Tips From The Pros.   A set of shaded boxes that highlight useful technical points and tricks used by more professional programmers.

Bit of Background Notes.   To make the study of computer science even more rewarding and to provide breadth material, these notes are carefully placed throughout the book. These notes supplement the technical material with historical, biographical, and other interesting factual asides.

Enrichment Sections.   Given the many different emphases that can be applied in teaching C, I have included a number of Enrichment Sections. These allow you to provide different emphases with different students or different C class sections.

APPENDICES AND SUPPLEMENTS

An extensive set of appendicies is provided. These include appendices on operator precedence, ASCII codes, program entry, compilation and execution, I/0 redirection, floating point storage concepts, and a C reference guide are provided. Additionally a Function and Macro reference are provided on the inside front and back covers. Solutions to selected odd-numbered exercises are also provided.

A more extensive solutions manual is available to adopters on request. Additionally, an IBM-PC compatible source code diskette for all example programs is packaged with the text.

Acknowledgements

This book began as an idea. It became a reality only due to the encouragement, skills, and efforts supplied by many people. I would like to acknowledge their contribution.

First, I would like to thank Jerry Westby, my editor at West Publishing Company. In addition to his continuous faith, encouragement, attention to detail and relentless challenges, he has turned out to be what all authors hope for: a true partner. Additionally, I would like to thank Dean DeChambeau for his handling of numerous review details that permitted me to concentrate on the actual writing of the text. I would also like to express my gratitude to the individual reviewers listed on the next page. Each of these individuals supplied extremely detailed and constructive reviews of both the original manuscript and a number of revisions. Their suggestions, attention to detail, and comments were extraordinarily helpful to me as the manuscript evolved and matured through the editorial process.

Once the review process was completed, the task of turning the final manuscript into a textbook depended on many people other than myself. For this I especially want to thank the production editor, Stephanie Syata, the copy editor, Lorretta Palagi, and the compositor, Carlisle Communications, Ltd. The dedication of these people was incredible and very important to me. Almost from the moment the book moved to the production stage these individuals seemed to take personal ownership of the text and I am very grateful to them. I am also very appreciative of the suggestions and work of the promotion manager at West, Ellen Stanton.

Special acknowledgement goes to two of my colleagues who provided material for this text. In addition to numerous contributions made to this text by R. Kenneth Walter of Weber State University, I am especially grateful for his graciously providing The Bit of Background notes as well as numerous end-of-chapter exercises. I also wish to acknowledge John Lyon of The University of Arizona who originally provided the analogy used in the introduction to Chapter 6, the material on stub functions, as well as the Age-Norms application and exercises in Section 7.5 for my FORTRAN text with Scott/Jones Publishers. This material is used in this text by permission of the publisher. As always, any errors in the text rests solely on my shoulders.

Finally, the direct encouragement and support of Fairleigh Dickinson University is also gratefully acknowledged. Specifically, this includes the direct encouragement and support provided by Dr. Geoffrey Weinman, the Vice President of Academic Affairs, my dean, Dr. Paul Lerman, and my chairman, Ron Heim. Without their support this text could not have been written.

Finally, I deeply appreciate the patience, understanding, and love provided by my friend, wife, and partner, Rochelle.

Gary Bronson

Stephen J. Allan
Utah State University

Robert Anderson
University of Houston

Ben A. Blake
Cleveland State University

Natasa Bozovic
San Jose State University

Jacobo Carrasquel
Carnegie Mellon University

John Carroll
San Diego State University

William L. Clark
University of Alaska Anchorage

Michael L. Collard
Kent State University

John S. DaPonte
Southern Connecticut State University

Herbert E. Dunsmore
Purdue University

Peggy S. Eaton
Plymouth State University

Rhonda Ficek
Moorhead State University

Jesse M. Heines
University of Massachusetts Lowell

Mike Holland
Northern Virginia Community College

Erh-Wen Hu
William Paterson College

Joseph Hurley
Texas A & M University

Peter Isaacson
University of North Colorado

Stephen P. Leach
Florida State University

Lester I. McCann
University of Central Oklahoma

Robert E. Norton
San Diego Mesa Community College

Margaret Anne Pierce
Georgia Southern University

Joan Ramuta
College of Saint Francis

Larry Ruzzo
University of Washington

Ali R. Salehnia
South Dakota State University

Robert Signorile
Boston College

Winnie Y. Yu
Southern Connecticut State University

Contents

1

Introduction to Computers and Programming

1.1 HARDWARE AND SOFTWARE

The process of using a machine to add and subtract is almost as old as recorded history. The earliest "machine" was the abacus (Figure 1.1) — a device as common in China as hand-held calculators are in the United States. Both of these machines, however, require direct human involvement as they are being used. To add two numbers with an abacus requires the movement of beads on the device, while adding two numbers with a calculator requires that the operator push both the number and the addition operator keys.

It is worth distinguishing between these two distinct types of input: the operations to be performed, such as addition and subtraction, and the actual data that is being operated on, because the distinction forms the basis for programming a computer. As we will see shortly, the operations to be performed constitute the basis for a computer program, while the data becomes the input on which the program works.

The idea of constructing a computing machine that separates these two types of input (operations and data) and permits the loading and prestoring of operations separately from the data originated in the early 1800s, or likely even earlier. Figure 1.2 illustrates the conceptual design of such a machine. As illustrated by this hypothetical machine, space is allocated for a set of instructions that can be loaded into the machine separately from the data. The instructions might be as simple as:

Instruction 1: Accept a number from the input device and store it.

Instruction 2: Add the next number entered to the stored number.

1

FIGURE 1.1   An Abacus

Instruction 3: Multiply the result of instruction 2 by the next number entered.

Instruction 4: Subtract the result of instruction 3 by the next number entered.

Instruction 5: Display the result of instruction 4.

The added feature of the hypothetical machine illustrated in Figure 1.2 over a simple calculator is that it permits a set of instructions to be preloaded into the machine before any data is entered. Once the instructions have been loaded, the machine will operate when it is given any four numbers. For example, if the numbers 2, 3, 6, and 8 are entered, the machine would display the number 22.

The first recorded attempt at creating such a machine was made by Charles Babbage, in England, in 1822. The set of instructions to be input to this machine, which Babbage called an analytical engine (Figure 1.3), was developed by Ada Byron, the daughter of the poet Lord Byron. Although Babbage's machine was not successfully built in his lifetime, the concept developed by him was partly realized in 1937 at Iowa State University by Dr. John V. Atanasoff and a graduate student named Clifford Berry. The machine was known as the ABC, which stood for Atanasoff-Berry Computer. This computer manipulated binary numbers, but required external wiring of the machine to perform the desired operations. Thus, the goal of internally storing a replaceable set of instructions had still not been achieved.

Due to the impetus provided by the impending outbreak of World War II, more concentrated work on the development of the computer began in late 1939. One of the pioneers of this work was Dr. John W. Mauchly, of the Moore School of Engineering at the University of Pennsylvania. Dr. Mauchly, who had visited Dr. Atanasoff, began working with J. Presper Eckert in 1939 on a computer called ENIAC (for Electrical Numerical Integrator and Computer, Figure 1.4). Funding for this project was provided by the U.S. government, and one of the early functions performed by this machine was the calculation of trajectories for ammunition fired from large guns. When completed in 1946 ENIAC contained 18,000 vacuum tubes, weighed approximately 30 tons, and could perform 5000 additions or 360 multiplications in one second.

A BIT OF BACKGROUND

The "Turing Machine"

In the 1930s and 1940s, Alan Mathison Turing (1912–1954) and others developed the theory of what a computing machine should be able to do. Turing invented a theoretical, pencil-and-paper machine, which is referred to as the Turing machine, that contains the minimum set of operations for solving programming problems. Turing had hoped to prove that all problems could be solved by a set of instructions to such a hypothetical computer.

What he succeeded in proving was that some problems cannot be solved by any machine, just as some problems cannot be solved by any person.

Alan Turing's work formed the foundation of computer theory before the first electronic computer was built. His contributions to the team that developed the critical code-breaking computers during World War II led directly to the practical implementation of his theories.

FIGURE 1.2   Conceptual Design of a Self-Operating Calculating Machine

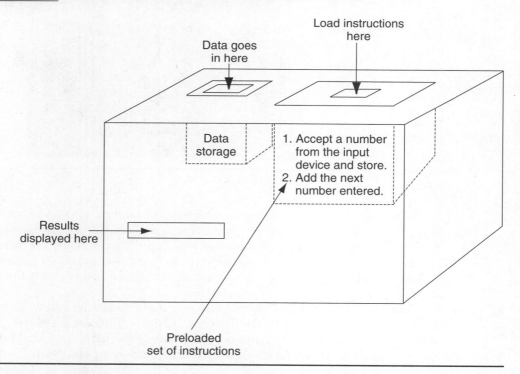

FIGURE 1.3   Charles Babbage's Analytical Engine (Crown Copyright)

While work was progressing on ENIAC with vacuum tubes, work on a computer named the Mark I (Figure 1.5) was being done at Harvard University using mechanical relay switches. The Mark I was completed in 1944, but could only perform six multiplications in one second. Both of these machines, however, like the Atanasoff-Berry computer, required external wiring to perform the desired operations.

The final goal of a stored program computer was achieved at Cambridge University in England, with the design of EDSAC (Electronic Delayed Storage Automatic Computer). In addition to performing calculations, EDSAC permitted storage of instructions that directed the computer's operation. The means of using the computer's memory to store both instructions and data, and the design to accomplish this so that the computer first retrieved an instruction and then the data needed by the instruction, was developed by John Von Neumann. This same design and operating principle is still used by the majority of computers manufactured today. The only things that have significantly changed are

FIGURE 1.4   ENIAC (Courtesy IBM Archives)

the size and speeds of the components used to make a computer and the types of programs that are stored internal to it. Collectively, the components used to make a computer are referred to as *hardware*, while the programs are known as *software*.

Computer Hardware

All computers, from large supercomputers costing millions of dollars to smaller desktop personal computers must perform a minimum set of functions and provide the capability to:

1. Accept input
2. Display output
3. Store information in a logically consistent format (traditionally binary)
4. Perform arithmetic and logic operations on either the input or stored data
5. Monitor, control, and direct the overall operation and sequencing of the system.

FIGURE 1.5 The Mark I (Courtesy IBM Archives)

Figure 1.6 illustrates the computer components that support these capabilities. These physical components are collectively referred to as *hardware*.

Memory Unit   This unit stores information in a logically consistent format. Typically, both instructions and data are stored in memory, usually in separate and distinct areas.

Each computer contains memory of two fundamental types: RAM and ROM. *RAM*, which is an acronym for random-access memory, is usually volatile, which means that whatever is stored there is lost when the computer's power is turned off. Your programs and data are stored in RAM while you are using the computer. The size of a computer's RAM memory is usually specified in terms of how many bytes of RAM are available to the user. Personal computer (PC) memories currently consist of from 1 to 32 million bytes (denoted as megabytes or MB).

ROM, which is an acronym for read-only memory, contains fundamental instructions that cannot be lost or changed by the casual computer user. These instructions include those necessary for loading anything else into the machine when it is first turned on and any other instructions the manufacturer requires to be permanently accessible when the computer is turned on. ROM is nonvolatile; its contents are not lost when the power goes off.

FIGURE 1.6   Basic Hardware Units of a Computer

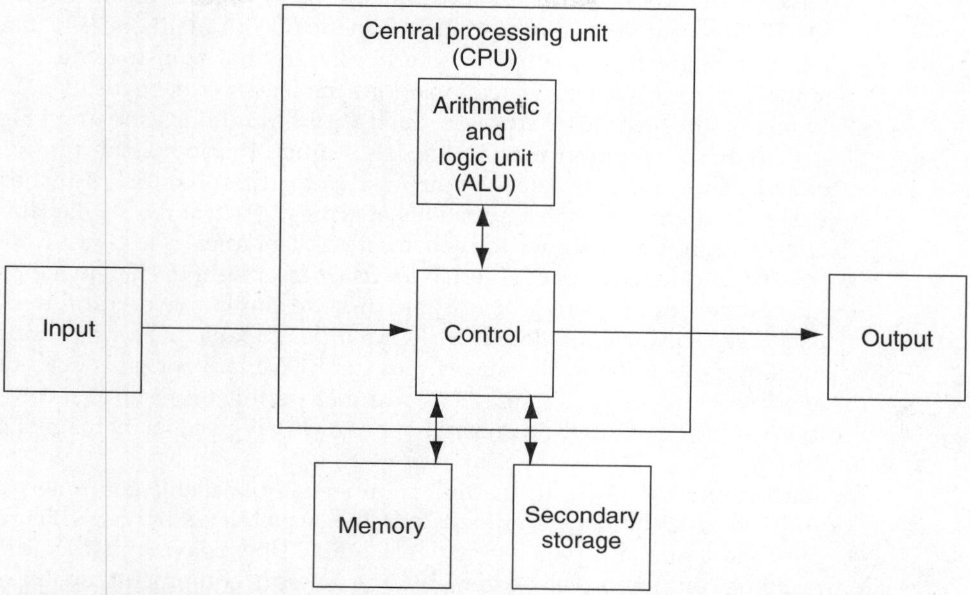

Control Unit   The control unit directs and monitors the overall operation of the computer. It keeps track of where in memory the next instruction resides, issues the signals needed to both read data from and write data to other units in the system, and executes all instructions.

Arithmetic and Logic Unit (ALU)   The ALU performs all the arithmetic and logic functions, such as addition, subtraction, comparison, etc., provided by the system.

Input/Output (I/O) Unit   This unit provides access to and from the computer. It is the interface to which peripheral devices such as keyboards, cathode-ray screens, and printers are attached.

Secondary Storage   Because RAM memory in large quantities is still relatively expensive and volatile, it is not practical as a permanent storage area for programs and data. Secondary or auxiliary storage devices are used for this purpose. Although data have been stored on punched cards, paper tape, and other media in the past, virtually all secondary storage is now stored on magnetic tape, magnetic disks, and optical storage media.

The surfaces of magnetic tapes and disks are coated with a material that can be magnetized by a write head, and the stored magnetic field can be detected by a read head. Current tapes are capable of storing thousands of characters per inch of tape, and a single tape may store up to hundreds of megabytes. Tapes, by nature, are sequential storage media, which means that they allow data to be written or read in one sequential stream from beginning to end. Should you desire access to a block of data in the middle of the tape, you must scan all preceding data on the tape to find the block of interest. Because of this, tapes are primarily used for mass backup of the data stored on large-capacity disk drives.

A more convenient method of rapidly accessing stored data is provided by a direct access storage device (DASD), where any one file or program can be written or read independent of its position on the storage medium. The most popular DASD in recent years has been the magnetic disk. A magnetic *hard disk* consists of either a single rigid platter or several platters that spin together on a common spindle. A movable access arm positions the read/write heads over, but not quite touching, the recordable surfaces. Such a configuration is shown in Figure 1.7.

Another common magnetic disk storage device is the removable *floppy diskette*. Currently, the most popular sizes for these are 5 1/4 inches and 3 1/4 inches in diameter, with respective capacities of 1.2 and 1.44 megabytes, respectively. Figure 1.8 illustrates the construction of a typical 5 1/4-inch floppy diskette.

In optical media, data is stored by using laser light to change the reflective surface properties of a single removable diskette similar or identical to a video compact disk. The disk is called a CD-ROM and is capable of storing several thousand megabytes.[1] Although the majority of CD-ROMS are currently read-only devices, erasable methods are coming into use that permit the user to record, erase, and reuse optical disks in the same manner as a very high capacity magnetic disk.

Hardware Evolution   In the first commercially available computers of the 1940s and 1950s, all hardware units except the secondary storage, which consisted of punched cards and paper tape, were built using relays and vacuum tubes. The resulting computers were extremely large pieces of equipment, capable of thousands of calculations per second, and costing millions of dollars (Figure 1.9). With the commercial introduction of transistors in the 1960s both the size and cost of computer hardware was reduced. The transistor was approximately one-twentieth the size of its vacuum tube counterpart, which allowed manufacturers to combine the arithmetic and logic unit with the control unit into a single new unit. This combined unit was called the *central processing unit* (CPU). The combination of the ALU and control units into one CPU made sense because a majority of control signals generated by a

---

FIGURE 1.7   **Internal Structure of a Hard Disk Drive**

Disk Pack, Showing Tracks, Sectors, and Cylinders

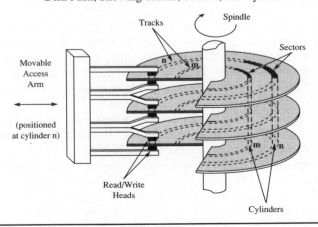

---

[1]A thousand megabytes is referred to as a gigabyte.

FIGURE 1.8   Construction of a 5¼-inch Floppy Diskette

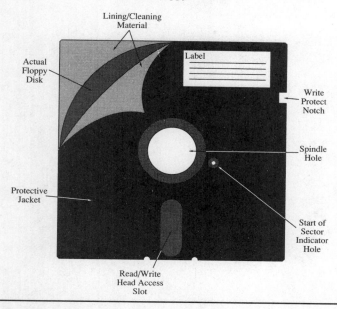

5¼ inch Floppy Diskette

program are directed to the ALU in response to arithmetic and logic instructions within the program. Combining the ALU with the control unit simplified the interface between these two units and provided improved processing speed.

The mid-1960s saw the introduction of integrated circuits (ICs), which resulted in still another significant reduction in the space required to produce a CPU. Initially, integrated circuits were manufactured with up to 100 transistors on a single 1-cm^2 chip of silicon. Such devices are referred to as small-scale integrated (SSI) circuits. From the 1960s to the mid-1970s, medium scale integrated (MSI) chips predominated, with each chip containing from 10 to 1000 transistors. Large scale integrated (LSI) circuits, one of which is shown in Figure 1.10, contained more than 1000 transistors and were introduced in the mid-1970s. The actual integrated circuit chip illustrated in Figure 1.10 is in the center of the figure and is electrically connected to the larger pins shown on the side of the package by gold wires, which are also visible in the figure. The package itself is referred to as a dual in-line package (DIP). In actual use the chip at the center of the DIP would be covered and hermetically sealed.

Current versions of integrated circuit chips contain hundreds of thousands to over a million transistors and are referred to as *very large scale integrated (VLSI)* chips. VLSI chip technology has provided the means of transforming the giant computers of the 1950s into today's desktop personal computers. Each individual unit required to form a computer (CPU, memory, and I/O) is now manufactured on individual VLSI chips, respectively, and the single-chip CPU is referred to as a *microprocessor*. Figure 1.11 illustrates the actual size and internal structure of a state-of-the art VLSI microprocessor chip. The chip itself is in the center of the square on the right and the cover for the package is on the left. Internally the chip is connected with wires to the pins on the outside of the package. The underside of these pins appear as a series of silver dots in the square on the right side of the figure.

FIGURE 1.9   An IBM 701 in 1952 (Countesy IBM Archives)

Figure 1.12 illustrates how the complete set of chips needed for a computer is put on boards and connected internally to create a computer, such as the early Compaq and IBM-PCs of the 1980s (Figure 1.13). Figure 1.14 illustrates a more current notebook computer (Figure 1.14).

Concurrent with the remarkable reduction in computer hardware size has been an equally dramatic decrease in cost and increase in processing speeds. The equivalent computer hardware that cost more than a million dollars in 1950 can now be purchased for less than 500 dollars. If the same reductions occurred in the automobile industry, for example, a Rolls-Royce could now be purchased for 10 dollars! The processing speeds of current computers have also increased by a factor of a thousand over their 1950s predecessors, with the computational speeds of current machines being measured in both millions of instructions per second (MIPS) and billions of instructions per second (BIPS).

Computer Software

As we have seen, a computer is a machine made of physical components. In this regard it is the same as any other machine, such as an automobile or lawn mower. Like these other machines, it must be turned on and then driven, or controlled,

FIGURE 1.10 An Integrated Circuit within a DIP (Courtesy Data General Corporation)

FIGURE 1.11 Internal Picture of a Pentium Microprocesser Chip

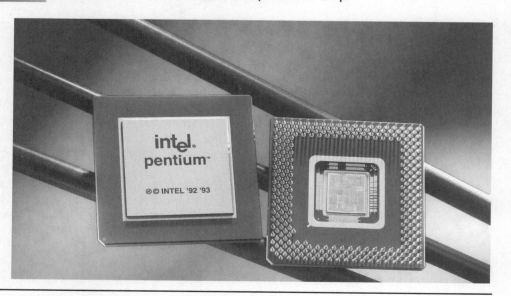

FIGURE 1.12   Internal and External Components of a Desktop Personal Computer
(Courtesy Compaq Corporation)

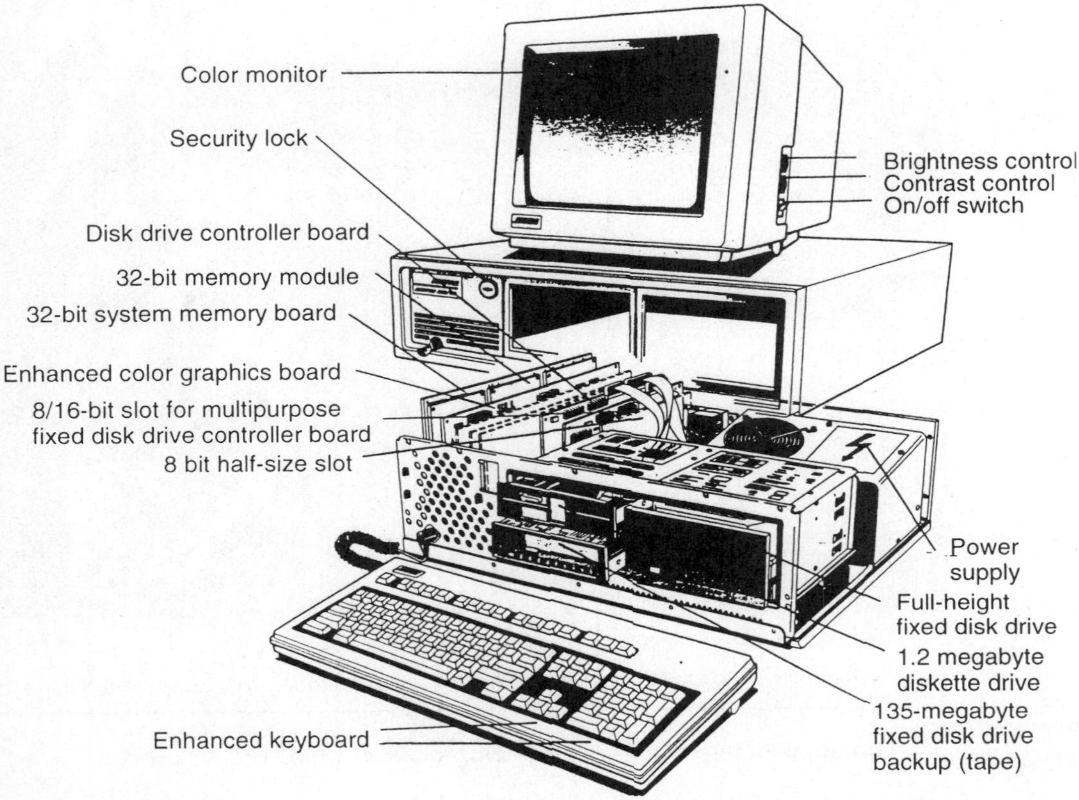

Color monitor

Security lock

Disk drive controller board

32-bit memory module

32-bit system memory board

Enhanced color graphics board

8/16-bit slot for multipurpose
fixed disk drive controller board

8 bit half-size slot

Enhanced keyboard

Brightness control
Contrast control
On/off switch

Power
supply

Full-height
fixed disk drive

1.2 megabyte
diskette drive

135-megabyte
fixed disk drive
backup (tape)

---

before it can do the task it was meant to do. How this gets done is what distinguishes a computer from other types of machinery.

In an automobile, for example, control is provided by the driver, who sits inside of and directs the car. In a computer, the driver is a set of instructions, called a program. More formally, a *computer program* is a self-contained set of instructions used to operate a computer to produce a specific result. Another term for a program or set of programs is *software*, and we will use both terms interchangeably throughout the text.[2]

The process of writing a program, or software, is called *programming*, while the set of instructions that can be used to construct a program is called a *programming language*. Available programming languages come in a variety of forms and types.

Machine Language   At its most fundamental level the only programs that can actually be used to operate a computer are *machine language* programs.

---

[2]The term *software* is sometimes also used to denote both the programs and the data on which the programs will operate.

A BIT OF BACKGROUND

Ada Augusta Byron, Countess of Lovelace

Ada Byron, the daughter of Lord Byron, was a colleague of Charles Babbage in his attempt throughout the mid 1800s to build an analytical engine. It was Ada's task to develop the algorithms - solutions to problems in the form of step-by-step instructions - that would allow the engine to compute the values of mathematical functions. Babbage's machine was not successfully built in his lifetime, primarily because the technology of the time did not allow mechanical parts to be constructed with necessary tolerances. Nonetheless, Ada is recognized as the first computer programmer. She published a collection of notes that established the basis for computer programming; and the modern Ada programming language is named in her honor.

Such programs, which are also referred to as executable programs, or executables for short, consist of a sequence of instructions composed of binary numbers such as[3]:

```
11000000   000000000001   000000000010

11110000   000000000010   000000000011
```

FIGURE 1.13   An Original (1980s) IBM Personal Computer (Courtesy IBM Corporation)

---

[3]Review Section 1.7 at the end of this chapter if you are unfamiliar with binary numbers.

FIGURE 1.14 A Current Texas Instrument Travelmate Notebook Computer atop its Docking Station (Courtesy Texas Instrument)

Such machine language instructions consist of two parts: an instruction part and an address part. The instruction part, which is referred to as the opcode (short for operation code), is usually the leftmost set of bits in the instruction and tells the computer the operation to be performed, such as add, subtract, multiply, etc., while the rightmost bits specify the memory addresses of the data to be used. For example, assuming that the eight leftmost bits of the first instruction listed above is the operation code to add, and the next two groups of twelve bits are the addresses of the two operands to be added, this instruction would be a command to "add the data in memory location 1 to the data in memory location 2."[4] Similarly, assuming that the opcode 11110000 means multiply, the next instruction is a command to "multiply the data in memory location 2 by the data in location 3."

---

[4]To obtain the address values as decimal numbers, convert the binary values to decimal using the method presented in Section 1.7.

Assembly Languages   Although each class of computer, such as IBM PCs, Apple Macintoshes, and DEC VAX computers, has its own particular machine language, it is very tedious and time consuming to write such machine language programs. One of the first advances in programming was the substitution of word-like symbols, such as ADD, SUB, MUL, for the binary opcodes and both decimal numbers and labels for memory addresses. For example, using these symbols and decimal values for memory addresses, the previous two machine language instructions can be written:

```
ADD 1, 2

MUL 2, 3
```

Programming languages that use this type of symbolic notation are referred to as *assembly languages*. Since computers can only execute machine language programs, the set of instructions contained within an assembly language program must be translated into a machine language program before it can be executed on a computer (Figure 1.15). Translator programs that perform this function for assembly language programs are known as *assemblers*.

Low- and High-Level Languages   Both machine level and assembly languages are classified as *low-level languages*. This is because both of these language types use instructions that are directly tied to one type of computer. As such, an assembly language program is limited in that it can only be used with the specific computer type for which the program is written. Such programs do, however, permit the use of special features of a particular computer and generally execute at the fastest level possible.

In contrast to low-level languages are languages that are classified as high-level. A *high-level language* uses instructions that resemble written languages, such as English, and can be run on a variety of computer types. FORTRAN, BASIC, Pascal, and C are all examples of high-level languages.[5] Using C, an instruction to add two numbers together and multiply by a third number can be written:

```
result = (first + second) * third;
```

Programs written in a computer language (high or low level) are referred to interchangeably as both source programs and *source code*. Once a program is written in a high-level language it must also, like a low-level assembly program, be

---

FIGURE 1.15   Assembly Programs Must Be Translated

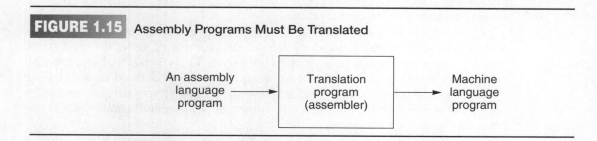

An assembly language program → Translation program (assembler) → Machine language program

---

[5]C is sometimes classified as a middle-level language to convey the fact that although C is written as a high-level language, it can also take advantage of machine features that historically could only be accessed with assembly or machine languages.

translated into the machine language of the computer on which it will run. This translation can be accomplished in two ways.

When each statement in a high-level source program is translated individually and executed immediately upon translation, the programming language used is called an interpreted language, and the program doing the translation is called an *interpreter*.

When all of the statements in a high-level source program are translated as a complete unit before any one statement is executed, the programming language used is called a compiled language. In this case, the program doing the translation is called a *compiler*. Both compiled and interpreted versions of a language can exist, although typically one predominates. For example, although compiled versions of BASIC do exist, BASIC is predominantly an interpreted language. Similarly, although interpreted versions of C exist, C is predominantly a compiled language.

Procedure and Object Orientations   In addition to classifying programming languages as high or low level, they are also classified by orientation as either procedure or object oriented. In a *procedure-oriented language* the available instructions are used to create self-contained units, referred to as procedures. The purpose of a procedure is to accept data as input and transform the data in some manner to produce a specific result as an output. For the last 25 years most high-level programming languages have all been procedure oriented. From an orientation standpoint, C is a procedure-oriented programming language.

Within the past few years a second orientation, referred to as object oriented, has evolved. One of the motivations for *object-oriented languages* was the development of graphical screens capable of displaying multiple windows. In such an environment each window on the screen can conveniently be considered an object, with associated characteristics, such as color, position, and size. Using an object approach, a program must first define the characteristics of the objects it will be manipulating and then be constructed of units that pass information to each object to produce the desired results.

Application and System Software   Two logical categories of computer programs are application software and system software. *Application software* consists of those programs written to perform particular tasks required by the users. Most of the examples in this book would be called application software. *System software* is the collection of programs that must be readily available to any computer system in order for it to operate at all.

In the early computer environments of the 1950s and 1960s, the user had to load a few system instructions by hand—using rows of switches on a front panel—to prepare the computer to do anything at all. Those initial, hand-entered commands were said to *boot* the computer, an expression derived from "pulling oneself up by the bootstraps." Today the so-called bootstrap loader is internally contained in ROM and is a permanent, automatically executed component of the computer's system software.

Additionally, before the 1960s, it was not uncommon for the user to have to load a separate set of programs necessary for reading from and writing to the input and output devices that were being used. Similarly, it was the user's responsibility to find the code that would translate an application program to the computer's internal machine language so that it could be executed. Typically,

TABLE 1.1 Common Operating System Commands

Task	DOS Command	UNIX Command
Display the directory of all files available	DIR	dir
Delete a specified file or group of files	ERASE or DELETE filename(s)	rm filename(s)
List the contents of a program to the monitor	TYPE filename	cat filename
Print the contents of a program to the printer	PRINT filename	lp or lptr filename
Copy a file	COPY source destination	cp source destination
Rename a file	RENAME oldname newname	mv oldname newname
Force a permanent halt to a running program	CTRL Break or CTRL Z or CTRL C	Del key, CTRL Break, or \
Force a temporary suspension of the current operation	CTRL S or Pause	CTRL S
Resume the current operation (recover from a CTRL S)	CTRL S	CTRL S

most of these *utilities* are now kept on either a hard disk or floppy diskette and are booted into the computer either automatically when the system is powered up or on command by the user.

Various terms are used by different manufacturers for the collection of system programs called the operating system. Often, the system software name ends with OS or DOS (for Disk Operating System). Additional tasks handled by modern operating systems include memory, input and output, and secondary storage management. Many systems handle very large programs, as well as multiple users concurrently, by dividing programs into segments or pages that are moved between the disk and memory as needed. Such operating systems create a virtual memory, which appears to be as large as necessary to handle any job; and a multiuser environment is produced that gives each user the impression that the computer and peripherals are his or hers alone. Additionally, many operating systems, including windowed environments, permit each user to run multiple programs. Such operating systems are referred to as multitasking systems.

Most system operations are transparent to the user; that is, they take place internally without user intervention. However, some operating system commands are provided intentionally for you to interact directly with the system. The most common of these commands are those that allow the handling of data files on disk. Some of these are listed in Table 1.1 by the names with which they are implemented in both MS-DOS and UNIX operating systems.

Exercises 1.1

1. Define the following terms:

    a. computer program

    b. programming

    c. programming language

    d. high-level language

    e. low-level language

    f. machine language

    g. assembly language

    h. procedure-oriented language

    i. object-oriented language

    j. source program

    k. compiler

    l. interpreter

2. Describe the accomplishments of the following people:

    a. Charles Babbage

    b. Ada Byron

    c. John Atanasoff

    d. Clifford Berry

    e. John W. Mauchly

    f. J. Presper Eckert

    g. John Von Neumann

3. Describe where the following machines were designed and the advancement in computer technology provided by them:

    a. analytic engine

    b. ABC

    c. ENIAC

    d. Mark I

    e. EDSAC

4. Describe the hardware units of a computer and the purpose of each unit.

5. a. Describe the difference between high- and low-level languages.

    b. Describe the difference between procedure and object-oriented languages.

6. Describe the similarities and differences between assemblers, interpreters, and compilers.

7. a. Assume the following operation codes:

    11000000 means add the 1st operand to the 2nd operand

    10100000 means subtract the 1st operand from the 2nd operand

    11110000 means multiply the 2nd operand by the 1st operand

    11010000 means divide the 2nd operand by the 1st operand

Translate the following instructions into English:

Opcode	Address of 1st Operand	Address of 2nd Operand
11000000	000000000001	0000000000010
11110000	000000000010	0000000000011
10100000	000000000100	0000000000011
11010000	000000000101	0000000000011

    b. Assuming the following locations contain the following data, determine the result produced by the instructions listed in Exercise 7a.

Address	Initial Value (in decimal) Stored at This Address
00000000001	5
00000000010	3
00000000011	6
00000000100	16
00000000101	4

8. Rewrite the machine-level instructions listed in Exercise 7a using assembly language notation. Use the symbolic names ADD, SUB, MUL, and DIV for addition, subtraction, multiplication, and division operations, respectively. In writing the instructions use decimal values for the addresses.

1.2 PROGRAMMING LANGUAGES

On a fundamental level, all procedure-oriented computer programs do the same thing (Figure 1.16); they direct a computer to accept data (input), to manipulate the data (process), and to produce reports (output). This implies that all procedure-oriented computer programming languages must provide essentially the same capabilities for performing these operations. These capabilities are provided either as specific instruction types, or "prepackaged" groups of instructions that can be called to do specific tasks. In C, the "prepackaged" groups of instructions are called library functions. Table 1.2 lists the fundamental set of instructions and library functions provided by FORTRAN, BASIC, COBOL, Pascal, and C for performing input, processing, and output tasks.

If all programming languages provide essentially the same features, why are there so many of them? The answer is that there are vast differences in the types of input data, calculations needed, and output reports required by various applications. For example, scientific and engineering applications require high-precision numerical outputs, accurate to many decimal places. In addition, these applications typically use many algebraic or trigonometric formulas to produce their results. For example, calculating the bacterial concentration level in a polluted pond, as illustrated in Figure 1.17, requires the evaluation of an exponential equation to a high degree of numerical accuracy. For such applications, the FORTRAN programming language, with its algebra-like instructions, was initially developed. FORTRAN, whose name is an acronym derived from FORmula TRANslation, was introduced in 1957. It was the first commercially available high-level language and is the oldest high-level language still in use.

FIGURE 1.16 All Programs Perform the Same Operations

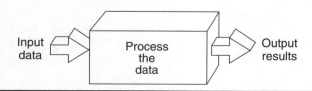

TABLE 1.2 Fundamental Programming Language Instruction Summary

Operation	FORTRAN	BASIC	COBOL	Pascal	C
Input (get the data)	READ	INPUT READ/DATA	READ ACCEPT	READ READLN	getchar() gets() scanf() sscanf() fscanf()
Processing (use the data)	= IF/ELSE DO	LET IF/ELSE FOR WHILE UNTIL	COMPUTE IF/ELSE PERFORM	:= IF/ELSE FOR WHILE REPEAT	= if/else for while do
	+ − * / **	+ − * / ^	ADD SUBTRACT MULTIPLY DIVIDE	+ − * / **	+, =+, ++ −, =−, −− *, =* /, =/ pow()
Output (display the data)	WRITE PRINT	PRINT PRINT/ USING	WRITE DISPLAY	WRITE WRITELN	putchar() puts() printf() sprintf() fprintf()

Business applications usually deal in whole numbers, representing inventory quantities, for example, or dollar and cents data accurate to only two decimal places. These applications require simpler mathematical calculations than are needed for scientific applications. The outputs required from business programs frequently consist of reports containing extensive columns of neatly formatted dollar and cents numbers and totals. For these applications the COBOL programming

FIGURE 1.17   FORTRAN was Developed for Scientific and Engineering Applications

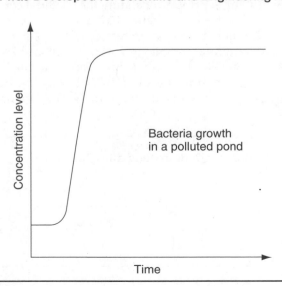

Bacteria growth in a polluted pond

FIGURE 1.18   COBOL Is Ideal for Many Business Applications

```
                        INVENTORY REPORT

    Item                                In     On     Unit
    No.          Description         Stock   Order    Cost

    10365    360KB - Diskette          20       0     5.95
    10382    720KB - Diskette          10      50    10.70
    10420    1.2MB - Diskette           2      60     8.40
    10436   1.44MB - Diskette           6
    10449     20MB - Cartridge
    10486     40MB - Cartridge
```

language, with its picture output formats is an ideal language (Figure 1.18). COBOL, which was commercially introduced in the 1960s, stands for COmmon Business Oriented Language.

Teaching programming to students has its own set of requirements. Here, a relatively straightforward, easy-to-understand language is needed that does not require detailed knowledge of a specific application. Both the BASIC and Pascal programming languages were developed for this purpose. BASIC stands for Beginners All-purpose Symbolic Instruction Code, and was developed in the 1960s at Dartmouth College. BASIC is ideal for creating small, easily developed, interactive programs.

Pascal was developed in the 1971 to provide students with a firmer foundation in modular and structured programming than was provided by early versions of BASIC.[6] Modular programs consist of many small subprograms, each of which performs a clearly defined and specific task that can be tested and modified without disturbing other sections of the program. Pascal is not an acronym, like the words FORTRAN, COBOL, and BASIC, but is named after the seventeenth-century mathematician, Blaise Pascal. The Pascal language is so rigidly structured, however, that there are no escapes from the structured modules when such escapes would be useful. This is unacceptable for many real-world projects, and is one of the reasons why Pascal did not become widely accepted in the scientific, engineering, and business fields. The design philosophy, called structured programming, that lead to the development of Pascal is, however, very relevant to C programmers. Using a structured programming approach results in readable, reliable, and maintainable programs. We introduce the elements of this program design philosophy in the next section, and continue to expand on it and use it throughout the text.

The C language was initially developed in the 1970s by Ken Thompson, Dennis Ritchie, and Brian Kernighan at AT&T Bell Laboratories. C evolved from a language called B, which was itself developed from the language BCPL. C has an extensive set of capabilities and is a true general-purpose programming language. As such, it can be used for everything from simple, interactive programs to highly sophisticated and complex engineering and scientific programs, within

---

[6]Current versions of both BASIC and FORTRAN do provide the same type of structures found in Pascal.

the context of a truly structured language. An indication of C's richness of library and instruction capabilities is clearly evident from Table 1.2. Not only does C initially provide many "tools" with which to build programs, it also provides the programmer with the ability to easily create new "tools" to add to the existing library routines. It is for this reason that C has become known as the professional programmer's language.

1.3 PROBLEM SOLUTION AND SOFTWARE DEVELOPMENT

No matter what field of work you choose or what your lifestyle may be, you will have to solve problems. Many of these, such as adding up the change in your pocket, can be solved quickly and easily. Others, such as riding a bicycle, require some practice but soon become automatic. Still others require considerable planning and forethought if the solution is to be appropriate and efficient. For example, constructing a cellular telephone network or creating an inventory management system for a department store are problems for which trial-and-error solutions could prove expensive and disastrous.

Creating a program is no different, because a program is a solution developed to solve a particular problem. As such, writing a program is almost the last step in a process of first determining what the problem is and the method that will be used to solve the problem. Each field of study has its own name for the systematic method used to solve problems by designing suitable solutions. In science and engineering the approach is referred to as the *scientific method*, while in quantitative analysis the approach is referred to as the *systems approach*.

The technique used by professional software developers for understanding the problem that is being solved and for creating an effective and appropriate software solution is called the *software development procedure*. This procedure, as illustrated in Figure 1.19 consists of three overlapping phases:

- Development and Design
- Documentation
- Maintenance

As a discipline, software engineering is concerned with creating readable, efficient, reliable, and maintainable programs and systems. The software development procedure is used to achieve this goal.

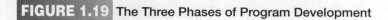

FIGURE 1.19 The Three Phases of Program Development

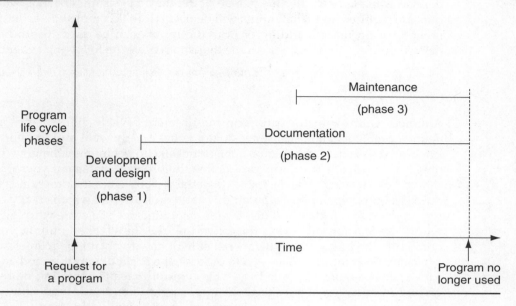

Phase I. Development and Design

Phase I begins with either a statement of a problem or a specific request for a program, which is referred to as a program requirement. Once a problem has been stated or a specific request for a program solution has been made, the development and design phase begins. This phase consists of the four well-defined steps illustrated in Figure 1.20 and summarized next. Each of these steps is elaborated upon at the end of this section.

FIGURE 1.20 The Development and Design Steps

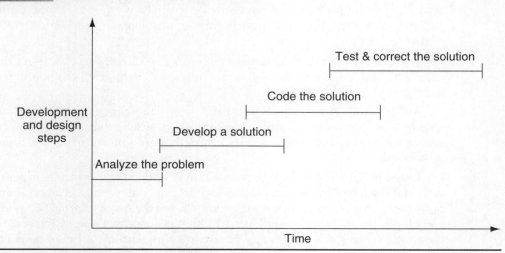

1. Analyze the Problem: This step is required to ensure that the problem is clearly defined and understood. The determination that the problem is clearly defined is made only after the person doing the analysis understands what outputs are required and what inputs will be needed. To accomplish this, the analyst must have an understanding of how the inputs can be used to produce the desired output. For example, assume that you receive the following assignment:

Write a program that gives the information we need about circles. Complete by tomorrow.

—Management

A simple analysis of this program requirement reveals that it is not a well-defined problem at all because we do not know exactly what output information is required. As such, it would be a major mistake to begin immediately writing a program to solve it. To clarify and define the problem statement your first step should be to contact "Management" to define exactly what the program is to produce (its outputs). Suppose you do this and you learn that what is really desired is a program to calculate and display the circumference of a circle when given the radius. Since a formula exists for converting the input to the output, you may proceed to the next step. If you are not sure of how to obtain the required output or exactly what inputs are needed to produce the desired output, a more in-depth background analysis is called for. This typically means obtaining more background information about the problem or application. It also frequently entails doing one or more hand calculations to ensure that you understand what inputs are needed and how they must be combined to achieve the desired output.

2. Develop a Solution: In this step we determine and select a solution for solving the problem. The solution is typically obtained by a series of refinements, starting with a preliminary solution found in the analysis step, until an acceptable and complete solution is obtained. This solution must be checked, if this was not already done in the analysis step, to ensure that it correctly produces the desired outputs. The check is typically done by doing one or more hand calculations.

Sometimes the selected solution is quite easy, and sometimes it is quite complex. For example, the solution to determine the dollar value of the change in one's pocket or to determine the circumference of a circle is quite simple and consists of a simple calculation. The construction of an inventory tracking and control system for a computer store, however, is more complex. Techniques for solving these more complex problems are presented at the end of this section.

3. Code the Solution: This step, which is also referred to as writing the program and implementing the solution, consists of translating the solution into a computer program.

4. Test and Correct the Solution: As its name suggests, this step requires testing of the completed computer program to ensure that it does, in fact, provide a solution to the problem. Any errors that are found during the tests must be corrected.

Listed in Table 1.3 is the relative amount of effort that is typically expended on each of these four development and design steps in large commercial programming projects. As this listing demonstrates, coding is not the major effort in this phase.

Many new programmers have trouble because they spend the majority of their time writing the program, without spending sufficient time understanding

TABLE 1.3 Effort Expended in Phase I

Step	Effort
Analysis	10%
Design	20%
Coding	20%
Testing and correcting	50%

the problem or designing an appropriate solution. In this regard, it is worthwhile to remember the programming proverb, "It is impossible to write a successful program for a problem or application that is not fully understood." A somewhat equivalent and equally valuable proverb is "The sooner you start coding a program the longer it usually takes to complete."

Phase II: Documentation

In practice, most programmers forget many of the details of their own programs a few months after they have finished working on them. If they, or other programmers must subsequently make modifications to the program much valuable time can be lost figuring out just how the original code works. Good documentation prevents this from occurring.

So much work becomes useless or lost, and so many tasks must be repeated because of inadequate documentation that it could be argued that documenting your work is the most important step in problem solving. Actually, many of the critical documents are created during the analysis, design, coding, and testing steps. Completing the documentation requires collecting these documents, adding additional material, and presenting it in a form that is most useful to you and your organization.

Although not everybody classifies them in the same way, there are essentially five documents for every problem solution:

1. Program description
2. Algorithm development and changes
3. Well-commented program listing
4. Sample test runs
5. Users' manual.

"Putting yourself in the shoes" of a member of a large organization's team that might use your work — anyone from the secretary to the programmer/analysts and management — should help you to make the content and design of the important documentation clear. The documentation phase formally begins in the Development and Design phase and continues into the Maintenance phase.

Phase III: Maintenance

This phase is concerned with ongoing correction of problems, revisions to meet changing needs, and addition of new features. Maintenance is often the major effort, the primary source of revenue, and the longest lasting of the three major phases. While development may take days or months, maintenance may continue for years or decades. The better the documentation is, the more efficiently this phase can be performed and the happier the customer and user will be.

A Closer Look at Phase I

Because the majority of this text is concerned with phase I of the software development procedure, we elaborate further on the four steps required for this phase. The use of these steps forms the central focus of our work in creating useful programming solutions.

Step 1: Analyze the Problem   Countless hours have been spent writing computer programs that either have never been used or have caused considerable animosity between programmer and user because the programmer did not produce what the user needed or expected. Successful programmers understand and avoid this by ensuring that the problem's requirements are understood. This is the first step in creating a program and the most important, because in it the specifications for the final program solution are determined. If the requirements are not fully and completely understood before programming begins, the results are almost always disastrous.

Imagine designing and building a house without fully understanding the architect's specifications. After the house is completed, the architect tells you that a bathroom is required on the first floor, where you have built a wall between the kitchen and the dining room. In addition, that particular wall is one of the main support walls for the house and contains numerous pipes and electrical cables. In this case, adding one bathroom requires a rather major modification to the basic structure of the house.

Experienced programmers understand the importance of analyzing and understanding a program's requirements before coding, if for no other reason than that they too have constructed programs that later had to be entirely dismantled and redone. The following exercise should give you a sense of this experience.

Figure 1.21 illustrates the outlines of six individual shapes from a classic children's puzzle. Assume that as one or more shapes are given, starting with shapes A and B, an easy-to-describe figure must be constructed. Typically, shapes A and B are initially arranged to obtain a square, as illustrated in Figure 1.22. Next, when shape C is considered, it is usually combined with the existing square to form a rectangle, as illustrated in Figure 1.23. Then when pieces D and E are added, they are usually arranged to form another rectangle, which is placed alongside the existing rectangle to form a square, as shown in Figure 1.24.

The process of adding new pieces onto the existing structure is identical to constructing a program and then adding to it as each subsequent requirement is understood, rather than completely analyzing the problem before a solution is undertaken. The problem arises when the program is almost finished and a requirement is

FIGURE 1.21   Six Individual Shapes

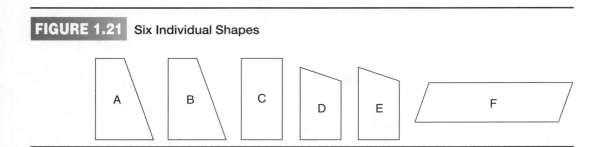

FIGURE 1.22 Typical First Figure

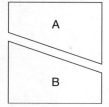

FIGURE 1.23 Typical Second Figure

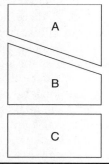

---

added that does not fit easily into the established pattern. For example, assume that the last shape (shape F; see Figure 1.25) is now to be added. This last piece does not fit into the existing pattern that has been constructed. In order to include this piece with the others, the pattern must be completely dismantled and restructured.

Unfortunately, many programmers structure their programs in the same sequential manner used to construct Figure 1.24. Rather than taking the time to understand the complete set of requirements, new programmers frequently start coding based on the understanding of only a small

---

FIGURE 1.24 Typical Third Figure

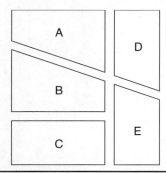

FIGURE 1.25 The Last Piece

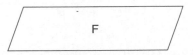

subset of the total requirements. Then, when a subsequent requirement does not fit the existing program structure, the programmer is forced to dismantle and restructure either parts or all of the program.

Now, let's approach the problem of creating a figure from another view. If we started by arranging the first set of pieces as a parallelogram, all the pieces could be included in the final figure, as illustrated in Figure 1.26. It is worthwhile observing that the piece that caused us to dismantle the first figure (Figure 1.24) actually sets the pattern for the final figure illustrated in Figure 1.26. This is often the case with programming requirements. The requirement that seems to be the least clear is frequently the one that determines the main interrelationships of the program. It is worthwhile to include and understand all the known requirements before beginning coding. Thus, before any solution is attempted the analysis step must be completed.

The person performing the analysis must initially take a broad perspective, see all of the pieces, and understand the main purpose of what the program or system is meant to achieve. The key to success here, which ultimately determines the success of the final program, is to determine the main purpose of the system as seen by the person making the request. For large systems, the analysis is usually conducted by a systems analyst. For smaller systems or individual programs, the analysis is typically performed directly by the programmer.

Regardless of how the analysis is done, or by whom, at its conclusion there should be a clear understanding of:

FIGURE 1.26 Including All the Pieces

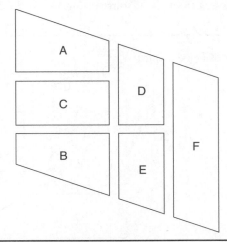

- What the system or program must do
- What reports or outputs must be produced
- What inputs are required to create the desired outputs.

Step 2: Develop (Design) a Solution   Once the problem is clearly understood a solution can be developed. In this regard the programmer is in a similar position to that of an architect who must draw up the plans for a house: The house must conform to certain specifications and meet the needs of its owner, but can be designed and built in many possible ways. So too for a program.

For small programs the selected solution may be extremely simple and consist of only one or more calculations that must be performed. More typically, the initial solution must be refined and organized into smaller subsystems, with specifications for how the subsystems will interface with each other. To achieve this goal, the description of the algorithm starts from the highest level (topmost) requirement and proceeds downward to the parts that must be constructed to achieve this requirement. To make this more meaningful, consider a computer program that is required to track the number of parts in inventory. The required output for this program is a description of all parts carried in inventory and the number of units of each item in stock; the given inputs are the initial inventory quantity of each part, the number of items sold, the number of items returned, and the number of items purchased.

For these specifications, a designer could initially organize the requirements for the program into the three sections illustrated in Figure 1.27. This is called a first-level structure diagram because it represents the first overall structure of the program selected by the designer.

Once an initial structure is developed, it is refined until the tasks indicated in the boxes are completely defined. For example, both the data entry and report subsections shown in Figure 1.27 would be further refined as follows: The data entry section certainly must include provisions for entering the data. Since it is the system designer's responsibility to plan for contingencies and human error, provisions must also be made for changing incorrect data after an entry has been made and for deleting a previously entered value altogether. Similar subdivisions for the report section can also be made. Figure 1.28 illustrates a second-level structure diagram for an inventory tracking system that includes these further refinements.

FIGURE 1.27   **First-Level Structure Diagram**

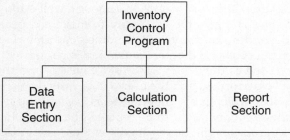

FIGURE 1.28 Second-Level Refinement Structure Diagram

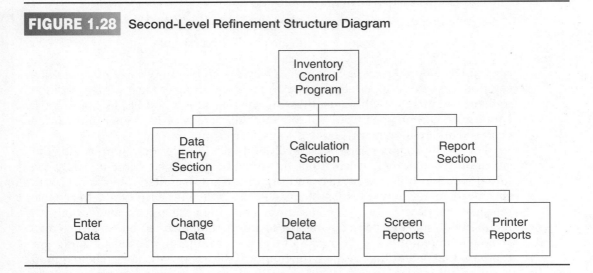

The process of refining a solution continues until the smallest requirement is included within the solution. Notice that the design produces a treelike structure where the levels branch out as we move from the top of the structure to the bottom. When the design is complete each task designated in a box is typically coded with separate sets of instructions that are executed as they are called on by tasks higher up in the structure.

Step 3: Code the Solution   Coding involves translating the chosen design solution into a computer program. If the analysis and solution steps have been correctly performed, the coding step becomes rather mechanical in nature. In a well-designed program, the statements making up the program will, however, conform to certain well-defined patterns, or structures, that have been defined in the solution step. These structures control how the program executes and consist of the following types:

1. Sequence
2. Selection
3. Iteration
4. Invocation.

Sequence defines the order in which instructions are executed by the program. The specification of which instruction comes first, which comes second, and so on, is essential if the program is to achieve a well-defined purpose.

Selection provides the capability to make a choice between different operations, depending on the result of some condition. For example, the value of a number can be checked before a division is performed. If the number is not zero, it can be used as the denominator of a division operation; otherwise the division will not be performed and the user will be issued a warning message.

Iteration, which is also referred to as *looping* and *repetition*, provides the ability for the same operation to be repeated based on the value of a condition. For example, grades might be repeatedly entered and added until a negative grade is entered. In this case the entry of a negative grade is the condition that signifies

---

A BIT OF BACKGROUND

Niklaus Wirth

Niklaus Wirth received an M.S. degree from the University of Quebec in 1962 and a Ph.D. from the University of California at Berkeley in 1963. He then returned to his undergraduate alma mater, the Swiss Federal Institute of Technology, to teach. While serving there in 1971, he announced a new language he had designed and named Pascal. Pascal became very popular in the 1970s and early 1980s because of its emphasis on the sequence, selection, iteration, and invocation control structures.

---

the end of the repetitive input and addition of grades. At that point a calculation of an average for all the grades entered could be performed.

Invocation involves invoking, or summoning, a set of statements as it is needed. For example, the computation of a person's net pay involves the tasks of obtaining pay rates and hours worked, calculating the net pay, and providing a report or check for the required amount. Each of these individual tasks would typically be coded as separate units that are called into execution, or invoked, as they are needed.

Step 4: Test and Correct the solution   The purpose of testing is to verify that a program works correctly and actually fulfills its requirements. In theory, testing would reveal all existing program errors (in computer terminology, a program error is called a bug[7]). In practice, this would require checking all possible combinations of statement execution. Because of the time and effort required, this is usually an impossible goal except for extremely simple programs. (We illustrate why this is generally an impossible goal in Section 4.8)

Because exhaustive testing is not feasible for most programs, different philosophies and methods of testing have evolved. At its most basic level, however, testing requires a conscious effort to ensure that a program works correctly and produces meaningful results. This means that careful thought must be given to what the test is meant to achieve and the data that will be used in the test. If testing reveals an error (bug), the process of debugging, which includes locating, correcting, and verifying the correction, can be initiated. It is important to realize that although testing may reveal the presence of an error, it does not necessarily indicate the absence of one. Thus, the fact that a test revealed one bug does not indicate that another one is not lurking somewhere else in the program.

To catch and correct errors in a program it is important to develop a set of test data that determines whether the program gives correct answers. In fact, an accepted step in formal software development many times is to plan the test procedures and create meaningful test data before writing the code. This tends to

---

[7]The derivation of this term is rather interesting. When a program stopped running on the Mark I at Harvard University in September 1945, Grace Hopper traced the malfunction to a dead insect that had gotten into the electrical circuits. She recorded the incident in her logbook at 15:45 hours as "Relay #70 . . . (moth) in relay. First actual case of bug being found."

help the person be more objective about what the program must do, because it essentially circumvents any subconscious temptation after coding to avoid test data that will not work. The procedures for testing a program should examine every possible situation under which the program will be used. The program should be tested with data in a reasonable range as well as at the limits and in areas where the program should tell the user that the data are invalid. In fact, developing good test procedures and data for sophisticated problems can be more difficult than writing the program code itself.

Backup   Although not part of the formal design process, it is critical to make and keep backup copies of the program at each step of the programming and debugging process. It is easy to delete or change the current working version of a program beyond recognition. Backup copies allow the recovery of the last stage of work with a minimum of effort. The final working version of a useful program should be backed up at least twice. In this regard, another useful programming proverb is "Backup is unimportant if you don't mind starting all over again." The three most fundamental rules of maintaining program and data integrity are:

1. backup!
   2. Backup!
      3. BACKUP!

Many organizations keep at least one backup on site, where it can be easily retrieved, and another backup copy either in a fireproof safe or at a remote location.

Exercises 1.3

1. a. List and describe the four steps required in the design and development stage of a program.

   b. In addition to the design and development stage, what are the other two stages required in producing a program and why are they required?

2. A note from your supervisor, Ms. J. Williams, says:

   Solve our payroll deduction problems.
   —J. Williams

   a. What should be your first task?

   b. How would you accomplish this task?

   c. How long would you expect this to take, assuming everyone cooperates?

3. Program development is only one phase in the overall software development procedure. Assuming that documentation and maintenance require 60% of the total software effort in designing a system, and using Table 1.3, determine the amount of effort required for initial program coding as a percentage of total software effort.

4. Many people requesting a program or system for the first time consider coding to be the most important aspect of program development. They feel that they know what they need and think that the programmer can begin coding with minimal time spent in analysis. As a programmer, what pitfalls can you envision in working with such people?

5. Many first-time computer users try to contract with programmers for a fixed fee (total amount to be paid is fixed in advance). What is the advantage to the user in having this arrangement? What is the advantage to the programmer in having this arrangement? What are some disadvantages to both user and programmer in this arrangement?

6. Many programmers prefer to work on an hourly rate basis. Why do you think this is so? Under what conditions would it be advantageous for a programmer to give a client a fixed price for the programming effort?

7. Experienced users generally want a clearly written statement of programming work to be done, including a complete description of what the program will do, delivery dates, payment schedules, and testing requirements. What is the advantage to the user in requiring this? What is the advantage to a programmer in working under this arrangement? What disadvantages does this arrangement have for both user and programmer?

8. Assume that a computer store makes, on average, 15 sales per day. Assuming that the store is open six days a week and that each sale requires an average of 100 characters, determine the minimum storage that the system must have to keep all sales records for a two-year period.

9. Assume that you are creating a sales recording system for a client. Each sale input to the system requires that the operator type in a description of the item sold, the name and address of the firm buying the item, the value of the item, and a code for the person making the trade. This information consists of a maximum of 300 characters. Estimate the time it would take for an average typist to input 200 sales. (*Hint:* To solve this problem you must make an assumption about the number of words per minute that an average typist can type and the average number of characters per word.)

10. Most commercial printers for personal computers can print at a speed of 165 characters per second. Using such a printer, determine the time it would take to print out a complete list of 10,000 records. Assume that each record consists of 300 characters.

1.4 ALGORITHMS

Before a program is written, the programmer must clearly understand what data are to be used, the desired result, and the procedure to be used to produce this result. The procedure, or solution, selected in the design step is referred to as an algorithm. More precisely, an *algorithm* is defined as a step-by-step sequence of instructions that must terminate and describes how the data is to be processed to produce the desired outputs. In essence, an algorithm answers the question, "What method will you use to solve this problem?"

Only after we clearly understand the data that we will be using and select an algorithm (the specific steps required to produce the desired result) can we code

The Young Gauss

German mathematical genius Johann Carl Fredrich Gauss (1777–1855) professed that he could "reckon" before he could talk. When only two years old he discovered an error in his father's business records.

One day in school, young Johann's teacher asked his class to add up the numbers between 1 and 100. To the chagrin of the teacher, who had thought the task would keep the class busy for a while, Gauss almost instantly wrote the number on his slate and exclaimed, "There it is!" He had reasoned that the series of numbers could be written forward and backward and added term-by-term to get 101 one hundred times. Thus, the sum was 100(101) /2; and Gauss, at the age of 10, had discovered that

$$1 + 2 + \ldots + n = n\,(n + 1)\,/2.$$

the program. Seen in this light, *programming* is the translation of a selected algorithm into a language that the computer can use.

To illustrate an algorithm, we shall consider a simple problem. Assume that a program must calculate the sum of all whole numbers from 1 through 100. Figure 1.29 illustrates three methods we could use to find the required sum. Each method constitutes an algorithm. Clearly, most people would not bother to list the possible alternatives in a detailed step-by-step manner, as we have done here, and then select one of the algorithms to solve the problem. But then, most people do not think algorithmically; they tend to think intuitively. For example, if you had to change a flat tire on your car, you would not think of all the steps required — you would simply change the tire or call someone else to do the job. This is an example of intuitive thinking.

Unfortunately, computers do not respond to intuitive commands. A general statement such as "add the numbers from 1 to 100" means nothing to a computer, because the computer can only respond to algorithmic commands written in an acceptable language such as C. To program a computer successfully, you must clearly understand this difference between algorithmic and intuitive commands. A computer is an "algorithm-responding" machine; it is not an "intuitive-responding" machine. You cannot tell a computer to change a tire or to add the numbers from 1 through 100. Instead, you must give the computer a detailed step-by-step set of instructions that, collectively, forms an algorithm. For example, the following set of instructions

Set n equal to 100
Set $a = 1$
Set b equal to 100
Calculate sum $= \dfrac{n(a + b)}{2}$
Print the sum

forms a detailed method, or algorithm, for determining the sum of the numbers from 1 through 100. Notice that these instructions are not a computer program. Unlike a program, which must be written in a language the computer can respond to, an algorithm can be written or described in various ways. When English-like phrases are used to describe the algorithm (the processing steps), as in this example, the description is called *pseudocode*. When mathematical equations are used, the description is called a formula. When diagrams that employ the symbols shown in Figure 1.30 are used, the description is referred to as a *flowchart*. Figure 1.31 illustrates the use of these symbols in depicting an algorithm for determining the average of three numbers.

Because flowcharts are cumbersome to revise and can easily support unstructured programming practices, they have fallen out of favor by professional programmers, while the use of pseudocode to express the logic of algorithms has gained increasing acceptance. In describing an algorithm using pseudocode,

---

FIGURE 1.29   Summing the Numbers 1 Through 100

Method 1 — Columns: Arrange the numbers from 1 to 100 in a column and add them

$$
\begin{array}{r}
1 \\
2 \\
3 \\
4 \\
\bullet \\
\bullet \\
\bullet \\
98 \\
99 \\
+\ 100 \\
\hline
5050
\end{array}
$$

Method 2 — Groups: Arrange the numbers in groups that sum to 100. Multiply the number of groups by 100 and add in any unused numbers.

$$
\begin{array}{l}
1 +\ 100 = 100 \\
2 +\ \ 99 = 100 \\
3 +\ \ 98 = 100 \\
4 +\ \ 97 = 100 \\
\bullet \qquad \bullet \\
\bullet \qquad \bullet \\
\bullet \qquad \bullet \\
49 +\ \ 51 = 100 \\
50 +\ \ \ 0 =\ \ 50
\end{array}
$$

50 groups

$(50 \times 100) + 50 = 5050$

One unused number

Method 3 — Formula: Use the formula

$$\text{Sum 5} = \frac{n(a+b)}{2}$$

where

$n=$ number of terms to be added (100)
$a=$ first number to be added (1)
$b=$ last number to be added (100)

$$\text{Sum 5} = \frac{100(1+100)}{2} = 5050$$

FIGURE 1.30 Flowchart Symbols

SYMBOL	NAME	DESCRIPTION
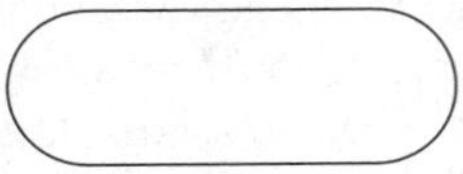	Terminal	Indicates the beginning or end of an algorithm
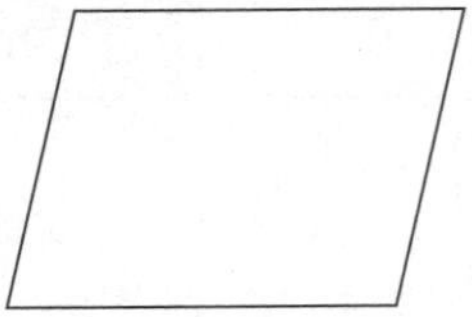	Input/Output	Indicates an Input or Output operation
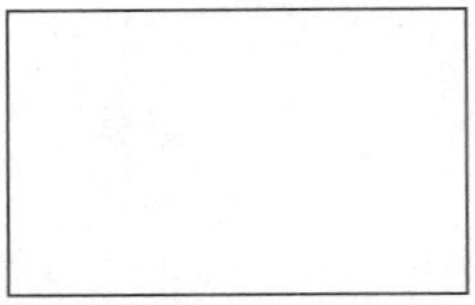	Process	Indicates computation or data manipulation
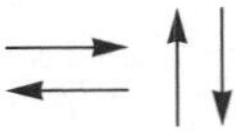	Flow Lines	Used to connect the flowchart symbols and indicates the logic flow
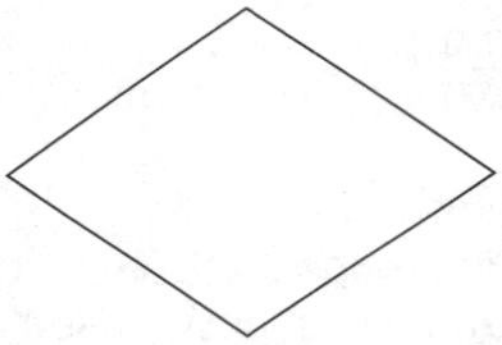	Decision	Indicates a decision point in the algorithm
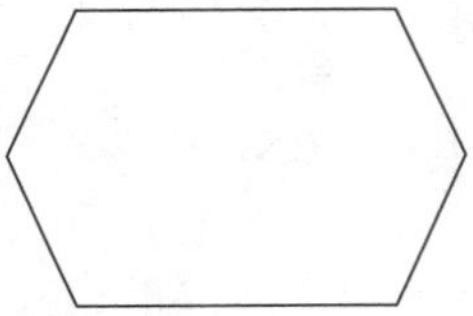	Loop	Indicates the initial, final, and increment values of a loop
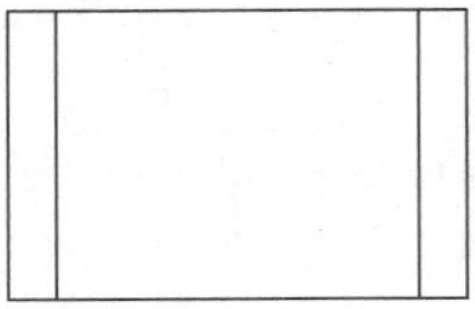	Predefined Process	Indicates a predefined process, as in calling a sorting process
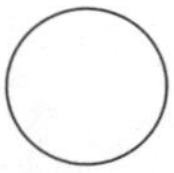	Connector	Indicates an entry to, or exit from, another part of the flowchart

FIGURE 1.31   Flowchart for Calculating the Average of Three Numbers

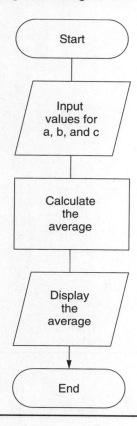

short English phrases are used. For example, acceptable pseudocode for describing the steps needed to compute the average of three numbers is:

Input the three numbers into the computer's memory.
Calculate the average by adding the numbers and dividing the sum by three.
Display the average.

Only after an algorithm has been selected and the programmer understands the steps required can the algorithm be written using computer-language statements. The writing of an algorithm using computer-language statements is called coding the algorithm, which is the third step in our program development procedure (see Figure 1.32). Most of the remainder of this text is devoted to showing you how to develop and then code algorithms into C.

FIGURE 1.32   Coding an Algorithm

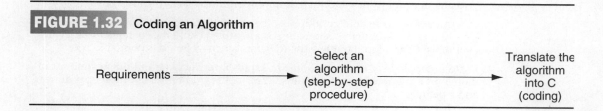

FIGURE 1.33   A Simple Paint-by-Number Figure

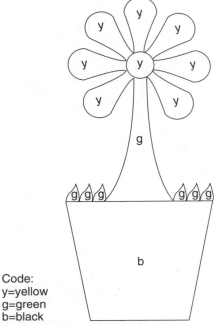

Code:
y=yellow
g=green
b=black

Exercises 1.4

1. Determine a step-by-step procedure (list the steps) to do the following tasks. (*Note:* There is no one single correct answer for each of these tasks. The exercise is designed to give you practice in converting intuitive-type commands into equivalent algorithms and making the shift between the thought processes involved in the two types of thinking.)

   a. Fix a flat tire.

   b. Make a telephone call.

   c. Go to the store and purchase a loaf of bread.

   d. Roast a turkey.

2. a. Determine the six possible step-by-step procedures (list the steps) to paint the flower shown in Figure 1.33, with the restriction that each color must be completed before a new color can be started. (*Hint:* one of the algorithms is "Use yellow first, green second, black last.")

   b. Which of the six painting algorithms (series of steps) is best if we are limited to using one paintbrush and there is no turpentine to clean the brush.

3. Determine and write an algorithm (list the steps) to interchange the contents of two cups of liquid. Assume that a third cup is available to hold the contents of either cup temporarily. Each cup should be rinsed before any new liquid is poured into it.

4. Write a detailed set of instructions, in English, to calculate the dollar amount of money in a piggybank that contains h half-dollars, q quarters, n nickels, d dimes, and p pennies.

5. Write a set of detailed, step-by-step instructions, in English, to find the smallest number in a group of three integer numbers.

6. a. Write a set of detailed, step-by-step instructions, in English, to calculate the change remaining from a dollar after a purchase is made. Assume that the cost of the goods purchased is less than a dollar. The change received should consist of the smallest number of coins possible.

   b. Repeat Exercise 6a, but assume the change is to be given only in pennies.

7. a. Write an algorithm to locate the first occurrence of the name WESTBY in a list of names arranged in random order.

   b. Discuss how you could improve your algorithm for Exercise 7a if the list of names was arranged in alphabetical order.

8. Write an algorithm to determine the total occurrences of the letter *e* in any sentence.

9. Determine and write an algorithm to sort four numbers into ascending (from lowest to highest) order.

1.5 ENRICHMENT STUDY: DIGITAL STORAGE CONCEPTS

The physical components used in manufacturing a computer require that the numbers and letters stored by the computer are not stored using the same symbols that people use. The number that we know as 126, for example, is not stored using the symbols 126. Neither is the letter that we recognize as A stored using this symbol. In this section, we will see why this is so, and how most computers store numbers. In Chapter 2 we will see how letters are stored.

The smallest and most basic data item in a computer is called a bit. Physically, a bit is really a switch that can be either open or closed. By convention, the open and closed positions of each switch are represented as a 0 and a 1, respectively.

A single bit that can represent the values 0 and 1, by itself, has limited usefulness. All computers, therefore, group a set number of bits together, both for storage and transmission. The grouping of eight bits to form a larger unit is an almost universal computer standard. Such groups are commonly referred to as bytes. A single byte consisting of eight bits, where each bit is either a 0 or 1, can represent any one of 256 distinct patterns. These consist of the pattern 00000000 (all eight switches open) to the pattern 11111111 (all eight switches closed), and all possible combinations of 0's and 1's between. Each of these patterns can be used to represent either a letter of the alphabet, other single characters, such as a dollar sign, comma, etc., a single digit, or numbers containing more than one digit. The patterns of 0's and 1's used to represent letters, single digits, and other single characters are called character codes (two such codes, called the ASCII and EBCDIC codes, are presented in Section 2.3). The patterns used to store numbers are called number codes, one of which is presented next.

Two's Complement Numbers

The most common number code for storing integer values inside a computer is called the two's complement representation. Using this code, the integer equivalent of any bit pattern, such as 10001101, is easy to determine and can be found for either positive or negative integers with no change in the conversion method. For convenience we will assume byte-sized bit patterns consisting of a set of eight bits each, although the procedure carries directly over to larger size bit patterns.

FIGURE 1.34   An Eight-Bit Value Box

−128	64	32	16	8	4	2	1

The easiest way to determine the integer represented by each bit pattern is to first construct a simple device called a value box. Figure 1.34 illustrates such a box for a single byte. Mathematically, each value in the box illustrated in Figure 1.34 represents an increasing power of two. Since two's complement numbers must be capable of representing both positive and negative integers, the leftmost position, in addition to having the largest absolute magnitude, also has a negative sign.

Conversion of any binary number, for example, 10001101, simply requires inserting the bit pattern in the value box and adding the values having ones under them. Thus, as illustrated in Figure 1.35, the bit pattern 10001101 represents the integer number -115.

The value box can also be used in reverse, to convert a base 10 integer number into its equivalent binary bit pattern. Some conversions, in fact, can be made by inspection. For example, the base 10 number -125 is obtained by adding 3 to -128. Thus, the binary representation of -125 is 10000011, which equals -128 + 2 + 1. Similarly, the two's complement representation of the number 40 is 00101000, which is 32 plus 8.

Although the value box conversion method is deceptively simple, the method is directly related to the underlying mathematical basis of two's complement binary numbers. The original name of the two's complement code was the weighted-sign code, which correlates directly to the value box. As the name weighted sign implies, each bit position has a weight, or value, of two raised to a power and a sign. The signs of all bits except the leftmost bit are positive and the sign of the leftmost bit is negative.

In reviewing the value box, it is evident that any two's complement binary number with a leading 1 represents a negative number, and any bit pattern with a leading 0 represents a positive number. Using the value box it is easy to determine the most positive and negative values capable of being stored. The most negative value that can be stored in a single byte is the decimal number -128, which has the bit pattern 10000000. Any other nonzero bit will simply add a positive amount to the number. Additionally, it is clear that a positive number must

FIGURE 1.35   Converting 10001101 to a Base 10 Number

−128	64	32	16	8	4	2	1	
1	0	0	0	1	1	0	1	
−128 +	0 +	0 +	0 +	8 +	4 +	0 +	1	= −115

have a 0 as its leftmost bit. From this you can see that the largest positive eight-bit two's complement number is 01111111 or 127.

Words and Addresses

One or more bytes may themselves be grouped into larger units, called words, which facilitate faster and more extensive data access. For example, retrieving a word consisting of four bytes from a computer's memory results in more information than that obtained by retrieving a word consisting of a single byte. Such a retrieval is also considerably faster than four individual byte retrievals. This increase in speed and capacity, however, is achieved by an increase in the computer's cost and complexity.

Early personal computers, such as the Apple IIe and Commodore machines, internally stored and transmitted words consisting of single bytes. AT&T 6300 and IBM-PC/XTs use word sizes consisting of two bytes, while Digital Equipment, and Intel 486 computers process words consisting of four bytes each. Super computers, such as the CRAY-1 and Control Data 7000, have six- and eight-byte words, respectively.

The arrangement of words in a computer's memory can be compared to the arrangement of suites in a very large hotel, where each suite is made up of rooms of the same size. Just as each suite has a unique room number to locate and identify it, each word has a unique numeric address. In computers that allow each byte to be individually accessed, each byte has its own address. Like room numbers, word and byte addresses are always non-negative, whole numbers that are used for location and identification purposes. Also, like hotel rooms with connecting doors for forming larger suites, words can be combined to form larger units for the accommodation of different size data types.

1.6 COMMON PROGRAMMING ERRORS

The most common errors associated with the material presented in this chapter are as follows:

1. A major programming error made by most beginning programmers is the rush to write and run a program before fully understanding what is required and the algorithms that will be used to produce the desired result. A symptom of this haste to get a program entered into the computer is the lack of any documentation or even a program outline or a written program itself. Many problems can be caught just by checking a copy of the program or even a description of the algorithm written in pseudocode.

2. A second major error is not backing up a program. Almost all new programmers make this mistake until they lose a program that has taken considerable time to code.

3. The third error made by many new programmers is the lack of understanding that computers respond only to explicitly defined algorithms. Telling a computer to add a group of numbers is quite different than telling a friend to add the numbers. The computer must be given the precise instructions for doing the addition in a programming language.

1.7 CHAPTER REVIEW

Key Terms

algorithm
ALU
analysis
application software
assembler
assembly language
backup copies
boot
coding
central processing unit
compiler
control unit
development
documentation
floppy diskette
flowchart
hard disk
hardware
high-level language
input/output unit
invocation
iteration
low-level language
machine language
maintenance
memory unit

microprocessor
object-oriented
 language
procedure-oriented
 language
programming
programming
 language
pseudocode
RAM
refinement
repetition
ROM
secondary storage
selection
sequence
software
software development
 procedure
software engineering
software maintenance
source code
system software
testing
VLSI

Summary

1. The first recorded attempt at creating a self-operating computational machine was made by Charles Babbage in 1822. The concept became a reality with the Atanasoff-Berry Computer built in 1937 at Iowa State University, which was the first computer to use a binary numbering scheme to store and manipulate data. Two of the earliest large-scale digital computers were the Mark I, built at Harvard University in 1944, and the ENIAC, built in 1946 at the Moore School of Engineering at the University of Pennsylvania. All of these machines, however, required external wiring to perform the desired operations. The first computer to employ the concept of a stored program was the EDSAC, built at Cambridge University in England. The design and operating principles used in the design of this machine, developed by the mathematician John Von Neumann, are still used by the majority of computers manufactured today.

2. The physical components used in constructing a computer are called its *hardware*. These components include input, processing, output, memory, and storage units.

3. The programs used to operate a computer are referred to as *software*.

4. Programming languages come in a variety of forms and types. Machine-language programs, also known as executable programs, contain the binary codes that can be executed by a computer. Assembly languages permit the use of

A BIT OF BACKGROUND

Binary ABC

Dr. John V. Atanasoff agonized several years over the design of a computing machine to help his Iowa State University graduate students solve complex equations. He considered building a machine based on binary numbers—the most natural system to use with electromechanical equipment that had one of two easily recognizable states, on and off—but feared people would not use a machine that was not based on the familiar and comfortable decimal system.

Finally, on a cold evening at a road-house in Illinois in 1937, he determined that it had to be done the simplest and least expensive way, with binary digits (bits). During the next two years he and graduate student Clifford Berry built the first electronic digital computer, called the ABC (for Atanasoff-Berry Computer). Since that time the vast majority of computers have been binary machines.

---

symbolic names for mathematical operations and memory addresses. Programs written in assembly languages must be converted to machine language, using translator programs called assemblers, before the programs can be executed. Assembly and machine languages are referred to as *low-level languages*.

Compiler and interpreter languages are referred to as *high-level languages*. This means that they are written using instructions that resemble a written language, such as English, and can be run on a variety of computer types. Compiler languages require a compiler to translate the program into a binary language form, while interpreter languages require an interpreter to do the translation.

5. As a discipline, software engineering is concerned with creating readable, efficient, reliable, and maintainable programs and systems.

6. The software development procedure consists of three phases:
   - Program development and design
   - Documentation
   - Maintenance.

7. The program development and design phase consists of four well-defined steps:
   - Analyze the problem
   - Develop a solution
   - Code the solution
   - Test and debug the solution.

8. An algorithm is step-by-step procedure that must terminate and describes how a computation or task is to be performed.

9. A computer program is a self-contained unit of instructions used to operate a computer to produce a specific result. More formally, a computer program is a description of an algorithm written in a language that can be processed by a computer.

10. The four fundamental control structures are:
    - Sequence
    - Selection
    - Iteration
    - Invocation.

CHAPTER

2 | Problem Solving Using C

2.1 INTRODUCTION TO C

A well-designed program is constructed using a design philosophy similar to that used in constructing a well-designed building. It doesn't just happen; it depends on careful planning and execution of the final design to accomplish its intended purpose. Just as an integral part of the design of a building is its structure, the same is true for a program.

In programming, the term *structure* has two interrelated meanings. The first meaning refers to the program's overall construction, which is the topic of this section. The second meaning refers to the sequence, selection, and repetition forms used to code individual tasks within a program, which is the topic of Chapters 4 and 5. In relation to its first meaning, programs whose structure consists of interrelated segments, arranged in a logical and easily understandable order to form an integrated and complete unit, are referred to as modular programs (Figure 2.1). Modular programs are noticeably easier to develop, correct, and modify than programs constructed otherwise. In programming terminology, the smaller segments used to construct a modular program are referred to as *modules*.

Each module is designed and developed to perform a specific task, and is really a small subprogram all by itself. A complete C program is constructed

44

FIGURE 2.1   A Well-Designed Program Is Built Using Modules

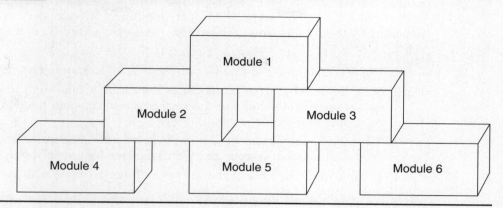

by combining as many modules as necessary to produce the desired result. The advantage of modular construction is that the overall design of the program can be developed before any single module is written. Once the requirements for each module are finalized, it can be programmed and integrated within the overall program as the module is completed. A module performs operations that are very limited in nature and are meant to handle at most one or two tasks required by the complete program. In C these modules are called *functions*. A function is a module that contains a sequence of operations encapsulated as a single unit.

It helps to think of a function as a small machine that transforms the data it receives into a finished product. For example, Figure 2.2 illustrates a function that accepts two numbers as inputs and multiplies the two numbers to produce one output. As illustrated, the interface to the function from the outside is its inputs and results. How the inputs are converted to results are both encapsulated and hidden within the function. In this regard the function can be thought of as a single unit providing a special-purpose operation.

FIGURE 2.2   A Multiplying Function

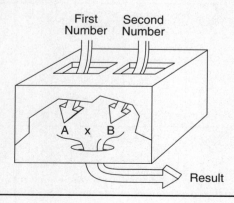

One important requirement for designing a good function is to give it a name that conveys to the reader some idea about what the function does. The names permissible for functions are also used to name other elements of the C language, and are collectively referred to as *identifiers*. Identifiers are composed of any combination of letters, digits, and underscores (_) selected according to the following rules.

1. The first character of the name must be a letter or underscore (_).
2. Only letters, digits, or underscores may follow the initial letter. Blank spaces are not allowed; use the underscore to separate words in a name consisting of multiple words.
3. A function name cannot be one of the keywords listed in Table 2.1. (A *keyword* is a word that is set aside by the language for a special purpose.[1])
4. The maximum number of characters in a function name is 31 characters.

Examples of valid C identifiers are:

```
deg_to_rad     intersect     add_nums     slope
bessel1        mult_two      find_max     density
```

Examples of invalid identifiers are:

```
1AB3     ◄──────────  (Begins with a number, which violates rule 1.)
E*6      ◄──────────  Contains a special character, which violates rule 2.)
while    ◄──────────  (This is a keyword, which violates rule 3.)
```

In addition to conforming to C's identifier rules, a C function name must always be followed by parentheses (the reason for these will be seen shortly). Also, a good function name should be a mnemonic. A *mnemonic* is a word or name designed as a memory aid. For example, the function name deg_to_rad() (note that we have included the required parentheses after the identifier, which clearly marks this as a function name) is a mnemonic if it is the name of a function that converts degrees to radians. Here, the name itself helps to identify what the function does.

Examples of valid function names that are not mnemonics are:

```
easy()    c3po()    r2d2()    theforce()    mike()
```

TABLE 2.1 Keywords

auto	default	float	register	struct	volatile
break	do	for	return	switch	while
case	double	goto	short	typedef	
char	else	if	signed	union	
const	enum	int	sizeof	unsigned	
continue	extern	long	static	void	

---

[1]Keywords in C are also reserved words, which means they must be used only for their specified purpose. Attempts to use them for any other purpose will generate an error message.

Nonmnemonic function names, however, should not be used because they convey no information about what the function does. Notice that all function names have been typed in lowercase letters. This is traditional in C, although it is not absolutely necessary. Uppercase letters are usually reserved for symbolic constants, a topic covered in Chapter 3, and for separating words in an identifier when underscores are not used. Thus, for example, the name `deg_to_rad` without underscores would be written as `degToRad`.

Note that C is a case-sensitive language. This means that the compiler distinguishes between uppercase and lowercase letters. Thus, in C, the names `TOTAL`, `total`, and `TotaL` represent three distinct and different names. For this reason, we will type function names predominantly in lower case, and reserve capitals for symbolic constants and multiple word names.

The main() Function

A distinct advantage of using functions in C is that the overall structure of the program, in general, and that of individual modules, in particular, can be planned in advance, including provision for testing and verifying each module's operation. Thus, we can plan what functions are needed and how they will interact with one another before writing them. Only then will we write each function to perform the task it is required to do.

Typically a `main()` function is used to provide for the orderly placement and execution of all other functions. Because the reserved word `main` tells the compiler where program execution is to begin, each C program must have one and only one function called `main()`. As the `main()` function is commonly used to invoke other functions by calling them in the sequence in which they are to operate (see Figure 2.3), this function is sometimes referred to as a driver function.[2]

Figure 2.4 illustrates a complete `main()` function. The first line of the function, in this case `void main(void)`, is referred to as a function header line. A function header line, which is always the first line of a function, contains three pieces of information:

1. What type of data, if any, is returned from the function
2. The name of the function
3. What type of data, if any, is sent into the function.

The keyword before the function name defines the type of value the function returns when it has completed operating. When placed before the function's name the keyword `void` (see Table 2.1) designates that the function will return no value. Similarly, when placed within the parentheses following the function name, `void` signifies that no data will be transmitted into the function when it is run. (Data transmitted into a function at run time are referred to as *arguments* of the function.) The braces, { and }, determine the beginning and end of the function body and enclose the statements making up the function. The statements inside the braces determine what the function does. Each statement inside the function must end with a semicolon (;).

You will be naming and writing many of your own C functions. In fact, the rest of this book is primarily about how to determine what functions are required

---

[2]Modules executed from `main()` may, in turn, execute other modules. Each module, however, always returns to the module that initiated its execution. This is true even for `main()`, which returns control to the operating system in effect when `main()` was initiated.

FIGURE 2.3   The main ( ) FunctionDirect All Other Functions

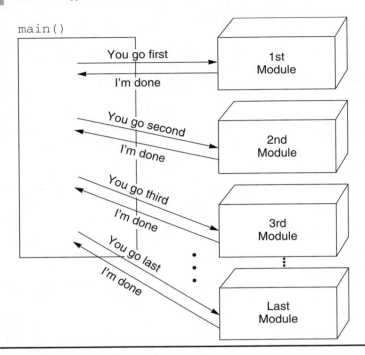

and how to write the functions. Each program, however, must have one and only one `main()` function. Until we learn how to pass data into a function and return data from a function (the topics of Chapter 6), the header line illustrated in Figure 2.4 will serve us for all the programs we need to write. In addition, many useful functions have already been written for us. We will now see how to use one of these functions to create our first working C program.

FIGURE 2.4   The structure of a main( ) Function

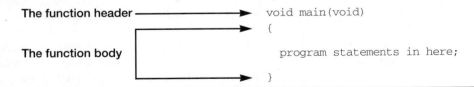

The printf() Function

One of the most versatile and commonly used functions provided by all C compilers is named `printf()`. This function, as its name suggests, is a print function that formats data given to it and sends it to the standard system display device. For most systems this display device is a video screen. This function prints out whatever is transmitted to it. For example, if the data *Hello there world!* is sent to `printf()`, this data is printed (or displayed) on your terminal by the `printf()` function.

FIGURE 2.5   Passing Data to a Function

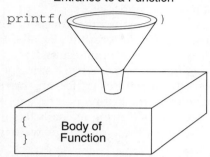

Entrance to a Function

printf( )

{
} Body of
Function

Inputting data to a function is called passing data to the function. The data *Hello there world!* is passed to the printf() function by surrounding the data within double quotes ("data in here") and "placing it within the parentheses in the function's name as follows.

```
printf("Hello there world!");
```

The purpose of the parentheses after a function's name is to provide a funnel through which information can be passed to the function (see Figure 2.5). As noted earlier, the items that are passed to the function through the parentheses are referred to as the function's arguments.Now let's put all this together into a working C program that can be run on your computer. Consider Program 2.1.

PROGRAM 2.1

```
#include <stdio.h>
void main(void)
{
   printf("Hello there world!");
}
```

The first line of the program:

```
#include <stdio.h>
```

is a preprocessor command. Preprocessor commands begin with a pound sign, # , and perform some action before the compiler translates the source program into machine code. Specifically, the #include preprocessor command causes the contents of the named file, in this case stdio.h, to be inserted where the #include command appears. The file stdio.h is referred to as a header file because it is placed at the top, or head, of a C program using the #include command. In particular, the stdio.h file provides a proper interface to the printf() function, and must be included in all programs using printf(). As indicated in Program 2.1, preprocessor commands do not end with a semicolon.

Following the preprocessor command is the start of the program's `main()` function. The `main()` function itself has only one statement. Remember that statements end with a semicolon (;). The statement in `main()` calls the function `printf()` and passes one argument to it. The argument is the string of characters `Hello there world!`

Since `printf()` is a prewritten function, we do not have to write it; it is available for use just by calling it correctly. Like all C functions, `printf()` was written to do a specific task, which is to print results. It is a very versatile function that can print results in many different forms. When a string of characters is passed to `printf()`, the function sees to it that the characters are correctly printed on your screen.

As we have seen, the beginning and end of a string of characters is marked by using double quotes ("string of characters in here") and passing such a string to `printf()` requires these quotes, as we have done in Program 2.1. The program's output is:

```
Hello there world!
```

Let us write another program to illustrate `printf()`'s versatility. Read Program 2.2 to determine what it does.

PROGRAM 2.2

```c
#include <stdio.h>
void main(void)
{
  printf("Computers, computers everywhere");
  printf("\n   as far as I can C\n");
}
```

When Program 2.2 is run, the following is displayed:

```
Computers, computers everywhere
      as far as I can C
```

You might be wondering why the `\n` did not appear in the output. The two characters `\` and `n`, when used together, are called a newline escape sequence. They tell `printf()` to start on a new line. In C, the backslash (`\`) character provides an "escape" from the normal interpretation of the character following it by altering the meaning of the next character. If the backslash was omitted from the second `printf()` call in Program 2.2, the n would be printed as the letter n and the program would print out:

```
Computers, computers everywheren    as far as I can C
```

Newline escape sequences can be placed anywhere within the message passed to `printf()`. See if you can determine what the following program prints:

```c
#include <stdio.h>
void main(void)
{
  printf("Computers everywhere\n as far as\n\nI can see\n");
}
```

The output for this program is:

```
Computers everywhere
 as far as

I can see
```

1. State whether the following are valid function names. If they are valid, state whether they are mnemonic names. (Recall that a mnemonic function name conveys some idea about the function's purpose.) If they are invalid names, state why.

m1234()	new_bal()	abcd()	A12345()	1A2345()
power()	abs_val()	mass()	do()	while()
add_5()	taxes()	net_pay()	12345()	int()
cosine()	a2b3c4d5()	netPay()	amount()	$sine()
oldBalance()	nevValue()	salestax()	1stApprox()	float()

2. Assume that the following functions have been written:

   retrieve_old_bal(), enter_sold_amt(), calc_ new_bal(), report()

   a. From the functions' names, what do you think each function might do?

   b. In what order do you think a main() function might execute these functions, based on their names?

3. Assume that the following functions have been written:

   input_bill(), calc_salestax(), calc_balance()

   a. From the functions' names, what do you think each function might do?

   b. In what order do you think a main() function might execute these functions, based on their names?

4. Determine names for functions that do the following:

   a. Find the average of a set of numbers.

   b. Find the area of a rectangle.

   c. Find the minimum value in a set of numbers.

   d. Convert a lowercase letter to an uppercase letter.

   e. Convert an uppercase letter to a lowercase letter.

   f. Sort a set of numbers from lowest to highest.

   g. Alphabetize a set of names.

5. Just as the keyword void can be used to signify that a function will return no value, the keywords int, char, float, and double can be used to signify that a function will return an integer, character, floating-point number, and double precision number. Using this information, write header lines for a main() function that will receive no arguments but will return:

   a. an integer

   b. a character

   c. a floating-point number

   d. a double precision number

6. a. Using the printf() function, write a C program that prints your name on one line, your street address on a second line, and your city, state, and zip code on the third line.

b. Compile and run the program you wrote for Exercise 6a. (*Hint:* To do this you must understand the procedures for entering, compiling, and running a C program on the particular computer you are using.)

7. a. Write a C program to print the following:

```
Computers, computers everywhere
    as far as I can see
I really, really like these things,
    Oh joy, Oh joy for me!
```

b. Compile and run the program you wrote for Exercise 7a.

8. a. How many printf() statements should be used to display the following?:

```
DEGREES    RADIANS
   0       0.0000
  90       1.5708
 180       3.1416
 270       4.7124
 360       6.2832
```

b. What is the minimum number of `printf()` statements that could be used to print the table in Exercise 8a? Why would you not write a program using the minimum number of `printf()` function calls?

c. Write a complete C program to produce the output illustrated in Exercise 8a.

d. Run the program you have written for Exercise 8c on a computer.

9. In response to a newline escape sequence, `printf()` positions the next displayed character at the beginning of a new line. This positioning of the next character actually represents two distinct operations. What are they?

10. a. Most computer operating systems provide the capability for redirecting the output produced by `printf()` either to a printer or directly to a floppy or hard disk file. Read the first part of Appendix D for a description of this redirection capability.

b. If your computer supports output redirection, run the program written for Exercise 7a using this feature. Have your program's display redirected to a file named poem.

c. If your computer supports output redirection to a printer, run the program written for Exercise 7a using this feature.

Note: Most projects, both programming and nonprogramming, can be structured into smaller subtasks or units of activity. These smaller subtasks can often be delegated to different people so that when all the tasks are finished and integrated, the project or program is completed. For Exercises 11 through 16, determine a set of subtasks that, taken together, complete the required task. (The purpose of these exercises is to have you consider the different ways that complex tasks can be structured. Although there is no one correct solution to these exercises, there are incorrect solutions and solutions that are better than others. An incorrect solution is one that does not complete the task correctly. One solution is better than another if it more clearly or easily identifies what must be done or does it more efficiently.)

11. You are given the task of wiring and installing lights in the attic of your house. Determine a set of subtasks that, taken together, accomplishes this. (*Hint:* The first subtask would be to determine the placement of the light fixtures.)

12. You are given the job of preparing a complete meal for five people next weekend. Determine a set of subtasks, that taken together, accomplishes this. (*Hint:* One subtask, not necessarily the first one, would be to buy the food.)

13. You are a sophomore in college and are planning to go to law school after graduation. List a set of major objectives that you must fulfill to meet this goal. (*Hint:* One objective is "Take the right courses.")

14. You are given the job of planting a vegetable garden. Determine a set of subtasks that accomplishes this. (*Hint:* One such subtask would be to plan the layout of the garden.)

15. You are responsible for planning and arranging the family camping trip this summer. List a set of subtasks that, taken together, accomplishes this. (*Hint:* One subtask would be to select the camp site.)

16. a. A national electrical supply distribution company desires a computer system to prepare its customer invoices. The system must, of course, be capable of creating each day's invoices. Additionally, the company wants the capability to retrieve and output a printed report of all invoices that meet certain criteria, for example, all invoices sent in a particular month with a net value of more than a given dollar amount, all invoices sent in a year to a particular client, or all invoices sent to firms in a particular state. For this system, determine three or four major program units into which the system could be separated. (*Hint:* One program unit is "Prepare invoices" to create each day's invoices.)

    b. Suppose someone enters incorrect data for a particular invoice, which is discovered after the data has been entered and stored by the system. What program unit is needed to take care of correcting this problem? Discuss why such a program unit might or might not be required by most business systems.

    c. Assume a program unit exists that allows a user to alter or change data that has been incorrectly entered and stored. Discuss the need for including an "audit trail" that would allow for later reconstruction of the changes made, when they were made, and who made them.

2.2 PROGRAMMING STYLE

C programs start execution at the beginning of the `main()` function. Since a program can have only one starting point, every C language program must contain one and only one `main()` function. As we have seen, all of the statements that make up the `main()` function are then included within the braces { } following the function name. Although the `main()` function must be present in every C program, C does not require that the word `main`, the parentheses (), or the braces { } be placed in any particular form. The form used in the last section

```
void main(void)
{
    program statements in here;
}
```

was chosen strictly for clarity and ease in reading the program. For example, the following general form of a `main()` function would also work:

```
void main
(void
){ first statement;second statement;
third statement;fourth
statement;}
```

Notice that more than one statement can be put on a line, or one statement can be written across lines. Except for strings of characters contained within double quotes, function names, and keywords, C ignores all whitespace (*whitespace* refers to any combination of one or more blank spaces, tabs, or new lines). For example, changing the whitespace in Program 2.1 and making sure not to split the string `Hello there world!` or the function names `printf` and `main` across two lines results in the following valid program:

```
#include <stdio.h>
void main
(void
){printf
("Hello there world!"
);}
```

Although this version of `main()` does work, it is an example of extremely poor programming style. It is difficult to read and understand. For readability, the `main()` function should always be written in standard form as:

```
#include <stdio.h>
void main(void)
{
    program statements in here;
}
```

In this standard form the function name starts in column 1 and is placed with the required parentheses on a line by itself. The opening brace of the function body follows on the next line and is placed under the first letter of the function name. Similarly, the closing function brace is placed by itself in column 1 as the last line of the function. This structure serves to highlight the function as a single unit.

Within the function itself, all program statements are typically indented at least two spaces, although indentation is not required. Indentation is another sign of good programming practice, especially if the same indentation is used to align similar groups of statements. Review Program 2.2 to see that the same indentation was used for both `printf()` function calls.

As you progress in your understanding and mastery of C, you will develop your own indentation standards. Just keep in mind that the final form of your programs should be consistent and should always serve as an aid to the reading and understanding of your programs.

Comments

Comments are explanatory remarks made within a program. When used carefully, comments can be very helpful in clarifying what the complete program is about, what a specific group of statements is meant to accomplish, or what one line is intended to do.

The symbols `/*`, with no whitespace between them, designate the start of a comment. Similarly, the symbols `*/`, as a single unit with no intervening whitespace, designate the end of a comment.[3] For example,

```
/* this is a comment */
/* this program prints out a message */
/* this program calculates a square root */
```

are all comment lines.

___

[3]Additionally, some compilers permit the start of a comment to be designated by double slashes (`//`). Such comments extend only to the end of the line on which they are written.

Comments can be placed anywhere within a program and have no effect on program execution. The computer ignores all comments—they are there strictly for the convenience of anyone reading the program.

A comment can be written either on a line by itself or on the same line containing a program statement. Program 2.3 illustrates the use of comments within a program.

PROGRAM 2.3

```
#include <stdio.h>
/* this program prints a message */
void main(void)
{
  printf("Hello there world!\n"); /* a call to printf() */
}
```

The first comment appears on a line by itself above the main() function and describes what the program does. This is generally a good location to include a short comment describing the program's purpose. The second comment appears on the same line as that containing the printf() function call. If a comment is too long to be contained on one line, it can be continued across two or more lines as illustrated below:

```
/* this comment is used to illustrate a
   comment that extends over two lines */
```

Under no circumstances can comments be nested—one comment containing another comment within itself. For example,

```
/* this nested comment is /* always */ invalid */
```

Typically, many comments are required when using nonstructured programming languages. These comments are necessary to clarify the purpose of either the program itself or individual sections and lines of code within the program. In C, the program's structure is intended to make the program readable, making the use of extensive comments unnecessary. This is reinforced if both function names and variable names, described in the next chapter, are carefully selected to convey their meaning to anyone reading the program. However, if the purpose of a function or any of its statements is still not clear from its structure, name, or context, include comments where clarification is needed.

Exercises 2.2

1. a. Will the following program work?

```
#include <stdio.h>
void main(void){printf("Hello there world!");}
```

   b. Why is the program given in Exercise 1a not a good program?

2. Rewrite the following programs to conform to good programming practice.

   a. #include <stdio.h>

```
void main(void
) {
printf
(
"The time has come\n"
);}
```

b. ```
   #include <stdio.h>
   void main
   (void){printf("Newark is a city\n");printf(
   "In New Jersey\n"); printf
   (It is also a city\n"
   ); printf(In Delaware\n"
   );}
   ```

c. ```
   #include <stdio.h>
   void main(void){printf("Reading a program\n");printf(
   "is much easier\n"
   );printf("if a standard form for main is used\n")
   ;printf
   ("and each statement is written\n");printf(
   "on a line by itself\n")
   ;}
   ```

d. ```
   #include <stdio.h>
   void main
   (void){printf("Every C program"
   );printf
   ("\nmust have one and only one"
   );
   printf("main function"
   );
   printf(
   "\n the escape sequence of characters")
   ;printf
   "\nfor a newline can be placed anywhere"
   );printf
   ("\n within the message passed to printf()"
   );}
   ```

3. a. When used in a message, the backslash character alters the meaning of the character immediately following it. If we wanted to print the backslash character, we would have to tell printf() to escape from the way it normally interprets the backslash. What character do you think is used to alter the way a single backslash character is interpreted?

   b. Using your answer to Exercise 3a, write the escape sequence for printing a backslash.

4. a. A *token* of a computer language is any sequence of characters that, as a unit, with no intervening characters or whitespace, has a unique meaning. Using this definition of a token, determine whether escape sequences, function names, and the keywords listed in Table 2.1 are tokens of the C language.

   b. Discuss whether adding whitespace to a message alters the message. Discuss whether messages can be considered tokens of C.

   c. Using the definition of a token given in Exercise 4a, determine whether the statement "Except for tokens of the language, C ignores all whitespace" is true.
   ```

2.3 DATA CONSTANTS AND ARITHMETIC OPERATIONS

C programs can process different types of data in different ways. For example, calculating the bacteria growth in a polluted pond requires mathematical operations on numerical data, while sorting a list of names requires comparison operations using alphabetical data. In this section we introduce C's elementary data types and the operations that can be performed on them. Additionally, we show how to use the `printf()` function to display the results of these operations.

The three basic data values used in C are integers, floating-point numbers, and character values. Each of these data values is described in the following subsections.

Integer Numbers

An *integer number* or integer value is zero or any positive or negative number without a decimal point. Examples of valid integer values are:

$$0 \quad 5 \quad -10 \quad +25 \quad 1000 \quad 253 \quad -26351 \quad +36$$

As these examples illustrate, integers may be signed (have a leading + or − sign) or unsigned (no leading + or − sign). No commas, decimal points, or special symbols, such as the dollar sign, are allowed. Examples of invalid integer values are:

$$\$255.62 \quad 2,523 \quad 3. \quad 6,243,892 \quad 1,492.89 \quad +6.0$$

Different computer types have their own internal limit on the largest (most positive) and smallest (most negative) integer values that can be used in a program. These limits depend on the amount of storage each computer sets aside for an integer; as such, they are said to be implementation dependent. The more commonly used storage allocations are listed in Table 2.2. (Review Section 1.5 if you are unfamiliar with the concept of a byte.) By referring to your computer's reference manual or using the `sizeof` operator introduced in the next section you can determine the actual number of bytes allocated by your computer for each integer value.

Sometimes larger integer numbers are required than those supported by the memory allocations shown in Table 2.2. For example, many applications use dates, such as 7/12/96. Typically such dates are converted to the number of days

TABLE 2.2 Integer Values and Word Size*

Word Size	Maximum Integer Value	Minimum Integer Value
1 byte	127	−128
2 bytes	32,767	−32,768
4 bytes	2,147,483,647	−2,147,483,648

*It is interesting to note that in all cases the magnitude of the most negative integer allowed is always one more than the magnitude of the most positive integer. This is due to the method most commonly used to represent integers, called two's complement representation. For an explanation of two's complement representation see Section 1.5.

from the turn of the century, which makes it possible to store and sort dates using a single number for each date. Unfortunately, for dates after 1987, the number of days from the turn of the century is larger than the maximum of 32,767 allowed by some compilers.

To accommodate real application requirements such as this, C provides for long integer data values. This is done by appending the letter L (either uppercase or lowercase) to the number. For example, 57682L indicates a long integer value.

As with integer values, the amount of storage allocated for a long integer is compiler dependent. Although you would expect that a long integer value would be allocated more space than a standard integer, this may not be the case, especially for computers that reserve more than two bytes for normal integer values. About all that can be said is that long integers will provide no less space than regular integers. The actual amount of storage allocated by your computer should be checked by the `sizeof` operator described at the end of Section 2.4.

Floating-Point Numbers

A *floating-point number*, which is also called a *real number*, is any signed or unsigned number having a decimal point. Examples of floating-point numbers are:

```
+10.625    5.    -6.2    3251.92    0.0    0.33    -6.67    +2.
```

Notice that the numbers `5.`, `0.0`, and `+2.` are classified as floating-point numbers, while the same numbers written without a decimal point (`5`, `0`, `+2`) would be integer values. As with integer values, special symbols, such as the dollar sign and the comma, are not permitted in real numbers. Examples of invalid real numbers are:

```
5,326.25    24    123    6,459    $10.29
```

C supports two different categories of floating-point numbers: floats and doubles. The difference between these numbers is the amount of storage that a computer uses for each type. Most computers use twice the amount of storage for doubles than for floats, which allows a double to have approximately twice the precision of a float (for this reason floats are sometimes referred to as single-precision numbers and doubles as *double-precision numbers*). The actual storage allocation for each data type, however, depends on the particular computer. In computers that use the same amount of storage for both single- and double-precision numbers, these two data types become identical. The `sizeof` operator introduced in Section 2.4 will allow you to determine the amount of storage reserved by your computer for each of these data types. A double number is indicated to the computer by appending an L (either uppercase or lower case) to the number. In the absence of these suffixes, a floating-point number is considered as a float (single-precision) value. For example:

9.234 indicates a float (single precision) value

9.234L indicates a double (double precision) value

The only difference in these numbers is the amount of storage the computer may use to store them. For numbers having more than six decimal places to the right of the decimal point, this storage becomes important. Appendix E describes the binary storage format typically used for real values and its impact on number precision. As previously noted, the exact difference, if any, in allocated storage is computer dependent. The only requirement made by C is that a double cannot provide any less precision than a float.

Exponential Notation   Floating-point numbers can be written in exponential notation, which is similar to scientific notation and is commonly used to express both very large and very small numbers in a compact form. The following examples illustrate how numbers with decimals can be expressed in exponential and scientific notation.

Decimal Notation	Exponential Notation	ScientificNotation
1625.	1.625e3	1.625×10^3
63421.	6.3421e4	6.3421×10^4
.00731	7.31e−3	7.31×10^{-3}
.000625	6.25e−4	6.25×10^{-4}

In exponential notation, the letter e stands for exponent. The number following the e represents a power of 10 and indicates the number of places the decimal point should be moved to obtain the standard decimal value. The decimal point is moved to the right if the number after the e is positive, or to the left if the number after the e is negative. For example, the e3 in the number 1.625e3 means move the decimal place three places to the right, so that the number becomes 1625. The e-3 in the number 7.31e-3 means move the decimal point three places to the left, so that 7.31e-3 becomes .00731.

Character Values

The third basic type of data recognized by C are characters. *Characters* include the letters of the alphabet (both uppercase and lowercase), the ten digits 0 through 9, and special symbols such as $+$ \$. , $-$!. A single character value is any one letter, digit, or special symbol enclosed by single quotes. Examples of valid character values are:

```
'A'     '$'     'b'     '7'     'y'     '!'     'M'     'q'
```

   Character values are typically stored in a computer using either the ASCII or EBCDIC codes. *ASCII* (pronounced "ass-key") is an acronym for American Standard Code for Information Interchange. *EBCDIC* (pronounced either as ebb-sah-dick or ebb-see-dick) is an acronym for Extended Binary Coded Decimal Interchange Code. Each of these codes assigns individual characters to a specific pattern of 0's and 1's. Table 2.3 lists the correspondence between bit patterns and the uppercase letters of the alphabet used by the ASCII and EBCDIC codes.

   Using Table 2.3, we can determine how the characters 'W', 'E', 'S', 'T', 'B', and 'Y', for example, are stored inside a computer that uses the ASCII character code. Using the ASCII code, this sequence of characters requires six bytes of storage (one byte for each letter) and would be stored as illustrated in Figure 2.6.

Escape Sequences

When a backslash (\) is used directly in front of a select group of characters, the backslash tells the computer to escape from the way these characters would normally be interpreted. For this reason, the combination of a backslash and these specific characters is called an *escape sequence*. We have already encountered an example of this in the newline escape sequence, \n. Table 2.4 lists C's most commonly used escape sequences.

TABLE 2.3 The ASCII and EBCDIC Uppercase Letter Codes

Letter	ASCII Code	EBCDIC Code	Letter	ASCII Code	EBCDIC Code
A	01000001	11000001	N	01001110	11010101
B	01000010	11000010	O	01001111	11010110
C	01000011	11000011	P	01010000	11010111
D	01000100	11000100	Q	01010001	11011000
E	01000101	11000101	R	01010010	11011001
F	01000110	11000110	S	01010011	11100010
G	01000111	11000111	T	01010100	11100011
H	01001000	11001000	U	01010101	11100100
I	01001001	11001001	V	01010110	11100101
J	01001010	11010001	W	01010111	11100110
K	01001011	11010010	X	01011000	11100111
L	01001100	11010011	Y	01011001	11101000
M	01001101	11010100	Z	01011010	11101001

Although each escape sequence listed in Table 2.4 is made up of two distinct characters, the combination of the two characters with no intervening whitespace causes the computer to store one character code. Table 2.5 lists the ASCII code byte patterns for the escape sequences listed in Table 2.4.

FIGURE 2.6   The Letters WESTBY Stored Inside a Computer

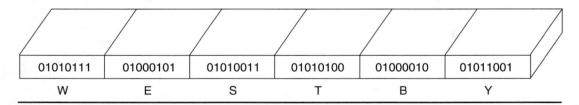

6 bytes of storage

01010111	01000101	01010011	01010100	01000010	01011001
W	E	S	T	B	Y

Arithmetic Operations

Integers and real numbers can be added, subtracted, multiplied, and divided. Although it is usually better not to mix integers and real numbers when performing arithmetic operations, predictable results are obtained when different data types are used in the same arithmetic expression. Somewhat surprising is the fact that character data can also be added and subtracted with both character and integer data to produce useful results.

TABLE 2.4 Escape Sequences

Escape Sequence	Meaning
\b	Move back one space
\f	Move to next page
\n	Move to next line
\r	Carriage return
\t	Move to next tab setting
\\	Backslash character
\'	Single quote
\nnn	Treat nnn as an octal number

The operators used for arithmetic operations are called arithmetic operators, and are listed next:

Operation	Operator
Addition	+
Subtraction	−
Multiplication	*
Division	/
Modulus division	%

A *simple arithmetic expression* consists of an arithmetic operator connecting two operands in the form:

operand *operator* operand

Examples of arithmetic expressions are:

```
3 + 7
18 - 3
12.62 + 9.8
0.08 * 12.2
12.6 / 2.
```

The spaces around the arithmetic operators in these examples are inserted strictly for clarity and can be omitted without affecting the value of the expression.

TABLE 2.5 The ASCII Escape Sequence Codes

C Escape Sequence	Meaning	Computer Code
\b	Backspace	00001000
\f	Form feed	00001100
\n	Newline	00001010
\r	Carriage return	00001101
\\	Backslash	01011100
\'	Single quote	00100111
\"	Double quote	00100010

The value of any arithmetic expression can be displayed using the `printf()` function. Doing this requires passing two items to `printf()`: a control string that tells the function where and in what form the result is to be displayed, and the expression that we wish to evaluate. For example, the value of the expression `6 * 14` can be displayed using the statement:

```
printf("The value of 6 times 14 is %d\n", 6 * 14);
```

This statement passes two arguments to the `printf()` function. The first argument is the message `The value of 6 times 14 is %d\n` and the second argument is the value of the expression `6 * 14`.

The first argument passed to `printf()` must always be a message. A message that also includes a conversion control sequence, such as %d, is termed a control string.[4] Conversion control sequences have a special meaning to the `printf()` function. They tell the function what type of value is to be displayed and where to display it. Conversion control sequences are also referred to as conversion specifications and format specifiers. A conversion control sequence always begins with a `%` symbol and ends with a conversion character (`c`, `d`, `f`, etc.). As we will see, additional formatting characters can be placed between the `%` symbol and the conversion character.

The percent sign % in a conversion sequence tells `printf()` that we wish to print an argument value at the place in the message where the `%` is located. The `d`, placed immediately after the `%`, tells `printf()` that the value should be printed as an integer.

When `printf()` sees the conversion control sequence in its control string, it substitutes the value of the next argument in place of the conversion control sequence. Since this next argument is the expression `6 * 14`, which has a value of 84, it is this value that is displayed. Also, as indicated in the example, all arguments passed to the `printf()` function must be separated by commas. Thus, the statement

```
printf("The value of 6 times 14 is %d\n", 6 * 14);
```

causes the printout

```
The value of 6 times 14 is 84
```

Just as the `%d` conversion control sequence alerts `printf()` that an integer value is to be displayed, the conversion control sequence `%f` (the `f` stands for floating point) indicates that a number with a decimal point is to be displayed. For example, the statement

```
printf("The value of 0.06 times 14.8 is %f\n", 0.06 * 14.8);
```

causes the display

```
The value of 0.06 times 14.8 is .888000
```

As this display shows, the `%f` conversion control sequence causes `printf()` to display six digits to the right of the decimal place. If the number does not have six decimal digits, zeros are added to the number to fill the fractional part. If the number has more than six decimal digits, the fractional part is rounded to six decimal digits.

One caution should be mentioned here. The `printf()` function does not check the values it is given. If an integer conversion control sequence is used

---

[4]More formally, a control string is referred to as a control specifier. We will use the more descriptive term, control string, to emphasize that a string is being referenced.

(%d, for example) and the value given the function is either a floating-point or double-precision number, there is no telling what value will be displayed. Similarly, if a floating-point conversion control sequence is used and the corresponding number is an integer, an unanticipated result will occur.

Character data is displayed using the %c conversion control sequence.[5] For example, the statement

```
printf("The first letter of the alphabet is an %c.",'a');
```

causes the display

```
The first letter of the alphabet is an a.
```

Program 2.4 illustrates using printf() to display the results of an expression within the statements of a complete program.

PROGRAM 2.4

```
#include <stdio.h>
void main(void)
{
  printf("%f plus %f equals %f\n", 15.0, 2.0, 15.0 + 2.0);
  printf("%f minus %f equals %f\n",15.0, 2.0, 15.0 - 2.0);
  printf("%f times %f equals %f\n",15.0, 2.0, 15.0 * 2.0);
  printf("%f divided by %f equals %f\n",15.0, 2.0, 15.0 / 2.0);
}
```

The output of Program 2.4 is:

```
15.000000 plus 2.000000 equals 17.000000
15.000000 minus 2.000000 equals 13.000000
15.000000 times 2.000000 equals 30.000000
15.000000 divided by 2.000000 equals 7.500000
```

Notice that each statement in Program 2.4 passes four arguments to the printf() function consisting of one control string and three values. Within each control string there are three %f conversion control sequences (one for each value that is to be displayed).

Expression Types   An *expression* that contains only integer operands is called an integer expression, and the result of the expression is an integer value. Similarly, an expression containing only floating-point operands (single and double precision) is called a floating-point expression, and the result of such an expression is a floating-point value. An expression containing both integer and floating-point operands is called a *mixed-mode* expression. Although it is usually better not to mix integer and floating-point operands in an arithmetic operations, the data type of each operation is determined by the following rules:

---

[5]It can also be printed using the %s conversion control sequence. More precisely, the %c sequence designates exactly one character value, where %s designates a string of one or more characters. Thus, printf("Hello World!") is equivalent to printf("%s","Hello World!").

1. If both operands are integers, the result of the operation is an integer.
2. If one operand is a floating point value, the result of the operation is a double precision value.

Notice that the result of an arithmetic expression is never a single-precision (float) number. This is because the computer temporarily converts all floats to double-precision numbers when arithmetic is being done.

Integer Division

The division of two integers can produce rather strange results for the unwary. For example, dividing the integer 15 by the integer 2 yields an integer result. Since integers cannot contain a fractional part, the possibly expected result, 7.5, is not obtained. In C, the fractional part of the result obtained when dividing two integers is dropped (truncated). Thus, the value of 15/2 is 7, the value of 9/4 is 2, and the value of 19/5 is 3.

There are times when we would like to retain the remainder of an integer division. To do this C provides an arithmetic operator that captures the remainder when two integers are divided. This operator, called the *modulus operator,* has the symbol %. The modulus operator can be used only with integers. For example,

9 % 4 is 1

17 % 3 is 2

14 % 2 is 0

A Unary Operator (Negation)

Besides the binary operators for addition, subtraction, multiplication, and division, C also provides unary operators. One of these unary operators uses the same symbol that is used for binary subtraction ($-$). The minus sign used in front of a single numerical operand negates (reverses the sign of) the number.

Table 2.6 summarizes the six arithmetic operations we have described so far and lists the data type of the result produced by each operator based on the data type of the operands involved.

TABLE 2.6 Summary of Arithmetic Operators

Operation	Operator	Type	Operand	Result
Addition	+	Binary	Both integers	Integer
			One operand not an integer	Double precision
Subtraction	−	Binary	Both integers	Integer
			One operand not an integer	Double precision
Multiplication	*	Binary	Both integers	Integer
			One operand not an integer	Double precision
Division	/	Binary	Both integers	Integer
			One operand not an integer	Double precision
Modulus negation	%	Binary	Both integers	Integer
Negation	−	Unary	One integer	Integer
			One floating-point or double-precision operand	Double precision

Operator Precedence and Associativity

Besides such simple expressions as 5 + 12 and .08 * 26.2, we frequently need to create more complex arithmetic expressions. C, like most other programming languages, requires that certain rules be followed when writing expressions containing more than one arithmetic operator:

1. Two binary arithmetic operator symbols must never be placed side by side. For example, 5 * %6 is invalid because the two operators * and % are placed next to each other.

2. Parentheses should be used to form groupings, and all expressions enclosed within parentheses are evaluated first. For example, in the expression (6 + 4) / (2 + 3), the 6 + 4 and 2 + 3 are evaluated first to yield 10 / 5. The 10 / 5 is then evaluated to yield 2.

3. Sets of parentheses may also be enclosed by other parentheses. For example, the expression (2 * (3 + 7)) / 5 is valid. When parentheses are used within parentheses, the expressions in the innermost parentheses are always evaluated first. The evaluation continues from innermost to outermost parentheses until the expressions of all parentheses have been evaluated. The number of right-facing parentheses, (, must always equal the number of left-facing parentheses,), so that there are no unpaired sets.

4. Parentheses cannot be used to indicate multiplication. The multiplication operator, *, must be used. For example, the expression (3 + 4) (5 + 1) is invalid. The correct expression is (3 + 4) * (5 + 1).

Parentheses should be used to specify logical groupings of operands and to indicate clearly to both the computer and programmers the intended order of arithmetic operations. In the absence of parentheses, expressions containing multiple operators are evaluated by the priority, or *precedence*, of the operators. Table 2.7 lists both the precedence and *associativity* of the operators considered in this section.

TABLE 2.7 Operator Precedence and Associativity

Operator	Associativity
unary −	Right to left
* / %	Left to right
+ −	Left to right

The precedence of an operator establishes its priority relative to all other operators. Operators at the top of Table 2.7 have a higher priority than operators at the bottom of the table. In expressions with multiple operators, the operator with the higher precedence is used before an operator with a lower precedence. For example, in the expression 6 + 4 / 2 + 3, the division is done before the addition, yielding an intermediate result of 6 + 2 + 3. The additions are then performed to yield a final result of 11.

Expressions containing operators with the same precedence are evaluated according to their associativity. This means that evaluation is either from left to right or from right to left as each operator is encountered. For example, in the expression `8 + 5 * 7 % 2 * 4`, the multiplication and modulus operator are of higher precedence than the addition operator and are evaluated first. Both of these operators, however, are of equal precedence. Therefore, these operators are evaluated according to their left-to-right associativity, yielding

```
8 + 5 * 7 % 2 * 4 =
8 + 35 % 2 * 4 =
    8 + 1 * 4 =
    8 + 4 = 12
```

Exercises 2.3

1. Determine data types appropriate for the following data:

   a. the average of four grades

   b. the number of days in a month

   c. the length of the Golden Gate Bridge

   d. the numbers in a state lottery

   e. the distance from Brooklyn, NY to Newark, NJ

   f. the names in a mailing list

2. Convert the following numbers into standard decimal form:

   6.34e5   1.95162e2   8.395e1   2.95e-3   4.623e-4

3. Write the following decimal numbers using exponential notation:

   126.   656.23   3426.95   4893.2   .321   .0123   .006789

4. Listed below are correct algebraic expressions and incorrect C expressions corresponding to them. Find the errors and write corrected C expressions.

	Algebra	*C Expression*
a.	(2)(3) + (4)(5)	(2)(3) + (4)(5)
b.	$\frac{6 + 18}{2}$	6 + 18 / 2
c.	$\frac{4.5}{12.2 - 3.1}$	4.5 / 12.2 - 3.1
d.	4.6(3.0 + 14.9)	4.6(3.0 + 14.9)
e.	(12.1 + 18.9)(15.3 − 3.8)	(12.1 + 18.9)(15.3 - 3.8)

5. Determine the value of the following integer expressions:

   a. `3 + 4 * 6`

   b. `3 * 4 / 6 + 6`

   c. `2 * 3 / 12 * 8 / 4`

   d. `10 * (1 + 7 * 3)`

   e. `20 - 2 / 6 + 3`

   f. `20 - 2 / (6 + 3)`

   g. `(20 - 2) / 6 + 3`

   h. `(20 - 2) / (6 + 3)`

    i. 50 % 20

    j. (10 + 3) % 4

6. Determine the value of the following floating point expressions:

    a. 3.0 + 4.0 * 6.0

    b. 3.0 * 4.0 / 6.0   6.0

    c. 2.0 * 3.0 / 12.0 * 8.0 / 4.0

    d. 10.0 * (1.0 + 7.0 * 3.0)

    e. 20.0 - 2.0 / 6.0 + 3.0

    f. 20.0 - 2.0 / (6.0 + 3.0)

    g. (20.0 - 2.0) / 6.0 + 3.0

    h. (20.0 - 2.0) / (6.0 + 3.0)

7. Assume that amount has the integer value 1, m has the integer value 50, n has the integer value 10, and p has the integer value 5; evaluate the following expressions:

    a. n / p + 3

    b. m / p + n - 10 * amount

    c. m - 3 * n + 4 * amount

    d. amount / 5

    e. 18 / p

    f. -p * n

    g. -m / 20

    h. (m + n) / (p + amount)

    i. m + n / p + amount

8. Using the system reference manuals for your computer, determine the character code used by your computer.

9. Determine the output of the following program:

```
#include <stdio.h>
void main(void)   /* a program illustrating integer truncation */
{
    printf("answer1 is the integer %d\n", 9/4);
    printf("\nanswer2 is the integer %d\n", 17/3);
}
```

10. Determine the output of the following program:

```
#include <stdio.h>
void main(void)   /* a program illustrating the % operator */
{
    printf("The remainder of 9 divided by 4 is %d\n", 9 % 4);
    printf("The remainder of 17 divided by 3 is %d\n", 17 % 3);
}
```

11. Write a C program that displays the results of the expressions 3.0 * 5.0, 7.1 * 8.3 - 2.2, and 3.2 / (6.1 * 5). Calculate the value of these expressions manually to verify that the displayed values are correct.

12. Write a C program that displays the results of the expressions 15 / 4, 15 % 4, and 5 * 3 - (6 * 4). Calculate the value of these expressions manually to verify that the displayed values are correct.

13. a. Show how the name KINGSLEY would be stored inside a computer that uses the ASCII code. That is, draw a figure similar to Figure 2.8 for the letters KINGSLEY.

    b. Show how the name KINGSLEY would be stored inside a computer that uses the EBCDIC code.

14. a. Repeat Exercise 13a using the letters of your own last name.

    b. Repeat Exercise 13b using the letters of your own last name.

15. Enter, compile, and run Program 2.1 on your computer system.

16. Since computers use different representations for storing integer, floating-point, double-precision, and character values, discuss how a program might alert the computer to the data types of the various values it will be using.

17. Although we have concentrated on operations involving integer and floating-point numbers, C allows characters and integers to be added or subtracted. This can be done because C always converts a character to an equivalent integer value whenever a character is used in an arithmetic expression. Thus, characters and integers can be freely mixed in such expressions. For example, if your computer uses the ASCII code, the expression 'a' + 1 equals 'b', and 'z' - 1 equals 'y'. Similarly, 'A' + 1 is 'B', and 'Z' - 1 is 'Y'. With this as background, determine the character results of the following expressions (assume that all characters are stored using the ASCII code).

    a. 'm' - 5

    b. 'm' + 5

    c. 'G' + 6

    d. 'G' - 6

    e. 'b' - 'a'

    f. 'g' - 'a' + 1

    g. 'G' - 'A' + 1

    Note: For the following exercise the reader should have an understanding of basic computer storage concepts. Specifically, if you are unfamiliar with the concept of a byte, refer to Section 1.5 before doing the next exercise.

18. Although the total number of bytes varies from computer to computer, memory sizes of 65,536 to more than several million bytes are not uncommon. In computer language, the letter K is used to represent the number 1024, which is 2 raised to the 10th power and M is used to represent the number 1,048,576, which is 2 raised to the 20th power. Thus, a memory size of 640K is really 64 times 1024, or 655,360 bytes, and a memory size of 4M is really 4 times 1,048,576, which is 4,194,304 bytes. Using this information, calculate the actual number of bytes in:

    a. a memory containing 512K bytes

    b. a memory containing 2M bytes

    c. a memory containing 8M bytes

    d. a memory containing 16M bytes

    e. a memory consisting of 4M words, where each word consists of 2 bytes

    f. a memory consisting of 4M words, where each word consists of 4 bytes

    g. a floppy diskette that can store 1.44M bytes

2.4 VARIABLES AND DECLARATION STATEMENTS

All integer, floating-point, and other values used in a computer program are stored and retrieved from the computer's memory unit. Conceptually, individual memory locations in the memory unit are arranged like the rooms in a large hotel. Like hotel rooms, each memory location has a unique address ("room number"). Before high-level languages such as C existed, memory locations were referenced by their addresses. For example, to store the integer values 45 and 12 in the memory locations 1652 and 2548 (see Figure 2.7), respectively, required instructions equivalent to

Put a 45 in location 1652.
Put a 12 in location 2548.

To add the two numbers just stored and save the result in another memory location, for example at location 3000, required a statement comparable to

Add the contents of location 1652
to the contents of location 2548
and store the result into location 3000.

Clearly this method of storage and retrieval is a cumbersome process. In high-level languages like C, symbolic names are used in place of actual memory addresses. These symbolic names are called *variables*. A variable is simply a name given by the programmer that is used to refer to computer storage locations. The term variable is used because the value stored in the variable can change, or vary. For each name that the programmer uses, the computer keeps track of the actual memory address corresponding to that name. In our hotel room analogy, this is equivalent to putting a name on the door of a room and referring to the room by this name, such as the BLUE room, rather than using the actual room number.

In C the selection of variable names is left to the programmer, as long as the following rules are observed:

1. The variable name must begin with a letter or underscore (_), and may contain only letters, underscores, or digits. It cannot contain any blanks, commas, or special symbols, such as ( ) & , $ # . ! \ ?
2. A variable name cannot be a keyword (see Table 2.1).
3. The variable name cannot consist of more than 31 characters.

These rules are similar to those used for selecting function names. As with function names, variable names should be mnemonics that give some indication of the variable's use. For example, a good name for a variable used to store a value that is the total of some other values would be sum or total. Variable names

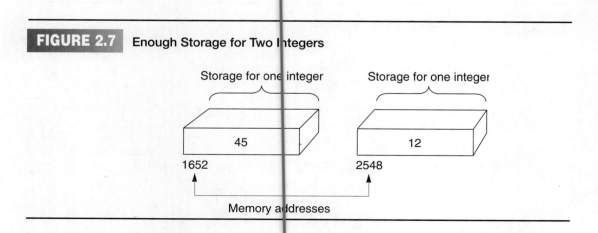

FIGURE 2.7   Enough Storage for Two Integers

Storage for one integer   Storage for one integer

45   12

1652   2548

Memory addresses

that give no indication of the value stored, such as `r2d2`, `linda`, `bill`, and `getum`, should not be selected. As with function names, all variable names are typed in lowercase letters. This again is traditional in C, although not required.

Now assume that the first memory location illustrated in Figure 2.9, which has address 1652, is given the name `num1`. Also assume that memory location 2548 is given the variable name `num2`, and memory location 3000 is given the variable name `total`, as illustrated in Figure 2.8. Using these variable names, the operation of storing 45 in location 1652, storing 12 in location 2548, and adding the contents of these two locations is accomplished by the C statements

```
num1 = 45;
num2 = 12;
total = num1 + num2;
```

Each of these three statements is called an *assignment statement* because it tells the computer to assign (store) a value into a variable. Assignment statements always have an equal (=) sign and one variable name immediately to the left of this sign. The value on the right of the equal sign is determined first and this value is assigned to the variable on the left of the equal sign. The blank spaces in the assignment statements are inserted for readability. We will have much more to say about assignment statements in the next chapter, but for now we can use them to store values in variables.

A variable name is useful because it frees the programmer from concern over where data is physically stored inside the computer. We simply use the variable name and let the compiler worry about where in memory the data is actually stored. Before storing a value into a variable, however, C requires that we clearly declare the type of data that is to be stored in it. We must tell the compiler, in advance, the names of the variables that will be used for characters, the names that will be used for integers, and the names that will be used to store the other C data types.

Declaration Statements

Naming a variable and specifying the data type that can be stored in it are accomplished using declaration statements. A *declaration statement* has the general form:

```
data-type variable name;
```

FIGURE 2.8   Naming Storage Locations

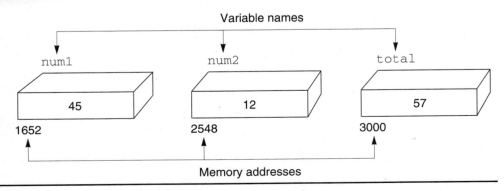

where `data-type` designates a valid C data type and `variable name` is a user-selected variable name. For example, variables used to hold integer values are declared using the keyword `int` to specify the data type and have the form:

```
int variable-name;
```

Thus, the declaration statement

```
int total;
```

declares `total` as the name of a variable capable of storing an integer value.

In addition to the reserved word `int` used to specify an integer, the reserved word `long`, which is considered a data type qualifier, is used to specify a long integer.[6] For example, the statement

```
long int datenum;
```

declares `datenum` as a variable that will be used to store a long integer. When using the long qualifier the keyword `int` can be omitted. Thus, the previous declaration can be written as:

```
long datenum;
```

Variables used to hold single-precision, floating-point values are declared using the keyword `float`, whereas variables that will be used to hold double-precision values are declared using the keyword `double`. For example, the statement

```
float firstnum;
```

declares `firstnum` as a variable that will be used to store a floating-point number. Similarly, the statement

```
double secnum;
```

declares that the variable `secnum` will be used to store a double-precision number.

Declaration statements within a function must appear immediately after the opening brace of a function and, like all C statements, must end with a semicolon. A C function containing declaration statements has the general form:

```
function name()
{
declaration statements
other statements
}
```

Program 2.5 illustrates the declaration and use of four floating-point variables. The `printf()` function is then used to display the contents of one of these variables.

---

[6]Additionally, the reserved words `unsigned int` are used to specify an integer that can only store non-negative numbers and the reserved words `short int` are used to specify a short integer. Long integers and unsigned integers are displayed using the `%ld` and `%u` control sequences, respectively, in the `printf()` function.

◆ A CLOSER LOOK ◆

Atomic Data

The variables we have declared have all been used to store atomic data values. An *atomic data value* is a value that is considered a complete entity by itself and is not decomposable into a smaller data type supported by the language. For example, although an integer can be decomposed into individual digits, C does not have a numerical digit data type. Rather, each integer is regarded as a complete value by itself and, as such, is considered atomic data. Similarly, since the integer data type only supports atomic data values, it is said to be an *atomic data type.* As you might expect, floats and chars are atomic data types also.

PROGRAM 2.5

```c
#include <stdio.h>
void main(void)
{
   float grade1;  /* declare grade1 as a float variable */
   float grade2;  /* declare grade2 as a float variable */
   float total;   /* declare total as a float variable */
   float average; /* declare average as a float variable */

   grade1 = 85.5;
   grade2 = 97.0;
   total = grade1 + grade2;
   average = total/2.0;
   printf("The average grade is %f\n",average);
}
```

The placement of the declaration statements in Program 2.5 is straightforward, although we will see shortly that individual declaration statements for the same data type are typically combined into a single declaration statement. When Program 2.5 is run, the following output is displayed:

> The average grade is 91.250000

Two comments with respect to the printf() function call made in Program 2.5 should be mentioned here. If a variable name is one of the arguments passed to a function, as it is to printf() in Program 2.5, the function only receives a copy of the value stored in the variable. It does not receive the variable's name. When the program sees a variable name in the function parentheses, it first goes to the variable and retrieves the value stored. It is this value that is passed to the function. Thus, when a variable is included in the printf() argument list, printf() receives the value stored in the variable and then displays this value. Internally, printf() has no knowledge of where the value it receives came from or the variable name under which the value was stored.

Although this procedure for passing data into a function may seem surprising, it is really a safety procedure for ensuring that a called function does not have access to the original variable. This guarantees that the called function cannot inadvertently change data in a variable declared outside itself. We will have more to say about this when we see how to write our own functions.

The second comment concerns the use of the `%f` conversion control sequence in Program 2.5. Although this conversion control sequence works for both floating-point and double-precision numbers, the conversion control sequence `%lf` may also be used for displaying the values of double-precision variables. The letter `l` indicates that the number is a long floating-point number, which is what a double-precision number really is. Omitting the `l` conversion character has no effect on the `printf()` function when double-precision values are displayed. As we shall see, however, it is essential in entering double-precision values when the input function `scanf()`, introduced in the next chapter, is used.

Just as integers, floating-point, and double-precision variables must be declared before they can be used, a variable used to store a character must also be declared. Character variables are declared using the keyword `char`. For example, the declaration

```
char ch;
```

declares `ch` to be a character variable.

Multiple Declarations

Variables having the same data type can always be grouped together and declared using a single declaration statement. The common form of such a declaration is:

```
data-type variable-list
```

For example, the four separate declarations:

```
float grade1;
float grade2;
float total;
float average;
```

can be replaced by the single declaration statement[7]:

```
float grade1, grade2, total, average;
```

Similarly, the two integer declarations

```
int num1;
int num2;
```

can be replaced with the single declaration statement:

```
int num1, num2;
```

---

[7]There are two schools of thought on using multiple declarations: Some programmers insist that variables of the same data type should always be multiply declared; others insist, with equal vehemence, that each variable should be declared on an individual line with an optional comment as to its purpose. We prefer a middle ground. Where multiple declarations can be used to save space they are used. If a comment on an individual variable is advantageous, we will use a single declaration.

Notice that declaring multiple variables in a single declaration requires that the data type of the variables be given only once, that all the variables names be separated by commas, and that only one semicolon be used to terminate the declaration. The space after each comma is inserted for readability, and is not required.

Declaration statements can also be used to store an initial value into each declared variable. For example, the declaration statement

```
int num1 = 15;
```

both declares the variable num1 as an integer variable and sets the value of 15 into the variable. When a declaration statement is used to store a value into the variable, the variable is said to be *initialized*. Thus, in this example, it is correct to say that the variable num1 has been initialized to 15. Similarly, the declaration statement

```
float grade1 = 87.0, grade2 = 93.5, total;
```

declares three floating-point variables and initializes two of them. Constants, expressions using only constants (such as 87.0 + 12.2), and expressions using constants and previously initialized variables can all be used as initializers within a declaration statement. For example, Program 2.5 with initialization of the variables within their declaration statements would appear as:

```
#include <stdio.h>
void main(void)
{
   float grade1 = 85.5, grade2 = 97.0, total, average;

   total = grade1 + grade2;
   average = total/2.0;
   printf("The average grade is %f\n",average);
}
```

Notice the blank line after the declaration statement. Placing a blank line after variable declarations is a common programming practice that improves both a program's appearance and readability; we will adopt this practice for all of our programs.

Specifying Storage Allocation

Declaration statements perform both software and hardware tasks. From a software perspective, declaration statements always provide a convenient, up-front list of all variables and their data types. In this software role, variable declarations also eliminate an otherwise common and troublesome error caused by the misspelling of a variable's name within a program. For example, assume that a variable named distance is declared and initialized using the statement

```
int distance = 26;
```

Now assume that this variable is inadvertently misspelled in the statement

```
mpg = distnce / gallons;
```

In languages that do not require variable declarations, the program would treat `distnce` as a new variable and either assign an initial value of zero to the variable or use whatever value happened to be in the variable's storage area. In either case a value would be calculated and assigned to `mpg`, and finding the error or even knowing that an error occurred could be extremely troublesome. Such errors are impossible in C, because the compiler will flag `distnce` as an undeclared variable. The compiler cannot, of course, detect when one declared variable is typed in place of another declared variable.

In addition to their software role, declaration statements can also perform a distinct hardware task. Since each data type has its own storage requirements, the compiler can allocate sufficient storage for a variable only after knowing the variable's data type. Because variable declarations provide this information, they can be used to force the compiler to reserve sufficient physical memory storage for each variable. Declaration statements used for this hardware purpose are also called *definition statements*, because they define or tell the compiler how much memory is needed for data storage.

All the declaration statements we have encountered so far have also been definition statements. Later, we will see cases of declaration statements that do not cause any new storage to be allocated and are used simply to declare or alert the program to the data types of previously created and existing variables.

Figure 2.9 illustrates the effect produced by declaration statements that also perform a definition role. The figure shows that definition statements (or, if you prefer, declaration statements that also cause memory to be allocated) "tag" the first byte of each set of reserved bytes with a name. This name is, of course, the variable's name and is used by the program to correctly locate the starting byte of each variable's reserved memory area.

After a variable has been declared within a program, it is typically used by a programmer to refer to the contents of the variable (that is, the variable's value). Where in memory this value is stored is generally of little concern to the programmer. The compiler, however, must be concerned with where each value is stored and with correctly locating each variable. In this task the compiler uses the variable name to locate the first byte of storage previously allocated to the variable. Knowing the variable's data type then allows the computer to store or retrieve the correct number of bytes.

Determining Storage Allocation Size

C provides an operator for determining the amount of storage allocated for each data type. This operator, called the `sizeof()` operator, returns the number of bytes of the variable or data type following it. Examples of the `sizeof()` operator are:

```
sizeof(num1)    sizeof(int)    sizeof(float)
```

If the item within the parentheses is a variable, as in the example `sizeof(num1)`, the `sizeof()` operator returns the number of bytes of storage that the computer reserved for the variable. If the item within the parentheses is a data type, such as `int` or `float`, `sizeof()` will return the number of bytes of storage that the computer uses for the given data type. Using either approach, we can use `sizeof()` to determine the amount of storage used by different data types. Consider Program 2.6:

FIGURE 2.9a   Defining the Integer Variable Named Total

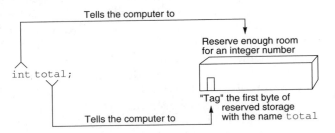

FIGURE 2.9b   Defining the Floating-Point Variable Named Firstnum

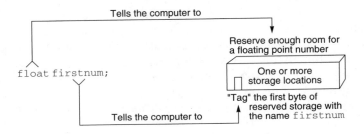

FIGURE 2.9c   Defining the Double-Precision Variable Named Secnum

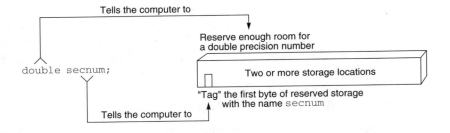

FIGURE 2.9d   Defining the Character Variable Named Ch

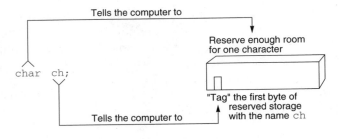

PROGRAM 2.6

```c
#include <stdio.h>
void main(void)
{
  int num1;

  printf("Bytes of storage used by an integer: %d\n", sizeof(num1));
}
```

Program 2.6 declares that the variable num1 is used to store an integer. The sizeof() operator is then used to tell us how much room the computer actually set aside for the variable num1. The sizeof() operator itself is used as an argument to the printf() function. When Program 2.6 is compiled using a Borland version 2.0 C compiler, the following output is obtained:

```
Bytes of storage used by an integer: 4
```

In using the sizeof() operator, one caution should be noted. The number of bytes given by the sizeof() operator is in terms of the storage reserved for one character. Since almost all computers store one character in one byte, the value given by sizeof() is normally a true byte count. If, however, a computer uses two bytes to store one character (possible, but not very likely), the number given by the sizeof() operator would have to be multiplied by two to obtain a true byte count.

Exercises 2.4

1. State whether the following variable names are valid or not. If they are invalid, state the reason why.

prod_a	c1234	abcd	_c3	12345
newbal	while	$total	new bal	a1b2c3d4
9ab6	sum.of	average	grade1	fin_grad

2. State whether the following variable names are valid or not. If they are invalid, state the reason why. Also indicate which of the valid variable names should not be used because they convey no information about the variable.

salestax	a243	r2d2	first_num	cc_a1
harry	sue	c3p0	average	sum
maximum	okay	a	awesome	goforit
3sum	for	tot.a1	c$five	netpay

3. a. Write a declaration statement to declare that the variable count will be used to store an integer.

   b. Write a declaration statement to declare that the variable grade will be used to store a floating-point number.

   c. Write a declaration statement to declare that the variable yield will be used to store a double-precision number.

   d. Write a declaration statement to declare that the variable initial will be used to store a character.

4. Write declaration statements for the following variables.

   a. num1, num2, and num3 used to store integer numbers

b. grade1, grade2, grade3, and grade4 used to store single-precision float-ing-point numbers

c. tempa, tempb, and tempc used to store double-precision floating-point num-bers

d. ch, let1, let2, let3, and let4 used to store character types

5. Write declaration statements for the following variables.

a. firstnum and secnum used to store integers

b. price, yield, and coupon used to store floating-point numbers

c. maturity used to store a double-precision number

6. Rewrite each of these declaration statements as three individual declarations.

a. int month, day = 30, year;

b. double hours, rate, otime = 15.62;

c. float price, amount, taxes;

d. char in_key, ch, choice = 'f';

7. a. Determine the effect of each statement in the following program:

```
#include stdio.h
void main(void)
{
    int num1, num2, total;

    num1 = 25;
    num2 = 30;
    total = num1 + num2;
    printf("The total of %d and %d is %d\n.",num1,num2,total);
}
```

b. What output will be printed when the program listed in Exercise 7a is run?

8. Write a C program that stores the sum of the integer numbers 12 and 33 in a vari-able named sum. Have your program display the value stored in sum.

9. Write a C program that stores the value 16 in the integer variable length and the value 18 in the integer variable width. Have your program calculate the value assigned to the variable perimeter, using the assignment statement

perimeter = length + length + width + width;

and print the value stored in the variable perimeter. Make sure you declare all the variables as integers at the beginning of the main() function.

10. Write a C program that stores the integer value 16 in the variable num1 and the inte-ger value 18 in the variable num2. (Make sure you declare the variables as integers.) Have your program calculate the total of these numbers and their average. The total should be stored in an integer variable named total and the average in an integer variable named average. (Use the statement average = total/2.0; to calculate the average.) Use the printf() function to display the total and average.

11. Repeat Exercise 10, but store the number 15 in num1 instead of 16. With a pencil, write down the average of num1 and num2. What do you think your program will store in the integer variable that you used for the average of these two numbers? How can you ensure that the correct answer will be printed for the average?

12. Write a C program that stores the number 105.62 in the variable firstnum, 89.352 in the variable secnum, and 98.67 in the variable thirdnum. (Make sure you declare the variables first as either float or double.) Have your program calculate the total of the three numbers and their average. The total should be stored in the variable total and the average in the variable average. (Use the state-ment average = total /3.0; to calculate the average.) Use the printf() function to display the total and average.

13. Using the `sizeof()` operator, write a C program that displays the number of bytes that your compiler uses for storing integer, long integer, floating-point, double-precision, and character data.

14. Every variable has at least two items associated with it. What are these two items?

15. a. A statement used to clarify the relationship between squares and rectangles is "All squares are rectangles but not all rectangles are squares." Write a similar statement that describes the relationship between definition and declaration statements.

   b. Why must a variable be defined before any other C statement that uses the variable?

   Note for Exercises 16 through 18: Assume that a character requires one byte of storage, an integer two bytes, a floating-point number four bytes, a double-precision number eight bytes, and that variables are assigned storage in the order they are declared.

16. a. Using Figure 2.12 and assuming that the variable name `rate` is assigned to the byte having memory address 159, determine the addresses corresponding to each variable declared in the following statements. Also fill in the appropriate bytes with the initialization data included in the declaration statements (use letters for the characters, not the computer codes that would actually be stored).

```
float rate;
char ch1 = 'w', ch2 = 'o', ch3 = 'w', ch4 = '!';
double taxes;
int num, count = 0;
```

FIGURE 2.10 Memory Bytes for Exercises 16, 17, and 18

Address:	159	160	161	162	163	164	165	166

Address:	167	168	169	170	171	172	173	174

Address:	175	176	177	178	179	180	181	182

Address:	183	184	185	186	187	188	189	190

---

b. Repeat Exercise 16a, but substitute the actual byte patterns that a computer using the ASCII code would use to store the characters in the variables ch1, ch2, ch3, and ch4. (*Hint:* Use Table 2.3.)

17. a. Using Figure 2.10 and assuming that the variable named cn1 is assigned to the byte at memory address 159, determine the addresses corresponding to each variable declared in the following statements. Also fill in the appropriate bytes with the initialization data included in the declaration statements (use letters for the characters and not the computer codes that would actually be stored).

```
char cn1 = 'a', cn2 = ' ', cn3 = 'b', cn4 = 'u', cn5 = 'n';
char cn6 = 'c', cn7 = 'h', key = '\\', sch = '\'', inc = 'o';
char inc1 = 'f';
```

b. Repeat Exercise 17a, but substitute the actual byte patterns that a computer using the ASCII code would use to store the characters in each of the declared variables. (*Hint:* Use Table 2.3.)

18. Using Figure 2.10 and assuming that the variable name miles is assigned to the byte at memory address 159, determine the addresses corresponding to each variable declared in the following statements:

```
float miles;
int count, num;
double dist, temp;
```

2.5 APPLYING THE SOFTWARE DEVELOPMENT PROCEDURE

Recall from Section 1.3 that writing a C program is the third step in the programming process. The first two steps in the process are determining what is required and selecting the algorithm to be coded into C. In this section, we show how the steps presented in Section 1.3 are applied in practice when converting programming problems into working C programs. To review, once a program requirement or problem is stated, the software development procedure consists of the following steps.

Step 1: Analyze the Problem

The analysis can consist of up to two parts. The first is a basic analysis that must be performed on all problems and consists of extracting the complete input and output information supplied by the problem. That is, you must (1) determine and understand the desired output items that the program must produce and (2) determine the required input items.

Together these two items are referred to as the problem's input/output, or I/O for short. Only after a problem's I/O has been determined is it possible to select an initial algorithm for transforming the inputs into the desired outputs. At this point it is sometimes necessary and/or useful to perform a hand calculation to verify that the output can indeed be obtained from the inputs. Clearly, if a formula is given that relates the inputs to the output, this step can be omitted at this stage. If the required inputs are available and the desired output(s) can be produced, the problem is said to be clearly defined and can be solved.

For a variety of reasons it may not be possible to complete a basic analysis. If this is the case, an extended analysis may be necessary. An extended analysis simply means that you must obtain additional information about the problem so that you thoroughly understand what is being asked for and how to achieve the result. In this text any additional information required for an understanding of the problem will be supplied along with the problem statement.

Step 2: Develop a Solution

This step is frequently referred to as the design step, and we will use the terms *development* and *design* interchangeably. In this step you must settle on an algorithm for transforming the input items into the desired outputs and refine it as necessary so that it adequately defines all of the features that you want your program to have. If you haven't performed a hand calculation using the algorithm in the analysis step, you should do so here, using specific input values.

In designing a solution, the specific approach we will take is referred to as the top-down approach. This approach consists of starting with the most general solution and refining it in the manner presented in Section 1.3 such that the final program solution consists of clearly defined tasks that can be accomplished by individual program functions.

Step 3: Code the Solution into C

At this point you actually write the C program that corresponds to the solution developed in step 2.

Step 4: Test and Correct the Program

This is done by means of selected test data and is used to make corrections to the program when errors are found. One set of test data that should always be used is the data used in your previous hand calculation.

To see how each of these steps can be implemented in practice, we now apply it to a simple programming problem.

> The circumference, C, of a circle is given by the formula $C = 2\pi r$, where π
> is the constant 3.1416 (accurate to four decimal places), and r is the
> radius of the circle. Using this information, write a C program to calcu-
> late the circumference of a circle that has a 2-inch radius.

Step 1: Analyze the Problem   The first step in developing a program for this problem statement is to perform a basic analysis. We begin by determining the required outputs. Frequently, the statement of the problem will use such words as *calculate, print, determine, find,* or *compare,* which can be used to determine the desired outputs.

For our sample problem statement, the key phrase is "to calculate the circumference of a circle." This clearly identifies an output item. Since there are no other such phrases in the problem, only one output item is required.

After we have clearly identified the desired output, the basic analysis step continues with the identification of all input items. It is essential at this stage to distinguish between input items and input values. An *input item* is the name of an input quantity, while an *input value* is a specific number or quantity that the input item can be. For example, in our sample problem statement, the input item is the radius of the circle (the known quantity). Although this input item has a specific numerical value in this problem (the value 2), actual input item values are generally not of importance at this stage.

The reason that input values are not needed at this point is the initial selection of an algorithm is typically independent of specific input values. The algorithm depends on knowing what the output and input items are and if there are any special limits. Let us see why this is so.

From the problem statement it is clear that the algorithm for transforming the input items to the desired output is given by the formula $C = 2\pi r$. Notice that this formula can be used regardless of the specific values assigned to r. Although we cannot produce an actual numerical value for the output item (circumference) unless we have an actual numerical value for the input item, the correct relationship between inputs and outputs is expressed by the formula. Recall that this is precisely what an algorithm provides: a description of how the inputs are to be transformed into outputs that works for all inputs.

Step 2: Develop a Solution   The basic algorithm for transforming the inputs into the desired output is provided by the given formula. We must now refine it by listing, in detail, how the inputs, outputs, and algorithm are to be combined to produce a solution. This listing indicates the steps that will be taken by the program to solve the problem. As such it constitutes an outline of the final form that will be followed by the program code. Using pseudocode, the complete algorithm for solving this problems is:

Assign a value to r.
Calculate the circumference using the formula C $= 2\pi$ r.
Display the result.

Notice that the structure of this algorithm conforms to the sequential control structure presented in Section 1.3.

Having selected and refined the algorithm, the next step in the design (if it was not already done in the analysis step) is to check the algorithm by hand using specific data. Performing a manual calculation, either by hand or using a calculator, helps to ensure that you really do understand the problem. An added feature of doing a manual calculation is that the results can be used later to verify program operation in the testing phase. Then, when the final program is used with other data, you will have established a degree of confidence that a correct result is being calculated.

Doing a manual calculation requires that we have specific input values that can be assigned and used by the algorithm to produce the desired output. For this problem one input value is given: a radius of 2 inches. Substituting this value into the formula, we obtain a circumference of 2 (3.1416)(2) = 12.5664 inches.

Step 3: Code the Solution   Since we have carefully developed a program solution, all that remains is to code the solution algorithm in C. This means declaring appropriate input and output variables, initializing the input variables appropriately, computing the circumference, and printing the calculated circumference value. Program 2.7 performs these steps.

PROGRAM 2.7

```
#include <stdio.h>
void main(void)
{
```

(continued on next page)

(continued from previous page)

```
  float radius, circumference;

  radius = 2.0;
  circumference = 2.0 * 3.1416 * radius;
  printf("The circumference of the circle is %f\n", circumference);
}
```

When program 2-7 is executed, the following output is produced:

```
              The circumference of the circle is 12.566400
```

Now that we have a working program that produces a result, the final step in the development process, testing the program, can begin.

Step 4: Test and Debug the Program   The purpose of testing is to verify that a program works correctly and actually fulfills its requirements. Once testing has been completed the program can be used to calculate outputs for differing input data without the need for retesting. This is, of course, one of the real values in writing a program; the same program can be used over and over with new input data.

The simplest test method is to verify the program's operation for carefully selected sets of input data. One set of input data that should always be used is the data that was selected for the hand calculation made previously in step 2 of the development procedure. In this case the program is relatively simple and performs only one calculation. Because the output produced by the test run agrees with our hand calculation we have a good degree of confidence that it can be used to calculate correctly the circumference for any input radius.

Exercises 2.5

Note: In each of these exercises a programming problem is given. Read the problem statement first and then answer the questions pertaining to the problem.

1. Consider the following programming problem: A C program is required that calculates the amount, in dollars, contained in a piggybank. The bank contains half dollars, quarters, dimes, nickels, and pennies.

   a. For this programming problem, how many outputs are required?

   b. How many inputs does this problem have?

   c. Determine an algorithm for converting the input items into output items.

   d. Test the algorithm written for Exercise 1c using the following sample data: half dollars = 0, quarters = 17, dimes = 24, nickels = 16, pennies = 12.

2. Consider the following programming problem: A C program is required to calculate the value of distance, in miles, given the relationship

   ```
   distance = rate * elapsed time
   ```

   a. For this programming problem, how many outputs are required?

   b. How many inputs does this problem have?

   c. Determine an algorithm for converting the input items into output items.

    d. Test the algorithm written for Exercise 2c using the following sample data: Rate is 55 miles per hour and elapsed time is 2.5 hours.

    e. How must the algorithm you determined in part (c) be modified if the elapsed time is given in minutes instead of hours?

3. Consider the following programming problem: A C program is required to determine the value of Ergies, given the relationships

$$\text{Ergies} = \text{Fergies} * \sqrt{\text{Lergies}}$$

    a. For this programming problem, how many outputs are required?

    b. How many inputs does this problem have?

    c. Determine an algorithm for converting the input items into output items.

    d. Test the algorithm written for Exercise 3c using the following sample data: Fergies = 14.65 and Lergies = 4.

4. Consider the following programming problem: A C program is required to display the following name and address:

        Mr. S. Hazlet
        63 Seminole Way
        Dumont, NJ 07030

    a. For this programming problem, how many lines of output are required?

    b. How many inputs does this problem have?

    c. Determine an algorithm for converting the input items into output items.

5. Consider the following program problem: A C program is required to determine how far a car has traveled after 10 seconds assuming the car is initially traveling at 60 miles per hour and the driver applies the brakes to decelerate uniformly at a rate of 12 miles/sec^2. Use the fact that distance $= s - (1/2)dt^2$, where s is the initial speed of the car, d is the deceleration, and t is the elapsed time.

    a. For this programming problem, how many outputs are required?

    b. How many inputs does this problem have?

    c. Determine an algorithm for converting the input items into output items.

    d. Test the algorithm written for Exercise 5c using the data given in the problem.

6. Consider the following programming problem: In 1627, Manhattan Island was sold to the Dutch settlers for approximately $24. If the proceeds of that sale had been deposited in a Dutch bank paying 5% interest, compounded annually, what would the principle balance be at the end of 1995? A display is required as follows:

```
Balance as of December 31, 1990 is: xxxxxx
```

where xxxxxx is the amount calculated by the program.

    a. For this programming problem, how many outputs are required?

    b. How many inputs does this problem have?

    c. Determine an algorithm for converting the input items into output items.

    d. Test the algorithm written for Exercise 6c using the data given in the problem statement.

7. Consider the following programming problem: A C program is required that calculates and displays the weekly gross pay and net pay of two individuals. The first individual is paid an hourly rate of $8.43 and the second individual is paid an hourly rate of $5.67. Both individuals have 20% of their gross pay withheld for income tax purposes and both pay 2% of their gross pay, before taxes, for medical benefits.

a. For this programming problem, how many outputs are required?

b. How many inputs does this problem have?

c. Determine an algorithm for converting the input items into output items.

d. Test the algorithm written for Exercise 7c using the following sample data: The first person works 40 hours during the week and the second person works 35 hours.

8. Consider the following programming problem: The formula for the standard normal deviate, z, used in statistical applications is

$$z = \frac{X - \mu}{\sigma}$$

where μ refers to a mean value and σ to a standard deviation. Using this formula, write a program that calculates and displays the value of the standard normal deviate when $X = 85.3$, $\mu = 80$, and $\sigma = 4$.

a. For this programming problem, how many outputs are required?

b. How many inputs does this problem have?

c. Determine an algorithm for converting the input items into output items.

d. Test the algorithm written for Exercise 8c using the data given in the problem.

9. Consider the following programming problem: The equation describing exponential growth is:

$$y = e^x$$

Using this equation, a C program is required to calculate the value of y.

a. For this programming problem, how many outputs are required?

b. How many inputs does this problem have?

c. Determine an algorithm for converting the input items into output items.

d. Test the algorithm written for Exercise 9c assuming $e = 2.718$ and $x = 10$.

2.6 FOCUS ON PROBLEM SOLVING

In this section the software development procedure introduced in Section 1.3 and expanded upon in the previous section is applied to two specific programming problems. Although each problem is different, the top-down development procedure works for both situations. This procedure can be applied to any programming problem to produce a completed program and forms the foundation for all programs developed in this text.

Problem 1: Pendulum Clocks

Pendulums used in clocks, such as grandmother and grandfather clocks, keep fairly accurate time for the following reason: when the length of a pendulum is relatively large compared to the maximum arc of its swing, the time to complete one swing is independent of both the pendulum's weight and the maximum displacement of the swing. When this condition is satisfied, the relationship between the time to complete one swing and the length of the pendulum is given by the formula

$$length = g[time/(2\ \pi)]^2,$$

where π, accurate to four decimal places, is equal to 3.1416 and g is the gravitational constant equal to 32.2 ft/sec^2. When the time of a complete swing is given in seconds, the length of the pendulum is in feet. Using the given formula, write a C program to calculate and display the length of a pendulum needed to produce a swing that will be completed in one second. The length should be displayed in inches.

We now apply the top-down software development procedure to this problem.

Step 1: Analyze the Problem For this problem a single output is required by the program: the length of the pendulum. Additionally, the problem specifies that the actual value be displayed be in units of inches. The input items required to solve for the length are the time to complete one swing, the gravitational constant, g, and π.

Step 2: Develop a Solution The algorithm given for transforming the three input items into the desired output item is given by the formula length = g[time/(2 π)]^2. Since this formula calculates the length in feet and the problem specifies that the result should be displayed in inches, we will have to multiply the result of the formula by 12. Thus, the complete algorithm for our program solution is:

Assign values to g, π, and time.
Calculate the length (in inches) using the formula length = 12 * g[time/(2 π)].
Display the result.

A hand calculation, using the data that g = 32.2, time = 1, and π = 3.1416, yields a length of 9.79 inches for the pendulum.

Step 3: Code the Solution Program 2.8 provides the necessary code.

PROGRAM 2.8

```
#include <stdio.h>
void main(void)
{
    float time, length, pi;

    pi = 3.1416;
    time = 1.0;
    length = 12.0 * 32.2 * time/(2.0*pi) * time/(2.0*pi);
    printf("The length is %4.2f inches.\n", length);
}
```

Program 2.8 begins with an `#include` preprocessor command followed by a `main()` function. This function starts with the header line `void main(void)` and ends with the closing brace, `}`. Additionally, Program 2.8 contains one declaration statement, three assignment statements, and one output statement. The assignment statements `pi = 3.1416` and `time = 1.0` are used to initialize the `pi` and `time` variables, respectively. The assignment statement

```
length = 12.0 * 32.2 * time/(2.0*pi) * time/(2.0*pi);
```

calculates a value for the variable `length`. Notice that the `12.0` is used to convert the calculated value from feet into inches. Also notice the placement of parentheses in the expression `time/(2.0*pi)`. The parentheses ensures that the value of `pi` is multiplied by 2.0 before the division is performed. If these parentheses were not included, the value of `time` would first be divided by 2.0, and then the quantity `time/2.0` would be multiplied by pi. Finally, this same quantity is multiplied by itself to obtain the necessary squared value. (In the next chapter, we will see how to use C's power function to obtain the same result.) When Program 2.8 is compiled and executed the following output is produced:

```
The length is 9.79 inches.
```

Step 4: Test and Debug the Program The last step in the development procedure is to test the output. Because the displayed value agrees with the previous hand calculation, we have established a degree of confidence in the program. This permits us to use the program for different values of time. Note that if the parentheses were not correctly placed in the assignment statement that calculated a value for length, the displayed value would not agree with our previous hand calculation. This would have alerted us to the fact there was an error in the program.

Problem 2: Telephone Switching Networks

A directly connected telephone network is one in which all telephones in the network are directly connected and do not require a central switching station to establish calls between two telephones. For example, financial institutions on Wall Street use such a network to maintain direct and continuously open phone lines between firms.

The number of direct lines needed to maintain a directly connected network for n telephones, is given by the formula

$$lines = n(n-1)/2.$$

For example, directly connecting four telephones requires 6 individual lines (see Figure 2.11). Adding a fifth telephone to the network illustrated in Figure 2.11 would require an additional 4 lines for a total of 10 lines.

Using the given formula, write a C program that determines the number of direct lines required for 100 telephones, and the additional lines required if 10

FIGURE 2.11 Directly Connecting Four Telephones

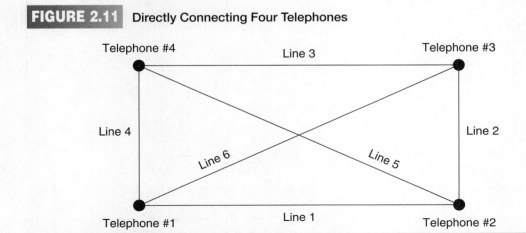

new telephones were added to the network. Use the top-down software development procedure.

Step 1: Analyze the Problem For this program two outputs are required: the number of direct lines for 100 telephones and the additional number of lines needed when 10 new telephones are added to the existing network. The input item required for this problem is the number of telephones, which is denoted as n in the formula.

Step 2: Develop a Solution The first output is easily obtained using the formula lines = $n(n-1)/2$. Although there is no formula given for additional lines, we can use the given formula to determine the total number of lines needed for 110 subscribers. Subtracting the number of lines for 100 subscribers from the number of lines needed for 110 subscribers will then yield the number of additional lines required. Thus, the complete algorithm for our program, in pseudocode, is

Calculate the number of direct lines for 100 subscribers.
Calculate the number of direct lines for 110 subscribers.
Calculate the additional lines needed, which is the difference between the
  second and first calculation.
Display the number of lines for 100 subscribers.
Display the additional lines needed.

Checking our algorithm by hand, using the given data, yields that lines = $100(100 - 1)/2 = 100(99)/2 = 4950$ lines for 100 telephones and that lines = 5995 direct lines are needed for 110 telephones. Thus, an additional 1045 lines would be needed to directly connect the ten additional telephones into the existing network.

Step 3: Code the Solution Program 2.9 provides the necessary code.

PROGRAM 2.9

```c
#include <stdio.h>
void main(void)
{
   int numin1, numin2, lines1, lines2;

   numin1 = 100;
   numin2 = 110;
   lines1 = numin1 * (numin1 - 1)/2;
   lines2 = numin2 * (numin2 - 1)/2;
   printf("The number of initial lines is %d.\n", lines1);
   printf("There are %d additional lines needed.\n", lines2 - lines1);
}
```

As before, the C program includes the `stdio.h` header file and consists of one `main()` function. The body of this function begins with the opening brace, {, and ends with the closing brace, }. Since the number of lines between subscribers must be an integer (a fractional line is not possible) the variables `lines1` and `lines2` are specified as integer variables. The first two assignment statements initialize the variables `numin1` and `numin2`. The next assignment statement calculates the number of lines needed for 100 subscribers and the last assignment statement calculates the number of lines for 110 subscribers. The first call to `printf()` is used to display a message and the result of the first calculation. The second call to `printf()` is used to display the difference between the two calculations. The following output is produced when Program 2.13 is compiled and executed.

```
The number of initial lines is 4950.
There are 1045 additional lines needed.
```

Step 4: Test and Debug the Program   Because the displayed value agrees with the previous hand calculation, we have established a degree of confidence in the program.

Exercises 2.6

1. a. Modify Program 2.8 to calculate the length of a pendulum that produces an arc that takes two seconds to complete.

   b. Compile and execute the program written for Exercise 1a on a computer.

2. a. Modify Program 2.8 to determine the time it takes a 3-foot pendulum to complete one swing. Your program should produce the following display:

   ```
   The time to complete one swing (in seconds) is: _____
   ```

   where the underscore is replaced by the actual value calculated by your program.

   b. Compile and execute the program written for Exercise 2a on a computer. Make sure to do a hand calculation so that you can verify the results produced by your program.

   c. After you have verified the results of the program written in Exercise 2a, modify the program to calculate the time it takes a 4-foot pendulum to complete one swing.

3. a. Modify Program 2.9 to calculate and display the total number of lines needed to connect 1000 individual phones directly to each other.

   b. Compile and execute the program written for Exercise 3a on a computer.

4. a. Modify Program 2.9 so that the variable `numfin` is initialized to 10, which is the additional number of subscribers to be connected to the existing network. Make any other changes in the program so that the program produces the same display as Program 2.9.

   b. Compile and execute the program written for Exercise 4a on a computer. Check that the display produced by your program matches the display shown in the text.

5. a. Write, compile, and execute a C program to convert temperature in degrees Fahrenheit to degrees Celsius. The equation for this conversion is

   $$\text{Celsius} = 5.0/9.0\ (\text{Fahrenheit} - 32.0).$$

   Have your program convert and display the Celsius temperature corresponding to 98.6 degrees Fahrenheit. Your program should produce the display:

   ```
   For a fahrenheit temperature of _____ degrees,
   the equivalent celsius temperature is _____ degrees.
   ```

where appropriate values are inserted by your program in place of the underscores.

    b. Check the values computed by your program by hand. After you have verified that your program is working correctly, modify it to convert 86.5 degrees Fahrenheit into its equivalent Celsius value.

6. a. Write, compile, and execute a C program to calculate the dollar amount contained in a piggy bank. The bank currently contains 12 half-dollars, 20 quarters, 32 dimes, 45 nickels, and 27 pennies.

    b. Check the values computed by your program by hand. After you have verified that your program is working correctly, modify it to determine the dollar value of a bank containing no half-dollars, 17 quarters, 19 dimes, 10 nickels, and 42 pennies.

7. a. Write, compile, and execute a C program to calculate the elapsed time it took to make a 183.67-mile trip. The equation for computing elapsed time is

$$\text{elapsed time} = \text{total distance} \, / \, \text{average speed}.$$

Assume that the average speed during the trip was 58 miles per hour.

    b. Check the values computed by your program by hand. After you have verified that your program is working correctly, modify it to determine the elapsed time it takes to make a 372-mile trip at an average speed of 67 miles per hour.

8. a. Write, compile, and execute a C program to calculate the sum of the numbers from 1 to 100. The formula for calculating this sum is

$$\text{sum} = (n/2) \, (\, 2a + (n\text{-}1)d \,),$$

where n = number of terms to be added, a = the first number, and d = the difference between each number.

    b. Check the values computed by your program by hand. After you have verified that your program is working correctly, modify it to determine the sum of the integers from 100 to 1000.

Note: Exercises 9, 10, and 11 require raising a number to a power. This can be accomplished using C's power function `pow()`. For example, the statement `pow(2.0,5.0);` raises the number 2.0 to the fifth power, and the statement `pow(num1,num2);` raises the variable num1 to the num2 power. To use the power function either place an `#include math.h` preprocessor command on a line by itself after the `#include stdio.h` command or include the declaration statement `double pow();` with the variable declaration statements used in your program. The power function is explained in more detail in Section 3.3.

9. a. Newton's law of cooling states that when an object with an initial temperature T is placed in a surrounding substance of temperature A, it will reach a temperature *TFIN* in t minutes according to the formula

$$TFIN = (T - A) \, e^{-kt} + A.$$

In this formula e is the irrational number 2.71828 rounded to five decimal places, commonly known as Euler's number, and k is a thermal coefficient, which depends on the material being cooled. Using this formula write, compile, and execute a C program that determines the temperature reached by an object after 20 minutes when it is placed in a glass of water whose temperature is 60 degrees. Assume that the object initially has a temperature of 150 degrees and has a thermal constant of 0.0367.

    b. Check the value computed by your program by hand. After you have verified that your program is working correctly, modify it to determine the temperature reached after 10 minutes when it is placed in a glass of water whose temperature is 50 degrees.

10. a. Given an initial deposit of money, denoted as A, in a bank that pays interest annually, the amount of money at a time N years later is given by the formula

$$AMOUNT = A * (1 + I)^N$$

where I is the interest rate as a decimal number (e.g., 9.5% is .095). Using this formula write, compile, and execute a C program that determines the amount of money that will be available in four years if $10,000 is deposited in a bank that pays 10% interest annually. (*See the note prior to Exercise 9 for information on C's power function.*)

b. Check the value computed by your program by hand. After you have verified that your program is working correctly, modify it to determine the amount of money available if $24 dollars is invested at 4% for 300 years.

11. a. If an initial deposit of A dollars is made in a bank and the interest, I, is compounded M times a year, the amount of money available after N years is given by the expression

$$A * (1 + I/M)^{M*N.}$$

Using this expression write, compile, and run a C program to determine the amount of money available after 10 years if $5000 is invested in a bank paying 6% interest compounded quarterly ($M = 4$). (*See the note prior to Exercise 9 for information on C's power function.*)

b. Check the value computed by your program by hand. After you have verified that your program is working correctly, modify it to determine the amount of money available if $1000 dollars is invested at 8%, compounded quarterly, for 10 years.

2.7 ENRICHMENT STUDY: VARIABLE ADDRESSES AND MEMORY STORAGE

Every variable has three major items associated with it: the value stored in the variable, and address of the variable, and its data types. In C, the value stored in a variable is referred to as the variable's contents, while the address of the first memory location used for the variable constitutes its address. How many memory locations are actually used by the variable depends on the variable's data type. The relationship between those three items is illustrated in Figure 2.12.

Programmers are usually concerned only with the value assigned to a variable (its contents, or rvalue) and give little attention to where the value is stored (its address, or lvalue). For example, consider Program 2.10.

PROGRAM 2.10

```c
#include <stdio.h>
void main(void)
{
  int num;

  num = 22;
  printf("The value stored in num is %d.\n",num);
}
```

Program 2.10 merely prints the value 22, which was assigned to the integer variable num (its contents). We can go further, however, and ask "Where is the number 22 actually stored?" Although the answer is "In num," this is only half of the answer. The variable name num is simply a convenient symbol for real, physical locations in memory, as illustrated in Figure 2.13.

FIGURE 2.12   **A Typical Variable**

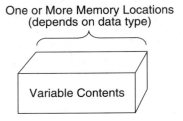

One or More Memory Locations
(depends on data type)

Variable Contents

Variable Address

To determine the address of num, we can use C's address operator, &, which means "the address of," directly in front of the variable name (no space between & and the variable). For example, &num means the address of num, &total means the address of total, and &price means the address of price. Program 2.11 uses the address operator to display the address of the variable num.

PROGRAM 2.11

```c
#include <stdio.h>
void main(void)
{
    int num;

    num = 22;
    printf("num = %d   The address of num = %p.\n", num, &num);
}
```

The output of Program 2.11 is

```
num = 22   The address of num = FFEO.
```

FIGURE 2.13   **Somewhere in Memory**

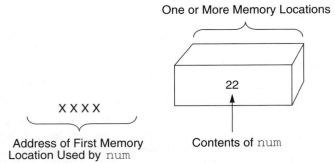

One or More Memory Locations

22

X X X X

Address of First Memory
Location Used by num

Contents of num

FIGURE 2.14   A More Complete Picture of the Variable num

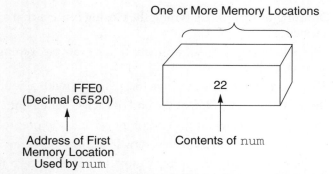

Figure 2.14 illustrates the additional address information provided by the output of Program 2.11.

Clearly, the address output by Program 2.11 depends on the computer used to run the program. Every time Program 2.11 is executed, however, it displays a representation of the address of the first byte used to store the variable num. Note also that the address is printed using the conversion sequence %p. The %p conversion sequence simply provides us with a convenient way of displaying an address. The display has no impact on how addresses are used internal to the program and merely provides us with a useful representation that is helpful in understanding what addresses are.[8]

As we shall see, using addresses as opposed to only displaying them provides the C programmer with an extremely powerful programming tool. They provide the ability to penetrate directly into the inner workings of the computer and access the computer's basic storage structure. This ability, which is more important to systems programmers than applications programmers, gives C programmers capabilities and programming power that are just not available in most other computer languages.

2.8 COMMON PROGRAMMING ERRORS

Part of learning any programming language is making the elementary mistakes commonly encountered as you begin to use the language. These mistakes tend to be quite frustrating, since each language has its own set of common programming errors waiting for the unwary. The more common errors made when initially programming in C are as follows:

---

[8]In non-ANSI C, the %p conversion sequence may not be available. For these compilers, use the conversion sequence %u, which forces the address to be treated as an unsigned integer data type, and what is displayed is printf()'s representation of the address in this format. An address, however, is not an unsigned integer data type—it is a unique data type that may or may not require the same amount of storage as an unsigned integer. The use of the %u conversion sequence simply provides us with a convenient way of displaying an address when the %p is unavailable.

1. Incorrectly typing the `void main(void)` header line.

2. Omitting or incorrectly typing the opening brace { that signifies the start of a function body.

3. Omitting or incorrectly typing the closing brace } that signifies the end of a function.

4. Misspelling the name of a function; for example, typing `pint()` instead of `printf()`.

5. Forgetting to close the message to `printf()` with a double quote symbol.

6. Omitting the semicolon at the end of each C statement.

7. Adding a semicolon at the end of the `#include` preprocessor command.

8. Forgetting the `\n` to indicate a new line.

9. Incorrectly typing the letter O for the number zero (0), or vice versa. Incorrectly typing the letter l for the number 1, or vice versa.

10. Forgetting to declare all the variables used in a program. This error is not detected by the compiler and an error message is generated for all undeclared variables.

11. Storing an inappropriate data type in a declared variable. This error is not detected by the compiler and the assigned value is converted to the data type of the variable it is assigned to.

12. Using a variable in an expression before a value has been assigned to the variable. Here, whatever value happens to be in the variable will be used when the expression is evaluated, and the result will be meaningless.

13. Dividing integer values incorrectly. This error is usually disguised within a larger expression and can be a very troublesome error to detect. For example, the expression

$$3.425 + 2/3 + 7.9$$

yields the same result as the expression

$$3.425 + 7.9$$

because the integer division of 2/3 is 0.

14. Mixing data types in the same expression without clearly understanding the effect produced. Since C allows expressions with "mixed" data types, it is important to understand the order of evaluation and the data type of all intermediate calculations. As a general rule it is better never to mix data types in an expression unless a specific effect is desired.

15. Not including the correct number and type of conversion control sequences in `printf()` function calls for the data types of the remaining arguments.

16. Not closing off the control string in `printf()` with a double quote symbol " followed by a comma when additional arguments are passed to `printf()`.

17. Forgetting to separate all arguments passed to `printf()` with commas.

The third, fifth, sixth, seventh, and eighth errors in this list are initially the most common. It is worthwhile for you to write a program and specifically introduce each of these errors, one at a time, to see what error messages are produced by your compiler. Then, when these error messages appear due to inadvertent errors, you will have had experience in understanding the messages and correcting the errors.

On a more fundamental level, a major programming error made by all beginning programmers is the rush to code and run a program before fully understanding what is required and the algorithms and procedures that will be used to produce the desired result. A symptom of this haste to get a program entered into the computer is the lack of either an outline of the proposed program or a written program itself. Many problems can be caught just by checking a copy of the program, either handwritten or listed from the computer, before it is ever compiled.

2.9 CHAPTER REVIEW

Key Terms

argument	identifier
ASCII	int
associativity	integer number
declaration statement	keyword
definition statement	long
double	main
double-precision number	mixed-mode
EBCDIC	mnemonic
escape sequence	module
expression	modulus operator
float	precedence
floating-point number	printf
function	variable

Summary

1. A C program consists of one or more modules called functions. One of these functions must be called `main()`. The `main()` function identifies the starting point of a C program.

2. Many functions, like `printf()`, are supplied in a standard library of functions provided with each C compiler.

3. When the `printf()` function is used within a program, the preprocessor command `#include <stdio.h>` must be placed at the top of the program. Preprocessor commands do not end with a semicolon.

4. The simplest C program consists of the single function `main()`.

5. Following the function header line, the body of a function has the general form:

```
{
    All program statements in here;
}
```

6. All C statements must be terminated by a semicolon.

7. The `printf()` function is used to display text or numerical results. The first argument to `printf()` can be a message, which is enclosed in double quotes. The text in the message is displayed directly on the screen and may include new line escape sequences for format control.

8. Three types of data were introduced in this chapter: integer, floating point, and character data. Each of these types of data is typically stored in a computer using different amounts of memory. C recognizes each of these data types, in addition to other types yet to be presented.

9. The `printf()` function can be used to display all of C's data types. The conversion control sequences for displaying integer, single-precision floating-point, double-precision floating-point, and character values are `%d`, `%f`, `%lf`, and `%c`, respectively. The `%f` conversion control sequence can be used in place of the `%lf` sequence for double-precision values.

10. Every variable in a C program must be declared as to the type of value it can store. Declarations within a function must be placed as the first statements after a left brace {. Variables may also be initialized when they are declared. Additionally, variables of the same type may be declared using a single declaration statement.

11. Declaration statements always play a software role of informing the compiler of a function's valid variable names. When a variable declaration also causes the compiler to set aside memory storage locations for the variable, the declaration statement is also called a definition statement. All of the declarations we have encountered have also been definition statements.

12. A simple C program containing declaration statements has the form:

```
#include <stdio.h>
void main(void)
{
    declaration statements;
    other statements;
}
```

13. An expression is any combination of constants and/or variables that can be evaluated to yield a value.

14. Expressions are evaluated according to the precedence and associativity of the operators used in the expression.

Exercises

1. Given the following variable declarations, determine which statements and commands are legal and which are illegal. If illegal, explain why.

```
int numOfApples, numOfOranges;
int vector, digitialTemp;
float average, distance;
char letter, symbol;
```

a. `average = 89.4;`

b. `distyance= 130;`

c. `numOfOranges = (54 * numOfApples) % 3;`

d. `vector = numOfApples;`

e. `digitalTemp = (float) average;`

f. `numOfApples = numOfOranges + letter;`

g. `symbol = letter;`

h. `distance = distance % average;`

i. `vector = distance / average;`

j. `numOfApples = (int)average;`

k. `numOfOranges = (int) distance;`

l. `average = (float) vector;`

m. `distance = float(numOfApples);`

n. `numOfApples = numOfOranges - distance;`

o. `numOfOragnes = -17;`

2. Evaluate the following mixed-mode expressions and list the data type of the result. In evaluating the expressions be aware of the data types of all intermediate calculations.

a. `10.0 + 15 / 2 + 4.3`

b. `10.0 + 15.0 / 2 + 4.3`

c. `3.0 * 4 / 6 + 6`

d. `3 * 4.0 / 6 + 6`

e. `20.0 - 2 / 6 + 3`

f. `10 + 17 * 3 + 4`

g. `10 + 17 / 3. + 4`

h. `3.0 * 4 % 6 + 6`

i. `10 + 17 % 3 + 4.`

3. Repeat Exercise 7 in Section 2.3 assuming that `amount` has the real value 1.0, m has the real value 50.0, n has the real value 10.0, and p has the real value 5.0.

4. Analyze the following problem statements and determine if the problem statement is well defined. If the problem is not well defined, explain why.

   a. In a list consisting of 50 test grades, find the grade that appears most frequently.

   b. If a person can only pay $600 to $750 for house payments, what range of houses should be considered?

   c. Determine the smallest number such that the difference of its digits is 31.

   d. Find the first 10 sets of integer numbers a, b, and c such that $a^2 + b^2 = c^2$.

5. Determine if the given algorithm solves the following problem.

   Problem: Determine the largest value for any two given numbers.

   Algorithm: Compute the difference, D, between the two numbers A and B as $D = A - B$. If D is greater than 1, the first number is larger; otherwise the second number is larger.

6. Write a C program that determines which letter lies halfway between any two letters of the alphabet. Test your program using the following letters:

   A and C

   A and Z

   M and Q

   M and P

   Z and Z

7. a. The table in Appendix B lists the integer values corresponding to each letter stored using the ASCII code. Using this table, notice that the uppercase letters consist of contiguous codes starting with an integer value of 65 for A and ending with 90 for the letter Z. Similarly, the lowercase letters begin with the integer value of 97 for the letter a and end with 122 for the letter z. With this as background, determine the character value of the expressions 'A' + 32 and 'Z' + 32.

   b. Using Appendix B, determine the integer value of the expression 'a' - 'A'.

   c. Determine the character value of the following expression, where `upper-case letter` can be any uppercase letter from A to Z:

      `uppercase letter + 'a' - 'A'`

8. You decide to make your company's logo—a red circle surrounded by a concentric blue ring—a well-recognized symbol. To do this you intend to pay farmers throughout the country to paint the logo on their barns. The problem is to determine, for a given-size barn, how much red paint and how much blue paint will be required. From experience, the number of quarts of paint is equal to the area to be painted (in square feet) divided by 125. Using this information construct a structure chart for determining the quarts of red and blue paint that will be needed. (*Hint:* You will have to determine the area of the inner circle and outer ring. Assume that the outer circle has a radius of b, and the inner circle has a radius of a.)

9. Write, test, and run a C program to do the following: Given the current time (hours and minutes) on a 24-hour clock, add a whole number of hours and tell what the new clock reading is and how many days later it will be. (*Hint:* Use `/24` and `%24`, and designate midnight as 0:00 hours instead of 24:00 hours. Example: 17:30 + 37 hours is 6:30, two days later.

10. In a game of Woodenbleevit, three players make up a team. At the end of each round, the team score is the total points accumulated by the team divided by 3 and truncated to the next smaller whole number. For example, if your team received 76 points in a round, the team score for that round would be 25 (76/3 = 25.333 = 25 truncated). A game consists of five rounds.

    Write, test, and run a C program that uses the following team scores:

    Round 1: 14 points (still learning)
    Round 2: 292 points (beginners luck)
    Round 3: 77 points
    Round 4: 82 points
    Round 5: 45 points

    Your program should divide each round's score by 3 and truncate to get the team score for the round. Add the team scores for the five rounds to get the team score for the game. Determine how many points the team lost because of the truncation process. (*Hint:* Use both the division and modular operations.)

11. Hap's Hazard County Phone Company, Inc., charges for phone calls by distance (miles) and length of time (minutes). The cost of a call (in dollars) is computed as 0.30 * (time + 0.05 * distance). Write, test, and run a C program that calculates the cost for three phone calls and the total cost of all three calls using the following data:

Call 1:   3 miles, 20 minutes

Call 2:   2 miles, 15 minutes

Call 3:   6 miles, 4 minutes

The output of your program should include the time, distance, and cost of each call.

Note: Exercises 12 and 13 require raising a number to a power. This can be accomplished using C's power function `pow()`. For example, the statement `pow(2.0,5.0);` raises the number 2.0 to the fifth power, and the statement `pow(num1,num2);` raises the variable `num1` to the `num2` power. To use the power function, either place an `#include math.h` preprocessor command on a line by itself after the `#include stdio.h` command or include the declaration statement `double pow();` with the variable declaration statements used in your program. The power function is explained in more detail in Section 3.3.

12. a. Effective annual interest is the rate that must be compounded annually to generate the same interest as a stated rate compounded over a stipulated conversion period. For example, a stated rate of 8% compounded quarterly is equivalent to an effective annual rate of 8.24%. The relationship between the effective annual rate, E, and the stated rate, I, compounded M times a year is $E = (1 + I/M)^M - 1$. Using this formula, write, compile, and execute a C program to determine the effective annual rate for a stated rate of 6% compounded four times a year (quarterly).

    b. Check the value computed by your program by hand. After you have verified that your program is working correctly, modify it to determine the effective annual rate for a stated rate of 8% compounded monthly.

13. a. The present value of a dollar amount is the amount of money that must be deposited in a bank account today to yield a specified dollar amount in the future. For example, if a bank is currently paying 8% interest annually, you would have to deposit $6947.90 in the bank today to have $15,000 in 10 years. Thus, the present value of the $15,000 is $6947.90. Using this information, write, compile, and execute a C program that calculates how much must be deposited in a bank today to provide exactly $8000 in 9 years at an annual interest rate of 8%. Use the formula

    present value = future amount / (1.0 + annual interest rate)^{years}

    b. Check the value computed by your program by hand. After you have verified that your program is working correctly, modify it to determine the amount of money that must be invested in a bank today to yield $15,000 in 18 years at an annual rate of 6%.

14. a The set of linear equations

$$a_{11}X_1 + a_{12}X_2 = c_1$$
$$a_{21}X_1 + a_{22}X_2 = c_2$$

can be solved using Cramer's rule as

$$X_1 = \frac{c_1 a_{22} - a_{12} c_2}{a_{11} a_{22} - a_{12} a_{21}}$$

$$X_2 = \frac{a_{11} c_2 - c_1 a_{21}}{a_{11} a_{22} - a_{12} a_{21}}$$

Using these equations, write, compile, and execute a C program to solve for the X_1 and X_2 values that satisfy the following equations:

$$3X_1 + 4X_2 = 40$$
$$5X_1 + 2X_2 = 34$$

b. Check the values computed by your program by hand. After you have verified that your program is working correctly, modify it to solve the following set of equations:

$$3X_1 + 12.5X_2 = 22.5$$
$$4.2X_1 - 6.3X_2 = 30$$

CHAPTER

3

Completing
the Basics

In the previous two chapters we explored how results are displayed using C's `printf()` function and how numerical data is stored and processed using variables and assignment statements. In this chapter we complete our introduction to C by presenting additional processing and input capabilities.

3.1 ASSIGNMENT OPERATIONS

The most basic C statement for both assigning values to variables and performing computations is the assignment statement. This statement has the general form

```
variable = operand;
```

The simplest operand in C is a single constant, and in each of the following assignment statements, the expression to the right of the equal sign is a constant:

```
length = 25;
width = 17.5;
```

In each of these assignment statements the value of the constant to the right of the equal sign is assigned to the variable on the left side of the equal sign. It is extremely important to note that the equal sign in C does not have the same meaning as an equal sign in algebra. The equal sign in an assignment statement tells the computer to first determine the value of the operand to the right of the equal sign and then to store (or assign) that value in the variable to the left of the equal sign. In this regard, the C statement `length = 25;` is read "length is assigned the value 25." The blank spaces in the assignment statement are inserted for readability only.

101

A   BIT   OF   BACKGROUND

Napier's Bones

Scottish mathematician John Napier, born near Edinburgh, England, in 1550, spent most of his life creating methods and devices to make mathematical calculations easier. One of his early inventions was a set of square rods, made of bone, that were used for multiplying whole numbers. Napier is also credited with the discovery that the weight of any object can be found by balancing the object on a scale against weights of relative size 1, 2, 4, 8, ...

His most valuable invention, however, was the natural logarithm, which replaced multiplication and division problems with the addition and subtraction of loga-

rithms. For 25 years beginning in 1490, Napier devoted himself almost entirely to generating tables of logarithms.

The contribution of the logarithmic technique to science and technology is immeasurable. Until the advent of electronic calculators and computers, logarithms were *the* approach to lengthy calculations. The logarithmic slide rule, invented by William Oughtred early in the seventeenth century, was the only reasonably affordable computing tool for engineers, scientists, and students until the mid-1970s.

In most modern high-level languages, including C, you will find a function, such as *log (x)*, for calculating logarithms.

Recall from the Section 2.4 that an initial value can be assigned to a variable when it is declared. If an initialization is not done from within the declaration statement, the variable is initialized the first time a value is assigned using an assignment statement. Subsequent assignment statements can, of course, be used to change the value assigned to a variable. For example, assume the following statements are executed one after another and that no value has been assigned to length previously:

```
length = 3.7;
length = 6.28;
```

The first assignment statement assigns the value of 3.7 to the variable named length. Since this is the first time a value is assigned to this variable it is also correct to say that "length is initialized to 3.7." The next assignment statement causes the computer to assign a value of 6.28 to length. The 3.7 that was in length is overwritten with the new value of 6.28, because a variable can only store one value at a time. In this regard, it is sometimes useful to think of the variable to the left of the equal sign as a temporary parking spot in a huge parking lot. Just as an individual parking spot can only be used by one car at a time, each variable can only store one value at a time. The "parking" of a new value in a variable automatically causes the computer to remove any value previously parked there.

In addition to being a constant, the operand to the right of the equal sign in an assignment statement can be a variable or any valid C expression. An *expression* is any combination of constants and variables that can be evaluated to yield a result. Thus, the expression in an assignment statement can be used to perform calculations using the arithmetic operators introduced in Section 2.3 (see Table 2.6). Examples of assignment statements using expressions containing these operators are:

```
sum = 3 + 7;
diff = 15 - 6;
```

```
product = .05 * 14.6;
tally = count + 1;
newTotal = 18.3 + total;
taxes = .06 * amount
totalWeight = weight * factor;
average = sum /items;
slope = (y2 - y1) / (x2 - x1);
```

As always in an assignment statement, the computer first calculates the value of the expression to the right of the equal sign and then stores this value in the variable to the left of the equal sign. For example, in the assignment statement `totalWeight = weight * factor;` the expression `weight * factor` is first evaluated to yield a result. This result, which is a number, is then stored in the variable totalWeight.

In writing assignment statements, you must be aware of two important considerations. Since the expression to the right of the equal sign is evaluated first, all variables used in the expression must be initialized if the result is to make sense. For example, the assignment statement `totalWeight = weight * factor;` will only cause a valid number to be stored in `totalWeight` if the programmer first takes care to put valid numbers in `weight` and `factor`. Thus, the sequence of statements

```
weight = 155.0;
factor = 1.06;
totalWeight = weight * factor;
```

ensures that we know the values being used to obtain the result that will be stored in the variable to the left of the equal sign. Figure 3.1 illustrates the values stored in the variables `weight`, `factor`, and `totalWeight`.

The second consideration to keep in mind is that since the value of an expression is stored in the variable to the left of the equal sign, only one variable can be listed in this position. For example, the statement

```
amount + 1769 = 1462 + 10 - 24;
```

is an invalid assignment statement. The right-side expression evaluates to the integer 1448, which can only be stored in a variable. Since `amount + 1769` is not the valid name of a memory location (it is not a valid variable name), the computer does not know where to store the value 1448. Program 3.1 illustrates the use of assignment statements to calculate the volume of a cylinder. As illustrated in Figure 3.2, the volume of a cylinder is determined by the formula, $Volume = \pi r^2 h$, where r is the radius of the cylinder, h is the height, and π is the constant 3.1416 (accurate to four decimal places).

FIGURE 3.1   **Values Stored in the Variables**

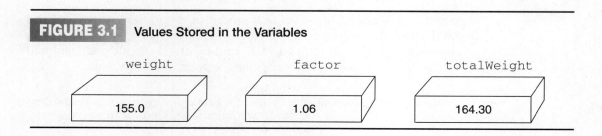

weight
155.0

factor
1.06

totalWeight
164.30

FIGURE 3.2   Determining the Volume of a Cylinder

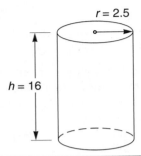

PROGRAM 3.1

```
#include <stdio.h>
void main(void)
{
/*    this program calculates the volume of a cylinder, */
/*       given its radius and height                    */
   float radius, height, volume;

   radius = 2.5;
   height = 16.0;
   volume = 3.1416 * radius * radius * height;
   printf("The volume of the cylinder is %f\n", volume);
}
```

When Program 3.1 is compiled and executed, the output is

        The volume of the cylinder is 314.160000

Notice the order in which statements are executed in Program 3.1. The program begins with the keyword `main` and continues sequentially, statement by statement, until the closing brace is encountered. All computer programs execute in this manner. The computer works on one statement at a time, executing that statement with no knowledge of what the next statement will be. This explains why all variables used in an expression must have values assigned to them before the expression is evaluated. When the computer executes the statement

        volume = 3.1416 * radius * radius * height;

in Program 3.1, it uses whatever value is stored in the variables `radius` and `height` at the time the assignment statement is executed.[1] If no values have been specifically assigned to these variables before they are used in the assignment statement, the computer uses whatever values happen to occupy these variables

---

[1]Since C does not have an exponentiation operator, the square of the radius is obtained by the term `radius * radius`. In Section 3.3 we introduce C's power function `pow()`, which allows us to raise a number to a power.

when they are referenced (on some systems all variables are automatically initial-ized to zero). The computer does not "look ahead" to see if you assign values to these variables later in the program.

It is important to realize that in C the equal sign, =, used in assignment state-ments is itself an operator, *which differs from the way most other high-level languages process this symbol.* In C, the = symbol is called the *assignment operator.* Since the equal sign is an operator in C, multiple assignments are possible in the same statement. For example, in the statement a = b = c = 25; all the assignment operators have the same precedence. Since the assignment operator has a right-to-left associativity, the final evaluation proceeds in the sequence

```
c = 25;
b = c;
a = b;
```

This has the effect of assigning the number 25 to each of the variables individual-ly, and can be represented as

```
a = (b = (c = 25));
```

Thus, the single statement a = b = c = 25; is equivalent to the three individ-ual statements

```
c = 25;
b = 25;
a = 25;
```

Assignment Variations

Although only one variable is allowed immediately to the left of an equal sign in an assignment expression, the variable on the left of the equal sign can also be used on the right of the equal sign. For example, the assignment expression sum = sum + 10 is valid. Clearly, as an algebra equation sum could never be equal to itself plus 10. But in C, the expression sum = sum + 10 is not an equation—it is an expression that is evaluated in two major steps. The first step is to calcu-late the value of sum + 10. The second step is to store the computed value in sum. See if you can determine the output of Program 3.2.

PROGRAM 3.2

```c
#include <stdio.h>
void main(void)
{
   int sum;

   sum = 25;
   printf("The number stored in sum is %d.\n",sum);
   sum = sum + 10;
   printf("The number now stored in sum is %d.\n",sum);
}
```

The assignment statement sum = 25; tells the computer to store the number 25 in sum, as shown in Figure 3.3. The first call to printf() causes the value

---

FIGURE 3.3 **The Integer** 25 **Is Stored in** sum

sum

25

---

stored in sum to be displayed by the message The number stored in sum is 25. The second assignment statement in Program 3–2, sum = sum + 10; causes the computer to retrieve the 25 stored in sum and add 10 to this number, yielding the number 35. The number 35 is then stored in the variable on the left side of the equal sign, which is the variable sum. The 25 that was in sum is simply overwritten with the new value of 35, as shown in Figure 3.4.

Assignment expressions like sum = sum + 25, which use the same variable on both sides of the assignment operator, can be written using the following assignment operators:

$$+= \quad -= \quad *= \quad /= \quad \%=$$

For example, the expression sum = sum + 10 can be written as sum += 10. Similarly, the expression price *= rate is equivalent to the expression price = price * rate.

In using these new assignment operators it is important to note that the variable to the left of the assignment operator is applied to the complete expression on the right. For example, the expression price *= rate + 1 is equivalent to the expression price = price * (rate + 1), not price = price * rate + 1.

Accumulating

Assignment expressions like sum += 10 or its equivalent, sum = sum + 10, are very common in programming. These expressions are required in accumulating subtotals when data is entered one number at a time. For example, if we want to add the numbers 96, 70, 85, and 60 in calculator fashion, the following statements could be used:

Statement	Value in sum
sum = 0;	0
sum = sum + 96;	96
sum = sum + 70;	166
sum = sum + 85;	251
sum = sum + 60;	311

FIGURE 3.4   sum = sum + 10; **Causes a New Value to be Stored in** sum

sum

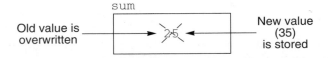

Old value is overwritten ———→ 25 ←——— New value (35) is stored

---

The first statement clears sum by storing 0 in the variable. This removes any number ("garbage" value) in sum that would invalidate the final total. As each number is added, the value stored in sum is increased accordingly. After completion of the last statement, sum contains the total of all the added numbers. Program 3.3 illustrates the effect of these statements by displaying sum's contents after each addition is made.

PROGRAM 3.3

```c
#include <stdio.h>
void main(void)
{
  int sum;

  sum = 0;
  printf("The value of sum is initially set to %d.\n", sum);
  sum = sum + 96;
  printf("  sum is now %d.\n", sum);
  sum = sum + 70;
  printf("  sum is now %d.\n", sum);
  sum = sum + 85;
  printf("  sum is now %d.\n", sum);
  sum = sum + 60;
  printf("  The final sum is %d.\n", sum);
}
```

The output displayed by Program 3.3 is:

```
The value of sum is initially set to 0.
  sum is now 96.
  sum is now 166.
  sum is now 251.
  The final sum is 311.
```

Although Program 3.3 is not a practical program (it is easier to add the numbers by hand), it does illustrate the subtotaling effect of repeated use of statements having the form

```
variable = variable + new_value;
```

We will find many uses for this type of statement when we become more familiar with the repetition statements introduced in Chapter 5.

Counting

An assignment statement that is very similar to the accumulating statement is the *counting* statement. Counting statements have the form

```
variable = variable + fixed_number;
```

Examples of counting statements are:

```
i = i + 1;
n = n + 1;
count = count + 1;
```

```
j = j + 2;
m = m + 2;
kk = kk + 3;
```

In each of these examples the same variable is used on both sides of the equal sign. After the statement is executed, the value of the respective variable is increased by a fixed amount. In the first three examples the variables i, n, and count have all been increased by one. In the next two examples the respective variables have been increased by two, and in the final example the variable kk has been increased by three.

For the special case in which a variable is either increased or decreased by one, C provides two unary operators. Using the increment operator ++, the expression variable = variable + 1 can be replaced by the expression ++variable. Examples of the increment operator are:

Expression	Alternative
i = i + 1	++i
n = n + 1	++n
count = count + 1	++count

Program 3.4 illustrates the use of the increment operator.

PROGRAM 3.4

```
#include <stdio.h>
void main(void)
{
  int count;

  count = 0;
  printf("The initial value of count is %d.\n", count);
  ++count;
  printf("    count is now %d.\n", count);
  ++count;
  printf("    count is now %d.\n", count);
  ++count;
  printf("    count is now %d.\n", count);
  ++count;
  printf("    count is now %d.\n", count);
}
```

The output displayed by Program 3.4 is:

```
The initial value of count is 0.
    count is now 1.
    count is now 2.
    count is now 3.
    count is now 4.
```

In addition to the increment operator, C also provides a decrement operator, --. As you might expect, the expression--variable is equivalent to the expression variable = variable - 1. Examples of the decrement operator are:

Expression	Alternative
`i = i - 1`	`--i`
`n = n - 1`	`--n`
`count = count - 1`	`--count`

When `++` appears before a variable, it is called a prefix increment operator. Besides appearing before (pre) a variable, the increment operator can also be applied after a variable; for example, in the expression `n++`. When the increment appears after a variable it is called a postfix increment. Both of these expressions, `++n` and `n++`, correspond to the longer expression `n = n + 1`. The distinction between a prefix and postfix increment operator occurs when the variable being incremented is used in an assignment expression. For example, the expression `k = ++n` does two things in one expression. Initially the value of `n` is incremented by one, and then the new value of `n` is assigned to the variable `k`. Thus, the statement `k = ++n;` is equivalent to the two statements

```
n = n + 1;  /* increment n first     */
k = n;      /* assign n's value to k */
```

The assignment expression `k = n++`, which uses a postfix increment operator, reverses this procedure. A postfix increment operates after the assignment is completed. Thus, the statement `k = n++;` first assigns the current value of `n` to `k` and then increments the value of `n` by one. This is equivalent to the two statements

```
k = n;      /* assign n's value to k */
n = n + 1;  /* and then increment n  */
```

Just as there are prefix and postfix increment operators, C also provides prefix and postfix decrement operators. For example, both of the expressions `--n` and `n--` reduce the value of `n` by one. These expressions are equivalent to the longer expression `n = n - 1`. As with the increment operator, however, the prefix and postfix decrement operators produce different results when used in assignment expressions. For example, the expression `k = --n` first decrements the value of `n` by one before assigning the value of `n` to `k`. But the expression `k = n--` first assigns the current value of `n` to `k` and then reduces the value of `n` by one.

The increment and decrement operators can often be used advantageously to reduce program storage requirements and increase execution speed. For example, consider the following three statements:

```
count = count + 1;
count += 1;
++count;
```

All perform the same function; however, when these instructions are compiled for execution on an IBM personal computer the storage requirements for the instructions are 9, 4, and 3 bytes, respectively. Using the assignment operator `=` instead of the increment operator results in using three times the storage space for the instruction, with an accompanying decrease in execution speed.

Type Conversions

We have already seen the conversion of an operand's data type within mixed arithmetic expressions (see Section 2.3). For example, if `val` is a double precision variable and num is an integer variable, num's value is converted to double precision in the expression val + num.

The general rules for converting operands in mixed arithmetic expressions were presented in the previous chapter. A more complete set of conversion rules for arithmetic operators is listed in Table 3.1.

TABLE 3.1 Conversion Rules for Arithmetic Operators

Rule 1: All character and short integer operands are converted to integer values and all floating-point operands are converted to double precision values within arithmetic expressions.

Rule 2: If one operand is a double precision value, then the other operand is converted to a double precision value and the result of the expression is a double precision value.

Rule 3: If one operand is a long integer value, then the other operand is converted to a long integer value and the resulting value of the expression is a long integer value.

Rule 4: If one operand is an unsigned integer value, then the other operand is converted to an unsigned integer value and the resulting value of the expression is an unsigned value.

Rule 5: If both operands are of type int, no conversions occur and the resulting value of the expression is an integer value.

Data type conversions also take place across assignment operators. Here the value of the expression on the right side of the equal sign is converted to the data type of the variable to the left of the equal sign. For example, consider the evaluation of the expression

$$a = b * d$$

where a and b are integer variables and d is a floating-point variable. Referring to rule 1 in Table 3.1, the value of d used in the expression is converted to a double precision number for purposes of computation. (It is important to note that the value stored in d remains a floating-point number.) Since one of the operands is a double-precision variable, rule 2 calls for b's value to be converted to a double precision number for the computation (again, the value stored in b remains an integer) and the resulting value of the expression b * d is a double precision number. Finally, since the left side of the assignment operator is an integer variable, the double precision value of the expression (b * d) is truncated to an integer value and stored in the variable a.

In addition to data type conversions that are made automatically to operands in mixed arithmetic expressions, C also provides for user-specified type conversions. The operator used to force the conversion of a value to another type is the *cast* operator. This is a unary operator having the form (*data_type*), where data_type is the desired data type of the operand following the cast. For example, the expression

$$(int) (a * b)$$

ensures that the value of the expression a * b is converted to an integer value. The parentheses around the expression (a * b) are required because the cast operator has a higher precedence than the multiplication operator.

As a last example, consider the expression (int) a * b, where both a and b are double precision variables. Here, only a's value is cast into an integer before multiplication by b. The cast into an integer value causes the fractional part of a's value to be truncated. Since b is a double precision operand, the value of the operand (int) a is converted back to a double precision number (rule 2 in Table 3.1). The forced conversion back to a double precision number, however, does not restore the fractional part of a. As before, the value stored in a is not affected and remains a double precision number; only the value of a used to evaluate the expression is truncated.

Exercises 3.1

1. Write an assignment statement to calculate the circumference of a circle having a radius of 3.3 inches. The equation for determining the circumference c of a circle is $c = 2\pi r$, where r is the radius and π equals 3.1416.

2. Write an assignment statement to calculate the area of a circle. The equation for determining the area a of a circle is $a = \pi r^2$, where r is the radius and $\pi = 3.1416$.

3. Write an assignment statement to convert temperature in degrees Fahrenheit to degrees Celsius. The equation for this conversion is *Celsius = 5/9(Fahrenheit - 32)*.

4. Write an assignment statement to calculate the round trip distance d, in feet, of a trip that is s miles long, one way.

5. Write an assignment statement to calculate the elapsed time, in minutes, that it takes to make a trip. The equation for computing elapsed time is *Elapsed time = total distance/average speed.* Assume that the distance is in miles and the average speed is in miles/hour.

6. Write an assignment statement to calculate the nth term in an arithmetic sequence. The formula for calculating the value v of the nth term is $v = a + (n-1)d$, where a is the first number in the sequence and d is the difference between any two numbers in the sequence.

7. Determine the output of the following program:

```
#include <stdio.h>
void main(void) /* a program illustrating integer truncation */
{
    int num1, num2;

    num1 = 9/2;
    num2 = 17/4;
    printf("the first integer displayed is %d\n", num1);
    printf("the second integer displayed is %d\n", num2);
}
```

8. Determine the output of the following program:

```
#include <stdio.h>
void main(void)
{
    float average = 26.27;

    printf("the average is %f\n", average);
    average = 682.3;
    printf("the average is %f\n", average);
    average = 1.968;
    printf("the average is %f\n", average);
}
```

9. Determine the output of the following program:

```
#include <stdio.h>
void main(void)
```

```
{
  float sum;

  sum = 0.0;
  printf("the sum is %f\n", sum);
  sum = sum + 26.27;
  printf("the sum is %f\n", sum);
  sum = sum + 1.968;
  printf("the final sum is %f\n", sum);
}
```

10. a. Determine what each statement causes to happen in the following program:

```
#include <stdio.h>
void main(void)
{
  int num1, num2, num3, total;

  num1 = 25;
  num2 = 30;
  total = num1 + num2;
  printf(" %d + %d = %d\n", num1, num2, total);
}
```

   b. What output will be produced when the program listed in Exercise 10.a is compiled and executed?

11. Determine and correct the errors in the following programs:

   a.
```
#include <stdio.h>
void main(void)
{
  width = 15
  area = length * width;
  printf("The area is %d\n",area
}
```

   b.
```
#include <stdio.h>
void main(void)
{
  int length, width, area;

  area = length * width;
  length = 20;
  width = 15;
  printf("The area is %d\n",area);
```

   c.
```
#include <stdio.h>
void main(void)
{
  int length = 20; width = 15, area;

  length * width = area;
  printf("The area is %d\n",area);
}
```

12. By mistake a student reordered the statements in Program 3.3 as follows:

```
#include <stdio.h>
void main(void)
{
  int sum;
  sum = 0;
  sum = sum + 96;
  sum = sum + 70;
```

```
sum = sum + 85;
sum = sum + 60;
printf("The value of sum is initially set to %d.\n", sum);
printf("   sum is now %d.\n", sum);
printf("   sum is now %d.\n", sum);
printf("   sum is now %d.\n", sum);
printf("   The final sum is %d.\n", sum);
}
```

Determine what output this program produces.

13. Using Program 3.1, determine the volume of cylinders having the following radii and heights:

Radius (in.)	Height (in.)
1.62	6.23
2.86	7.52
4.26	8.95
8.52	10.86
12.29	15.35

14. The area of an ellipse (see Figure 3.5) is given by the formula $Area = \pi ab$. Using this formula, write a C program to calculate the area of an ellipse having a minor axis of 2.5 inches and a major axis of 6.4 inches.

FIGURE 3.5   The Minor Axis *a* and the Major Axis *b* of an Ellipse

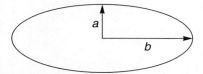

3.2 FORMATTING NUMBERS FOR PROGRAM OUTPUT

Besides displaying correct results, it is extremely important that a program present its results attractively. Most programs are judged, in fact, on the perceived ease of data entry and the style and presentation of their output. For example, displaying a monetary result as 1.897000 is not in keeping with accepted report conventions. The display should be either $1.90 or $1.89, depending on whether rounding or truncation is used.

The format of values displayed by `printf()` can be controlled by *field width specifiers* included as part of each conversion control sequence. For example, the statement

```
printf("The sum of%3d and%4d is%5d.\n", 6, 15, 21);
```

causes the printout

```
        The sum of   6 and   15 is   21.
```

The numbers 3, 4, and 5 in the control string are the field width specifiers. The 3 causes the first number to be printed in a total field width of three spaces, in this case two blank spaces followed by the number 6. The field width specifier for the second conversion control sequence, %4d, causes two blank spaces and the number 15 to be printed for a total field width of four spaces. The last field width specifier causes the 21 to be printed in a field of five spaces, which includes three blanks and the number 21. As illustrated, each integer is right-justified within the specified field.

Field width specifiers are useful in printing columns of numbers so that the numbers in each column align correctly. For example, Program 3.5 illustrates how a column of integers would align in the absence of field width specifiers.

PROGRAM 3.5

```
#include <stdio.h>
void main(void)
{
  printf("%d\n", 6);
  printf("%d\n", 18);
  printf("%d\n", 124);
  printf("---\n");
  printf("%d\n", 6+18+124);
}
```

The output of Program 3.5 is

```
6
18
124
---
148
```

Since no field widths are given, the `printf()` function allocates enough space for each number as it is received. To force the numbers to align on the units digit requires a field width wide enough for the largest displayed number. For Program 3.5, a width of three suffices. The use of this field width is illustrated in Program 3.6.

PROGRAM 3.6

```
#include <stdio.h>
void main(void)
{
  printf("%3d\n", 6);
  printf("%3d\n", 18);
  printf("%3d\n", 124);
  printf("---\n");
  printf("%3d\n", 6+18+124);
}
```

The output of Program 3.6 is

```
            6
           18
          124
          ---
          148
```

Formatted floating-point numbers require the use of two field width speci-fiers. The first specifier determines the total width of the display, including the decimal point and possible sign; the second determines how many digits are printed to the right of the decimal point. For example, the statement

```
printf("|%10.3f|\n",25.67);
```

causes the printout

```
|    25.670|
```

The bar symbol, |, is used to clearly mark the beginning and end of the display field. The field width specifier 10.3 tells printf() to display the number in a total field of 10, which includes one decimal point and three digits to the right of the decimal point. Since the number contains only two digits to the right of the decimal point, the decimal part of the number is padded with a trailing zero.

For all numbers (integers, floating point, and double precision), printf() ignores the specified field width if the total field width is too small, and allocates enough space for the integer part of the number to be printed. The fractional part of both floating point and double precision numbers is always displayed with the number of specified digits. If the fractional part contains fewer digits than specified, the number is padded with trailing zeros; if the fractional part contains more digits than called for in the specifier, the number is rounded to the indicated number of decimal places. Table 3.2 illustrates the effect of various field width specifiers.

TABLE 3.2 Effect of Field Width Specifiers

Specifier	Number	Display	Comments
|%2d|	3	|3|	Number fits in field
|%2d|	43	|43|	Number fits in field
|%2d|	143	|143|	Field width ignored
|%2d|	2.3	Machine dependent	Floating point in an integer field
|%5.2f|	2.366	| 2.37|	Field of 5 with 2 decimal digits
|%5.2f|	42.3	|42.30|	Number fits in field
|%5.2f|	142.364	|142.36|	Field width ignored but fractional specifier used
|%5.2f|	142	Machine dependent	Integer in a floating point field

Format Modifiers

In addition to the conversion control sequences (%d, %f, etc.) and the field width specifiers that may be used with them, C also provides a set of format modifiers that provide additional format control, such as left and right field justification. Format modifiers, if used, must always be placed immediately after the % sym-bol. The more commonly used format modifiers are discussed next.

Left Justification   Numbers displayed using the `printf()` function are normally displayed right-justified with leading spaces inserted to fill the selected field width. To force the output to left-justify the display, a minus sign (-) format modifier can be used. For example, the statement

```
printf("|%-10d|\n",59);
```

causes the display

```
|59        |
```

Again, we have used the bar symbol, |, to identify clearly the beginning and end of the designated display. Notice that the displayed number, 59, is printed at the beginning of the field (left-justification within the field), rather than at the end of the field, as would occur in the absence of the format modifier. Also notice that the format modifier within the `printf()` function is placed immediately after the % symbol.

Explicit Sign Display   Normally, the sign of a number is only displayed for negative numbers. To force both positive and negative signs to be displayed, a plus (+) format modifier must be used. For example, the statement

```
printf("|%+10d|\n",59);
```

causes the display

```
|       +59|
```

If there were no plus sign immediately after the % symbol in the `printf()` function call, the output would not contain the sign of the positive number.

Format modifiers may be combined. For example, the conversion control sequence `%-+10d` would cause an integer number to both display its sign and be left-justified in a field width of 10 spaces. Because the order of the format modifiers is not critical, this conversion control sequence could just as well have been written `%+-10d`.

Other Number Bases[2]

When outputting integers, several display conversions are possible. As we have seen, the conversion control sequence `%d`, with or without a field width specifier, causes integers to be displayed in decimal (base 10) form. To display the value of an integer as either a base 8 (*octal*) or a base 16 (*hexadecimal*) number, we need to use the conversion control sequences `%o` and `%x`, respectively. Program 3.7 illustrates each of these conversion control sequences.

PROGRAM 3.7

```
#include <stdio.h>
void main(void)  /* a program to illustrate output conversions */
{
  printf("The decimal (base 10) value of 15 is %d.\n", 15);
  printf("The octal (base 8) value of 15 is %o.\n", 15);
  printf("The hexadecimal (base 16) value of 15 is %x.\n", 15);
}
```

---

[2]This topic may be omitted on first reading without loss of subject continuity.

The output produced by Program 3.7 is:

```
The decimal (base 10) value of 15 is 15.
The octal (base 8) value of 15 is 17.
The hexadecimal (base 16) value of 15 is F.
```

The display of integer values in one of the three possible number systems (decimal, octal, and hexadecimal) does not affect how the number is actually stored inside a computer. All numbers are stored using the computer's own internal codes. The conversion control sequences used in `printf()` simply tell the function how to convert the internal code for output display purposes.

Besides displaying integers in octal or hexadecimal form, integer constants can also be written in a program in these forms. To designate an octal integer constant, the number must have a leading zero. The number 023, for example, is an octal number in C. Hexadecimal numbers are denoted using a leading 0x. The use of octal and hexadecimal integer constants is illustrated in Program 3.8.

PROGRAM 3.8

```c
#include <stdio.h>
void main(void)
{
  printf("The decimal value of 025 is %d.\n",025);
  printf("The decimal value of 0x37 is %d.\n",0x37);
}
```

When Program 3.8 is run, the following output is obtained:

```
The decimal value of 025 is 21.
The decimal value of 0x37 is 55.
```

The relationship between the input, storage, and display of integers is illustrated in Figure 3.6. To force both octal and hexadecimal numbers to be printed with a leading 0 and 0x, respectively, the # format modifier must be used. For example, the statement:

```c
printf("The octal value of decimal 21 is %#o\n",21);
```

produces the display

```
The octal value of decimal 21 is 025
```

Without the inclusion of the # format modifier within the conversion control sequence %o, the displayed octal value would be 25, with no leading 0. Similarly, the statement

```c
printf("The hexadecimal value of decimal 55 is %#x\n",55);
```

produces the display

```
The hexadecimal value of decimal 55 is 0x37
```

Without the inclusion of the # format modifier within the conversion control sequence %x, the displayed hexadecimal value would be 37, with no leading 0x.

FIGURE 3.6   Input, Storage, and Display of Integers

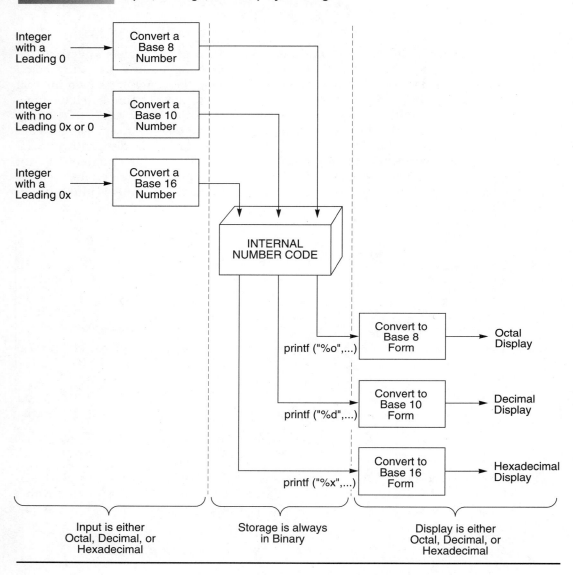

Exercises 3.2

1. Determine the output of the following program:

```
#include <stdio.h>
void main(void) /* a program illustrating integer truncation */
{
    printf("answer1 is the integer %d\n", 9/4);
    printf("answer2 is the integer %d\n", 17/3);
}
```

2. Determine the output of the following program:

```
#include <stdio.h>
void main(void)  /* a program illustrating the % operator */
{
   printf("The remainder of 9 divided by 4 is %d\n", 9 % 4);
   printf( "The remainder of 17 divided by 3 is %d\n", 17 % 3);
}
```

3. Write a C program that displays the results of the expressions `3.0 * 5.0`, `7.1 * 8.3 - 2.2`, and `3.2 / (6.1 * 5)`. Calculate the value of these expressions manually to verify that the displayed values are correct.

4. Write a C program that displays the results of the expressions `15 / 4`, `15 % 4`, and `5 * 3 - (6 * 4)`. Calculate the value of these expressions manually to verify that the display produced by your program is correct.

5. Determine the errors in each of the following statements:

a. `printf("%d,\n" 15)`

b. `printf("%f\n", 33);`

c. `printf("%5d\n", 526.768);`

d. `printf("a b c\n", 26, 15, 18);`

e. `printf("%3.6f\n", 47);`

f. `printf("%3.6\n", 526.768);`

g. `printf(526.768, 33,"%f %d\n");`

6. Determine and write out the display produced by the following statements:

a. `printf("|%d|\n",5);`

b. `printf("|%4d|\n",5);`

c. `printf("|%4d|\n",56829);`

d. `printf("|%5.2f|\n",5.26);`

e. `printf("|%5.2f|\n",5.267);`

f. `printf("|%5.2f|\n",53.264);`

g. `printf("|%5.2f|\n",534.264);`

h. `printf("|%5.2f|\n",534.);`

7. Write out the display produced by the following statements.

a. `printf("The number is %6.2f\n",26.27);`
`printf("The number is %6.2f\n",682.3);`
`printf("The number is %6.2f\n",1.968);`

b. `printf("$%6.2f\n",26.27);`
`printf(" %6.2f\n",682.3);`
`printf(" %6.2f\n",1.968);`
`printf("--------\n");`
`printf("$%6.2f\n", 26.27 + 682.3 + 1.968);`

c. `printf("$%5.2f\n",26.27);`
`printf(" %5.2f\n",682.3);`
`printf(" %5.2f\n",1.968);`
`printf("--------\n");`
`printf("$%5.2f\n", 26.27 + 682.3 + 1.968);`

d. `printf("%5.2f\n",34.164);`
`printf("%5.2f\n",10.003);`
`printf("-----\n");`
`printf("%5.2f\n", 34.164 + 10.003);`

8. a. Rewrite the `printf()` function calls in the following program to produce the display:

```
The sales tax is $ 1.80
The total bill is $37.80
```

```
#include <stdio.h>
void main(void)
{
  printf("The sales tax is %f\n", 0.05 * 36);
  printf("The total bill is %f\n", 37.80);
}
```

   b. Run the program written for Exercise 8.a to verify the output display.

9. The following table lists the correspondence between the decimal numbers 1 through 15 and their octal and hexadecimal representation:

Decimal:	1	2	3	4	5	6	7	8	9	10	11	12	13	14	15
Octal:	1	2	3	4	5	6	7	10	11	12	13	14	15	16	17
Hexadecimal:	1	2	3	4	5	6	7	8	9	A	B	C	D	E	F

Using the above table, determine the output of the following program:

```
#include <stdio.h>
void main(void)
{
  printf("The value of 14 in octal is %o.\n",14);
  printf("The value of 14 in hexadecimal is %x.\n",14);
  printf("The value of 0xA in decimal is %d.\n",0xA);
  printf("The value of 0xA in octal is %o.\n",0xA);
}
```

10. a. Write a program that uses the `%d` control sequence to display the integer values of the lowercase letters a, m, and n, respectively. Do the displayed values for these letters match the values listed in Appendix B?

   b. Expand the program written for Exercise 10.a to display the integer value corresponding to the internal computer code for a newline escape sequence.

3.3 USING MATHEMATICAL LIBRARY FUNCTIONS

As we have seen, assignment statements can be used to perform arithmetic computations. For example, the assignment statement

$$tax = rate * income;$$

multiplies the value in `rate` times the value in `income` and then assigns the resulting value to `tax`. Although addition, subtraction, multiplication, and division are easily accomplished using C's arithmetic operators, no such operators exist for raising a number to a power, finding the square root of a number, or other mathematical values. To facilitate the calculation of powers, square roots, logarithmic, and other mathematical calculations, C provides standard preprogrammed functions that can be included in a program. Like the `printf()` function with which you are already familiar, the available mathematical functions are stored in a mathematics library that contains the collection of standard and tested functions available on your system.

Before using one of C's mathematical functions, you must know

- The name of the desired mathematical function
- What the mathematical function does
- The type of data required by the mathematical function
- The data type of the result returned by the mathematical function.

To illustrate the use of C's mathematical functions, consider the mathematical function named `sqrt`, which calculates the square root of a number. The square root of a number is computed using the expression

$$\texttt{sqrt(number)}$$

where the function's name, in this case `sqrt`, is followed by parentheses containing the number for which the square root is desired. The parentheses following the function name effectively provide a "funnel" through which data can be passed to the function (see Figure 3.7). The items that are passed to the function through the parentheses are called *arguments* of the function and constitute its input data. For example, the following expressions are used to compute the square root of the arguments 4.0, 17.0, 25.0, 1043.29, and 6.4516:

```
sqrt(4.0)
sqrt(17.0)
sqrt(25.0)
sqrt(1043.29)
sqrt(6.4516)
```

The argument to the function named `sqrt` must be a double precision value. The `sqrt` function computes the square root of its argument and the returned result is itself a double precision value. The values returned by the previous expressions are

Expression	Value returned
sqrt(4.0)	2.000000
sqrt(17.0)	4.123106
sqrt(25.0)	5.000000
sqrt(1043.29)	32.300000
sqrt(6.4516)	2.540000

FIGURE 3.7   Passing Data to the `sqrt()` Function

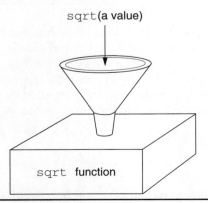

sqrt(a value)

sqrt function

TABLE 3.3 Common C Functions

Function name and argument(s)	Argument type(s)	Returned value	Description
`int abs(int i)`	integer	integer	Absolute value of *i*
`double fabs(double d)`	double	double	Absolute value of *d*
`double pow(double d1, double d2)`	double	double	*d*1 raised to the *d*2 power
`double exp(double d)`	double	double	*e* raised to the *d* power
`double sqrt(double d)`	double	double	Square root of *d*
`double sin(double d)`	double	double	Sine of *d* (*d* in radians)
`double cos(double d)`	double	double	Cosine of *d* (*d* in radians)
`double log(double d)`	double	double	Natural log of *d*
`double log10(double d)`	double	double	Common log (base 10) of *d*

In addition to the `sqrt` function, Table 3.3 lists the more commonly used mathematical functions provided in C. Although some of the mathematical functions listed require more than one argument, all functions, by definition, return a single value. Table 3.4 lists the value returned by selected functions using example arguments. Note that the argument types for the examples agree with those given in Table 3.3 for the specified function.

TABLE 3.4 Selected Functions Examples

Example	Returned value
`abs (-7.362)`	7.362000
`abs (-3)`	3
`pow(2.0, 5.0)`	32.000000
`sqrt(16.0)`	4.000000
`exp(-3.2)`	0.040762
`pow (10, 3)`	1000.000000
`log (18.697)`	2.928363
`log10 (18.697)`	1.271772

For each case in which a mathematical function is used, it is called into action by giving the name of the function and passing any data to it within parentheses following the function's name (see Figure 3.8). The arguments that are passed to a function need not be single constants. Expressions can also be arguments provided that the expression can be computed to yield a value of the required data type. For example, the following arguments are valid for the given functions:

```
sqrt(4.0 + 5.3 * 4.0)
sqrt(16.0 * 2.0 - 6.7)
sqrt(x * y - z/3.2)
abs(2.3 * 4.6)
```

The expressions in parentheses are first evaluated to yield a specific value. Thus, values would have to be assigned to the variables x, y, and z before their use

---

FIGURE 3.8   Using and Passing Data to a Function

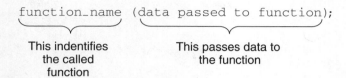

```
function_name (data passed to function);
```

This indentifies   This passes data to
the called   the function
function

---

in the preceding expressions. After the value of the argument is calculated, it is passed to the function.

Functions may be included as part of larger expressions. For example,

```
4 * sqrt(4.5 * 10.0 - 9.0) - 2.0 =
      4 * sqrt(36.000000) - 2.0 =
            4 * 6.000000 - 2.0 = 24.000000 - 2.0 = 22.000000
```

and

```
3.0 * log(30 * .514) =
      3.0 * log(15.42) =
            3.0 * 2.735665 = 8.206995
```

The step-by-step evaluation of

```
3.0 * sqrt(5 * 33 - 13.71) / 5
```

is:

Step	Result
1. Perform multiplication in argument	`3.0 * sqrt(165 - 13.71) / 5`
2. Complete argument calculation	`3.0 * sqrt(151.290000) / 5`
3. Return a function value	`3.0 * 12.300000 / 5`
4. Perform the multiplication	`36.900000 / 5`
5. Perform the division	`7.380000`

Program 3.9 illustrates the use of the sqrt function to determine the time it takes a ball to hit the ground after it has been dropped from an 800-foot tower. The mathematical formula used to calculate the time, in seconds, that it takes to fall a given distance, in feet, is:

$$Time = sqrt(2 * distance / g)$$

where g is the gravitational constant equal to 32.2 ft/sec^2.

Notice that Program 3.9 contains a declaration statement for the sqrt() function. Although the actual code for the sqrt() function is contained within a standard mathematics library, the proper declaration for the function must be provided by the programmer within any program using the function.[3] Alternatively, all compilers have a standard *mathematical header* file named math.h that contains appropriate declaration statements for the supplied mathematical library functions. To include the information in this file in your program, which allows you to use all of the mathematical functions without explicitly

PROGRAM 3.9

```c
#include <stdio.h>
void main(void)
{
  double time, height;
  double sqrt();

  height = 800.0;
  time = sqrt(2.0 * height / 32.2);
  printf("It will take %4.2lf seconds\n", time);
  printf("to fall %7.3lf feet.\n", height);
}
```

typing declaration statements for each function, the following preprocessor statement must be included with your program:

```
#include <math.h>   ◄──── no semicolon
```

Thus, using this statement, we can rewrite Program 3.9 as Program 3.10. (The order of the two #include commands can be reversed.)

PROGRAM 3.10

```c
#include <stdio.h>
#include <math.h>
void main(void)
{
  double time, height;

  height = 800.0;
  time = sqrt(2.0 * height / 32.2);
  printf("It will take %4.2lf seconds\n", time);
  printf("to fall %7.3lf feet.\n", height);
}
```

Notice in Program 3.10 that the declaration statement double sqrt(); used in Program 3.9 has been eliminated. The output of both Programs 3.9 and 3.10 is:

```
It will take 7.05 seconds
to fall 800.00 feet.
```

As used in both programs, the value returned by the sqrt function is assigned to the variable time. In addition to assigning a function's returned value to a vari-

---

[3]Additionally, if you are using a UNIX based system, the compile command must be changed to cc filename -lm. The -lm provides an argument to the compiler to search the mathematics library. The Microsoft and Borland DOS- and Windows-based compilers do not require any additional arguments.

able, the returned value may be included within a larger expression, or even used as an argument to another function. For example, the expression

```
sqrt(pow(10,abs(num)))
```

is valid. Because parentheses are present, the computation proceeds from the inner to the outer pairs of parentheses. Thus, the absolute value of num is computed first and used as an argument to the pow function. The value returned by the pow function is then used as an argument to the sqrt function.

Note that the arguments of all mathematical trigonometric functions (sin, cos, etc.) must be in radians. Thus, to obtain the sine of an angle that is given in degrees the angle must first be converted to radian measure. This is easily accomplished by multiplying the angle by the term (3.1416/180.). For example, to obtain the sine of 30 degrees, the expression sin(30 * 3.1416/180.) should be used.

Exercises 3.3

1. Write function calls to determine:

   a. The square root of 6.37.

   b. The square root of x - y.

   c. The sine of 30 degrees.

   d. The sine of 60 degrees.

   e. The absolute value of a^2 - b^2.

   f. The value of e raised to the third power.

2. For $a = 10.6$, $b = 13.9$, $c = -3.42$, determine the value of:

   a. `(int) a`

   b. `(int) b`

   c. `(int) c`

   d. `(int) a + b`

   e. `(int) a + b + c`

   f. `(int) (a + b) + c`

   g. `(int) (a + b + c)`

   h. `(float) (int) a + b`

   i. `(float) (int) (a + b)`

   j. `abs(a) + abs(B)`

   k. `sqrt(abs(a - B))`

3. Write C statements for the following:

   a. $b = \sin x - \cos x$

   b. $b = \sin^2 x - \cos^2 x$

   c. area = $(c * b * \sin a)/2$

   d. $c = \sqrt{a^2 + b^2}$

   e. $p = \sqrt{|m - n|}$

   f. sum $= \dfrac{a(r^n - 1)}{r - 1}$

4. Write, compile, and execute a program that calculates and returns the fourth root of the number 81.0, which is 3. When you have verified that your program works correctly, use it to determine the fourth root of 1,728.896400. Your program should make use of the sqrt function.

5. Write, compile, and execute a C program that calculates the distance between two points whose coordinates are (7,12) and (3,9). Use the fact that the distance between two points having coordinates (x1,y1) and (x2,y2) is *Distance = sqrt([x1 - x2]² + [y1 - y2]²)*. When you have verified that your program works correctly by calculating the distance between the two points manually, use your program to determine the distance between the points (-12,-15) and (22,5).

6. If a 20-foot ladder is placed on the side of a building at a 75-degree angle, as illustrated in Figure 3.9, the height at which the ladder touches the building can be calculated as *height = 20 * sin 75°*. Calculate this height by hand and then write, compile, and execute an C program that determines and displays the value of the height. When you have verified that your program works correctly, use it to determine the height of a 25-foot ladder placed at an angle of 85 degrees.

FIGURE 3.9   Calculating the Height at Which a Ladder Touches a Building

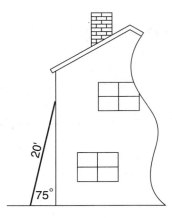

7. A model of worldwide population, in billions of people, after 1990 is given by the equation

$$Population = 5.5(1 + e^{0.02 [year - 1990]})$$

Using this formula, write, compile, and execute a C program to estimate the worldwide population in the year 1995. Verify the result displayed by your program by calculating the answer manually. After you have verified your program is working correctly, use it to estimate the world's population in the year 2012.

3.4 PROGRAM INPUT USING THE scanf() FUNCTION

Data for programs that are only going to be executed once may be included directly in the program. For example, if we wanted to multiply the numbers 300.0 and 0.05, we could use Program 3.11.

PROGRAM 3.11

```c
#include <stdio.h>
void main(void)
{
  float num1, num2, product;

  num1 = 300.0;
  num2 = 0.05;
  product = num1 * num2;
  printf("%f times %f is %f\n", num1, num2, product);
}
```

The output displayed by Program 3.11 is:

```
300.000000 times 0.050000 is 15.000000
```

Program 3.11 can be shortened, as illustrated in Program 3.12. Both programs, however, suffer from the same basic problem in that they must be rewritten in order to multiply different numbers. Both programs lack the facility for entering different numbers on which to be operated.

PROGRAM 3.12

```c
#include <stdio.h>
void main(void)
{
  printf("%f times %f is %f\n", 300.0, .05, 300.0*.05);
}
```

Except for the practice provided to the programmer of writing, entering, and running the program, programs that do the same calculation only once, on the same set of numbers, are clearly not very useful. After all, it is simpler to use a calculator to multiply two numbers than to enter and run either Program 3.11 or 3.12.

This section presents the `scanf()` function, which is used to enter data into a program while it is executing. Just as the `printf()` function displays a copy of the value stored inside a variable, the `scanf()` function allows the user to enter a value at the terminal (see Figure 3.10). The value is then stored directly in a variable.

Like the `printf()` function, the `scanf()` function requires a control string as the first argument inside the function name parentheses. The control string tells the function the type of data being input and uses the same conversion control sequences as the `printf()` function. Unlike the control string used in a `printf()` function, however, the control string passed to `scanf()` cannot contain a message. Also, unlike `printf()` where a list of variable names can follow the control string, `scanf()` requires that a list of variable addresses follow the control string. For the variables we have been using (integer, floating point, double, and character), the

---

FIGURE 3.10 scanf() **Is Used to Enter Data;** printf() **Is Used to Display Data**

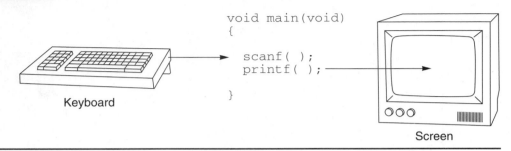

```
void main(void)
{
   scanf( );
   printf( );
}
```

Keyboard

Screen

---

variable addresses are obtained by writing an ampersand symbol, &, immediately before the variable's name. For example, whereas num1, num2, num3 is a list of three variable names, &num1, &num2, &num3 is a list of three variable addresses. The ampersand symbol, &, is C's address operator, which means "the address of." Thus, if num1 is a variable name, &num1 means "the address of num1," and the statement scanf("%d", &num1); is a call to the scanf() function.[4] The conversion control sequence %d in this statement is identical to the conversion control sequence used in printf() in that it tells the scanf() function that it will be dealing with an integer number, and the address operator & in front of the variable num1, as already noted, is required for scanf().

When a statement such as scanf("%d",&num1); is encountered, the computer stops program execution and continuously scans the keyboard for data (scanf is short for "scan function" and "formatted scan"). When a data item is typed, the scanf() function stores the item using the address it was given. The program then continues execution with the next statement after the call to scanf(). To see this, consider Program 3.13.

PROGRAM 3.13

```
#include <stdio.h>
void main(void)
{
  float num1, num2, product;

  printf("Please type in a number: ");
  scanf("%f",&num1);
  printf("Please type in another number: ");
  scanf("%f",&num2);
  product = num1 * num2;
  printf("%f times %f is %f\n",num1, num2, product);
}
```

---

[4]The interested reader may review Section 2.7, which contains more detailed introductory material on the address operator. We will encounter the address operator again, and be much more specific about its purpose in Chapters 6 and 10.

The first call to `printf()` in Program 3.13 prints a message that tells the person at the terminal what should be typed. When a message is used in this manner it is called a *prompt*. In this case the prompt tells the user to type a number. The computer then executes the next statement, which is a call to `scanf()`. The `scanf()` function puts the computer into a temporary pause (or wait) state for as long as it takes the user to type a value. Then the user signals the `scanf()` function by pressing the return key after the value has been typed. The entered value is stored in the variable whose address was passed to `scanf()`, and the computer is taken out of its paused state. Program execution then proceeds with the next statement, which in Program 3.13 is another call to `printf()`. This call causes the next message to be displayed. The second call to `scanf()` again puts the computer into a temporary wait state while the user types a second value. This second number is stored in the variable num2 .

The following sample run was made using Program 3.13.

```
Please type in a number: 300.
Please type in another number: .05
300.000000 times .050000 is 15.000000
```

In Program 3.13, each call to `scanf()` is used to store one value into a variable. The `scanf()` function, however, can be used to enter and store as many values as there are conversion control sequences in the control string. For example, the statement

```
scanf("%f %f",&num1,&num2);
```

results in two values being read from the terminal and assigned to the variables num1 and num2 . If the data entered at the terminal was

```
0.052 245.79
```

the variables num1 and num2 would contain the values 0.052 and 245.79, respectively. The space in the control string between the two conversion control sequences, "%f %f", is strictly for readability. The control string "%f%f" would work equally well. When actually entering numbers such as 0.052 and 245.79, however, you should leave at least one space between the numbers, regardless of which control string, "%f %f" or "%f%f", is used. The space between the entered numbers clearly indicates where one number ends and the next begins and is called a *delimiter*. Inserting more than one space between numbers has the same effect on `scanf()` as inserting a single space.

The only time that a space can affect the value being entered is when `scanf()` is expecting a character data type. For example, the statement `scanf("%c%c%c",&ch1,&ch2,&ch3);` causes `scanf()` to store the next three characters typed in the variables ch1, ch2, and ch3, respectively. If you type x y z, the x is stored in ch1, a blank is stored in ch2, and y is stored in ch3 . If, however, the statement `scanf("%c  %c  %c",&ch1,&ch2,&ch3);` was used, `scanf()` looks for three characters, each separated by exactly one space.

Any number of `scanf()` function calls can be made in a program, and any number of values can be input using a single `scanf()` function. Just be sure that a conversion control sequence is used for each value to be entered and that the address operator is used in front of the variable name where the value is to be stored.[5] Program 3.14 illustrates use of the `scanf()` function to input three numbers from the keyboard. The program then calculates and displays the average of the numbers entered.

---

[5]As we will see, for character strings the address operator is *not* used. This is because a character string name is a pointer.

PROGRAM 3.14

```c
#include <stdio.h>
void main(void)
{
    int num1, num2, num3; float average;

    printf("Enter three integer numbers: ");
    scanf("%d %d %d", &num1, &num2, &num3);
    average = (num1 + num2 + num3)/3.0;
    printf("The average of the numbers is %f\n", average);
}
```

The following sample run was made using Program 3.14:

```
Enter three integer numbers: 22 56 73
The average of the numbers is 50.333333
```

Note that the data typed at the keyboard for this sample run consists of the input:

```
22 56 73
```

In response to this line of input, Program 3.14 stores the value 22 in the variable num1, the value 56 in the variable num2, and the value 73 in the variable num3 (see Figure 3.11). Since the average of three integer numbers can be a floating-point number, the variable average, which is used to store the average, is declared as a floating-point variable. Note also that the parentheses are needed in the assignment statement average = (num1+num2+num3)/3.0. Without

FIGURE 3.11 Inputting Data into the Variables num1, num2, **and** num3

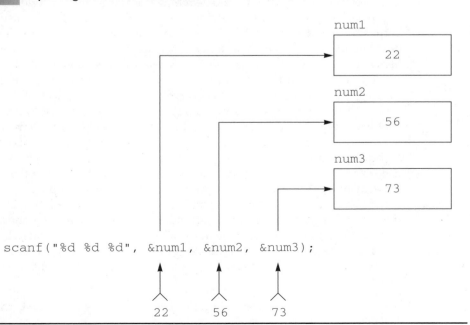

these parentheses, the only value that would be divided by three would be the integer in num3 (since division has a higher precedence than addition).

The conversion control sequences used in a scanf() control string are the same as those used in printf() calls, with one caution. When printing a double precision number using printf(), the conversion control sequence for a floating-point variable, %f, can be used. This is not true when using scanf(). If a double precision number is to be entered, the conversion control sequence %lf must be used.

The scanf() function, again like the printf() function, does not test the data type of the values being entered. It is up to the user to ensure that all variables are declared correctly and that any numbers entered are of the correct type. However, scanf() is "clever" enough to make a few data type conversions. For example, if an integer is entered in place of a floating point or double precision number, the scanf() function automatically supplies a decimal point at the end of the integer before storing the number. Similarly, if a floating point or double precision number is entered when an integer is expected, the scanf() function only uses the integer part of the number. For example, assume the following numbers are typed in response to the function call scanf("%f %d %f", &num1, &num2, &num3);

56 22.879 33.923

scanf() converts the 56 to 56.0 and stores this value in the variable num1. The function continues scanning the input, expecting an integer value. As far as scanf() is concerned, the decimal point after the 22 in the number 22.879 indicates the end of an integer and the start of a decimal number. Thus, the number 22 is stored in num2. Continuing to scan the typed input, scanf() takes the .879 as the next floating-point number and stores this value in num3. As far as scanf() is concerned, 33.923 is extra input and is ignored until the next scanf() is encountered. If, however, you do not initially type enough data, the scanf() function will continue to make the computer pause until sufficient data has been entered.

scanf() **with Buffered Input**[6]

Seemingly strange results are sometimes obtained when the scanf() function is used to accept characters. To see how this can occur, consider Program 3.15, which uses scanf() to accept the next character entered at the keyboard and store the character in the variable fkey.

PROGRAM 3.15

```c
#include <stdio.h>
void main(void)
{
  char fkey;

  printf("Type in a character: ");
  scanf("%c", &fkey);
  printf("The key just accepted is %d\n", fkey);
}
```

---

[6]This section contains supplementary material on the scanf() function and can be omitted on first reading without loss of subject continuity.

When Program 3.15 is run, the character entered in response to the prompt `Type in a character:` is stored in the character variable fkey and the decimal code for the character is displayed by the last `printf()` function call. The following sample run illustrates this:

```
Type in a character: m
The key just accepted is 109
```

At this point, everything seems to be working just fine, although you might be wondering why we displayed the decimal value of m rather than the character itself. The reason for this will soon become apparent.

In typing m, two keys are usually pressed, the m key and the ENTER key. On most computer systems these two characters are stored in a temporary holding area called a *buffer* immediately after they are pressed, as illustrated in Figure 3.12. The first key pressed, m in this case, is taken from the buffer and stored in `fkey`. This, however, still leaves the code for the ENTER key in the buffer. Any subsequent call to `scanf()` for character input will automatically pick up the code for the ENTER key as the next character. For example, consider Program 3.16.

PROGRAM 3.16

```c
#include <stdio.h>
void main(void)
{
  char fkey, skey;

  printf("Type in a character: ");
  scanf("%c", &fkey);
  printf("The key just accepted is %d\n", fkey);
  printf("Type in another character: ");
  scanf("%c", &skey);
  printf("The key just accepted is %d\n", skey);
}
```

FIGURE 3.12 Typed Keyboard Characters Are First Stored in a Buffer

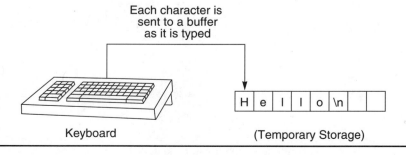

Each character is
sent to a buffer
as it is typed

| H | e | l | l | o | \n | | |

Keyboard   (Temporary Storage)

The following is a sample run for Program 3.16.

```
Type in a character: m
The key just accepted is 109
Type in another character: The key just accepted is 10
```

Let us review what has happened. In entering m in response to the first prompt, the ENTER key is also pressed. From a character standpoint this represents the entry of two distinct characters. The first character is m, which is stored as 109. The second character also gets stored in the buffer with the numerical code for the ENTER key. The second call to scanf() picks up this code immediately, without waiting for any additional key to be pressed. The last call to printf() displays the code for this key. The reason for displaying the numerical code rather than the character itself is because the ENTER key has no printable character associated with it that can be displayed.

Remember that every key has a numerical code, including the ENTER, SPACE, ESCAPE, and CONTROL keys. These keys generally have no effect when entering numbers, because scanf() ignores them as leading or trailing whitespace input with numerical data. Nor do these keys affect the entry of a single character requested as the first user data to be input, as is the case in Program 3.16. Only when a character is requested after the user has already input some other data, as in Program 3.16, does the usually invisible ENTER key become noticeable.

There is a quick solution to avoid having the ENTER key accepted as legitimate character input. All we have to do is clear the input buffer after we accept the desired input. This is accomplished by the fflush(stdin) statement, which flushes the standard input device (the keyboard) of any data. Program 3.17 illustrates use of this technique. The ENTER key, which is accepted along with the first character typed, is flushed from the buffer after the first character is stored into fkey.

PROGRAM 3.17

```c
#include <stdio.h>
void main(void)
{
  char fkey, skey;

  printf("Type in a character: ");
  scanf("%c", &fkey);
  fflush(stdin);          /* this flushes out the buffer */
  printf("The key just accepted is %d\n", fkey);
  printf("Type in another character: ");
  scanf("%c", &skey);   /* accept another code */
  printf("The key just accepted is %d\n", skey);
}
```

In reviewing Program 3.17, observe that the first scanf() function call stores only one character. Now when the user types an m and presses the ENTER key, the m is assigned to fkey and the code for the ENTER key remains in the buffer. The fflush() call then clears the buffer. The next call to scanf() stores the code for the next key pressed in the variable skey. The following is a sample run for Program 3.17.

```
Type in a character: m
The key just accepted is 109
Type in another character: b
The key just accepted is 98
```

The solution to the "phantom" ENTER key used in Program 3.17 is not the only solution possible. (There is never just one way of doing something in C.)[7] All solutions, however, center on the fact that the ENTER key is a legitimate character input and must be treated as such when using a buffered system.

Exercises 3.4

1. For the following declaration statements, write a `scanf()` function call that will cause the computer to pause while the appropriate data is typed by the user.

   a. `int firstnum;`

   b. `float grade;`

   c. `double secnum;`

   d. `char keyval;`

   e. `int month years;`
   `float average;`

   f. `char ch;`
   `int num1,num2;`
   `double grade1,grade2;`

   g. `float interest, principal, capital;`
   `double price,yield;`

   h. `char ch,letter1,letter2;`
   `int num1,num2,num3;`

   i. `float temp1,temp2,temp3;`
   `double volts1,volts2;`

2. For the following `scanf()` function calls, write appropriate declaration statements for the variables.

   a. `scanf("%d",&day);`

   b. `scanf("%c",&fir_char);`

   c. `scanf("%f",&grade);`

   d. `scanf("%lf",&price);`

   e. `scanf("%d %d %c",&num1,&num2,&ch1);`

   f. `scanf("%f %f d",&firstnum,&secnum,&count);`

   g. `scanf("%c %c %d %lf",&ch1,&ch2,&flag,&average);`

3. Given the following declaration statements,

   ```
   int num1,num2;
   float firstnum,secnum;
   double price,yield;
   ```

---

[7]Another solution is remove the `fflush()` call and replace the first `scanf()` call with the statement `scanf("%c%c", &fkey, &skey)`. This stores the ENTER key code into `skey`, which is then overwritten by the second `scanf()` call. Alternatively, if the `flush()` call is removed, the last `scanf()` call in Program 3.17 can be replaced with the statement `scanf("\n%c", &skey)`.

determine and correct the errors in the following `scanf()` function calls:

a. `scanf("%d",num1);`

b. `scanf("%f %f %f",&num1,firstnum,&price);`

c. `scanf("%c %lf %f",&num1,&secnum,&price);`

d. `scanf("%d %d %lf",num1,num2,yield);`

e. `scanf(&num1,&num2);`

f. `scanf(&num1,"%d");`

4. a. Write a C program that first displays the following prompt:

    `Enter the temperature in degrees Celsius:`

    Have your program accept a value entered from the keyboard and convert the temperature entered to degrees Fahrenheit, using the equation *Fahrenheit = (9.0 / 5.0) * Celsius + 32.0*. Your program should then display the temperature in degrees Celsius, using an appropriate output message.

   b. Compile and execute the program written for Exercise 4.a. Verify your program by calculating by hand, and then by using your program, the Fahrenheit equivalent of the following test data:

    `Test data set 1: 0 degrees Celsius.`
    `Test data set 2: 50 degrees Celsius`
    `Test data set 3: 100 degrees Celsius`

    When you are sure your program is working correctly, use it to complete the following table:

Celsius	Fahrenheit
45	
50	
55	
60	
65	
70	

5. Write, compile, and execute a C program that displays the following prompt:

    `Enter the radius of a circle:`

    After accepting a value for the radius, your program should calculate and display the area of the circle. (*Hint: Area = 3.1416 * radius².*) For testing purposes, verify your program using a test input radius of 3 inches. After manually determining that the result produced by your program is correct, use your program to complete the following table:

Radius (in.)	Area (sq. in.)
1.0	
1.5	
2.0	
2.5	
3.0	
3.5	

6. a. Write, compile, and execute a C program that displays the following prompts:

    `Enter the miles driven:`
    `Enter the gallons of gas used:`

After each prompt is displayed, your program should use a scanf() statement to accept data from the keyboard for the displayed prompt. After the gallons of gas used number has been entered, your program should calculate and display miles per gallon. This value should be included in an appropriate message and calculated using the equation *Miles per gallon = miles / gallons used.* Verify your program using the following test data:

```
Test data set 1: Miles = 276, Gas = 10 gallons.
Test data set 2: Miles = 200, Gas = 15.5 gallons.
```

When you have completed your verification, use your program to complete the following table:

Miles driven	Gallons used	MPG
250	16.00	
275	18.00	
312	19.54	
296	17.39	

b. For the program written for Exercise 6.a, determine how many verification runs are required to ensure the program is working correctly and give a reason supporting your answer.

7. a. Write, compile, and execute a C program that displays the following prompts:

```
Enter a number:
Enter a second number:
Enter a third number:
Enter a fourth number:
```

After each prompt is displayed, your program should use a scanf() statement to accept a number from the keyboard for the displayed prompt. After the fourth number has been entered, your program should calculate and display the average of the numbers. The average should be included in an appropriate message. Check the average displayed by your program using the following test data:

```
Test data set 1: 100, 100, 100, 100
Test data set 2: 100, 0, 100, 0
```

When you have completed your verification, use your program to complete the following table:

Numbers	Average
92, 98, 79, 85	
86, 84, 75, 86	
63, 85, 74, 82	

b. Repeat Exercise 7.a, making sure that you use the same variable name, number, for each number input. Also use the variable sum for the sum of the numbers. (*Hint:* To do this, you may use the statement sum = sum + number after each number is accepted. Review the material on accumulating presented in Section 3.1.)

8. a. Write, compile, and execute a C program that computes and displays the value of the second-order polynomial $ax^2 + bx + c$ for any user input values of the coefficients a, b, c, and the variable x. Have your program first display a message informing the user as to what the program will do, and then display suitable prompts to alert the user to enter the desired data. (*Hint:* Use a prompt such as *Enter the coefficient of the x squared term:*)

b. Check the result produced by the program written for Exercise 8.a using the following test data:

```
Test data set 1: a = 0, b = 0, c = 22, x = 56
Test data set 2: a = 0, b = 22, c = 0, x = 2
Test data set 3: a = 22, b = 0, c = 0, x = 2
Test data set 4: a = 2, b = 4, c = 5, x = 2
Test data set 5: a = 5, b = -3, c = 2, x = 1
```

When you have completed your verification, use your program to complete the following table:

a	b	c	x	Polynomial Value
2.0	17.0	-12.0	1.3	
3.2	2.0	15.0	2.5	
3.2	2.0	15.0	-2.5	
-2.0	10.0	0.0	2.0	
-2.0	10.0	0.0	4.0	
-2.0	10.0	0.0	5.0	
-2.0	10.0	0.0	6.0	
5.0	22.0	18.0	8.3	
4.2	-16	-20	-5.2	

9. The number of bacteria, B, in a certain culture that is subject to refrigeration can be approximated by the equation $B = 300,000\, e^{-0.032t}$, where e is the irrational number 2.71828 rounded to five decimal places, known as Euler's number, and t is the time, in hours, that the culture has been refrigerated. Using this equation, write, compile, and execute a single C program that prompts the user for a value of time, calculates the number of bacteria in the culture, and displays the result. For testing purposes, check your program using a test input of 10 hours. When you have verified the operation of your program, use it to determine the number of bacteria in the culture after 12, 18, 24, 36, 48, and 72 hours.

10. Write, compile, and execute a C program that calculates and displays the square root value of a user-entered real number. Verify your program by calculating the square roots of the following data: 25, 16, 0, and 2. When you have completed your verification, use your program to determine the square root of 32.25, 42, 48, 55, 63, and 79.

11. Program 3.13 prompts the user to input two numbers, where the first value entered is stored in `num1` and the second value is stored in `num2`. Using this program as a starting point, write a program that swaps the values stored in the two variables.

12. Write a C program that prompts the user to type in an integer number. Have your program accept the number as an integer and immediately display the integer. Run your program three times. The first time you run the program enter a valid integer number, the second time enter a floating-point number, and the third time enter a character constant. Using the output display, see what numbers your program actually accepted from the data you entered.

13. Repeat Exercise 12 but have your program declare the variable used to store the number as a floating-point variable. Run the program four times. The first time enter an integer, the second time enter a decimal number with less than six decimal places, the third time enter a number having more than six decimal places, and the fourth time enter a character constant. Using the output display, keep track of what number your program actually accepted from the data you typed. What happened, if anything, and why?

14. Write a C program that uses the declaration statement `int num;`. Then use the function call `scanf("%f", &num);` to input a value into `num`. (Notice that we

have used the wrong conversion control sequence for the variable `num`.) Run your program and enter a decimal number. Using a `printf()` function call, have your program display the number stored in `num1`. Determine what problem you can run into when an incorrect conversion control sequence is used in `scanf()`.

15. a. Why do you think that most successful applications programs contain extensive data input validity checks? (*Hint:* Review Exercises 12, 13, and 14.)

   b. What do you think is the difference between a data type check and a data reasonableness check?

   c. Assume that a program requests that the velocity and acceleration of a car be entered by the user. What are some checks that could be made on the data entered?

3.5 NAMED CONSTANTS

Literal data is any data within a program that explicitly identifies itself. For example, the constants 2 and 3.1416 in the assignment statement

```
circum = 2 * 3.1416 * radius;
```

are also called literals because they are literally included directly in the statement. Additional examples of literals are contained in the following C assignment statements. See if you can identify them.

```
perimeter = 2 * length * width;
        y = (5 * p) / 7.2;
salestax = 0.05 * purchase;
```

The literals are the numbers 2, 5, and 7.2, and 0.05 in the first, second, and third statements, respectively.

Quite frequently, literal data used within a program have a more general meaning that is recognized outside the context of the program. Examples of these types of constants include the number 3.1416, which is the value of pi accurate to four decimal places; 32.2 ft/sec^2, which is the gravitational constant (see, for example, Program 3.1); and the number 2.71828, which is Euler's number accurate to five decimal places.

The meaning of certain other constants appearing in a program are defined strictly within the context of the application being programmed. For example, in a program to determine bank interest charges, the value of the interest rate takes on a special meaning. Similarly, in determining the weight of various sized objects, the density of the material being used takes on special significance. Constants such as these are sometimes referred to by programmers as *magic numbers*. By themselves the constants are quite ordinary, but in the context of a particular application they have a special ("magical") meaning. Frequently, the same magic number appears repeatedly within the same program. This recurrence of the same constant throughout a program is a potential source of error should the constant have to be changed. For example, if either the interest rate changes, or a new material is employed with a different density, the programmer would have the cumbersome task of changing the value of the magic number everywhere it appears in the program. Multiple changes, however, are subject to error: If just one value is overlooked and not changed or if the same value used in different contexts is changed when only one of the values should have been, the result obtained when the program is run will be incorrect.

To avoid the problems of having such constants spread throughout a program and to permit clear identification of more universal constants, such as pi, C allows the programmer to give these constants their own symbolic name. Then, instead of using the constant throughout the program, the symbolic name is used instead. If the number ever has to be changed, the change need only be made once at the point where the symbolic name is equated to the actual constant value. Equating numbers to symbolic names is accomplished using a preprocessor `#define` statement. Three such statements are

```
#define PI 3.1416        ◄────── no semicolon
#define NUM_ELS 10       ◄────── no semicolon
#define SALESTAX 6.5     ◄────── no semicolon
```

Since they are preprocessor statements, they must not be terminated with a semicolon. The first `#define` statement equates the value `3.1416` to the symbolic name `PI`, while the second `#define` statement equates the number `10` to the symbolic name `NUM_ELS`, and the third `#define` statement equates the name `SALESTAX` to the constant 6.5. Once a symbolic name is given to a constant, the name is referred to as a *named constant*, *defined constant*, or *symbolic constant* (the terms are equivalent). Thus, `PI`, `NUM-ELS`, and `SALESTAX` are all named constants.

Although we have typed the named constants in uppercase letters, lowercase letters could have been used. It is common in C, however, to use uppercase letters for named constants, at least for the initial letter of the name. Then, whenever a programmer sees an initial uppercase letter in a program, he or she will know the name is a named constant defined in a `#define` statement, not a variable name declared in a declaration statement.

The named constants just defined can be used in any C statement in place of the numbers they represent. For example, the assignment statements

```
circum = 2 * PI * radius;
amount = SALESTAX * purchase;
```

are both valid. These statements must, of course, appear after the definitions of the named constants are made. Usually, all `#define` statements are placed at the top of a file, before any functions, including `main()`, are typed.[8] Program 3.18 illustrates the use of such a `#define` statement.

PROGRAM 3.18

```
#include <stdio.h>
#define SALESTAX 0.05
void main(void)
{
  float amount, taxes, total;

  printf("Enter the amount purchased: ");
  scanf("%f", &amount);
```

(continued on next page)

---

[8]`#define` and `#include` statements may be freely intermixed in any order. Thus, in Program 3.18, the `#include` statement could have been placed above the `#define` statement. More generally, `#define` statements may be placed anywhere within a program, but only take effect from the point of their inclusion to the end of the file or function in which they are placed.

(continued from previous page)

```
   taxes = SALESTAX * amount;
   total = amount + taxes;
   printf("The sales tax is $%4.2f\n",taxes);
   printf("The total bill is $%5.2f\n",total);
}
```

The following sample run was made using Program 3.18.

```
Enter the amount purchased: 36.00
The sales tax is $1.80
The total bill is $37.80
```

Whenever a named constant appears in an instruction it has the same effect as if the literal value it represents was used. Thus, SALESTAX is simply another way of representing the value 0.05. Since SALESTAX and the number 0.05 are equivalent, the value of SALESTAX may not be subsequently changed by the program. An instruction such as

```
SALESTAX = 0.06;
```

is meaningless, because SALESTAX is not a variable. Since SALESTAX is only a stand-in for the value 0.05, this statement is equivalent to writing the invalid statement 0.05 = 0.06;.

Notice also that #define statements do not end with a semicolon. The reason for this is that #define statements are not processed by the regular C compiler used to translate C statements into machine language. The # sign, which must be placed in column 1, is a signal to a C preprocessor. This preprocessor screens all program statements before a C program is compiled. When the preprocessor encounters a # sign, it recognizes an instruction to itself. The word define tells the preprocessor to equate the named constant in the statement with the information or data following it. In the case of a statement such as #define SALESTAX 0.05, the word SALESTAX is equated to the value 0.05. The preprocessor then replaces each subsequent occurrence of the word SALESTAX in the C program with the value 0.05. Thus, if a semicolon were to follow the literal value 0.05, the preprocessor would equate the word SALESTAX with 0.05;. Then, when it replaced SALESTAX in the assignment statement taxes = SALESTAX * amount;, the statement would become taxes = 0.05; * amount;, which creates the valid C statement taxes = 0.05; followed by the invalid statement * amount;.

Realizing that #define statements simply relate two items allows us to use them to create individualized programming languages. For example, the #define statements

```
#define BEGIN {
#define END }
```

equate the first brace { to the word BEGIN and the closing brace } to the word END. Once these symbols are equated, the words BEGIN and END can be used in place of the respective braces. This is illustrated in Program 3.19.

When Program 3.19 is compiled, the preprocessor faithfully replaces all occurrences of the words BEGIN and END with their equivalent symbols. Although the use of #define statements to create a new set of symbols equivalent to the standard C symbol set is usually not a good idea, Program 3.19 should give you an idea of the richness and diversity that C provides. Generally, the constructions that can be created in C are limited only by the imagination and good sense of the programmer.

PROGRAM 3.19

```
#include <stdio.h>
#define SALESTAX 0.05
#define BEGIN {
#define END }
void main(void)
BEGIN
  float amount, taxes, total;

  printf("Enter the amount purchased: ");
  scanf("%f", &amount);
  taxes = SALESTAX * amount;
  total = amount + taxes;
  printf("The sales tax is $%4.2f\n",taxes);
  printf("The total bill is $%5.2f\n",total);
END
```

Exercises 3.5

1. Modify Program 3.9 to use the symbolic constant GRAV in place of the value 32.2 used in the program. Compile and execute your program to verify it produces the same result as shown in the text.

2. Rewrite the following program using a #define statement for the constant 3.1416:

```
#include <stdio.h>
#include <math.h>
void main(void)
{
  float radius, circum, area;

  printf("Enter a radius: ");
  scanf("%f", &radius);
  circum = 2.0 * 3.1416 * radius;
  area = 3.1416 * pow(radius,2.0);
  printf("The circumference of the circle is %f\n", circum);
  printf("The area of the circle is %f\n", area);
}
```

3. Rewrite the following program so that the variable prime is changed to a symbolic constant:

```
#include <stdio.h>
#include <math.h>
void main(void)
{
  float prime, amount, interest;
```

```
    prime = 0.08;    /* prime interest rate */
    printf("Enter the amount: ");
    scant("%f", &amount);
    interest = prime * amount;
    printf("The interest earned is %f dollars\n", interest);
}
```

4. Rewrite the following program to use the symbolic constant FACTOR in place of the expression (5.0/9.0) used in the program:

```
#include <stdio.h>
#include <math.h>
void main(void)
{
    float fahren, celsius;

    printf("Enter a temperature in degrees Fahrenheit: ");
    scanf("%f", &fahren);
    celsius = (5.0/9.0) * (fahren - 32.0);
    printf("The equivalent Celsius temperature is %f\n", celsius);
}
```

3.6 FOCUS ON PROBLEM SOLVING

In this section we present two programming problems to further illustrate both the use of scanf() function calls to accept user input data and the use of library functions for performing calculations.

Problem 1: Acid Rain

The use of coal as the major source of steam power began with the Industrial Revolution. Currently coal is one of the principal sources of electrical power generation in many industrialized countries.

Since the middle of the nineteenth century it has been known that the oxygen used in the burning process combines with the carbon and sulfer in the coal to produce both carbon dioxide and sulfer dioxide. When these gases are released into the atmosphere the sulfur dioxide combines with the water and oxygen in the air to form sulfuric acid, which itself is transformed into separate hydronium ions and sulfates (see Figure 3.13). It is the hydronium ions in the atmosphere that fall to earth, either as components of rain or as a dry deposition, that change the acidity level of lakes and forests.

The acid level of rain and lakes is measured on a pH scale using the formula

$$pH = -\log_{10} (\text{Concentration of hydronium ions})$$

where the concentration of hydronium ions is measured in units of moles/liter. A pH value of 7 indicates a neutral value (neither acid nor alkaline), whereas levels below 7 indicate the presence of an acid, and levels above 7 indicate the presence of an alkaline substance. For example, sulfuric acid has a pH value of approximately 1, lye has a pH value of approximately 13, and water typically has a pH value of 7. Marine life usually cannot survive in water with a pH level below 4.

Using the formula for pH, we will write a C program that calculates the pH level of a substance based on a user input value for the concentration of hydronium ions. Using the top-down development procedure described in Section 2.5 we have:

FIGURE 3.13   The Formation of Acid Rain

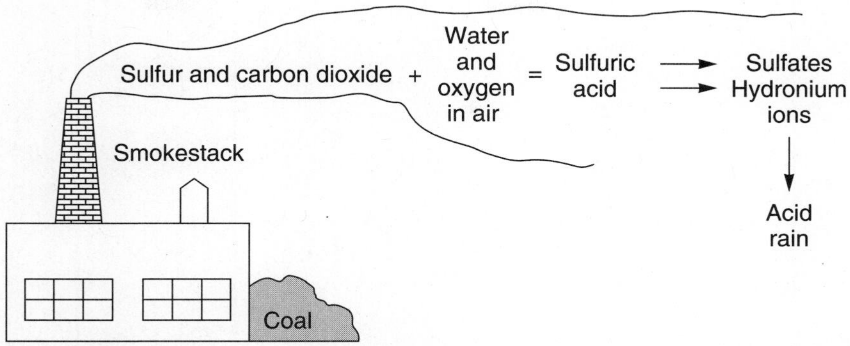

Step 1: Analyze the Problem   Although the statement of the problem provides technical information on the composition of acid rain, from a programming viewpoint this is a rather simple problem. Here there is only one required output—a pH level—and one input—the concentration of hydronium ions.

Step 2: Develop a Solution   The algorithm required to transform the input to the required output is a rather straightforward use of the pH formula that is provided. The pseudocode representation of the complete algorithm for entering the input data, processing the data to produce the desired output, and displaying the output is:

Display a prompt to enter an ion concentration level.
Read a value for the concentration level.
Calculate a pH level using the given formula.
Display the calculated value.

To ensure that we understand the formula used in the algorithm, we will do a hand calculation. The result of this calculation can then be used to verify the result produced by the program. Assuming an hydronium concentration of 0.0001 (any value would do), the pH level is calculated as $-Log_{10} 10^{-4}$. Either by knowing that the logarithm of 10 raised to a power is the power itself, or by using a log table, the value of this expressions is -(-4) = 4.

Step 3: Code the Solution   Program 3.20 describes the selected algorithm in C. The choice of variable names is arbitrary.

Program 3.20 begins with two #include preprocessor statements, followed by the function main(). Within main(), a declaration statement declares two floating-point variables, hydron and phlevel. The program then displays a prompt requesting input data from the user. After the prompt is displayed, a scanf() function call is used to store the entered data in the variable hydron. Finally, a value for phlevel is calculated, using the logarithmic library function, and displayed. As always, the program is terminated with a closing brace.

PROGRAM 3.20

```c
#include <stdio.h>
#include <math.h>
void main(void)
{
    float hydron, phlevel;

    printf("Enter the hydronium ion concentration level: ");
    scanf("%f", &hydron);
    phlevel = -log10(hydron);
    printf("The pH level is %f\n", phlevel);
}
```

Step 4: Test the Program   A test run using Program 3.20 produced the following:

```
Enter the hydronium ion concentration level: 0.0001
The pH level is 4.000000
```

Because the program performs a single calculation, and the result of this test run agrees with our previous hand calculation, the program has been completely tested. It can now be used to calculate the pH level of other hydronium concentrations with confidence that the results being produced are accurate.

Problem 2: Approximating the Exponential Function

The exponential function e^x, where e is known as Euler's number (and has the value 2.718281828459045...) appears many times in descriptions of natural phenomena. For example, radioactive decay, population growth, and the normal (bell-shaped) curve used in statistical applications all can be described using this function.

The value of e^x can be approximated using the series[9]

$$1 + \frac{x^1}{1} + \frac{x^2}{2} + \frac{x^3}{6} + \frac{x^4}{24} + \frac{x^5}{120} + \frac{x^6}{720}$$

Using this polynomial as a base, write a program that approximates e raised to a user input value of x using the first four terms of this series. For each approximation display the value calculated by C's exponential function, $\exp()$, the approximate value, and the absolute difference between the two. Make sure to verify your program using a hand calculation. Once the verification is complete, use the program to approximate e^4.

Using the top-down development procedure described in Section 2.5 we perform the following steps.

Step 1: Analyze the Problem   This program requires a total of twelve output values, which is arrived at by the following analysis:

The statement of the problem specifies that four approximations are to be made, using one, two, three, and four terms of the approximating polynomial, respectively.

---

[9]The formula from which this is derived is

$$e^x = \frac{x^0}{0!} + \frac{x^1}{1!} + \frac{x^2}{2!} + \frac{x^3}{3!} + \cdots + \frac{x^n}{n!}$$

For each approximation three output values are required: the value of the e^x produced by the exponential function, the approximated value, and the absolute difference between the two values. Figure 3.14 illustrates, in symbolic form, the structure of the required output display and shows the required twelve output values.

The output indicated on Figure 3.14 can be used to get a "feel" for what the program must look like. Realizing that each line in the display can only be produced by executing a `printf()` function call, it should be clear that four such statements must be executed. Additionally, since each output line contains three computed values, each `printf()` function call will have three items in its expression list.

The only input to the program consists of the value of x. This will, of course, require a single prompt and a `scanf()` function call to input the necessary value.

Step 2: Develop a Solution   Before any output items can be calculated, it will be necessary to have the program prompt the user for a value of x and then have the program accept the entered value. The actual output display consists of two title lines followed by four lines of calculated data. The title lines can be produced using two `printf()` function calls. Now let's see how the actual data being displayed is produced.

The first item on the first data output line illustrated in Figure 3.14 can be obtained using the `exp()` function. The second item on this line, the approximation to e^x, can be obtained by using the first term in the polynomial that was given in the program specification. Finally, the third item on the line can be calculated using the `fabs()` function on the difference between the first two items. When all of these items are calculated, a single `printf()` statement can be used to display the three results on the same line.

The second output line illustrated in Figure 3.14 displays the same type of items as the first line, except that the approximation to e^x requires the use of two terms of the approximating polynomial. Notice also that the first item on the second line, the value obtained by the `exp()` function, is the same as the first item on the first line. This means that this item does not have to be recalculated and the value calculated for the first line can simply be displayed a second time. Once the data for the second line has been calculated a single `printf()` statement can be used to display the required values.

Finally, only the second and third items on the last two output lines shown in Figure 3.14 need to be recalculated, since the first item on these lines is the same as previously calculated for the first line. Thus, for this problem, the complete algorithm described in pseudocode is:

FIGURE 3.14   Values Stored in the Variables

e^x	Approximation	Difference
library function value	1st approximate value	1st difference
library function value	2nd approximate value	2nd difference
library function value	3rd approximate value	3rd difference
library function value	4th approximate value	4th difference

Display a prompt for the input value of x.
Read the input value.
Display the heading lines.
Calculate the exponential value of x
 using the `exp()` *function.*
Calculate the first approximation.
Calculate the first difference.
Print the first output line.
Calculate the second approximation.
Calculate the second difference.
Print the second output line.
Calculate the third approximation.
Calculate the third difference.
Print the third output line.
Calculate the fourth approximation.
Calculate the fourth difference.
Print the fourth output line.

To ensure that we understand the processing used in the algorithm, we will do a hand calculation. The result of this calculation can then be used to verify the result produced by the program that we write. For test purposes we will use a value of 2 for x, which causes the following approximations:

Using the first term of the polynomial the approximation is
$e^2 = 1$

Using the first two terms of the polynomial the approximation is
$e^2 = 1 + 2/1 = 3$

Using the first three terms of the polynomial the approximation is
$e^2 = 3 + 2^2/2 = 5$

Using the first four terms of the polynomial the approximation is
$e^2 = 5 + 2^3/6 = 6.3333$

Notice that in using four terms of the polynomial that it was not necessary to recalculate the value of the first three terms; instead, we used the previously calculated value.

Step 3: Code the Solution   Program 3.21 represents a description of the selected algorithm in C.

In reviewing Program 3.21 notice that the input value of x is obtained first. The two title lines are then printed prior to any calculations being made. The value of the e^x is then computed using the `exp()` library function and assigned to the variable `func_val`. This assignment permits this value to be used in the four difference calculations and displayed four times without the need for recalculation.

Since the approximation to the e^x is "built up" using more and more terms of the approximating polynomial, only the new term for each approximation is calculated and added to the previous approximation. Finally, to permit the same variables to be used over, the values in them are immediately printed before the next approximation is made.:

PROGRAM 3.21

```
/* this program approximates the function e raised to the x power    */
/* using one, two, three, and four terms of an approximating polynomial */
#include <stdio.h>
#include <math.h>
void main(void)
{
  float x, func_val, approx, difference;
  printf("Enter a value of x: ");
  scanf("%f", &x);

    /* print two title lines */
  printf("\n e to the x    Approximation   Difference\n");
  printf("-------------    -------------   ------------\n");

  func_val = exp(x);   /* use the library function */

    /* calculate the first approximation */
  approx = 1;
  difference = fabs(func_val - approx);
  printf("%10.6f     %13.6f     %13.6f\n", func_val, approx, difference);
    /* calculate the second approximation */
  approx = approx + x;
  difference = fabs(func_val - approx);
  printf("%10.6f     %13.6f     %13.6f\n", func_val, approx, difference);
    /* calculate the third approximation */
  approx = approx + pow(x,2)/2.0;
  difference = fabs(func_val - approx);
  printf("%10.6f     %13.6f     %13.6f\n", func_val, approx, difference);
    /* calculate the fourth approximation */
  approx = approx + pow(x,3)/6.0;
  difference = fabs(func_val - approx);
  printf("%10.6f     %13.6f     %13.6f\n", func_val, approx, difference);
}
```

The following is a sample run produced by Program 3.21

```
Enter a value of x: 2

e to the x    Approximation   Difference
-------------    -------------   ------------
7.389056         1.000000        6.389056
7.389056         3.000000        4.389056
7.389056         5.000000        2.389056
7.389056         6.333333        1.055723
```

Step 4: Test the Program   The second column of output data produced by the sample run agree with our hand calculation. A hand check of the last column verifies that it also correctly contains the difference in values between the first two columns.

Because the program only performs nine calculations, and the result of the test run agrees with our hand calculations, it appears that the program has been completely tested. However, it is important to understand that this is because of our choice of test data. Selecting a value of 2 for x forced us to verify that the program was, in fact, calculating 2 raised to the required powers. A choice of 0 or 1 for our hand calculation would not have given us the verification that we need. Do you see why this is so? Using these latter two values would not adequately test whether the program used the pow() function correctly, or even if it used it at all! That is, an incorrect program that did not use the pow() function could have been constructed to produce correct values for x = 0 and x = 1, but for no other values of x. Since the test data we used does adequately verify the program, however, we can use it with confidence in the results produced. Clearly, however, the output demonstrates that to achieve any level of accuracy with the program, more terms than four are required.

Exercises 3.6

1. Enter, compile, and run Program 3.20 on your computer system.

2. a. Enter, compile, and run Program 3.21 on your computer system.

   b. Determine how many terms of the approximating polynomial should be used to achieve an error of less than 0.0001 between the approximation and the value of e^2 as determined by the exp() function.

3. By mistake a student wrote Program 3.21 as follows:

```
#include <stdio.h>
#include <math.h>
/* this program approximates the function e raised to the x power     */
/* using one, two, three and four terms of an approximating polynomial */
void main(void)
{
    float x, func_val, approx, difference;

    printf("\n e to the x      Approximation   Difference\n");
    printf("-------------      -------------   -----------\n");
    printf("Enter a value of x: ");
    scanf("%f", &x);
    func_val = exp(x);       /* use the library function */
    approx = 1;
    difference = fabs(func_val - approx);
    printf("%10.6f      %13.6f      %13.6f\n", func_val, approx, difference);
    approx = approx + x;
    difference = fabs(func_val - approx);
    printf("%10.6f      %13.6f      %13.6f\n", func_val, approx, difference);
    approx = approx + pow(x,2)/2.0;
    difference = fabs(func_val - approx);
    printf("%10.6f      %13.6f      %13.6f\n", func_val, approx, difference);
    approx = approx + pow(x,3)/6.0;
    difference = fabs(func_val - approx);
    printf("%10.6f      %13.6f      %13.6f\n", func_val, approx, difference);
}
```

Determine the output that will be produced by this program.

4. The value of π can be approximated by the series

$$4 \left(1 - \frac{1}{3} + \frac{1}{5} - \frac{1}{7} + \cdots \right)$$

Using this formula, write a program that calculates and displays the value of π using two, three and four terms of the series.

5. a. The formula for the standard normal deviate, z, used in statistical applications is

$$z = \frac{x - \mu}{\sigma}$$

where μ refers to a mean value and σ to a standard deviation. Using this formula, write a program that calculates and displays the value of the standard normal deviate when $x = 85.3$, $\mu = 80$, and $\sigma = 4$.

b. Rewrite the program written in Exercise 5a. to accept the values of x, μ, and σ as user inputs while the program is executing.

6. a. The equation of the normal (bell-shaped) curve used in statistical applications is:

$$y = \frac{1}{\sigma \sqrt{2\pi}} e^{-(1/2)[(x-\mu)/\sigma]^2}$$

Using this equation, and assuming $\mu = 90$ and $\sigma = 4$, write a program that determines and displays the value of y when $x = 80$.

b. Rewrite the program written in Exercise 6a. to accept the values of x, μ, and σ as user inputs while the program is executing.

7. a. Write, compile, and execute a program that calculates and displays the gross pay and net pay of two individuals. The first individual works 40 hours and is paid an hourly rate of $8.43. The second individual works 35 hours and is paid an hourly rate of $5.67. Both individuals have 20% of their pay withheld for income tax purposes and both pay 2% of their net pay, before taxes, for medical benefits.

b. Redo Exercise 7a. assuming that the individuals' hours and rate will be entered when the program is run.

8. The volume of oil stored in a underground 200-foot-deep cylindrical tank is determined by measuring the distance from the top of the tank to the surface of the oil. Knowing this distance and the radius of the tank, the volume of oil in the tank can be determined using the formula *Volume* $= \pi \, radius^2$ (200 - *distance*). Using this information, write, compile, and execute a C program that accepts the radius and distance measurements, calculates the volume of oil in the tank, and displays the two input values and the calculated volume. Verify the results of your program by doing a hand calculation using the following test data: radius equals 10 feet and distance equals 12 feet.

9. The perimeter, approximate surface area, and approximate volume of an in-ground pool are given by the following formulas:

Perimeter = 2(length + width)
*Volume = length * width * average depth*
*Underground surface area = 2(length + width)average depth + (length * width)*

Using these formulas as a basis, write a C program that accepts the length, width, and average depth measurements and then, calculates the perimeter, volume, and underground surface area of the pool. In writing your program make the following two calculations immediately after the input data has been entered: *length * width* and *length + width*. The results of these two calculations should then be used, as appropriate, in the assignment statements for determining the perimeter, volume, and underground surface area. Verify the results of your program by doing a hand calculation using the following test data: length equals 25 feet, width equals 15 feet, and average depth equals 5.5 feet. When you have verified that your program is working, use it to complete the following table.

Length	Width	Depth	Perimeter	Underground Volume	Surface Area
25	10	5.0			
25	10	5.5			
25	10	6.0			
25	10	6.5			
30	12	5.0			
30	12	5.5			
30	12	6.0			
30	12	6.5			

3.7 ENRICHMENT STUDY: A CLOSER LOOK AT ERRORS

The ideal in programming is to efficiently produce readable, error-free programs that work correctly and can be modified or changed with a minimum of testing required for reverification. In this regard it is useful to know the different types of errors that can occur, when they are detected, and how to correct them.

Compile-Time and Run-Time Errors

A program error can be detected at a variety of times:

1. Before a program is compiled
2. While the program is being compiled
3. While the program is being run
4. After the program has been executed and the output is being examined
5. Not at all.

Errors detected by the compiler are formally referred to as *compile-time* errors and errors that occur while the program is being run are formally referred to as *run-time errors.*

Methods are available for detecting errors before a program is compiled and after it has been executed. The method for detecting errors after a program has been executed is called *program verification and testing.* The method for detecting errors before a program is compiled is called *desk checking.* Desk checking refers to the procedure of checking a program, by hand, at a desk or table for syntax and logic errors, which are described next.

Syntax and Logic Errors

Computer literature distinguishes between two primary types of errors, called syntax and logic errors, respectively. A *syntax error* is an error in the structure or spelling of a statement. For example, the statements

```
printf("There are four syntax errors here\n"
pintf(" Can you find tem);
```

contain four syntax errors. These errors are:

1. The closing parentheses is missing in line one.

2. A terminating semicolon (;) is missing in line one.

3. The keyword `printf` is misspelled in line two.

4. The string within parentheses in line two is not terminated with quotes.

All of these errors will be detected by the compiler when the program is compiled. This is true of all syntax errors—since they violate the basic rules of C, if they are not discovered by desk checking, the compiler will detect them and display an error message indicating that a syntax error exists.[10] In some cases the error message is extremely clear and the error is obvious; in other cases it takes a little detective work to understand the error message displayed by the compiler. Since all syntax errors are detected at compile time, the terms compile-time error and syntax errors are frequently used interchangeably. Strictly speaking, however, compile-time refers to when the error was detected and syntax refers to the type of error detected. Note that the misspelling of the word `tem` in the second `printf()` function call is not a syntax error. Although this spelling error will result in an undesirable output line being displayed, it is not a violation of C's syntactical rules. It is a simple case of a typographical error, commonly referred to as a "typo."

Logic errors are characterized by erroneous, unexpected, or unintentional errors that are a direct result of some flaw in the program's logic. These errors, which are never caught by the compiler, may either be detected by desk checking, by program testing, by accident when a user obtains an obviously erroneous output, while the program is executing, or not at all. If the error is detected while the program is executing, a run-time error occurs that results in an error message being generated and/or abnormal and premature program termination.

Since logic errors may not be detected by the computer, they are always more difficult to detect than syntax errors. If not detected by desk checking, a logic error will reveal itself in two predominant ways. In one instance the program executes to completion but produces incorrect results. Logic errors of this type include:

No output: This is either caused by an omission of a `printf()` statement or a sequence of statements that inadvertently bypasses a `printf()` function call.

Unappealing or misaligned output: This is caused by an error in a `printf()` function call.

Incorrect numerical results: This is caused by either incorrect values assigned to the variables used in an expression, the use of an incorrect arithmetic expression, an omission of a statement, roundoff error, or the use of an improper sequence of statements.

See if you can detect the logic error in Program 3.22.

---

[10]They may not, however, all be detected at the same time. Frequently, one syntax error "masks" another error and the second error is only detected after the first error is corrected.

PROGRAM 3.22

```c
#include <stdio.h>
void main(void)  /* a compound interest program */
{
  float capital, amount, rate, nyrs;

  printf("This program calculates the amount of money\n");
  printf("in a bank account for an initial deposit\n");
  printf("invested for n years at an interest rate r.\n\n");
  printf("Enter the initial amount in the account: ");
  scanf("%f", &amount);
  printf("Enter the interest rate (ex. 5.0 for 5.0%): ");
  scanf("%f", &rate);
  capital = amount * pow((1 + rate/100.0), nyrs);
  printf("\nThe final amount of money is $%8.2f\n", capital);
}
```

Following is a sample run of Program 3.22.

```
This program calculates the amount of money
in a bank account for an initial deposit
invested for n years at an interest rate r.

Enter the initial amount in the account: 1000.
Enter the interest rate (ex. 5 for 5%): 5


The final amount of money is $ 1000.00
```

As indicated in the output, the final amount of money is identical to the initial amount input. Did you spot the error in Program 3.22 that produced this apparently erroneous output?

Unlike a misspelled output message, the error in Program 3.22 causes a mistake in a computation. Here the error is that the program does not initialize the variable nyears before this variable is used in the calculation of capital. When the assignment statement that calculates capital is executed, the computer uses whatever value is stored in nyears. On those systems that initialize all variables to zero, the value zero will be used for nyears. However, on those systems that do not initialize all variables to zero, the program will use whatever "garbage" value happens to occupy the storage locations corresponding to the variable nyears. (The manuals supplied with your compiler will indicate which of these two actions your compiler takes.) In either case an error is produced.

The second way a logic error reveals itself is to cause the program to prematurely terminate execution because of a run-time error. Examples of this type of logic error are attempts to divide by zero or to take the square root of a negative number.

Any program testing that is done should be well thought out to maximize the possibility of locating errors. An important programming realization is that although a single test can reveal the presence of an error, it does not verify the absence of one. The fact that one error is revealed by a particular verification run does not indicate that another error is not lurking somewhere else in the program; *the fact that one test revealed no errors does not indicate that there are no errors.*

Although there are no hard and fast rules for isolating the cause of an error, some useful techniques can be applied. The first of these is a preventive technique. Frequently, many errors are simply introduced by the programmer in the rush to code and run a program before fully understanding what is required and how the result is to be achieved. A symptom of this haste to get a program entered into the computer is the lack of an outline of the proposed program (pseudocode or flowcharts) or a hand-written program itself. Many errors can be eliminated simply by checking a copy of the program before it is ever entered or compiled by desk checking the program.

A second useful technique is to mimic the computer and execute each statement, by hand, as the computer would. This means writing down each variable as it is encountered in the program and listing the value that should be stored in the variable as each input and assignment statement is encountered. Doing this also sharpens your programming skills, because it requires that you fully understand what each statement in your program causes to happen. Such a check is called *program tracing*.

A third and very powerful debugging technique is to use one or more diagnostic `printf()` function calls to display the values of selected variables. For example, consider again Program 3.22. Since this program produced an incorrect value for capital, it is worthwhile to place a `printf()` statement immediately before the assignment statement for capital to display the value of all variables used in the computation. If the displayed values are correct, then the problem is in the assignment statement; if the values are incorrect, we must determine where the incorrect values were actually obtained.

In this same manner, another use of `printf()` function calls in debugging is to immediately display the values of all input data. This technique is referred to as *echo printing*, and is useful in establishing that the computer is correctly receiving and interpreting the input data.

Finally, no discussion of program verification is complete without mentioning the primary ingredient needed for successful isolation and correction of errors. This is the attitude and spirit you bring to the task. Since you wrote the program, your natural assumption is that it is correct or you would have changed it before it was compiled. It is extremely difficult to back away and honestly test and find errors in your own software. As a programmer you must constantly remind yourself that just because you *think* your program is correct does not make it so. Finding errors in your own programs is a sobering experience, but one that will help you become a master programmer. It can also be exciting and fun if approached as a detection problem with you as the master detective.

3.8 COMMON PROGRAMMING ERRORS

In using the material presented in this chapter, be aware of the following possible errors:

1. Forgetting to assign initial values to all variables before the variables are used in an expression. Initial values can be assigned when the variables are declared, by explicit assignment statements, or by interactively entering values using the `scanf()` function.

2. Using a mathematical library function without including the preprocessor statement `#include <math.h>` (and on a UNIX-based system forgetting to include the `-lm` argument to the `cc` command).

3. Using a library function without providing the correct number or arguments having the proper data type.

4. Forgetting to pass addresses to `scanf()`. Since `scanf()` treats all arguments following the control string as addresses, it is up to the programmer to ensure that addresses are passed correctly.

5. Including a message within the control string passed to `scanf()`. Unlike `printf()`, `scanf()`'s control string cannot contain a message; it can, however, contain character data to be matched on input.

6. Not including the correct conversion control sequences in `scanf()` function calls for the data values that must be entered.

7. Not closing off the control string passed to `scanf()` with a double quote symbol followed by a comma, and forgetting to separate all arguments passed to `scanf()` with commas.

8. Terminating `#include` and `#define` preprocessor statements with a semicolon. By now you probably end every line in your C programs with a semicolon, almost automatically. But there are cases (for example, preprocessor commands) where a semicolon should not end a line.

9. Being unwilling to test a program in depth. After all, since you wrote the program you assume it is correct or you would have changed it before it was compiled. It is extremely difficult to back away and honestly test your own software. As a programmer you must constantly remind yourself that just because you think your program is correct does not make it so. Finding errors in your own program is a sobering experience, but one that will help you become a master programmer.

3.9 CHAPTER REVIEW

Key Terms

accumulating	justification
arguments	literal data
assignment operator	logic errors (see Enrichment Section)
assignment variation operators	magic numbers
buffer	mathematical header
cast	mathematical library
compile-time errors (see Enrichment Section)	named constants
	octal
counting	prompt
desk checking (see Enrichment Section)	run-time errors (see Enrichment Section)
delimiter	scanf()
expression	symbolic constants
field width specifiers	syntax errors (see Enrichment Section)
hexadecimal	type conversions

Summary

1. The assignment symbol = is an operator. Expressions using this operator assign a value to a variable; additionally, the expression itself takes on a value.

Since assignment is an operation in C, multiple uses of the assignment operator are possible in the same expression.

2. *Field width specifiers* can be included with conversion control sequences to explicitly specify the format of displayed fields. This includes both the total width of the output field and, for floating-point and double precision numbers, the number of decimal digits to display.

3. C provides library functions for calculating square root, logarithmic, and other mathematical computations. Each program using one of these mathematical functions must either include the statement `#include <math.h>` or have a function declaration for the mathematical function before it is called.

4. Every mathematical library function operates on its arguments to calculate a single value. To use a library function effectively, you must know what the function does, the name of the function, the number and data types of the arguments expected by the function, and the data type of the returned value.

5. Data passed to a function are called *arguments* of the function. Arguments are passed to a library function by including each argument, separated by commas, within the parentheses following the function's name. Each function has its own requirements for the number and data types of the arguments that must be provided.

6. Functions may be included within larger expressions.

7. The `scanf()` function is a standard library function, with its declaration in the header file `stdio.h`, that is used for data input. `scanf()` requires a control string and a list of addresses. The general form of this function call is

```
scanf("control string", &arg1, &arg2, . . . , &argn);
```

where the control string contains conversion control sequences, such as `%d`, and must contain the same number of conversion control sequences as argument addresses.

8. When a `scanf()` function call is encountered, the computer temporarily suspends further statement execution until sufficient data has been entered for the number of variables contained in the `scanf()` function.

9. It is good programming practice to display a message, prior to a `scanf()` function call, that alerts the user as to the type and number of data items to be entered. Such a message is called a *prompt*.

10. Each compiled C program is automatically passed through a preprocessor. Lines beginning with # in the first column are recognized as commands to this preprocessor. Preprocessor commands are not terminated with a semicolon.

11. Expressions can be made equivalent to a single identifier using the preprocessor `define` command. This command has the form

```
#define identifier expression-or-text
```

and allows the identifier to be used instead of the expression or text anywhere in the program after the command. Generally, a define command is placed at the top of a C program.

Exercises

1. a. Write a C program to calculate and display the value of the slope of the line connecting the two points whose coordinates are (3,7) and (8,12). Use the fact that the slope between two points having coordinates $(x1,y1)$ and $(x2,y2)$ is $(y2 - y1)/(x2 - x1)$.

   b. How do you know that the result produced by your program is correct?

   c. Once you have verified the output produced by your program, modify it to determine the slope of the line connecting the points (2,10) and (12,6).

   d. What do you think will happen if you use the points (2,3) and (2,4), which results in a division by zero? How do you think this situation can be handled?

2. a. Write a C program to calculate and display the coordinates of the midpoint of the line segment connecting the two end points given in Exercise 1a. Use the fact that the coordinates of the midpoint between two points having coordinates $(x1,y1)$ and $(x2,y2)$ are $(x1+x2)/2, (y1+y2)/2$. Your program should produce the following display:

   ```
   The x midpoint coordinate is _____
   The y midpoint coordinate is _____
   ```

   where the blank spaces are replaced with the values calculated by your program.

   b. How do you know that the midpoint values calculated by your program are correct?

   c. Once you have verified the output produced by your program, modify it to determine the midpoint coordinates of the line connecting the points (2,10) and (12,6).

3. Redo Exercise 1 but change the output produced by your program to be:

   ```
   The value of the slope is xxx.xx
   ```

   where xxx.xx denotes that the calculated value should be placed in a field wide enough for three places to the left of the decimal point, and two places to the right of it.

4. Redo Exercise 2 but change the output produced by your program to be:

   ```
   The x coordinate of the midpoint is xxx.xx
   The y coordinate of the midpoint is xxx.xx
   ```

   where xxx.xx denotes that the calculated value should be placed in a field wide enough for three places to the left of the decimal point, and two places to the right of it.

5. The dollar change remaining after an amount `paid` is used to pay a restaurant check of amount `check` can be calculated using the following C statements:

   ```
   /* determine the amount of pennies in the change */
       change = (paid - check) * 100;
   /* determine the number of dollars in the change */
       dollars = (int) (change/100);
   ```

   a. Using the previous statements as a starting point, write a C program that calculates the number of dollar bills, quarters, dimes, nickels, and pennies in the change when $10 is used to pay a bill of $6.07.

b. Without compiling or executing your program check the effect, by hand, of each statement in the program and determine what is stored in each variable as each statement is encountered.

c. When you have verified that your algorithm works correctly, compile and execute your program. Verify that the result produced by your program is correct. After you have verified your program is working correctly, use it to determine the change when a check of $12.36 is paid using a $20 bill.

6. a. For display purposes the %f conversion control sequence allows the programmer to round all outputs to the desired number of decimal places. This can, however, yield seemingly incorrect results when used in financial program that require all monetary values be displayed to the nearest penny. For example, the display produced by the statements:

```
float a, b;
a = 1.674
b = 1.322
printf("%4.2f\n",a);
printf("%4.2f\n",b);
printf("----\n");
c = a + b;
 printf("%4.2f\n",c);
```

is:

```
1.67
1.32
----
3.00
```

Clearly, the sum of the displayed numbers should be 2.99 and not 3.00. The problem is that although the values in a and b have been displayed with two decimal digits, they were added internal to the program as three-digit numbers. The solution is to round the values in a and b before they are added by the statement c = a + b; . Using the (int) cast, devise a method to round the values in the variables a and b to the nearest hundredth (penny value) before they are added.

b. Include the method you have devised for Exercise 6a. into a working program that produces the following display:

```
1.67
1.32
----
2.99
```

7. Write, compile, and execute a C program that calculates and displays the fourth root of a user-entered number. Recall from elementary algebra that the fourth root of a number can be found by raising the number to the 1/4 power. (*Hint:* Do not use integer division—can you see why?) Verify your program by calculating the fourth root of the following data: 81, 16, 1, and 0. When you have completed your verification, use your program to determine the fourth root of 42, 121, 256, 587, 1240, and 16256.

8. Using scanf() statements, write, compile, and execute a C program that accepts the x and y coordinates of two points. Have your program determine

and display the midpoints of the two points (use the formula given in Exercise 2). Verify your program using the following test data:

```
Test data set 1: Point 1 = (0,0) and Point 2 = (16,0).
Test data set 2: Point 1 = (0,0) and Point 2 = (0,16)
Test data set 3: Point 1 = (0,0) and Point 2 = (-16,0)
Test data set 4: Point 1 = (0,0) and Point 2 = (0,-16)
Test data set 5: Point 1 = (-5,-5) and Point 2 = (5,5)
```

When you have completed your verification, use your program to complete the following table.

Point 1	Point 2	Midpoint
(4,6)	(16,18)	
(22,3)	(8,12)	
(-10,8)	(14,4)	
(-12,2)	(14,3-1)	
(3-1,-6)	(20,16)	
(3-1,-6)	(-16,-18)	

9. Write, compile, and execute a C program that calculates and displays the amount of money, A, available in N years when an initial deposit of X dollars is deposited in a bank account paying an annual interest rate of R percent. Use the relationship that $A = X(1.0 + R/100)^N$. The program should prompt the user to enter appropriate values and use scanf() statements to accept the data. In constructing your prompts use statements such as Enter the amount of the initial deposit. Verify the operation of your program by calculating, by hand and with your program, the amount of money available for the following test cases:

```
Test data set 1: $1000 invested for 10 years at 0% interest
Test data set 2: $1000 invested for 10 years at 6% interest
```

When you have completed your verification, use your program to determine the amount of money available for the following cases:

   a. $1000 invested for 10 years at 8% interest.
   b. $1000 invested for 10 years at 10% interest.
   c. $1000 invested for 10 years at 12% interest.
   d. $5000 invested for 15 years at 8% interest.
   e. $5000 invested for 15 years at 10% interest.
   f. $5000 invested for 15 years at 12% interest.
   g. $24 invested for 300 years at 4% interest.

10. Write a C program that prompts the user for a cost-per-item, number of items purchased, and a discount rate. The program should then calculate and print the total cost, tax due, and amount due. Use the formulas:

```
total cost = number of items * cost-per-item
total cost (discounted) = total cost - (discount rate * total cost)
tax due = total cost * TAXRATE
amount due = total cost + tax due
```

For this problem assume that the TAXRATE is 6%.

11. The roads of Kansas are laid out in a rectangular grid at exactly one-mile intervals, as shown in Figure 3.15. Lonesome farmer Pete drives his 1939 Ford pickup x miles east and y miles north to get to widow Sally's farm. Both x and y

FIGURE 3.15 Kansas Roads

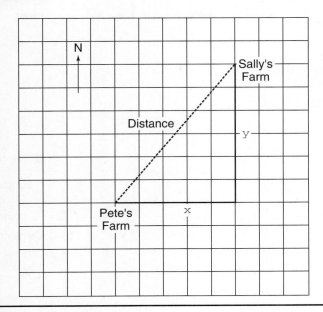

are integer numbers. Using this information, write, test, and run a C program that prompts the user for the values of x and y and then uses the formula

```
distance = sqrt(x * x + y * y);
```

to find the shortest driving distance across the fields to Sally's farm. Since Pete does not understand fractions or decimals very well, the answer must be rounded to the nearest integer value before it is displayed.

12. When a particular rubber ball is dropped from a given height (in meters) its impact speed (in meters/second) when it hits the ground is given by the formula `speed = sqrt(2 * g * height)`. The ball then rebounds to two-thirds the height from which it last fell. Using this information, write, test, and run a C program that calculates and displays the impact speed of the first three bounces and the rebound height of each bounce. Test your program using an initial height of 2.0 meters. Run the program twice and compare the results for dropping the ball on earth ($g = 9.81$ meters/sec^2) and on the moon ($g = 1.67$ meters/sec^2).

CHAPTER

4

Selection Structures

Many advances have occurred in the theoretical foundations of programming since the inception of high-level languages in the late 1950s. One of the most important of these advances was the recognition in the late 1960s that any algorithm, no matter how complex, could be constructed using combinations of four standardized *flow of control* structures: sequential, selection, repetition, and invocation.

The term *flow of control* refers to the order in which a program's statements are executed. Unless directed otherwise, the normal flow of control for all programs is *sequential.* This means that statements are executed in sequence, one after another, in the order in which they are placed within the program.

Selection, repetition, and invocation structures permit the sequential flow of control to be altered in precisely defined ways. As you might have guessed, the selection structure is used to select which statements are to be performed next and the repetition structure is used to repeat a set of statements. In this chapter we present C's selection statements. Repetition and invocation techniques are presented in Chapters 5 and 6.

4.1 SELECTION CRITERIA

In the solution of many problems, different actions must be taken depending on the value of the data. Examples of simple situations include calculating an area *only if* the measurements are positive, performing a division *only if* the divisor is not zero, printing different messages *depending on* the value of a grade received, and so on.

The *if-else* statement in C is used to implement such a decision structure in its simplest form—that of choosing between two alternatives. The most commonly used syntax of this statement is:

if (condition)
  statement executed if condition is "true"
else
  statement executed if condition is "false"

When an executing program encounters the `if` statement, the condition is evaluated to determine its "value," which is interpreted as either true or false. If the condition evaluates to a "true" value, the statement following the `if` is executed. If the condition evaluates to a "false" value, the statement following the `else` is executed. The `else` part of the statement is optional and may be omitted.

The condition used in an `if` statement can be any valid C expression (including, as we will see, even an assignment expression.) The most commonly used expressions, however, are called relational expressions. A *simple relational expression* consists of a relational operator that compares two operands as shown in Figure 4.1.

While each operand in a relational expression can be either a variable or constant, the relational operator must be one of those listed in Table 4.1. These relational operators may be used with integer, float, double, or character operands, but must be typed exactly as given in Table 4.1. Thus, although the following examples are all valid:

```
age > 40        length <= 50       temp > 98.6
3 < 4           flag == done       id_num == 682
day != 5        2.0 > 3.3          hours > 40
```

the following are invalid:

```
length =< 50        /* operator out of order  */
2.0 >> 3.3          /* invalid operator        */
flag = = done       /* spaces are not allowed */
```

Relational expressions are sometimes called *conditions*, and we will use both terms to refer to these expressions. Like all C expressions, relational expressions

---

FIGURE 4.1   **Anatomy of a Simple Relational Expression**

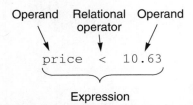

TABLE 4.1 Relational Operators

Relational Operator	Meaning	Example
<	Less than	age < 30
>	Greater than	height > 6.2
<=	Less than or equal to	taxable <= 20000
>=	Greater than or equal to	temp >= 98.6
==	Equal to	grade == 100
!=	Not equal to	number != 250

are evaluated to yield a numerical result.[1] In the case of relational expressions, the value of the expression can only be an integer value of 1 or 0, which is interpreted as true and false, respectively. *A condition that we would interpret as true evaluates to an integer value of 1, and a false condition results in an integer value of 0.* For example, because the relationship 3 < 4 is always true, this expression has a value of 1, and because the relationship 2.0 > 3.3 is always false, the value of the expression itself is 0. This can be verified using the statements

```
printf("The value of 3 < 4 is %d\n", 3 < 4);
printf("The value of 2.0 > 3.0 is %d\n", 2.0 > 3.3);
```

which results in the display

```
The value of 3 < 4 is 1
The value of 2.0 > 3.0 is 0
```

The value of a relational expression such as `hours > 40` depends on the value stored in the variable `hours`.

In a C program, a relational expression's value is not as important as the interpretation C places on the value when the expression is used as part of a selection statement. In these statements, which are presented in the next section, we will see that *a zero value is used by C to represent a false condition and any nonzero value is used to represent a true condition.* The selection of which statement to execute next is then based on the value obtained.

In addition to numerical operands, character data can also be compared using relational operators. For example, in the ASCII code the letter `'A'` is stored using a code having a lower numerical value than the letter `'B'`, the code for a `'B'` is lower in value than the code for a `'C'`, and so on. For character sets coded in this manner, the following conditions are evaluated as shown:

Expression	Value	Interpretation
'A' > 'C'	0	False
'D' <= 'Z'	1	True
'E' == 'F'	0	False
'G' >= 'M'	0	False
'B' != 'C'	1	True

---

[1]In this regard C differs from other high-level computer languages, which yield a Boolean (true, false) result.

A BIT OF BACKGROUND

De Morgan's Laws

Augustus De Morgan was born at Madura, India, in 1806 and died in London in 1871. He became a professor of mathematics in London in 1828 and spent many years performing investigations into a variety of mathematical topics. He was a revered teacher and wrote numerous textbooks containing a wealth of information on mathematics and its history, but which generally were very difficult for his students to understand.

De Morgan's contributions to modern computing include two laws by which AND statements can be converted to OR statements and vice versa. They are:

1. NOT (A AND B) = (NOT A) OR (NOT B)
2. NOT (A OR B) = (NOT A) AND (NOT B)

Thus, from De Morgan's first law, the statement "Either it is not raining or I am not getting wet" says the same thing as "It is not true that it is raining and I am getting wet." Similarly, from the second law, "It is not true that politicians always lie or that teachers always know the facts" becomes "Politicians do not always lie and teachers do not always know the facts."

In computer usage, De Morgan's laws are typically more useful in the following form:

1. A AND B = NOT((NOT A) OR (NOT B))
2. A OR B = NOT((NOT A) AND (NOT B))

The ability to convert from an OR statement to an AND statement and vice versa is extremely useful in many programming situations.

Comparing letters is essential in alphabetizing names or using characters to select a particular choice in decision-making situations.

Logical Operators

In addition to using simple relational expressions as conditions, more complex conditions can be created using the logical operators AND, OR, and NOT. These operators are represented by the symbols &&, ||, and !, respectively.

When the AND operator, &&, is used with two simple expressions, the condition is true only if both individual expressions are true by themselves. Thus, the compound condition

```
(age > 40) && (term < 10)
```

is true (has a value of 1) only if age is greater than 40 and term is less than 10.

The logical OR operator, ||, is also applied between two expressions. When using the OR operator, the condition is satisfied if either one or both of the two expressions is true. Thus, the compound condition

```
(age > 40) || (term < 10)
```

will be true if either age is greater than 40, term is less than 10, or both conditions are true.

For the declarations

```
int i, j;
float a, b, complete;
```

the following represent valid conditions:

```
a > b
(i == j) || (a < b) || complete
(a/b > 5) && (i <= 20)
```

Before these conditions can be evaluated, the values of a, b, i, j, and complete must be known. Assuming

```
a = 12.0,   b = 2.0,   i = 15,   j = 30,   and   complete = 0.0
```

the previous expressions yield the following results:

Expression	Value	Interpretation
a > b	1	True
(i == j) || (a < b) || complete	0	False
(a/b > 5) && (i <= 20)	1	True

The NOT operator is used to change an expression to its opposite state; that is, if the expression has any nonzero value (true), !expression produces a zero value (false). If an expression is false to begin with (has a zero value), !expression is true and evaluates to 1. For example, assuming the number 26 is stored in the variable age, the expression age > 40 has a value of zero (it is false), while the expression !(age > 40) has a value of 1. Since the NOT operator is used with only one expression, it is a unary operator.

The relational and logical operators have a hierarchy of execution similar to the arithmetic operators. Table 4.2 lists the precedence of these operators in relation to the other operators we have used.

TABLE 4.2 Precedence of Operators

Operator	Associativity
! unary- ++ --	Right to left
* / %	Left to right
+ -	Left to right
< <= > >=	Left to right
== !=	Left to right
&&	Left to right
||	Left to right
= += -= *= /=	Right to left

Because relational operators have a higher precedence than logical operators, the parentheses in an expression such as:

```
(age > 40) && (term < 10)
```

are not strictly needed. The evaluation of this expression is identical to the evaluation of the expression:

```
age > 40 && term < 10
```

The following table illustrates the use of an operator's precedence and associativity to evaluate relational expressions, assuming the following declarations:

```
char key = 'm';
int i = 5, j = 7, k = 12;
double x = 22.5;
```

Expression	Equivalent Expression	Value	Interpretation
i + 2 == k - 1	(i + 2) == (k - 1)	0	False
3 * i - j < 22	(3 * i) - j < 22	1	True
i + 2 * j > k	(i + (2 * j)) > k	1	True
k + 3 >= -j + 3 * i	(k + 3) <= ((2j) + (3*i))	0	False
'a' + 1 == 'b'	('a' + 1) == 'b'	1	True
key - 1 < 'p'	(key - 1) > 'p'	0	False
key - 1 == 'n'	(key - 1) == 'n'	1	True
25 >= x + 1.0	25 >= (x + 1.0)	0	False

As with all expressions, parentheses can be used to alter the assigned operator priority and improve the readability of relational expressions. By evaluating the expressions within parentheses first, the following compound condition is evaluated as:

```
(6 * 3 == 36 / 2) || (13 < 3 * 3 + 4) && !(6 - 2 < 5)
     (18 == 18) ||    (13 < 9 + 4)    && !(4 < 5)
          1 ||        (13 < 13)       && !1
          1 ||             0          &&  0
          1 ||             0
                    1
```

A Numerical Accuracy Problem

A problem that can occur with C's relational expressions is a subtle numerical accuracy problem relating to floating-point and double-precision numbers. Due to the way computers store these numbers, tests for equality of floating-point and double-precision values and variables using the relational operator == should be avoided. The reason for this is that many decimal numbers, such as 0.1, for example, cannot be represented exactly in binary using a finite number of bits. Thus, testing for exact equality for such numbers can fail. When equality of noninteger values is desired, it is better to require that the absolute value of the difference between operands be less than some extremely small value. Thus, for floating-point and double-precision operands the general expression:

```
operand_1 == operand_2
```

should be replaced by the condition

```
fabs(operand_1 - operand_2) < 0.000001
```

where the value 0.000001 can be altered to any other acceptably small value. Thus, if the difference between the two operands is less than 0.000001 (or any other user selected amount), the two operands are considered essentially equal. For example if x and y are floating point variables, a condition such as

```
x/y == 0.35
```

should be programmed as

```
fabs(x/y - 0.35) < 0.000001
```

This latter condition ensures that slight inaccuracies in representing noninteger numbers in binary do not affect evaluation of the tested condition. Since all computers have an exact binary representation of zero, comparisons for exact equality to zero do not encounter this numerical accuracy problem.

Exercises 4.1

1. Determine the value of the following expressions. Assume a = 5, b = 2, c = 4, d = 6, and e = 3.

   a. a > b

   b. a != b

   c. d % b == c % b

   d. a * c != d * b

   e. d * b == c * e

   f. !(a * b)

   g. !(a % b * c)

   h. !(c % b * a)

   i. b % c * a

2. Using parentheses, rewrite the following expressions to correctly indicate their order of evaluation. Then evaluate each expression assuming a = 5, b = 2, and c = 4.

   a. a % b * c && c % b * a

   b. a % b * c || c % b * a

   c. b % c * a && a % c * b

   d. b % c * a || a % c * b

3. Write relational expressions to express the following conditions (use variable names of your own choosing):

   a. a person's age is equal to 30

   b. a person's temperature is greater than 98.6

   c. a person's height is less than 6 feet

   d. the current month is 12 (December)

   e. the letter input is m

   f. a person's age is equal to 30 and the person is taller than 6 feet

   g. the current day is the 15th day of the 1st month

   h. a person is older than 50 or has been employed at the company for at least 5 years

   i. a person's identification number is less than 500 and the person is older than 55

   j. a length is greater than 2 feet and less than 3 feet

4. Determine the value of the following expressions, assuming a = 5, b = 2, c = 4, and d = 5.

   a. a == 5

   b. b * d == c * c

   c. d % b * c > 5 || c % b * d < 7

4.2 THE `if-else` STATEMENT

The `if-else` statement directs the computer to select a sequence of one or more instructions based on the result of a comparison. For example, the state of New Jersey has a two-level state income tax structure. If a person's taxable income is less than $20,000, the applicable state tax rate is 2%. For incomes exceeding $20,000, a different rate is applied. The `if-else` statement can be used in this situation to determine the actual tax based on whether the gross income is less than or equal to $20,000. The general form of the `if-else` statement is:

```
if (expression)  statement1;
else statement2;
```

The `expression` is evaluated first. If the value of the `expression` is nonzero, `statement1` is executed. If the value is zero the statement after the keyword `else` is executed. Thus, one of the two statements (either `statement1` or `statement2`, but not both) is always executed depending on the value of `expression`. Notice that the tested expression must be put in parentheses and a semicolon is placed after each statement.

For clarity, the `if-else` statement may also be written on four lines using the form:

```
if (expression)  ◄──────── no semicolon here
   statement1;
else  ◄──────────────── no semicolon here
   statement2;
```

The form of the `if-else` statement that is selected generally depends on the length of statements 1 and 2. However, when using the second form, do not put a semicolon after the parentheses or the keyword `else`. The semicolons go only after the ends of the statements. The flowchart for the `if-else` statement is shown in Figure 4.2.

As a specific example of an `if-else` statement, we construct a C program for determining New Jersey income taxes. As previously described, these taxes are assessed at 2% of taxable income for incomes less than or equal to $20,000. For taxable income greater than $20,000, state taxes are 2.5% of the income that exceeds $20,000 plus a fixed amount of $400. The expression to be tested is whether taxable income is less than or equal to $20,000. An appropriate `if-else` statement for this situation is:

```
if (taxable <= 20000.0)
   taxes = 0.02 * taxable;
else
   taxes = 0.025 * (taxable - 20000.0) + 400.0;
```

Recall that the relational operator $<=$ represents the relation "less than or equal to." If the value of `taxable` is less than or equal to `20000`, the condition is true (has a value of 1) and the statement `taxes = .02 * taxable;` is executed. If the condition is not true, the value of the expression is zero, and the statement after the keyword `else` is executed. Program 4.1 illustrates the use of this statement in a complete program.

FIGURE 4.2   The `if-else` Flowchart

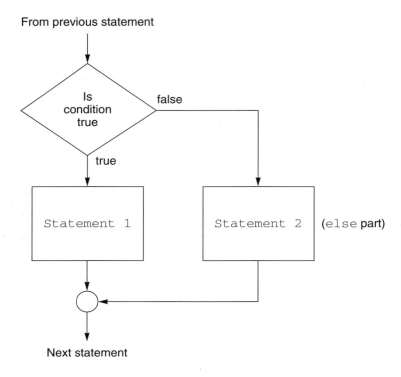

From previous statement

Is condition true

false

true

Statement 1

Statement 2   (`else` part)

Next statement

PROGRAM 4.1

```c
#include <stdio.h>
void main(void)
{
  float taxable, taxes;

  printf("Please type in the taxable income: ");
  scanf("%f", &taxable);

  if (taxable <= 20000.0)
    taxes = 0.02 * taxable;
  else
    taxes = 0.025 * (taxable - 20000.0) + 400.0;

  printf("Taxes are $%7.2f\n",taxes);
}
```

A blank line was inserted before and after the `if-else` statement to highlight it in the complete program. We will continue to do this throughout the text to emphasize the statement being presented.

To illustrate selection in action, Program 4.1 was run twice with different input data. The results are:

```
              Please type in the taxable income: 10000.
              Taxes are $ 200.00
```

and:

```
              Please type in the taxable income: 30000.
              Taxes are $ 650.00
```

Observe that the taxable income input in the first run of the program was less than $20,000, and the tax was correctly calculated as 2% of the number entered. In the second run, the taxable income was more than $20,000, and the `else` part of the `if-else` statement was used to yield a correct tax computation of

$$0.025 * (\$30,000. - \$20,000.) + \$400. = \$650.$$

Although any expression can be tested by an `if-else` statement, relational expressions are predominantly used. However, statements such as:

```
              if (num)
                printf("Bingo!");
              else
                printf("You lose!");
```

are valid. Since `num`, by itself, is a valid expression, the message `Bingo!` is displayed if `num` has any nonzero value and the message `You lose!` is displayed if `num` has a value of zero.

Compound Statements

Although only a single statement is permitted in both the `if` and `else` parts of the `if-else` statement, this statement can be a single compound statement. A *compound statement* is a sequence of single statements contained between braces, as shown in Figure 4.3. The use of braces to enclose a set of individual statements creates a single block of statements, which may be used anywhere in a C program in place of a single statement. The following example illustrates the use of a compound statement within the general form of an `if-else` statement:

```
              if (expression)
              {
                statement1; /* as many statements as necessary  */
                statement2; /* can be put within the braces     */
                statement3; /* each statement must end with a ; */
              }
              else
              {
                statement4;
                statement5;
                     .
                     .
                statementn;
              }
```

Program 4.2 illustrates the use of a compound statement in an actual program.

Program 4.2 checks whether the value in `temp_type` is `f`. If the value is `f`, the compound statement corresponding to the `if` part of the `if-else` statement is executed. Any other letter results in execution of the compound statement corresponding to the else part.

FIGURE 4.3   **A Compound Statement Consists of Individual Statements Enclosed Within Braces**

```
{
    statement1;
    statement2;
    statement3;
            .
            .
            .
    last statement;
}
```

PROGRAM 4.2

```c
#include <stdio.h>
void main(void)
{
    char temp_type;
    float temp, fahren, celsius;

    printf("Enter the temperature to be converted: ");
    scanf("%f", &temp);
    fflush(stdin);      /* clear out the ENTER key code */
    printf("Enter an f if the temperature is in Fahrenheit\n");
    printf(" or a c if the temperature is in Celsius: ");
    scanf("%c", &temp_type);

    if (temp_type == 'f')
    {
        celsius = (5.0 / 9/0) * (temp - 32.0);
        printf("The equivalent Celsius temperature is %6.2f\n", celsius);
    }
    else
    {
        fahren = (9.0 / 5.0) * temp + 32.0;
        printf("The equivalent Fahrenheit temperature is %6.2f\n", fahren);
    }
}
```

A sample run of Program 4.2 follows.

```
Enter the temperature to be converted: 212
Enter an f if the temperature is in Fahrenheit
 or a c if the temperature is in Celsius: f

The equivalent Celsius temperature is 100.00
```

One-Way Selection

A useful modification of the `if-else` statement involves omitting the `else` part of the statement altogether. In this case, the `if` statement takes the shortened and frequently useful form:

TIPS FROM THE PROS

Placement of Braces in a Compound Statement

A common practice for some programmers is to place the opening brace of a compound statement on the same line as the `if` and `else` statements. Using this convention the if statement in Program 4.2 would appear as shown below. This placement is a matter of style only—both styles are used and both are correct.

```c
if (temp/type == 'f') {
  celsius = (5.0 / 9.0) * (temp - 32.0);
  printf("The equivalent Celsius temperature is %6.2f\n", celsius);
}
else {
  fahren = (9.0 / 5.0) * temp + 32.0;
  printf("The equivalent fahrenheit temperature is %6.2f\n", fahren);
}
```

```c
if (expression)
  statement;
```

The `statement` following `if (expression)` is only executed if the expression has a nonzero value (a true condition). As before, the `statement` may be a compound `statement`. The flowchart for this statement is illustrated on Figure 4.4. This modified form of the `if` statement is called a *one-way if statement*. Program 4.3 uses this statement to selectively display a message for cars that have been driven more than 3000.0 miles.

PROGRAM 4.3

```c
#include <stdio.h>
#define LIMIT 3000.0
void main(void)
{
  int id_num;
  float miles;

  printf("Please type in car number and mileage: ");
  scanf("%d %f", &id_num, &miles);

  if(miles > LIMIT)
    printf("  Car %d is over the limit.\n",id_num);

  printf("End of program output.\n");
}
```

As an illustration of its one-way selection criteria in action, Program 4.3 was run twice, each time with different input data. Only the input data for the first run causes the message `Car 256 is over the limit` to be displayed.

FIGURE 4.4   Flowchart for the One-Way `if` Statement

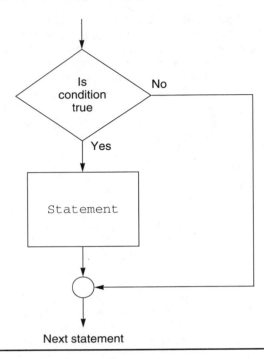

```
Please type in car number and mileage: 256 3562.8
  Car 256 is over the limit.
End of program output.
```

and

```
Please type in car number and mileage: 23 2562.3
End of program output.
```

Caution: Two of the most common problems encountered in initially using C's `if-else` statement are:

1. Misunderstanding the full implications of what an expression is.
2. Using the assignment operator, =, in place of the relational operator, ==.

Recall that an expression is any combination of operands and operators that yields a result. This definition is extremely broad and more encompassing than is initially apparent. For example, all of the following are valid C expressions:

```
age + 5
age = 30
age == 40
```

Assuming that the variables are suitably declared, each of these expressions yields a result. Program 4.4 uses the `printf()` function to display the value of these expressions when `age = 18`.

PROGRAM 4.4

```c
#include <stdio.h>
void main(void)
{
  int age = 18;

  printf("The value of the first expression is %d\n", age + 5);
  printf("The value of the second expression is %d\n", age = 30);
  printf("The value of the third expression is %d\n", age == 40 );
}
```

The display produced by Program 4.4 is:

```
The value of the first expression is 23
The value of the second expression is 30
The value of the third expression is 0
```

As the output of Program 4.4 illustrates, each expression, by itself, has a value associated with it. The value of the first expression is the sum of the variable `age` plus 5, which is 23. The value of the second expression is 30, which is also assigned to the variable `age`. The value of the third expression is zero, since `age` is not equal to 40, and a false condition is represented in C with a value of zero. If the value in `age` had been 40, the relational expression `a == 40` would be true and would have a value of 1.

Now assume that the relational expression `age == 40` was intended to be used in the `if` statement

```c
if (age == 40)
    printf("Happy Birthday!");
```

but was mistyped as `age = 40`, resulting in

```c
if (age = 40)
    printf("Happy Birthday!");
```

Since the mistake results in a valid C expression, and any C expression can be tested by an `if` statement, the resulting `if` statement is valid and will cause the message `Happy Birthday!` to be printed regardless of what value was previously assigned to `age`. Can you see why?

The condition tested by the `if` statement does not compare the value in `age` to the number 40, but assigns the number 40 to `age`. That is, the expression `age = 40` is not a relational expression at all, but an assignment expression. At the completion of the assignment, the expression itself has a value of 40. Since C treats any nonzero value as true, the call to `printf()` is made. Another way of looking at this is to realize that the `if` statement is equivalent to the following two statements:

```c
age = 40;       /* assign 40 to age */
if (age)        /* test the value of age */
  printf("Happy Birthday!");
```

Since a C compiler has no means of knowing that the expression being tested is not the desired one, you must be especially careful when writing conditions.

Exercises 4.2

1. Write appropriate `if` statements for each of the following conditions:

   a. If `angle` is equal to 90 degrees print the message `The angle is a right angle`, else print the message that `The angle is not a right angle`.

   b. If the temperature is above 100 degrees display the message `above the boiling point of water`, else display the message `below the boiling point of water`.

   c. If the number is positive add the number to `possum`, else add the number to `negsum`.

   d. If `slope` is less than .5 set the variable `flag` to zero, else set `flag` to one.

   e. If the difference between `num1` and `num2` is less than .001, set the variable `approx` to zero, else calculate `approx` as the quantity `(num1 - num2) / 2.0`.

   f. If the difference between `temp1` and `temp2` exceeds 2.3 degrees, calculate `error` as `(temp1 - temp2) * factor`.

   g. If x is greater than y and z is less than 20, read in a value for p.

   h. If `distance` is greater than 20 and it is less than 35, read in a value for `time`.

2. Write if statements corresponding to the conditions illustrated by each of the following flow charts.

   a.

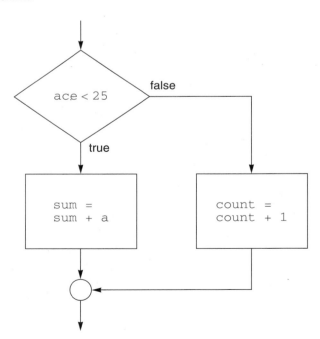

b.

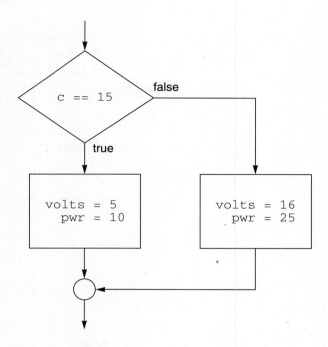

c.

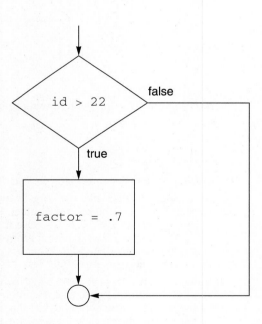

d.

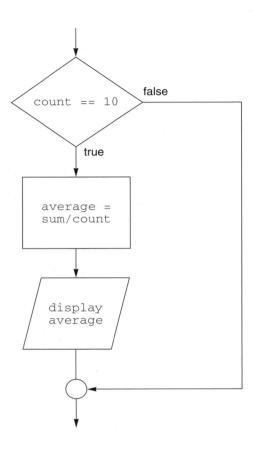

3. Rewrite Program 4.1 using the following preprocessor statements:

```
#define LIMIT 20000
#define REGRATE 0.02
#define HIGHRATE 0.025
#define FIXED 400
```

(If necessary, review Section 3.5 for the use of the named constants.)

4. Write a C program that asks the user to input two numbers. If the first number entered is greater than the second number, the program should print the message `The first number is greater`, else it should print the message `The first number is smaller`. Test your program by entering the numbers 5 and 8 and then using the numbers 11 and 2. What do you think your program will display if the two numbers entered are equal? Test this case.

5. a. If money is left in a particular bank for more than two years, the interest rate given by the bank is 8.5%, else the interest rate is 7%. Write a C program that uses the `scanf()` function to accept the number of years into the variable `nyrs` and display the appropriate interest rate depending on the input value.

   b. How many runs should you make for the program written in Exercise 5a to verify that it is operating correctly? What data should you input in each of the program runs?

6. a. In a pass/fail course, a student passes if the grade is greater than or equal to 70 and fails if the grade is lower. Write a C program that accepts a grade and prints the message `A passing grade` or `A failing grade`, as appropriate.

b. How many runs should you make for the program written in Exercise 6a to verify that it is operating correctly? What data should you input in each of the program runs?

4.3 NESTED if STATEMENTS

As we have seen, an if-else statement can contain simple or compound statements. Any valid C statement can be used, including another if-else statement. Thus, one or more if-else statements can be included within either part of an if-else statement. The inclusion of one or more if statements within an existing if statement is called a *nested if* statement. For example, substituting the one-way if statement

```
if (distance > 500)
    printf("snap");
```

for statement1 in the following if statement

```
if (hours < 9)
    statement1;
else
    printf("pop");
```

results in the nested if statement

```
if (hours < 9)
{
    if (distance > 500)
        printf("snap");
}
else
    printf("pop");
```

The braces around the inner one-way if are essential, because in their absence C associates an else with the closest unpaired if. Thus, without the braces, the preceding statement is equivalent to

```
if (hours < 9)
    if (distance > 500)
        printf("snap");
    else
        printf("pop");
```

Here the else is paired with the inner if, which destroys the meaning of the original if-else statement. Notice also that the indentation is irrelevant as far as the compiler is concerned. Whether the indentation exists or not, *the statement is compiled by associating the last else with the closest unpaired if, unless braces are used to alter the default pairing.*

The process of nesting if statements can be extended indefinitely, so that the printf("snap"); statement could itself be replaced by either a complete if-else statement or another one-way if statement.

Figure 4.5 illustrates the general form of a nested if-else statement when an if-else statement is nested within the if part of an if-else statement [Figure 4.5(a)] and within the else part of an if-else statement [Figure 4.5(b)].

FIGURE 4.5a If–else Nested Within the IF Part

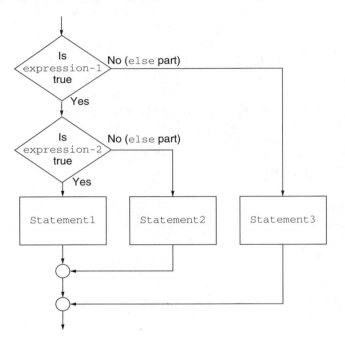

FIGURE 4.5b If–else Nested Within the ELSE Part

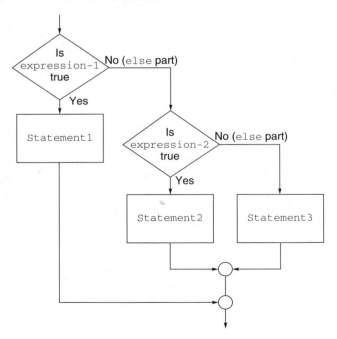

The if-else **Chain**

In general, the nesting illustrated in Figure 4.5(a) tends to be confusing and is best avoided in practice. However, an extremely useful construction occurs for the nesting illustrated in Figure 4.5(b), which has the form:

```
if (expression_1)
    statement1;
else
    if (expression_2)
        statement2;
    else
        statement3;
```

As with all C programs, the indentation we have used is not required. Since whitespace is ignored in C, the preceding construction can be rewritten using the following arrangement:

```
if (expression_1)
    statement1;
else if (expression_2)
    statement2;
else
    statement3;
```

This form of a nested if statement is extremely useful in practice, and is formally referred to as an *if-else* chain. Each condition is evaluated in order, and if any condition is true the corresponding statement is executed and the remainder of the chain is terminated. The statement associated with the final else is only executed if none of the previous conditions is satisfied. This serves as a default or catch-all case that is useful for detecting an impossible or error condition.

The chain can be continued indefinitely by repeatedly making the last statement another if-else statement. Thus, the general form of an if-else chain is:

```
if (expression_1)
    statement1;
else if (expression_2)
    statement2;
else if (expression_3)
    statement3;
          .
          .
          .
else if (expression_n)
    statement_n;
else
    last_statement;
```

Each condition is evaluated in the order in which it appears in the statement. For the first condition that is true, the corresponding statement is executed, and the remainder of the statements in the chain are not executed. Thus, if expression_1 is true, only statement1 is executed; otherwise expression_2 is tested. If expression_2 is then true, only statement2 is executed; otherwise expression_3 is tested, and so on. The final else in the chain is optional, and `last_statement` is only executed if none of the previous expressions was true. As a specific example, consider the following `if-else` chain:

```
if (marcode == 'M')
  printf("Individual is married.\n");
else if (marcode == 'S')
  printf("Individual is single.\n");
else if (marcode == 'D')
  printf("Individual is divorced.\n");
else if (marcode == 'W')
  printf("Individual is widowed.\n")
else
  printf("An invalid code was entered.\n");
```

Execution through this chain begins with a test of the expression `marcode == 'M'`. If the value in `marcode` is an `M` the message `Individual is married` is displayed, no further expressions in the chain are evaluated, and execution resumes with the next statement immediately following the chain. If the value in `marcode` is not an `M`, the expression `marcode == 'S'` is tested, and so on, until a true condition is found. If none of the conditions in the chain is true, the message `An invalid code was entered` would be displayed. In all cases, execution resumes with whatever statement immediately follows the chain. Program 4.5 uses this `if-else` chain within a complete program.

PROGRAM 4.5

```
#include <stdio.h>
void main(void)
{
  char marcode;

  printf("Enter a marital code: ");
  scanf("%c", &marcode);

  if (marcode == 'M')
    printf("Individual is married.\n");
  else if (marcode == 'S')
    printf("Individual is single.\n");
  else if (marcode == 'D')
    printf("Individual is divorced.\n");
  else if (marcode == 'W')
    printf("Individual is widowed.\n");
  else
    printf("An invalid code was entered.\n");

  printf("Thanks for participating in the survey.\n");
}
```

In reviewing Program 4.5 note that the message `Thanks for participating in the survey` is always printed. This is the statement immediately after the `if-else` chain to which execution is transferred once the chain completes its execution. Which message is printed within the `if-else` chain depends on the value entered into `marcode`.

As a final example illustrating the `if-else` chain, let us calculate the monthly income of a computer salesperson using the following commission schedule:

Monthly Sales	Income
Greater than or equal to $50,000	$375 plus 16% of sales
Less than $50,000 but greater than or equal to $40,000	$350 plus 14% of sales
Less than $40,000 but greater than or equal to $30,000	$325 plus 12% of sales
Less than $30,000 but greater than or equal to $20,000	$300 plus 9% of sales
Less than $20,000 but greater than or equal to $10,000	$250 plus 5% of sales
Less than $10,000	$200 plus 3% of sales

The following `if-else` chain can be used to determine the correct monthly income, where the variable `mon_sales` is used to store the salesperson's current monthly sales:

```
if (mon_sales >= 50000.00)
   income = 375.00 + .16 * mon_sales;
else if (mon_sales >= 40000.00)
   income = 350.00 + .14 * mon_sales;
else if (mon_sales >= 30000.00)
   income = 325.00 + .12 * mon_sales;
else if (mon_sales >= 20000.00)
   income = 300.00 + .09 * mon_sales;
else if (mon_sales >= 10000.00)
   income = 250.00 + .05 * mon_sales;
else
   income = 200.000 + .03 * mon_sales;
```

Notice that this example makes use of the fact that the chain is stopped once a true condition is found. This is accomplished by checking for the highest monthly sales first. If the salesperson's monthly sales is less than $50,000, the `if-else` chain continues checking for the next highest sales amount until the correct category is obtained.

Program 4.6 uses this `if-else` chain to calculate and display the income corresponding to the value of monthly sales input in the `scanf()` function.

PROGRAM 4.6

```
#include <stdio.h>
void main(void)
{
  float mon_sales, income;

  printf("Enter the value of monthly sales: ");
  scanf("%f", &mon_sales);
  if (mon_sales >= 50000.00)
    income = 375.00 + .16 * mon_sales;
  else if (mon_sales >= 40000.00)
```

(continued on next page)

(continued from previous page)

```
    income = 350.00 + .14 * mon_sales;
  else if (mon_sales >= 30000.00)
    income = 325.00 + .12 * mon_sales;
  else if (mon_sales >= 20000.00)
    income = 300.00 + .09 * mon_sales;
  else if (mon_sales >= 10000.00)
    income = 250.00 + .05 * mon_sales;
  else
    income = 200.00 + .03 * mon_sales;
  printf("The income is $%7.2f\n",income);
}
```

A sample run using Program 4.6 is illustrated below:

```
        Enter the value of monthly sales: 36243.89
        The income is $4674.27
```

As with all C statements, each individual statement within an `if-else` chain can be replaced by a compound statement bounded by the braces `{` and `}`.

Exercises 4.3

1. Modify Program 4.5 to accept both lowercase and uppercase letters as marriage codes. For example, if a user enters either an m or an M, the program should display the message `Individual is married`.

2. Write nested `if` statements corresponding to the conditions illustrated in each of the following flowcharts.

   a.

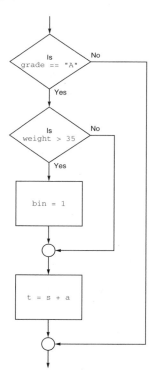

b.

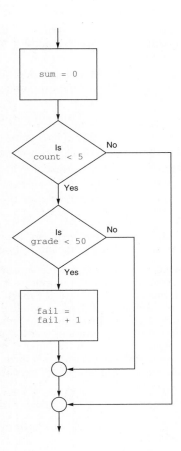

3. An angle is considered acute if it is less than 90 degrees, obtuse if it is greater than 90 degrees, and a right angle if it is equal to 90 degrees. Using this information, write a C program that accepts an angle, in degrees, and displays the type of angle corresponding to the degrees entered.

4. The grade level of undergraduate college students is typically determined according to the following schedule:

Number of Credits Completed	Grade Level
Less than 32	Freshman
32 to 63	Sophomore
64 to 95	Junior
96 or more	Senior

Using this information, write a C program that accepts the number of credits a student has completed, determines the student's grade level, and displays the grade level.

5. A student's letter grade is calculated according to the following schedule:

Numerical Grade	Letter Grade
Greater than or equal to 90	A
Less than 90 but greater than or equal to 80	B
Less than 80 but greater than or equal to 70	C
Less than 70 but greater than or equal to 60	D
Less than 60	F

Using this information, write a C program that accepts a student's numerical grade, converts the numerical grade to an equivalent letter grade, and displays the letter grade.

6. The interest rate used on funds deposited in a bank is determined by the amount of time the money is left on deposit. For a particular bank, the following schedule is used:

Time on Deposit	Interest Rate
Greater than or equal to 5 years	0.095
Less than 5 years but greater than or equal to 4 years	0.09
Less than 4 years but greater than or equal to 3 years	0.085
Less than 3 years but greater than or equal to 2 years	0.075
Less than 2 years but greater than or equal to 1 year	0.065
Less than 1 year	0.055

Using this information, write a C program that accepts the time that funds are left on deposit and displays the interest rate corresponding to the time entered.

7. Write a C program that accepts a number followed by one space and then a letter. If the letter following the number is f, the program is to treat the number entered as a temperature in degrees Fahrenheit, convert the number to the equivalent degrees Celsius, and print a suitable display message. If the letter following the number is c, the program is to treat the number entered as a temperature in Celsius, convert the number to the equivalent degrees Fahrenheit, and print a suitable display message. If the letter is neither an f or a c, the program is to print a message that the data entered is incorrect and terminate. Use an if-else chain in your program and make use of the conversion formulas:

```
Celsius = (5.0 / 9.0) * (Fahrenheit - 32.0)
Fahrenheit = (9.0 / 5.0) * Celsius + 32.0
```

8. Using the commission schedule from Program 4.6, the following program calculates monthly income:

```
void main(void)
{
  float mon_sales, income;

  printf("Enter the value of monthly sales: ");
  scanf("%f",mon_sales);
  if (mon_sales >= 50000.00)
    income = 375.00 + .16 * mon_sales;
  if (mon_sales >= 40000.00 && mon_sales < 50000.00)
    income = 350.00 + .14 * mon_sales;
  if (mon_sales >= 30000.00 && mon_sales < 40000.00)
    income = 325.00 + .12 * mon_sales;
  if (mon_sales >= 20000.00 && mon_sales < 30000.00)
    income = 300.00 + .09 * mon_sales;
  if (mon_sales >= 10000.00 && mon_sales < 20000.00)
    income = 250.00 + .05 * mon_sales;
  if (mon_sales < 10000.00)
    income = 200.00 + .03 * mon_sales;
  printf("The income is $%7.2f\n",income);
}
```

a. Will this program produce the same output as Program 4.6?

b. Which program is better and why?

9. The following program was written to produce the same result as Program 4.6:

```
void main(void)
{
  float mon_sales, income;
```

```
        printf("Enter the value of monthly sales: ");
        scanf("%f",mon_sales);
        if (mon_sales < 10000.00)
           income = 200.00 + .03 * mon_sales;
        else if (mon_sales >= 10000.00)
           income = 250.00 + .05 * mon_sales;
        else if (mon_sales >= 20000.00)
           income = 300.00 + .09 * mon_sales;
        else if (mon_sales >= 30000.00)
           income = 325.00 + .12 * mon_sales;
        else if (mon_sales >= 40000.00)
           income = 350.00 + .14 * mon_sales;
        else if (mon_sales >= 50000.00)
           income = 375.00 + .16 * mon_sales;
        printf("The income is $%7.2f\n",income);
     }
```

a. Will this program run?

b. What does this program do?

c. For what values of monthly sales does this program calculate the correct income?

4.4 THE switch STATEMENT

The if-else chain is used in programming applications where one set of instructions must be selected from many possible alternatives. The *switch statement* provides an alternative to the if-else chain for cases that compare the value of an integer expression to a specific value. The general form of a switch statement is:

```
switch (expression)
{                        /* start of compound statement */
   case value_1:   ◀─────────────── terminated with a colon
      statement1;
      statement2;

        .

        .

      break;
   case value_2:   ◀─────────────── terminated with a colon
      statementm;
      statementn;

        .

        .

      break;

        .

        .

   case value_n:   ◀─────────────── terminated with a colon
      statementw;
      statementx;

        .

        .

      break;
   default:        ◀─────────────── terminated with a colon
      statementaa;
      statementbb;

        .

}                        /* end of switch and compound statement */
```

The switch statement uses four new keywords: `switch`, `case`, `default`, and `break`. Let's see what each of these words does.

The keyword `switch` identifies the start of the `switch` statement. The expression in parentheses following this word is evaluated and the result of the expression compared to various alternative values contained within the compound statement. The expression in the `switch` statement must evaluate to an integer result or a compilation error results.

Internal to the switch statement, the keyword `case` is used to identify or label individual values that are compared to the value of the `switch` expression. The `switch` expression's value is compared to each of these case values in the order in which these values are listed until a match is found. When a match occurs, execution begins with the statement immediately following the match. Thus, as illustrated in Figure 4.6, the value of the expression determines where in the `switch` statement execution actually begins.

Any number of case labels may be contained within a `switch` statement, in any order. If the value of the expression does not match any of the case values, however, no statement is executed unless the keyword `default` is encountered. The word `default` is optional and operates the same as the last `else` in an if-else chain. If the value of the expression does not match any of the case values, program execution begins with the statement following the word `default`.

Once an entry point has been located by the `switch` statement, all further `case` evaluations are ignored and execution continues through the end of the compound statement unless a `break` statement is encountered. This is the reason for the `break` statement, which identifies the end of a particular case and causes an immediate exit from the `switch` statement. Thus, just as the word `case` identifies possible starting points in the compound statement, the `break` statement determines terminating points. If the `break` statements are omitted, all `cases` following the matching `case` value, including the `default` case, are executed.

When we write a `switch` statement, we can use multiple `case` values to refer to the same set of statements; the `default` label is optional. For example, consider the following:

```
switch (number)
{
  case 1:
    printf("Have a Good Morning\n");
    break;
  case 2:
    printf("Have a Happy Day\n");
    break;
  case 3:
  case 4:
  case 5:
    printf("Have a Nice Evening\n");
}
```

If the value stored in the variable `number` is 1, the message `Have a Good Morning` is displayed. Similarly, if the value of `number` is 2, the second message is displayed. Finally, if the value of `number` is 3 or 4 or 5, the last message is displayed. Since the statement to be executed for these last three cases is the same, the cases for these values can be "stacked together" as shown in the example. Also, since there is no default, no message is printed if the value of `number` is not one of the listed `case` values. Although it is good programming practice to list

---

FIGURE 4.6   The Expression Determines an Entry Point

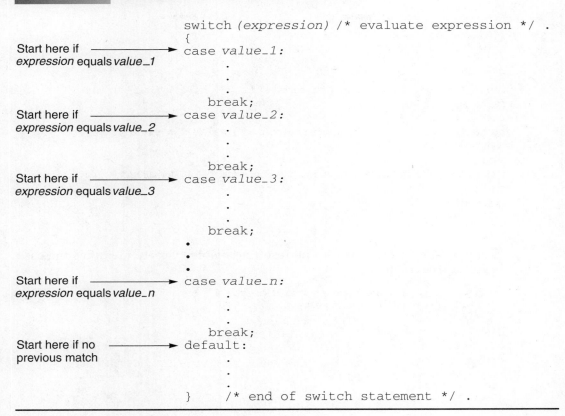

```
                      switch (expression) /* evaluate expression */ .
                      {
Start here if  ────────► case value_1:
expression equals value_1    .

                             .

                             .
                        break;
Start here if  ────────► case value_2:
expression equals value_2    .

                             .

                             .
                        break;
Start here if  ────────► case value_3:
expression equals value_3    .

                             .

                             .
                        break;
                        •

                        •

                        •
Start here if  ────────► case value_n:
expression equals value_n    .

                             .

                             .
                        break;
Start here if no  ─────► default:
previous match               .

                             .

                             .
                      }     /* end of switch statement */ .
```

---

case values in increasing order, this is not required by the switch statement. A switch statement may have any number of case values, in any order; only the values being tested for need to be listed.

Program 4.7 uses a switch statement to select the arithmetic operation (addition, multiplication, or division) to be performed on two numbers depending on the value of the variable opselect.

    PROGRAM 4.7

```c
#include <stdio.h>
void main(void)
{
  int opselect;
  double fnum, snum;

  printf("Please type in two numbers: ");
  scanf("%lf %lf", &fnum, &snum);
  printf("Enter a select code: \n");
```

(continued on next page)

(continued from previous page)

```
  printf("         1 for addition\n");
  printf("         2 for multiplication\n");
  printf("         3 for division : ");
  scanf("%d", &opselect);
  switch (opselect)
  {
    case 1:
      printf("The sum of the numbers entered is %6.3lf\n", fnum+snum);
      break;
    case 2:
      printf("The product of the numbers entered is %6.3lf\n",fnum*snum);
      break;
    case 3:
      printf("The first number divided by the second is %6.3lf\n", fnum/snum);
      break;
  }     /* end of switch */
}   /* end of main() */
```

Program 4.7 was run twice. The resulting display clearly identifies the case selected. The results are:

```
Please type in two numbers: 12 3
Enter a select code:
        1 for addition
        2 for multiplication
        3 for division : 2
The product of the numbers entered is  36.000
```

and

```
Please type in two numbers: 12 3
Enter a select code:
        1 for addition
        2 for multiplication
        3 for division : 3
The first number divided by the second is  4.000
```

In reviewing Program 4.7 notice the break statement in the last case. Although this break is not necessary, it is a good practice to terminate the last case in a switch statement with a break. This prevents a possible program error later, if an additional case is subsequently added to the switch statement. With the addition of a new case, the break between cases becomes necessary; having the break in place ensures you will not forget to include it at the time of the modification.

Since character data types are always converted to integers in an expression, a switch statement can also be used to "switch" based on the value of a character expression. For example, assuming that choice is a character variable, the following switch statement is valid:

```
switch(choice)
{
  case 'a':
  case 'e':
  case 'i':
```

```
      case 'o':
      case 'u':
        printf("The character in choice is a vowel\n");
        break;
      default:
        printf("The character in choice is not a vowel\n");
        break;    /* this break is optional */
   }    /* end of switch statement */
```

Exercises 4.4

1. Rewrite the following if-else chain using a switch statement:

```
if (let_grad == 'A')
  printf("The numerical grade is between 90 and 100\n");
else if (let_grad == 'B')
  printf("The numerical grade is between 80 and 89.9\n");
else if (let_grad == 'C')
  printf("The numerical grade is between 70 and 79.9\n");
else if (let_grad == 'D');
  printf("How are you going to explain this one\n");
else
{
  printf("Of course I had nothing to do with my grade.\n");
  printf("It must have been the professor's fault.\n");
}
```

2. Rewrite the following if-else chain using a switch statement:

```
if (res_typ == 1)
{
  in_data();
  check();
}
else if (res_typ == 2)
{
  capacity();
  devtype();
}
else if (res_typ == 3)
{
  volume();
  mass();
}
else if (res_typ == 4)
{
  area();
  weight();
}
else if (res_typ == 5)
{
  files();
  save();
}
else if (res_typ == 6)
{
  retrieve();
  screen();
}
```

3. Each disk drive in a shipment of these devices is stamped with a code from 1 through 4, which indicates a drive of the following type:

Code	Disk Drive Type	
1	360-kilobyte drive	(5 ½ inch)
2	1.2-megabyte drive	(5 ½ inch)
3	722-kilobyte drive	(3 ¼ inch)
4	1.4-megabyte drive	(3 ¼ inch)

Write a C program that accepts the code number as an input, and based on the value entered, displays the correct disk drive type.

4. Rewrite Program 4.5 using a `switch` statement.

5. Determine why the `if-else` chain in Program 4.6 cannot be replaced with a `switch` statement.

6. Rewrite Program 4.7 using a character variable for the select code. (*Hint:* Review Section 3.4 if your program does not operate as you think it should.)

4.5 FOCUS ON PROBLEM SOLVING

Two major uses of C's `if` statements are to select appropriate processing paths and to prevent undesirable data from being processed at all. In this section examples of both uses are provided.

Problem 1: Data Validation

An important use of C's `if` statements is to validate data by checking for clearly invalid cases. For example, a date such as 5/33/86 contains an obviously invalid day. Similarly, the division of any number by zero within a program, such as 14/0, should not be allowed. Both of these examples illustrate the need for a technique called *defensive programming,* in which the program includes code to check for improper data before an attempt is made to process it further. The defensive programming technique of checking user input data for erroneous or unreasonable data is referred to as *input data validation.*

Consider the case where we are to write a C program to calculate the square root and the reciprocal of a user-entered number. Before calculating the square root, validate that the number is not negative, and before calculating the reciprocal, check that the number is not zero.

Step 1: Analyze the Problem   The statement of the problem requires that we accept a single number as an input, validate the entered number, and based on the validation produce two possible outputs: If the number is non-negative we are to determine its square root and if the input number is not zero we are to determine its reciprocal.

Step 2: Develop a Solution   Since the square root of a negative number does not exist as a real number and the reciprocal of zero cannot be taken, our program must contain input data validation statements to screen the user input data and avoid these two cases. The pseudocode describing the processing required is:

Display a program purpose message
Accept a user input number
If the number is negative
  print a message that the square root cannot be taken
Else
  calculate and display the square root
Endif
If the number is zero then
  print a message that the reciprocal cannot be taken
Else
  calculate and display the reciprocal
Endif

Step 3: Code the Solution   The C code corresponding to our pseudocode solution is listed in Program 4.8.

PROGRAM 4.8

```c
#include <stdio.h>
#include <math.h>
void main(void)
{
    double usenum;

    printf("This program calculates the square root and\n");
    printf("reciprocal (1/number) of a number\n");
    printf("\nPlease enter a number: ");
    scanf("%lf", &usenum);
    if (usenum < 0.0)
        printf("The square root of a negative number does not exist.\n");
    else
        printf("The square root of %lf is %lf\n", usenum, sqrt(usenum));
    if (usenum == 0.0)
        printf("The reciprocal of zero does not exist.\n");
    else
        printf("The reciprocal of %lf is %lf\n", usenum, 1/usenum);
}
```

Program 4.8 is a rather straightforward program containing two separate (non-nested) if statements. The first if statement checks for a negative input number; if the number is negative a message indicating that the square root of a negative number cannot be taken is displayed, else the square root is taken. The second if statement checks whether the entered number is zero; if it is, a message indicating that the reciprocal of zero cannot be taken is displayed, else the reciprocal is taken.

Step 4: Test and Debug the Program   Test values should include an appropriate value for the input, such as 5, and values for the limiting cases, such as a negative and zero input value. Test runs follow for two of these cases:

```
        This program calculates the square root and
        reciprocal (1/number) of a number

        Please enter a number: 5

        The square root of 5.000000 is 2.236068
        The reciprocal of 5.000000 is 0.200000
```

and

```
        This program calculates the square root and
        reciprocal (1/number) of a number

        Please enter a number: −6

        The square root of a negative number does not exist
        The reciprocal of −6.000000 is −0.166667
```

Problem 2: Solving Quadratic Equations

A *quadratic equation* is an equation that has the form $ax^2 + bx + c = 0$ or that can be algebraically manipulated into this form. In this equation, x is the unknown variable, and a, b, and c are known constants. Although the constants b and c can be any numbers, including zero, the value of the constant a cannot be zero (if a is zero, the equation would become a *linear equation* in x). Examples of quadratic equations are:

$$5x^2 + 6x + 2 = 0$$

$$x^2 - 7x + 20 = 0$$

$$34x^2 + 16 = 0$$

In the first equation $a = 5$, $b = 6$, and $c = 2$; in the second equation $a = 1$, $b = -7$, and $c = 20$; and in the third equation $a = 34$, $b = 0$, and $c = 16$.

The real roots of a quadratic equation can be calculated using the quadratic formula as:

$$\text{root 1} = \frac{-b + \sqrt{b^2 - 4ac}}{2a}$$

and:

$$\text{root 2} = \frac{-b - \sqrt{b^2 - 4ac}}{2a}$$

Using these equations we will write a C program to solve for the roots of a quadratic equation.

Step 1: Analyze the Problem   The problem requires that we accept three inputs—the coefficients a, b, and c of a quadratic equation—and compute the roots of the equation using the given formulas.

Step 2: Develop a Solution   A first attempt at a solution would be to use the user-entered values of a, b and c to calculate directly a value for each of the roots. Thus, our first solution would be:

Display a program purpose message.
Accept user-input values for a, b, and c.
Calculate the two roots.
Display the values of the calculated roots.

However, this solution must be refined further to account for a number of possible input conditions. For example, if a user entered a value of 0 for both *a* and *b*, the equation is neither quadratic or linear and has no solution (this is referred to as a degenerate case). Another possibility is that the user supplies a non-zero value for *b* but makes *a* zero. In this case the equation becomes a linear one with a single solution of $-c/b$. A third possibility is that the value of the term $b^2 - 4ac$, which is called the *discriminant,* is negative. Since the square root of a negative number cannot be taken, this case will have no real roots. Finally, when the discriminant is zero, both roots are the same (this is referred to as the repeated roots case).

Taking into account all four of these limiting cases, a refined solution for correctly determining the roots of a quadratic equation is expressed by the following pseudocode:

Display a program purpose message
Accept user-input values for a, b, and c
If a = 0 and b = 0 then
  display a message saying that the equation has no solution.
Else if a = zero then
  calculate the single root equal to $-c/b$
  display the single root
Else
  calculate the discriminant
  if the discriminant > 0 then
    solve for both roots using the given formulas
    display the two roots
  else if the discriminant < 0 then
    display a message that there are no real roots
  else
    calculate the repeated root equal to $-b/(2a)$
    display the repeated root
  Endif
Endif

Notice in the pseudocode that we have used nested `if-else` structures. The outer `if-else` structure is used to validate the entered coefficients and determine that we have a valid quadratic equation. The inner `if-else` structure is then used to determine if the equation has two real roots (discriminant > 0) two imaginary roots (discriminant < 0) or repeated roots (discriminant = 0).

Step 3: Code the Solution   The equivalent C code corresponding to our pseudocode solution is listed in Program 4.9.

PROGRAM 4.9

```
/* this program solves for the roots of a quadratic equation */
#include <stdio.h>
#include <math.h>
void main(void)
```

(continued on next page)

(continued from previous page)

```
{
  double a, b, c, disc, root1, root2;

  printf("This program calculates the roots of a\n");
  printf("    quadratic equation of the form\n");
  printf("              2\n");
  printf("          ax + bx + c = 0\n\n");
  printf("Please enter values for a, b, and c: ");
  scanf("%lf %lf %lf", &a, &b, &c);
  if ( a == 0.0 && b == 0.0)
     printf("The equation is degenerate and has no roots.\n");
  else if (a == 0.0)
     printf("The equation has the single root x = %lf\n", -c /b);
  else
  {
    disc = pow(b,2.0) - 4 * a * c;    /* calculate discriminant */
    if (disc > 0.0)
    {
       disc = sqrt(disc);
       root1 = (-b + disc) / (2 * a);
       root2 = (-b - disc) / (2 * a);
       printf("The two real roots are %lf and %lf\n", root1, root2);
    }
    else if (disc < 0.0)
       printf("Both roots are imaginary.\n");
    else
       printf("Both roots are equal to %lf\n", -b / (2 * a));
  }
}
```

Step 4: Test and Debug the Program   Test values should include values for a, b, and c that result in two real roots, plus limiting values for a and b that result in either a linear equation ($a = 0$, $b \neq 0$), a degenerate equation ($a = 0$, $b = 0$), and a negative and zero discriminant. Two such test runs of Program 4.9 follow:

```
This program calculates the roots of a
    quadratic equation of the form
           ax² + bx + c = 0
Please enter values for a, b, and c: 1 2 -35

The two real roots are 5.000000 and -7.000000
```

and:

```
This program calculates the roots of a
    quadratic equation of the form
           ax² + bx + c = 0
Please enter values for a, b, and c: 0 0 16

The equation is degenerate and has no roots
```

The first run solves the quadratic equation $x^2 + 2x - 35 = 0$, which has the real roots $x = 5$ and $x = -7$. The input data for the second run results in the equation $0x^2 + 0x + 16 = 0$. Because this degenerates into the mathematical impossibility of $16 = 0$, the program correctly identifies this as a degenerate equation. We leave it as an exercise to create test data for the other limiting cases checked for by the program.

Exercises 4.5

1. a. Write a program that accepts two real numbers from a user and a select code. If the entered select code is 1, have the program add the two previously entered numbers and display the result; if the select code is 2, the numbers should be multiplied; and if the select code is 3, the first number should be divided by the second number.

   b. Determine what the program written in Exercise 1a does when the entered numbers are 3 and 0, and the select code is 3.

   c. Modify the program written in Exercise 1a so that division by 0 is not allowed and an appropriate message is displayed when such a division is attempted.

2. a. Write a program to display the following two prompts:

   ```
   Enter a month (use a 1 for Jan, etc.):
   Enter a day of the month:
   ```

   Have your program accept and store a number in the variable month in response to the first prompt, and accept and store a number in the variable day in response to the second prompt. If the month entered is not between 1 and 12 inclusive, print a message informing the user that an invalid month has been entered. If the day entered is not between 1 and 31, print a message informing the user that an invalid day has been entered.

   b. What will your program do if the user types a number with a decimal point for the month? How can you ensure that your if statements check for an integer number?

   c. In a non–leap year February has 28 days, the months January, March, May, July, August, October, and December have 31 days, and all other months have 30 days. Using this information, modify the program written in Exercise 2a to display a message when an invalid day is entered for a user-entered month. For this program ignore leap years.

3. a. The quadrant in which a line drawn from the origin resides is determined by the angle that the line makes with the positive X axis as follows:

Angle from the Positive X Axis	Quadrant
Between 0 and 90 degrees	I
Between 90 and 180 degrees	II
Between 180 and 270 degrees	III
Between 270 and 360 degrees	IV

   Using this information, write a C program that accepts the angle of the line as user input and determines and displays the quadrant appropriate to the input data. (*Note:* If the angle is exactly 0, 90, 180, or 270 degrees the corresponding line does not reside in any quadrant but lies on an axis.)

   b. Modify the program written for Exercise 3a so that a message is displayed that identifies an angle of zero degrees as the positive X axis, an angle of 90 degrees as the positive Y axis, an angle of 180 degrees as the negative X axis, and an angle of 270 degrees as the negative Y axis.

4. a. All years that are evenly divisible by 400 or are evenly divisible by four and not evenly divisible by 100 are leap years. For example, since 1600 is evenly divisible by 400, the year 1600 was a leap year. Similarly, since 1988 is evenly divisible by four but not by 100, the year 1988 was also a leap year. Using this informa-

tion, write a C program that accepts the year as user input, determines if the year is a leap year, and displays an appropriate message that tells the user if the entered year is or is not a leap year.

b. Using the code written in Exercise 4a redo Exercise 2c such that leap years are taken into account.

5. Based on an automobile's model year and weight the state of New Jersey determines the car's weight class and registration fee using the following schedule:

Model Year	Weight	Weight Class	Registration Fee
1970 or earlier	Less than 2,700 lbs	1	$16.50
	2,700 to 3,800 lbs	2	25.50
	More than 3,800 lbs	3	46.50
1971 to 1979	Less than 2,700 lbs	4	27.00
	2,700 to 3,800 lbs	5	30.50
	More than 3,800 lbs	6	52.50
1980 or later	Less than 3,500 lbs	7	19.50
	3,500 or more lbs	8	52.50

Using this information write a C program that accepts the year and weight of an automobile and determines and displays the weight class and registration fee for the car.

6. Modify Program 4.9 so that the imaginary roots are calculated and displayed when the discriminant is negative. For this case the two roots of the equation are:

$$x_1 = \frac{-b}{2a} + \frac{\sqrt{-(b^2 - 4ac)}}{2a} i$$

and

$$x_2 = \frac{-b}{2a} - \frac{\sqrt{-(b^2 - 4ac)}}{2a} i$$

where i is the imaginary number symbol for the square root of -1. (*Hint:* Calculate the real and imaginary parts of each root separately.)

7. In the game of Blackjack the cards 2 through 10 are counted at their face values, regardless of suit, all face cards (jack, queen, and king) are counted as 10, and an ace is counted as either a 1 or an 11, depending on the total count of all the cards in a player's hand. The ace is counted as 11 only if the resulting total value of all cards in a player's hand does not exceed 21, else it is counted as a 1. Using this information write a C program that accepts three card values as inputs (a 1 corresponding to an ace, a 2 corresponding to a two, and so on), calculates the total value of the hand appropriately, and displays the value of the three cards with a printed message.

4.6 ENRICHMENT STUDY: A CLOSER LOOK AT PROGRAM TESTING

In theory, a comprehensive set of test runs would reveal all possible program errors and ensure that a program will work correctly for any and all combinations of input and computed data. In practice this requires checking all possible combinations of statement execution. Due to the time and effort required, this is an impossible goal except for extremely simple programs. Let us see why this is so. Consider Program 4.10.

PROGRAM 4.10

```c
#include <stdio.h>
void main(void)
{
  int num;

  printf("Enter a number:");
  scanf("%d", &num);
  if (num == 5)
    printf("Bingo!\n");
  else
    printf("Bongo!\n");
}
```

Program 4.10 has two paths that can be traversed from when the program is run to when the program reaches its closing brace. The first path, which is executed when the input number is 5, is in the sequence:

```c
printf("Enter a number");
scanf("%d", &num);
printf("Bingo!\n");
```

The second path, which is executed whenever any number except 5 is input, includes the sequence of instructions:

```c
printf("Enter a number");
scanf("%d", &num);
printf("Bongo!\n");
```

To test each possible path through Program 4.10 requires two runs of the program, with a judicious selection of test input data to ensure that both paths of the `if` statement are exercised. The addition of one more `if` statement in the program increases the number of possible execution paths by a factor of two and requires four (2^2) runs of the program for complete testing. Similarly, two additional `if` statements increase the number of paths by a factor of four and require eight (2^3) runs for complete testing and three additional `if` statements would produce a program that required sixteen (2^4) test runs.

Now consider a modestly sized application program consisting of only ten modules, each module containing five `if` statements. Assuming the modules are always called in the same sequence, there are 32 possible paths through each module (2 raised to the fifth power) and more than 1,000,000,000,000,000 (2 raised to the fiftieth power) possible paths through the complete program (all modules executed in sequence). The time needed to create individual test data to exercise each path and the actual computer run time required to check each path make the complete testing of such a program impossible to achieve.

The inability to fully test all combinations of statement execution sequences has led to the programming saying that "there is no error-free program." It has also led to the realization that any testing that is done should be well thought out to maximize the possibility of locating errors. At a minimum, test data should include appropriate values for input values, illegal input values that the program should reject, and limiting values that are checked by selection statements within the program.

4.7 COMMON PROGRAMMING ERRORS

Three programming errors are common to C's selection statements:

1. *Using the assignment operator, =, in place of the relational operator, ==:* This can cause an enormous amount of frustration because any expression can be tested by an if-else statement. For example, the statement:

```
if (opselect = 2)
    printf("Happy Birthday");
else
    printf("Good Day");
```

always results in the message Happy Birthday being printed, regardless of the initial value in the variable opselect. The reason for this is that the assignment expression opselect = 2 has a value of 2, which is considered a true value in C. The correct expression to determine the value in opselect is opselect == 2.

2. *Letting the if-else statement appear to select an incorrect choice:* In this typical debugging problem, the programmer mistakenly concentrates on the tested condition as the source of the problem. For example, assume that the following if-else statement is part of your program:

```
if (key == 'F')
{
    contemp = (5.0/9.0) * (intemp - 32.0);
    printf("Conversion to Celsius was done");
}
else
{
    contemp = (9.0/5.0) * intemp + 32.0;
    printf("Conversion to Fahrenheit was done");
}
```

This statement will always display Conversion to Celsius was done when the variable key contains an F. Therefore, if this message is displayed when you believe key does not contain F, investigation of key's value is called for. As a general rule, whenever a selection statement does not act as you think it should, test your assumptions about the values assigned to the tested variables by displaying their values. If an unanticipated value is displayed, you have at least isolated the source of the problem to the variables themselves, rather than the structure of the if-else statement. From there you will have to determine where and how the incorrect value was obtained.

3. *Using nested if statements without including braces to indicate the desired structure:* Without braces the compiler defaults to pairing elses with the closest unpaired ifs, which sometimes destroys the original intent of the selection statement. To avoid this problem and to create code that is readily adaptable to change, it is useful to write all if-else statements as compound statements in the form:

```
if (expression)
{
    one or more statements in here
}
else
{
    one or more statements in here
}
```

By using this form, no matter how many statements are added later, the original integrity and intent of the `if` statement are maintained.

4.8 CHAPTER REVIEW

Key Terms

compound statement	nested `if`
condition	one-way selection
false condition	simple relational expression
`if-else` chain	`switch` statement
`if-else` statement	true condition

Summary

1. Relational expressions, which are also called *simple conditions* are used to compare operands. If a relational expression is true, the value of the expression is the integer 1. If the relational expression is false, it has an integer value of 0. Relational expressions are created using the following relational operators:

Relational Operator	Meaning	Example
`<`	Less than	`age < 30`
`>`	Greater than	`height > 6.2`
`<=`	Less than or equal to	`taxable <= 20000`
`>=`	Greater than or equal to	`temp >= 98.6`
`==`	Equal to	`grade == 100`
`!=`	Not equal to	`number ! 250`

2. More complex conditions can be constructed from relational expressions using C's logical operators, `&&` `(AND)`, `||` `(OR)`, and `!` `(NOT)`.

3. An `if-else` statement is used to select between two alternative statements based on the value of an expression. Although relational expressions are usually used for the tested expression, any valid expression can be used. In testing an expression, `if-else` statements interpret a nonzero value as true and a zero value as false. The general form of an `if-else` statement is:

```
if (expression)
    statement1;
else
    statement2;
```

This is a two-way selection statement. If the expression has a nonzero value it is considered as true, and `statement1` is executed; otherwise `statement2` is executed.

4. An `if-else` statement can contain other `if-else` statements. In the absence of braces, each `else` is associated with the closest preceding unpaired `if`.

5. The `if-else` chain is a multiway selection statement having the general form:

```
                    if (expression_1)
                        statement_1;
                    else if (expression_2)
                        statement_2;
                    else if (expression_3)
                        statement_3;

                                .
                                .
                                .

                    else if (expression_m)
                        statement_m;
                    else
                        statement_n;
```

Each expression is evaluated in the order in which it appears in the chain. Once an expression is true (has a nonzero value), only the statement between that expression and the next else if or else is executed, and no further expressions are tested. The final else is optional, and the statement corresponding to the final else is only executed if none of the previous expressions is true.

6. A compound statement consists of any number of individual statements enclosed within the brace pair, { and }. Compound statements are treated as a single unit and can be used anywhere a single statement is used.

7. The switch statement is a multiway selection statement. The general form of a switch statement is:

```
switch (expression)
{                          /* start of compound statement */
    case value_1:     ◄——————— terminated with a colon
        statement1;
        statement2;

                  .
                  .

        break;
    case value_2:     ◄——————— terminated with a colon
        statementm;
        statementn;

                  .
                  .

        break;

                  .
                  .

    case value_n:     ◄——————— terminated with a colon
        statementw;
        statementx;

                  .
                  .

        break;
    default:          ◄——————— terminated with a colon
        statementaa;
        statementbb;

          .
          .
}                          /* end of switch and compound statement */
```

For this statement the value of an integer expression is compared to a number of integer or character constants or constant expressions. Program execution is transferred to the first matching case and continues through the end of the `switch` statement unless an optional `break` statement is encountered. The `cases` in a `switch` statement can appear in any order and an optional `default case` can be included. The `default case` is executed if none of the other cases is matched.

Exercises

1. Write C code sections to make the following decisions.
   a. Ask for two integer temperatures. If their values are equal, display the temperature; otherwise do nothing.
   b. Ask for character values `letter1` and `letter2`, representing capital letters of the alphabet, and display them in alphabetical order.
   c. Ask for three integer values, `Num1`, `Num2`, and `Num3`, and display them in decreasing order.

2. a. Write a C program to compute and display a person's weekly salary as determined by the following conditions: If the hours worked are less than or equal to 40, the person receives $8.00 per hour; else the person receives $320.00 plus $12.00 for each hour worked over 40 hours. The program should request the hours worked as input and should display the salary as output.
   b. How many runs should you make for the program written in Exercise 2a to verify that it is operating correctly? What data should you input in each of the program runs?

3. a. Write a program that displays either the message `I FEEL GREAT TODAY!` or `I FEEL DOWN TODAY #$*!` depending on the input. If the character u is entered in the variable code, the first message should be displayed; else the second message should be displayed.
   b. How many runs should you make for the program written in Exercise 3a to verify that it is operating correctly? What data should you input in each of the program runs?

4. a. A senior engineer is paid $1000 a week and a junior engineer $600 a week. Write a C program that accepts as input an engineer's status in the character variable `status`. If `status` equals `'S'`, the senior person's salary should be displayed, else the junior person's salary should be output.
   b. How many runs should you make for the program written in Exercise 4a to verify that it is operating correctly? What data should you input in each of the program runs?

5. Write a C program that accepts a character as input data and determines if the character is an uppercase letter. An uppercase letter is any character that is greater than or equal to `'A'` and less than or equal to `'Z'`. If the entered character is an uppercase letter, display the message `The character just entered is an uppercase letter`. If the entered letter is not uppercase, display the message `The character just entered is not an uppercase letter`.

6. Repeat Exercise 5 to determine if the character entered is a lowercase letter. A lowercase letter is any character greater than or equal to `'a'` and less than or equal to `'z'`.

7. The following program displays the message `Hello there!` regardless of the letter input. Determine where the error is.

```c
#include <stdio.h>
void main(void)
{
  char letter;

  printf("Enter a letter: ");
  scanf("%c",&letter);
  if (letter = 'm')
    printf("Hello there!\n");
}
```

8. a. Write, run, and test a C program that accepts a user input integer number and determines whether it is even or odd. Display the entered number and the message `Even` or `Odd`.

   b. Modify the program written for Exercise 8a to determine if the entered number is exactly divisible by a value specified by the user. That is, is it divisible by 3, 7, 13, or any other user-specified value.

9. As a part-time student, you took two courses last term. Write, run, and test a C program that calculates and displays your gradepoint average (GPA) for the term. Your program should prompt the user to enter the grade and credit hours for each course. These should then be displayed with the lower grade first. The gradepoint average for the term should be calculated and displayed. A warning message should be printed if the GPA is less than 2.0 and a congratulatory message if the GPA is 3.5 or above.

10. Write a program that will give the user only three choices: `Convert from Fahrenheit to Celsius`, `Convert from Celsius to Fahrenheit`, or `Quit`. If the third choice is chosen, the program stops. If one of the first two choices is selected, the program should prompt the user for either a Fahrenheit or Celsius temperature, as appropriate, and then calculate and display the corresponding temperature. Use the conversion equations

$$F = (9/5)\ C + 32$$
$$C = (5/9)\ (F - 32)$$

CHAPTER

5 | Repetition Structures

The programs examined so far have illustrated the programming concepts involved in input, output, assignments, and selection capabilities. By this time you should have gained enough experience to be comfortable with these concepts and the mechanics of implementing them using C. Many problems, however, require a repetition capability, in which the same calculation or sequence of instructions is repeated, over and over, using different sets of data. Examples of such repetition include continual checking of user data entries until an acceptable entry, such as a valid password, is entered, counting and accumulating running totals, and acceptance of input data and recalculation of output values that only stops upon entry of a sentinel value.

This chapter explores the different methods that programmers use in constructing repeating sections of code and how they can be implemented in C. More commonly, a section of code that is repeated is referred to as a *loop*, because after the last statement in the code is executed the program branches, or loops back to the first statement and starts another repetition through the code. Each repetition is also referred to as an iteration or pass through the loop.

5.1 INTRODUCTION

Constructing a repetitive section of code requires that four elements be present. The first necessary element is a repetition statement. This *repetition statement* both defines the boundaries containing the repeating section of code and controls

203

whether the code will be executed or not. In general there are three different forms of repetition structures, all of which are provided in C:

a. `while` structure
b. `for` structure
c. `do` structure

Each of these structures requires a condition that must be evaluated, which is the second required element for constructing repeating sections of code. Valid conditions are identical to those used in selection statements. If the condition is true, the code is executed; otherwise, it is not.

The third required element is a statement that initially sets the condition. This statement must always be placed before the condition is first evaluated to ensure correct loop execution the first time the condition is evaluated.

Finally, there must be a statement within the repeating section of code that allows the condition to become false. This is necessary to ensure that, at some point, the repetitions stop.

Pretest and Posttest Loops

The condition being tested can be evaluated at either the beginning or the end of the repeating section of code. Figure 5.1 illustrates the case where the test occurs at the beginning of the loop. This type of loop is referred to as a *pretest loop* because the condition is tested before any statements within the loop are executed. If the condition is true, the executable statements within the loop are executed. If the initial value of the condition is false, the executable statements within the loop are never executed at all and control transfers to the first statement after the loop. To avoid infinite repetitions, the condition must be updated within the loop. Pretest loops are also referred to as *entrance-controlled loops*. Both the `while` and `for` loop structures are examples of such loops.

FIGURE 5.1   A Pretest Loop

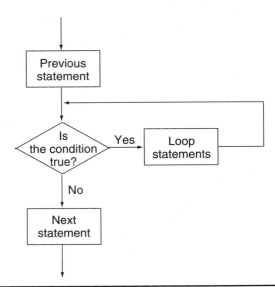

A loop that evaluates a condition at end of the repeating section of code, as illustrated in Figure 5.2, is referred to as a *posttest* or *exit-controlled loop*. Such loops always execute the loop statements at least once before the condition is tested. Since the executable statements within the loop are continually executed until the condition becomes false, there always must be a statement within the loop that updates the condition and permits it to become false. The do construct is an example of a posttest loop.

Fixed Count Versus Variable Condition Loops

In addition to where the condition is tested (pretest or posttest), repeating sections of code are also classified as to the type of condition being tested. In a *fixed count loop*, the condition is used to keep track of how many repetitions have occurred. For example, we might want to produce a table of 10 numbers, including their squares and cubes or a fixed design such as:

In each of these cases, a fixed number of calculations is performed or a fixed number of lines are printed, at which point the repeating section of code is exited. All of C's repetition statements can be used to produce fixed count loops.

In many situations the exact number of repetitions is not known in advance or the items are too numerous to count beforehand. For example, when entering a

---

FIGURE 5.2   A Posttest Loop

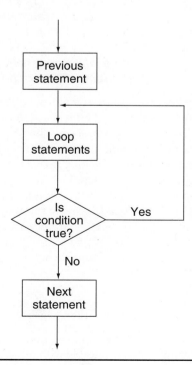

large amount of market research data we might not want to take the time to count the number of actual data items that are to be entered. In cases like this, a variable condition loop is used. In a *variable condition loop*, the tested condition does not depend on a count being achieved, but rather on a variable that can change interactively with each pass through the loop. When a specified value is encountered, regardless of how many iterations have occurred, repetitions stop. All of C's repetition statements can be used to create variable condition loops.[1] In this chapter we will encounter examples of both fixed count and variable condition loops.

5.2 while LOOPS

In C, a `while` loop is constructed using a `while` statement. The general form of this statement is:

```
while (expression)
    statement;
```

The expression contained within parentheses is the condition tested to determine if the statement following the parentheses is executed. The expression is evaluated in exactly the same manner as that contained in an `if-else` statement—the difference is in how the expression is used. As we have seen, when the expression is true (has a nonzero value) in an `if-else` statement, the statement following the expression is executed once. In a `while` statement, the statement following the expression is executed repeatedly as long as the expression evaluates to a nonzero value. Considering just the expression and the statement following the parentheses, the process used by the computer in evaluating a while statement is:

1. **Test the expression**
2. **If the expression has a nonzero (true) value**
   a. *execute the statement following the parentheses*
   b. *go back to step 1*
   else
   exit the while statement and execute the next executable statement following the while statement

Notice that step 2b forces program control to be transferred back to step 1. This transfer of control back to the start of a `while` statement in order to reevaluate the expression is what forms the program loop. The `while` statement literally loops back on itself to recheck the expression until it evaluates to zero (becomes false). This naturally means that somewhere in the loop provision must be made that permits the value of the tested expression to be altered. As we will see, this is indeed the case.

This looping process produced by a `while` statement is illustrated in Figure 5.3. A diamond shape is used to show the two entry and two exit points required in the decision part of the `while` statement. To make this a little more tangible, consider the relational expression `count <= 10` and the statement `printf("%d ",count);`. Using these, we can write the following valid `while` statement:

---

[1]In this C differs from most other languages such as BASIC, FORTRAN, and Pascal. In each of these languages the FOR structure (which is implemented using a DO statement in FORTRAN) can only be used to produce fixed count loops. C's for structure, as we will see shortly, is virtually interchangeable with its while structure.

FIGURE 5.3 Anatomy of a WHILE Loop

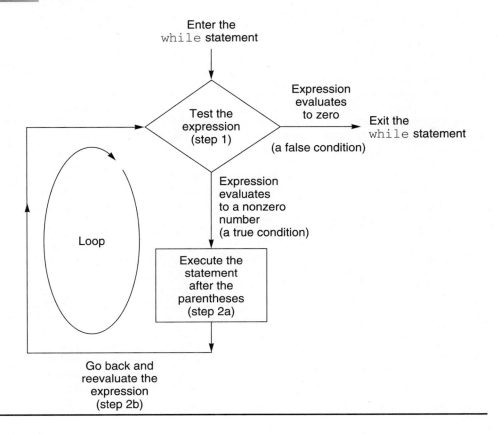

```
while (count <= 10)
    printf("%d  ",count);
```

Although this statement is valid, the alert reader will realize that we have created a situation in which the printf() function either is called forever (or until we stop the program) or is not called at all. Let us see why this happens.

If count has a value less than or equal to 10 when the expression is first evaluated, a call to printf() is made. The while statement then automatically loops back on itself and retests the expression. Since we have not changed the value stored in count, the expression is still true and another call to printf() is made. This process continues forever, or until the program containing this statement is prematurely stopped by the user. However, if count starts with a value greater than 10, the expression is false to begin with and the printf() function call is never made.

How do we set an initial value in count to control what the while statement does the first time the expression is evaluated? The answer, of course, is to assign values to each variable in the tested expression before the while statement is encountered. For example, the following sequence of instructions is valid:

```
count = 1;
while (count <= 10)
    printf("%d  ",count);
```

A BIT OF BACKGROUND

Comptometer Arithmetic

In the early 1900's, mechanical calculators, called *comptometers*, performed only addition. Since multiplication is only a quick method of addition (for example, 5 times 4 is really 5 added 4 times), producing multiplication results presented no problems—answers were obtained using repeated additions. Subtraction and division, however, initially did present a problem. Clever accountants soon discovered that subtraction and division were possible. Subtraction was accomplished by writing the nine's complement on each numeric key. That is, 9 was written on the 0 key, 8 on the 1 key, 7 on the 2 key, and so on. Subtraction was then performed by adding the nine's complement numbers, then adding 1 to the result. For example, consider the subtraction problem

$$637 - 481 = 156$$

Then nine's complement of 481 is 518, and

$$637 + 518 + 1 = 1,156$$

which gives the answer (156) to the problem when the leftmost carry digit is ignored.

It did not take the accountants long to solve division problems using repeated subtractions—all on a machine designed to handle only additions.

Early computers, which had only the facilities for doing addition, used similar algorithms for performing subtraction, multiplication, and division. They used, however, two's complement numbers rather than nine's complement. (See Section 1.5 for an introduction to two's complement numbers.)

Although many computers now come with special-purpose hardware, called floating-point processors, to perform multiplication and division directly, they still use two's complement number representation internally and perform subtraction using two's complement addition. And when a floating-point processor is not used, sophisticated software algorithms are employed that perform multiplications and divisions based on repeated additions and subtractions.

Using this sequence of instructions, we have ensured that count starts with a value of 1. We could assign any value to count in the assignment statement—the important thing is to assign some value. In practice, the assigned value depends on the application.

We must still change the value of count so that we can finally exit the while statement. To do so, we need an expression such as count = count + 1 to increment the value of count each time the while statement is executed. The fact that a while statement provides for the repetition of a single statement does not prevent us from including an additional statement to change the value of count. All we have to do is replace the single statement with a compound statement. For example:

```
count = 1;                /* initialize count */
while (count <= 10)
{
  printf("%d  ",count);
  count = count + 1;      /* increment count */
}
```

Note that, for clarity, we have placed each statement in the compound statement on a different line. This is consistent with the convention adopted for compound statements in the last chapter. Let us now analyze the preceding sequence of instructions.

The first assignment statement sets `count` equal to 1. The `while` statement is then entered and the expression is evaluated for the first time. Since the value of `count` is less than or equal to 10, the expression is true and the compound statement is executed. The first statement in the compound statement is a call to the `printf()` function to display the value of `count`. The next statement adds 1 to the value currently stored in `count`, making this value equal to 2. The `while` statement now loops back to retest the expression. Since `count` is still less than or equal to 10, the compound statement is again executed. This process continues until the value of `count` reaches 11. Program 5.1 illustrates these statements in an actual program.

PROGRAM 5.1

```c
#include <stdio.h>
void main(void)
{
    int count;

    count = 1;                  /* initialize count */
    while (count <= 10)
    {
        printf("%d  ",count);
        count = count + 1;      /* add 1 to count */
    }
}
```

The output for Program 5.1 is:

```
1  2  3  4  5  6  7  8  9  10
```

There is nothing special about the name `count` used in Program 5.1. Any valid integer variable could have been used.

Before we consider other examples of the `while` statement, two comments concerning Program 5.1 are in order. First, the statement `count = count + 1` can be replaced with any statement that changes the value of `count`. A statement such as `count = count + 2`, for example, would cause every second integer to be displayed. Second, it is the programmer's responsibility to ensure that `count` is changed in a way that ultimately leads to a normal exit from the `while` loop. For example, if we replace the expression `count = count + 1` with the expression `count = count - 1`, the value of `count` will never exceed 10 and an infinite loop will be created. An *infinite loop* is a loop that never ends. The computer will not reach out, touch you, and say, "Excuse me, you have created an infinite loop." It just keeps displaying numbers until you realize that the program is not working as you expected.

Now that you have some familiarity with the `while` statement, see if you can read and determine the output of Program 5.2:

PROGRAM 5.2

```c
#include <stdio.h>
void main(void)
{
  int i, count;

  i = 10;
  while (i >= 1)
  {
    printf("%d  ",i);
    count = count - 1;
  }
}
```

The assignment statement in Program 5.2 initially sets the `int` variable i to 10. The `while` statement then checks to see if the value of i is greater than or equal to 1. While the expression is true, the value of i is displayed by the call to `printf()` and the value of i is decremented by 1. When i finally reaches zero, the expression is false and the program exits the `while` statement. Thus, the following display is obtained when Program 5.2 is run:

```
10  9  8  7  6  5  4  3  2  1
```

To illustrate the power of the `while` statement, consider the task of printing a table of numbers from 1 to 10 with their squares and cubes. This can be done with a simple `while` statement as illustrated by Program 5.3:

PROGRAM 5.3

```c
#include <stdio.h>
void main(void)
{
  int num;

  printf("NUMBER SQUARE CUBE\n");
  printf("------ ------ ----\n");
  num = 1;
  while (num < 11)
  {
    printf("%3d    %3d  %4d\n", num, num*num, num*num*num);
    num = num + 1;
  }
}
```

Note that the expression used in Program 5.3 is `num < 11`. For the integer variable `num`, this expression is exactly equivalent to the expression `num <= 10`. The choice of which to use is entirely up to you.

If we want to use Program 5.3 to produce a table of 1000 numbers, all we do is change the expression in the `while` statement from `i < 11` to `i < 1001`. Changing the `11` to `1001` produces a table of 1000 lines—not bad for a simple five-line `while` statement.

When Program 5.3 is run, the following display is produced:

NUMBER	SQUARE	CUBE
1	1	1
2	4	8
3	9	27
4	16	64
5	25	125
6	36	216
7	49	343
8	64	512
9	81	729
10	100	1000

All the program examples illustrating the while statement are examples of fixed count loops, because the tested condition is a counter that checks for a fixed number of repetitions. A variation on the fixed count loop can be made where the counter is not incremented by one each time through the loop, but by some other value. For example, consider the task of producing a Celsius to Fahrenheit temperature conversion table. Assume that Fahrenheit temperatures corresponding to Celsius temperatures ranging from 5 to 50 degrees are to be displayed in increments of five degrees. The desired display can be obtained with the following series of statements:

```
celsius = 5;        /* starting Celsius value */
while (celsius <= 50)
{
   fahren = (9.0/5.0) * celsius + 32.0;
   printf("%5d%12.2f\n",celsius, fahren);
   celsius = celsius + 5;
}
```

As before, the while statement consists of everything from the word while through the closing brace of the compound statement. Prior to entering the while loop we have made sure to assign a value to the counter being evaluated, and there is a statement to alter the value of the counter within the loop (in increments of 5) to ensure an exit from the while loop. Program 5.4 illustrates the use of this code in a complete program.

PROGRAM 5.4

```
#include <stdio.h>
#define MAX_CELSIUS 50
#define START_VAL 5
#define STEP_SIZE 5
void main(void) /* program to convert Celsius to Fahrenheit */
{
  int celsius;
  float fahren;

  printf("DEGREES    DEGREES\n");
  printf("CELSIUS  FAHRENHEIT\n");
  printf("-------  ----------\n");
  celsius = START_VAL;
  while (celsius <= MAX_CELSIUS)
  {
     fahren = (9.0/5.0) * celsius + 32.0;
     printf("%5d%12.2f\n",celsius, fahren);
     celsius = celsius + STEP_SIZE;
  }
}
```

The display obtained when Program 5.4 is executed is:

DEGREES CELSIUS	DEGREES FAHRENHEIT
5	41.00
10	50.00
15	59.00
20	68.00
25	77.00
30	86.00
35	95.00
40	104.00
45	113.00
50	122.00

Exercises 5.1

1. Rewrite Program 5.1 to print the numbers 2 to 10 in increments of two. The output of your program should be:

   ```
   2   4   6   8   10
   ```

2. Rewrite Program 5.4 to produce a table that starts at a Celsius value of −10 and ends with a Celsius value of 60, in increments of 10 degrees.

3. a. For the following program determine the total number of items displayed. Also determine the first and last numbers printed.

   ```c
   #include <stdio.h>
   void main(void)
   {
      int num = 0;

      while (num <= 20)
      {
         num++;
         printf("%d   ",num);
      }
   }
   ```

   b. Enter and run the program from Exercise 3a on a computer to verify your answers to the exercise.

   c. How would the output be affected if the two statements within the compound statement were reversed (that is, if the printf() call were made before the num++ statement)?

4. Write a C program that converts gallons to liters. The program should display gallons from 10 to 20 in one-gallon increments and the corresponding liter equivalents. Use the relationship: liters = 3.785* gallons.

5. Write a C program to produce the following display:

   ```
   0
    1
     2
      3
       4
        5
         6
          7
           8
            9
   ```

6. Write a C program to produce the following displays:

```
a.  ****      b.       ****
      ****           ****
        ****       ****
          ****   ****
```

7. Write a C program that converts feet to meters. The program should display feet from 3 to 30 in three-foot increments and the corresponding meter equivalents. Use the relationship: meters = feet / 3.28.

8. A machine purchased for $28,000 is depreciated at a rate of $4000 a year for seven years. Write and run a C program that computes and displays a depreciation table for seven years. The table should have the form:

Year	Depreciation	End-of-Year Value	Accumulated Depreciation
1	4000	24000	4000
2	4000	20000	8000
3	4000	16000	12000
4	4000	12000	16000
5	4000	8000	20000
6	4000	4000	24000
7	4000	0	28000

9. An automobile travels at an average speed of 55 miles per hour for four hours. Write a C program that displays the distance driven, in miles, that the car has traveled after 0.5, 1, 1.5, etc., hours until the end of the trip.

10. a. An approximate conversion formula for converting Fahrenheit to Celsius temperatures is

$$Celsius = (Fahrenheit - 30) / 2$$

Using this formula, and starting with a Fahrenheit temperature of zero degrees, write a C program that determines when the approximate equivalent Celsius temperature differs from the exact equivalent value by more than four degrees. (*Hint:* Use a while loop that terminates when the difference between approximate and exact Celsius equivalents exceeds four degrees.)

b. Using the approximate Celsius conversion formula given in Exercise 10a, write a C program that produces a table of Fahrenheit temperatures, exact Celsius equivalent temperatures, approximate Celsius equivalent temperatures, and the difference between the correct and approximate equivalent Celsius values. The table should begin at zero degrees Fahrenheit, use two-degree Fahrenheit increments and terminate when the difference between exact and approximate values differs by more than four degrees.

11. Write a C program to find the sum, sum of squares, and the sum of cubes of the first n integer, beginning with 1 and ending with $n = 100$. Verify that in each case

$$1 + 2 + 3 + \dots + n = n(n+1)/2$$
$$1^2 + 2^2 + 3^2 + \dots + n^2 = n(n+1)(2n+1)/6$$
$$1^3 + 2^3 + 3^3 + \dots + n^3 = n^2(n+1)^2/4$$

12. Write a C program to find the sum of the first 100 terms in this series

$$1/(1 * 2) + 1/(2 * 3) + 1/(3 * 4) + \dots + 1/[n*(n+1)]$$

Verify that the sum equals $n/(n + 1)$. Determine the value that the sum approaches as n gets infinitely large.

5.2 INTERACTIVE while LOOPS

Combining interactive data entry with the repetition capabilities of the while statement produces very adaptable and powerful programs. To understand the concept involved, consider Program 5.5, where a while statement is used to accept and then display four user-entered numbers, one at a time. Although it uses a very simple idea, the program highlights the flow of control concepts needed to produce more useful programs.

PROGRAM 5.5

```c
#include <stdio.h>
#define MAXNUMS 4
void main(void)
{
  int count;
  float num;

  printf("This program will ask you to enter some numbers.\n\n");
  count = 1;
  while (count <= MAXNUMS)
  {
    printf("Enter a number: ");
    scanf("%f", &num);
    printf("The number entered is %f\n", num);
    count = count + 1;
  }
}
```

The following is a sample run of Program 5.5. The italicized items were input in response to the appropriate prompts.

```
This program will ask you to enter some numbers.

Enter a number: 26.2
The number entered is 26.200000
Enter a number: 5
The number entered is 5.000000
Enter a number: 103.456
The number entered is 103.456000
Enter a number: 1267.89
The number entered is 1267.890000
```

Let us review the program so we understand clearly how the output was produced. The first message displayed is caused by execution of the first printf() function call. This call is outside and before the while statement, so it is executed once before any statement in the while loop.

Once the while loop is entered, the statements within the compound statement are executed while the tested condition is true. The first time through the compound statement, the message Enter a number: is displayed. The pro-

FIGURE 5.4   Flow of Control Diagrams for Program 5.5

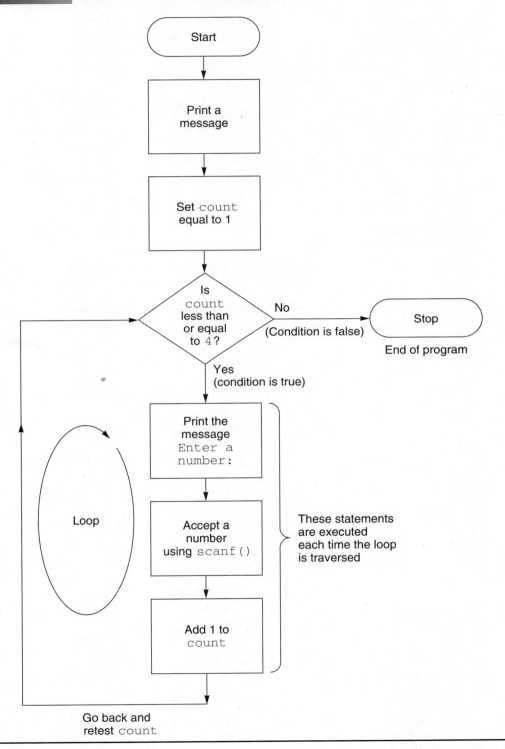

gram then calls scanf(), which forces the computer to wait for a number to be entered at the keyboard. Once a number is typed and the RETURN or ENTER key is pressed, the call to printf() displaying the number is executed. The variable count is then incremented by one. This process continues until four passes through the loop have been made and the value of count is 5. Each pass causes the message Enter a number: to be displayed, causes one call to scanf() to be made, and causes the message The number entered is to be displayed. Figure 5.4 illustrates this flow of control.

Rather than simply displaying the entered numbers, Program 5.5 can be modified in order to use the entered data. For example, let us add the numbers entered and display the total. To do this, we must be very careful about how we add the numbers, since the same variable, num, is used for each number entered. Because of this the entry of a new number in Program 5.5 automatically causes the previous number stored in num to be lost. Thus, each number entered must be added to the total before another number is entered. The required sequence is:

Enter a number
Add the number to the total

How do we add a single number to a total? A statement such as total = total + num does the job perfectly. This is the accumulating statement introduced

---

FIGURE 5.5   Accepting and Adding a Number to a Total

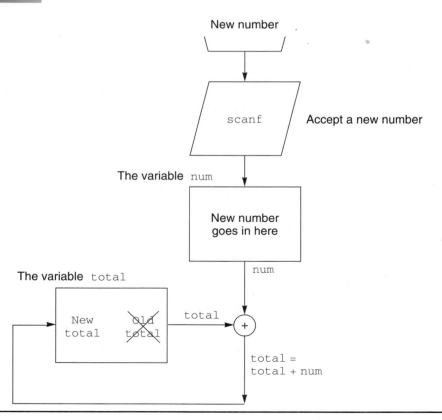

in Section 3.1. After each number is entered, the accumulating statement adds the number into the total, as illustrated in Figure 5.5. The complete flow of control required for adding the numbers is illustrated in Figure 5.6. In reviewing Figure 5.6, observe that we have made a provision for initially setting the total to zero before the while loop is entered. If we were to clear the total inside the while loop, it would be set to zero each time the loop was executed and any value previously stored would be erased.

Program 5.6 incorporates the necessary modifications to Program 5.5 to total the numbers entered. As indicated in the flow diagram shown in Figure 5.6, the statement total = total + num; must be placed immediately after the scanf() function call. Putting the accumulating statement at this point in the program ensures that the entered number is immediately "captured" into the total.

PROGRAM 5.6

```
#include <stdio.h>
#define MAXNUMS 4
void main(void)
{
  int count;
  float num, total;

  printf("This program will ask you to enter some numbers.\n\n");
  count = 1;
  total = 0;
  while (count <= MAXNUMS)
  {
    printf("Enter a number: ");
    scanf("%f", &num);
    total = total + num;
    printf("The total is now %f\n", total);
    count = count + 1;
  }
  printf("\nThe final total is %f\n",total);
}
```

Let us review Program 5.6. The variable total was created to store the total of the numbers entered. Prior to entering the while statement the value of total is set to zero. This ensures that any previous value present in the storage location(s) assigned to the variable total is erased. Within the while loop the statement total = total + num; is used to add the value of the entered number into total. As each value is entered, it is added into the existing total to create a new total. Thus, total becomes a running subtotal of all the values entered. Only when all numbers are entered does total contain the final sum of all the numbers. After the while loop is finished, the last printf() function call is used to display this sum.

Using the same data that was entered in the sample run for Program 5.5, the following sample run of Program 5.6 was made:

```
This program will ask you to enter some numbers.

Enter a number: 26.2
The total is now 26.200000
Enter a number: 5
The total is now 31.200000
Enter a number: 103.456
The total is now 134.656000
Enter a number: 1267.89
The total is now 1402.546000

The final total is 1402.546
```

FIGURE 5.6   Accumulation Flow of Control

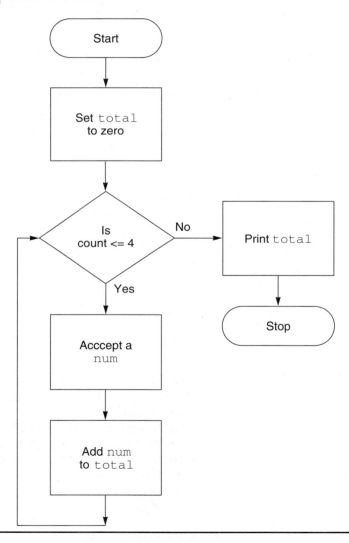

Having used an accumulating assignment statement to add the numbers entered, we can now go further and calculate the average of the numbers. Where do we calculate the average—within the `while` loop or outside of it?

In the case at hand, calculating an average requires that both a final sum and the number of items in that sum be available. The average is then computed by dividing the final sum by the number of items. At this point, we must ask, "At what point in the program is the correct sum available, and at what point is the number of items available?" In reviewing Program 5.6 we see that the correct sum needed for calculating the average is available after the `while` loop is finished. In fact, the whole purpose of the `while` loop is to ensure that the numbers are entered and added correctly to produce a correct sum. After the loop is finished, we also have a count of the number of items used in the sum. However, due to the way the `while` loop was constructed, the number in `count` (5) when the loop is finished is one more than the number of items (4) used to obtain the total. Knowing this, we simply subtract 1 from `count` before using it to determine the average. With this as background, see if you can read and understand Program 5.7.

PROGRAM 5.7

```c
#include <stdio.h>
#define MAXNUMS 4
void main(void)
{
  int count;
  float num, total,average;

  printf("This program will ask you to enter some numbers.\n");
  count = 1;
  total = 0;
  while (count <= MAXNUMS)
  {
    printf("Enter a number: ");
    scanf("%f", &num);
    total = total + num;
    count = count + 1;
  }
  count = count - 1;
  average = total / count;
  printf("The average of the numbers is %f\n",average);
}
```

Program 5.7 is almost identical to Program 5.6, except for the calculation of the average. We have also removed the constant display of the total within and after the `while` loop. The loop in Program 5.7 is used to enter and add four numbers. Immediately after the loop is exited, the average is computed and displayed. A sample run of Program 5.7 follows:

```
This program will ask you to enter some numbers.

Enter a number: 26.2
Enter a number: 5
Enter a number: 103.456
Enter a number: 1267.89

The average of the numbers is 350.636500
```

Sentinels

All of the loops we have created thus far have been examples of fixed count loops, where a counter has been used to control the number of loop iterations. By means of a `while` statement variable condition loops may also be constructed. For example, when entering grades we may not want to count the number of grades that will be entered, but would prefer to enter the grades continuously and, at the end, type in a special data value to signal the end of data input.

In computer programming, data values used to signal either the start or end of a data series are called *sentinels*. The *sentinel values* must, of course, be selected so as not to conflict with legitimate data values. For example, if we were constructing a program to process a student's grades, and assuming that no extra credit is given that could produce a grade higher than 100, we could use any grade higher than 100 as a sentinel value. Program 5.8 illustrates this concept. In Program 5.8 data is continuously requested and accepted until a number larger than 100 is entered. Entry of a number higher than 100 alerts the program to exit the `while` loop and display the sum of the numbers entered.

PROGRAM 5.8

```
#include <stdio.h>
#define HIGHGRADE 100
void main(void)
{
  float grade = 0;
  float total = 0;

  printf("To stop entering grades, type in any number\n");
  printf(" greater than 100.\n\n");
  while (grade <= HIGHGRADE)
  {
    printf("Enter a grade: ");
    scanf("%f", &grade);
    total = total + grade;
  }
  printf("\nThe total of the grades is %f\n",total-grade);
}
```

We show a sample run using Program 5.8 below. As long as grades less than or equal to 100 are entered, the program continues to request and accept additional data. When a number greater than 100 is entered, the program adds this number to the total and exits the `while` loop. Outside of the loop and within the `printf()` function call, the value of the sentinel that was added to the total is subtracted and the sum of the legitimate grades that were entered is displayed.

```
To stop entering grades, type in any number greater than 100.

Enter a grade: 95
Enter a grade: 100
Enter a grade: 82
Enter a grade: 101


The total of the grades is 277.000000
```

One of the most useful sentinels provided in C is the named constant `EOF`, which stands for end of file. The actual value of `EOF` is compiler dependent, but is always assigned a code that is not used by any other character. How `EOF` works is explained next.

Each computer operating system has its own code for an end-of-file mark. In the UNIX operating system, this mark is generated whenever the CON-TROL and D keys are pressed simultaneously, while in the IBM DOS operating system the mark is generated whenever the CONTROL and Z keys are pressed simultaneously. When a C program detects this combination of keys as an input value, it converts the input value into its own `EOF` code, as illustrated in Figure 5.7.

The actual definition of the `EOF` constant, using the `#define` statement previously described in Section 3.4, is defined in the compiler source file `stdio.h`. Thus, the `EOF` named constant can be used in all programs that have included `stdio.h`. For example, consider Program 5.9.

PROGRAM 5.9

```
#include <stdio.h>
void main(void)
{
  float grade, total = 0;          /* note the initialization  here */

  printf("To stop entering grades, press either the F6 key\n");
  printf(" or the ctrl and z keys simultaneously on IBM computers\n");
  printf(" or the ctrl and d keys for UNIX operating systems.\n\n");
  printf("Enter a grade: ");
  while (scanf("%f", &grade) != EOF)
  {
    total = total + grade;
    printf("Enter a grade: ");
  }
  printf("\nThe total of the grades is %f\n",total);
}
```

FIGURE 5.7   Generation of the `EOF` Constant by the `scanf()` Function

---

Notice that the first line in Program 5.9 is the `#include <stdio.h>` statement. Since the `stdio.h` file contains the definition of `EOF`, this constant may now be referenced in the program.

EOF is used in Program 5.9 to control the `while` loop. The expression `scanf("%f", &grade) != EOF` makes use of the fact that the `scanf()` function returns an `EOF` value if an attempt is made to read an end-of-file mark. From a user's viewpoint, assuming an IBM computer is being used, pressing both the CONTROL and Z keys simultaneously generates an end-of-file mark, which is converted to the `EOF` constant by `scanf()`. The following is a sample run using Program 5.9:

```
To stop entering grades, press either the F6 key
 or the ctrl and z keys simultaneously on IBM computers
 or the ctrl and d keys for UNIX operating systems.

Enter a grade: 100
Enter a grade: 200
Enter a grade: 300
Enter a grade: ^Z

The total of the grades is 600.000000
```

One distinct advantage of Program 5.9 over Program 5.8 is that the sentinel value is never added to the total, so it does not have to be subtracted later. One disadvantage of Program 5.9, however, is that it requires the user to type in an unfamiliar combination of keys to terminate data input.

The `break` and `continue` Statements

Two useful statements in connection with repetition statements are the `break` and `continue` statements. We have already encountered the `break` statement in relation to the `switch` statement. The general form of this statement is:

```
break;
```

A `break` statement, as its name implies, forces an immediate break, or exit, from the `switch`, `while`, and the `for` and `do-while` statements presented in the next sections.

For example, execution of the following `while` loop is immediately terminated if a number greater than 76 is entered.

```
while(count <= 10)
{
  printf("Enter a number: ");
  scanf("%f", &num);
  if (num > 76)
  {
    printf("You lose!\n");
    break;          /* break out of the loop */
  }
  else
    printf("Keep on trucking!\n");
}
/* break jumps to here */
```

The break statement violates pure structured programming principles because it provides a second, nonstandard exit from a loop. Nevertheless, the break statement is extremely useful and valuable for breaking out of loops when an unusual condition is detected. The break statement is also used to exit from a switch statement, but this is because the desired case has been detected and processed.

The continue statement is similar to the break statement but applies only to loops created with while, do-while, and for statements. The general format of a continue statement is:

```
continue;
```

When continue is encountered in a loop, the next iteration of the loop is immediately begun. For while loops this means that execution is automatically transferred to the top of the loop and reevaluation of the tested expression is initiated. Although the continue statement has no direct effect on a switch statement, it can be included within a switch statement that itself is contained in a loop. Here the effect of continue is the same: The next loop iteration is begun.

As a general rule the continue statement is less useful than the break statement, but it can be used for skipping over data that should not be processed while remaining in a loop. For example, invalid grades are simply ignored in the following section of code and only valid grades are added to the total[2]:

```
while (count < 30)
{
  printf("Enter a grade: ");
  scanf("%f", &grade);
  if(grade < 0 || grade > 100)
    continue;
  total = total + grade;
  count++;
}
```

---

[2]The continue is not essential, however, and the selection could have been written as :

```
If (grade >= 0 && grade <= 100)
{
  total = total + grade
  count++;
}
```

The Null Statement

Statements are always terminated by a semicolon. A semicolon with nothing preceding it is also a valid statement, called the null statement. Thus, the statement

                                    ;

is a null statement. This is a do-nothing statement that is used where a statement is syntactically required, but no action is called for. Null statements typically are used with either `while` or `for` statements. An example of a for statement using a null statement is found in Program 5.11c in the next section.

Exercises 5.2

1. Rewrite Program 5.6 to compute the total of eight numbers.

2. Rewrite Program 5.6 to display the prompt:

   ```
   Please type in the total number of data values to be added:
   ```

   In response to this prompt, the program should accept a user-entered number and then use this number to control the number of times the `while` loop is executed. Thus, if the user enters 5 in response to the prompt, the program should request the input of five numbers and display the total after five numbers have been entered.

3. a. Write a C program to convert Celsius degrees to Fahrenheit. The program should request the starting Celsius value, the number of conversions to be made, and the increment between Celsius values. The display should have appropriate headings and list the Celsius value and the corresponding Fahrenheit value. Use the relationship Fahrenheit = (9.0 / 5.0) * Celsius + 32.0.

   b. Run the program written in Exercise 3a on a computer. Verify that your program starts at the correct starting Celsius value and contains the exact number of conversions specified in your input data.

4. a. Modify the program written in Exercise 3 to request the starting Celsius value, the ending Celsius value, and the increment. Thus, instead of the condition checking for a fixed count, the condition will check for the ending Celsius value.

   b. Run the program written in Exercise 4a on a computer. Verify that your output starts at the correct beginning value and ends at the correct ending value.

5. Rewrite Program 5.7 to compute the average of ten numbers.

6. Rewrite Program 5.7 to display the prompt:

   ```
   Please type in the total number of data values to be averaged:
   ```

   In response to this prompt, the program should accept a user-entered number and then use this number to control the number of times the `while` loop is executed. Thus, if the user enters 6 in response to the prompt, the program should request the input of six numbers and display the average of the next six numbers entered.

7. By mistake, a programmer put the statement `average = total / count;` within the `while` loop immediately after the statement `total = total + num;` in Program 5.7. Thus, the `while` loop becomes:

   ```c
   while (count <= MAXNUMS)
   {
     printf("Enter a number: ");
     scanf("%f", &num);
     total = total + num;
     average = total / count;
     count = count + 1;
   }
   ```

Will the program yield the correct result with this `while` loop? From a programming perspective, which `while` loop is better to use, and why?

8. An arithmetic series is defined by

$$a + (a + d) + (a + 2d) + (a + 3d) + ... + (a + (n-1)d)$$

where a is the first term, d is the "common difference," and n is the number of terms to be added. Using this information write a C program that uses a `while` loop to both display each term and determine the sum of the arithmetic series having $a = 1$, $d = 3$, and $n = 100$. Make sure that your program displays the value it has calculated.

9. A geometric series is defined by

$$a + ar + ar^2 + ar^3 + ... + ar^{n-1}$$

where a is the first term, r is the "common ratio," and n is the number of terms in the series. Using this information write a C program that uses a `while` loop to both display each term and determine the sum of a geometric having $a = 1$, $r = 0.5$, and $n = 100$. Make sure that your program displays the value it has calculated.

10. In addition to the arithmetic average of a set of numbers both a geometric and harmonic mean can be calculated. The geometric mean of a set of n numbers x_1, x_2, ... x_n is defined as

$$\sqrt[n]{x_1 \cdot x_2 \cdot .... .x_n}$$

and the harmonic mean as

$$\frac{n}{\dfrac{1}{x_1} + \dfrac{1}{x_2} + ... + \dfrac{1}{x_n}}$$

Using these formulas, write a C program that continues to accept numbers until the number 999 is entered, and then calculates and displays both the geometric and harmonic means of the entered numbers. (*Hint:* It will be necessary for your program to correctly count the number of values entered.)

11. a. The following data were collected on a recent automobile trip.

	Mileage	Gallons
Start of trip:	22495	Full tank
	22841	12.2
	23185	11.3
	23400	10.5
	23772	11.0
	24055	12.2
	24434	14.7
	24804	14.3
	25276	15.2

Write a C program that accepts a mileage and gallons value and calculates the miles per gallon (mpg) achieved for that segment of the trip. The miles per gallon is obtained as the difference in mileage between fill-ups divided by the number of gallons of gasoline used in the fill-up.

b. Modify the program written for Exercise 11a to additionally compute and display the cumulative mpg achieved after each fill-up. The cumulative mpg is calculated as the difference between each fill-up mileage and the mileage at the start of the trip divided by the sum of the gallons used to that point in the trip.

12. a. Write a C program to convert Celsius degrees to Fahrenheit. The program should request the starting Celsius value, the number of conversions to be made, and the increment between Celsius values. The display should have appropriate headings and list the Celsius value and the corresponding Fahrenheit value. Use the relationship Fahrenheit = (9.0 / 5.0) * Celsius + 32.0.

b. Run the program written in Exercise 12a on a computer. Verify that your program starts at the correct starting Celsius value and contains the exact number of conversions specified in your input data.

13. a. Modify the program written in Exercise 12 to request the starting Celsius value, the ending Celsius value, and the increment. Thus, instead of the condition checking for a fixed count, the condition will check for the ending Celsius value.

b. Run the program written in Exercise 13a on a computer. Verify that your output starts at the correct beginning value and ends at the correct ending value.

14. a. A bookstore summarizes its monthly transactions by keeping the following information for each book in stock:

Book identification number
Inventory balance at the beginning of the month
Number of copies received during the month
Number of copies sold during the month

Write a C program that accepts this data for each book and then displays the book identification number and an updated book inventory balance using the relationship:

New balance = Inventory balance at the beginning of the month
        + Number of copies received during the month
        − Number of copies sold during the month

Your program should use a while loop with a fixed count condition so that information on only three books is requested.

b. Run the program written in Exercise 14a on a computer. Review the display produced by your program and verify that the output produced is correct.

15. Modify the program you wrote for Exercise 14a to keep requesting and displaying results until a sentinel identification value of 999 is entered. Run the program on a computer.

5.3 for LOOPS

In C, a for loop is constructed using a for statement. This statement performs the same functions as the while statement, but uses a different form. In many situations, especially those that use a fixed count condition, the for statement format is easier to use than its while statement equivalent.

The general form of the for statement is:

```
for (initializing list; expression; altering list) statement;
```

Although the for statement looks a little complicated, it is really quite simple if we consider each of its parts separately.

Within the parentheses of the for statement are three items, separated by semicolons. Each of these items is optional and can be described individually, but the semicolons must be present.

In its most common form, the initializing list consists of a single statement used to set the starting (initial value) of a counter; the expression contains the maximum or minimum value the counter can have and determines when the loop is finished; and the altering list provides the increment value that is added to or subtracted from the counter each time the loop is executed. Examples of simple `for` statements having this form are:

```
for (count = 1; count < 10; count = count + 1)
   printf("%d ", count);
```

and

```
for (i = 5; i <= 15; i = i + 2)
   printf("%d ", i);
```

In the first `for` statement, the counter variable is named `count`, the initial value assigned to `count` is 1, the loop continues as long as the value in `count` is less than 10, and the value of `count` is incremented by one each time through the loop. In the next `for` statement, the counter variable is named `i`, the initial value assigned to `i` is 5, the loop continues as long as `i`'s value is less than or equal to 15, and the value of `i` is incremented by 2 each time through the loop. In both cases, a `printf()` function call is used to display the value of the counter. Another example of a `for` loop is given in Program 5.10.

PROGRAM 5.10

```
#include <stdio.h>
#include <math.h>
#define MAXCOUNT 5
void main(void)
{
  int count;

  printf("NUMBER    SQUARE ROOT\n");
  printf("------    -----------\n");
  for (count = 1; count  <= MAXCOUNT; count = count +1)
    printf("  %d        %f\n",count,  sqrt(count));
}
```

When Program 5.10 is executed, the following display is produced:

NUMBER	SQUARE ROOT
1	1.000000
2	1.414214
3	1.732051
4	2.000000
5	2.236068

The first two lines displayed by the program are produced by the two `printf` statements placed before the `for` statement. The remaining output is produced by the `for` loop. This loop begins with the `for` statement and is executed as follows.

The initial value assigned to the counter variable `count` is 1. Since the value in `count` does not exceed the final value of 5, the execution of the `printf` statement within the loop produces the display

```
                              1 1.000000
```

Control is then transferred back to the `for` statement, which then increments the value in `count` to 2, and the loop is repeated, producing the display

```
                              2 1.414214
```

This process continues until the value in `count` exceeds the final value of 5, producing the complete output table. For comparison purposes, a `while` loop that is equivalent to the `for` loop contained in Program 5.10 is:

```
            count = 1
            while (count <= MAXCOUNT)
            {
                printf("  %d         %f\n", count, sqrt(count));
                count = count + 1;
            }
```

As seen in this example, the difference between the `for` and `while` loops is the placement of the initialization, condition test, and incrementing items. The grouping of these items in the `for` statement is very convenient when fixed count loops must be constructed. See if you can determine the output produced by Program 5.11.

PROGRAM 5.11

```
#include <stdio.h>
void main(void)
{
    int count;

    for (count = 2; count <= 20; count = count + 2)
        printf("%d  ",count);
}
```

Did you figure it out? The loop starts with a count initialized to 2, stops when `count` exceeds 20, and increments `count` in steps of 2. The output of Program 5.11 is:

```
2   4   6   8   10   12   14   16   18   20
```

The `for` statement does not require that any of the items in parentheses be present or that they be used for initializing or altering the values in the expression statements. However, the two semicolons must be present within the `for`'s parentheses. For example, the construction `for ( ; count <= 20 ; )` is valid.

If the initializing list is missing, the initialization step is omitted when the `for` statement is executed. This, of course, means that the programmer must provide the required initializations before the `for` statement is encountered. Similarly, if the altering list is missing, any expressions needed to alter the evaluation of the tested expression must be included directly within the statement part of the loop. The `for` statement only ensures that all expressions in the initializing list are executed once, before evaluation of the tested expression, and that all expressions in the altering list are executed at the end of the loop before the tested expression is rechecked. Thus, Program 5.11 can be rewritten in any of the three ways shown in Programs 5.11a, 5.11b, and 5.11c.

PROGRAM 5.11a

```c
#include <stdio.h>
void main(void)
{
  int count;

  count = 2; /* initializer outside for statement */
  for ( ; count <= 20; count = count + 2)
    printf("%d ",count);
}
```

PROGRAM 5.11b

```c
#include <stdio.h>
void main(void)
{
  int count;

  count = 2; /* initializer outside for loop */
  for( ; count <= 20; )
  {
    printf("%d ",count);
    count = count + 2;          /* alteration statement */
  }
}
```

PROGRAM 5.11c

```c
#include <stdio.h>
void main(void)     /* all expressions within the for's parentheses */
{
  int count;

  for (count = 2; count <= 20; printf("%d  ",count), count = count + 2);
}
```

In Program 5.11a, `count` is initialized outside the `for` statement and the first list inside the parentheses is left blank. In Program 5.11b, both the initializing list and the altering list are removed from within the parentheses. Program 5.11b also uses a compound statement within the `for` loop, with the expression-altering statement included in the compound statement. Finally, Program 5.11c has included all items within the parentheses, so there is no need for any useful state-

▷▷▷ TIPS FROM THE PROS ◁◁◁

Where to Place the Opening Braces

There are two styles of writing `for` loops that are used by professional C programmers. These styles only come into play when the `for` loop contains a compound statement. The style illustrated and used in the text takes the form:

```
for (expression)
{
  compound statement in here
}
```

An equally acceptable style that is used by many programmers places the initial brace of the compound statement on the first line. Using this style a `for` loop appears as:

```
for (expression) {
  compound statement in here
}
```

The advantage of the first style is that the braces line up under one another, making it easier to locate brace pairs. The advantage of the second style is that it makes the code more compact and saves a display line, permitting more code to be viewed in the same display area. Both styles are used but are almost never intermixed. Select whichever style appeals to you and be consistent in its use. As always, the indentation you use within the compound statement (two or four spaces, or a tab) should also be consistent throughout all of your programs. The combination of styles that you select becomes a "signature" for your programming work.

ment following the parentheses. Here the null statement satisfies the syntactical requirement of one statement to follow the `for`'s parentheses.

Observe also in Program 5.11c that the altering list (last set of items in parentheses) consists of two items, and that a comma has been used to separate these items. The use of commas to separate items in both the initializing and altering lists is required if either of these two lists contains more than one item. Last, note the fact that Programs 5.11a, 5.11b, and 5.11c are all inferior to Program 5.11. The `for` statement in Program 5.11 is much clearer since all the expressions pertaining to the tested expression are grouped within the parentheses.

Although the initializing and altering lists can be omitted from a `for` statement, omitting the tested expression results in an infinite loop. For example, such a loop is created by the statement

```
for (count = 2; ; count = count + 1)
   printf("%d",count);
```

As with the `while` statement, both `break` and `continue` statements can be used within a `for` loop. The `break` forces an immediate exit from the `for` loop, as it does in the `while` loop. The `continue`, however, forces control to be passed to the altering list in a `for` statement, after which the tested expression is reevaluated. This differs from the action of `continue` in a `while` statement, where control is passed directly to the reevaluation of the tested expression.

FIGURE 5.8 A for **Loop Flowchart**

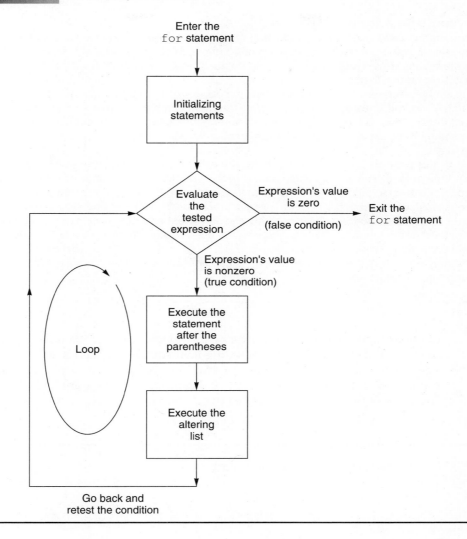

Figure 5.8 illustrates the internal workings of a for loop. As shown, when the for loop is completed, control is transferred to the first executable statement following the loop. To avoid the necessity of always illustrating these steps, a simplified set of flowchart symbols is available for describing for loops. Using the fact that a for statement can be represented by the flowchart symbol

complete for loops can alternatively be illustrated as shown in Figure 5.9.

> ▶ TIPS FROM THE PROS ◀

Do You Use a for or while Loop?

A commonly asked question by beginning programmers is which loop structure should they use—a `for` or `while` loop? This is a good question because both of these loop structures are pretest loops that, in C, can be used to construct both fixed count and variable condition loops.

In almost all other computer languages, including BASIC and Pascal, the answer is relatively straightforward, because the `for` statement can only be used to construct fixed count loops. Thus, in these languages `for` statements are used to construct fixed count loops and `while` statements are generally used only when constructing variable condition loops.

In C, this easy distinction does not hold, since each statement can be used to create each type of loop. The answer in C, then, is really a matter of style. Since `for` and `while` loops are interchangeable in C, either loop is appropriate. Some professional programmers always use a `for` statement for every pretest loop they create and almost never use a `while` statement—others always use a while statement and rarely use a `for` statement. Still a third group tends to retain the convention used in other languages—a `for` loop is generally used to create fixed count loops and a `while` loop is used to create variable condition loops. In C it is all a matter of style and you will encounter all three styles in your programming career.

To understand the enormous power of `for` loops, consider the task of printing a table of numbers from 1 to 10, including their squares and cubes, using this statement. Such a table was previously produced using a `while` loop in Program 5.3. You may wish to review Program 5.3 and compare it to Program 5.12 to get a further sense of the equivalence between `for` and `while` loops.

FIGURE 5.9   A Simplified `for` Loop Flowchart

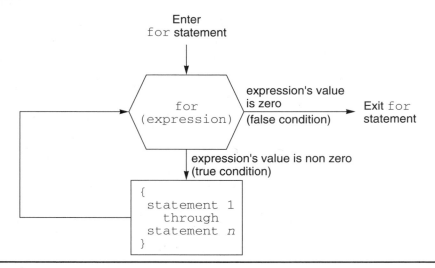

PROGRAM 5.12

```
#include <stdio.h>
void main(void)
{
  int num;

  printf("NUMBER    SQUARE    CUBE\n");
  printf("------    ------    ----\n");
  for (num = 1; num <= 10; ++num)
    printf("%3d         %3d        %4d\n", num, num*num, num*num*num);
}
```

When Program 5.12 is run, the display produced is:

NUMBER	SQUARE	CUBE
1	1	1
2	4	8
3	9	27
4	16	64
5	25	125
6	36	216
7	49	343
8	64	512
9	81	729
10	100	1000

Simply changing the number 10 in the `for` statement of Program 5.12 to a 1000 creates a loop that is executed 1000 times and produces a table of numbers from 1 to 1000. As with the `while` statement, this small change produces an immense increase in the processing and output provided by the program. Notice also that the expression `++num` was used in the altering list in place of the usual `num = num + 1`.

Exercises 5.3

1. Write individual `for` statements for the following cases:

   a. Use a counter named `i` that has an initial value of 1, a final value of 20, and an increment of 1.

   b. Use a counter named `icount` that has an initial value of 1, a final value of 20, and an increment of 2.

   c. Use a counter named `J` that has an initial value of 1, a final value of 100, and an increment of 5.

   d. Use a counter named `icount` that has an initial value of 20, a final value of 1, and an increment of −1.

   e. Use a counter named `icount` that has an initial value of 20, a final value of 1, and an increment of −2.

   f. Use a counter named `count` that has an initial value of 1.0, a final value of 16.2, and an increment of 0.2.

g. Use a counter named xcnt that has an initial value of 20.0, a final value of 10.0, and an increment of -0.5.

2. Determine the number of times each for loop is executed for the for statements written for Exercise 1.

3. Determine the value in total after each of the following loops is executed:

a.
```
total = 0;
   for (i = 1; i <= 10; i = i + 1)
      total = total + 1;
```

b.
```
total = 1;
   for (count = 1; count <+ 10; count = count + 1)
      total = total * 2;
```

c.
```
total = 0
   for ( i = 10; i <= 15; i = i + 1)
      total = total + i;
```

d.
```
total = 50
   for (i = 1; i <=10; i = i + 1)
      total = total - i;
```

e.
```
total = 1
   for (icnt = 1; icnt <= 8; ++icnt)
      total = total * icnt;
```

f.
```
total = 1.0
   for (j = 1; j <= 5; ++j)
      total = total / 2.0;
```

4. Determine the output of the following program.

```
#include <stdio.h>
void main(void)
{
   int i;

   for (i = 20; i >= 0; i = i - 4)
      printf("%d ",i);
}
```

5. Modify Program 5.12 to produce a table of the numbers 0 through 20 in increments of 2, with their squares and cubes.

6. Modify Program 5.12 to produce a table of numbers from 10 to 1, instead of 1 to 10 as it currently does.

7. Write and run a C program that displays a table of 20 temperature conversions from Fahrenheit to Celsius. The table should start with a Fahrenheit value of 20 degrees and be incremented in values of 4 degrees. Recall that Celsius = (5.0/9.0) * (Fahrenheit − 32).

8. Modify the program written for Exercise 7 to initially request the number of conversions to be made.

9. A programmer starts with a salary of $25,000 and expects to receive a $1500 raise each year.

a. Write a C program to compute and print the programmer's salary for each of the first 10 years and the total amount of money the programmer would receive over the 10-year period.

b. Write a C program to compute and print the programmer's salary for 10 years if the programmer begins at $25,000 and receives a 5% raise each year.

10. The probability that an individual telephone call will last less than t minutes can be approximated by the exponential probability function

Probability that a call lasts less than t minutes = $1 - e^{-t/a}$

where a is the average call length and e is Euler's number (2.71828). For example, assuming that the average call length is 2.5 minutes, the probability that a call will last less than one minute is calculated as $1 - e^{-1/2.5} = 0.3297$.

Using this probability function, write a C program that calculates and displays a list of probabilities of a call lasting less than 1 to less than 10 minutes, in one-minute increments.

11. The arrival rate of customers in a busy New York bank can be estimated using the Poisson probability function

$$P(x) = \frac{\lambda^x\, e^{-\lambda}}{x!}$$

where x = the number of customer arrivals per minute; λ = the average number of arrivals per minute; and e = Euler's number (2.71828). For example, if the average number of customers entering the bank is three customers per minute, then λ is equal to three.

Thus,

probability of 1 customer arriving in any one minute =

$$P(x=1) = \frac{3^1 e^{-3}}{1!} = 0.149561$$

and

Probability of 2 customers arriving in any one minute =

$$P(x=1) = \frac{3^2 e^{-3}}{2!} = 0.224454$$

a. Using the Poisson probability function, write a C program that calculates and displays the probability of 1 to 10 customer arrivals in any one minute when the average arrival rate is 3 customers per minute.

b. The formula given in Exercise 11a is also applicable for estimating the arrival rate of planes at a busy airport (here, an arriving "customer" is an incoming airplane). Using this same formula modify the program written in Exercise 11a to accept the average arrival rate as an input data item. Then run the modified program to determine the probability of 0 to 10 planes attempting to land in any one-minute period at an airport during peak arrival times. Assume that the average arrival rate for peak arrival times is two planes per minute.

12. Write and run a program that calculates and displays the amount of money available in a bank account that initially has $1000 deposited in it and that earns 8% interest a year. Your program should display the amount available at the end of each year for a period of 10 years. Use the relationship that the money available at the end of each year equals the amount of money in the account at the start of the year plus 0.08 times the amount available at the start of the year.

13. The Fibonacci sequence is 0, 1, 1, 2, 3, 5, 8, 13, . . ., where the first two terms are 0 and 1, and each term thereafter is the sum of the two preceding terms; that is Fib(n) = Fib(n-1) + Fib(n-2). Using this information, write a C program that calcu-

A BIT OF BACKGROUND

The Blockhead

One mathematician of the Middle Ages who has had a profound influence on modern science is Leonardo of Pisa (1170–1250). In his youth he was called *Filus Bonacci*, which means "son of (Guglielmo) Bonacci," and the name "stuck." Hence, he is commonly known today as Fibonacci. He traveled widely, met with scholars throughout the Mediterranean area, and produced four very significant works on arithmetic and geometry. One of his discoveries is the sequence of numbers that bears his name: 0,1, 1,2,3,5,8,13, ... After the first two values, 0 and 1, each number of the Fibonacci sequence is obtained from the sum of the preceding two numbers.

Fibonacci often referred to himself as Leonardo Bigollo, probably because *bigollo* is Italian for "traveler." However, another meaning of *bigollo* in Italian is "blockhead." Some people suspect he may have adopted this name to show the professors of his time what a blockhead—a person who had not been educated in their schools—could accomplish.

Some blockhead! The Fibonacci sequence alone describes such natural phenomena as the spiraling pattern of nautilus shells, elephant tusks, sheep horns, bird's claws, pine apples, and branching patterns of plants *and* the proliferation of rabbits. The ratio of successively higher adjacent terms in the sequence also approaches the "golden section," a ratio that describes an aesthetically pleasing proportion used in the visual arts.

lates the nth number in a Fibonacci sequence, where n is interactively entered into the program by the user. For example, if $n = 6$, the program should display the value 5.

14. A machine purchased for $28,000 is depreciated at a rate of $4000 a year for seven years. Write and run a C program that uses a for loop to compute and display a depreciation table for seven years. The table should have the form:

Depreciation Schedule

Year	Depreciation	End-of-Year Value	Accumulated Depreciation
----	------------	-----------	-------------
1	4000	24000	4000
2	4000	20000	8000
3	4000	16000	12000
4	4000	12000	16000
5	4000	8000	20000
6	4000	4000	24000
7	4000	0	28000

15. A well-regarded manufacturer of widgets has been losing 4% of its sales each year. The annual profit for the firm is 10% of sales. This year the firm has had $10 million in sales and a profit of $1 million. Determine the expected sales and profit for the next 10 years. Your program should complete and produce a display as follows:

| | Sales and Profit Projection | |
Year	Expected Sales	Projected Profit
1	$10000000.00	$1000000.00
2	$ 9600000.00	$ 960000.00
3	.	.
.	.	.
.	.	.
.	.	.
10	.	.
Totals:	$	$

5.4 LOOP PROGRAMMING TECHNIQUES

In this section we present four common programming techniques associated with pretest (for and while) loops. All of these techniques are common knowledge to experienced programmers.

Technique 1: Interactive Input Within a Loop

In Section 5.2 we presented the effect of including a scanf() statement within a while loop. Interactively entering data within a loop is a general technique that is equally applicable to for loops. For example, in Program 5.13 a scanf() statement is used to allow a user to interactively input a set of numbers. As each number is input, it is added to a total. When the for loop is exited, the average is calculated and displayed.

PROGRAM 5.13

```c
#include <stdio.h>
#define MAXCOUNT 5
void main(void)
/* this program calculates the average of MAXCOUNT  user-entered numbers */
{
  int count;
  float num, total, average;

  for(total = 0.0, count = 1; count <= MAXCOUNT; ++count)
  {
    printf("Enter a number: ");
    scanf("%f", &num);
    total = total + num;
  }
  average = total / MAXCOUNT;
  printf("The average of the data entered is %f\n",average);
}
```

The for statement in Program 5.13 creates a loop that is executed five times. The user is prompted to enter a number each time through the loop. After each number is entered, it is immediately added to the total. Notice that total is initialized to zero as part of the initializing list of the `for` statement is executed. The loop in Program 5.13 is executed as long as the value in `count` is less than or equal to five, and is terminated when count becomes six (the increment to six, in fact, is what causes the loop to end).

Technique 2: Selection Within a Loop

Another common programming technique is to use either a `for` or `while` loop to cycle through a set of numbers and select those numbers that meet one or more criteria. For example, assume that we want to find both the positive and negative sum of a set of numbers. The criterion here is whether the number is positive or negative, and the logic for implementing this program is given by the following pseudocode:

for Maxnum numbers
    Enter a number
    If the number is greater than zero
        add the number to the positive sum
    else
        add the number to the negative sum
    End if
End for

Program 5.14 describes this algorithm in C for a fixed count loop where five numbers are to be entered.

PROGRAM 5.14

```c
#include <stdio.h>
#define MAXNUMS 5
void main(void)
/* this program computes the positive and negative sums of a set */
/* of MAXNUMS user entered numbers                               */
{
  int i;
  float usenum, postot, negtot;

  postot = 0; /* this initialization can be done in the declaration */
  negtot = 0; /* this initialization can be done in the declaration */
  for (i = 1; i <= MAXNUMS; ++i)
  {
    printf("Enter a number (positive or negative) : ");
    scanf("%f", &usenum);
    if (usenum > 0)
      postot = postot + usenum;
  else
    negtot = negtot + usenum;
  }
  printf("The positive total is %f\n", postot);
  printf("The negative total is %f\n", negtot);
}
```

The following is a sample run using Program 5.14.

```
Enter a number (positive or negative) : 10
Enter a number (positive or negative) : -10
Enter a number (positive or negative) : 5
Enter a number (positive or negative) : -7
Enter a number (positive or negative) : 11
The positive total is 26.000000
The negative total is -17.000000
```

Technique 3: Evaluating Functions of One Variable

Loops can be conveniently constructed to determine and display the values of a single variable mathematical function for a set of values over any specified interval. For example, assume that we want to know the values of the function

$$y = 10x^2 + 3x - 2$$

for x between 2 and 6. Assuming that x has been declared as an integer variable, the following for loop can be used to calculate the required values:

```
for (x = 2; x <= 6; ++x)
{
  y = 10 * pow(x,2.0) + 3 * x - 2;
  printf(" %3d         %3d\n", x, y);
}
```

For this loop we have used the variable x as both the counter variable and the unknown (independent variable) in the function. For each value of x from two to five a new value of y is calculated and displayed. This for loop is contained within Program 5.15, which also displays appropriate headings for the values printed.

PROGRAM 5.15

```
#include <stdio.h>
#include <math.h>
void main(void)
{
  int x, y;

  printf("x value    y value\n");
  printf("-------    --------\n");
  for (x = 2; x <= 6; ++x)
  {
    y = 10 * pow(x,2) + 3 * x - 2;
    printf(" %3d         %3d\n", x, y);
  }
}
```

The following is displayed when Program 5.15 is executed:

x value	y value
2	44
3	97
4	170
5	263
6	376

Two items are of importance here. The first is that any equation with one unknown can be evaluated using a single `for` or an equivalent `while` loop. The method requires substituting the desired equation into the loop in place of the equation used in Program 5.15, and adjusting the counter values to match the desired solution range.

The second item of note is that we are not constrained to using integer values for the counter variable. For example, by specifying a noninteger increment, solutions for fractional values can be obtained. This is shown in Program 5.16, where the equation $y = 10x^2 + 3x - 2$ is evaluated in the range $x = 2$ to $x = 6$ in increments of 0.5:

PROGRAM 5.16

```c
#include <stdio.h>
#include <math.h>
void main(void)
{
  float x, y;

  printf("x value       y value\n");
  printf("--------      ----------\n");
  for (x = 2.0; x <= 6.0; x = x + 0.5)
  {
    y = 10.0 * pow(x,2.0) + 3.0 * x - 2.0;
    printf("%8.6f    %10.6f\n", x, y);
  }
}
```

Notice that x and y have been declared as floating-point variables in Program 5.16 to allow these variables to take on fractional values. The following is the output produced by this program:

x value	y value
2.000000	44.000000
2.500000	68.000000
3.000000	97.000000
3.500000	131.000000
4.000000	170.000000
4.500000	214.000000
5.000000	263.000000
5.500000	317.000000
6.000000	376.000000

Technique 4: Interactive Loop Control

Values used to control a loop may be set using variables rather than constant values. For example, the four statements

```
i = 5;
j = 10;
k = 1;
for (count = i; count <= j; count = count + k)
```

produce the same effect as the single statement

```
for (count = 5; count <=10; count = count + 1)
```

Similarly, the statements

```
i = 5;
j = 10;
k = 1;
count = i;
while (count <= j)
    count = count + k;
```

produce the same effect as the following while loop

```
count = 5;
while (count <= 10)
    count = count + 1;
```

The advantage of using variables in the initialization, condition, and altering expressions is that it allows us to assign values for these expressions external to either the for or while statement. This is especially useful when a scanf() function call is used to set the actual values. To make this a little more tangible, consider Program 5.17.

PROGRAM 5.17

```c
#include <stdio.h>
void main(void)
/* this program displays a table of numbers, their squares and cubes */
/* starting from the number 1. The final number in the table is   */
/* input by the user */
{
  int num, final;

  printf("Enter the final number for the table: ");
  scanf("%d", &final);

  printf("NUMBER SQUARE CUBE\n");
  printf("------ ------ ----\n");

  for (num = 1; num <= final; ++num)
    printf("%3d     %3d    %4d\n", num, num*num, num*num*num);
}
```

In Program 5.17, we have used a variable name within the condition (middle) expression only. Here a `scanf()` statement has been placed before the loop to allow the user to decide what the final value should be. Notice that this arrangement permits the user to set the size of the table at run time, rather than having the programmer set the table size at compile time. This also makes the program more general, since it now can be used to create a variety of tables without the need for reprogramming and recompiling.

Exercises 5.4

1. **`scanf()` within a loop:** Write and run a C program that accepts six Fahrenheit temperatures, one at a time, and converts each value entered to its Celsius equivalent before the next value is requested. Use a `for` loop in your program. The conversion required is Celsius = (5.0/9.0) * (Fahrenheit − 32).

2. **`scanf()` within a loop:** Write and run a C program that accepts 10 individual values of gallons, one at a time, and converts each value entered to its liter equivalent before the next value is requested. Use a `for` loop in your program. Use the relationship that there are 3.785 liters in one gallon.

3. **Interactive loop control:** Modify the program written for Exercise 2 to initially request the number of data items that will be entered and converted.

4. **Interactive loop control:** Modify Program 5.14 so that the number of entries to be input is specified by the user when the program is executed.

5. **Selection:** Modify Program 5.14 so that it displays the average of the positive and negative numbers. (*Hint:* Be careful not to count the number zero as a negative number.) Test your program by entering the numbers 17, −10, 19, 0 −4. The positive average displayed by your program should be 18.5 and the negative average, −7.

6. a. **Selection:** Write a C program that selects and displays the maximum value of five numbers that are to be entered when the program is executed. (*Hint:* Use a `for` loop with both a `scanf()` and `if` statement internal to the loop.).

   b. Modify the program written for Exercise 6a so that it displays both the maximum value and the position in the input set of numbers where the maximum occurs.

7. **Selection:** Write a C program that selects and displays the first 20 integer numbers that are evenly divisible by 3.

8. **Selection:** A child's parents promised to give the child $10 on her 12th birthday and double the gift on every subsequent birthday until the gift exceeded $1000. Write a C program to determine how old the girl will be when the last amount is given, and the total amount she received including the last gift.

9. **Mathematical functions:** Modify Program 5.16 to produce a table of y values for the following:

   a. $y = 3x^5 - 2x^3 + x$

   for x between 5 and 10 in increments of .2

   b. $y = 1 + x + \dfrac{x^2}{2} + \dfrac{x^3}{6} + \dfrac{x^4}{24}$

   for x between 1 and 3 in increments of 0.1.

c. $y = 2e^{.8t}$ for t between 4 and 10 in increments of 0.2.

10. **Mathematical Functions:** A model of worldwide population, in billions of people, is given by the equation

$$\text{Population} = 5.5(1 + e^{0.02*t})$$

where t is the time in years ($t = 0$ represents January 1995 and $t = 1$ represents January 1996). Using this formula, write a C program that displays a yearly population table for the years January 1999 through January 2005.

11. **Mathematical functions:** The height, as a function of time, t, of a projectile fired with an initial velocity v straight into the air is given by

$$height = vt - \tfrac{1}{2}gt^2$$

Using these formulas, write a C program that displays a table of heights for a projectile fired with an initial velocity of 500 ft/sec. g is the gravitational constant equal to 32.2 ft/sec^2. The table should contain values corresponding to the time interval 0 to 10 seconds in increments of one-half seconds.

12. **Interactive loop control:** Modify Program 5.17 to accept the starting and increment values of the table produced by the program.

13. **Interactive loop control:** Write a C program that converts Fahrenheit to Celsius temperature in increments of 5 degrees. The initial value of the Fahrenheit temperature and the total conversions to be made are to be requested as user input during program execution. Recall that Celsius = (5.0/9.0) * (Fahrenheit − 32.0)

14. a. **Interactive loop control:** Modify the program written for Exercise 12 of Section 5.3 to initially prompt the user for the amount of money deposited in the account.

b. Modify the program written for Exercise 14a to additionally prompt the user for the number of years that should be used.

c. Modify the program written for Exercise 14a to additionally prompt the user for both the interest rate and the number of years to be used.

5.5 NESTED LOOPS

In many situations it is convenient to use a loop contained within another loop. Such loops are called *nested loops*. A simple example of a nested loop is:

```
for(i = 1; i <= 5; ++i)        /* start of outer loop  ◄---------------┤ */
{                              /*                                      │ */
  printf("i is now %d\n",i);/*                                       │ */
    for(j = 1; j <= 4; ++j)      /* start of inner loop  ◄---┤        │ */
      printf("  j = %d", j);     /* end of inner loop  ◄------┤        │ */
}                              /* end of outer loop  ◄----------------┤ */
```

The first loop, controlled by the value of i, is called the outer loop. The second loop, controlled by the value of j, is called the inner loop. Notice that all statements in the inner loop are contained within the boundaries of the outer loop and that we have used a different variable to control each loop. For each single trip through the outer loop, the inner loop runs through its entire sequence.

Thus, each time the i counter increases by 1, the inner `for` loop executes completely. This situation is illustrated in Figure 5.10 (page 245).

Program 5.18 includes the preceding code in a working program.

PROGRAM 5.18

```
#include <stdio.h>
void main(void)
{
  int i,j;

  for(i = 1; i <= 5; ++i)          /* start of outer loop ◄---------- */
  {                                /*                                 */
    printf("i is now %d\n",i);/*                                      */
    for(j = 1; j <= 4; ++j)        /* start of inner loop ◄-+         */
      printf("  j = %d", j);       /* end of inner loop ◄-----+       */
  }                                /* end of outer loop ◄------------- */
}
```

The output of a sample run of Program 5.18 is:

```
i is now 1
    j = 1  j = 2  j = 3  j = 4
i is now 2
    j = 1  j = 2  j = 3  j = 4
i is now 3
    j = 1  j = 2  j = 3  j = 4
i is now 4
    j = 1  j = 2  j = 3  j = 4
i is now 5
    j = 1  j = 2  j = 3  j = 4
```

To illustrate the usefulness of a nested loop, we will use one to compute the average grade for each student in a class of 20 students. Each student has taken four exams during the course of the semester. The final grade is calculated as the average of these examination grades. The pseudocode describing how this computation can be done is:

for 20 times
    Set the student grade total to zero
    for 4 times
        Input a grade
        Add the grade to the total
    End for /* end of inner for loop */
    Calculate student's average grade
    Print the student's average grade
End for /* end of outer for loop */

As described by the pseudocode, an outer loop consisting of 20 passes will be used to compute the average grade for each student. The inner loop will consist of four passes. One examination grade is entered in each inner loop pass. As each grade is entered, it is added to the total for the student, and at the end of the loop the average is calculated and displayed. Since both outer and inner loops are fixed count loops of 20 and 4, respectively, we will use `for` statements to create these loops (see Tips from the Pros on page 232). Program 5.19 provides the C code corresponding to the pseudocode.

FIGURE 5.10 For Each *i, j* Loop

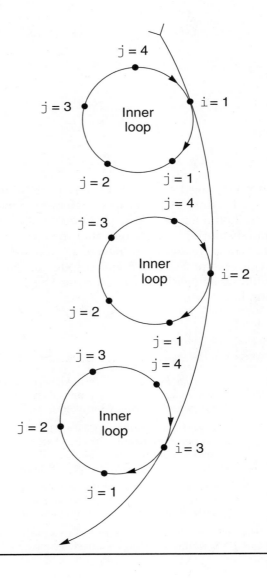

PROGRAM 5.19

```c
#include <stdio.h>
#define NUMGRADES 4
#define NUMSTUDENTS 20
void main(void)
{
  int i,j;
  float grade, total, average;

  for (i = 1; i <= NUMSTUDENTS; i++)     /* start of outer  loop */
  {
    total = 0;   /* clear the total for this student */
    for ( j = 1; j <= NUMGRADES; j++)   /* start of inner loop */
    {
      printf("Enter examination grade %d for student %d: ", j, i);
      scanf("%f", &grade);
      total = total + grade;   /* add the grade into the total */
    }                          /* end of the inner for loop */
    average = total / NUMGRADES;   /* calculate the average  */
    printf("  The average for student %d is %f\n\n",i, average);
  }                                /* end of the outer for loop */
}
```

In reviewing Program 5.19, pay particular attention to the initialization of `total` within the outer loop, before the inner loop is entered. `total` is initialized 20 times, once for each student. Also notice that the average is calculated and displayed immediately after the inner loop is finished. Since the statements that compute and print the average are also contained within the outer loop, 20 averages are calculated and displayed. The entry and addition of each grade within the inner loop use techniques we have seen before, which should now be familiar to you.

Exercises 5.5

1. Four experiments are performed, each experiment consisting of six test results. The results for each experiment are given below. Write a program using a nested loop to compute and display the average of the test results for each experiment.

1st experiment results:	23.2	31.5	16.9	27.5	25.4	28.6
2nd experiment results:	34.8	45.2	27.9	36.8	33.4	39.4
3rd experiment results:	19.4	16.8	10.2	20.8	18.9	13.4
4th experiment results:	36.9	39.5	49.2	45.1	42.7	50.6

2. Modify the program written for Exercise 1 so that the number of test results for each experiment is entered by the user. Write your program so that a different number of test results can be entered for each experiment.

3. a. A bowling team consists of five players. Each player bowls three games. Write a C program that uses a nested loop to enter each player's individual scores and

then computes and displays the average score for each bowler. Assume that each bowler has the following scores:

1st bowler: 286   252   265
2nd bowler: 212   186   215
3rd bowler: 252   232   216
4th bowler: 192   201   235
5th bowler: 186   236   272

b. Modify the program written for Exercise 3a to calculate and display the average team score. (*Hint:* Use a second variable to store the total of all the players' scores.)

4. Rewrite the program written for Exercise 3a to eliminate the inner loop. To do this, you will have to input three scores for each bowler rather than one at a time.

5. Write a program that calculates and displays values for Y when

$$Y = XZ/(X-Z)$$

Your program should calculate y for values of x ranging between 1 and 5 and values of z ranging between 2 and 6. x should control the outer loop and be incremented in steps of 0.2 and z should be incremented in steps of 0.5. Your program should also display the message "FUNCTION UNDEFINED" when the x and z values are equal.

6. Write a program that calculates and displays the yearly amount available if $1000 is invested in a bank account for 10 years. Your program should display the amounts available for interest rates from 6% to 12% inclusively, in 1% increments. Use a nested loop, with the outer loop controlling the interest rate and the inner loop controlling the years. Use the relationship that the money available at the end of each year equals the amount of money in the account at the start of the year, plus the interest rate times the amount available at the start of the year.

7. In the Duchy of Upenchuck, the fundamental unit of currency is the Upenchuck Dragon (UD). Income tax deductions are based on salary in units of 10,000 UD and on the number of dependents the employee has. The formula, designed to favor low-income families, is

Deduction (UD) = Dependents * 500 + 0.05 *(50,000 − Salary)

Beyond five dependents and beyond 50,000 UD, the deduction does not change. There is no tax, hence no deduction, on incomes of less than 10,000 UD. Based on this information, create a table of Upenchuck income tax deductions, with dependents 0 to 5 as the column headings and salary 10000, 20000, 30000, 40000, and 50000 as the rows.

5.6 do LOOPS

Both the `while` and `for` statements evaluate an expression at the start of the repetition loop; as such they are always used to create pretest loops. Posttest loops, which are also referred to as exit-controlled loops, can also be constructed in C. The basic structure of such a loop, which is referred to as a `do` loop is illustrated in Figure 5.11. Notice that a `do` loop continues iterations through the loop while the condition is true and exits the loop when the condition is false. Let's see how this is done.

In C, the posttest `do` loop is created using a `do` statement. As its name implies, this statement allows us to do some statements before an expression is evaluated at the end of the loop. The general form of C's `do` statement is:

```
do
   statement;
while (expression);  ◄───────  don't forget the final ;
```

As with all C programs, the single statement in the do may be replaced with a compound statement. A flow control diagram illustrating the operation of the do statement is shown in Figure 5.12. As illustrated, all statements within the do statement are executed at least once before the expression is evaluated. Then, if the expression has a nonzero value, the statements are executed again. This process continues until the expression evaluates to zero (becomes false). For example, consider the following do statement:

```
do
{
   printf("Enter a price: ");
   scanf("%f", &price);
   salestax = RATE * price;
   printf("The sales tax is $%5.2f\n", salestax);
}
while (price != SENTINEL);
```

Here the compound statement within the loop will always be executed at least once, regardless of the value of the tested condition. They will then be repeatedly executed as long as the condition remains true. Notice that in this section of code the loop processes the sentinel value.

As with all repetition statements, the do statement can always replace or be replaced by an equivalent while or for statement. The choice of which statement to

---

FIGURE 5.11 do Loop Structure

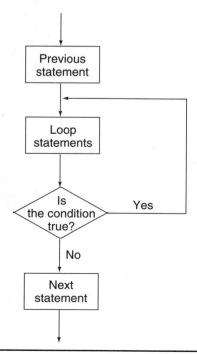

FIGURE 5.12   The do Statement's Flow of Control

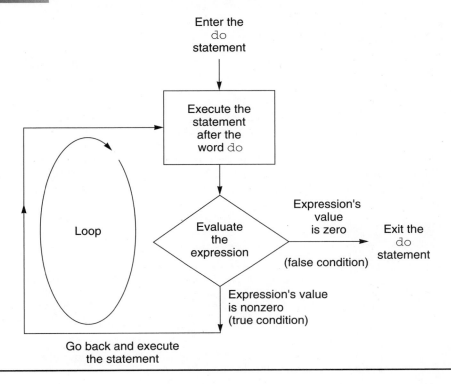

use depends on the application and the style preferred by the programmer. In general, the while and for statements are preferred because they clearly let anyone reading the program know what is being tested "right up front" at the top of the program loop.

Validity Checks

The do statement is particularly useful in filtering user-entered input and providing *data validiation* checks. For example, assume that an operator is required to enter a valid customer identification number between the numbers 1000 and 1999. A number outside this range is to be rejected and a new request for a valid number made. The following section of code provides the necessary data filter to verify the entry of a valid identification number:

```
do
{
   printf("Enter an identification number: ");
   scanf("%f", &id_num);
}
while (id_num < 1000 || id_num > 1999);
```

Here, a request for an identification number is repeated until a valid number is entered. This section of code is "bare bones" in that it neither alerts the operator to the cause of the new request for data nor allows premature exit from the loop if a valid identification number cannot be found. An alternative removing the first drawback is:

```
do
{
  printf("Enter an identification number: ");
  scanf("%f", &id_num);
  if (id_num < 1000 || id_num > 1999)
  {
    printf(" An invalid number was just entered\n");
    printf("Please check the ID number and re-enter\n");
  }
  else
    break;/* break if a valid id num was entered */
} while(1);   /* this expression is always true */
```

Here we have used a break statement to exit from the loop. Since the expression being evaluated by the do statement is always 1 (true), an infinite loop has been created that is only exited when the break statement is encountered.

Exercises 5.6

1. a. Using a do statement, write a program to accept a grade. The program should request a grade continuously as long as an invalid grade is entered. An invalid grade is any grade less than 0 or greater than 100. After a valid grade has been entered, your program should display the value of the grade entered.

   b. Modify the program written for Exercise 1a so that the user is alerted when an invalid grade has been entered.

   c. Modify the program written for Exercise 1b so that it allows the user to exit the program by entering the number 999.

   d. Modify the program written for Exercise 1b so that it automatically terminates after five invalid grades are entered.

2. a. Write a program that continuously requests a grade to be entered. If the grade is less than 0 or greater than 100, your program should print an appropriate message informing the user that an invalid grade has been entered, else the grade should be added to a total. When a grade of 999 is entered, the program should exit the repetition loop and compute and display the average of the valid grades entered.

   b. Run the program written in Exercise 2a on a computer and verify the program using appropriate test data.

3. a. Write a program to reverse the digits of a positive integer number. For example, if the number 8735 is entered, the number displayed should be 5378. (Hint: Use a do statement and continuously strip off and display the units digit of the number. If the variable num initially contains the number entered, the units digit is obtained as (num % 10). After a units digit is displayed, dividing the number by 10 sets up the number for the next iteration. Thus, (8735 % 10) is 5 and (8735 / 10) is 873. The do statement should continue as long as the remaining number is not zero.)

   b. Run the program written in Exercise 3a on a computer and verify the program using appropriate test data.

4. Repeat any of the exercises in Section 5.3 using a do statement rather than a for statement.

5. Given a number n, and an approximation for its square root, a closer approximation to the actual square root can be obtained using the formula:

$$New\ approximation = \frac{(n/Previous\ approximation) + Previous\ approximation}{2}$$

Using this information, write a C program that prompts the user for a number and an initial guess at its square root. Using this input data your program should calculate an approximation to the square root that is accurate to 0.00001. (*Hint:* Stop the loop when the difference between two approximations is less than 0.00001.)

6. Here is a challenging problem for those who know a little calculus. The Newton-Raphson method can be used to find the roots of any equation $y(x) = 0$. In this method the $(i + 1)st$ approximation, x_{i+1}, to a root of $y(x) = 0$ is given in terms of the ith approximation, x_i, by the formula

$$x_{i+1} = x_i - y(x_i) / y'(x_i)$$

For example, if $y(x) = 3x^2 + 2x - 2$, then $y'(x) = 6x + 2$, and the roots are found by making a reasonable guess for a first approximation x_1, and iterating using the equation

$$x_{i+1} = x_i - (3x_i^2 + 2x_i - 2) / (6x_i + 2)$$

a. Using the Newton-Raphson method, find the two roots of the equation $3x^2 + 2x - 2 = 0$. (*Hint:* There is one positive root and one negative root.)

b. Extend the program written for Exercise 6a so that it will find the roots of any function $y(x) = 0$, when the function for $y(x)$ and the derivative of $y(x)$ are placed in the code.

5.7 COMMON PROGRAMMING ERRORS

Five errors are commonly made by beginning C programmers when using repetition statements. Two of these pertain to the tested expression and have already been encountered with the `if` and `switch` statements. The first is the inadvertent use of the assignment operator, `=`, for the equality operator, `==`, in the tested expression. An example of this error is typing the assignment expression `a = 5` instead of the desired relational expression `a == 5`. Since the tested expression can be any valid C expression, including arithmetic and assignment expressions, this error is not detected by the compiler.

As with the `if` statement, repetition statements should not use the equality operator, `==`, when testing floating-point or double-precision operands. For example, the expression `fnum == 0.01` should be replaced by an equivalent test requiring that the absolute value of `fnum - 0.01` be less than an acceptable amount. The reason for this is that all numbers are stored in binary form. Using a finite number of bits, decimal numbers such as 0.01 have no exact binary equivalent, so that tests requiring equality with such numbers can fail.

The next two errors are particular to the `for` statement. The most common is to place a semicolon at the end of the `for`'s parentheses, which frequently produces a do-nothing loop. For example, consider the statements

```
for(count = 0; count < 10; ++ count);
    total = total + num;
```

Here the semicolon at the end of the first line of code is a null statement. This has the effect of creating a loop that is executed 10 times with nothing done except the incrementing and testing of count. This error tends to occur because C programmers are used to ending most lines with a semicolon.

The next error occurs when commas are used to separate the items in a for statement instead of the required semicolons. An example of this is the statement

```
for (count = 1, count < 10, ++count)
```

Commas must be used to separate items within the initializing and altering lists, and semicolons must be used to separate these lists from the tested expression.

The last error occurs when the final semicolon is omitted from the do statement. This error is usually made by programmers who have learned to omit the semicolon after the parentheses of a while statement and carry over this habit when the reserved word while is encountered at the end of a do statement.

5.8 CHAPTER REVIEW

Key Terms

counter
data validation
fixed count loop
for loop
infinite loop
nested loop
posttest loop

pretest loop
do loop
repetition statement
sentinel values
variable condition loop
while loop

Summary

1. A section of repeating code is referred to as a *loop*. The loop is controlled by a repetition statement that tests a condition to determine whether the code will be executed. Each pass through the loop is referred to as a *repetition* or *iteration*. The tested condition must always be explicitly set prior to its first evaluation by the repetition statement. Within the loop there must always be a statement that permits altering of the condition so that the loop, once entered, can be exited.

2. There are three basic type of loops:

   a. while
   b. for
   c. do

   The while and for loops are *pretest* or *entrance-controlled loops*. In this type of loop, the tested condition is evaluated at the beginning of the loop, which requires that the tested condition be explicitly set prior to loop entry. If the condition is true, loop repetitions begin; otherwise the loop is not entered. Iterations continue as long as the condition remains true. In C, while and for loops are constructed using while, and for statements, respectively.

   The do loop is a *posttest* or *exit-controlled loop*, where the tested condition is evaluated at the end of the loop. This type of loop is always executed at least once. do loops continue to execute as long as the tested condition remains true.

3. Loops are also classified as to the type of tested condition. In a *fixed count loop*, the condition is used to keep track of how many repetitions have occurred. In a *variable condition loop* the tested condition is based on a variable that can change interactively with each pass through the loop.

4. In C, a `while` loop is constructed using a `while` statement. The most commonly used form of this statement is:

```
while (expression)
{
      statements;
}
```

The expression contained within parentheses is the condition tested to determine if the statement following the parentheses, which is generally a compound statement, is executed. The expression is evaluated in exactly the same manner as that contained in an `if-else` statement; the difference is how the expression is used. In a `while` statement the statement following the expression is executed repeatedly as long as the expression retains a nonzero value, rather than just once, as in an `if-else` statement. An example of a `while` loop is:

```
count = 1;                 /* initialize count */
while (count <= 10)
{
   printf("%d  ",count);
   count = count + 1;    /* increment count */
}
```

The first assignment statement sets `count` equal to 1. The `while` statement is then entered and the expression is evaluated for the first time. Since the value of `count` is less than or equal to 10, the expression is true and the compound statement is executed. The first statement in the compound statement is a call to the `printf()` function to display the value of `count`. The next statement adds 1 to the value currently stored in `count`, making this value equal to 2. The `while` statement now loops back to retest the expression. Since count is still less than or equal to 10, the compound statement is again executed. This process continues until the value of `count` reaches 11.

The `while` statement always checks its expression at the top of the loop. This requires that any variables in the tested expression must have values assigned before the `while` is encountered. Within the `while` loop there must be a statement that alters the tested expression's value.

5. In C, a `for` loop is constructed using a `for` statement. This statement performs the same functions as the `while` statement, but uses a different form. In many situations, especially those that use a fixed count condition, the `for` statement format is easier to use than its `while` statement equivalent. The most commonly used form of the for statement is:

```
for (initializing list; expression; altering list)
{
   statements;
}
```

Within the parentheses of the `for` statement are three items, separated by semicolons. Each of these items is optional but the semicolons must be present.

The initializing list is used to set any initial values before the loop is entered; generally it is used to initialize a counter. Statements within the initializing list are only executed once. The expression in the `for` statement is the condition being tested: It is tested at the start of the loop and prior to each iteration. The altering list contains loop statements that are not contained within the compound statement: generally it is used to increment or decrement a counter each time the loop is executed. Multiple statements within a list are separated by commas. An example of a `for` loop is:

```
for (total = 0, count = 1; count < 10; count = count + 1)
{
  printf("Enter a grade: ");
  total = total + grade;
}
```

In this for statement, the initializing list is used to initialize both `total` and `count`. The expression determines that the loop will execute as long as the value in `count` is less than 10, and the value of count is incremented by one each time through the loop.

6. The `for` statement is extremely useful in creating fixed count loops. This is because the initializing statements, the tested expression, and statements affecting the tested expression can all be included in parentheses at the top of a `for` loop for easy inspection and modification.

7. The `do` statement is used to create posttest loops because it checks its expression at the end of the loop. This ensures that the body of a `do` loop is executed at least once. Within a `do` loop there must be at least one statement that alters the tested expression's value.

Exercises

1. Write sections of C code to do the following:

   a. Display the multiples of 3 backward from 33 to 3, inclusive.

   b. Display the capital letters of the alphabet backward from Z to A.

2. Write, run, and test a C program to find the value of 2^n using a for loop, where n is an integer value entered by the user at the keyboard. (*Hint:* Initialize result = 1. Accumulate result = 2 * result.)

3. The value of Euler's number e, can be approximated using the formula

$$e = 1 + 1/1! + 1/2! + 1/3! + 1/4! + 1/5! + \ldots$$

   Using this formula, write a C program that approximates the value of e using a `while` loop that terminates when the difference between two successive approximations differs by less than 1.0e−6.

4. Using the formula provided in Exercise 3 formula, determine how many terms are needed to approximate the value returned by the `exp()` function with an error less than 1.0e-6. [*Hints:* Use a `while` loop that terminates when the difference between the value returned by the `exp()` function and the approximation is less than 1 E-6.

5. a. The outstanding balance on Rhona Karp's car loan is $8000. Each month Rhona is required to make a payment of $300, which includes both interest

and principal repayment of the car loan. The monthly interest is calculated as 0.10/12 of the outstanding balance of the loan. After the interest is deducted, the remaining part of the payment is used to pay off the loan. Using this information, write a C program that produces a table indicating the beginning monthly balance, the interest payment, the principal payment, and the remaining loan balance after each payment is made. Your output should resemble and complete the entries in the following table until the outstanding loan balance is zero.

Beginning Balance	Interest Payment	Principal Payment	Ending Loan Balance
8000.000000	66.666667	233.333333	7766.666667
7766.666667	64.722223	235.277777	7531.388889
7531.388889	.	.	.
.	.	.	
.	.	.	
.	.	.	0.000000

b. Modify the program written in Exercise 5a to display the total of the interest and principal paid at the end of the table produced by your program.

6. The monthly payment due on an outstanding car loan is typically calculated using the formula:

$$\text{Monthly payment} = \frac{(\text{Loan amount})\,(\text{Monthly interest rate})}{1.0 - (1.0 + \text{Monthly interest rate})^{-(\text{Number of months})}}$$

where

$$\text{Monthly interest rate} = \text{Annual percentage rate}/(12.0 * 100)$$

Using these formulas write, run, and test a C program that prompts the user for the amount of the loan, the annual percentage rate, and the number of years of the loan. From this input data produce a loan amortization table similar to the one shown below for the following inputs:

What is the amount of the loan? $ 1500.00
What is the annual percentage rate? 14.0
How many years will you take to pay back the loan? 1.0

Amount, 1500.00;   Annual %, Interest 14.00;   Years, 1;   Monthly Payment, 134.68

Payment Number	Interest Paid	Principal Paid	Cumulative Interest	Total Paid to Date	New Balance Due
1	17.50	117.18	17.50	134.68	1382.82
2	16.13	118.55	33.63	269.36	1264.27
3	14.75	119.93	48.38	404.04	1144.34
4	13.35	121.33	61.73	538.72	1023.01
5	11.94	122.75	73.67	673.40	900.27
6	10.50	124.18	84.17	808.08	776.09
7	9.05	125.63	93.23	942.76	650.46
8	7.59	127.09	100.81	1077.45	523.37
9	6.11	128.57	106.92	1212.13	394.79
10	4.61	130.07	111.53	1346.81	264.72
11	3.09	131.59	114.61	1481.49	133.13
12	1.55	133.13	116.17	1616.1	70.00

In constructing the loop necessary to produce the body of the table, the following initializations must be made:

New balance due = Original loan amount
Cumulative Interest = 0.0
Paid to date = 0.0
Payment number = 0

Within the loop the following calculations and accumulations should be used:

Payment number = Payment number + 1
Interest paid = New balance due * Monthly interest rate
Principal paid = Monthly payment - Interest paid
Cumulative interest = Cumulative interest + Interest paid
Paid to date = Paid to date + Monthly payment
New balance due = New balance due - Principal paid

7. Modify the program written for Exercise 6 to prevent the user from entering an illegal value for the interest rate. That is, write a loop that asks the user repeatedly for the annual interest rate until a value between 1.0 and 25.0 is entered.

8. In the hypothetical Republic of Dwump, the basic unit of currency is the dwork, and the exchange rate at present is 2.57 dworks per U.S. dollar. Develop, run, and test a C program to create a table of dollars versus dworks in steps of $0.25 from `MinDollars` to `MaxDollars`, where values for these two variables will be entered by the user at the keyboard. The exchange rate (2.57 dworks per dollar) and the step value (0.25) should be declared as named constants, so that they can be found and changed easily. The exchange rate should be displayed at the head of the output table, and the columns `Dollars` and `Dworks` should be labeled.

9. Develop, test, and execute a C program that uses a `while` loop to determine the smallest integer power of 3 that exceeds 30,000. That is, find the smallest value of n such that $3^n < 30{,}000$. (*Hint:* Initialize `PowerOfThree = 1`. Accumulate `PowerOfThree = 3 * PowerOfThree`.)

10. A prime integer number is one that has exactly two different divisors, namely 1 and the number itself. Write, run, and test a C program that finds and prints all the prime numbers less than 100. [*Hint:* 1 is a prime number. For each number from 2 to 100, find `Remainder = Number % n`, where n ranges from 2 to `sqrt(number)`. If n is greater than `sqrt(number)`, then the number is not equally divisible by n (why?). If any `Remainder` equals 0, then the number is not a prime number.]

11. Print the decimal, octal, and hexadecimal values of all characters between the start and stop characters entered by a user. For example, if the user enters an `'a'` and a `'z'`, the program should print all the characters between a and z and their respective values. Make sure that the second character entered by the user occurs later in the alphabet then the first character. If it does not, write a loop that asks the user repeatedly for a valid second character.

12. Create a table of selling price versus purchase price. Have the user enter the range of purchase prices (from lowest to highest), the percent markup, and the increment between purchase prices. Display the table of purchase prices and selling prices on the screen, with appropriate headings. The formula for calculating the selling price from the purchase price are:

Markup fraction = Percent markup / 100.0
Selling price = (1.0 + Markup fraction) * Purchase price

13. The quotient in long division is the number of times the divisor can be sub-tracted from the dividend. The remainder is what is left over after the last subtraction. Write a C program that performs division using this method.

14. Write a C program that uses iteration to accumulate the sum $1 + 2 + 3 + \ldots + N$, where N is a user-entered integer number. Then evaluate the expression $N(N + 1)/2$ to verify that this expression yields the same result as the itera-tion.

15. a. An old Arabian legend has it that a fabulously wealthy but unthinking king agreed to give a beggar one cent and double the amount for 64 days. Using this information write, run, and test a C program that displays how much the king must pay the beggar on each day. The output of your pro-gram should appear as follows:

```
DAY          AMOUNT OF BET
 1               0.01
 2               0.02
 3               0.04
 .                .
 .                .
 .                .
64                .
```

b. Modify the program you wrote for Exercise 15b to determine on which day the king will have paid a total of one million dollars to the beggar.

16. According to legend the island of Manhattan was purchased from the native Indian population in 1626 for $24. Assuming that this money was invested in a Dutch bank paying 5% simple interest per year, construct a table showing how much money the Indians would have at the end of each 20-year period starting in 1626 and ending in 2006.

CHAPTER

6 Modularity Using Functions: Part 1

Professional programs are designed, coded, and tested very much like hardware—as a set of modules that are integrated to perform a completed whole. A good analogy of this is an automobile where one major module is the engine, another is the transmission, a third the braking system, a fourth the body, and so on. Each of these modules is linked together and ultimately placed under the control of the driver, which can be compared to a supervisor or main program module. The whole now operates as a complete unit, able to do useful work, such as driving to the store. During the assembly process, each module is individually constructed, tested, and found to be free of defects (bugs) before it is installed in the final product.

Now think of what you might do if you wanted to improve your car's performance. You might alter the existing engine or remove it altogether and bolt in a new engine. Similarly, you might change the transmission or tires or shock absorbers, making each modification individually as your time and budget allowed. In each case the majority of the other modules can stay the same, but the car now operates differently.

In this analogy, each of the major components of a car can be compared to a function. For example, the driver calls on the engine when the gas pedal is pressed. The engine accepts inputs of fuel, air, and electricity to turn the driver's request into a useful product—power—and then sends this output to the transmission for further processing. The transmission receives the output of the engine and converts it to a form that can be used by the drive axle. An additional input to the transmission is the driver's selection of gears (drive, reverse, neutral, etc.).

In each case, the engine, transmission, and other modules only "know" the universe bounded by their inputs and outputs. The driver need know nothing of the internal operation of the engine, transmission, drive axle, and other modules that are being controlled. The driver simply "calls" on a module, such as the engine, brakes, air conditioning, and steering when that module's output is required. Communication between modules is restricted to passing needed inputs to each module as it is called on to perform its task, and each module operates internally in a relatively independent manner. This same modular approach is used by engineers to create and maintain reliable C programs using functions.

As we have seen, each C program must contain a main function. In addition to this required function, C programs may also contain any number of additional functions. In this chapter we learn how to write these functions, pass data to them, process the passed data, and return a result.

6.1 FUNCTION AND ARGUMENT DECLARATIONS

In creating C functions we must be concerned with both the function itself and how it interfaces with other functions, such as `main`. This includes correctly passing data into a function when it is called and returning a value from a function. In this section we describe the first part of the interface, passing data to a function and having the function correctly receive, store, and process the transmitted data.

As we have already seen with mathematical functions, a function is called, or used, by giving the function's name and passing any data to it in the parentheses following the function name (see Figure 6.1). The called function must be able to accept the data passed to it by the function doing the calling. Only after the called function successfully receives the data can the data be manipulated to produce a useful result.

To clarify the process of sending and receiving data, consider Program 6.1, which calls a function named `find_max`. The program, as shown, is not yet complete. Once the function `find_max` is written and included in Program 6.1, the completed program, consisting of the functions `main` and `find_max`, can be run.

FIGURE 6.1   Calling and Passing Data to a Function

```
function_name(data passed to function);
```

This indentifies
the called
function

This passes data to
the function

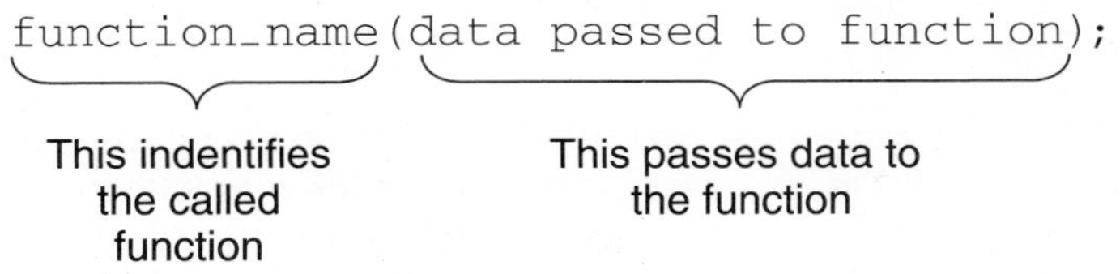

A BIT OF BACKGROUND

Subprograms

Although the concepts are similar, user-defined program units are generically referred to as *subprograms*, but are called by different names in different programming languages. C language subprograms are all referred to as *functions*.

In Pascal they are named *procedures* and *functions.* Modula-2 names them PROCE-DURES (even though some of them are actual functions). COBOL refers to them as paragraphs, while FORTRAN and BASIC refer to them as *subroutines* and *functions.*

PROGRAM 6.1

```c
#include <stdio.h>
void main(void)
{
  int firstnum, secnum;
  void find_max(int, int);  /* the function prototype */

  printf("\nEnter a number: ");
  scanf("%d", &firstnum);
  printf("Great! Please enter a second number: ");
  scanf("%d", &secnum);

  find_max(firstnum, secnum); /* the function is called here */
}
```

Let us examine declaring and calling the function find_max from the main function. We will then write find_max to accept the data passed to it and determine the largest or maximum value of the two passed values.

The function find_max is referred to as the *called function,* because it is called or summoned into action by its reference in main. The function that does the calling, in this case main, is referred to as the *calling function.* The terms *called* and *calling* come from standard telephone usage, where one party calls the other on a telephone. The party initiating the call is referred to as the calling party, and the party receiving the call is referred to as the called party. The same terms describe function calls. Within main, the called function, in this case find_max, is declared as a function that expects to receive two integer numbers and return no value (a void) back to main. This declaration is formally referred to as a function prototype. The function is then called by the last statement in the program.

Function Prototypes

Before a function can be called, it must be declared to the function that will do the calling. The declaration statement for a function is referred to as a *function prototype.* The function prototype tells the calling function the type of value that will be formally returned, if any, and the data type of the values that the calling function should transmit to the called function. For example, the function prototype previously used in Program 6.1:

```
void find_max(int, int);
```

declares that the function `find_max` expects two integer values to be sent to it, and that this particular function formally returns no value (`void`). Function prototypes may be placed with the variable declaration statements of the calling function, as in Program 6.1, or above the calling function name. Thus, the function prototype for `find_max` could have been placed either before or after the statement `#include <stdio.h>`, prior to `main`, or within `main`, as in Program 6.1. (The reasons for the choice of placement are presented in Section 6.4). The general form of function prototype statements is:

```
return-data-type   function-name(list of argument data types);
```

The data-type refers to the data type of the value that will be formally returned by the function. Examples of function prototypes are:

```
int fmax(int, int);
float swap(int, char, char, double);
void display(double, double);
```

The function prototype for `fmax` declares that this function expects to receive two integer arguments and will formally return an integer value. The function prototype for `swap` declares that this function requires four arguments consisting of an integer, two characters, and a double-precision argument, in this order, and will formally return a floating-point number. Finally, the function prototype for `display` declares that this function requires two double-precision arguments and does not return any value. Such a function might be used to display the results of a computation directly, without returning any value to the called function.

The use of function prototypes permits error checking of data types by the compiler. If the function prototype does not agree with data types defined when the function is written, an error message (typically `Declaration syntx error`) will occur. The prototype also serves another task; it ensures conversion of all arguments passed to the function to the declared argument data type when the function is called.

Calling a Function

Calling a function is a rather trivial process. All that is required is that the name of the function be used and that any data passed to the function be enclosed within the parentheses following the function name. The items enclosed within the parentheses are called *actual arguments* of the called function (see Figure 6.2).

FIGURE 6.2   Calling and Passing Two Values to `find_max`

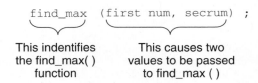

FIGURE 6.3   `find_max` **Receives Actual Values**

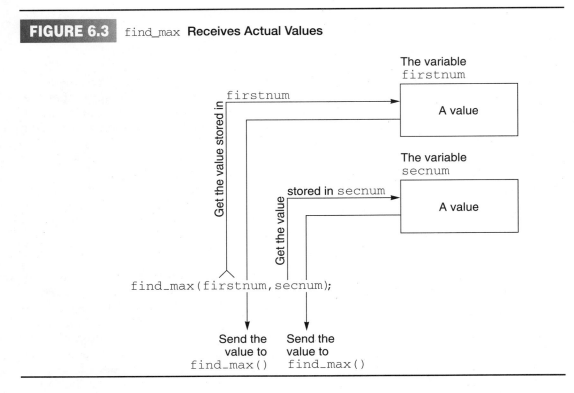

If a variable is one of the actual arguments in a function call, the called function receives a copy of the value stored in the variable. For example, the statement

`find_max(firstnum,secnum);`

calls the function `find_max` and causes the values currently residing in the variables `firstnum` and `secnum` to be passed to `find_max`. The variable names in parentheses are actual arguments that provide values to the called function. After the values are passed, control is transferred to the called function.

As illustrated in Figure 6.3, *the function* `find_max` *does not receive the variable names* `firstnum` *and* `secnum` *and has no knowledge of these variable names.*[1] The function simply receives the values in these variables and must itself determine where to store these values before it does anything else. Although this procedure for passing data to a function may seem surprising, it is really a safety procedure for ensuring that a called function does not inadvertently change data stored in a variable. The function gets a copy of the data to use. It may change its copy and, of course, change any variables or arguments declared inside itself. However, unless specific steps are taken to do so, a function is not allowed to change the contents of variables declared in other functions.

Let us now begin writing the function `find_max` to process the values passed to it.

---

[1]This is significantly different from computer languages such as FORTRAN, where functions and subroutines receive access to the variable and can pass data back through them. In Section 6.3 we will see, using pointer variables, that C also permits direct access to the calling function's variables.

FIGURE 6.4   General Format of a Function

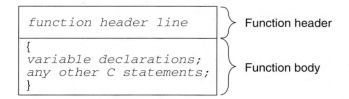

Defining a Function

A function is defined when it is written. Each function is defined once (that is, written once) in a program and can then be used by any other function in the program that suitably declares it.

Like the `main` function, every C function consists of two parts, a *function header* and a *function body*, as illustrated in Figure 6.4. The purpose of the function header is to identify the data type of the value returned by the function, provide the function with a name, and specify the number, order, and type of arguments expected by the function. The purpose of the function body is to operate on the passed data and directly return, at most, one value back to the calling function. (We will see, in Section 7.3, how a function can be made to return multiple values through the argument list.)

The function header is always the first line of a function and contains the function's returned value type, its name, and the names and data types of its arguments. Since `find_max` will not formally return any value and is to receive two integer arguments, the following header line can be used:

```
void find_max(int x, int y)  ◄─────── no semicolon
```

The argument names in the header line are formally referred to as *parameters* or *formal arguments,* and we will use these terms interchangeably.[2] Thus, the argument `x` will be used to store the first value passed to `find_max` and the argument `y` will be used to store the second value passed at the time of the function call. The function does not know where the values come from when the call is made from `main`. The first part of the call procedure executed by the computer involves going to the variables `firstnum` and `secnum` and retrieving the stored values. These values are then passed to `find_max` and ultimately stored in the formal arguments `x` and `y` (see Figure 6.5).

The function name and all parameter names in the header line, in this case `find_max`, `x`, and `y`, are chosen by the programmer. Any names selected according to the rules used to choose variable names can be used. All parameters listed in the function header line must be separated by commas and must have their individual data types declared separately.

Now that we have written the function header for the `find_max` function, we can construct the body of this function. Let us assume that the `find_max` function selects and displays the larger of the two numbers passed to it.

---

[2]The portion of the function header that contains the function name and parameters is formally referred to as a *function declarator,* which should not be confused with a function declaration (prototype).

FIGURE 6.5   Storing Values into Arguments

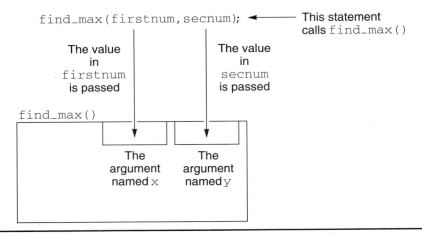

As illustrated in Figure 6.6, a function body begins with an opening brace, { , contains any necessary variable declarations and other C statements, and ends with a closing brace, } . This should be familiar to you because it is the same structure used in the main functions we have written. This should come as no surprise because main is itself a function and must adhere to the rules required for constructing all legitimate functions.

In the body of the function find_max, we will declare one variable to store the maximum of the two numbers passed to it. We will then use an if-else statement to find the maximum of the two numbers. Finally, a printf() function call will be used to display the maximum. The complete function definition for the find_max function is:

```
void find_max(int x, int y)
{                       /* start of function body */
   int maxnum;          /* variable declaration */

   if (x >= y)          /* find the maximum number */
     maxnum = x;
   else
     maxnum = y;

   printf("\nThe maximum of the two numbers is %d\n" , maxnum);

}   /* end of function body and end of function */
```

FIGURE 6.6   Structure of a Function Body

```
{

      Variable declarations and
      other C statements

}
```

Notice that the argument declarations are made within the header line and the variable declaration is made immediately after the opening brace of the function's body. This is in keeping with the concept that argument values are passed to a function from outside the function, and that variables are declared and assigned values from within the function body.

Program 6.2 includes the `find_max` function within the program code previously listed in Program 6.1.

PROGRAM 6.2

```c
#include <stdio.h>
void main(void)
{
  int firstnum, secnum;
  void find_max(int, int);  /* the function prototype */

  printf("\nEnter a number: ");
  scanf("%d", &firstnum);
  printf("Great! Please enter a second number: ");
  scanf("%d", &secnum);

  find_max(firstnum, secnum);  /* the function is called here */

}

/* following is the function find_max() */

void find_max(int x, int y)
{                     /* start of function body */
  int maxnum;         /* variable declaration */

  if (x >= y)         /* find the maximum number */
    maxnum = x;
  else
    maxnum = y;

  printf("\nThe maximum of the two numbers is %d\n", maxnum);
}   /* end of function body and end of function */
```

Program 6.2 can be used to select and print the maximum of any two integer numbers entered by the user. A sample run using Program 6.2 follows:

```
Enter a number: 25
Great! Please enter a second number: 5

The maximum of the two numbers is 25
```

The placement of the `find_max` function after the `main` function in Program 6.2 is a matter of choice. Some programmers prefer to put all called functions at the top of a program and make `main` the last function listed. We prefer to list `main` first because it is the driver function that should give anyone reading the program an idea of what the complete program is about before encountering the details of each function. Either placement approach is acceptable and you will encounter both styles in your programming work. In no case, however, can find_max be placed inside main. This is true for all C functions, which must be defined by themselves outside any other function. Each C function is a separate and independent entity with its own arguments and variables; nesting of functions is never permitted.

Program Stubs

An alternative to completing each function required in a complete program, is to write the main function first, and add the functions later, as they are developed. The problem that arises with this approach, however, is the same problem that occurred with Program 6.1—that is, the program cannot be run until all of the functions are included. For convenience we have reproduced the code for Program 6.1 below.

```c
#include <stdio.h>
void main(void)
{
  int firstnum, secnum;
  void find_max(int, int);   /* the function prototype */

  printf("\nEnter a number: ");
  scanf("%d", &firstnum);
  printf("Great! Please enter a second number: ");
  scanf("%d", &secnum);

  find_max(firstnum, secnum); /* the function is called here */
}
```

This program would be complete if there were a function definition for find_max. But we really don't need a *correct* find_max function to test and run what has been written, we just need a function that *acts* like it is; a "fake" find_max that accepts the proper number and types of arguments and returns values of the proper form for the function call is all we need to allow initial testing. This fake function is called a stub. A *stub* is the beginning of a final function that can be used as a placeholder for the final unit until the unit is completed. A stub for find_max is as follows:

```c
void find_max(int x, int y)
{
  printf("In find_max()\n");
  printf("The value of x is %d\n", x);
  printf("The value of x is %d\n", y);
}
```

This stub function can now be compiled and linked with the previously completed code to obtain an executable program. The code for the function can then be further developed, with the "real" code, when it is completed, replacing the stub portion. As illustrated, a stub should always display the name of the function that it represents.

The minimum requirement of a stub function is that it compile and link with its calling module. In practice, it is a good idea to have a stub display a message that it has been entered successfully and the value(s) of its received arguments, as in the stub for find_max.

As the function is refined, you let it do more and more, perhaps allowing it to return intermediate or incomplete results. This incremental, or stepwise, refinement is an important concept in efficient program development that provides you with the means to run a program that does not yet meet all of its final requirements.

Exercises 6.1

1. For the following function headers, determine the number, type, and order (sequence) of the values that must be passed to the function:

   a. `void factorial(int n)`

   b. `void price(int type, double yield, double maturity)`

   c. `void yield(int type, double price, double maturity)`

   d. `void interest(char flag, float price, float time)`

   e. `void total(float amount, float rate)`

   f. `void roi(int a, int b, char c, char d, float e, float f)`

   g. `void get_val(int item, int iter, char decflag, char delim)`

2. a. Write a function named `check` that has three arguments. The first argument should accept an integer number, the second argument a floating-point number, and the third argument a double-precision number. The body of the function should just display the values of the data passed to the function when it is called. (*Note:* When tracing errors in functions, it is very helpful to have the function display the values it has been passed. Quite frequently, the error is not in what the body of the function does with the data, but in the data received and stored.)

   b. Include the function written in Exercise 2a in a working program. Make sure your function is called from `main`. Test the function by passing various data to it.

3. a. Write a function named `find_abs` that accepts a double-precision number passed to it, computes its absolute value, and displays the absolute value. The absolute value of a number is the number itself if the number is positive, and the negative of the number if the number is negative.

   b. Include the function written in Exercise 3a in a working program. Make sure your function is called from `main`. Test the function by passing various data to it.

4. a. Write a function called `mult` that accepts two-floating point numbers as arguments, multiplies these two numbers, and displays the result.

   b. Include the function written in Exercise 4a in a working program. Make sure your function is called from `main`. Test the function by passing various data to it.

5. a. Write a function named `sqr_it` that computes the square of the value passed to it and displays the result. The function should be capable of squaring numbers with decimal points.

   b. Include the function written in Exercise 5a in a working program. Make sure your function is called from `main`. Test the function by passing various data to it.

6. a. Write a function named `powfun` that raises an integer number passed to it to a positive integer power and displays the result. The positive integer should be the second value passed to the function. Declare the variable used to store the result as a long integer data type to ensure sufficient storage for the result.

   b. Include the function written in Exercise 6a in a working program. Make sure your function is called from `main`. Test the function by passing various data to it.

7. a. Write a function that produces a table of the numbers from 1 to 10, their squares, and cubes. The function should produce the same display as that produced by Program 5.10.

b. Include the function written in Exercise 7a in a working program. Make sure your function is called from `main`. Test the function by passing various data to it.

8. a. Modify the function written for Exercise 7 to accept the starting value of the table, the number of values to be displayed, and the increment between values. Name your function `sel_tab`. A call to `sel_tab(6,5,2);` should produce a table of five lines, the first line starting with the number 6 and each succeeding number increasing by 2.

   b. Include the function written in Exercise 8a in a working program. Make sure your function is called from `main`. Test the function by passing various data to it.

6.2 RETURNING VALUES

Using the method of passing data into a function presented in the previous section, the called function only receives copies of the values contained in the arguments at the time of the call (review Figure 6.3 if this is unclear to you). This method of calling a function and passing values to it is referred to as a *call by value,* and is a distinct advantage of C. Since the called function does not have direct access to any of the calling function's variables, it cannot inadvertently alter the value stored in one of these variables.

When a function is called by value it may process the data sent to it in any fashion desired and directly return at most one, and only one, "legitimate" value to the calling function (see Figure 6.7). In this section we see how such a value is returned to the calling function. As you might expect, given C's flexibility, there is a way of returning more than a single value, but that is the topic of the next section.

As with the calling of a function, directly returning a value requires that the interface between the called and calling functions be handled correctly. From its side of the return transaction, the called function must provide the following items:

• The data type of the returned value
• The actual value being returned

FIGURE 6.7 A Function Returns at Most One Value

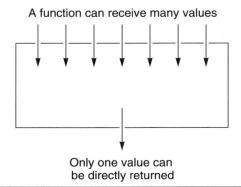

A function can receive many values

Only one value can
be directly returned

A function returning a value must specify, in its header line, the data type of the value that will be returned. Recall that the function header line is the first line of the function, which includes both the function's name and a list of argument names. As an example, consider the `find_max` function written in the last section. It determined the maximum value of two numbers passed to the function. For convenience, the original `find_max` code is listed below.

```
void find_max(int x, int y)
{                         /* start of function body */
   int maxnum;           /* variable declaration */

   if (x >= y)       /* find the maximum number */
     maxnum = x;
   else
     maxnum = y;
   printf("\nThe maximum of the two numbers is %d\n", maxnum);
}  /* end of function body and end of function */
```

As written, the function's header line is `void find_max(int x, int y)`, where `x` and `y` are the names chosen for the function's formal arguments.

If `find_max` is now to return a value, the function's header line must be amended to include the data type of the value being returned. For example, if an integer value is to be returned, the proper function header line is

```
int find_max(int x, int y)
```

Similarly, if the function is to return a floating-point value, the correct function header line is

```
float find_max(int x, int y)
```

and if the function is to return a double-precision value the header line would be

```
double find_max(int x, int y)
```

Let us now modify the function `find_max` to return the maximum value of the two numbers passed to it. To do this, we must first determine the data type of the value that is to be returned and include this data type in the function's header line.

Since the maximum value determined by `find_max` is stored in the integer variable `maxnum`, it is the value of this variable that the function should return. Explicitly specifying that an integer value will be returned from `find_max` requires that the function declaration be `int find_max(int x, int y)`. Observe that this is the same as the original function header line for `find_max` with the substitution of the keyword `int` for the keyword `void`.

Having declared the data type that `find_max` will return, all that remains is to include a statement within the function to cause the return of the correct value. To return a value, a function must use a *return statement*, which has the form:

```
return(expression);
```

When the return statement is encountered, the expression is evaluated first. The value of the expression is then automatically converted to the data type declared in the function header before being sent back to the calling function (the parentheses surrounding the expression are optional). After the value is returned, program control reverts to the calling function. Thus, to return the value stored in maxnum, all we need to do is add the statement return (maxnum); before the closing brace of the find_max function. The complete function code is:

```
       ┌──► int find_max(int x, int y)  /* function header line */
       │    {                           /* start of function body */
These  │      int maxnum;               /* variable declaration */
should │
be the │      if (x >= y)
same   │        maxnum = x;
data   │      else
type   │        maxnum = y;
       │
       │      return(maxnum);           /* return statement */
       └────}
```

In the new code for the function find_max, note that the data type of the expression contained within the parentheses of the return statement correctly matches the data type in the function's header line. It is up to the programmer to ensure that this is so for every function returning a value. Failure to exactly match the return value with the function's declared data type may not result in an error when your program is compiled, but it may lead to undesired results since the return value is always converted to the data type declared in the function declaration. Usually this is a problem only when the fractional part of a returned floating-point or double-precision number is truncated because the function was declared to return an integer value.

Having taken care of the sending side of the return transaction, we must now prepare the calling function to receive the value sent by the called function. On the calling (receiving) side, the calling function must:

- Be alerted to the type of value to expect
- Properly use the returned value

Alerting the calling function as to the type of return value to expect is properly taken care of by the function prototype. For example, including the function prototype

```
int find_max(int, int);
```

with main's variable declarations is sufficient to alert main that find_max is a function that will return an integer value.

To actually use a returned value we must either provide a variable to store the value or use the value directly in an expression. Storing the returned value in a variable is accomplished using a standard assignment statement. For example, the assignment statement

```
max = find_max(firstnum, secnum);
```

can be used to store the value returned by find_max in the variable named max. This assignment statement does two things. First the right-hand side of the assignment statement calls find_max, then the result returned by find_max is stored in the variable max. Since the value returned by find_max is an integer, the variable max must also be declared as an integer variable within the calling function's variable declarations.

The value returned by a function need not be stored directly in a variable, but can be used wherever an expression is valid. For example, the expression 2 * find_max(firstnum, secnum) multiplies the value returned by find_max by two, and the statement printf("%d", find_max(firstnum, secnum)); displays the returned value.

Program 6.3 illustrates the inclusion of both prototype and assignment statements for `main` to correctly declare, call, and store a returned value from `find_max`. As before, and in keeping with our convention of placing the `main` function first, we have placed the `find_max` function after `main`.

PROGRAM 6.3

```
#include <stdio.h>
void main(void)
{
  int firstnum, secnum, max;
  int find_max(int, int);  /* the function prototype */

  printf("\nEnter a number: ");
  scanf("%d", &firstnum);
  printf("Great! Please enter a second number: ");
  scanf("%d", &secnum);

  max = find_max(firstnum, secnum); /* the function is called here */

  printf("\nThe maximum of the two numbers is %d\n", max);
}

 /* following is the function find_max() */

int find_max(int x, int y)
{                    /* start of function body */
  int maxnum;        /* variable declaration */

  if (x >= y)        /* find the maximum number */
    maxnum = x;
  else
    maxnum = y;

  return(maxnum);
}   /* end of function body and end of function */
```

In reviewing Program 6.3 it is important to note the four items we have introduced in this section. The first item is the prototype for `find_max` within `main`. This statement, which ends with a semicolon as all declaration statements do, alerts `main` to the data type that `find_max` will be returning. The parentheses after the name `find_max` inform `main` that `find_max` is a function rather than a variable. The second item to notice in `main` is the use of an assignment statement to store the returned value from the `find_max` call into the variable `maxnum`. We have also made sure to correctly declare `maxnum` as an integer within `main`'s variable declarations so that it matches the data type of the returned value.

The last two items of note concern the coding of the `find_max` function. The first line of `find_max` declares that the function will return an integer value, and the expression in the return statement evaluates to a matching data type. Thus, find_max is internally consistent in sending an integer value back to main, and main has been correctly alerted to receive and use the returned integer.

In writing your own functions you must always keep these four items in mind. For another example, see if you can identify these four items in Program 6.4.

PROGRAM 6.4

```
#include <stdio.h>
#define MAXCOUNT 4
void main(void)
{
  int count;                    /* start of declarations */
  double fahren;

  double tempvert(double);   /* function prototype */

  for(count = 1; count <= MAXCOUNT; count++)
  {
    printf("\nEnter a Fahrenheit temperature: ");
    scanf("%lf", &fahren);
    printf("The Celsius equivalent is %5.2lf\n", tempvert(fahren));
  }
}

/* convert fahrenheit to celsius */
double tempvert(double in_temp)
{
  return( (5.0/9.0) * (in_temp - 32.0) );
}
```

In reviewing Program 6.4 let us first analyze the function tempvert. The complete definition of the function begins with the function's header line and ends with the closing brace after the return statement. The function is declared as a double; this means the expression in the function's return statement must evaluate to a double-precision number, which it does. Since a function header line is not a statement but the start of the code defining the function, the function header line does not end with a semicolon.

On the receiving side, main has a prototype for the function tempvert that agrees with tempvert's function definition. As with all declaration statements, multiple declarations of the same type may be made within the same statement. Thus, we could have used the same declaration statement to declare both the variable fahren and the function tempvert as double-precision data types. If we had done so, the single declaration statement double fahren, tempvert(double); could have been used to replace the two individual declarations for fahren and tempvert. For clarity, however, we will always keep function prototype statements apart from variable declaration statements. No additional variable is declared in main to store the returned value from tempvert because the returned value is immediately passed to printf() for display.

One further point is worth mentioning here. One of the purposes of declarations, as we learned in Chapter 2, is to alert the computer to the amount of internal storage reserved for the data. The prototype within `main` for `tempvert` performs this task and tells the compiler how much storage area must be accessed by `main` when the returned value is retrieved. Had we placed the `tempvert` function before `main`, however, the function header line for `tempvert` would suffice to alert the compiler to the type of storage needed for the returned value. In this case, the function prototype for `tempvert`, within `main`, could be eliminated. Since we have chosen always to list `main` as the first function in a file, we must include function prototypes for all functions called by `main`. This style also serves to document what functions will be accessed by `main`.

Exercises 6.2

1. Rewrite Program 6.3 so that the function `find_max` accepts two floating-point arguments and returns a floating-point value to `main`. Make sure to modify `main` in order to pass two floating-point values to `find_max` and accept and store the floating-point value returned by `find_max`.

2. For the following function headers, determine the number, type, and order (sequence) of values that should be passed to the function when it is called and the data type of the value returned by the function.

   a. `int factorial(int n)`

   b. `double price(int type, double yield, double maturity)`

   c. `double yield(int type, double price, maturity)`

   d. `char interest(char flag, float price, float time)`

   e. `int total(float amount, float rate)`

   f. `float roi(int a, int b, char c, char d, float e, float f)`

   g. `void get_val(int item, int iter, char decflag)`

3. Write function headers for the following:

   a. A function named `check` that has three arguments. The first argument should accept an integer number, the second argument a floating-point number, and the third argument a double-precision number. The function returns no value.

   b. A function named `find_abs` that accepts a double-precision number passed to it and returns its absolute value.

   c. A function named `mult` that accepts two floating-point numbers as arguments, multiplies these two numbers, and returns the result.

   d. A function named `sqr_it` that computes and returns the square of the integer value passed to it.

   e. A function named `powfun` that raises an integer number passed to it to a positive integer power and returns the result.

   f. A function that produces a table of the numbers from 1 to 10, their squares, and cubes. No arguments are to be passed to the function and the function returns no value.

4. a. Write a C function named `find_abs` that accepts a double-precision number passed to it, computes its absolute value, and returns the absolute value to the calling function. The absolute value of a number is the number itself if the number is positive, and the negative of the number if the number is negative.

b. Include the function written in Exercise 4a in a working program. Make sure your function is called from `main` and correctly returns a value to `main`. Have `main` use a `printf()` function call to display the value returned. Test the function by passing various data to it.

5. a. Write a C function called `mult` that accepts two double-precision numbers as arguments, multiplies these two numbers, and returns the result to the calling function.

   b. Include the function written in Exercise 5a in a working program. Make sure your function is called from `main` and correctly returns a value to `main`. Have `main` use a `printf()` function call to display the value returned. Test the function by passing various data to it.

6. a. Write a C function named `powfun` that raises an integer number passed to it to a positive integer power and returns the result to the calling function. Declare the variable used to return the result as a long integer data type to ensure sufficient storage for the result.

   b. Include the function written in Exercise 6a in a working program. Make sure your function is called from `main` and correctly returns a value to `main`. Have `main` use a `printf()` function call to display the value returned. Test the function by passing various data to it.

7. A second-degree polynomial in x is given by the expression $ax^2 + bx + c$, where a, b, and c are known numbers and a is not equal to zero. Write a C function named `poly_two(a,b,c,x)` that computes and returns the value of a second-degree polynomial for any passed values of a, b, c, and x.

8. a. Rewrite the function `tempvert` in Program 6.4 to accept a temperature and a character as arguments. If the character passed to the function is the letter `f`, the function should convert the passed temperature from Fahrenheit to Celsius, else the function should convert the passed temperature from Celsius to Fahrenheit.

   b. Modify the `main` function in Program 6.4 to call the function written for Exercise 8a. Your main function should ask the user for the type of temperature being entered and pass the type (`f` or `c`) into `tempvert`.

9. a. An extremely useful programming algorithm for rounding a real number to n decimal places is:

   Step 1: Multiply the number by 10n.
   Step 2: Add .5.
   Step 3: Delete the fractional part of the result.
   Step 4: Divide by 10^n.

   For example, using this algorithm to round the number 78.374625 to three decimal places yields:

   Step 1: $78.374625 \times 10^3 = 78374.625$
   Step 2: $78374.625 + .5 = 78375.125$
   Step 3: Retaining the integer part = 78375
   Step 4: 78375 divided by $10^3 = 78.375$

   Using this algorithm, write a C program that accepts a user-entered value of money, multiplies the entered amount by an 8.675% interest rate, and displays the result rounded to two decimal places.

   b. Enter, compile, and execute the program written for Exercise 9a.

10. a. Write a C function named `whole` that returns the integer part of any number passed to the function. (*Hint:* Assign the passed argument to an integer variable.)

    b. Include the function written in Exercise 10a in a working program. Make sure your function is called from `main` and correctly returns a value to `main`. Have `main` use a `printf()` function call to display the value returned. Test the function by passing various data to it.

11. a. Write a C function named fracpart that returns the fractional part of any number passed to the function. For example, if the number 256.879 is passed to fracpart, the number .879 should be returned. Have the function fracpart call the function whole that you wrote in Exercise 10. The number returned can then be determined as the number passed to fracpart less the returned value when the same argument is passed to whole. The completed program should consist of main followed by fracpart followed by whole.

   b. Include the function written in Exercise 11a in a working program. Make sure your function is called from main and correctly returns a value to main. Have main use a print() function call to display the value returned. Test the function by passing various data to it.

12. a. Write a function named totamt that accepts four actual integer arguments named quarters, dimes, nickels, and pennies, which represent the number of quarters, dimes, nickels, and pennies in a piggybank. The function should determine the dollar value of the number of quarters, dimes, nickels, and pennies passed to it and display the calculated value.

   b. Include the totamt function written for Exercise 12a in a working program. The main function should correctly call and pass the values of 26 quarters, 80 dimes, 100 nickels, and 216 pennies to totamt. Make sure to do a hand calculation to verify the result displayed by your program.

6.3 FOCUS ON PROBLEM SOLVING

In many mathematical and simulation problems, probability must be considered or statistical sampling techniques must be used. For example, in simulating automobile traffic flow or telephone usage patterns, statistical models are required. Additionally, applications such as simple computer games and more involved "strategy games" in business and science can only be described statistically. All of these statistical models require the generation of *random numbers*, that is, a series of numbers whose order cannot be predicted.

In practice, there are no truly random numbers. Dice never are perfect; cards are never shuffled completely randomly; the supposedly random motions of molecules are influenced by the environment; and digital computers can handle numbers only within a finite range and with limited precision. The best one can do is generate *pseudorandom numbers*, which are sufficiently random for the task at hand.

Some computer languages contain a library function that produces random numbers; other do not. Although a random number generator is not defined for C, almost all C compilers provide a library function named rand for generating random numbers and srand for setting the initial "seed" value. Similarly, Pascal and Modula-2 contain no standard random number generator, although some Pascal and Modula-2 compilers do provide one. Here we present one algorithm for creating our own random numbers. We will use this algorithm in three problems: The first problem will be to simulate the tossing of a coin to determine the number of resulting heads and tails; the second problem will be to create a game of HiLo; and the third problem will be to find an approximation to the area under a curve using Monte Carlo simulation.

Generating Pseudorandom Numbers

Many algorithms have been developed for generating pseudorandom numbers. Some of these algorithms utilize a counting scheme, such as counting bits beginning at some arbitrary location in a changing memory. Another scheme, used here, creates pseudorandom numbers by performing a calculation. A version of this scheme is the *power residue method*.

The power residue method begins with an odd n digit integer, which is referred to as the "seed" number. The seed is multiplied by the value $(10^{n/2} - 3)$. Using the lowest n digits of the result (the "residue") produces a new seed. Continuing this procedure produces a series of random numbers, with each new number used as the seed for the next number. If the original seed has four or more digits (n equal to or greater than 4) and is not divisible by either 2 or 5, this procedure yields $5 \times 10^{(n-2)}$ random numbers before a sequence of numbers repeats itself. For example, starting with a six-digit seed ($n = 6$), such as 654321, a series of $5 \times 10^4 = 50,000$ random numbers can be generated. Using a power residue algorithm we will write a random number generator function.

As an algorithm then, the specific power residue algorithm we will use consists of the following steps:

Step 1: Have a user enter a six-digit integer seed that is not divisible by 2 or 5; this means the number should be an odd number not ending in 5.

Step 2: Multiply the seed number by 997, which is $10^3 - 3$.

Step 3: Extract the lower 6 digits of the result produced by step 2. Use this random number as the next seed.

Step 4: Repeat steps 2 and 3 for as many random numbers as needed.

Thus, if the user-entered seed number is 654321 (step 1), the first random number generated is calculated as follows:

Step 2: 654321 * 997 = 652358037

Step 3: Extract the lower 6 digits of the number obtained in step 2. This is accomplished using a standard programming "trick."

The trick involves these steps:

Step 3a: Divide the number by $10^6 = 1000000$. For example, 652358037 / 1000000 = 652.358037.

Step 3b: Take the integer part of the result of Step 3a. For example, the integer part of 652.358037 = 652.

Step 3c: Multiply the previous result by 10^6. For example, $652 \times 10^6 = 652000000$.

Step 3d: Subtract this result from the original number. For example, 652358037 − 652000000 = 358037.

The integer part of a floating-point number can either be taken by assigning the floating-point number to an integer variable or by a C *cast* (see Section 3.1). In our procedure we will use the cast mechanism. Thus, the algorithm for producing a random number can be accomplished using the following code:

```
i = (int) (997.0 * x / 1.e6);    /* take the integer part */
x = 997.0 * x - i * 1.e6;
```

Incorporating this code into a function, which we have named `randnum`, results in the following:

```
float randnum(float x)
{
  int i;
```

```
      i = (int) (997.0 * X / 1.e6);     /* take the integer part */
      x = 997.0 * x - i * 1.e6;
      return(x);
   }
```

Program 6.5 uses this random number generator function to produce a series of 10 random numbers.

PROGRAM 6.5

```
#include <stdio.h>
#define NUMBERS 10
void main(void)
/* this program generates ten pseudo-random numbers from */
/* a user input "seed" value                             */
{
  int i;
  float seed;
  float randnum(float);    /* this is the name of our random number */
               /* generator function */
  printf("Enter an odd 6-digit number not ending in 5: ");
  scanf("%f", &seed);

  for (i = 1; i <= NUMBERS; ++i)
  {
    seed = randnum(seed);
    printf("%14.6f\n",seed);
  }
}

/* here is the random number generator function */
float randnum(float x)
{
  int i;

  i = (int) (997.0 * x / 1.e6);     /* take the integer part */
  x = 997.0 * x - i * 1.e6;
  return(x);
}
```

A sample run of Program 6.5 follows.

```
        Enter an odd 6-digit number not ending in 5: 654321
        358037.000000
        962889.000000
           333.000000
        332001.000000
          4997.000000
        982009.000000
         62973.000000
        784081.000000
        728757.000000
        570729.000000
```

You should verify that this function does indeed return different sets of random numbers depending on the initially entered seed value.

One slight modification to the `rand` function can be made. Conventionally, random number generators are used to produce values within the range of 0.0 to 1.0. To produce such numbers using the `rand` function, we simply divide the computed value by 10^6 before it is returned from the function.

Having created a random number generator, we will now use it to solve three different problems.

Problem 1: Create a Coin Toss Simulation

A common use of random numbers is to simulate events using a program, rather than going through the time and expense of constructing a real-life experiment. For example, statistical theory tells us that the probability of having a single tossed coin turn up heads is 50%. Similarly, there is a 50% probability of having a single tossed coin turn up tails.

Using these probabilities we would expect a single coin that is tossed 1000 times to turn up heads 500 times and tails 500 times. In practice, however, this is never exactly realized for a single experiment consisting of 1000 tosses. Instead of actually tossing a coin 1000 times we can use a random number generator to simulate these tosses. In particular, we will use the random number function developed in the previous application.

Analyze the Problem for Input/Output Requirements   For this problem two outputs are required: the percentage of heads and the percentage of tails that result when a simulated coin is tossed 1000 times. Additionally, one input item will be required for us to use our random number generator function: an odd six-digit user-input integer that does not end in the digit 5. We will have to prompt the user to enter this number.

Develop a Solution   The percentage of heads and tails are determined as:

$$\text{Percentage of heads} = \frac{\text{Number of heads}}{1000} \times 100\%$$

$$\text{Percentage of tails} = \frac{\text{Number of tails}}{1000} \times 100\%$$

To determine the number of heads and tails, we will have to simulate 1000 random numbers in such a manner that we can define a result of "heads" or "tails" from each generated number. There are a number of ways to do this.

One way is to use our random number generator to generate integers between 0 and 1,000,000 by truncating the returned number. Knowing that any single toss has a 50% chance of being either a head or a tail, we could designate a "head" as an even random number and a "tail" as an odd random number. Another identification scheme would be to designate "head" as any random number between 0 and 55,555, and a "tail" as any random number between 55,556 and 100,000. A third method would be to modify our random number generator to return a random number between 0 and 1 as described earlier. Then we could define a "head" as any number greater than 0.5 and any other result as a "tail." This is the algorithm we will adopt. Since the rand function created in the previous application returns a random number between 0 and 999,999, we will divide the returned number by 1,000,000 to produce a random number between 0 and 1.

Having defined how we will create a single toss that has a 50% chance of turning up heads or tails, the generation of 1000 tosses is rather simple: We use a fixed count loop that generates 1000 random numbers. For each generation we identify the result as either a head or tail, and accumulate the results in a heads and tails counter. Thus, the complete simulation algorithm is given by the pseudocode:

Initialize a heads count to zero.
Initialize a tails count to zero.
For 1000 times
    Generate a random number between 0 and 1
    If the random number is greater than .5
        Consider this as a head and
        Add one to the heads count
    Else
        Consider this as a tail and
        Add one to the tails count
    End if
End for
Calculate the percentage of heads as
    the number of heads divided by 1000 × 100%.
Calculate the percentage of tails as
    the number of tails divided by 1000 × 100%.
Print the percentage of heads and tails obtained.

Code the Solution   Program 6.6 codes this algorithm in C.
Two sample runs of Program 6.6 follow.

```
Enter an odd 6-digit number not ending in 5: 654321

       Heads came up 49.599998 percent of the time
       Tails came up 50.400002 percent of the time
```

and

```
Enter an odd 6-digit number not ending in 5: 876543

       Heads came up 51.299999 percent of the time
       Tails came up 48.700001 percent of the time
```

Writing and executing Program 6.6 is certainly easier than manually tossing a coin 1000 times. It should be noted that the validity of the results produced by the program depends on how random the numbers produced by the random number function actually are.

Test and Debug the Program   Program 6.6 must pass two tests. The more important test concerns the randomness of each generated number. This, of course, is really a test of the random number

PROGRAM 6.6

```c
#include <stdio.h>
#define NUMTOSSES 1000
void main(void)
/* a program to simulate the tossing of a coin NUMTOSSES times */
{
  int heads, tails, i;
  float seed, x, flip, perheads, pertails;
  float randnum(float);        /* function prototype */

  printf("Enter an odd 6-digit number not ending in 5: ");
  scanf("%f", &seed);
  heads = 0;         /* initialize heads count */
  tails = 0;         /* initialize tails count */

  /* simulate NUMTOSSES tosses of a coin */
  for (i = 1; i <= NUMTOSSES; ++i)
  {
    seed = randnum(seed);
    flip = seed / 1.e6;    /* normalize the number between 0 and 1 */
    if (flip > 0.5)
      heads = heads + 1;
    else
      tails = tails + 1;
  }
  perheads = (heads / (float) NUMTOSSES) * 100.0;  /* calculate heads percentage */
  pertails = (tails / (float) NUMTOSSES) * 100.0;  /* calculate tails percentage */
  printf("\nHeads came up %f percent of the time\n", perheads);
  printf("Tails came up %f percent of the time\n", pertails);
}

float randnum(float x)
{
  int i;

  i = 997.0 * x / 1.e6;     /* take the integer part */
  x = 997.0 * x - i * 1.e6;
  return(x);
}
```

function. For our purposes, we have used a previously written function using an algorithm that ensures generation of a series of 50,000 random numbers before the sequence of numbers repeats. So at this point we accept the "randomness" of the generator (see Exercise 4 at the end of this section for a method of verifying the function's randomness.)

Once the question of the random number generator has been settled, the second test requires that we correctly generate 1000 numbers and accumulate a head and tail count. That this process is correctly accomplished is adequately verified by a simple desk check of the for loop within Program 6.6. Also, we do know that the result of the simulation must be close to 50% heads and 50% tails. The results of the simulation verify this to be the case.

Problem 2: Write a HiLo Computer Game

For this problem a computer game named HiLo is required. In this game the computer chooses an integer number between 0 and 100 and asks the user/player to guess its value. Guesses are counted and the player is told after each incorrect guess whether the guess was too high or too low, and is asked for another guess. When the player has found the number, he or she is told how many guesses it took.

Analyze the Problem for Input/Output Requirements   The generation of a random number will require that the user be asked for an odd six-digit seed number not ending in 5. Additionally, the user will repeatedly be asked to input a guess until the randomly generated number is found. When the correct guess is made, the program is required to display the number of guesses.

Develop a Solution   Upon entry of the user-selected seed, a random number between 0 and 100 must be generated. This is easily accomplished by generating a random number between 0 and 1, multiplying it by 100, and taking the integer part of the result. That is,

$$number = (int)(100.0 * random\ number)$$

A loop, beginning with a count of 0, can then be used to ask for the guess, increment count, compare the guess with the number, and repeat until the guess equals the number. A do structure ensures that the player gets to guess at least once. The pseudocode describing this procedure is:

Ask for the seed.
Generate a random number.
Initialize count = 0.
Do
    Ask for guess
    Increment count
    If guess < random number
       Print "Too Low"
    Else If guess > random number
       Print "Too High"
While guess does not equal random number
Write count.

Code the Solution   Program 6.7 presents the algorithm written as C code:

PROGRAM 6.7

```c
#include <stdio.h>
#define DEBUG 0
void main(void)
{
  int guess, count, val;
  float seed;
  float randnum(float);

  printf("Enter an odd 6-digit number not ending in 5: ");
  scanf("%f", &seed);

  seed = randnum(seed);
  val = (int) ((seed/1.e6) * 100);
  if (DEBUG)
    printf("seed = %f  val = %d", seed, val);
  count = 0;

  do
  {
    printf("\nEnter your guess: ");
    scanf("%d", &guess);
    count++;
    if (guess < val)
      printf("\nYour guess was too low - guess again!");
    else if (guess > val)
      printf("\nYour guess was too high - guess again!");
  } while (guess != val);

  printf("\nCongratulations! You did it in %d guesses\n", count);
}
float randnum(float x)
{
  int i;

  i = (int)(997.0 * x / 1.e6);
  x = 997.0 * x - i * 1.e6;
  return(x);
}
```

Test and Debug the Program   Included within Program 6.7 is the named constant, DEBUG. When this constant is set to 1, the program will display its randomly generated number. Using this display, we can run the program and select guesses that are known to be too high and too low to see that the program reacts correctly. Once this testing is done, the debug constant should be set to 0. Here is a sample run.

```
Enter an odd 6-digit number not ending in 5: 456789

Enter your guess: 50
```

```
Your guess was too high - guess again!
Enter your guess: 25

Your guess was too low - guess again!
Enter your guess: 37

Your guess was too low - guess again!
Enter your guess: 41

Congratulations! You did it in 4 guesses
```

Problem 3: Use Monte Carlo Simulation to Estimate the Area Under a Curve

Here is a more serious application of random numbers. It uses a technique called the *Monte Carlo method,* by which large numbers of experiments involving random outcomes are performed to find an approximate solution to a problem.

The area under a curve can be approximated by using Monte Carlo simulation. To understand how this simulation works, consider that we wish to determine the area under the curve $y = f(x)$ shown in Figure 6.8, between the limits $x = a$ and $x = b$. On top of this curve we build a rectangular box bounded by the x axis, the lines $x = a$, $x = b$, and the line defined by the curve at its highest y value.

Now assume that we toss N darts at random into the rectangular box and that M of these darts land between the curve and the x axis. Calculate the ratio M/N as

$$\frac{M}{N} = \frac{\text{Number of darts between the curve and the } x \text{ axis}}{\text{Total number of darts in the box}}$$

The ratio M/N will be approximately equal to the ratio of the shaded area under the curve to the total area of the box; that is:

$$\frac{M}{N} \approx \frac{\text{Area under the curve (shaded area)}}{\text{Total area of the box}}$$

FIGURE 6.8   A General Curve $y = f(x)$

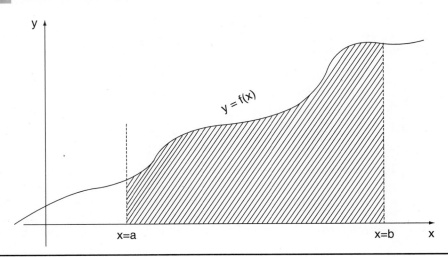

A BIT OF BACKGROUND

Monte Carlo

Monte Carlo is a community within the principality of Monaco on the Mediterranean coast of France. Monte Carlo's fame as a gambling resort is responsible for its name being adopted for mathematical methods involving random numbers.

Monte Carlo techniques involve creating random numbers within given limits and determining what percentage of those numbers meet certain criteria. They can be used to calculate the area between curves (as in this section), to estimate the arrival of airplanes at an airport, to predict the percentage of manufactured parts that will be defective, to project the growth and decline of populations with fixed resources, to specify the need thickness of nuclear-reactor shielding, and so forth.

Monte Carlo calculations were hardly feasible before the development of high-speed computers. In many cases, billions of random numbers must be generated in order to achieve statistically accurate results. If, on a superfast computer, one random number selection and test calculation required a microsecond, then a billion calculations would take about 1000 seconds (roughly 17 minutes). On a typical 486-style personal computer, where the same calculation could take a millisecond, a billion such calculations would require a million seconds (or eleven and a half days).

Clearly the speed and capacity of a computer are critical for effective application of Monte Carlo techniques. It has not been unusual for a single highly accurate computation of this nature to monopolize a ten-million-dollar computer for hours. However, new parallel-processing machines, which can handle many operations concurrently, are reducing the time required for Monte Carlo calculations using large data samples.

From this, we can calculate the area under the curve as:

$$\text{Area under the curve (shaded area)} \approx \text{Total area of the box} \left(\frac{M}{N}\right)$$

where the total area of the box is found by multiplying the length by the width. The problem is to write a computer program that effectively tosses darts and determines the area under any curve $y = f(x)$ between the limits $x = a$ and $x = b$.

Analyze the Problem for Input/Output Requirements   The inputs required for this problem will be

1. The equation of the curve we want the area for
2. The lower x limit, a, between which the area is to be calculated
3. The upper x limit, b, between which the area is to be calculated
4. A user-entered seed number to generate the series of random numbers that will be used to simulate the throwing of "darts"

The output will be the approximate area under the curve.

Develop a Solution   We will restrict ourselves to functions and ranges in which the curve is generally increasing or decreasing within the desired range, and in which the curve lies entirely above the x axis. These restrictions are not necessary

FIGURE 6.9 Structure Chart for Monte Carlo Estimation of Curve Area

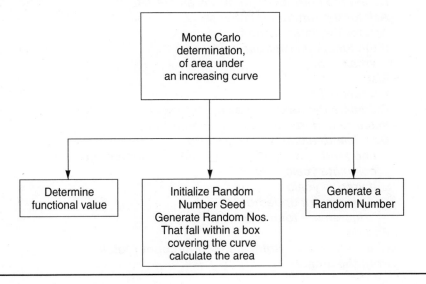

to find the area, but help to simplify the solution. The increasing/decreasing restriction makes it easy to locate the maximum y value, because for increasing curves the maximum y value occurs at $x = b$ and has the value $f(b)$. For decreasing curves the maximum y value occurs at $x = a$ and has the value $f(a)$. Requiring that the curve lie above the x axis removes the problem of assessing which parts of the curve are above and below the x axis.

The equation $y = f(x)$ for the curve will be written in a function that finds y for a given argument value of x. For example, if the function is $y = 3x^2 + 2x + 1$, the function is simply:

```
float fcn(float x)
{
   return (3.0 * pow(x,2) + 2.0 * x + 1.0);
}
```

For any other function $y = f(x)$, just replace the content of the return statement with the expression defining $f(x)$.

The formula for determining the total area of the box is $width * length = (b - a) * ymax$, where $ymax = f(b)$ for an increasing curve and $f(a)$ for a decreasing curve.

Now choose a pair of random numbers, xrnd and yrnd such that $a \leq$ xrnd $\leq b$ and $0 \leq$ yrnd $\leq$ ymax to simulate the coordinates where a dart would land in the box. A random number between a and b can be found using the equation $(b-a) * random\ number + a$. Using xrnd, determine ycalc = f(xrnd), and then determine if yrnd lies under the curve; that is, whether yrnd $\leq$ ycalc. If so, increment the count of numbers under the curve. Increment the count of total number of points selected. Repeat this process for a large number of randomly selected points. Then calculate and display the area under the curve.

A structure chart for the solution is shown in Figure 6.9. The pseudocode for this solution is:

Define the function fcn(x).
Define whether the function is increasing or decreasing.
Define the number of iterations as MAXREPS.
Ask for the random number seed.
Ask for the limits a and b.
If the function is increasing
  ymax = f(b)
Else
  ymax = f(a)
Calculate the total area as (b−a)(ymax).
Initialize undercount and totalcount to zero.
Do while totalcount ≤ MAXREPS
  find xrnd and yrnd using the random number generator
  calculate ycalc = f(xrnd)
  If yrnd ≤ ycalc
    increment undercount
    increment totalcount
End do.
Calculate area = (total area)(undercount / totalcount).
Print the area.

Code the Solution   Program 6.8 presents the algorithm written as C code:

PROGRAM 6.8

```c
#include <stdio.h>
#include <math.h>
#define MAXCOUNT 1000
#define INCREASE 1     /* this is an increasing curve */

float fcn(float x)
{
  return (3.0*pow(x,2) + 2.0*x + 1.0);
}

void main(void)
{
  int undercount = 0, totalcount = 0;
  float x, seed, val, xrnd, yrnd, ymax, ycalc, a, b, boxarea, area;
  float randnum(float), fcn(float);

  printf("\nEnter an odd 6-digit number not ending in 5: ");
  scanf("%f", &seed);
  printf("What is the lower limit on x? ");
  scanf("%f", &a);
  printf("What is the upper limit on x? ");
  scanf("%f", &b);

  if (INCREASE)
    ymax = fcn(b);
```

(continued on next page)

```
(continued from previous page)
    ymax = fcn(b);
  else
    ymax = fcn(a);
  boxarea = (b - a) * ymax;

  while (totalcount < MAXCOUNT)
  {
    seed = randnum(seed);   /* get a random x value */
    val = seed/1.e6;        /* creates a number between 0 and 1 */
    xrnd = (b - a) * val + a;
    seed = randnum(seed);   /* get a random y value */
    val = seed/1.e6;
    yrnd = ymax * val;
    if (yrnd <= fcn(xrnd))
      undercount++;
    totalcount++;
  }

  area = boxarea * (float)undercount/(float)totalcount;

  printf("\nFor the curve defined in the function fcn(x),\n");
  printf("between x = %5.2f and x = %5.2f\n", a, b);
  printf("The area is approximately %f\n", area);
}

float randnum(float x)
{
  int i;

  i = (int)(997.0 * x / 1.e6);   /* take the integer part */
  x = 997.0 * x - i * 1.e6;
  return(x);
}
```

Notice that we have placed the `fcn` function, which defines the curve, at the top of the program. This is to alert us that this function must be changed for each curve $y = f(x)$.

Test and Debug the Program   During the testing phase statements could be inserted into the code to display the values of `xrnd`, `yrnd`, `ycalc`, `undercount`, and `totalcount` during each iteration. If you assign a very large value to `MAXREPS`, you may want to print a message during each iteration that tells the user that the program is executing. Test the program for various values of *a* and *b*. Increase `MAXREPS` for greater accuracy. Alter the function $f(x)$ to find the area under a different curve. If you are comfortable with calculus, compare your answers with the integral of the function; otherwise, sketch the curve on graph paper and estimate the area to see if you are getting reasonable results. A sample run looks like:

```
Enter an odd 6-digit number not ending in 5: 456789
What is the lower limit on x? 2.0
What is the upper limit on x? 4.0
For the curve defined in the function fcn(x),
between x =   2.00 and x =   4.00
The area is approximately 69.084000

The true area under the curve between x = 2.0 and x = 4.0 is
70.0.
```

Exercises 6.3

1. Modify Program 6.6 so that it requests the number of tosses from the user. (*Hint:* Make sure the program correctly determines the percentages of heads and tails obtained.)

2. (Central limit theorem simulation) Modify Program 6.6 so that it automatically generates 20 simulations, with each simulation having 1000 tosses. Print the percentage for each run and the percentages for the 20 runs combined.

3. Modify the Program 6.7 to allow the user to run the game again after a game has been completed. The program should display the message "WOULD YOU LIKE TO PLAY AGAIN - 'Y'/'N'?: " and restart if the user enters either 'Y' or 'y'.

4. a. Write a program that tests the effectiveness of the random number generator used in Program 6.5. Start by initializing 10 counters, such as zerocount, onecount, twocount, ... ninecount to 0. Then generate a large number of pseudorandom integers between 0 and 9. Each time a 0 occurs, increment zerocount; when a 1 occurs, increment onecount; etc. Finally, print the percentage of the time each number occurred.

   b. Rerun the program you wrote for Exercise 4a using different seed values. Try some even seed values and some odd seed values that end in 5 to determine whether these affect the randomness of the numbers.

5. Redo Exercise 4 using the srand and rand library functions that come with almost all C compilers. These functions are provided to create new "seed" values and generate sequences of pseudorandom numbers.

6. In the game of Blackjack the cards 2 through 10 are counted at their face values, regardless of suit, all picture cards (jack, queen, and king) are counted as 10, and an ace is counted as either a 1 or 11, depending on the total count of all the cards in a player's hand. The ace is counted as 11 only if the total value of all cards in a player's hand does not exceed 21, else it is counted as a 1. Using this information write a C program that uses a random number generator to select three cards (a 1 initially corresponding to an ace, a 2 corresponding to a face card of two, and so on), calculate the total value of the hand appropriately, and display the value of the three cards with a printed message.

7. Write a C function that determines the quadrant in which a line drawn from the origin resides. The determination of the quadrant is made using the angle that the line makes with the positive X as follows:

Angle from the Positive X Axis	**Quadrant**
Between 0 and 90 degrees	1
Between 90 and 180 degrees	2
Between 180 and 270 degrees	3
Between 270 and 360 degrees	4

Note: If the angle is exactly 0, 90, 180, or 270 degrees, the corresponding line does not reside in any quadrant but lies on an axis. For this situation, your function should return a zero. An invalid angle should result in a return value of –1.

8. All years that are evenly divisible by 400 or are evenly divisible by 4 and not evenly divisible by 100 are leap years. For example, since 1600 is evenly divisible by 400, the year 1600 was a leap year. Similarly, since 1988 is evenly divisible by 4 but not by 100, the year 1988 was also a leap year. Using this information, write a C function that accepts the year as an input, and returns a 1 if the passed year is a leap year or a 0 if it is not.

9. Based on an automobile's model year and weight the State of New Jersey determines the car's weight class and registration fee using the following schedule:

Model Year	Weight	Registration Fee
1970 or earlier	Less than 2700 lbs	$16.50
	2700 to 3800 lbs	25.50
	More than 3800 lbs	46.50
1971 to 1979	Less than 2700 lbs	27.00
	2700 to 3800 lbs	30.50
	More than 3800 lbs	52.50
1980 or later	Less than 3500 lbs	19.50
	3500 or more lbs	52.50

Using this information, write a C subprogram function that accepts the year and weight of an automobile and returns the registration fee for the car.

10. Deal and display a hand of four different cards that can come from four different suits (heart, club, diamond, spade) of 13 cards each named ACE = 1, 2, 3, 4, 5, 6, 7, 8, 9, 10, Jack = 11, Queen = 12, King = 13. [*Hint:* Use the expressions `suit = (int)(4.0 * random number + 1.0)` and `card = (int)(13.0 * random number + 1)`, where the random number is between 0 and 1.]

11. It has been suggested that a monkey pushing keys at random on a typewriter could produce the works of Shakespeare, given sufficient time. Simulate this by having a program select and display letters at random. Count the number of letters typed until the program produces one of the two-letter words *at, is, he, we, up,* or *on.* When one of these words is produced, stop the program and display the total number of letters typed. (*Hint:* Choose a letter by selecting a random integer number between 1 and 26.)

12. Write a program to simulate the rolling of two dice. If the total of the two dice is 7 or 11 you win; otherwise, you lose. Embellish this program as much as you like, with betting, different odds, different combinations for win or lose, stopping play when you have no money left or reach the house limit, displaying the dice, etc. [*Hint:* Calculate the dots showing on each die by the expression `dots = (int)(6.0 * random number + 1)`, where the random number is between 0 and 1.]

13. Modify the value of the named constant MAXCOUNT to 10, 100, and 10,000, respectively, and rerun Program 6.8 to see how these values affect the accuracy of the result. For each of these values, run the program with seed values of 123457, 234567, and 456789. Fill in the following table with the area reported by each run of the program. Comment on what did occur and what you think should have occurred. If there were any differences between what did occur and what you expected, comment on what you think the differences were caused by.

	MAXCOUNT			
	10	100	1000	10000
Seed = 123457				
Seed = 234567				
Seed = 456789				

14. Use the Monte Carlo algorithm developed in Program 6.8 to find an approximate value for π, which is 3.14159 accurate to five decimal places. In Figure 6.10, the

FIGURE 6.10 Calculation of π

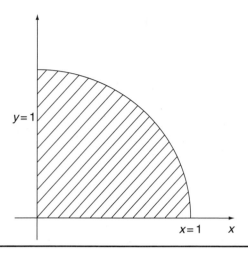

shaded area represents one quarter of a circle having a radius, r, of 1 unit. The area of the box bounded by the axes and the lines $x = 1$ and $y = 1$ is 1 square unit. The area of the quarter-circle is $1/4\ \pi\ r^2$, but since $r = 1$ this area equals $\pi/4$ square units. Therefore,

$$\frac{\pi}{4} = \frac{\text{Area of quarter circle}}{\text{Area of the box}} \approx \frac{M}{N}$$

where M is the number of random numbers that fall under the curve and N is the total number of random numbers selected within the box. Generate random points inside the box (xrnd, yrnd) such that $0 \le$ xrnd ≤ 1 and $0 \le$ yrnd ≤ 1, and test to see if yrnd $\le$ ycalc, where ycalc $=$ f(xrnd), and $f(x)$ is the curve defined by the circle

$$y = f(x) = \text{sqrt}(1 - x^2)$$

15. Here is a version of a problem called "the random walk." It can be extended to two or three dimensions and used to simulate molecular motion, to determine the effectiveness of reactor shielding, or to calculate a variety of other probabilities.

Assume that your very tired and sleepy pet dog leaves his favorite lamp post on warm summer evenings and staggers randomly either 2 steps in the direction towards home or 1 step in the opposite direction. After the first step the dog again staggers randomly two steps toward home or one step backward, and does this again, and again. If the pet reaches a total distance of 10 steps from the lamp post in the direction toward home, you find him and take him home. If the dog arrives back at the lamp post before reaching 10 steps in the direction toward home, he lies down and spends the night at the foot of the lamp post.

Write a C program that simulates 500 summer evenings, and calculate and print the percentage of the time your pet sleeps at home for these evenings. [*Hint:* In a loop, determine forward or backward based on the value of a random number. Accumulate the distance the dog has reached toward your home. If the distance reaches 10, stop the loop and increment the home count. If the distance reaches 0 before it reaches 10, stop the loop but do not increment the home count. Repeat this loop 500 times and find the ratio of (home count)/500.]

6.4 ENRICHMENT STUDY: INTRODUCTION TO ABSTRACTION

A very important programming concept, and one that you will increasingly encounter as you progress in your studies, is the idea of abstraction. This concept is fundamentally applied to three areas: data type abstraction, procedural abstraction, and abstract data types—all of which you now have the background to understand. In this section we first introduce the concept of abstraction and then use it to define these three types of abstractions.

In its most general usage, an abstraction is simply an idea or term that identifies general qualities or characteristics of a group of objects, independent of any one specific object in the group. For example, consider the term "car." As a term this is an abstraction: It refers to a group of objects that individually contain the characteristics associated with a car, such as a motor, passenger compartment, wheels, steering capabilities, brakes, etc. A particular instance of a car, such as my car or your car are not abstractions—they are real objects that are classified as "type car" because they have the attributes associated with a car.

Although we use abstract concepts all the time, we tend not to think of them as such. For example, the words tree, dog, cat, table, and chair are all abstractions, just as a car is. Each of these terms refers to a set of qualities that are met by a group of particular things. For each of these abstractions there are many individual trees, dogs, and cats, each instance of which conforms to the general characteristics associated with the abstract term.

In programming, especially in more advanced work, we are much more careful to label appropriate terms as abstractions than we are in everyday life. The first such term that is really an abstraction is a data type. Let us see why this is so.

Just as "my car" is a particular instance or object of the more abstract "type car," a particular integer, say, 5 for example, is a specific object or instance of the more abstract "type integer," where an integer is a signed or unsigned number having no decimal point. As such, each type—integer, character, and floating point—is considered an abstraction that defines a general type of which specific instances can be realized. Such types, then, simply identify common qualities of each group and make it reasonable to speak of integer types, character types, and floating-point types.

Having defined what we mean by a type, we can now create the definition of a data type. In programming terminology a data type consists of *both* an acceptable range of values of a particular type *and* a set of operations that can be applied to those values. Thus, the integer data type not only defines range of acceptable integer values, but also defines what operations can be applied to those values.

Although users of programming languages such as C ordinarily assume that mathematical operations such as addition, subtraction, multiplication, and division will be supplied for integers, the designers of C had to consider carefully what operations would be provided as part of the integer data type. For example, the designers of C did not include an exponentiation operator as part of the integer data type, while this operation is included in FORTRAN's data abstraction of integers (in C, exponentiation is supplied as a library function).

To summarize then, a data type is an abstraction that consists of *a set of values of a particular type* and *a set of operations that can be applied to those values.*

The set of allowed values is more formally referred to as the data type's *domain*. Table 6.1 lists the domain and the most common operations defined for the data types int, float, and char.[3]

Built-in and Abstract Data Types (ADTs)

All of the data type listed in Table 6.1 are provided as part of the C language. As such, they are formally referred to as *built-in* or *primitive* data types (the two terms are synonyms). In contrast to built-in data types, some programming languages permit programmers to create their own data types; that is, define a type of value with an associated domain and operations that can be performed on the acceptable values. Such user-defined data types are formally referred to as *abstract data types*. Although C does not provide the capability to create abstract data types, it is provided in C++. In C++ abstract data types are called *classes*, and the ability to create classes is the major enhancement provided to C by C++ (in fact, the original name for C++ was *C with Classes*.)

Procedural Abstraction

The assigning of a name to a data type, as we have seen, refers to data abstraction. In addition to this type of abstraction, all programming languages permit assigning a name to a procedure or function. As a specific example, consider the printf() function. This function internally consists of a sequence of instructions that provide for the formatted display of data. The instructions, however, are invoked as a unit using the single name printf.

The assigning of a name to a function or procedure in such a way that the function is invoked by simply using a name with appropriate arguments is formally referred to as *procedural abstraction*. In writing your own user-named functions you are actually creating procedural abstractions.

Notice that procedural abstraction effectively hides the implementation details of how a function actually performs its task. This hiding of the details is one of the hallmarks and strengths of abstraction. By thinking of tasks on an abstract procedural level, programmers can solve problems at a higher level without immediately being concerned with the nitty-gritty details of the actual solution implementation.

6.5 COMMON PROGRAMMING ERRORS

An extremely common programming error related to functions is passing incorrect data types. The values passed to a function must correspond to the data types of the arguments declared for the function. One way to verify that correct values have been received is to display all passed values within a function's body before any calculations are made. Once this verification has taken place, the display can be dispensed with.[4]

---

[3]The actual domain for integers can be found in the <limits.h> header file supplied by your compiler. Similarly, the domain for floating-point numbers can be found in the header file <float.h>.

[4]The practice, a good debugger program should be used. The use of debuggers is beyond the scope of this text.

Another common error is omitting the called function's prototype within the calling function. The called function must be alerted to the type of value that will be returned, and this information is provided by the function prototype. The prototype can be omitted if the called function is physically placed in a program before its calling function. Although it is also permissible to omit the prototype and return type for functions returning an integer, it is poor documenting practice to do so. The actual value returned by a function can be verified by displaying it both before and after it is returned.

The last two common errors are terminating a function's header line with a semicolon and forgetting to include the data type of a function's arguments within the header line.

6.6 CHAPTER REVIEW

Key Terms

actual arguments	function header
call by value	function prototype
called function	parameters
calling function	return statement
formal arguments	stubs
function body	

Summary

1. A function is called by giving its name and passing any data to it in the parentheses following the name. If a variable is one of the arguments in a function call, the called function receives a copy of the variable's value.

2. The commonly used form of a user-written function is:

```
return-type function-name(argument declarations)
{
    declarations and other C statements;
    return(expression);
}
```

The first line of the function is called the *function header.* The opening and closing braces of the function and all statements in between these braces constitute the function's *body.*

3. A function's return type is the data type of the value returned by the function. If no type is declared, the function is assumed to return an integer value. If the function does not return a value, it should be declared as a void type.

4. Functions can directly return at most a single data type value to their calling functions. This value is the value of the expression in the return statement.

5. Functions can be declared to all calling functions by means of a *function prototype.* The prototype provides a declaration for a function that specifies the data type returned by the function, its name, and the data types of the arguments expected by the function. As with all declarations, a function prototype is terminated with a semicolon and may be included within local variable declarations or as a global declaration. The most common form of a function prototype is:

```
data-type function-name(argument data types);
```

If the called function is placed physically above the calling function, no further declaration is required, since the function's definition serves as a global declaration to all following functions.

Exercises

1. A function is defined by the following code:

```
float fraction-to-decimal (float numerator, float denominator)
{
  return(numerator/denominator);
}
```

Write the shortest driver program module you can to test this function and check the passing of parameters.

2. A formula to raise a real number a to the real power b is given by the formula

$$a^b = e^{[(b * \ln(a))]}$$

where a must be positive and b must be positive or zero. Using this formula, write a function named power that accepts a and b as real values and returns a^b.

3. A fraction handling program contains this menu:

   A. Add two fractions
   B. Convert a fraction to decimal
   C. Multiply two fractions
   Q. Quit

   a. Write C code for the program with stub functions for the choices. All functions should return a floating point value.

   b. Insert the function FractionToDecimal from Exercise 1 into the code with appropriate commands to pass and display the parameters.

   c. Complete the program by replacing the stub functions with functions that perform appropriate operations.

4. a. The time in hours, minutes, and seconds is to be passed to a function named totsec. Write totsec to accept these values, determine the total number of seconds in the passed data, and display the calculated value.

   b. Include the totsec function written for Exercise 4a in a working program. The main function should correctly call totsec and display the value returned by the function. Use the following test data to verify your program's operation: hours = 10, minutes = 36, and seconds = 54. Make sure you do a hand calculation to verify the result displayed by your program.

5. A value that is sometimes useful is the greatest common divisor of two integers $n1$ and $n2$. A famous mathematician, Euclid, discovered an efficient method to do this over two thousand years ago (See Exercise 6). Right now, however, we'll settle for a stub. Write the integer function stub gcd(n1, n2). Simply have it return a value that suggests it received its arguments correctly. (*Hint:* $n1$ + $n2$ is a good choice of return values. Why isn't $n1$ / $n2$ a good choice?)

6. Euclid's method for finding the greatest common divisor (GCD) of two positive integers consists of the following steps:

   Divide the larger number by the smaller and retain the remainder.

   Divide the smaller number by the remainder, again retaining the remainder.

Continue dividing the prior remainder by the current remainder until the remainder is zero, at which point the last nonzero remainder is the greatest common divisor.

For example, assume the two positive integers are 84 and 49. We then have:

Step a: 84/49 yields a remainder of 35.

Step b: 49/35 yields a remainder of 14.

Step c: 35/14 yields a remainder of 7.

Step c: 14/7 yields a remainder of 0.

Thus, the last nonzero remainder, which is 7, is the greatest common divisor of 84 and 49.

Using Euclid's algorithm, replace the stub function written for Exercise 5 with an actual function that determines and returns the GCD of its two integer arguments.

7. a. Write a function named `tax` that accepts a dollar amount and a tax rate as formal arguments, and returns the tax due on the dollar amount. For example, if the numbers 100.00 and .06 are passed to the function, the value returned should be 6.00, which is 100.00 times .06.

   b. Include the `tax` function written for Exercise 7a in a working program. The `main` function should correctly call `tax` and display the value returned by the function.

8. a. Write a function named `daycount` that accepts a month, day, and year as its input arguments, calculates an integer representing the total number of days from the turn of the century corresponding to the passed date, and returns the calculated integer to the calling function. For this problem assume that each year has 365 days and each month has 30 days. Test your function by verifying that the date 1/1/00 returns a day count of one.

   b. Include the `daycount` function written for Exercise 8a in a working program. The `main` function should correctly call `daycount` and display the integer returned by the function.

9. a. A clever and simple method of preparing to sort dates into either ascending (increasing) or descending (decreasing) order is to first convert a date having the form month/day/year into an integer number using the formula *date = year * 10000 + month * 100 + day*. For example, using this formula the date 12/6/88 converts to the integer 881206 and the date 2/28/90 converts to the integer 900228. Sorting the resulting integer numbers automatically puts the dates into the correct order. Using this formula, write a function named `convertdays` that accepts a month, day, and year, converts the passed data into a single date integer, and returns the integer to the calling function.

   b. Include the `convertdays` function written for Exercise 9a in a working program. The `main` function should correctly call `convertdays` and display the integer returned by the function.

10. The following program uses the same variable names in both the calling and called function. Determine if this causes any problem for the compiler.

```
#include <stdio.h>
void main(void)
{
    int min, hour, sec;
    int time(int, int);   /* function prototype */

    printf("Enter two numbers: ");
    scanf("%d %d", &min, &hour);
    sec = time(min, hour);
    printf("The total number of seconds is %d", sec);

}
int time(int min, int hour)
{
    int sec;

    sec = (hour * 60 + min) * 60;
    return (sec);
}
```

11. Write a program that reads a key pressed on the keyboard and displays its code on the screen. Use the program to determine the code for the ENTER key. Then write a function named ReadOneChar that reads a character and ignores any succeeding characters until the ENTER key is pressed. The entered character should be returned by the function.

12. Write a function named pass() that returns a reject or accept code depending on whether the mean tolerance of a group of parts is less than or greater than 1.0% The tolerances should be passed to the function as an array and the function should calculate the average of the passed values. If the average is less than 1.0%, the function should return an A, for accept, else it should return an R, for reject.

13 a. Write and test a C function MakeMilesKmTable to display a table of miles converted to kilometers. The arguments to the function should be the starting and stopping values of miles and the increment. The output should be a table of miles and their equivalent kilometer values. Use the relationship that one mile is 1.61 kilometers.

   b. Modify the function written for Exercise 13a so that two columns are printed. For example, if the starting value is 1 mile, the ending value 20 miles, and the increment is 1, the display should look like:

Miles = Kilometer		Miles = Kilometers	
1	1.61	11	17.70
2	3.22	12	19.31
.	. .	.	.
.	.	.	.
10	16.09	20	32.18

   [*Hint:* Find split = (start + stop)/2. Let a loop execute from miles = start to split, and calculate and print across one line the values of miles and kilometers for both miles and (miles − start + split + 1).]

14. Heron's formula for the area A, of a triangle with sides of length a, b, and c is $A = sqrt[s(s-a)(s-b)(s-c)]$, where $s = (a + b + c)/2$. Write, test, and execute a function that accepts the values of a, b, and c as parameters from a calling function, and then calculates the values of s and $s(s − a)(s − b)(s − c)$. If this

FIGURE 6.11

```
Zzyz Corp.                              Date: (today's date)
1164 Sunrise Avenue
Kalispell, Montana

Pay to the order of: (first and last name)          $ (amount)

UnderSecurity Bank
Missoula, MT
                                        _____
                                        Authorized Signature
```

quantity is positive, the function calculates A. If the quantity is negative, a, b, and c do not form a triangle, and the function should set $A = -1$. The value of A should be returned by the function.

15. Write and test two functions EnterData and PrintCheck to produce the sample paycheck illustrated in Figure 6.11 on the screen. The items in parentheses should be accepted by EnterData and passed to PrintCheck for display.

16. Your company will soon open a new office in France. So that they can do business there, they have asked you to prepare a comprehensive package that will perform the following conversions on demand:

Measure	American	to	Metric	by	Formula
Distance	Inch		Centimeter		2.54 cm/in.
	Foot		Meter		0.305 m/ft
	Yard		Meter		0.9144 m/yd
	Mile		Kilometer		1.6909 km/mi
Temperature	Fahrenheit		Celsius		$C = (5/9)(F - 32)$
Weight	Pound		Kilogram		0.454 kg/lb
	Ounce		Gram		28.35 g/oz
Currency	Dollar		Franc		Entered by the user About 5 Franc/$
Capacity	Quart		Liter		0.946 liter/qt
	Teaspoon		Milliliter		4.9 ml/tsp
Math	Degree		Radian		$rad = (\pi/180)(degree)$
	Degree		Grad		$grad = (200/180)(degree)$

CHAPTER

7 | Modularity Using Functions: Part 2

Any project that requires a computer incurs both hardware and software costs. The costs associated with the hardware consist of all costs relating to the physical components used in the system. These components include the computer itself, peripherals, and any other items, such as air conditioning, cabling, and associated equipment required by the project. The software costs include all costs associated with initial program development and subsequent program maintenance. As illustrated in Figure 7.1, the major cost of most computer-based projects, whether for research, development, or final application, has become the software costs.

Software costs contribute so heavily to total project costs because these costs are closely related to human productivity (labor intensive), whereas hardware costs are more directly related to manufacturing technologies. For example, microchips that cost more than $500 per chip 10 years ago can now be purchased for less than $1 per chip.

It is far easier, however, to dramatically increase manufacturing productivity by a thousand, with the consequent decrease in hardware costs, than it is for people to double either the quantity or quality of their output. So as hardware costs have plummeted, software productivity and its associated costs have remained rather constant. Thus, the percentage of software costs to total system costs (hardware plus software) has increased dramatically.

Looking at just software costs (see Figure 7.2), we find that the maintenance of existing programs accounts for approximately 75% of total software costs. Maintenance includes the correction of newly found errors and the addition of new features and modifications to existing programs.

Students generally find it strange that maintenance is the predominant software cost because they are accustomed to solving a problem and moving on to a different

FIGURE 7.1   Software Is the Major Cost of Most Computer Projects

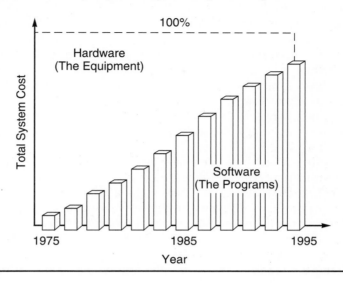

one. Commercial fields do not operate this way. In these fields, an application or idea typically builds on a previous one, and may require months or years of work. This is especially true in programming. Once a program is written, new features become evident. Advances in technology such as networking, fiber optics, genetic engineering, and graphical displays also open up new software possibilities.

How easily a program can be maintained (debugged, modified, or changed) is related to the ease with which the program can be read and understood. This,

FIGURE 7.2   Maintenance Is the Predominant Software Cost

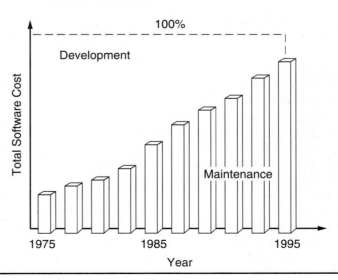

in turn, is directly related to the modularity with which the program was constructed. Modular programs, as we have seen, are constructed using one or more functions, each of which performs a clearly defined and specific task. If each function is clearly structured internally and the relationship between functions clearly specified, each function can be tested and modified with a minimum of disturbance or undesirable interaction with the other functions in the program.

Just as hardware designers frequently locate the cause of a hardware problem by using test methods designed to isolate the offending hardware subsystem, modular software permits the software engineer to similarly isolate program errors to specific software functions. We show how this accomplished in Section 7.5.

Once a bug has been isolated, or a new feature needs to be added, the required changes can be confined to appropriate functions, without radically affecting other functions. Only if the affected function requires different input data or produces different outputs are its surrounding functions affected. Even in this case the changes to the surrounding functions are clear; they must either be modified to output the data needed by the changed function or changed to accept the new output data. Functions help the programmer determine where the changes must be made, while the internal structure of the function determines how easy it will be to make the change.

In this chapter we continue our presentation of functions, providing additional information on specific features that are required for a full understanding of their capabilities.

7.1 VARIABLE SCOPE

Now that we have begun to write programs containing more than one function, we can look more closely at the variables declared within each function and their relationship to variables in other functions.

By their very nature, C functions are constructed to be independent modules. As we have seen, values are passed to a function using the function's argument list and a value is returned from a function using a return statement. Seen in this light, a function can be thought of as a closed box, with slots at the top to receive values and a single slot at the bottom of the box to return a value (see Figure 7.3).

The metaphor of a closed box is useful because it emphasizes the fact that what goes on inside the function, including all variable declarations within the function's body, are hidden from the view of all other functions. Since the variables created inside a function are conventionally available only to the function itself, they are said to be local to the function, or *local variables*. This term refers to the *scope* of a variable, where scope is defined as the section of the program where the variable is valid or "known." This section of the program is also referred to as where the variable is visible. A variable can have either a local scope or a global scope. A variable with a local scope is simply one that has had storage locations set aside for it by a declaration statement made within a function body. Local variables are only meaningful when used in expressions or statements inside the function that declared them. This

---

FIGURE 7.3   A Function Can Be Considered a Closed Box

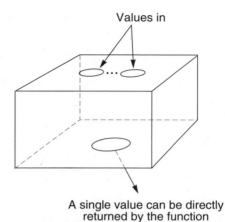

Values in

A single value can be directly
returned by the function

---

means that the same variable name can be declared and used in more than one function. For each function that declares the variable, a separate and distinct variable is created.

All the variables we have used until now have been local variables. This is a direct result of placing our declaration statements inside functions and using them as definition statements that cause the computer to reserve storage for the declared variable. As we shall see, declaration statements can be placed outside functions and need not act as definitions that cause new storage areas to be reserved for the declared variable.

A variable with *global scope,* more commonly termed a *global variable,* is one whose storage has been created for it by a declaration statement located outside any function. These variables can be used by all functions that are physically placed after the global variable declaration. This is shown in Program 7.1, where we have purposely used the same variable name inside both functions contained in the program.

The variable firstnum in Program 7.1 is a global variable because its storage is created by a definition statement located outside a function. Since both functions, main and valfun, follow the definition of firstnum, both of these functions can use this global variable with no further declaration needed.

Program 7.1 also contains two separate local variables, both named secnum. Storage for the secnum variable named in main is created by the definition statement located in main. A different storage area for the secnum variable in valfun is created by the definition statement located in the valfun function. Figure 7.4 illustrates the three distinct storage areas reserved by the three definition statements found in Program 7.1.

Each of the variables named secnum is local to the function in which their storage is created, and each of these variables can only be used from within the appropriate function. Thus, when secnum is used in main, the storage area reserved by main for its secnum variable is accessed, and when secnum is used in valfun, the storage area reserved by valfun for its

PROGRAM 7.1

```c
#include <stdio.h>
int firstnum;       /* create a global variable named firstnum */
void main(void)
{
  int secnum;             /* create a local variable named secnum */
  void valfun(void);    /* function prototype (declaration) */

  firstnum = 10; /* store a value into the global variable */
  secnum = 20;   /* store a value into the local variable */

  printf("From main: firstnum = %d\n", firstnum);
  printf("From main: secnum = %d\n", secnum);

  valfun();        /* call the function valfun */

  printf("\nFrom main again: firstnum = %d\n", firstnum);
  printf("From main again: secnum = %d\n", secnum);
}

void valfun(void)    /* no values are passed to this function */
{
  int secnum;  /* create a second local variable named secnum */

  secnum = 30; /* this only affects this local variable's value */

  printf("\nFrom valfun: firstnum = %d\n", firstnum);
  printf("From valfun: secnum = %d\n", secnum);

  firstnum = 40;     /* this changes firstnum for both functions */
  return;
}
```

secnum variable is accessed. The following output is produced when Program 7.1 is run:

```
From main: firstnum = 10
From main: secnum = 20

From valfun: firstnum = 10
From valfun: secnum = 30

From main again: firstnum = 40
From main again: secnum = 20
```

Let's analyze this output. Since firstnum is a global variable, both the main and valfun functions can use and change its value. Initially, both functions print the value of 10 that main stored in firstnum. Before returning, valfun changes the value of firstnum to 40, which is the value displayed when the variable firstnum is next displayed from within main.

Because each function only "knows" its own local variables, main can only send the value of its secnum to printf(), and valfun can only send the value of its secnum to printf(). Thus, whenever secnum is obtained from main the value of 20 is displayed, and whenever secnum is obtained from valfun the value 30 is displayed.

FIGURE 7.4   The Three Storage Areas Created by Program 7.1

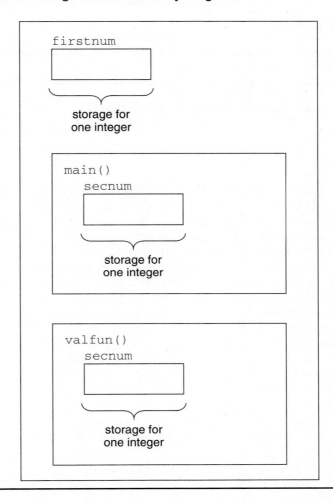

C does not confuse the two `secnum` variables because only one function can execute at a given moment. While a function is executing, only those variables and arguments that are "in scope" for that function (global and local) can be accessed.

The scope of a variable in no way influences or restricts the data type of the variable. Just as a local variable can be a character, integer, float, double, or any of the other data types (long/short) we have introduced, so can global variables be of these data types, as illustrated in Figure 7.5. The scope of a variable is determined by the placement of the definition statement that reserves storage for it and optionally by a declaration statement that makes it visible, whereas the data type of the variable is determined by using the appropriate keyword (`char`, `int`, `float`, `double`, etc.) before the variable's name in a declaration statement.

Misuse of Globals

Global variables allow the programmer to "jump around" the normal safeguards provided by functions. Rather than passing variables to a function, it is possible

◆ A CLOSER LOOK ◆

Storage Classes

`auto` and `register` variables are always local variables.

Only non-static global variables may be `extern`ed, which extends the variable's scope into another file or function.

Making a global variable `static` makes the variable private to the file in which it is declared. Thus, `static` variables cannot be `extern`ed. Except for `static` variables, all variables are initialized each time they come into scope.

to make all variables global ones. **Do not do this.** By indiscriminately making all variables global, you instantly destroy the safeguards C provides to make functions independent and insulated from each other, including the necessity of carefully designating the type of arguments needed by a function, the variables used in the function, and the value returned.

Using only global variables can be especially disastrous in larger programs that have many user-created functions. Since all variables in a function must be declared, creating functions that use global variables requires that you remember to write the appropriate global declarations at the top of each program using the function—they no longer come along with the function. More devastating than this, however, is the horror of trying to track down an error in a large program using global variables. Since a global variable can be accessed and changed by any function following the global declaration, it is a time-consuming and frustrating task to locate the origin of an erroneous value.

Global variables, however, are sometimes useful in creating variables that must be shared between many functions. Rather than passing the same variable to each function, it is easier to define the variable once as a global. Doing so also alerts anyone reading the program that many functions use the variable. Most large programs almost always make use of a few global variables. Smaller programs containing a few functions, however, should almost never contain globals.

FIGURE 7.5   Relating the Scope and Type of a Variable

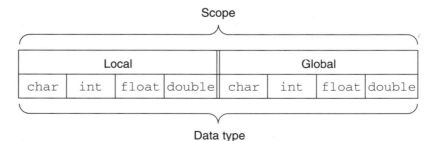

Exercises 7.1

1. a. For the following section of code, determine the data type and scope of all declared variables. To do this, use a separate sheet of paper and list the three column headings that follow (we have filled in the entries for the first variable):

Variable Name	Data Type	Scope
price	int	global to `main`, `roi`, and `step`

```
#include <stdio.h>
int price;
long int years;
double yield;

void main(void)
{
   int bondtype;
   double interest, coupon;
      .
      .
      .
}
double roi(int mat1, int mat2)
{
   int count;
   double eff_int;
      .
      .
      .
   return(eff_int);
}
int step(float first, float last)
{
   int numofyrs;
   float fracpart;
      .
      .
      .
   return(10*numofyrs);
}
```

   b. Draw boxes around the appropriate section of the above code to enclose the scope of each variable.

   c. Determine the data type of the arguments that the functions `roi` and `step` expect, and the data type of the value returned by these functions.

2. a. For the following section of code, determine the data type and scope of all declared variables. To do this, use a separate sheet of paper and list the three column headings that follow (we have filled in the entries for the first variable):

Variable Name	Data Type	Scope
key	char	global to `main`, `func1`, and `func2`

```
#include <stdio.h>
char key;
long int number;

void main(void)
{
```

```
      int a,b,c;
      double x,y;
          .
          .
          .

}

double secnum;

int func1(int num1, int num2)
{
  int o,p;
  float q;
      .
      .
      .

  return(p);
}

double func2(float first, float last)
{
  int a,b,c,o,p;
  float r;
  double s,t,x;
      .
      .
      .

  return(s * t);
}
```

    b. Draw a box around the appropriate section of the above code to enclose the scope of the variables key, secnum, y, and r.

    c. Determine the data type of the arguments that functions func1 and func2 expect, and the data type of the value returned by these functions.

3. Besides speaking about the scope of a variable, we can also apply the term to the arguments declared inside a function. What do you think is the scope of all function arguments?

4. Consider the following program structure:

```
#include <stdio.h>
int a, b;

void main(void)
{
  int c, d;
  float e, f;
    float One(float);
      .
      .
      .

}

float One(float p2)
{
    char m, n;
    void Two(void);
      .
      .
      .

}

void Two(void)
{
```

```
        int p, d;
        float q, r;
            .
            .
            .
    }
    Define the scope of the argument p2 and the variables a, b, c,
    d, m, n, p, d, q, and r.
```

5. Determine the values displayed by each call to printf in the following program:

```
#include <stdio.h>
int firstnum = 10;    /* declare and initialize a global variable */

void main(void)
{
    int firstnum = 20;   /* declare and initialize a local variable */
    void display(void); /* function prototype */
    printf("\nThe value of firstnum is %d", firstnum);
    display();
}

void display(void)
{
    printf("\nThe value of firstnum is now %d", firstnum);
}
```

7.2 VARIABLE STORAGE CLASS

The scope of a variable defines the location within a program where that variable can be used. Given a program, you could take a pencil and draw a box around the section of the program where each variable is valid. The space inside the box would represent the scope of a variable. From this viewpoint, the *scope of a variable* can be thought of as the space within the program where the variable is valid.

In addition to the space dimension represented by its scope, variables also have a time dimension. The time dimension refers to the length of time that storage locations are reserved for a variable. This time dimension is referred to as the variable's "lifetime." For example, all variable storage locations are released back to the computer when a program is finished running. However, while a program is still executing, interim variable storage areas are reserved and subsequently released back to the computer. Where and how long a variable's storage locations are kept before they are released can be determined by the storage class of the variable.

Besides having a data type and scope, every variable also has a *storage class*. The four available storage classes are called auto, static, extern, and register. If one of these class names is used, it must be placed before the variable's data type in a declaration statement. Examples of declaration statements that include a storage class designation are:

```
auto int num;       /* auto storage class and int data type */
static int miles;   /* static storage class and int data type */
register int dist;  /* register storage class and int data type */
extern int price;   /* extern storage class and int data type */
auto float coupon;  /* auto storage class and float data type */
static double yrs;  /* static storage class and double data type */
extern float yld;   /* extern storage class and float data type */
auto char in_key;   /* auto storage class and char variable */
```

To understand what the storage class of a variable means, we will first consider local variables (those variables created inside a function) and then global variables (those variables created outside a function).

Local Variable Storage Classes

Local variables can only be members of the auto, static, or register storage classes. If no class description is included in the declaration statement, the variable is automatically assigned to the auto class. Thus, *auto is the default class used by C*. All the local variables we have used, since the storage class designation was omitted, have been auto variables.

The term auto is short for *automatic*. Storage for automatic local variables is automatically reserved or created each time a function declaring automatic variables is called. As long as the function has not returned control to its calling function, all automatic variables local to the function are "alive"—that is, storage for the variables is available. When the function returns control to its calling function, its local automatic variables "die"—that is, the storage for the variables is released back to the computer. This process repeats itself each time a function is called. For example, consider Program 7.2, where the function testauto is called three times from main.

PROGRAM 7.2

```
#include <stdio.h>
void main(void)
{
  int count;              /* count is a local auto variable */
  void testauto(void);    /* function prototype */

  for(count = 1; count <= 3; count++)
    testauto();
}

void testauto(void)
{
  int num = 0;     /* num is a local auto variable initialized to 0 */

  printf("The value of the automatic variable num is %d\n", num);
  num++;
  return;
}
```

The output produced by Program 7.2 is:

```
The value of the automatic variable num is 0
The value of the automatic variable num is 0
The value of the automatic variable num is 0
```

Each time `testauto` is called, the automatic variable `num` is created and initialized to zero. When the function returns control to `main`, variable `num` is destroyed along with any value stored in `num`. Thus, the effect of incrementing `num` in `testauto`, before the function's return statement, is lost when control is returned to `main`.

For most applications, the use of automatic variables works just fine. There are cases, however, where we would like a function to remember values between function calls. This is the purpose of the `static` storage class. A local variable that is declared as static causes the program to keep the variable and its latest value even when the function that declared it is through executing. Examples of static variable declarations are:

```
static int rate;
static float taxes;
static double amount;
static char in_key;
static long years;
```

A local static variable is not created and destroyed each time the function declaring the static variable is called. Once created, local static variables remain in existence for the life of the program. This means that the last value stored in the variable when the function is finished executing is available to the function the next time it is called.

Because local static variables retain their values, they are not initialized within a declaration statement in the same way as automatic variables. To understand why, consider the automatic declaration int num = 0;, which causes the automatic variable `num` to be created and set to zero each time the declaration is encountered. This is called a *run-time initialization* because initialization occurs each time the declaration statement is encountered. This type of initialization would be disastrous for a static variable, because resetting the variable's value to zero each time the function is called would destroy the very value we are trying to save.

The initialization of static variables (both local and global) is done only once, when the program is compiled. At compilation time, the variable is created and any initialization value is placed in it.[1] Thereafter, the value in the variable is kept without further initialization each time the function is called. To see how this works, consider Program 7.3.

The output produced by Program 7.3 is:

```
The value of the static variable num is now 0
The value of the static variable num is now 1
The value of the static variable num is now 2
```

As illustrated by this output, the static variable `num` is set to zero only once. The function `teststat` then increments this variable just before returning control to `main`. The value that `num` has when leaving the function `teststat` is retained and displayed when the function is next called.

_____

[1]Some compilers force the initialization of static local variables the first time the definition statement is executed rather than when the program is compiled.

PROGRAM 7.3

```c
#include <stdio.h>
void main(void)
{
  int count;                /* count is a local auto variable */
  void teststat(void);      /* function prototype */

  for(count = 1; count <= 3; count++)
    teststat();
}

void teststat(void)
{
  static int num = 0;       /* num is a local static variable */

  printf("The value of the static variable num is now %d\n", num);
  num++;
  return;
}
```

Unlike automatic variables that can be initialized by either constants or expressions using both constants and previously initialized variables, static variables can only be initialized using constants or constant expressions, such as 3.2 + 8.0. Also, unlike automatic variables, all static variables are set to zero when no explicit initialization is given. Thus, the specific initialization of num to zero in Program 7.3 is not required.

The remaining storage class available to local variables, the register class, is not used as extensively as either automatic or static variables. Examples of register variable declarations are:

```c
register int time;
register double diffren;
register float coupon;
```

Register variables have the same time duration as automatic variables; that is, a local register variable is created when the function declaring it is entered, and is destroyed when the function completes execution. The only difference between register and automatic variables is where the storage for the variable is located.

Storage for all variables (local and global), except register variables, is reserved in the computer's memory area. Most computers have a few additional high-speed storage areas located directly in the computer's processing unit that can also be used for variable storage. These special high-speed storage areas are called *registers*. Since registers are physically located in the computer's processing unit, they can be accessed faster than the normal memory storage areas located in the computer's memory unit. Also, computer instructions that reference registers typically require less space than instructions that reference memory locations because there are fewer registers that can be accessed than there are memory locations.

For example, although the AT&T WE 32100 central processing unit has nine registers that can be used for local C program variables, it can be connected to memories that have more than four billion bytes. Most other computers have a similar set of user-accessible registers but millions of memory locations. When the compiler substitutes the location of a register for a variable during program compilation, less space in the instruction is needed than is required to address a memory having millions of locations.

Besides decreasing the size of a compiled C program, using register variables can also increase the execution speed of a C program, if the computer you are using supports this data type. Variables declared with the register storage class are automatically switched to the auto storage class if your computer does not support register variables or if the declared register variables exceed the computer's register capacity.

The only restriction in using the register storage class is that the address of a register variable, using the address operator &, cannot be taken. This is easily understood when you realize that registers do not have standard memory addresses.

Global Variable Storage Classes

Global variables are created by definition statements external to a function. By their nature, these externally defined variables do not come and go with the calling of any function. Once a global variable is created, it exists until the program in which it is declared is finished executing. Thus, global variables cannot be declared as either auto or register variables that are created and destroyed as the program is executing. Global variables may, however, be declared as members of the static or extern storage classes. Examples of declaration statements including these two class descriptions are:

```
extern int sum;
extern double price;
static double yield;
```

The static and extern classes affect only the scope, not the time duration, of global variables. As with static local variables, all global variables are initialized to zero at compile time.

The purpose of the extern storage class is to extend the scope of a global variable beyond its normal boundaries. To understand this, we must first note that all of the programs we have written so far have always been contained together in one file. Thus, when you have saved or retrieved programs you have only needed to give the computer a single name for your program. This is not required by C.

Larger programs typically consist of many functions that are stored in multiple files. An example of this is shown in Figure 7.6, where the three functions main, func1, and func2 are stored in one file and the two functions func3 and func4 are stored in a second file.

For the files illustrated in Figure 7.6, the global variables price, yield, and coupon declared in file1 can only be used by the functions main, func1, and func2 in this file. The single global variable, interest, declared in file2 can only be used by the functions func3 and func4 in file2.

Although the variable price has been created in file1, we may want to use it in file2. Placing the declaration statement extern int price; in file2, as shown in Figure 7.7, allows us to do this. Putting this statement at the top of file2 extends the scope of the variable price into file2 so that it may be used by both func3 and func4. Thus, the extern designation simply declares a global variable that is defined in another file. So placing the statement extern float yield; in func4 extends the scope of this global variable, created in file1, into func4, and the scope of the global variable interest, created in file2, is extended into func1 and func2 by the declaration statement extern double interest; placed before func1. Notice that interest is not available to main.

FIGURE 7.6   A Program May Extend Beyond One File

```
file1                              file2
int price;                         double interest;
float yield;                       void func3(void)
static double coupon;              {
void main(void)                        .
{                                      .
    func1( );                          .
    func2( );                      }
    func3( );                      void func4(void)
    func4( );                          .
}                                      .
void func1(void)                       .
{                                  }
    .
    .
    .
}
void func2(void)
{
    .
    .
    .
}
```

A declaration statement that specifically contains the word `extern` is different from every other declaration statement in that it does not cause the creation of a new variable by reserving new storage for the variable. An `extern` declaration statement simply informs the computer that the variable already exists and can now be used. The actual storage for the variable must be created somewhere else in the program using one, and only one, global declaration statement in which the word `extern` has not been used. Initialization of the global variable can, of course, be made with the original declaration of the global variable. Initialization within an `extern` declaration statement is not allowed and will cause a compilation error.

The existence of the `extern` storage class is the reason we have been so careful to distinguish between the creation and declaration of a variable. Declaration statements containing the word `extern` do not create new storage areas; they only extend the scope of existing global variables.

The last global class, static global, is used to prevent the extension of a global variable into a second file. Global static variables are declared in the same way as local static variables, except that the declaration statement is placed outside any function.

The scope of a global static variable *cannot* be extended beyond the file in which it is declared. This provides a degree of privacy for static global variables. Since they are only "known" and can only be used in the file in which they are declared, other files cannot access or change their values. Static global variables cannot be subsequently extended to a second file using an extern declaration statement. Trying to do so will result in a compilation error.

FIGURE 7.7	Extending the Scope of a Global Variable

file1

```
int price;
float yield;
static double coupon;
void main(void)
{
    func1( );
    func2( );
    func3( );
    func4( );
}
extern double interest;
void func1(void)
{
    .
    .
    .
}
void func2(void)
{
    .
    .
    .
}
```

file2

```
double interest;
extern int price;
void func3(void)
{
    .
    .
    .
}
void func4(void)
{
    extern float yield;
    .
    .
    .
}
```

Exercises 7.2

1. a. List the storage classes available to local variables.

   b. List the storage classes available to global variables.

2. Describe the difference between a local auto variable and a local static variable.

3. What is the difference between the following functions?:

```
void init1(void)
{
  static int yrs = 1;
  printf("\nThe value of yrs is %d", yrs);
  yrs = yrs + 2;
}

void init2(void)
{
  static int yrs;
  yrs = 1;
  printf("\nThe value of yrs is %d", yrs);
  yrs = yrs + 2;
}
```

4. a. Describe the difference between a static global variable and an extern global variable.

   b. If a variable is declared with an extern storage class, what other declaration statement must be present somewhere in the program?

5. The declaration statement static double years; can be used to create either a local or global static variable. What determines the scope of the variable years?

6. For the function and variable declarations illustrated in Figure 7.8, place an extern declaration to individually accomplish the following:

a. Extend the scope of the global variable choice into all of file2.

b. Extend the scope of the global variable flag into function pduction only.

c. Extend the scope of the global variable date into pduction and bid.

d. Extend the scope of the global variable date into roi only.

e. Extend the scope of the global variable coupon into roi only.

f. Extend the scope of the global variable b_type into all of file1.

g. Extend the scope of the global variable maturity into both price and yield.

FIGURE 7.8   **Files for Exercise 6**

```
file1                              file2

char choice;                       char b_type;
int flag;                          double maturity;
long date, time;                   void roi(void)
void main(void)                    {
{                                      .
    .                                  .
    .                                  .
    .                              }
}                                  void pduction(void)
double coupon;                     {
void price(void)                       .
{                                      .
    .                                  .
    .                              }
    .                              void bid(void)
}                                  {
void yield(void)                       .
{                                      .
    .                                  .
    .                              }
    .
}
```

7.3 RETURNING MULTIPLE FUNCTION VALUES

In the normal course of operation a called function receives values from its calling function, stores the passed values in its own local arguments, manipulates these arguments appropriately, and possibly returns a single value. Under this standard arrangement, the called function does not receive access to any variable used in the call; it only receives copies of the values stored in the variables. For example, in the function call

```
max = find_max(firstnum, secnum);
```

the find_max function receives copies of the values contained in firstnum and secnum when the call is made. As we have seen, this method of calling a function and passing values to it is referred to as a function *call by value.*

This call by value procedure is a distinct programming benefit. It allows functions to be written as independent entities without concern that altering an argument or variable in one function may inadvertently alter the value of a variable in another function. Under this approach, formal (receiving) arguments can be considered as either initialized variables or variables that will be assigned values when the function is called. At no time, however, does the called function have direct access to any variable contained in the calling function.

There are times, however, when it is desirable to give a function direct access to the local variables of its calling function. This allows the called function to access directly and change values in the variables of the called function, and effectively permits the called function to return multiple values. Doing this requires that a variable's address be passed to the called function. Once the called function has the variable's address, it "knows where the variable lives," so to speak, and can access the variable using the address and the indirection operator.

Passing an address is referred to as a *call by reference,* since the called function can reference, or access, the variable using the passed address. In this section we describe the technique required to pass addresses to a function and have the function accept and use the passed address:

Passing, Storing, and Using Addresses

To pass, store, and use addresses, we need to use the address operator (&), pointers, and the indirection operator (*). Let us review these topics before applying them to the process of writing a function.

The *address operator* is the ampersand symbol, &. Recall that the ampersand followed immediately by a variable means "the address of" the variable. Examples of this are:

&firstnum means "the address of firstnum"
&secnum means "the address of secnum"

Addresses themselves are values that can be stored in variables. The variables that store addresses are called *pointers*. Again, recall that pointers, like all variables, must be declared. In declaring pointers, the data type corresponding to the address being stored must be included in the declaration. Since all addresses appear the same, this additional information is needed by the compiler so it knows how many storage locations to access when it uses the address stored in the pointer. Examples of pointer declarations are:

```
char *in_addr;
int *num_pt;
float *dst_addr:
double *nm1_addr;
```

To understand pointer declarations, read them "backwards," starting with the indirection operator, the asterisk, *. Again, recall that an asterisk followed immediately by a variable or argument can be translated as either "the variable (or argument) whose address is stored in" or "the variable (or argument) pointed to by." Thus, *in_addr can be read as either "the variable whose address is stored in in_addr" or "the variable pointed to by in_addr." Applying this to pointer declarations, the declaration char *in_key;, for example, can be read as either "the variable whose address is stored in in_key is a character" or "the variable pointed to by in_key is a character." Both of these statements are frequently shortened to the simpler statement that "in_key points to a character." All three interpretations of the declaration statement are correct, so you can select and use whichever description makes a pointer declaration meaningful to you.

We now put all this together to pass two addresses to a function named newval. The function will be a stub, whose only task will be to verify correct receipt of the passed addresses. Passing addresses to a function should be familiar to you, because we have been using addresses each time we have called scanf. Consider Program 7.4.

PROGRAM 7.4

```
#include <stdio.h>
void main(void)
{
  float firstnum, secnum;
  void newval(float *, float *);  /* prototype to accept two pointers */

  printf("\nEnter two numbers: ");
  scanf("%f %f", &firstnum, &secnum);

  newval(&firstnum, &secnum);   /* call the function */
}
```

Observe in Program 7.4 that addresses are passed to both scanf and newval (also see Figure 7.9). The function prototype for newval declares that the function will not directly return a value and expects two pointer arguments (two addresses), each of which points to (is the address of) a floating-point variable.

Since addresses are stored in pointers, one of the first requirements in writing newval is to declare two arguments that can store passed addresses. The following argument declarations can be used:

```
float *num1_addr    /* num1_addr points to a floating point variable */
float *num2_addr    /* num2_addr points to a floating point variable */
```

The choice of the argument names num1_addr and num2_addr is, as with all argument names, up to the programmer.

Putting what we have together, the function header for newval is:

```
void newval(float *num1_addr, float *num2_addr) /* function declaration */
```

A stub version of newval is included in Program 7.5 to verify correct receipt of the addresses.

FIGURE 7.9   **Passing Addresses to** newval

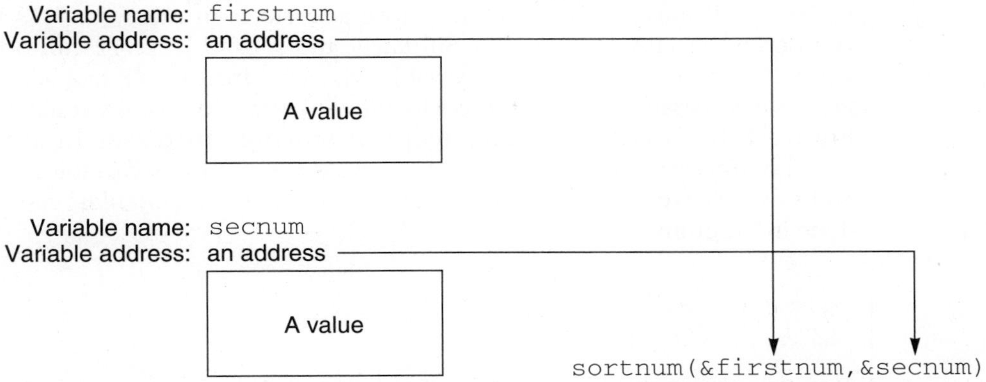

Variable name: firstnum
Variable address: an address ─────────────────────┐

```
┌─────────────────────┐
│                     │
│       A value       │
│                     │
└─────────────────────┘
```

Variable name: secnum
Variable address: an address ─────────────────────┐

```
┌─────────────────────┐
│                     │
│       A value       │
│                     │
└─────────────────────┘
```

sortnum(&firstnum,&secnum)

PROGRAM 7.5

```c
#include <stdio.h>
void main(void)
{
  float firstnum, secnum;
  void newval(float *, float *);  /* prototype to accept two pointers */

  printf("\nEnter two numbers: ");
  scanf("%f %f", &firstnum, &secnum);

  newval(&firstnum, &secnum);   /* call the function */
}

void newval(float *xnum_addr, float *ynum_addr)
{
  printf("\nThe value whose address is in num1_addr is %f\n", *xnum_addr);
  printf("The value whose address is in num2_addr is %f\n", *ynum_addr);
  return;
}
```

A sample run using Program 7.5 provided the following output:

```
Enter two numbers: 20.0   5.0
The value whose address is in num1_addr is 20.000000
The value whose address is in num2_addr is 5.000000
```

In reviewing Program 7.5 note two things. First, the function prototype void newval(*float *, float *) declares that newval returns no value directly and that its arguments are two pointers that "point to" floating-point variables. As such, when the function is called, it will require that two addresses be passed, and that each address is the address of a floating-point value. Second, within newval, the indirection operator is used to access the values stored in firstnum and `secnum`. `newval` itself has no knowledge of these variable names, but it does have the address of `firstnum` stored in `num1_addr` and the address of `secnum` stored in `num2_addr`. The expression `*num1_addr` used in the first `printf` call means "the variable whose address is in `num1_addr`." This is of course the variable `firstnum`. Similarly, the second `printf` call obtains the value stored in `secnum` as "the variable whose address is in `num2_addr`." Thus, we have successfully used pointers to allow `newval` to access variables in `main`. Figure 7.10 illustrates the concept of storing addresses in arguments.

Having verified that `newval` can access `main`'s local variables `firstnum` and `secnum`, we can now expand `newval` to alter these variables' values. This is done in Program 7.6.

PROGRAM 7.6

```c
#include <stdio.h>
void main(void)
{
  float firstnum, secnum;
  void newval(float *, float *);  /* prototype to accept two pointers */

  printf("\nEnter two numbers: ");
  scanf("%f %f", &firstnum, &secnum);
  printf("\nThe value in firstnum is %f\n", firstnum);
  printf("The value in secnum is %f\n", secnum);

  newval(&firstnum, &secnum);   /* call the function */

  printf("\nThe value in firstnum is now %f\n", firstnum);
  printf("The value in secnum is now %f\n", secnum);
}

void newval(float *num1_addr, float *num2_addr)
{
  printf("\nThe number whose address is in num1_addr is %f\n", *num1_addr);
  printf("The number whose address is in num2_addr is %f\n", *num2_addr);
  *num1_addr = 89.5;
  *num2_addr = 99.5;
  return;
}
```

In calling the `newval` function within Program 7.6 it is important to understand the significance of passing the addresses of `firstnum` and `secnum` to `newval`—they give `newval` the capability to access directly and alter the values stored in the variables `firstnum` and `secnum`. This is done within the function by the statements:

$$*num1\_addr = 89.5;$$
$$*num2\_addr = 99.5;$$

The first statement can be read as "store the value 89.5 into the variable whose address is in `num1_addr`." Similarly, the second statement can be read as "store

---

FIGURE 7.10 **Storing Addresses in Arguments**

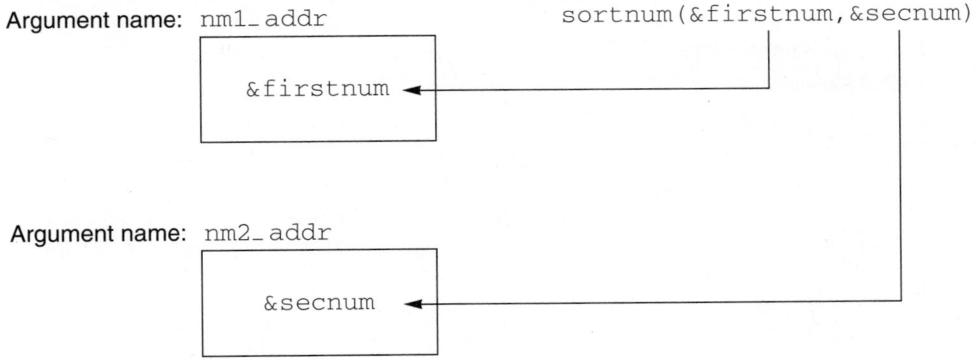

Argument name: `nm1_addr`   `sortnum(&firstnum,&secnum)`

`&firstnum`

Argument name: `nm2_addr`

`&secnum`

---

the value 99.5 into the variable whose address is in `num2_addr`." In `main()` these memory locations are referenced by the names `firstnum` and `secnum`, respectively, while in `newval()` the same locations are referenced using their actual memory addresses.

The following sample run was obtained using Program 7.6:

```
Enter two numbers: 10.0    20.0

The value in firstnum is 10.000000
The value in secnum is 20.000000

The number whose address is in num1_addr is 10.000000
The number whose address is in num2_addr is 20.000000

The value in firstnum is now 89.500000
The value in secnum is now 99.500000
```

As seen by this output, the values initially stored in `main`'s variables `firstnum` and `secnum` have been successfully altered from within `newval`.

The mechanism used in `newval` for altering the variables of its calling function provides the basis for returning multiple values from any function. For example, assume that a function is required to accept three values, compute these values' sum and product, and return these computed results to the calling routine. Naming the function `calc` and providing five formal arguments (three for the input data and two pointers for the returned values), the following function can be used:

```
void calc(float num1, float num2, float num3, float *tot_addr, float *prd_addr)
{
  *tot_addr = num1 + num2 + num3;
  *prd_addr = num1 * num2 * num3;
  return;
}
```

This function has five formal arguments, named `num1`, `num2`, `num3`, `total`, and `product`, of which only the last two are declared as pointers. Within the function only the last two arguments are altered. The value of the fourth argument, total, is calculated as the sum of the first three arguments; and the last argument, product, is computed as the product of the arguments num1, num2, and num3. Program 7.7 includes this function in a complete program.

PROGRAM 7.7

```
#include <stdio.h>
void main(void)
{
    float firstnum, secnum, thirdnum, sum, product;
    void calc(float, float, float, float *, float *);   /* prototype */

    printf("\nEnter three numbers: ");
    scanf("%f %f %f", &firstnum, &secnum, &thirdnum);

    calc(firstnum, secnum, thirdnum, &sum, &product);   /* function call */

    printf("\nThe sum of the numbers is: %f\n", sum);
    printf("The product of the numbers is: %f\n", product);
}

void calc(float num1, float num2, float num3, float *tot_addr, float *prd_addr)
{
    *tot_addr = num1 + num2 + num3;
    *prd_addr = num1 * num2 * num3;
    return;
}
```

The function calc is called from main using the five actual arguments firstnum, secnum, thirdnum, the address of sum, and the address of product. As required, these arguments agree in number and data type with the formal arguments declared by calc. Once calc is called, it uses its first three arguments to calculate values and place the results of this calculation directly into main's variables sum and product. It does this by using the addresses of these two variables. The following is a sample run using Program 7.5:

```
Enter three numbers: 2.5 6.0 10.0
The sum of the numbers is: 18.500000
The product of the numbers is: 150.000000
```

As a final example illustrating the usefulness of passing addresses to a called function, we construct a function named swap that exchanges the values of two of main's floating-point variables. Such a function is useful when sorting a list of numbers and will be used again in Chapter 8 for just such an application.

Since the value of more than a single variable is affected, swap cannot be written as a call by value function that returns a single value. The desired exchange of main's variables by swap can only be obtained by giving swap access to main's variables. One way of doing this is using pointer variables.

We have already seen how to pass addresses in Programs 7.4 through 7.7. Assuming that the names of the variables whose addresses we will pass are firstnum and secnum, the values stored in these variables can be interchanged from within swap by means of the three-step interchange algorithm:

1. Store firstnum's value in a temporary location.
2. Store secnum's value in firstnum.
3. Store the temporary value in secnum.

Using pointers from within swap, this takes the form:

1. Store the value held by the variable pointed to by num1_addr in a temporary location. The statement temp = *num1_addr; does this (see Figure 7.11).

FIGURE 7.11   Indirectly Storing firstnum's Value

num1_addr

| Address of firstnum |

(a) Go to the address for a value →

firstnum

| A value |

(b) Store the value found

temp

| firstnum's value |

---

2. Store the value held by the variable whose address is in num2_addr in the variable whose address is in num1_addr. The statement *num1_addr = *num2_addr; does this (see Figure 7.12).

FIGURE 7.12   Indirectly Changing firstnum's Value

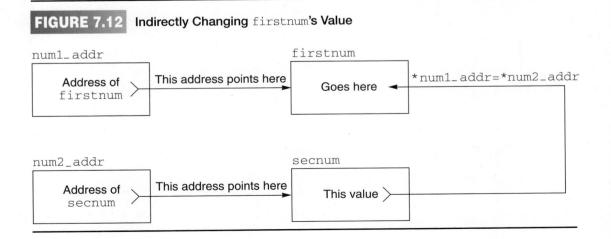

num1_addr

| Address of firstnum |

This address points here →

firstnum

| Goes here |

*num1_addr=*num2_addr

num2_addr

| Address of secnum |

This address points here →

secnum

| This value |

---

3. Move the value in the temporary location into the variable whose address is in
num2_addr. The statement *num2_addr = temp; does this (see Figure 7.13).

Here is the function swap written according to these specifications:

```
void swap(float *num1_addr, float *num2_addr)
{
  float temp;

  temp = *num1_addr;            /* save firstnum's value */
  *num1_addr = *num2_addr;      /* move secnum's value into firstnum */
  *num2_addr = temp;            /* change secnum's value */

  return;
}
```

Notice that the use of pointers in swap's argument list is what gives swap access
to the variables in the calling function whose addresses are passed into the pointer arguments. Program 7.8 contains swap in a complete program.

PROGRAM 7.8

```
#include <stdio.h>
void main(void)
{
  float firstnum = 20.5, secnum = 6.25;
  void swap(float *, float *);   /* function receives 2 pointers */

  printf("\nThe value stored in firstnum is: %f\n", firstnum);
  printf("The value stored in secnum is: %f\n\n",secnum);

  swap(&firstnum, &secnum);   /* call the function with pointers */

  printf("The value stored in firstnum is now: %f\n", firstnum);
  printf("The value stored in secnum is now: %f\n", secnum);
}

void swap(float *num1_addr, float *num2_addr)
{
  float temp;

  temp = *num1_addr;            /* save firstnum's value */
  *num1_addr = *num2_addr;      /* move secnum's value into firstnum */
  *num2_addr = temp;            /* change secnum's value */

  return;
}
```

The following sample run was obtained using Program 7.8:

```
The value stored in firstnum is: 20.500000
The value stored in secnum is: 6.250000

The value stored in firstnum is now: 6.250000
The value stored in secnum is now: 20.500000
```

FIGURE 7.13   Indirectly Changing secnum's Value

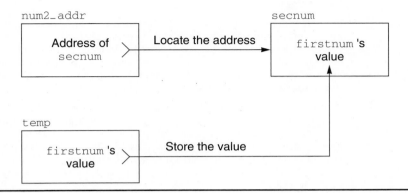

As illustrated in this output, the values stored in main's variables have been modified from within swap, which was made possible by the use of pointer arguments. If a call by value had been used instead, the exchange within swap would only affect swap's arguments and would accomplish nothing with respect to main's variables. Thus, a function such as swap can only be written using pointers that provide direct access to main's variables.

Exercises 7.3

1. Write argument declarations for the following:

   a. A formal argument named amount that will be a pointer to a floating-point value

   b. A formal argument named price that will be a pointer to a double-precision number

   c. A formal argument named minutes that will be a pointer to an integer number

   d. A formal argument named key that will be a pointer to a character

   e. A formal argument named yield that will be a pointer to a double-precision number

2. Suppose a program function contains these declarations:

   ```
   char m1, m2;
   float m3, m4;
   int m5;
   ```

   and that this function calls the whatnow() function. If changes made by WhatNow() to the variables m1, m2, m3, m4, and m5 are to be available to the calling function:

   a. What should the call to WhatNow() look like?

   b. Assuming that WhatNow() directly returns no value, what is its correct function header?

   c. What is the correct function prototype for WhatNow().

3. a. Three integer variables named seconds, minutes, and hours are to be used in a call to a function named time. Write a suitable function header for time, assuming that time accepts these variables as the pointer arguments sec, min, and hrs, and returns no value to its calling function.

   b. What should the call to time look like?

4. Rewrite the `find_max` function in Program 6.3 so that the variable max, declared in main, is used to store the maximum value of the two passed numbers. The value of max should be set directly from within `find_max` (*Hint:* A pointer to max will have to be accepted by `find_max`.)

5. Write a function named `change` that has a floating-point argument and four integer pointer arguments named `quarters`, `dimes`, `nickels`, and `pennies`, respectively. The function is to consider the floating-point passed value as a dollar amount and convert the value into an equivalent number of quarters, dimes, nickels, and pennies. Using the pointers, the function should directly alter the respective actual arguments in the calling function.

6. Write a function named `liquid` that has an integer number argument and pointer arguments named `gallons`, `quarts`, `pints`, and `cups`. The passed integer represents the total number of cups and the function is to determine the number of gallons, quarts, pints, and cups in the passed value. Using the pointers, the function should directly alter the respective actual arguments in the calling function. Use the relationships of 2 cups to a pint, 4 cups to a quart, and 16 cups to a gallon.

7. The following program uses the same argument names in both the calling and called function. Determine if this causes any problem for the computer.

```
#include <stdio.h>
void main(void)
{
  int min, hour;
  void time(int *, int *);  /* function prototype */

  printf("\nEnter two numbers :");
  scanf("%d %d", &min, &hour);
  time(&min, &hour);
}

void time(int *min, int *hour)
{
  int sec;

  sec = (*hour * 60 +* min) * 60;
  printf("\nThe total number of seconds is %d", sec);
}
```

7.4 RECURSION[2]

Because C allocates new memory locations for arguments and local variables each time a function is called, it is possible for a function to call itself. Functions that do so are referred to as *self-referential* or *recursive functions*. When a function invokes itself, the process is called *direct recursion*. Similarly, a function can invoke a second function, which it turn invokes the first function. This type of recursion is referred to as *indirect* or *mutual recursion*.

In 1936 Alan Turing showed that, although not every possible problem can be solved by computer, those problems that have recursive solutions also have computer solutions, at least in theory.

Mathematical Recursion

The recursive concept is that the solution to a problem can be stated in terms of "simple" versions of itself. Some problems can be solved using an algebraic

---

[2]This topic may be omitted on first reading with no loss of subject continuity.

A BIT OF BACKGROUND

The "Universal Algorithm Machine"

In the 1930s and 1940s, Alan Mathison Turing (1912–1954) and others studied in considerable depth the theory of what a computing machine should be able to do. Turing invented a theoretical, pencil-and-paper computer—now appropriately called a Turing machine—that he hoped would be a "universal algorithm machine." That is, he hoped to prove theoretically that all problems could be solved by a set of instructions to a hypothetical computer. What he succeeded in proving was that some problems cannot be solved by *any* machine, just as some

problems cannot be solved by any person. However, he did show that algorithms that can be defined recursively can indeed be solved by machine, though it may not be possible to predict how long it will take the machine to find the solution.

Alan Turing's work formed the foundation of computer theory before the first electronic computer was built. His contribution to the team that developed the critical code-breaking computers during World War II led directly to the practical implementation of his theories.

formula that shows recursion explicitly. For example, consider finding the factorial of a number n, denoted as $n!$, where n is a positive integer. This is defined as:

$$1! = 1$$
$$2! = 2 * 1 = 2 * 1!$$
$$3! = 3 * 2 * 1 = 3 * 2!$$
$$4! = 4 * 3 * 2 * 1 = 4 * 3!$$

and so on

The definition for $n!$ can be summarized by the following statements:

$$1! = 1$$
$$n! = n * (n-1)! \quad \text{for } n > 1$$

This definition illustrates the general considerations that must be specified in construction a recursive algorithm. These are:

1. What is the first case
2. How is the nth case related to the $(n-1)$st case

Although the definition seems to define a factorial in terms of a factorial, the definition is valid, because it can always be computed. For example, using the definition, 3! is first computed as:

$$3! = 3 * 2!$$

The value of 2! is determined from the definition as:

$$2! = 2 * 1!$$

Substituting this expression for 2! in the determination of 3! yields:

$$3! = 3 * 2 * 1!$$

1! is not defined in terms of the recursive formula, but is simply defined as being equal to 1. Substituting this value into the expression for 3! gives us

$$3! = 3 * 2 * 1 = 6$$

To see how a recursive function is defined in C, we construct the function factorial. In pseudocode, the processing required of this function is:

If n = 1
  factorial = n.
Else
  factorial = n * factorial(n − 1).

Notice that this algorithm is simply a restatement of the recursive definition previously given. In C, this can be written as:

```
int factorial(int n)
{
  if (n == 1)
    return (1);
  else
    return (n * factorial(n));
}
```

Program 7.9 illustrates this code in a complete program.

PROGRAM 7.9

```
#include <stdio.h>
void main(void)
{
  int n, result;
  int factorial(int);

  printf("Enter a number: ");
  scanf("%d", &n);
  result = factorial(n);
  printf("\nThe factorial of %d is %d\n", n, result);
}
int factorial(int n)
{
  if (n == 1)
    return(n);
  else
    return(n * factorial(n-1));
}
```

A sample run of Program 7.9 follows:

```
Enter a number: 3
The factorial of 3 is 6
```

How the Computation Is Performed

The sample run of Program 7.9 invoked `factorial` from `main` with a value of 3 using the call

$$\text{result = factorial(3n);}$$

Let's see how the computer actually performs the computation. The mechanism that makes it possible for a C function to call itself is that C allocates new memory locations for all function arguments and local variables as each function is called. This allocation is made dynamically, as a program is executed, in a memory area referred to as the stack.

A *stack* is simply an area of memory used for rapidly storing and retrieving data. It is conceptually similar to a stack of trays in a cafeteria, where the last tray placed on top of the stack is the first tray removed. This last-in/first-out mechanism provides the means for storing information in order of occurrence. Each function call simply reserves memory locations on the stack for its arguments, its local variables, a return value, and the address where execution is to resume in the calling program when the function has completed execution. Thus, when the function call `factorial(n)` is made, the stack is initially used to store the address of the instruction being executed [result = factorial(n);] the argument value for n, which is 3, and a space for the value to be returned by the factorial function. At this stage the stack can be envisioned as shown in Figure 7.14. From a program execution standpoint the function that made the call to factorial, in this case `main`, is suspended and the compiled code for the `factorial` function starts executing.

Within the `factorial` function itself, another function call is made. That this call is to `factorial` is irrelevant as far as C is concerned. The call is simply another request for stack space. In this case, the stack stores the address of the instruction being executed in `factorial`, the number 2, and a space for the value to be returned by the function. The stack can now be envisioned as shown in Figure 7.15. At this point a second version of the compiled code for `factorial` begins execution, while the first version is temporarily suspended.

Once again, the currently executing code, which is the second invocation of `factorial`, makes a function call. That this call is to itself is irrelevant in C. The call is once again handled in the same manner as any function call and begins with allocation of the stack's memory space. Here the stack stores the address of the instruction being executed in the calling function, which happens to be `factorial`, the number 1, and a space for the value to be returned by the function. The stack can now be envisioned as shown in Figure 7.16. At this point the third

FIGURE 7.14   **The Stack for the First Call to** factorial

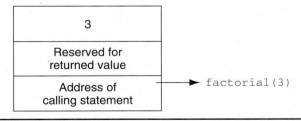

FIGURE 7.15   The Stack for the Second Call to factorial

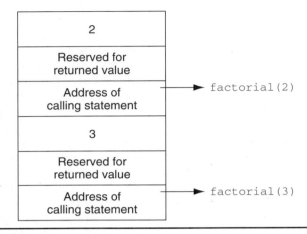

and final version of the compiled code for factorial begins execution, while the second version is temporarily suspended.

This third call to factorial results in a returned value of 1 being placed on the stack. This completes the set of recursive calls and permits the suspended calling functions to resume execution and be completed in reverse order. The value of 1 is used by the second invocation of factorial to complete its operation

FIGURE 7.16   The Stack for the Third Call to factorial

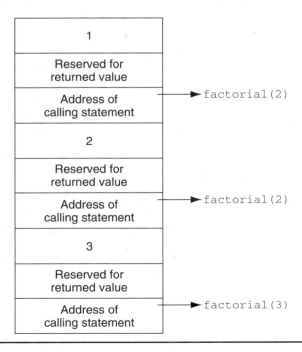

and place a return value of 2 on the stack. This value is then used by the first invocation of factorial to complete its operation and place a return value of 6 on the stack, with execution now returning to `main`. The original calling statement within `main` stores the return value of its invocation of `factorial` into the variable result.

Recursion Versus Iteration

The recursive method can be applied to any problem in which the solution is represented in terms of solutions to simpler versions of the same problem.

The most difficult tasks in implementing recursion are deciding how to create the process and visualizing what happens at each successive invocation.

Any recursive function can always be written in a nonrecursive manner using an iterative solution. For example, the factorial function can be written using an iteration algorithm as:

```
int factorial(int n)
{
    int fact;

    for(fact = 1; n > 0; n--)
        fact = fact * n;
    return(fact);
}
```

Since recursion is usually a difficult concept for beginning programmers, under what conditions would you use it in preference to a repetitive solution? The answer is rather simple.

If a problem solution can be expressed iteratively or recursively with equal ease, the iterative solution is preferable because it executes faster (there are no additional function calls, which consumes processing time) and uses less memory (the stack is not used for the multiple function calls needed in recursion). There are times, however, when recursive solutions are preferable.

First, some problems are simply easier to visualize using a recursive algorithm than a repetitive one. The Towers of Hanoi problem, which is a classic recursion problem, is an example of this (see Exercise 9 at the end of this chapter).

A second reason for using recursion is that it sometimes provides a much simpler solution. In these situations obtaining the same result using repetition requires extremely complicated coding that can be avoided by using recursion. An example of this is the quicksort sorting algorithm presented in Section 8.5.

Related to both of these reasons is a third. In many advanced applications recursion is both simpler to visualize and the only practical means of implementing a solution. Examples of these applications are the implementation of a quick sort algorithm (see Section 8.5) and in creating dynamically allocated data structures (see Section 11.5).

Exercises 7.4

1. The Fibonacci sequence is 0, 1, 1, 2, 3, 5, 8, 13, . . . such that the first two terms are 0 and 1, and each term thereafter is defined recursively as the sum of the two preceding terms; that is,

$$\text{Fib}(n) = \text{Fib}(n-1) + \text{Fib}(n-2)$$

Write a recursive function that returns the nth number in a Fibonacci sequence when n is passed to the function as an argument. For example, when $n = 8$, the function returns the 8th number in the sequence, which is 13.

2. The sum of a series of consecutive numbers from 1 to n can be defined recursively as:

```
sum(1) = 1;
sum(n) = n + sum(n - 1)
```

Write a recursive C function that accepts n as an argument and calculates the sum of the numbers from 1 to n.

3. a. The value of x^n can be defined recursively as:

$$x^0 = 1$$
$$x^n = x * x^{n-1}$$

Write a recursive function that computes and returns the value of x^n.

b. Rewrite the function written for Exercise 3a so that it uses a repetitive algorithm for calculating the value of x^n.

4. a. Write a function that recursively determines the value of the nth term of a geometric sequence defined by the terms

$$a, ar, ar^2, ar^3, \ldots, ar^{n-1}$$

The argument to the function should be the first term, a, the common ratio, r, and the value of n.

b. Modify the function written for Exercise 4a so that the sum of the first n terms of the sequence is returned.

5. a. Write a function that recursively determines the value of the nth term of an arithmetic sequence defined by the terms

$$a, a+d, a+2d, a+3d, \ldots, a+(n-1)d$$

The argument to the function should be the first term, a, the common difference, d, and the value of n.

b. Modify the function written for Exercise 5a so that the sum of the first n terms of the sequence is returned (*Note:* This is a more general form of Exercise 2.)

7.5 FOCUS ON PROBLEM SOLVING

A well-designed computer program starts like a well-designed term paper, with an outline. Just as a term paper begins with an initial outline that lists the paper's main topics, a computer program's initial outline provides a listing of the primary tasks that the program must accomplish. This is especially important when using functions, because each task required by the program is typically assigned to a function when it is coded.

As we have already seen, a computer program's initial outline is usually either a pseudocode description or a first-level structure diagram. This initial outline begins the process of defining a more complicated problem into a set of smaller, more manageable tasks. If it is required, each of these tasks can be further subdivided, or refined, into even smaller tasks. Once the tasks are well defined, the actual work of coding can begin, starting with any task, in any order. If there are more tasks than can be handled by one programmer, they can be distributed among as many programmers as required. This is equivalent to having many people work on a large research project, with each person responsible for an individual topic.

FIGURE 7.17   First-Level Structure Diagram of the Problem-Solver Algorithm

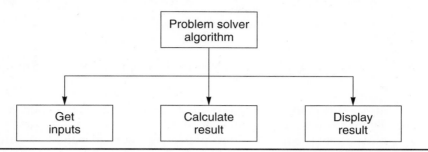

In its most general form, a typical outline applicable to most simple programs is the following algorithm:

Get the inputs to the problem.
Calculate the desired result.
Report the results of the calculation.

These three tasks are the primary responsibilities of every program, and we shall refer to this algorithm as the *problem-solver algorithm*. A first-level structure diagram of this algorithm is shown in Figure 7.17.

Each task in the problem-solver algorithm can be worked on independently and can, in turn, be refined and coded in any desired order, although completing the input section first usually makes testing and development easier. We now apply this refinement process to an actual programming problem. A new and very important aspect of this refinement will be the use of stubs (see Section 6.1) as "placeholder" functions. The stubs permit the construction of a working program while also providing for testing the transfer of data between functions. Once the overall program is constructed and running, each function is individually completed, integrated into the program in place of its stub, and tested. We show how this is accomplished with our next application.

Problem 1: Age Norms*

A fairly common procedure in child development is to establish normal ranges for height and weight as they relate to a child's age. These normal ranges are frequently referred to as *age norms*. In this application we develop a program for calculating both the expected height of a child between the ages of 6 and 11 and the deviation of this height norm to an actual child's height.

For our application, let us assume that as a part of a study on child development we have gathered various statistics on a group of normally maturing children between the ages of 6 and 11 years of age. From these data we have developed the following formula to predict the normal height, in inches, of a child in this age group:

$$\text{Normal height} = -0.25\,(\text{Age} - 6)^2 + 3.5\,(\text{Age} - 6) + 45$$

---

*This application as well as the problem-solver algorithm was provided by John Lyon of the University of Arizona for my Fortran text and is reprinted by permission of Scott/Jones publishers.

Using this formula we now develop a program to calculate and display the normal height for a child between 6 and 11 years old, and the percent difference from a child's actual height. The percent difference is given by the formula:

$$\text{Percent difference} = \frac{(100)\,(\text{Actual height} - \text{Normal height})}{\text{Normal Height}}$$

Next, we applying the software development process to this problem.

Analyze the Problem for Input/Output Requirements   At first glance it appears that this problem requires two inputs, the age and height of a child. There is one complication, however, because age is typically given in years and months, while the formula for the normal height requires age in years. Now we might be tempted to ask the user to enter an age, such as 10 years 6 months, as the number 10.5, but ultimately this will only cause resentment by the user. The correct approach is to permit the user to enter an age in years and months and have the computer convert the data entry into years. The conversion is easily accomplished using the formula *total years = years + months/12.0.*

Thus, the problem requires three inputs: a child's age in years and months, and the child's height. On the output side, two outputs are required: the "normal" height for a child of this age, and the percent difference between the child's actual height and the normal height. To ensure that we understand how the inputs will be converted into the required outputs, we do at least one hand calculation.

Assuming a child is 10 years and 6 months old, which converts to a yearly age of 10.5 years, the equation for calculating a normal height yields $-0.25\,*$ $(10.5 - 6)^2 + 3.5(1 - .5 - 6) + 45 = 55$ inches. Now assuming the child is actually 50 inches in height, the formula for percent difference yields $(100)(50 - 55)/50 =$ 9.09%. We will use these value as checks against those obtained from the completed program.

Develop a Solution   This problem, with the addition of a minor but important conversion issue, is a classic application of the problem-solver algorithm. For this particular application the problem solution takes the form:

Get the child's age and height as inputs.
Calculate a normal height and percent difference.
Display the calculated values.

The top-level structure diagram corresponding to this algorithm is shown in Figure 7.18. Using a modular design approach, each of the tasks specified in the structure is either coded as a function or is further developed and refined until all tasks are accounted for.

Although the modular approach permits us to develop functions in any order, the input section is typically constructed first to ensure that we understand the data with which we will be working. At this stage, it is convenient to accept these multiple inputs directly in the `main` function. Thus the requirement for the `main` function is that it first obtain the child's age and height. It must then convert the age value correctly and pass the child's age and height, as inputs, to a calculation module that must return a normal height and the

FIGURE 7.18 Top-Level Structure Diagram for Age Norms Program

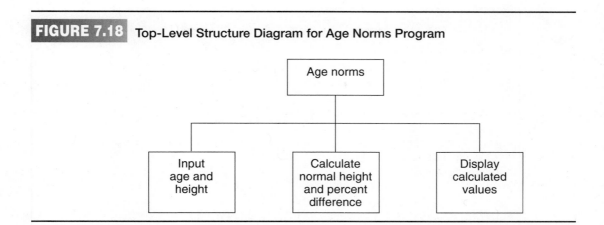

percent difference between the calculated normal height and actual height. Since a function can only return one direct value we must make a choice as to how we will implement the calculation module shown in Figure 7.18. We can either have the function return two values using pointers; or use two functions: one function to calculate and return the normal height, and the second function to calculate and return the percentage difference. We chose the two-function approach here and leave the one-function solution as an exercise (Exercise 2). Finally, the `main` function must pass the two calculated values to a display function. Figure 7.19 shows the refined, final structure diagram for this problem.

Code the Solution   Arbitrarily naming the calculation and display functions as `norms`, `pcdif`, and `showit`, respectively, and using stubs for these functions permits us to write a "skeleton" program, first, before completing the final program defined by Figure 7.19. This is a common practice when a program requires many functions, because it allows us to isolate and refine each function until all functions have been completed. Consider Program 7.10.

FIGURE 7.19 Refined Structure Diagram

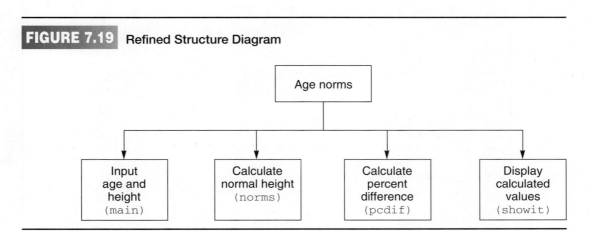

PROGRAM 7.10

```c
#include <stdio.h>
#include <math.h>
void main(void)
{
  int years, months, height, normht;
  float age, perdif;
  int norms(float);            /* here are the function prototypes */
  float pcdif(int, int);
  void showit(int, float);

  /* this is the input section */
  printf("\nHow old (in years) is this child? ");
  scanf("%d", &years);
  printf("How many months since the child's birthday? ");
  scanf("%d", &months);
  age = years + months/12.0;   /* convert to total years */
  printf("Enter the child's height (in inches): ");
  scanf("%d", &height);

  normht = norms(age);
  perdif = pcdif(height, normht);

  showit(normht, perdif);
}

/* the following is a stub for norms */
int norms(float age)
{
   printf("\nInto norms\n");
   printf("   age = %f\n", age);
   return(52);
}

/* the following is a stub for pcdif */
float pcdif(int childht, int avght)
{
  printf("\nInto pcdif\n");
  printf("   childht = %d     avght = %d\n", childht, avght);
  return(2.5);
}

/* the following is a stub for showit */
void showit(int normht, float perdif)
{
  printf("\nInto showit\n");
  printf("   normht = %d      perdif = %f\n", normht, perdif);
}
```

Notice that the input data required for the problem—year age, month age, and the child's height—are obtained from within main. The main function then calls norms with the single age argument that this function will need to calculate a "normal" height for this age. The pcdif function is then called with the two arguments it requires to calculate a percent difference. Finally it calls showit to display the values calculated in norms and pcdif. The program is then completed by the three stub functions, one for norms, one for pcdif, and one for showit.

Each stub function is constructed to display individually both a message indicating that the function has been called and the values of any passed arguments. Additionally, the stub for norms sets an arbitrary return value, as does the stub for pcdif. When these functions are fully developed, these values will be replaced by correctly calculated ones. For now, however, the values can be passed on to showit to verify correct argument transmission and receipt of all arguments.

Test and Debug the Program   Before proceeding with the development of each individual function, we test the program that we have. If the program works correctly, we can move on to function development; otherwise, we isolate the problem and retest until we are satisfied that what we have is working properly.

The following is the output from a sample run of Program 7.10.

```
How old (in years) is this child? 10
How many months since the child's birthday? 6
Enter the child's height (in inches): 50

Into norms
   age = 10.500000

Into pcdif
   childht = 50    avght = 52

Into showit
   normht = 52        perdif = 2.500000
```

This output verifies that the main function is working properly in obtaining an age and height, and converting an age of 10 years and 6 months to an equivalent decimal value of 10.5. Similarly, norms correctly receives the transmitted age and returns a value. The output also verifies that pcdif correctly receives the child's height and the "normal" height returned by norms. These values, in turn, are successfully passed to showit for display.

Having verified that the calling sequence of each function is correct, and that each function correctly receives its argument values, we can now develop them more completely to correctly calculate their return values. Because showit is the simpler of the three required functions, we will develop it first. This "out of order" development is not unusual; in fact, it is the same technique used by motion picture producers to complete a movie. Here we take advantage of the fact that displaying the results is rather trivial if someone else did the actual calculations. Besides, completing the output section gives us the means to verify the calculation section when it is completed. The showit function is:

```c
void showit(int normht, float perdif)
{
    printf("\nThe average height in inches is: %d\n", normht);
    printf("The actual height deviates by: %6.2f\%\n", perdif);
}
```

The showit function can either be placed in its own file and compiled separately, or placed directly into Program 7.10 as a replacement for the showit stub. In either case, the stub for showit is removed and the program rerun to test the completed showit function. This stub replacement procedure is a major testing technique used by all professional programmers. Its value is that it permits one to isolate and individually test each function as it is completed. Then, if the program does not act as we expect, we not only have a prior version to fall back on but have isolated the error to one particular function. This allows us either to continue working on the function or replace it with its stub and use the program as a test bed for one of the other functions. Assuming that our test of showit verifies its operation, we move on to completing the norms and pcdif functions.

We want norms to calculate and return the normal height given the child's age. A competed norms function that uses the formula previously given for calculating a "normal" height is:

```
#define MINAGE 6.0
int norm(float age)
{
    float agedif, avght;

    agedif = age - MINAGE;
    avght = (int)(-0.25*pow(agedif,2) + 3.5*agedif + 45.0);
    return(avght);
}
```

This function illustrates a typical calculation function. Also notice that norms uses a named constant, MINAGE, that defines the "base" age of six years old. Once again, having completed this function, we would use it in place of its stub and test it .

The last function, pcdif, is used to calculate the percent difference of the child's actual height from normal. Notice that the calculation of a percent difference is a general computation that can be used in other applications, so this is a useful function to have programmed. Here is the completed function:

```
float pcdif(int childht, int avght)
{
    return( fabs((float)(childht - avght)) / (float)(avght) * 100.0 );
}
```

Internally, the pcdif function uses no local variables and performs its calculation with the return statement. Since the function has two integer arguments, it uses explicit type conversion to avoid integer division and correctly return a floating-point value. Again, after completing this function, it should be used to replace its stub version and tested.

Program 7.11 illustrates the final evolution of Program 7.10 with all of the stubs replaced by their final versions.

A worthwhile feature of Program 7.11 is the use of the DEBUG constant. Setting this constant to 1 will force a display of the values returned by norms and pcdif. This display should be turned on when the norms and pcdif functions are completed to permit quick verification of their returned values. Once these functions pass their verification tests, DEBUG is set to 0.

PROGRAM 7.11

```c
#include <stdio.h>
#include <math.h>
#define DEBUG 0
main()
{
  int years, months, height, normht;
  float age, perdif;
  int norm(float);          /* here are the function prototypes */
  float pcdif(int, int);
  void showit(int, float);

  /* this is the input section */
  printf("\nHow old (in years) is this child? ");
  scanf("%d", &years);
  printf("How many months since the child's birthday? ");
  scanf("%d", &months);
  age = years + months/12.0;  /* convert to total years */
  printf("Enter the child's height (in inches): ");
  scanf("%d", &height);

  normht = norm(age);
  if (DEBUG)
    printf("normht = %d\n", normht);
  perdif = pcdif(height, normht);
  if (DEBUG)
    printf("perdif = %f\n", perdif);
  showit(normht, perdif);
}

#define MINAGE 6.0
int norm(float age)
{
  float agedif, avght;

  agedif = age - MINAGE;
  avght = (int)(-0.25*pow(agedif,2) + 3.5*agedif + 45.0);
  return (avght);
}

float pcdif(int childht, int avght)
{
  return (fabs((float)(childht - avght)) / (float)(avght) * 100.0 );
}

void showit(int normht, float perdif)
{
  printf("\nThe average height in inches is: %d\n", normht);
  printf("The actual height deviates by: %6.2f\%\n", perdif);
}
```

Here is a sample run of Program 7.11:

```
How old (in years) is this child? 10
How many months since the child's birthday? 6
Enter the child's height (in inches): 50

The average height in inches is: 55
The actual height deviates by: 9.09%
```

Because this result agrees with our previous hand calculation, and each function was individually tested for correct input in Program 7.10 and for correct output as the final version replaced the stub version, we have some degree of confidence that our program is correct.

Exercises 7.5

1. Modify Program 7.11 to calculate a child's normal weight and the percent weight difference in addition to the calculated height values. Assume the formula for predicting normal weight, in pounds, is:

   $$\text{Normal weight} = 0.5\,(\text{Age} - 6) + 5.0\,(\text{Age} - 6) + 48$$

2. Modify the function norms used in Program 7.11 to have it return both the normal height and the percentage difference. In doing so, retain the pcdif function, but have it be called from within norms.

3. Although useful functions having a void argument list are extremely limited, one such function can be constructed to return a value for π that is accurate to the maximum number of decimal places allowed by your computer. This value is obtained by taking the arcsine of 1.0, which is $\pi/2$, and multiplying the result by 2. In C, the required expression is $2.0 * asin(1.0)$, where the asin function is provided in the standard C mathematics library (remember to include math.h). Using this expression, write a C function named pi that returns the value of π.

4. The volume of a right circular cylinder is given by its radius squared times its height times pi. Assume you've written the function pi in Exercise 3. Now write a function that accepts two floating-point arguments, the radius of a cylinder and the cylinder's height, and returns the cylinder's volume. Use the function pi developed in Exercise 3 in your functions.

5. Write a function named distance that accepts the rectangular coordinates of two points (x_1, y_1) and (x_2, y_2), and calculates and returns the distance between the two points. The distance, d, between two points is given by the formula

   $$d = \sqrt{(x_2 - x_1)^2 + (y_2 - y_1)^2}$$

   Include your function in a complete working C program.

6. a. Write a function that calculates the area, a, of a circle when its circumference, c, is given. This function should call a second function, which returns the radius, r, of the circle, given c. The relevant formulas are $r = c/2\pi$ and $a = \pi r^2$.

   b. Write a structure chart for a program that accepts the value of the circumference from the user, calculates the radius and area, and displays the calculated values.

   c. Write and run a C program for the structure chart developed in Exercise 6b.

7. a. A recipe for making enough acorn squash for four people requires the following ingredients:

   2 acorn squashes
   2 teaspoons of lemon juice
   1/4 cup of raisins
   1½ cups of applesauce
   1/4 cup of brown sugar
   3 tablespoons of chopped walnuts

Using this information, write and test six functions that each accept the number of people that must be served and return the amount of each ingredient, respectively, that is required.

b. Write a structure chart for a program that accepts the number of people to be served, calculates the quantity of each ingredient needed, and displays the calculated values.

c. Write and run a C program for the structure chart developed in Exercise 7b.

8. The owner of a strawberry farm has made the following arrangement with a group of students: They may pick all the strawberries they want. When they are through picking, the strawberries will be weighed. The farm will retain 50% of the strawberries and the students will divide the remainder evenly between them. Using this information, write and test a C function named `straw` that accepts the number of students and the total pounds picked as input arguments, and returns the approximate number of strawberries each receives. Assume that a strawberry weighs approximately 1 ounce. There are 16 ounces to a pound. Include the `straw` function in a working C program.

9. a. The determinant of the 2 × 2 matrix

$$\begin{vmatrix} a_{11} & a_{12} \\ a_{21} & a_{22} \end{vmatrix}$$

is $a_{11}a_{22} - a_{21}a_{12}$. Similarly, the determinant of a 3 × 3 matrix

$$\begin{vmatrix} a_{11} & a_{12} & a_{13} \\ a_{21} & a_{22} & a_{23} \\ a_{31} & a_{32} & a_{33} \end{vmatrix} =$$

$$a_{11}\begin{vmatrix} a_{22} & a_{23} \\ a_{32} & a_{33} \end{vmatrix} - a_{21}\begin{vmatrix} a_{12} & a_{13} \\ a_{32} & a_{33} \end{vmatrix} + a_{31}\begin{vmatrix} a_{12} & a_{13} \\ a_{22} & a_{23} \end{vmatrix}$$

Using this information write and test two functions, named `det2` and `det3`. The `det2` function should accept the four coefficients of a 2 × 2 matrix and return its determinant. The `det3` function should accept the nine coefficients of a 3 × 3 matrix and return its determinant by calling `det2` to calculate the required 2 × 2 determinants.78

b. Write a structure chart for a program that accepts the nine coefficients of a 3 × 3 matrix in one function, passes these coefficients to `det3`, and uses a third function to display the calculated determinant.

c. Write and run a C program for the structure chart developed in Exercise 9b.

FIGURE 7.20 **Correspondence Between Polar (Distance and Angle) and Cartesian (x,y) Coordinates**

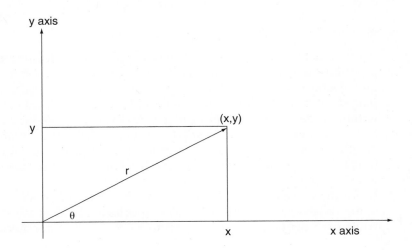

10. Assume that we must write a C program to convert the rectangular (*x,y*) coordinates of a point into polar form. That is, given an *x* and *y* position on a Cartesian coordinate system, as illustrated in Figure 7.20, we must calculate the distance from the origin, *r*, and the angle from the *x* axis, θ, specified by the point. The values of *r* and θ are referred to as the point's *polar coordinates*. When the *x* and *y* coordinates of a point are known, the equivalent *r* and θ coordinates can be calculated using the formulas:

$$r = \sqrt{x^2 + y^2}$$
$$\theta = \tan^{-1}(y/x), \quad x \neq 0$$

Using these formulas, write a function named polar that returns the *r* and θ values, respectively, as pointers, for a point having rectangular coordinates *x* and *y*.

7.6 COMMON PROGRAMMING ERRORS

A common error can occur when the same variable is declared locally within both the calling and called functions. Even though the variable name is the same, a change to one local variable *will* not alter the value in the other local variable.

Related to this error is the error caused when a local variable has the same name as a global variable. Within the function declaring it, the use of the local variable name only affects the local variable's contents.

Finally, for each function argument that has been declared as a pointer, you must remember to pass an address when the function is invoked.

7.7 CHAPTER REVIEW

Key Terms

address	program maintenance
auto	recursive functions
extern	register
global scope	scope
global variable	stack
local scope	static
local variable	storage class
pointer	variable scope

Summary

1. Every variable used in a program has a scope, which determines where in the program the variable can be used. The scope of a variable is either local or global and is determined by where the variable's definition statement is placed. A local variable is defined within a function and can only be used within its defining function or block. A global variable is defined outside a function and can be used in any function following the variable's definition. All global variables that are not specifically initialized by the user are initialized to zero by the compiler and can be shared between files using the keyword extern.

2. Every variable has a class. The class of a variable determines how long the value in the variable will be retained. auto variables are local variables that exist only while their defining function is executing. register variables are similar to

automatic variables but are stored in a computer's internal registers rather than in memory. static variables can be either global or local and retain their values for the duration of a program's execution. static variables are also set to zero when they are defined if they are not explicitly initialized by the user.

3. A function can be passed the address of a variable. If a called function is passed an address, it has the capability of directly accessing the respective calling function's variable. Using passed addresses permits a called function to return multiple values effectively.

4. A recursive solution is one in which the solution can be expressed in terms of a "simpler" version of itself. A recursive algorithm must always specify the first case or cases and how the *n*th case is related to the *(n −1)* case.

5. If a problem solution can be expressed repetitively or recursively with equal ease, the repetitive solution is preferable because it executes faster and uses less memory. In many advanced applications, recursion is simpler to visualize and the only practical means of implementing a solution.

Exercises

1. Write a function named time that has an integer argument named seconds and three integer pointer arguments named hours, min, and sec. The function is to convert the passed number of seconds into an equivalent number of hours, minutes, and seconds. Using the pointers, the function should directly alter the respective actual arguments in the calling function.

2. a. Write a function named date that accepts a long integer of the form yymmdd, such as 980412, determines the corresponding month, day, and year, and returns these three values to the calling function. For example, if date is called using the statement:

   date(980412, &month, &day, &year)

   the number 4 should be returned in month, the number 12 in day, and the number 98 in year. (*Hint*: See Exercise 9 in Section 6.5)

   b. Include the date subroutine written for Exercise 2a in a working program. The main function should correctly call date and display the three values returned by the function.

3. Assume there was no standard library function abs in C. Write the double-precision function dabsr that returns the absolute value of its double-precision argument.

4. Write the a function named payment that has three arguments: principal, which is the amount financed; int, which is the monthly interest rate; and months, which is the number of months the load exists. The function should return the monthly payment according to the following formula:

$$Payment = \frac{Principle}{\left[\dfrac{1 - (1 + Interest)^{-Months}}{Interest}\right]}$$

Note that the interest value used in this formula is a monthly rate, as a decimal. Thus if the yearly rate were 10%, the monthly rate is (.10/12). Test your function. What argument values cause it to malfunction (and should not be input)?

5. C's standard mathematical library functions sin, cos, and tan, sometimes need a little help. Angle measurements are often in degrees, not radians, and it's a nui-

sance (and potential source of error) to try to remember to apply the conversion factor. Write the functions `sindeg`, `cosdeg`, and `tandeg` that accept angle measurements in degrees and return the appropriate trigonometric relation. Use the function `pi` developed in Exercise 3 of Section 7.5 in your functions.

6. It is useful to have inverse trigonometric functions `asindeg`, `acosdeg`, and `atandeg` that return angle measurements in degrees instead of radians. Write these functions and use the pi function developed in Exercise 3 of Section 7.5.

Programming Pointer: We've used a "building-block" approach in these last two exercises. With the pi function developed in Exercise 3 of Section 7.5, it was simple to write the trigonometric functions that use degrees. With these functions completed, the rectangular-to-polar conversions are even more easily developed. Make free use of this technique as you develop programs. It simplifies program development, improves reliability, and provides a framework for future growth.

---

7. The following algorithm, discovered by Euclid, provides a simple means of determining the greatest common divisor (GCD) of two positive integers a and b:

Divide the larger number by the smaller and retain the remainder.

Divide the smaller number by the remainder, again retaining the remainder.

Continue dividing the prior remainder by the current remainder until the remainder is zero, at which point the last nonzero remainder is the greatest common divisor.

Write a recursive function named `GCD()` that implements this algorithm.

8. In the Fibonacci series 1, 1, 2, 3, 5, each element, after the first two elements, is simply the sum of the prior two values. In Exercise 1 of Section 7.4, you were asked to write a function that recursively computed the nth term of this series. For this exercise, write a function that uses repetition to calculate the nth term.

9. A classic recursion problem is represented by the Towers of Hanoi puzzle, which consists of three pegs and a set of disks initially set up as shown in Figure 7.21.

FIGURE 7.21   The Towers of Hanoi Puzzle

Peg A   Peg B   Peg C

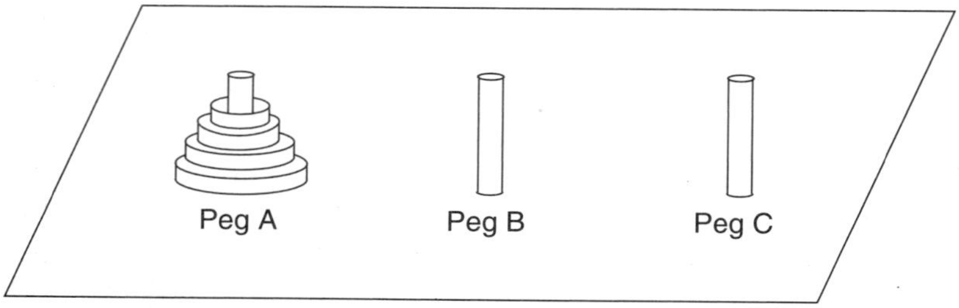

The object of the puzzle is to move all the disks from peg A to peg C, using peg B as needed, with the following constraints:

1. Only one disk may be moved at a time.

2. A larger disk can never be placed on a smaller disk.

The legend associated with this problem is that it was initially given, with 64 disks, to ancient monks in a monastery with the understanding that when the task was completed and all 64 disks reached peg C in the correct order, the world would end.

The solution to this puzzle is easily expressed as a recursive procedure where each n disk solution is defined in terms of an $n-1$ disk solution. To see how this works, first consider a one-disk puzzle. Clearly this has a simple solution, where we move the disk from peg A to peg C.

Now consider the two-disk problem. The solution to this puzzle is:

1. Use a one-disk solution to move the first disk to peg B.

2. Move the second disk to peg C.

3. Use a one-disk solution to move the disk on peg B to peg C.

The three-disk problem is slightly more complicated, but can be solved in terms of the two- and one-disk puzzle. The solution is:

1. Use a two-disk solution to get the first two disks in the right order on peg B.

2. Move the third disk to peg C.

3. Use a two-disk solution to correctly move the two disks from peg B to peg C.

Notice how the three-disk solution uses the two-disk solution and the two-disk solution uses the one-disk solution. Let's see if this same recursive reference holds for a four-disk puzzle. The solution to the four-disk puzzle is:

1. Use a three-disk solution to get the first three disks in the right order on peg B.

2. Move the fourth disk to peg C.

3. Use a three-disk solution to move the three disks from peg B to peg C.

At this stage we are ready to generalize the solution to n disks, which is:

1. Use an $n-1$ disk solution to get the first $n-1$ disks in the right order on peg B.

2. Move the nth disk to peg C.

3. Use the $n-1$ solution to move the $n-1$ disks from peg B to peg C.

Using this information, write a C program that asks the user how many disks to use and then prints the individual moves that must be made to solve the puzzle. For example, if the user responded with three for the number of disks, the program should display the following:

Move a disk from peg A to peg C
Move a disk from peg A to peg B
Move a disk from peg C to peg B
Move a disk from peg A to peg C
Move a disk from peg B to peg A
Move a disk from peg B to peg C
Move a disk from peg A to peg C

CHAPTER

8 | Arrays

The variables that we have used so far have all had a common characteristic: each variable could only be used to store a single value at a time. For example, although the variables `key`, `count`, and `grade` declared in the statements

```
char key;
int count;
float grade;
```

are of different data types, each variable can only store one value of the declared data type. These types of variables are called atomic variables. An *atomic variable*, which is also referred to as a *scalar variable*, is a variable whose value cannot be further subdivided or separated into a legitimate data type (see box page 72).

Frequently we may have a set of values, all of the same data type, that form a logical group. For example, Figure 8.1 illustrates three groups of items. The first group is a list of five floating-point temperatures, the second group is a list of four character codes, and the last group is a list of six integer grades.

FIGURE 8.1   Three Lists of Items

Temperatures	Codes	Grades
95.75	Z	98
83.0	C	87
97.625	K	92
72.5	L	79
86.25		85
		72

A simple list containing individual items of the same data type is called a *one-dimensional array*. In this chapter we describe how one-dimensional arrays are declared, initialized, stored inside a computer, and used. Additionally, we explore the use of one-dimensional arrays with example programs and present the procedures for declaring and using multidimensional arrays.

8.1 ONE-DIMENSIONAL ARRAYS

A one-dimensional array, which is also referred to as either a *single-dimensional array* or a *vector*, is a list of related values with the same data type that is stored using a single group name.[1] In C, as in other computer languages, the group name is referred to as the array name. For example, consider the list of temperatures illustrated in Figure 8.2. All the temperatures in the list are floating-point numbers and must be declared as such. However, the individual items in the list do not have to be declared separately. The items in the list can be declared as a single unit and stored under a common variable name called the array name. For convenience, we will choose temp as the name for the list shown in Figure 8.2. To specify that temp is to store five individual floating-point values requires the declaration statement float temp[5]. Notice that this declaration statement gives the array (or list) name, the data type of the items in the array, and the number of items in the array. Further examples of array declarations are:

```
int grades[5];
char code[4];
float amount[100];
```

Each array has sufficient memory reserved for it to hold the number of data items given in the declaration statement. Thus, the array named grades has storage reserved for five integers, the array named code has storage reserved for four characters, and the array named amount has storage reserved for 100 floating-point numbers. Figure 8.3 illustrates the storage reserved for the grades and code arrays. For illustrative purposes we have assumed that each character is stored using one byte and that each integer requires two bytes of storage.

FIGURE 8.2   A List of Temperatures

Temperatures

95.75
83.0
97.625
72.5
86.25

---

[1]Note that lists can be implemented in a variety of ways, some of which are further described in Chapter 14. An array is simply one implementation of a list in which all of the list elements are of the same type and each element is stored consecutively in a set of contiguous memory locations.

FIGURE 8.3 The grades and code Arrays in Memory

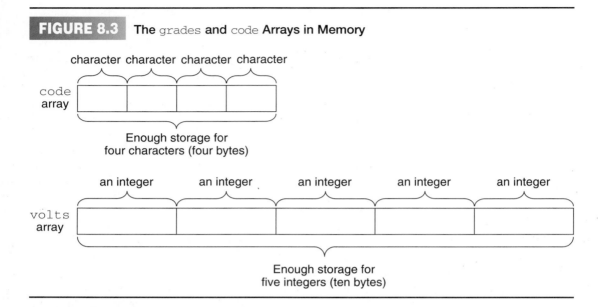

Each item in an array is called an *element* or *component* of the array. The individual elements stored in the arrays illustrated in Figure 8.3 are stored sequentially, with the first array element stored in the first reserved location, the second element stored in the second reserved location, and so on until the last element is stored in the last reserved location. This contiguous storage allocation for the list is a key feature of arrays because it provides a simple mechanism for easily locating any single element in the list.

Since elements in the array are stored sequentially, any individual element can be accessed by giving the name of the array and the element's position. This position is called the element's *index* or *subscript value* (the two terms are synonymous). For a single-dimensional array, the first element has an index of 0, the second element has an index of 1, and so on. In C, the array name and index of the desired element are combined by listing the index in braces after the array name. For example, given the declaration float temp[5],

temp[0] refers to the first temperature stored in the temp array

temp[1] refers to the second temperature stored in the temp array

temp[2] refers to the third temperature stored in the temp array

temp[3] refers to the fourth temperature stored in the temp array

temp[4] refers to the fifth temperature stored in the temp array

Figure 8.4 illustrates the temp array in memory with the correct designation for each array element. Each individual element is called an *indexed variable* or a *subscripted variable*, since both a variable name and an index or subscript value must be used to reference the element. Remember that the index or subscript value gives the position of the element in the array.

The subscripted variable, temp[0], is read as "temp sub zero." This is a shortened way of saying "the temp array subscripted by zero," and distinguishes the first element in an array from an atomic variable that could be declared as temp0. Similarly, temp[1] is read as "temp sub one," temp[2] as "temp sub two," and so on.

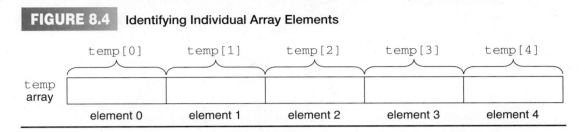

FIGURE 8.4   Identifying Individual Array Elements

Although it may seem unusual to reference the first element with an index of zero, the reason for doing so is as follows: Internally, unseen by the programmer, the computer uses the index as an offset from the array's starting position. As illustrated in Figure 8.5, the index tells the computer how many elements to skip, starting from the beginning of the array, to get to the desired element. From a programmer's viewpoint, then, it is sometimes easier to think of the first element in the array as element zero, the second element as element one, and so on. This makes the index value agree with the element number.

Subscripted variables can be used anywhere that scalar variables are valid. Examples using the elements of the `temp` array are:

```
temp[0] = 95.75;
temp[1] = temp[0] - 11.0;
temp[2] = 5.0 * temp[0];
temp[3] = 79.0;
temp[4] = (temp[1] + temp[2] - 3.1) / 2.2;
sum = temp[0] + temp[1] + temp[2] + temp[3] + temp[4];
```

The subscript contained within brackets need not be an integer constant; any expression that evaluates to an integer may be used as a subscript.[2] In each case, of course, the value of the expression must be within the valid subscript range

FIGURE 8.5   Accessing an Individual Array Element—Element 3

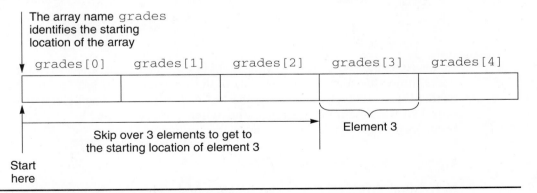

---

[2]Some compilers permit floating-point variables as subscripts; in these cases the floating-point value is truncated to an integer value.

defined when the array is declared. For example, assuming that i and j are int variables, the following subscripted variables are valid:

```
temp[i]
temp[2*i]
temp[j-i]
```

One extremely important advantage of using integer expressions as subscripts is that it allows sequencing through an array by using a loop. This makes statements like

```
sum = temp[0] + temp[1] + temp[2] + temp[3] + temp[4];
```

unnecessary. The subscript values in this statement can be replaced by a for loop counter to access each element in the array sequentially. For example, the code

```
sum = 0;                    /* initialize the sum to zero */
for (i = 0; i < 5; i++)
    sum = sum + temp[i];     /* add in a temperature */
```

sequentially retrieves each array element and adds the element to sum. Here the variable i is used both as the counter in the for loop and as a subscript. As i increases by one each time through the loop, the next element in the array is referenced. The procedure for adding the array elements within the for loop is similar to the accumulation procedure we have used many times before.

The advantage of using a for loop to sequence through an array becomes apparent when working with larger arrays. For example, if the temp array contained 100 values rather than just 5, simply changing the number 5 to 100 in the for statement is sufficient to sequence through the 100 elements and add each temperature to sum.

As another example of using a for loop to sequence through an array, assume that we want to locate the maximum value in an array of 1000 elements named grades. The procedure we will use to locate the maximum value is to assume initially that the first element in the array is the largest number. Then, as we sequence through the array, the maximum is compared to each element. When an element with a higher value is located, that element becomes the new maximum. The following code does the job.

```
maximum = grades[0];         /* set the maximum to element zero     */
for (i = 1; i < 1000; i++)   /* cycle through the rest of the array */
    if (grades[i] > maximum)  /* compare each element to the maximum */
        maximum = grades[i];   /* capture the new high value          */
```

In this code, the for statement consists of one if statement. The search for a new maximum value starts with element 1 of the array and continues through the last element. In a 1000-element array, the last element is 999. Each element is compared to the current maximum, and when a higher value is encountered it becomes the new maximum.

Input and Output of Array Values

Individual array elements can be assigned values interactively using the scanf() function. Examples of individual data entry statements are:

```
scanf("%f", &temp[0]);
scanf("%f %f %f", &temp[1], &temp[2], &temp[3]);
scanf("%f %f", &temp[4], &grades[6]);
```

In the first statement a single value will be read and stored in the variable named `temp[0]`. The second statement will cause three values to be read and stored in the variables `temp[1]`, `temp[2]`, and `temp[3]`, respectively. Finally, the last `scanf()` statement can be used to read values into the variables `temp[4]` and `grades[6]`.

Alternatively, a `for` loop can be used to cycle through the array for interactive data input. For example, the code

```
for (i = 0; i < 5; i++)
{
  printf("Enter a temperature: ");
  scanf("%f", &temp[i]);
}
```

prompts the user for five temperatures. The first temperature entered is stored in `temp[0]`, the second temperature entered in `temp[1]`, and so on until five temperatures have been input.

One caution should be mentioned about storing data in an array. C does not check the value of the index being used (called a *bounds check*). If an array has been declared as consisting of 10 elements, for example, and you use an index of 12, which is outside the bounds of the array, C will not notify you of the error when the program is compiled. The program will attempt to access element 12 by skipping over the appropriate number of bytes from the start of the array. Usually this results in a program crash—but not always. If the referenced location itself contains a value of the correct data type, the new value will simply overwrite the value in the referenced memory locations. This leads to more errors, which are particularly troublesome to locate when the variable legitimately assigned to the storage location is used at a different point in the program.

During output, individual array elements can be displayed using the `printf()` function or complete sections of the array can be displayed by including a `printf()` function call within a `for` loop. Examples using `printf()` to display subscripted variables are:

```
printf("%f", grades[6]);
```

and

```
printf("The value of element %d is %f", i, temp[i]);
```

and

```
for (n = 5; n <= 20; ++n)
  printf("%d %f\n", n, amount[n]);
```

The first `printf()` statement displays the value of the subscripted variable `grades[6]`. The second `printf()` statement displays the value of the subscript `i` and the value of `temp[i]`. Before this statement can be executed, `i` would have to have an assigned value. Finally, the last example includes a `printf()` statement within a `for` loop. Both the value of the index and the value of the elements from 5 to 20 are displayed.

◆ A CLOSER LOOK ◆

Structured Data Types

In contrast to atomic types (see box page 72), such as integer and floating-point data, there are structured types. A *structured type,* which is sometimes referred to as a *data structure,* is any type whose values can be decomposed and are related by some defined structure. Additionally, operations must be available for retrieving and updating individual values in the data structure.

Single-dimensional arrays are examples of a structured type. In a single-dimensional array, such as an array of integers, the array is composed of individual integer values where integers are related by their position in the list. Indexed variables provide the means of accessing and modifying values in the array.

Program 8.1 illustrates these input and output techniques using an array named `grades` that is defined to store five integer numbers. Included in the program are two `for` loops. The first `for` loop is used to cycle through each array element and allows the user to input individual array values. After five values have been entered, the second `for` loop is used to display the stored values.

PROGRAM 8.1

```c
#include <stdio.h>
#define MAXGRADES 5
void main(void)
{
  int i, grades[MAXGRADES];
  for (i = 0; i < MAXGRADES; i++)     /* Enter the grades */
  {
    printf("Enter a grade: ");
    scanf("%d", &grades[i]);
  }
  printf("\n");
  for (i = 0; i < MAXGRADES; i++)     /* Print the grades */
    printf("grades %d is %d\n", i, grades[i]);
}
```

A sample run of Program 8.1 follows:

```
Enter a grade: 85
Enter a grade: 90
Enter a grade: 78
Enter a grade: 75
Enter a grade: 92

grades 0 is 85
grades 1 is 90
grades 2 is 78
grades 3 is 75
grades 4 is 92
```

In reviewing the output produced by Program 8.1, pay particular attention to the difference between the index value displayed and the numerical value stored in the corresponding array element. *The index value refers to the location of the element in the array, while the subscripted variable refers to the value stored in the designated location.*

In addition to simply displaying the values stored in each array element, the elements can also be processed by appropriately referencing the desired element. For example, in Program 8.2, the value of each element is accumulated in a total, which is displayed upon completion of the individual display of each array element.

PROGRAM 8.2

```c
#include <stdio.h>
#define MAXGRADES 5
void main(void)
{
  int i, grades[MAXGRADES], total = 0;
  for (i = 0; i < MAXGRADES; i++) /* Enter the grades */
  {
    printf("Enter a grade: ");
    scanf("%d", &grades[i]);
  }
  printf("\nThe total of the grades ");
  for (i = 0; i < MAXGRADES; i++) /* Display and total the grades */
  {
    printf("%d   ", grades[i]);
    total =  total + grades[i];
  }
  printf("is  %d\n",total);
}
```

A sample run of Program 8.2 follows:

```
Enter a grade: 85
Enter a grade: 90
Enter a grade: 78
Enter a grade: 75
Enter a grade: 92

The total of the grades 85  90  78  75  92  is   420
```

Notice that in Program 8.2, unlike Program 8.1, only the values stored in each array element are displayed. Although the second for loop was used to accumulate the total of each element, the accumulation could also have been accomplished in the first loop by placing the statement total = total + grades[i]; after the scanf() call used to enter a value. Also notice that the printf() call used to display the total is made outside of the second for loop, so that the total is displayed only once, after all values have been added to the total. If this printf() call were placed inside of the for loop, five totals would be displayed, with only the last displayed total containing the sum of all of the array values.

Exercises 8.1

1. Write array declarations for the following:

    a. A list of 100 float grades

    b. A list of 50 floating-point temperatures

    c. A list of 30 characters, each representing a code

    d. A list of 100 integer years

    e. A list of 32 floating-point velocities

    f. A list of 1000 floating-point distances

    g. a list of 6 integer code numbers

2. Write appropriate notation for the first, third, and seventh elements of the following arrays:

    a. `int grades[20]`

    b. `float grades[10]`

    c. `float amps[16]`

    d. `int dist[15]`

    e. `float velocity[25]`

    f. `float time[100]`

3. a. Write individual `scanf()` statements that can be used to enter values into the first, third, and seventh elements of each of the arrays declared in Exercises 2a through 2f.

    b. Write a `for` loop that can be used to enter values for the complete array declared in Exercise 2a.

4. a. Write individual `printf()` statements that can be used to print the values from the first, third, and seventh elements of each of the arrays declared in Exercises 2a through 2f.

    b. Write a `for` loop that can be used to display values for the complete array declared in Exercise 2a.

5. List the elements that will be displayed by the following sections of code:

    a. ```
for (m = 1; m <= 5; m++)
    printf("%d ", a[m]);
```

    b. ```
for (k = 1; k <= 5; k = k + 2)
    printf("%d ", a[k]);
```

    c. ```
for (j = 3; j <= 10; j++)
    printf("%d ", b[j]);
```

    d. ```
for (k = 3; k <= 12; k = k + 3)
    printf("%d ", b[k]);
```

    e. ```
for (i = 2; i < 11; i = i + 2)
    printf("%d ", c[i]);
```

6. a. Write a program to input the following values into an array named prices: 10.95, 16.32, 12.15, 8.22, 15.98, 26.22, 13.54, 6.45, 17.59. After the data has been entered, have your program output the values.

    b. Repeat Exercise 6a, but after the data has been entered, have your program display it in the following form:
```

10.95	16.32	12.15
8.22	15.98	26.22
13.54	6.45	17.59

7. Write a program to input eight integer numbers into an array named `temp`. As each number is input, add the numbers into a total. After all numbers are input, display the numbers and their average.

8. a. Write a program to input 10 integer numbers into an array named `fmax` and determine the maximum value entered. Your program should contain only one loop and the maximum should be determined as array element values are being input. (*Hint:* Set the maximum equal to the first array element, which should be input before the loop used to input the remaining array values.)

   b. Repeat Exercise 8a, keeping track of both the maximum element in the array and the index number for the maximum. After displaying the numbers, print these two messages:

      The maximum value is: _____

      This is element number _____ in the list of numbers

   Have your program display the correct values in place of the underlines in the messages.

   c. Repeat Exercise 8b, but have your program locate the minimum of the data entered.

9. a. Write a program to input the following integer numbers into an array named grades: 89, 95, 72, 83, 99, 54, 86, 75, 92, 73, 79, 75, 82, 73. As each number is input, add the numbers to a total. After all numbers are input and the total is obtained, calculate the average of the numbers and use the average to determine the deviation of each value from the average. Store each deviation in an array named `deviation`. Each deviation is obtained as the element value less the average of all the data. Have your program display each deviation alongside its corresponding element from the `grades` array.

   b. Calculate the variance of the data used in Exercise 9a. The variance is obtained by squaring each individual deviation and dividing the sum of the squared deviations by the number of deviations.

10. Write a program that specifies three one-dimensional arrays named `prices`, `quantity`, and `amount`. Each array should be capable of holding 10 elements. Using a `for` loop, input values for the prices and quantity arrays. The entries in the `amount` array should be the product of the corresponding values in the prices and quantity arrays (thus, `amount[i]` = `price[i]` * `quantity[i]`). After all of the data has been entered, display the following output:

        Price   Quantity   Amount
        -----   --------   ------

    Under each column heading display the appropriate value.

11. a. Write a program that inputs 10 float numbers into an array named `raw`. After 10 user-input numbers are entered into the array, your program should cycle through `raw` 10 times. During each pass through the array, your program should select the lowest value in `raw` and place the selected value in the next available slot in an array named `sorted`. Thus, when your program is complete, the `sorted` array should contain the numbers in `raw` in sorted order from lowest to highest. (*Hint:* Make sure you reset the lowest value selected during each pass to a very high number so that it is not selected again. You will need a second `for` loop within the first `for` loop to locate the minimum value for each pass.)

b. The method used in Exercise 11a to sort the values in the array is very inefficient. Can you determine why? What might be a better method of sorting the
numbers in an array?

8.2 ARRAY INITIALIZATION

Array elements can be initialized within their declaration statements in the same
manner as scalar variables, except that the initializing elements must be included
in braces. Examples of such initializations are[3]:

```
int grades[5] = {98, 87, 92, 79, 85};
char codes[6] = {'s', 'a', 'm', 'p', 'l', 'e'};
double width[7] = {10.96, 6.43, 2.58, .86, 5.89, 7.56, 8.22};
```

Initializers are applied in the order in which they are written, with the first value
used to initialize element 0, the second value used to initialize element 1, and so
on, until all values have been used. Thus, in the declaration

```
int grades[5] = {98, 87, 92, 79, 85};
```

grades[0] is initialized to 98, grades[1] is initialized to 87, grades[2] is initialized to 92, grades[3] is initialized to 79, and grades[4] is initialized to 85.

Because whitespace is ignored in C, initializations may be continued across
multiple lines. For example, the declaration

```
int gallons[20] = {19, 16, 14, 19, 20, 18,   /* initializing values */
                   12, 10, 22, 15, 18, 17,   /* may extend across   */
                   16, 14, 23, 19, 15, 18,   /* multiple lines      */
                   21, 5};
```

uses four lines to initialize all of the array elements.

If the number of initializers is less than the declared number of elements listed in square brackets, the initializers are applied starting with array element
zero. Thus, in the declaration

```
float length[7] = {7.8, 6.4, 4.9, 11.2};
```

only length[0], length[1], length[2], and length[3] are initialized
with the listed values. The other array elements will be initialized to zero.

Unfortunately, there is no method of either indicating repetition of an initialization value or initializing later array elements without first specifying values
for earlier elements.

A unique feature of initializers is that the size of an array may be omitted
when initializing values are included in the declaration statement. For example,
the declaration

```
int gallons[] = {16, 12, 10, 14, 11};
```

reserves enough storage room for five elements. Similarly, the following two declarations are equivalent:

---

[3]Note that in older versions of C (non-ANSI) only global and local static arrays (see
Sections 7.1 and 7.2) could be initialized within their declaration statements. Local auto
arrays could not be initialized in this manner.

A BIT OF BACKGROUND

Handling Lists with LISP

Methods of handling lists have been especially important in the development of computer science and applications. In fact, in 1958 John McCarthy developed a language at the Massachusetts Institute of Technology specifically for manipulating lists. This language was named *LISP*, the acronym for *LISt Processing*. It has proved valuable for handling problems based on mathematical logic and is used extensively in artificial intelligence and pattern recognition projects.

One simple language related to LISP is named *Logo*, and has been made particularly user-friendly. It incorporates a technique called "turtle graphics," by which a pointer is moved around the screen to plot geometric figures. Logo has been used widely to teach programming fundamentals to children.

```
char codes[6] = {'s', 'a', 'm', 'p', 'l', 'e'};
char codes[] = {'s', 'a', 'm', 'p', 'l', 'e'};
```

Both of these declarations set aside six character locations for an array named `codes`. An interesting and useful simplification can also be used when initializing character arrays. For example, the declaration

```
char codes[] = "sample"; /* no braces or commas */
```

uses the string `"sample"` to initialize the codes array. Recall that a string is any sequence of characters enclosed in double quotes. This last declaration creates an array named `codes` having seven elements and fills the array with the seven characters illustrated in Figure 8.6. The first six characters, as expected, consist of the letters s, a, m, p, l, and e. The last character, which is the escape sequence \0, is called the *null character*. The null character is automatically appended to all strings by the C compiler. This character has an internal storage code that is numerically equal to zero (the storage code for the zero character has a numerical value of decimal 48, so the two cannot be confused by the computer), and is used as a marker, or sentinel, to mark the end of a string. As we shall see in Chapter 11, this marker is invaluable when manipulating strings of characters.

Once values have been assigned to array elements, either through initialization within the declaration statement or using the interactive input described in Section 7.2, the array elements can be processed as described in the previous section. For example, Program 8.3 illustrates the initialization of array elements within the declaration of the array and then uses a `for` loop to locate the maximum value stored in the array.

FIGURE 8.6 A String Is Terminated with a Special Sentinel

codes[0]	codes[1]	codes[2]	codes[3]	codes[4]	codes[5]	codes[6]
s	a	m	p	l	e	\0

PROGRAM 8.3

```c
#include <stdio.h>
#define MAXELS 5
void main(void)
{
  int i, max, nums[MAXELS] = {2, 18, 1, 27, 16};
  max = nums[0];
  for (i = 1; i < MAXELS; i++)
    if (max < nums[i])
      max = nums[i];
  printf("The maximum value is %d\n", max);
}
```

The output produced by Program 8.3 is:

```
The maximum value is 27
```

Exercises 8.2

1. Write array declarations, including initializers, for the following:

   a. A list of 10 integer grades: 89, 75, 82, 93, 78, 95, 81, 88, 77, 82

   b. A list of 5 double-precision amounts: 10.62, 13.98, 18.45, 12.68, 14.76

   c. A list of 100 double-precision interest rates; the first six rates are 6.29, 6.95, 7.25, 7.35, 7.40, 7.42

   d. A list of 64 floating-point temperatures; the first 10 temperatures are 78.2, 69.6, 68.5, 83.9, 55.4, 67.0, 49.8, 58.3, 62.5, 71.6

   e. A list of 15 character codes; the first seven codes are f, j, m, q, t, w, z

2. Write an array declaration statement that stores the following values in an array named `prices`: 16.24, 18.98, 23.75, 16.29, 19.54, 14.22, 11.13, 15.39. Include these statements in a program that displays the values in the array.

3. Write a program that uses an array declaration statement to initialize the following numbers in an array named `slopes`: 17.24, 25.63, 5.94, 33.92, 3.71, 32.84, 35.93, 18.24, 6.92. Your program should locate and display both the maximum and minimum values in the array.

4. Write a program that stores the following prices in an array named `prices`: 9.92, 6.32, 12.63, 5.95, 10.29. Your program should also create two arrays named `units` and `amounts`, each capable of storing five double-precision numbers. Using a `for` loop and a `scanf()` function call, have your program accept five user-input numbers into the `units` array when the program is run. Your program should store the product of the corresponding values in the `prices` and `units` arrays in the `amounts` array (for example, `amounts[1] = prices[1] * units[1]`) and display the following output (fill in the table appropriately):

Price	Units	Amount
-----	-----	------
9.92	.	.
6.32	.	.
12.63	.	.
5.95	.	.
10.29	.	.

Total:		.

5. The string of characters "Good Morning" is to be stored in a character array named goodstr1. Write the declaration for this array in three different ways.

6. a. Write declaration statements to store the string of characters "Input the Following Data" in a character array named messag1, the string "----------------------------" in an array named messag2, the string "Enter the Date: " in an array named messag3, and the string "Enter the Account Number: " in the array named messag4.

   b. Include the array declarations written in Exercise 6a in a program that uses the printf() function to display the messages. For example, the statement printf("%s", messag1); causes the string stored in the messag1 array to be displayed. Your program will require four such statements to display the four individual messages. Using the printf() function with the %s control sequence to display a string requires that the end-of-string marker \0 be present in the character array used to store the string.

7. a. Write a declaration to store the string "This is a test" into an array named strtest. Include the declaration in a program to display the message using the following loop:

   ```
   for (i = 0; i < NUMDISPLAY; i++)
     printf("%c", strtest[i]);
   ```

   where NUMDISPLAY is a named constant for the number 14.

   b. Modify the for statement in Exercise 7a to display only the array characters t, e, s, and t.

   c. Include the array declaration written in Exercise 7a in a program that uses the printf() function to display characters in the array. For example, the statement printf("%s", strtest); will cause the string stored in the strtest array to be displayed. Using this statement requires that the last character in the array be the end-of-string marker \0.

   d. Repeat Exercise 7a using a while loop. [*Hint:* Stop the loop when the \0 escape sequence is detected. The expression while (strtest[i] != '\0') can be used.]

8.3 ARRAYS AS FUNCTION ARGUMENTS

Individual array elements are passed to a called function in the same manner as individual scalar variables; they are simply included as subscripted variables when the function call is made. For example, the function call

```
find_min(grades[2], grades[6]);
```

passes the values of the elements grades[2] and grades[6] to the function find_min().

Passing a complete array of values to a function is in many respects an easier operation than passing individual elements. The called function receives access to the actual array, rather than a copy of the values in the array. For example, if grades is an array, the function call find_max(grades); makes the complete grades array available to the find_max() function. This is different from passing a single variable to a function.

Recall that when a single scalar argument is passed to a function, the called function only receives a copy of the passed value, which is stored in one of the function's parameters. If arrays were passed in this manner, a copy of the complete array would have to be created. For large arrays, making duplicate copies of the array for each function call would be wasteful of computer storage and would frustrate the effort to return multiple element changes made by the called program (recall that a function directly returns at most one value). To avoid these problems, the called function is given direct access to the original array. Thus, any changes made by the called function are made directly to the array itself. For the following specific examples of function calls, assume that the arrays nums, keys, units, and prices are declared as:

```
int nums[5];                         /* an array of five integers  */
char keys[256];                      /* an array of 256 characters */
double units[500], prices[500];      /* two arrays of 500 doubles  */
```

For these arrays, the following function calls can be made:

```
find_max(nums);
find_ch(keys);
calc_tot(nums, units, prices);
```

In each case, the called function receives direct access to the named array.

On the receiving side, the called function must be alerted that an array is being made available. For example, suitable function header lines for the previous functions are:

```
int find_max(int vals[5])
char find_ch(char in_keys[256])
void calc_tot(int arr1[5], double arr2[500], double arr3[500])
```

In each of these function header lines, the names in the parameter list are chosen by the programmer. However, the parameter names used by the functions still refer to the original array created outside the function. This is made clear in Program 8.4.

PROGRAM 8.4

```
#include <stdio.h>
#define MAXELS 5
void main(void)
{
  int nums[MAXELS] = {2, 18, 1, 27, 16};
  int find_max(int [MAXELS]); /* function prototype */

  printf("The maximum value is %d\n", find_max(nums));
}

int find_max(int vals[MAXELS])  /* find the maximum value */
{
  int i, max = vals[0];

  for (i = 1; i < MAXELS; i++)
    if (max < vals[i]) max = vals[i];
  return(max);
}
```

Notice that the function prototype for `find_max()` within `main()` declares that `find_max` will return an integer and expects an array of five integers as an actual argument. It is also important to know that only one array is created in Program 8.4. In `main()` this array is known as `nums`, and in `find_max()` the array is known as `vals`. As illustrated in Figure 8.7, both names refer to the same array. Thus, in Figure 8.7 `vals[3]` is the same element as `nums[3]`.

The parameter declaration in the `find_max()` header line actually contains extra information that is not required by the function. All that `find_max()` must know is that the argument `vals` references an array of integers. Since the array has been created in `main()` and no additional storage space is needed in `find_max()`, the declaration for `vals` can omit the size of the array. Thus, an alternative function header line is:

$$\text{int find\_max(int vals[])}$$

This form of the function header makes more sense when you realize that only one item is actually passed to `find_max` when the function is called, which is the starting address of the `num` array. This is illustrated in Figure 8.8. Since only the starting address of `vals` is passed to `find_max`, the number of elements in the array need not be included in the declaration for `vals`.[4] In fact, it is generally advisable to omit the size of the array in the function header line. For example, consider the more general form of

---

FIGURE 8.7   Only One Array Is Created

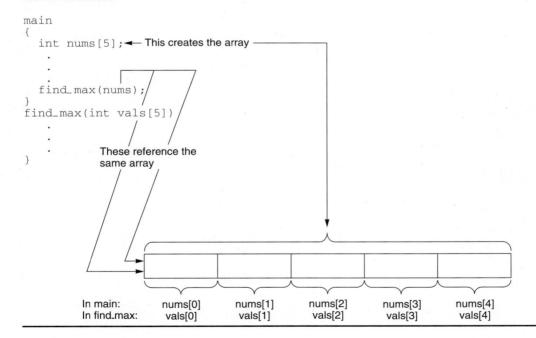

| In main: | nums[0] | nums[1] | nums[2] | nums[3] | nums[4] |
| In find_max: | vals[0] | vals[1] | vals[2] | vals[3] | vals[4] |

---

[4]An important consequence of this is that `find_max()` has direct access to the passed array. This means that any change to an element of the `vals` array actually is a change to the `nums` array. This is significantly different than the situation with scalar variables, where the called function does not receive direct access to the passed variable.

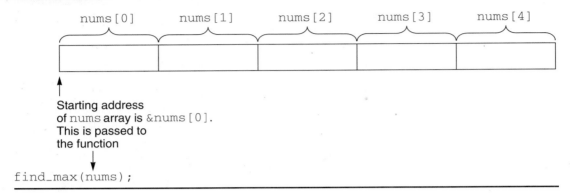

FIGURE 8.8   The Starting Address of the Array Is Passed

find_max(), which can be used to find the maximum value of an integer array of arbitrary size:

```c
int find_max(int vals[], int num_els)  /* find the maximum value */
{
  int i, max = vals[0];

  for (i = 1; i < num_els; i++)
   if (max < vals[i])
     max = vals[i];
  return(max);
}
```

Program 8.5 illustrates this function in a complete program.

PROGRAM 8.5

```c
#include <stdio.h>
#define MAXELS 5
void main(void)
{
  int nums[MAXELS] = {2, 18, 1, 27, 16};
  int find_max(int [], int); /* function prototype */

  printf("The maximum value is %d\n", find_max(nums, MAXELS));
}

int find_max(int vals[], int num_els)
{
  int i, max = vals[0];

  for (i = 1; i < num_els; i++)
    if (max < vals[i]) max = vals[i];

  return(max);
}
```

The more general form of find_max() used in Program 8.5 declares that the function returns an integer value. The function expects the starting address of an integer array and the number of elements in the array as arguments. Then, using the number of elements as the boundary for its search, the function's for loop causes each array element to be examined in sequential order to locate the maximum value. Since the highest subscript allowed is always one less than the total number of elements in the array, the expression (num_els - 1) is used to terminate the loop.

The output displayed by both Programs 8.4 and 8.5 is:

```
The maximum value is 27
```

Exercises 8.3

1. The following declaration was used to create the prices array:

   ```
   double prices[500];
   ```

   Write two different function header lines for a function named sort_arr() that accepts the prices array as an argument named in_array and returns no value.

2. The following declaration was used to create the keys array:

   ```
   char keys[256];
   ```

   Write two different function header lines for a function named find_key() that accepts the keys array as an argument named select and returns no value.

3. The following declaration was used to create the rates array:

   ```
   float rates[256];
   ```

   Write two different function header lines for a function named prime() that accepts the rates array as an argument named rates and returns a float.

4. a. Modify the find_max() function in Program 8.4 to locate the minimum value of the passed array.

   b. Include the function written in Exercise 4a in a complete program and run the program on a computer.

5. Write a program that has a declaration in main() to store the following numbers into an array named rates: 6.5, 7.2, 7.5, 8.3, 8.6, 9.4, 9.6, 9.8, 10.0. There should be a function call to show() that accepts the rates array as an argument named rates and then displays the numbers in the array.

6. a. Write a program that has a declaration in main() to store the string "Vacation is near" into an array named message.
   There should be a function call to display() that accepts message in an argument named strng and then displays the message.

   b. Modify the display() function written in Exercise 6a to display the first eight elements of the message array.

7. Write a program that declares three single-dimensional arrays named price, quantity, and amount. Each array should be declared in main() and should be capable of holding 10 double-precision numbers. The numbers that should be

stored in price are 10.62, 14.89, 13.21, 16.55, 18.62, 9.47, 6.58, 18.32, 12.15, 3.98. The numbers that should be stored in quantity are 4, 8.5, 6, 7.35, 9, 15.3, 3, 5.4, 2.9, 4.8. Your program should pass these three arrays to a function called extend(), which should calculate the elements in the amount array as the product of the corresponding elements in the price and quantity arrays (for example, amount[1] = price[1] * quantity[1]). After extend() has put values into the amount array, the values in the array should be displayed from within main().

8. Write a program that includes two functions named calc_avg() and variance(). The calc_avg() function should calculate and return the average of the values stored in an array named testvals. The array should be declared in main() and include the values 89, 95, 72, 83, 99, 54, 86, 75, 92, 73, 79, 75, 82, 73. The variance() function should calculate and return the variance of the data. The variance is obtained by subtracting the average from each value in testvals, squaring the values obtained, adding them, and dividing by the number of elements in testvals. The values returned from calc_avg() and variance should be displayed using printf() function calls in main().

8.4 FOCUS ON PROBLEM SOLVING

The next two applications are presented to illustrate using array processing and to further our understanding of using arrays as function arguments. In the first application, two statistical functions are created to determine the average and standard deviation, respectively, of an array of numbers. In the second application, a function is used to insert an identification number into an existing array that is maintained in a sorted order.

Application 1: Statistical Analysis

Two functions are to be developed to determine the average and standard deviation, respectively, of a list of integer numbers. Each function must be capable of accepting the numbers as an array and returning their calculated values to the calling function. We now apply the top-down development procedure to developing the required functions.

Analyze the Problem for Input/Output Requirements The statement of the problem indicates that two output values are required: an average and a standard deviation.

The input item defined in the problem statement is a list of integer numbers. Because the size of the list is not specified in the problem statement and to make our functions as general as possible, both functions will be designed to handle any size list passed to it. This requires that the exact number of elements in the array must also be passed to each function at the time of the function call. From each function's viewpoint this means that it must be capable of receiving at least two input items as arguments: an array of arbitrary size and an integer number corresponding to the number of elements in the passed array.

Develop a Solution The I/O specifications imply that the argument list of each function must be capable of receiving at least two items: one argument to

A BIT OF BACKGROUND

Statistics

The sum, sum of squares, and average of a list of numbers are commonly used quantities in statistics.

By all means take a course in statistics! Some of the most important applications of mathematics and computing to the real world are in the area of statistics. Whether you are in business, engineering, politics, government, weather forecasting, sports, education, or virtually any other field you can name, being able to handle statistics will give you a decided advantage. It has been claimed that "statistics don't lie, but some statisticians do," and this is true. Statistical methods and data are sometimes misused by people to convince others—people who do not understand statistics—of something the statistics really do not support.

accommodate the integer array and the second argument to accept an integer. The first function is to return the average of the numbers in the passed array and the second function the standard deviation. These items are determined as follows:

Calculate the average by adding the grades and dividing by the number of grades that were added.
Determine the standard deviation by:
1. *Subtracting the average from each individual grade. This results in a set of new numbers, each of which is called a deviation.*
2. *Square each deviation found in the previous step.*
3. *Add the squared deviations and divide the sum by the number of deviations.*
4. *The square root of the number found in the previous step is the standard deviation.*

Notice that the calculation of the standard deviation requires the average, which means that the standard deviation can only be calculated only after the average has been computed. Thus, in addition to requiring the array of integers and the number of values in the array, the standard deviation function also will require that the average be passed to it. This is the advantage of specifying the algorithm, in detail, before any coding is done; it ensures that all necessary inputs and requirements are discovered early in the programming process.

To ensure that we understand the required processing we will do a hand calculation. For this calculation we will arbitrarily assume that the average and standard deviation of the following 10 grades are to be determined: 98, 82, 67, 54, 78, 83, 95, 76, 68, and 63.

The average of this data is determined as

$$\text{Average} = (98 + 82 + 67 + 54 + 78 + 83 + 95 + 76 + 68 + 63)/10 = 76.4$$

The standard deviation is calculated by first determining the sum of the squared deviations. The standard deviation is then obtained by dividing the resulting sum by 10 and taking its square root.

$$\text{Sum of squared deviations} = (98 - 76.4)^2 + (82 - 76.4)^2$$
$$+ (67 - 76.4)^2 + (54 - 76.4)^2$$
$$+ (78 - 76.4)^2 + (83 - 76.4)^2$$
$$+ (95 - 76.4)^2 + (76 - 76.4)^2$$
$$+ (68 - 76.4)^2 + (63 - 76.4)^2$$
$$= 1730.400700$$

$$\text{Standard deviation} = \sqrt{1730.4007/10} = \sqrt{173.04007} = 13.154470$$

Having specified the algorithm required of each function, we are now in a position to code them.

Code the Solution   In writing functions it is convenient to initially concentrate on the header line. The body of the function can then be written to process the input arguments correctly to produce the desired results.

Naming our averaging function `find_avg()`, and arbitrarily selecting the argument names `nums` and `numel` for the passed array and the number of elements, respectively, the function header becomes

```
float find_avg(int nums[], int numel)
```

This begins the definition of the averaging function as accepting an array of integer values and an integer number. As illustrated by the hand calculation, the average of a set of integer numbers can be a floating-point number; therefore, the function is defined as returning a floating-point value. The body of the function calculates the average as described by the algorithm developed earlier. Thus, the completed `find_avg()` function becomes:

```
float find_avg(int nums[], int numel)
{
  int i;
  float sumnums = 0.0;

  for (i = 0; i < numel; i++)  /* calculate the sum of the grades */
    sumnums = sumnums + nums[i];

  return(sumnums / numel);     /* calculate and return the average */
}
```

In the body of the function is a `for` loop to sum the individual numbers. Notice also that the termination value of the loop counter in the `for` loop is `numel`, the number of integers in the array that are passed to the function through the argument list. The use of this argument gives the function its generality and allows it to be used for input arrays of any size. For example, calling the function with the statement

```
find_avg(values,10)
```

tells the function that `numel` is 10 and the `values` array consists of 10 values, while the statement

```
find_avg(values,1000)
```

tells `find_avg()` that `numel` is 1000 and that the `values` array consists of 1000 numbers. In both calls the actual argument named `values` corresponds to the parameter named `nums` within the `find_avg()` function.

Using similar reasoning as that for the averaging function, the function header for the standard deviation routine, which we will name `std_dev()`, becomes:

```
float std_dev(int nums[], int numel, float av)
```

This header begins the definition of the `std_dev()` function. It defines the function as returning a floating-point value and accepting an array of integers, an integer value, and a floating-point value as inputs to the function. The body of the `std_dev()` function must calculate the standard deviation as described in the development step. The complete standard deviation function becomes:

```
float std_dev(int nums[], int numel, float av)
{
  int i;
  float sumdevs = 0.0;

  for (i = 0; i < numel; i++)
    sumdevs = sumdevs + pow((nums[i] - av),2.0);

  return(sqrt(sumdevs/numel));
}
```

Test and Debug the Program   Testing a program's functions requires writing a main program unit to call the function and display the returned results. Program 8.6 uses such a main unit to set up a `grades` array with the data previously used in our hand calculation and to call the `find_avg` function.

A test run using Program 8.6 produced the following display:

```
The average of the numbers is 76.40
The standard deviation of the numbers is 13.15
```

Although this result agrees with our previous hand calculation, testing is really not complete without verifying the calculation at the boundary points. In this case such a test consists of checking the calculation with all of the same values, such as all 0's and all 100's. Another simple test would be to use five 0's and five 100's. We leave these tests as an exercise.

Application 2: List Maintenance

A common programming problem is to maintain a list in either numerical or alphabetical order. For example, telephone lists are traditionally kept in alphabetical order, whereas lists of part numbers are kept in numerical order.

As part of an overall maintenance program, a function is to be written that correctly inserts a three-digit identification code within a list of numbers. The list is maintained in increasing number order and duplicate identification codes are not allowed. In this application such a function will be written. A maximum list size of 100 values will be allowed and a sentinel value of 9999 will be used to indicate the end of the list. Thus, for example, if the current list contains nine identification codes, the tenth position in the list will contain the sentinel value.

We again apply the top-down function development approach to this problem.

PROGRAM 8.6

```c
#include <stdio.h>
#include <math.h>
#define NUM_ELS 10

void main(void)
{
  int values[NUM_ELS] = {98, 82, 67, 54, 78, 83, 95, 76, 68, 63};
  float average, stddev;
  float find_avg(int [], int);          /* function prototype */
  float std_dev(int [], int, float);   /* function prototype */

  average = find_avg(values, NUM_ELS); /* call the function */
  stddev = std_dev(values, NUM_ELS, average); /* call the function */

  printf("The average of the numbers is %5.2f\n", average);
  printf("The standard deviation of the numbers is %5.2f\n", stddev);
}

float find_avg(int nums[], int numel)
{
  int i;
  float sumnums = 0.0;

  for (i = 0; i < numel; i++)  /* calculate the sum of the grades */
    sumnums = sumnums + nums[i];

  return (sumnums / numel);    /* calculate and return the average */
}

float std_dev(int nums[], int numel, float av)
{
  int i;
  float sumdevs = 0.0;

  for (i = 0; i < numel; i++)
    sumdevs = sumdevs + pow((nums[i] - av),2);

  return(sqrt(sumdevs/numel));
}
```

Analyze the Problem for Input/Output Requirements   The required output is an updated list of three-digit codes in which the new code has been inserted correctly into the existing list.

The input items for this function are the existing array of identification codes and the new code that is to be inserted into the list.

Develop a Solution   Insertion of an identification code into the existing list requires the following processing:

Determine where in the list the new code should be placed.
  This is done by comparing the new code to each value in
    the current list until either a match is found, an identification
    code larger than the new code is located,
    or the end of the list is encountered.
If the new code matches an existing code
  Display a message that the code already exists.
Else
    To make room for the new element in the array move
      each element down one position. This is done by
      starting from the sentinel value and moving each
      item down one position until the desired position
      in the list is vacated.
    Insert the new code in the vacated position
Endif

For our hand calculation assume that the list of identification codes consists of the numbers illustrated in Figure 8.9(a). If the number code 142 is to be inserted into this list, it must be placed in the fourth position in the list, after the number 136. To make room for the new code, all of the codes from the fourth position to the end of the list must be moved one position down, as illustrated on Figure 8.9(b). The move is always started from the end of the list and proceeds from the sentinel value back until the desired position in the list is reached. (You can convince your-self that if the copy proceeded forward from the fourth element the number 144 would be reproduced in all subsequent locations until the sentinel value was reached.) After the movement of the necessary elements, the new code is inserted in the correct position. This creates the updated list shown in Figure 8.9(c).

Code the Solution   For this problem we will use the argument name `idcode` for the passed array of identification numbers and the argument name `newcode`

FIGURE 8.9   Updating an Ordered List of Identification Numbers

| 109 | 122 | 136 | 144 | 157 | 162 | 178 | 185 | 192 | 9999 | | | |

(a) Original list

| 109 | 122 | 136 | 144 | 144 | 157 | 162 | 178 | 185 | 192 | 9999 | | |

(b) Elements copied to make room for the new code

| 109 | 122 | 136 | 142 | 144 | 157 | 162 | 178 | 185 | 192 | 9999 | | |

(c) The updated list

for the new code number to be inserted into the array. Here, the passed array is used for both receiving the original array of numbers and as the final, updated array. Internal to the function we will use a variable named `newpos` to hold the position in the list where the new code is to be inserted and the variable named `trlpos` to hold the position value of the sentinel. The variable i will be used as a running index value.

Using these argument and variable names, the function named `insert()` performs the required processing. After accepting the array and the new code value as arguments, `insert` performs the four major tasks described by the pseudocode selected in the design step.

```c
void insert(int idcode[], int newcode)
{
  int i, newpos, trlpos;

  /* find correct position to insert the new code */
  i = 0;
  while (idcode[i] < newcode)
    i++;
  if (idcode[i] == newcode)
    printf("\nThis identification code is already in the list");
  else
  {
    newpos = i; /* position for the new code */

    /* find the end of the list */
    while (idcode[i] != 9999)
      i++;
    trlpos = i;

    /* move idcodes over one position */
    for (i = trlpos; i >= newpos; --i)
      idcode[i+1] = idcode[i];

    /* insert the new code */
    idcode[newpos] = newcode;
  }
}
```

The first task accomplished by the function is to determine the correct position for the new code. This is done by cycling through the list as long as each value encountered is less than the new code. Since the sentinel value of 9999 is larger than any new code, the looping must stop when the sentinel value is reached.

After the correct position is determined, the position of the sentinel value, which is the last element in the list, is found. Starting from this last position, each element in the list is moved down by one position, until the value in the required new position is reached. Finally, the new identification code is inserted in the correct position.

Test and Debug the Problem   Program 8.7 incorporates the `insert()` function within a complete program. This allows us to test the function with the same data used in our hand calculation.

PROGRAM 8.7

```c
#include <stdio.h>
#define MAXNUM 100
void main(void)
{
  int newcode, i;
  int id[MAXNUM] = {109, 122, 136, 144, 157, 162, 178, 185, 192, 9999};
  void insert(int [], int);        /* function prototype */

  printf("\nEnter the new identification code: ");
  scanf("%d", &newcode);

  insert(id, newcode);

  printf("\nThe updated list is: ");
  i = 0;
  while(id[i] != 9999)
  {
    printf("%d ",id[i]);
    i++;
  }
}

void insert(int idcode[], int newcode)
{
  int i, newpos, trlpos;

  /* find correct position to insert the new code */
  i = 0;
  while (idcode[i] < newcode)
    i++;
  if (idcode[i] == newcode)
    printf("\nThis identification code is already in the list");
  else
  {
    newpos = i;    /* position for the new code */

    /* find the end of the list */
    while (idcode[i] != 9999)
      i++;
    trlpos = i;

    /* move idcodes over one position */
    for (i = trlpos; i >= newpos; --i)
      idcode[i+1] = idcode[i];

    /* insert the new code */
    idcode[newpos] = newcode;
  }
}
```

A sample run of Program 8.7 follows:

```
Enter the new identification code: 142
The updated list is: 109 122 136 142 144 157 162 178 185 192
```

Although this result agrees with our previous hand calculation, it does not constitute full testing of the program. To be sure that the program works for all cases, test runs should be made that:

1. Duplicate an existing code.
2. Place a new identification code at the beginning of the list.
3. Place a new identification code at the end of the list.

Exercises 8.4

1. Modify Program 8.6 so that the grades are entered into the `values` array using a function named `entvals`.

2. Rewrite Program 8.6 to determine the average and standard deviation of the following list of 15 grades: 68, 72, 78, 69, 85, 98, 95, 75, 77, 82, 84, 91, 89, 65, 74.

3. Modify Program 8.6 so that a high function is called that determines the highest value in the passed array and returns this value to the main program unit for display.

4. Modify Program 8.6 so that a function named `sort` is called after the call to the `std_dev` function. The `sort` function should sort the grades into increasing order for display by `main`.

5. a. Test Program 8.7 using an identification code of 86, which should place this new code at the beginning of the existing list.

   b. Test Program 8.7 using an identification code of 200, which should place this new code at the end of the existing list.

6. a. Determine an algorithm for deleting an entry from an ordered list of numbers.

   b. Write a function named `delete()`, which uses the algorithm selected in Exercise 6a, to delete an identification code from the list of numbers illustrated in Figure 8.9a.

7. Assume the following letters are stored in an array named `alphabet`: B, J, K, M, S, Z. Write and test a function named `adlet()`, which accepts both the `alphabet` array and a new letter as arguments, and inserts the new letter in the correct alphabetical order in the `alphabet` array.

8.5 SEARCHING AND SORTING

Most programmers encounter the need to both sort and search a list of data items at some time in their programming careers. For example, experimental results might have to be arranged in either increasing (ascending) or decreasing (descending) order for statistical analysis, lists of names may have to be sorted in alphabetical order, or a list of dates may have to be rearranged in ascending date order. Similarly, a list of names may have to be searched to find a particular name in the list, or a list of dates may have to be searched to locate a particular date. In this section we introduce the fundamentals of both sorting and searching lists.

Note that it is not necessary to sort a list before searching it, although, as we shall see, much faster searches are possible if the list is in sorted order.

Search Algorithms

A common requirement of many programs is to search a list for a given element. For example, in a list of names and telephone numbers, we might search for a specific name so that the corresponding telephone number can be printed, or we might wish to search the list simply to determine if a name is there. The two most common methods of performing such searches are the linear and binary search algorithms.

Linear Search   In a *linear search*, which is also known as a *sequential search*, each item in the list is examined in the order in which it occurs in the list until the desired item is found or the end of the list is reached. This is analogous to looking at every name in the phone directory, beginning with Aardvark, Aaron, until you find the one you want or until you reach Zzxgy, Zora. Obviously, this is not the most efficient way to search a long alphabetized list. However, the linear search has these advantages:

1. The algorithm is simple.
2. The list need not be in any particular order.

In a linear search the search begins at the first item in the list and continues sequentially, item by item, through the list.

The pseudocode for a function performing a linear search is:

Set a "found" flag to FALSE.
Set an index value to −1.
Begin with the first item in the list.
While there are still items in the list AND the "found" flag is FALSE
    Compare the item with the desired item.
    If the item was found
      Set the index value to the item's position in the list
      Set the "found" flag to TRUE.
    Endif
EndWhile
Return the index value

Notice that the function's return value indicates whether the item was found or not. If the return value is −1, the item was not in the list; otherwise, the return value provides the index of where the item is located within the list.

The function linearSearch illustrates this procedure as a C function:

```
linearSearch(int list[], int size, int key)
/* this function returns the location of key in the list */
/* a -1 is returned if the value is not found           */
{
  int index, found, i;

  index = -1;
  found = FALSE;
```

```
i = 0;
while (i < size && !found)
{
  if (list[i] == key)
  {
    found = TRUE;
    index = i;
  }
  i++;      /* move to next item in the list */
}
return(index);
}
```

In reviewing linearSearch notice that the while loop is simply used to access each element in the list, from the first element to the last, until a match is found with the desired item. If the desired item is located, the logical variable FOUND is set to true, which causes the loop to terminate; otherwise, the search continues until the end of the list is encountered.

To test this function, we have written a main driver function to call it and display the results returned by linearSearch. The complete test program is illustrated in Program 8.8.

Sample runs of Program 8.8 follow:

```
Enter the item you are searching for: 101
The item was found at index location 9
```

and

```
Enter the item you are searching for: 65
The item was not found in the list
```

As has already been pointed out, an advantage of linear searches is that the list does not have to be in sorted order to perform the search. Another advantage is that if the desired item is toward the front of the list, only a small number of comparisons will be made. The worst case, of course, occurs when the desired item is at the end of the list. On average, however, and assuming that the desired item is equally likely to be anywhere within the list, the number of required comparisons will be $N/2$, where N is the list's size. Thus, for a 10-element list, the average number of comparisons needed for a linear search is 5, and for a 10,000 element list, the average number of comparisons needed is 5000. As we show next, this number can be significantly reduced using a binary search algorithm.

Binary Search   In a *binary search* the list must be in sorted order. Starting with an ordered list, the desired item is first compared to the element in the middle of the list (for lists with an even number of elements, either of the two middle elements can be used). Three possibilities present themselves once the comparison is made: The desired item may be equal to the middle element, it may be greater than the middle element, or it may be less than the middle element.

In the first case the search has been successful, and no further searches are required. In the second case, since the desired item is greater than the middle element, if it is found at all it must be in the upper part of the list. This means that the lower part of the list consisting of all elements from the first to the midpoint element can be discarded from any further search. In the third case, since the desired

PROGRAM 8.8

```c
#include <stdio.h>
#define TRUE 1
#define FALSE 0
#define NUMEL 10
void main(void)
{
  int nums[NUMEL] = {5,10,22,32,45,67,73,98,99,101};
  int item, location;
  int linearSearch(int [], int, int);

  printf("Enter the item you are searching for: ");
  scanf("%d", &item);

  location = linearSearch(nums, NUMEL, item);

  if (location > -1)
    printf("The item was found at index location %d\n", location);
  else
    printf("The item was not found in the list\n");
}

linearSearch(int list[], int size, int key)
/* this function returns the location of key in the list */
/* a -1 is returned if the value is not found           */
{
  int index, found, i;

  index = -1;
  found = FALSE;
  i = 0;
  while (i < size && !found)
  {
    if (list[i] == key)
    {
      found = TRUE;
      index = i;
    }
    i++;     /* move to next item in the list */
  }
  return(index);
}
```

item is less than the middle element, if it is found at all it must be found in the lower part of the list. For this case the upper part of the list consisting all elements from the midpoint element to the last element can be discarded from any further search.

The algorithm for implementing this search strategy is illustrated in Figure 8.10 (see p. 375) and defined by the following pseudocode:

Set a "found" flag to FALSE.
Set an index value to −1.
Set the lower index to 0.
Set the upper index to one less than the size of the list.
Begin with the first item in the list.
While the lower index is less than or equal to the upper index and a match is not yet found
  Set the midpoint index to the integer average of the lower and upper index values
  Compare the desired item to the midpoint element.
  If the desired element equals the midpoint element
    The item has been found.
  Else if the desired element is greater than the midpoint element
    Set the lower index value to the midpoint value plus 1.
  Else if the desired element is less than the midpoint element
    Set the upper index value to the midpoint value less 1.
  End If
End While
Return the index value

As illustrated by both the pseudocode and the flowchart of Figure 8.10, a `while` loop is used to control the search. The initial list is defined by setting the lower index value to 0 and the upper index value to one less than the number of elements in the list. The midpoint element is then taken as the integerized average of the lower and upper values. Once the comparison to the midpoint element is made, the search is subsequently restricted by moving either the lower index to one integer value above the midpoint, or by moving the upper index one integer value below the midpoint. This process is continued until the desired element is found or the lower and upper index values become equal. The function binarySearch presents the C version of this algorithm.

```
binarySearch(int list[], int size, int key)
/* this function returns the location of key in the list */
/* a -1 is returned if the value is not found          */
{
  int index, found, left, right, midpt;

  index = -1;
  found = FALSE;
  left = 0;
  right = size -1;
  while (left <= right && !found)
  {
    midpt = (int) ((left + right) / 2);
    if (key == list[midpt])
    {
      found = TRUE;
      index = midpt;
    }
    else if (key > list[midpt])
      left = midpt + 1;
    else
      right = midpt - 1;
  }
  return(index);
}
```

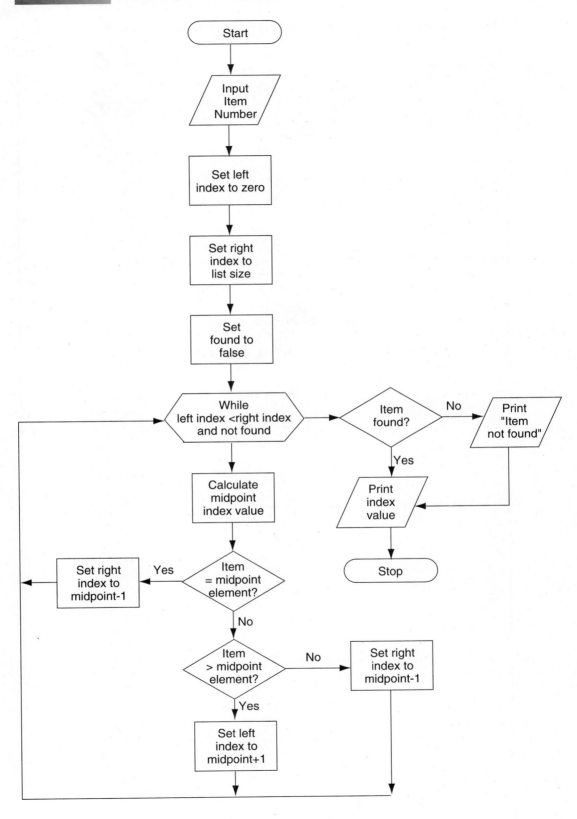

FIGURE 8.10 The Binary Search Algorithm

For purposes of testing this function, Program 8.9 is used.

PROGRAM 8.9

```c
#include <stdio.h>
#define TRUE 1
#define FALSE 0
#define NUMEL 10
main()
{
  int nums[NUMEL] = {5,10,22,32,45,67,73,98,99,101};
  int item, location;
  int binarySearch(int [], int, int);

  printf("Enter the item you are searching for: ");
  scanf("%d", &item);
  location = binarySearch(nums, NUMEL, item);
  if (location > -1)
    printf("The item was found at index location %d\n", location);
  else
    printf("The item was not found in the array\n");
}
binarySearch(int list[], int size, int key)
/* this function returns the location of key in the list */
/* a -1 is returned if the value is not found          */
{
  int index, found, left, right, midpt;

  index = -1;
  found = FALSE;
  left = 0;
  right = size -1;
  while (left <= right && !found)
  {
    midpt = (int) ((left + right) / 2);
    if (key == list[midpt])
    {
      found = TRUE;
      index = midpt;
    }
    else if (key > list[midpt])
      left = midpt + 1;
    else
      right = midpt - 1;
  }
  return(index);
}
```

A sample run using Program 8.9 yielded the following:

```
Enter the item you are searching for: 101
The item was found at index location 9
```

The value of using a binary search algorithm is that the number of elements that must be searched is cut in half each time through the `while` loop. Thus, the first time through the loop N elements must be searched; the second time through the loop $N/2$ of the elements have been eliminated and only $N/2$ remain. The third time through the loop another half of the remaining elements have been eliminated, and so on.

In general, after p passes through the loop, the number of values remaining to be searched is $N/(2^p)$. In the worst case, the search can continue until there is less than or equal to 1 element remaining to be searched. Mathematically, this can be expressed as $N/(2^p) \leq 1$. Alternatively, this may be rephrased as p is the smallest integer such that $2^p \geq N$. For example, for a 1000-element array, N is 1000 and the maximum number of passes, p, required for a binary search is 10. Table 8.1 compares the number of loop passes needed for a linear and binary search for various list sizes. As illustrated, the maximum number of loop passes for a 50-item list is almost 10 times more for a linear search than for a binary search, and the difference is even more spectacular for larger lists. As a rule of thumb, 50 elements are usually taken as the switchover point: For lists smaller than 50 elements, linear searches are acceptable; for larger lists, a binary search algorithm should be used.

Big-O Notation

On average, over a large number of linear searches with N items in a list, we would expect to examine half ($N/2$) of the items before locating the desired item. In a binary search the maximum number of passes, p, occurs when $(N/2)^p = 1$. This relationship can be algebraically manipulated to $2^p = N$, which yields $p = \log_2 N$, which approximately equals $3.33 \log_{10} N$.

For example, finding a particular name in an alphabetical directory with $N = 1000$ names would require an average of 500 ($N/2$) comparisons using a linear search. With a binary search, only about 10 ($\approx 3.33 \times \log_{10} 1000$) comparisons would be required.

A common way to express the number of comparisons required in any search algorithm using a list of N items is to give the order of magnitude of the

TABLE 8.1 A Comparison of `while` Loop Passes for Linear and Binary Searches

Array Size	10	50	500	5,000	50,000	500,000	5,000,000	50,000,000
Average linear search passes	5	25	250	2,500	25,000	250,000	2,500,000	25,000,000
Maximum linear search passes	10	50	500	5,000	50,000	500,000	5,000,000	50,000,000
Maximum binary search passes	4	6	9	13	16	19	23	26

number of comparisons required, on average, to locate a desired item. Thus, the linear search is said to be of order N and the binary search of order $\log_2 N$. Notationally, this is expressed as $O(N)$ and $O(\log_2 N)$, where the O is read as "the order of."

Sort Algorithms

For sorting data, two major categories of sorting techniques exist, called internal and external sorts, respectively. *Internal sorts* are used when the data list is not too large and the complete list can be stored within the computer's memory, usually in an array. *External sorts* are used for much larger data sets that are stored in large external disk or tape files and cannot be accommodated within the computer's memory as a complete unit. Here we present four internal sort algorithms that range from the simple and slow to the complex and fast. The first three algorithms presented are all quite commonly used when sorting lists with less than approximately 50 elements. For larger lists, more sophisticated sorting algorithms, such as the quicksort algorithm, are typically employed.

Selection Sort   One of the simplest sorting techniques is the selection sort. In a *selection sort* the smallest value is initially selected from the complete list of data and exchanged with the first element in the list. After this first selection and exchange, the next smallest element in the revised list is selected and exchanged with the second element in the list. Since the smallest element is already in the first position in the list, this second pass need only consider the second through last elements. For a list consisting of N elements, this process is repeated N-1 times, with each pass through the list requiring one less comparison than the previous pass.

For example, consider the list of numbers illustrated in Figure 8.11. The first pass through the initial list results in the number 32 being selected and exchanged with the first element in the list. The second pass, made on the reordered list, results in the number 155 being selected from the second through fifth elements. This value is then exchanged with the second element in the list. The third pass selects the number 307 from the third through fifth elements in the list and exchanges this value with the third element. Finally, the fourth and last pass through the list selects the remaining minimum value and exchanges it with

---

FIGURE 8.11   A Sample Selection Sort

Initial List	Pass 1	Pass 2	Pass 3	Pass 4
690	32	32	32	32
307	307	155	144	144
32	690	690	307	307
155	155	307	690	426
426	426	426	426	690

the fourth list element. Although each pass in this example resulted in an exchange, no exchange would have been made in a pass if the smallest value were already in the correct location.

In pseudocode, the selection sort is described as:

Set interchange count to zero (not required, but done just to keep track of the interchanges).
For each element in the list from first to next-to-last
  Find the smallest element from the current element being referenced to the last element by:
    Setting the minimum value equal to the current element
    Saving (storing) the index of the current element.
    For each element in the list from the current element + 1 to the last element in the list
      If element inner loop index] < minimum value
        Set the minimum value = element[inner loop index]
        Save the index the new found minimum value.
      End If
    End For
    Swap the current value with the new minimum value.
    Increment the interchange count.
End For
Return the interchange count.

The function `selection_sort` incorporates this procedure into a C function.

```c
int selection_sort(int num[], int numel)
{
   int i, j, min, minidx, temp, moves = 0;

   for ( i = 0; i < (numel - 1); i++)
   {
     min = num[i]; /* assume minimum is first element is sublist */
     minidx = i; /* index of minimum element */
     for(j = i + 1; j < numel; j++)
     {
       if (num[j] < min)    /* if we've located a lower value */
       {                     /* capture it */
         min = num[j];
         minidx = j;
       }
     }
     if (min < num[i])   /* check if we have a new minimum */
     {                    /* and if we do, swap values */
       temp = num[i];
       num[i] = min;
       num[minidx] = temp;
       moves++;
     }
   }
   return(moves);
}
```

The `selection_sort` function expects two arguments, the list to be sorted and the number of elements in the list. As specified by the pseudocode, a nested set of `for` loops performs the sort. The outer `for` loop causes one less pass through the list than the total number of data items in the list. For each pass, the variable `min` is initially assigned the value `num[i]`, where `i` is the outer `for` loop's counter variable. Since `i` begins at 0 and ends at one less than `numel`, each element in the list, except the last, is successively designated as the current element.

The inner loop is used in the function cycles through the elements below the current element to select the next smallest value. Thus, this loop begins at the index value `i+1` and continues through the end of the list. When a new minimum is found, its value and position in the list are stored in the variables named `min` and `minidx`, respectively. Upon completion of the inner loop, an exchange is made only if a value less than that in the current position was found.

For purposes of testing `selection_sort`, Program 8.10 was constructed. This program implements a selection sort for the same list of 10 numbers that was previously used to test our search algorithms. For later comparison to the other sorting algorithms that will be presented, the number of actual moves made by the program to get the data into sorted order is counted and displayed.

The output produced by Program 8.10 is as follows:

```
The sorted list, in ascending order, is:
5 10 22 32 45 67 73 98 99 101
 8 moves were made to sort this list
```

Clearly, the number of moves displayed depends on the initial order of the values in the list. An advantage of the selection sort is that the maximum number of moves that must be made is $N-1$, where N is the number of items in the list. Further, each move is a final move that results in an element residing in its final location in the sorted list.

A disadvantage of the selection sort is that $N(N-1)/2$ comparisons are always required, regardless of the initial arrangement of the data. This number of comparisons is obtained as follows: The last pass always requires one comparison, the next-to-last pass requires two comparisons, and so on, to the first pass, which requires $N-1$ comparisons. Thus, the total number of comparisons is:

$$1 + 2 + 3 + \ldots + N-1 = N(N-1)/2 = N^2/2 - N/2.$$

For large values of N the N^2 dominates, and the order of the selection sort is $O(N^2)$.

Exchange ("Bubble") Sort   In an exchange or *bubble sort*, elements of the list are exchanged with one another in such a manner that the list becomes sorted. One example of such a sequence of exchanges is provided by the bubble sort, where successive values in the list are compared, beginning with the first two elements. If the list is to be sorted in ascending (from smallest to largest) order, the smaller value of the two being compared is always placed before the larger value. For lists sorted in descending (from largest to smallest) order, the smaller of the two values being compared is always placed after the larger value.

For example, assuming that a list of values is to be sorted in ascending order, if the first element in the list is larger than the second, the two elements are interchanged. Then the second and third elements are compared. Again, if the second element is larger than the third, these two elements are interchanged. This pro-

PROGRAM 8.10

```c
#include <stdio.h>
#define NUMEL 10
void main(void)
{
  int nums[NUMEL] = {22,5,67,98,45,32,101,99,73,10};
  int i, moves;
  int selection_sort(int [], int);

  moves = selection_sort(nums, NUMEL);

  printf("The sorted list, in ascending order, is:\n");
  for (i = 0; i < NUMEL; ++i)
    printf("%d  ",nums[i]);
  printf("\n %d moves were made to sort this list\n", moves);
}

int selection_sort(int num[], int numel)
{
  int i, j, min, minidx, temp, moves = 0;

  for ( i = 0; i < (numel - 1); i++)
  {
    min = num[i];  /* assume minimum is the first array element */
    minidx = i;      /* index of minimum element */
    for(j = i + 1; j < numel; j++)
    {
      if (num[j] < min)    /* if we've located a lower value */
      {                    /* capture it */
        min = num[j];
        minidx = j;
      }
    }
    if (min < num[i])   /* check if we have a new minimum */
    {                   /* and if we do, swap values */
      temp = num[i];
      num[i] = min;
      num[minidx] = temp;
      moves++;
    }
  }
  return(moves);
}
```

cess continues until the last two elements have been compared and exchanged, if necessary. If no exchanges were made during this initial pass through the data, the data is in the correct order and the process is finished; otherwise, a second pass is made through the data, starting from the first element and stopping at the

---

FIGURE 8.12   The First Pass of an Exchange Sort

---

next-to-last element. The reason for stopping at the next-to-last element on the second pass is that the first pass always results in the most positive value "sinking" to the bottom of the list.

As a specific example of this process, consider the list of numbers illustrated in Figure 8.12. The first comparison results in the interchange of the first two element values, 690 and 307. The next comparison, between elements two and three in the revised list, results in the interchange of values between the second and third elements, 690 and 32. This comparison and possible switching of adjacent values is continued until the last two elements have been compared and possibly switched. This process completes the first pass through the data and results in the largest number moving to the bottom of the list. As the largest value sinks to its resting place at the bottom of the list, the smaller elements slowly rise, or "bubble," to the top of the list. This bubbling effect of the smaller elements is what gave rise to the name "bubble" sort for this sorting algorithm.

Because the first pass through the list ensures that the largest value always moves to the bottom of the list, the second pass stops at the next-to-last element. This process continues with each pass stopping at one higher element than the previous pass, until either $N-1$ passes through the list have been completed or no exchanges are necessary in any single pass. In both cases the resulting list is in sorted order. The pseudocode describing this sort is:

Set interchange count to zero (not required, but done just to
 keep track of the interchanges).
For the first element in the list to one less than the last element (i index)
  For the second element in the list to the last element (j index)
    If num[j] < num[j − 1]
    {
      swap num[j] with num[j − 1]
      increment interchange count
    }
  End For
End For
Return interchange count

This sort algorithm is coded in C as the function `bubble_sort`, which is included within Program 8.11 for testing purposes. This program tests `bubble_sort` with the same list of 10 numbers used in Program 8.10 to test `selection_sort`. For comparison to the earlier selection sort, the number of adjacent moves (exchanges) made by `bubble_sort` is also counted and displayed.

PROGRAM 8.11

```c
#include <stdio.h>
#define NUMEL 10
void main(void)
{
  int nums[NUMEL] = {22,5,67,98,45,32,101,99,73,10};
  int i, moves;
  int bubble_sort(int [], int);

  moves = bubble_sort(nums, NUMEL);

  printf("The sorted list, in ascending order, is:\n");
  for (i = 0; i < NUMEL; ++i)
    printf("%d  ",nums[i]);
  printf("\n %d moves were made to sort this list\n", moves);
}

int bubble_sort(int num[], int numel)
{
  int i, j, temp, moves = 0;

  for ( i = 0; i < (numel - 1); i++)
  {
    for(j = 1; j < numel; j++)
    {
      if (num[j] < num[j-1])
      {
        temp = num[j];
        num[j] = num[j-1];
        num[j-1] = temp;
        moves++;
      }
    }
  }
  return (moves);
}
```

Here is the output produced by Program 8.11:

```
The sorted list, in ascending order, is:
5 10 22 32 45 67 73 98 99 101
 18 moves were made to sort this list
```

As with the selection sort, the number of comparisons using a bubble sort is $O(N^2)$ and the number of required moves depends on the initial order of the values in the list. In the worst case, when the data is in reverse sorted order, the selection sort performs better than the bubble sort. Here both sorts require $N(N-1)/2$ comparisons, but the selection sort needs only $N-1$ moves while the bubble sort needs $N(N-1)/2$ moves. The additional moves required by the bubble sort result from the intermediate exchanges between adjacent elements to "settle" each element into its final position. In this regard the selection sort is superior, because no intermediate moves are necessary. For random data, such as that used in Programs 8.10 and 8.11, the selection sort generally performs equal to or better than the bubble sort. A modification to the bubble sort (see Exercise 4), which causes the sort to terminate when the list is in order regardless of the number of passes made, can make the bubble sort operate as an $O(N)$ sort in specialized cases.

Quick Sort   The selection and exchange sorts both require $O(N^2)$ comparisons, which make them very slow for long lists. The *quick sort* algorithm, which is also called a *partition sort,* divides a list into two smaller sublists and sorts each sublist by portioning into smaller sublists, and so on.[6] The order of a quick sort is $N \log_2 N$. Thus, for a 1000-item list, the total number of comparisons for a quick sort is in the order of $1000(3.3 \log_{10} 1000) = 1000(10) = 10,000$ compared to $1000(1000) = 1,000,000$ for a selection or exchange sort.

The quick sort puts a list into sorted order by a partitioning process. At each stage the list is partitioned into sublists so that a selected element, called the pivot, is placed in its correct position in the final sorted list. To understand the process consider the list illustrated in Figure 8.13. The original list shown consists of seven numbers. Designating the first element in the list, 98, as the pivot element, the list is rearranged as shown in the first partition. Notice that this partition results in all values less than 98 residing to its left and all values greater than 98 to its right. For now, disregard the exact order of the elements to the left and right of the 98 (in a moment we will see how the arrangement of the numbers came about).

The numbers to the left of the pivot constitute one sublist and the numbers to the right another sublist, which individually must be reordered by a partitioning process. The pivot for the first sublist is 67 and the pivot for the second sublist is 101. Figure 8.14 shows how each of these sublists is partitioned using their respective pivot elements. The partitioning process stops when a sublist has only

FIGURE 8.13   A First Quick Sort Partition

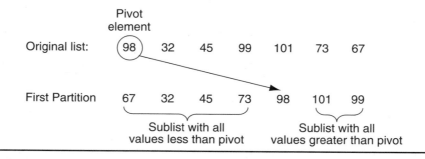

----

[6]This algorithm was developed by C. A. R. Hoare and first described by him in an article entitled "QuickSort" in *Computer Journal* (Vol. 5, pp. 10–15) in 1962. This sorting algorithm was so much faster than previous algorithms that it became known as the quick sort.

FIGURE 8.14   Completing the Quick Sort

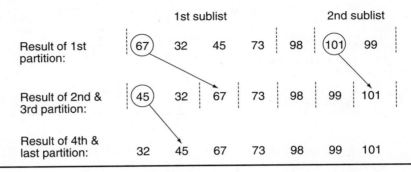

Result of 1st partition:

1st sublist: 67 32 45 73 98 | 2nd sublist: 101 99

Result of 2nd & 3rd partition:

45 32 | 67 | 73 | 98 | 99 | 101

Result of 4th & last partition:

32 45 67 73 98 99 101

one element. In the case illustrated in Figure 8.14, a fourth partition is required for the sublist containing the values 45 and 32, since all other sublists have only one element. Once this last sublist is partitioned, the Quick Sort is completed and the original list is in sorted order.

As we have illustrated, the key to the Quick Sort is its partitioning process. An essential part of this process is that each sublist is rearranged in place; that is, elements are rearranged within the existing list. This rearrangement is facilitated by first saving the value of the pivot, which frees its slot to be used by another element. The list is then examined from the right, starting with the last element in the list, for a value less than the pivot; when one is found it is copied to the pivot slot. This copy frees a slot at the right of the list for use by another element. The list is now examined from the left for any value greater than the pivot; when one is found it is copied to the last freed slot. This right-to-left and left-to-right scan is continued until the right and left index values meet. The saved pivot element is then copied into this slot. At that point all values to the left of the index are smaller than the pivot value and all values to the right are greater. Before providing the pseudocode for this process, we will show all of the steps required to complete one partition using our previous list of numbers.

Consider Figure 8.15, which shows our original list of Figure 8.13 and the positions of the initial left and right indexes. As shown in the figure, the pivot value has been saved into a variable named `pivot`, the right index points to the last list element and is the active index. Using this index the scan for elements less than the pivot value of 98 begins. Since 67 is less than the pivot value of 98, the 67 is moved into the pivot slot (the pivot value is not lost because it has

FIGURE 8.15   Start of the Scanning Process

Active scan direction
Right index element
(index value = 6)

pivot = 98

98 32 45 99 101 73 67

Left index element
(index value = 0)

FIGURE 8.16   List After the First Copy

```
pivot = 98
                                                    ┌─Right index element
            67   32   45   99  101   73   67          (index value = 6)

    Left index element ──┘
    (index value = 1)


    Active scan direction ────►
```

---

been assigned to the variable `pivot`) and the left index is incremented. This results in the arrangement shown in Figure 8.16.

Notice in Figure 8.16 that the element pointed to by the right index is now available for the next copy, since its value, 67, has been reproduced as the first element. (This will always be the case; when a scan stops, its index will indicate the position available for the next move.)

Scanning of the list shown in Figure 8.16 continues from the left for a search of all values greater than 98. This occurs when the 99 is reached. Since 99 is greater than the pivot value of 98, the scan stops and the 99 is copied into the position indicated by the right index. The right index is then incremented, which produces the situation illustrated in Figure 8.17.

Scanning of the list shown in Figure 8.17 now continues from the right in a search for values less than the pivot. Since 73 qualifies, the right scan stops, the 73 is moved into the position indicated by the left index, and the left index is incremented. This results in the list shown in Figure 8.18.

Scanning of the list shown in Figure 8.18 now resumes from the left in a search for values greater than 98. Since 101 qualifies this scan stops and the 101 is moved into the slot indicated by the right index, and the right index is incremented. This results in the list illustrated in Figure 8.19. Notice in this figure that left and right indices are equal. This is the condition that stops all scanning and indicates the position where the pivot should be placed. Doing so results in completion of this partition with the list in the order

67   32   45   73   98   101   99

Compare this list with the one previously shown for the first partition in Figure 8.13. As is seen, they are the same. Here the pivot has been placed so that all elements less than it are to its left and all values greater than it are to its right. The same partitioning process would now be applied to the sublists on either side of the partition.

FIGURE 8.17   Start of Second Right-Side Scan

```
                                        ◄──── Active scan direction

        pivot = 98                          ┌─Right index element
                                              (index value = 5)
            67   32   45   99  101   73   99

    Left index element ──┘
    (index value = 3)
```

FIGURE 8.18   Start of Second Left-Side Scan

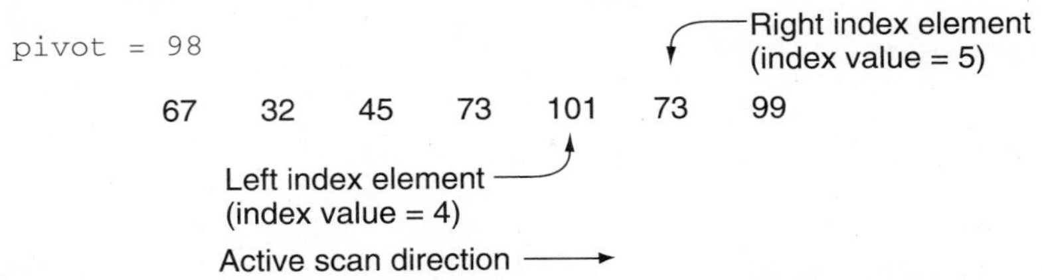

pivot = 98

```
        67    32    45    73    101    73    99
```

Right index element
(index value = 5)

Left index element
(index value = 4)

Active scan direction

The pseudocode describing this partitioning process is:

Set the pivot to the value of the first list element.
Initialize the left index to the index of the first list element.
Initialize the right index to the index of the last list element.
While (left index ≠ right index)
    / scan from the right, skipping over larger values */*
    While (right index element ≥ pivot) / skip over larger values */*
        Decrement right index.
    EndWhile
    If (right index ≠ left index)
        Move the lower value into the slot indicated by the left index
        Increment the left index.
    EndIf
    / scan from the left, skipping over smaller values */*
    While (left index element ≤ pivot) / skip over smaller values */*
        Increment left index.
    EndWhile
    If (left index ≠ right index)
        Move the higher value into the slot indicated by the right index
        Decrement the right index.
    EndIf
EndWhile
Move the pivot into the slot indicated by the left or right index (they are
    equal here).
Return the left (or right) index.

The function partition, contained within Program 8.12, codes this algorithm in C.

FIGURE 8.19   Position of List Elements After the 101 Is Moved

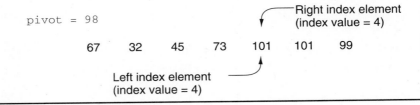

pivot = 98

```
        67    32    45    73    101    101    99
```

Right index element
(index value = 4)

Left index element
(index value = 4)

PROGRAM 8.12

```c
#include <stdio.h>
#define NUMEL 7

void main(void)
{
  int nums[NUMEL] = {98,32,45,99,101,73,67};
  int i, pivot;
  int partition(int [], int, int);

  pivot = partition(nums, 0, NUMEL-1);

  printf("\nThe returned pivot index is %d", pivot);
  printf("\nThe list is now in the order:\n");
  for (i = 0; i < NUMEL; i++)
    printf("%d ",nums[i]);
  printf("\n");
}

int partition(int num[], int left, int right)
{
  int pivot, temp;

  pivot = num[left]; /* "capture" the pivot value, which frees up one slot */
  while (left < right)
  {
    /* scan from right to left */
    while(num[right] >= pivot && left < right) /* skip over larger or equal values */
      right--;
    if (right != left)
    {
      num[left] = num[right]; /* move the higher value into the available slot */
      left++;
    }
    /* scan from left to right */
    while(num[left] <= pivot && left < right) /* skip over smaller or equal values */
      left++;
    if (right != left)
    {
      num[right] = num[left]; /* move the lower value into the available slot */
      right--;
    }
  }
  num[left] = pivot; /* move pivot into correct position */
  return(left);      /* return the pivot index */
}
```

Program 8.12 is simply used to test the function. Notice that it contains the same list that we used in our hand calculation. A sample run using Program 8.12 produced this output:

```
The returned pivot index is 4
The list is now in the order:
67 32 45 73 98 101 99
```

Notice that this output produces the result previously obtained by our hand calculation. The importance of the returned pivot index is that it defines the sublists that will be subsequently partitioned. The first sublist consists of all elements from the first list element to the element whose index is 3 (one less than the returned pivot index) and the second sublist consists of all elements starting at index value 5 (one more than the returned pivot index) and ending at the last list element.

The quicksort uses the returned pivot value in determining whether additional calls to partition are required for each sublist defined by the list segments to the left and right of the pivot index. This is done using the following recursive logic:

> *quicksort(list, lower index, upper index)*
>   *calculate a pivot index calling partition(list, lower index, upper index)*
>   *If (lower index < pivot index)*
>   *quicksort(list, lower, pivot index − 1)*
>   *If (upper index > pivot index)*
>   *quicksort(list, upper, pivot index + 1)*

The C code for this logic is described by the quicksort function contained within Program 8.13. As indicated, quicksort requires partition to both rearrange lists and return its pivot value.

 PROGRAM 8.13

```c
#include <stdio.h>
#define NUMEL 7

void main(void)
{
  int nums[NUMEL] = {67,32,45,73,98,101,99};
  int i;
  void quicksort(int [], int, int);

  quicksort(nums, 0, NUMEL-1);

  printf("\nThe sorted list, in ascending order, is:\n");
  for (i = 0; i < NUMEL; i++)
    printf("%d ",nums[i]);
  printf("\n");
}

void quicksort(int num[], int lower, int upper)
```

(continued on next page)

(continued from previous page)

```c
{
  int i, j, pivot;
  int partition(int [], int, int);

  pivot = partition(num,lower, upper);

  if (lower < pivot)
     quicksort(num, lower, pivot - 1);
  if (upper > pivot)
     quicksort(num, pivot + 1, upper);
}


int partition(int num[], int left, int right)
{
  int pivot, temp;

  pivot = num[left];  /* "capture" the pivot value, which frees up one slot */
  while (left < right)
  {
    /* scan from right to left */
    while(num[right] >= pivot && left < right)  /* skip over larger or equal values */
      right--;
    if (right != left)
    {
      num[left] = num[right]; /* move the higher value into the available slot */
      left++;
    }
    /* scan from left to right */
    while (num[left] <= pivot && left < right) /* skip over smaller or equal values */
      left++;
    if (right != left)
    {
      num[right] = num[left]; /* mover lower value into the available slot */
      right--;
    }
  }
  num[left] = pivot; /* move pivot into correct position */
  return(left);      /* return the pivot index */
}
```

Here is the output produced by Program 8.13:

```
The sorted list, in ascending order, is:
32 45 67 73 98 99 101
```

As indicated by this output, quicksort correctly sorts the test list of numbers. Figure 8.20 shows the sequence of calls made to quicksort by Program 8.13. In this figure left-pointing arrows indicate calls made because the first if condition (lower < pivot) was true and right-pointing arrows indicate calls made because the second if condition (upper > pivot) was true.

FIGURE 8.20   Sequence of Calls Made by Program 8.13

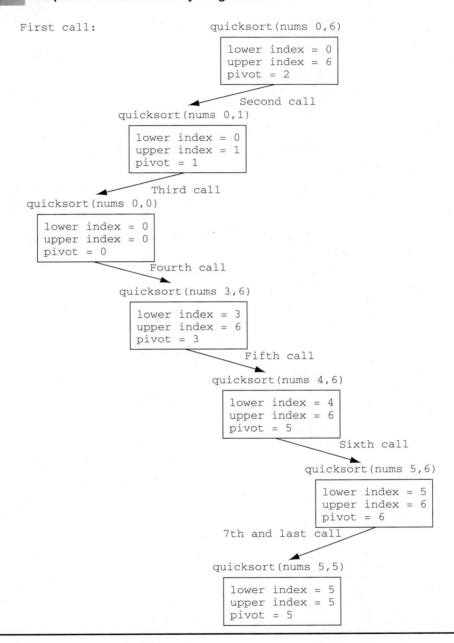

First call: quicksort(nums 0,6)

    lower index = 0
    upper index = 6
    pivot = 2

                                         Second call
             quicksort(nums 0,1)

    lower index = 0
    upper index = 1
    pivot = 1

                                  Third call
      quicksort(nums 0,0)

    lower index = 0
    upper index = 0
    pivot = 0

                          Fourth call
             quicksort(nums 3,6)

    lower index = 3
    upper index = 6
    pivot = 3

                                  Fifth call
                 quicksort(nums 4,6)

    lower index = 4
    upper index = 6
    pivot = 5

                                         Sixth call
                     quicksort(nums 5,6)

    lower index = 5
    upper index = 6
    pivot = 6

                          7th and last call
             quicksort(nums 5,5)

    lower index = 5
    upper index = 5
    pivot = 5

Exercises 8.5

1. a. Modify Program 8.10 to use a list of 100 randomly generated numbers and
      determine the number of moves required to put the list in order using a selec-
      tion sort. Display both the initial list and the reordered list.

   b. Redo Exercise 1a using a bubble sort.

2. For the functions selection_sort, bubble_sort, and quicksort, the sorting can be done in decreasing order by a simple modification. In each case identify the required changes and then rewrite each function to accept a flag indicating whether the sort should be in increasing or decreasing order. Modify each routine to correctly receive and use this flag argument.

3. a. The selection and bubble sort both use the same technique for swapping list elements. Replace the code in these two functions that performs the swap by a call to a function named swap. The prototype for swap should be

   ```
   void swap(int *, int*).
   ```

   swap itself should be constructed using the algorithm presented in Section 7.4.

   b. Describe why the quicksort function does not require the swapping algorithm used by the selection and bubble sorts.

4. An alternate form of the bubble sort is presented in the following program:

   ```
   #define TRUE 1
   #define FALSE 0
   void main(void)
   {
     int nums[10] = {22,5,67,98,45,32,101,99,73,10};
     int i, temp, moves, npts, outord;

     moves = 0;
     npts = 10;
     outord = TRUE;
     while (outord && npts > 0)
     {
       outord = FALSE;
       for ( i = 0; i < npts - 1; ++i)
         if (nums[i] > nums[i+1])
         {
           temp = nums[i+1];
         nums[i+1] = nums[i];
         nums[i] = temp;
           outord = TRUE;
         ++moves;
         }
       --npts;
     }
     printf("The sorted list, in ascending order, is:\n");
     for (i = 0; i < 10; ++i)
       printf("%d  ",nums[i]);
     printf("\n %d moves were made to sort this list\n", moves);
   }
   ```

   An advantage of this version of the bubble sort is that processing is terminated whenever a sorted list is encountered. In the best case, when the data is in sorted order to begin with, an exchange sort requires no moves (the same for the selection sort) and only $N-1$ comparisons [the selection sort always requires $N(N-1)/2$ comparisons].

   After you have run this program to convince yourself that it correctly sorts a list of integers, rewrite the sort algorithm it contains as a function named newbubbl, and test your function using the main function contained in Program 8.11.

5. a. Modify Program 8.13 to use a larger test list consisting of 20 numbers.

   b. Modify Program 8.13 to use a list of 100 randomly selected numbers.

6. A company currently maintains two lists of part numbers, where each part number is an integer. Write a C program that compares these lists of numbers and displays the numbers, if any, that are common to both. (*Hint:* Sort each list prior to making the comparison.)

7. Redo Exercise 6, but display a list of part numbers that are only on one list, but not both.

8. Rewrite the binary search algorithm to use recursion rather than iteration.

8.6 COMMON PROGRAMMING ERRORS

Four common errors are associated with using arrays:

1. Forgetting to declare the array. This error results in a compiler error message equivalent to "invalid indirection" each time a subscripted variable is encountered within a program.

2. Using a subscript that references a nonexistent array element. For example, declaring the array to be of size 20 and using a subscript value of 25. This error is not detected by most C compilers. It will, however, result in a run-time error that results either in a program crash or a value that has no relation to the intended element being accessed from memory. In either case it is usually an extremely troublesome error to locate. The only solution to this problem is to make sure, either by specific programming statements or by careful coding, that each subscript references a valid array element.

3. Not using a large enough conditional value in a `for` loop counter to cycle through all the array elements. This error usually occurs when an array is initially specified to be of size n and there is a `for` loop within the program of the form `for(i = 0; i < n; i++)`. The array size is then expanded but the programmer forgets to change the interior `for` loop parameters. Declaring an array's size using a named constant and consistently using the named constant throughout the function in place of the variable n eliminates this problem.

4. Forgetting to initialize the array. Although many compilers automatically set all elements of integer and real valued arrays to zero, and all elements of character arrays to blanks, it is up to the programmer to ensure that each array is correctly initialized before processing of array elements begins.

8.7 CHAPTER REVIEW

Key Terms

big-O notation
binary search
bubble sort
index value
indexed variable
linear (sequential) search
null character (`'\0'`)

one-dimensional array
quicksort
selection sort
single-dimensional array
subscript value
subscripted variable

Summary

1. A single-dimensional array is a data structure that can be used to store a list of values of the same data type. Such arrays must be declared by

giving the data type of the values that are stored in the array and the array size. For example, the declaration:

```
int num[100];
```

creates an array of 100 integers. A preferable approach is to first use a named constant to set the array size, and then use this constant in the definition of the array. For example:

```
#define MAXSIZE 100
```

and

```
int num[MAXSIZE];
```

2. Array elements are stored in contiguous locations in memory and referenced using the array name and a subscript, for example, `num[22]`. Any nonnegative integer value expression can be used as a subscript and the subscript 0 always refers to the first element in an array.

3. Arrays are passed to a function by passing the name of the array as an argument. The value actually passed is the address of the first array storage location. Thus, the called function receives direct access to the original array and not a copy of the array elements. Within the called function a formal argument must be declared to receive the passed array name. The declaration of the formal argument can omit the row size of the array.

4. The linear search is an $O(N)$ search. It examines each item in a list until the searched item is found or until it is determined that the item is not in the list.

5. The binary search is an $O(\log_2 N)$ search. It requires that a list be in sorted order before it can be applied.

6. The selection and bubble sort algorithms require an order of magnitude of N^2 comparisons for sorting a list of N items.

7. The Quick Sort algorithm requires an order of magnitude of $N \log_2 N$ comparisons to sort a list of N items.

Exercises

1. a. Write a C program that reads a list of floating-point grades from the keyboard into an array named `Grades`. The grades are to be counted as they are read, and entry is to be terminated when a negative value has been entered. Once all of the grades have been input, your program should find and display the sum and average of the grades. The grades should then be listed with an asterisk (*) placed in front of each grade that is below the average.

   b. Extend the program written for Exercise 1a to display each grade and its letter equivalent. Assume the following scale

   A grade between 90 and 100 is an A.

   A grade greater than or equal to 80 and less than 90 is a B.

   A grade greater than or equal to 70 and less than 80 is a C.

   A grade greater than or equal to 60 and less than 70 is a D.

   A grade less than 60 is an F.

2. Define an array named `PeopleTypes` that can store a maximum of 50 integer values that will be entered at the keyboard. Enter a series of 1's, 2's, 3's, and 4's into the array, where a 1 represents an infant, a 2 represents a child, a 3 represents a teenager, and a 4 represents an adult that was present at a local school function. Any other integer value should not be accepted as valid input and data entry should stop when a negative value has been entered.

   Your program should count the number of each 1, 2, 3, and 4 in the array and output a list of how many infants, children, teenagers, and adults were at the school function.

3. Given a one-dimensional array of integer numbers, write and test a function that prints the elements in reverse order.

4. Write and test a function that returns the position of the largest and smallest values in an array of floating-point numbers.

5. Read a set of numerical grades from the keyboard into an array. The maximum number of grades is 50 and data entry should be terminated when a negative number has been entered. Have your program sort and print the grades in *descending* order.

6. a. Write a C program that keeps track of the frequency of occurrence of each vowel as characters are typed at the keyboard. The end of the text should be signified by entry of an EOF (see Section 5.2) marker (ctrl Z for DOS and ctrl / for UNIX). The output of your program should be a count of each vowel encountered in the input text.

   b. Add a function to the program written for Exercise 6a that displays a histogram of the number of each vowel encountered. For example, if your program detected five a's, three e's, two i's, four o's, and 1 u, the histogram should appear as:

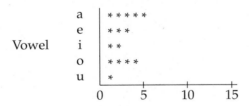

7. a. Define an array with a maximum of 20 integer values and either fill the array with numbers input from the keyboard or assigned by the program. Then write a function named `split()` that reads the array and places all zero or positive numbers into an array named `positive` and all negative numbers into an array named `negative`. Finally have your program call a function that displays the values in both the `positive` and `negative` arrays.

   b. Extend the program written for Exercise 7a to sort the `positive` and `negative` arrays into ascending order before they are displayed.

8. Using the `srand` and `rand` C library functions, fill an array of 1000 floating-point numbers with random numbers that have been scaled to the range 1 to 100. Then determine and display the number of random numbers having values between 1 and 50 and the number having values greater than 50. What do you expect the output counts to be?

9. In many statistical analysis programs, data values that are considerably outside the range of the majority of values are simply dropped from consideration. Using this information, write a C program that accepts up to 10 floating-point values from a user and determines and displays the average and standard deviation of the input values. All values that are more than four standard deviations away from the computed average are to be displayed and dropped from any further calculation, and a new average and standard deviation should be computed and displayed.

10. Given a one-dimensional array of floating-point numbers named num, write a function that determines the sum of the numbers
    a. using repetition
    b. using recursion. [*Hint:* If $n = 1$, then the sum is num[0]; otherwise, the sum is num[n] plus the sum of the first (n - 1) elements.

CHAPTER

9 | Multidimensional Arrays

In addition to one-dimensional arrays, all programming languages provide the capability of defining and using larger array sizes. In this chapter such arrays are presented, with the emphasis on two-dimensional arrays. Matrices, which are the mathematical equivalent of one- and two-dimensional arrays, are then introduced. After describing standard matrix operations, we show how they can be used with array processing techniques to solve systems of linear equations.

9.1 DECLARING AND PROCESSING TWO DIMENSIONAL ARRAYS

A *two-dimensional array*, which is also referred to as a table, consists of both rows and columns of elements. For example, the array of numbers

8	16	9	52
3	15	27	6
14	25	2	10

is called a two-dimensional array of integers. This array consists of three rows and four columns. To reserve storage for this array, both the number of rows and the number of columns must be included in the array's declaration. Calling the array val, the correct specification for this two-dimensional array is

```
int val[3][4];
```

397

Similarly, the declarations

```
float prices [10][5];
char code[6][26];
```

declare that the array `prices` consists of 10 rows and 5 columns of floating-point numbers and that the array code consists of 6 rows and 26 columns, with each element capable of holding one character.

To locate each element in a two-dimensional array, an element is identified by its position in the array. As illustrated in Figure 9.1, the term `val[1][3]` uniquely identifies the element in row 1, column 3. As with single-dimensional array variables, double-dimensional array variables can be used anywhere that scalar variables are valid. Examples using elements of the `val` array are:

```
amount = val[2][3];
val[0][0] = 62;
newnum = 4 * (val[1][0] - 5);
sum_row = val[0][0] + val[0][1] + val[0][2] + val[0][3];
```

The last statement causes the values of the four elements in row 0 to be added and the sum to be stored in the scalar variable `sum_row`.

As with single-dimensional arrays, two-dimensional arrays can be initialized from within their declaration statements. This is done by listing the initial values within braces and separating them by commas. Additionally, braces can be used to separate individual rows. For example, the declaration

```
int val[3][4] = { {8,16,9,52},
                  {3,15,27,6},
                  {14,25,2,10} };
```

declares `val` to be an array of integers with three rows and four columns, with the initial values given in the declaration. The first set of internal braces contains the values for row 0 of the array, the second set of internal braces contains the values for row 1, and the third set of braces the values for row 2.

Although the commas in the initialization braces are always required, the inner braces can be omitted. Thus, the initialization for val may be written as

```
int val[3][4] = { 8,16,9,52,
                  3,15,27,6,
                  14,25,2,10};
```

FIGURE 9.1   Each Array Element Is Identified by Its Row and Column Position

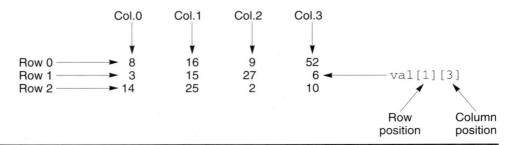

The separation of initial values into rows in the declaration statement is not necessary since the compiler assigns values beginning with the [0][0] element and proceeds row by row to fill in the remaining values. Thus, the initialization

```
int val[3][4] = {8,16,9,52,3,15,27,6,14,25,2,10};
```

is equally valid but does not clearly illustrate to another programmer where one row ends and another begins.

As illustrated in Figure 9.2, the initialization of a two-dimensional array is done in row order. First, the elements of the first row are initialized, then the elements of the second row are initialized, and so on, until the initializations are completed. This row ordering is also the same ordering used to store two-dimensional arrays. That is, array element [0][0] is stored first, followed by element [0][1], followed by element [0][2] and so on. Following the first row's elements are the second row's elements, and so on for all the rows in the array.

As with single-dimensional arrays, two-dimensional arrays may be displayed by individual element notation or by using loops (either while or for). This is illustrated by Program 9.1, which displays all of the elements of a 3 × 4 two-dimensional array using two different techniques. Notice in Program 9.1 that we have used named constants to define the array's rows and columns.

The display produced by Program 9.1 follows:

```
Display of val array by explicit element

 8    16    9    52
 3    15   27     6
14    25    2    10

Display of val array using a nested for loop

 8    16    9    52
 3    15   27     6
14    25    2    10
```

The first display of the val array produced by Program 9.1 is constructed by explicitly designating each array element. The second display of array element values, which is identical to the first, is produced using a nested for loop. Nested loops are especially useful when dealing with two-dimensional arrays because

---

FIGURE 9.2   **Storage and Initialization of the** val[] **Array**

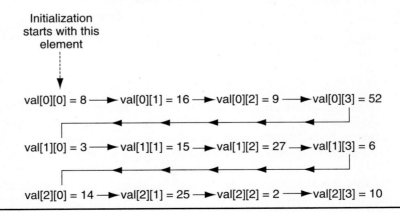

PROGRAM 9.1

```c
#include <stdio.h>
#define NUMROWS 3
#define NUMCOLS 4

void main(void)
{
  int i, j, val[NUMROWS][NUMCOLS] = {8,16,9,52,3,15,27,6,14,25,2,10};

  printf("\nDisplay of val array by explicit element");
  printf("\n%2d  %2d  %2d %2d",val[0][0],val[0][1],val[0][2],val[0][3]);
  printf("\n%2d  %2d  %2d %2d",val[1][0],val[1][1],val[1][2],val[1][3]);
  printf("\n%2d  %2d  %2d %2d",val[2][0],val[2][1],val[2][2],val[2][3]);
  printf("\nDisplay of val array using a nested for loop");
  for (i = 0; i < NUMROWS; i++)
  {
    printf("\n");        /* start each row on a new line */
    for (j = 0; j < NUMCOLS; j++)
      printf("%2d  ", val[i][j]);
  }
  printf("\n");
}
```

they allow the programmer to designate and cycle through each element easily. In Program 9.1, the variable i controls the outer loop and the variable j controls the inner loop. Each pass through the outer loop corresponds to a single row, with the inner loop supplying the appropriate column elements. After a complete row is printed, a new line is started for the next row. The effect is a display of the array in a row-by-row fashion.

Once two-dimensional array elements have been assigned, array processing can begin. Typically, for loops are used to process two-dimensional arrays because, as was previously noted, they allow the programmer to designate and cycle through each array element easily. For example, the nested for loop illustrated in Program 9.2 is used to multiply each element in the val array by the scalar number 10 and display the resulting value.

The output produced by Program 9.2 follows:

```
Display of multiplied elements
 80  160   90  520
 30  150  270   60
140  250   20  100
```

Passing two dimensional arrays into a function is a process identical to passing single-dimensional arrays. The called function receives access to the entire array. For example, the function call display(val); makes the complete val array available to the function named display( ). Thus, any changes made by display( ) will be made directly to the val array. Assuming that the following two-dimensional arrays named test, code, and stocks are declared as:

PROGRAM 9.2

```c
#include <stdio.h>
#define NUMROWS 3
#define NUMCOLS 4

void main(void)
{
  int i, j, val[NUMROWS][NUMCOLS] = {8,16,9,52,
                                     3,15,27,6,
                                     14,25,2,10};
  /* multiply each element by 10 and display it */
  printf("\nDisplay of multiplied elements");
  for (i = 0; i < NUMROWS; i++)
  {
    printf("\n");    /* start each row on a new line */
    for (j = 0; j < NUMCOLS; j++)
    {
      val[i][j] = val[i][j] * 10;
      printf("%3d  ", val[i][j]);
    } /* end of inner loop */
  }    /* end of outer loop */
  printf("\n");
}
```

```c
int test[7][9];
char code[26][10];
float stocks[256][52];
```

the following function calls are valid:

```c
find_max(test);
obtain(code);
price(stocks);
```

On the receiving side, the called function must be alerted that a two-dimensional array is being made available. For example, assuming that each of the previous functions returns an integer, suitable function header lines for the functions are:

```c
int find_max(int nums[7][9])
char obtain(char key[26][10])
void price(float names[256][52])
```

In each of these function header lines, the argument names chosen are local to the function. However, the internal local names used by the function still refer to the original array created outside the function. If the array is a global one, there is no need to pass the array because the function could reference the array by its global name. Program 9.3 illustrates passing a local, two-dimensional array into a function that displays the array's values.

PROGRAM 9.3

```c
#include <stdio.h>
#define ROWS 3
#define COLS 4

void main(void)
{
  int val[ROWS][COLS] = {8,16,9,52,
                         3,15,27,6,
                         14,25,2,10};
  void display(int [ROWS][COLS]); /* function prototype */
  display(val);
}

void display(int nums[ROWS][COLS])
{
  int row_num, col_num;
  for (row_num = 0; row_num < ROWS; row_num++)
  {
    for(col_num = 0; col_num < COLS; col_num++)
      printf("%4d",nums[row_num][col_num]);
    printf("\n");
  }
}
```

Only one array is created in Program 9.3. This array is known as val in main( ) and as nums in display( ). Thus, val[0][2] refers to the same element as nums[0][2].

Notice the use of the nested for loop in Program 9.3. Nested for statements are especially useful when dealing with multidimensional arrays because they allow the programmer to cycle through each element. In Program 9.3, the variable row_num controls the outer loop and the variable col_num controls the inner loop. For each pass through the outer loop, which corresponds to row, the inner loop makes one pass through the column elements. After a complete row is printed, the \n escape sequence causes a new line to be started for the next row. The effect is a display of the array in a row-by-row fashion:

```
 8  16   9  52
 3  15  27   6
14  25   2  10
```

The argument declaration for nums in display( ) contains extra information that is not required by the function. The declaration for nums can omit the row size of the array. Thus, an alternative function declaration is:

```
display(int nums[][4])
```

The reason why the column size must be included while the row size is optional becomes obvious when you consider how the array elements are stored in memory. Starting with element val[0][0], each succeeding element is stored consecutively, row by row, as val[0][0], val[0][1], val[0][2], val[0][3], val[1][0], val[1][1], etc., as illustrated in Figure 9.3.

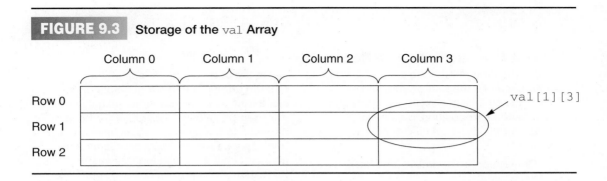

FIGURE 9.3 Storage of the `val` Array

As with all array accesses, an individual element of the `val` array is obtained by adding an offset to the starting location of the array. For example, assuming an integer requires 2 bytes of storage, the element `val[1][3]` is located at an offset of 14 bytes from the start of the array. Internally, the computer uses the row index, column index, and column size to determine this offset using the following calculation:

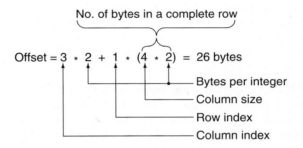

The number of columns is necessary in the offset calculation so that the computer can determine the number of positions to skip over in order to get to the desired row.

Larger Dimensional Arrays

Although arrays with more than two dimensions are not commonly used, C does allow any number of dimensions to be declared. This is done by listing the maximum size of all dimensions for the array. For example, the declaration `int response [4][10][[6]`; declares a three-dimensional array. The first element in the array is designated as `response [0][0][0]` and the last element as `response [3][9][5]`.

Conceptually, as illustrated in Figure 9.4, a three-dimensional array can be viewed as a book of data tables. Using this visualization, the first index can be thought of as the location of the desired row in a table, the second index value as the desired column, and the third index value, which is often called the "rank," as the page number of the selected table. Similarly, arrays of any dimension can be declared. Conceptually, a four-dimensional array can be represented as a shelf of books, where the fourth dimension is used to declare a desired book on the shelf, and a five-dimensional array can be viewed as a bookcase filled with books where the fifth dimension refers to a selected shelf in the bookcase. Using the same analogy, a six-dimensional array can be considered as a single row of book-

A BIT OF BACKGROUND

Deductive and Inductive Reasoning

Since the time of Aristotle (384–322 B.C.), a fundamental method of thought has been the syllogism. A *syllogism* consists of a general proposition, a specific proposition, and a specific conclusion, such as:

General proposition: *All cats have hair.*
Specific proposition: My pet is a cat.
Specific conclusion: My pet has hair.

This is an example of *deductive logic*, in which general rules lead to specific conclusions. Mathematics is based on deductive reasoning.

On the other hand, the scientific method attempts to draw general conclusions from specific experimental results. For example, a billion objects have been thrown into the air and they all have come back down. From these observations one might make the conclusion that everything that goes up must come down. This is *inductive logic.* Inductive conclusions can be verified repeatedly but never proved for certain unless the number of possible situations is finite. It takes only one contradictory experiment to disprove an inductive conclusion. For example, a *Voyager* spacecraft was thrown into the air and it did not come down.

cases where the sixth dimension references the desired bookcase in the row; a seven-dimensional array can be considered as multiple rows of bookcases where the seventh dimension references the desired row, and so on. Alternatively, arrays of three-, four-, five-, six-, etc.-dimensional arrays can be viewed as mathematical *n*-tuples of order three, four, five, six, etc., respectively.

FIGURE 9.4   Representation of a Three-Dimensional Array

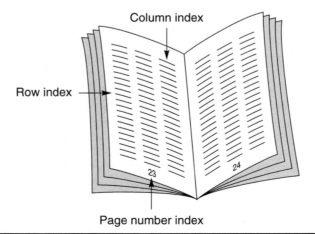

Exercises 9.1

1. Write appropriate specification statements for:

   a. An array of integers with 6 rows and 10 columns

   b. An array of integers with 2 rows and 5 columns

   c. An array of characters with 7 rows and 12 columns

   d. An array of characters with 15 rows and 7 columns

   e. An array of floating-point numbers with 10 rows and 25 columns

   f. An array of floating-point numbers with 16 rows and 8 columns

2. Determine the output produced by the following program:

```c
#include <stdio.h>
void main(void)
{
    int i, j, val[3][4] = {8,16,9,52,3,15,27,6,14,25,2,10};

    for (i = 0; i < 3; ++i)
        for (j = 0; j < 4; ++j)
            printf("%2d  ", val[i][j]);
}
```

3. a. Write a C program that adds the values of all elements in the val array used in Exercise 2 and displays the total.

   b. Modify the program written for Exercise 3a to display the total of each row separately.

4. Write a C program that adds equivalent elements of the two-dimensional arrays named first and second. Both arrays should have two rows and three columns. For example, element [1][2] of the resulting array should be the sum of first[1][2] and second[1][2]. The first and second arrays should be initialized as follows:

First			Second		
16	18	23	24	52	77
54	91	11	16	19	59

5. a. Write a C program that finds and displays the maximum value in a two-dimensional array of integers. The array should be declared as a 4 × 5 array of integers and initialized with the following data: 16, 22, 99, 4, 18, −258, 4, 101, 5, 98, 105, 6, 15, 2, 45, 33, 88, 72, 16, 3.

   b. Modify the program written in Exercise 5a so that it also displays the maximum value's row and column subscript numbers.

6. Write a C program to select the values in a 4 × 5 array of integers in increasing order and store the selected values in the single-dimensional array named sort. Use the data statement given in Exercise 5a to initialize the two-dimensional array.

7. a. A professor has constructed a two-dimensional array of float numbers having 3 rows and 5 columns. This array currently contains the test grades of the students in the professor's advanced compiler design class. Write a C program that reads 15 array values and then determine the total number of grades in the ranges less than 60, greater than or equal to 60 and less than 70, greater than or equal to 70 and less than 80, greater than or equal to 80 and less than 90, and greater or equal to 90.

   b. Entering 15 grades each time the program written for Exercise 7a is run is cumbersome. What method, therefore, is appropriate for initializing the array during the testing phase?

c. How might the program you wrote for Exercise 7a be modified to include the case of no grade being present? That is, what grade could be used to indicate an invalid grade and how would your program have to be modified to exclude counting such a grade?

8. a. Write a function that finds and displays the maximum value in a two-dimensional array of integers. The array should be declared as a 10 row by 20 column array of integers in `main()` and the starting address of the array should be passed to the function.

   b. Modify the function written in Exercise 8a so that it also displays the row and column number of the element with the maximum value.

   c. Can the function you wrote for Exercise 8a be generalized to handle any size two-dimensional array?

9.2 MATRIX OPERATIONS*

A *matrix* is mathematically defined as a rectangular array of elements arranged in horizontal rows and vertical columns that is enclosed within brackets. Examples of matrices are:

$$\mathbf{A} = \begin{bmatrix} 100 \\ 50 \\ 200 \end{bmatrix} \qquad \mathbf{B} = [21\ 0\ 0\ 5\ 4]$$

$$\mathbf{C} = \begin{bmatrix} 1 & 2 & 3 \\ 4 & 5 & 6 \\ 7 & 8 & 9 \end{bmatrix} \qquad \mathbf{D} = \begin{bmatrix} 2 & 4 \\ 0 & 8 \\ 1.7 & 1 \end{bmatrix} \qquad \mathbf{E} = \begin{bmatrix} 1 & 0 & 0 & 1 & 0 & 0 \\ 0 & 1 & 1 & 0 & 0 & 1 \\ 0 & 0 & 0 & 0 & 1 & 0 \end{bmatrix}$$

In this text, we designate matrices by uppercase, boldface, sans serif letters.

A matrix *per se* is nothing more than a table in which the horizontal and vertical lines usually used to separate the rows and columns have been deleted. Only the numbers themselves appear. As such, matrices are simply arrays that have been enclosed in brackets. When a matrix, such as **B**, consists of a single row it is referred to as a *row vector*. Similarly, when a matrix consists of a single column, as, for example, **A**, it is called a *column vector*. Thus, row and column vectors represent one-dimensional arrays, and all other matrices represent two-dimensional arrays.

By convention, the number of rows is given before the number of columns when discussing the *size* or *order* of a matrix. Matrix **A** above contains three rows and one column, so we say it has order 3×1 (read "three by one"). Matrix **B** has one row and five columns, so we say it has order 1×5. The orders of **C**, **D**, and **E**, are 3×3, 3×2, and 3×6, respectively.

As with arrays, the entries in a matrix are called *elements*. Since it is confusing to discuss elements in terms of their values (after all, if the zero element in matrix **E** was referred to, which element would be meant?), we use their positions in the matrix to identify them. We designate these elements by lowercase letters and use subscripts, starting with 1, to pinpoint their positions. The first subscript denotes the row, and the second subscript denotes the column. Accordingly, c_{23} represents the element in **C** located in the second row and third column, whereas e_{32} designates the element in **E** found in the third row and second column. For the particularmatrices given above $a_{31} = 200$, $b_{14} = 5$, $d_{22} = 8$, and c_{37} does not exist because **C** does not have a seventh column.

---

*This section may be omitted on first reading with no loss of subject continuity.

A BIT OF BACKGROUND

Matrices

A sophisticated theory for handling matrices was invented in 1858 by Arthur Cayley (1821–1895). Matrix theory is a comprehensive algebra for adding, multiplying, manipulating, and otherwise transforming two-dimensional arrays. One of its major applications has been for solving simultaneous linear equations.

Arthur Cayley's teachers considered him a "born mathematician" at an early age. He easily garnered top honors in mathematics at Cambridge University, but by the age of 25 he was studying law, a profession that would put bread on the table. After enduring 14 agonizing years of legal practice, Cayley was offered the Sadlerian professorship of mathematics at Cambridge. He eagerly accepted the offer, even though it meant a significant reduction in income. Thereafter, he spent his life in pursuit of mathematics.

In 1925, sixty-seven years after Cayley invented matrix algebra, Werner Heisenberg recognized its value as the exact tool he needed for developing the theory of quantum mechanics.

The *main diagonal* of a matrix is made up of all the elements whose row position equals their column position. Included on the main diagonal are the 1–1 element, the 2–2 element, the 3–3 element, and so on. Examples of main diagonals, indicated here by diagonal lines are:

$$\begin{bmatrix} 1 & 2 & 3 \\ 4 & 5 & 6 \\ 7 & 8 & 9 \end{bmatrix} \qquad \begin{bmatrix} 1 & 2 & 3 & 4 & 5 \\ 6 & 7 & 8 & 9 & 0 \end{bmatrix} \qquad \begin{bmatrix} 1 & 2 & 3 & 4 \\ 0 & 1 & 0 & 1 \\ 2 & 1 & 0 & 1 \\ 3 & 4 & 1 & 1 \\ 7 & 8 & 9 & 1 \end{bmatrix}$$

As we will see in the next section, a particularly important matrix is the identity matrix. An *identity matrix* is a square matrix having its diagonal elements equal to 1 and all other elements equal to 0. For example, the 3×3 and 4×4 identity matrices are, respectively:

$$\begin{bmatrix} 1 & 0 & 0 \\ 0 & 1 & 0 \\ 0 & 0 & 1 \end{bmatrix} \qquad \text{and} \qquad \begin{bmatrix} 1 & 0 & 0 & 0 \\ 0 & 1 & 0 & 0 \\ 0 & 0 & 1 & 0 \\ 0 & 0 & 0 & 1 \end{bmatrix}$$

Elementary Matrix Operations

Just as scalar numbers can be compared for equality, added, subtracted, and multiplied, similar operations are defined for matrices (matrix division is not defined). By extension, since matrices are really single and multidimensional arrays, these operations can be implemented using array processing techniques. Before seeing how these operations are applied, however, we must understand what they mean.

Two matrices are equal if they have the same order and if their corresponding elements are equal. It follows from this that two conditions must be satisfied before two matrices can be called equal: First, they must have exactly the same size and, second, every set of corresponding elements must match. In particular, the matrices:

$$\begin{bmatrix} 1 & 2 \\ 3 & 4 \end{bmatrix} \qquad \begin{bmatrix} 1 & 2 & 0 \\ 3 & 4 & 0 \end{bmatrix}$$

are not equal, since they do not have the same order. The matrices:

$$\begin{bmatrix} 1 & 2 \\ 3 & 4 \end{bmatrix} \qquad \begin{bmatrix} 2 & 3 \\ 1 & 4 \end{bmatrix}$$

have the same order but are still not equal, since their corresponding elements do not match.

The sum of two matrices of the same order is obtained by adding corresponding elements. For example, if

$$\mathbf{A} = \begin{bmatrix} 2 & 4 & -1 \\ 0 & 7 & 2 \\ 3 & 5 & 6 \end{bmatrix} \quad \text{and} \quad \mathbf{B} = \begin{bmatrix} -1 & 0 & -1 \\ 1 & 2 & .5 \\ 4 & -3 & 7 \end{bmatrix}$$

then:

$$\mathbf{C} = \mathbf{A} + \mathbf{B} = \begin{bmatrix} 1 & 4 & -2 \\ 1 & 9 & 2.5 \\ 7 & 2 & 13 \end{bmatrix}$$

Notice that the order of **C** is the same as that of **A** and **B** and that element $c_{ij} = a_{ij} + b_{ij}$, where i denotes the row subscript and j is the column subscript. Thus $c_{11} = a_{11} + b_{11}$, $c_{12} = a_{12} + b_{12}$, and so on. Program 9.4 illustrates how the addition of two matrices can be implemented in C.

The output provide by Program 9.4 is:

```
Display of added array elements
    1.00      1.00      7.00
    4.00      9.00      9.00
   -2.00      2.50     13.00
```

Matrix subtraction is defined similarly to matrix addition; the matrices must be of the same order, and the subtraction is performed on the corresponding elements. Thus,

$$\begin{bmatrix} 1 & 2 \\ 3 & 4 \end{bmatrix} - \begin{bmatrix} -1 & 2 \\ 0.5 & -2.1 \end{bmatrix} = \begin{bmatrix} 1-(-1) & 2-2 \\ 3-0.5 & 4-(-2.1) \end{bmatrix} = \begin{bmatrix} 2 & 0 \\ 2.5 & 6.1 \end{bmatrix}$$

In defining multiplication of matrices, there are two possibilities. The first is called *scalar multiplication* in which a matrix is multiplied by a number. The product of a number c with a matrix **A** is obtained by multiplying each element of **A** by c. Thus,

$$3 \begin{bmatrix} 2 & 1 \\ -1 & 3 \\ 4 & 5 \end{bmatrix} = \begin{bmatrix} 6 & 3 \\ -3 & 9 \\ 12 & 15 \end{bmatrix}$$

and

$$-\frac{1}{2}\begin{bmatrix} 1 & -2 \\ -3 & 4 \end{bmatrix} = \begin{bmatrix} -\dfrac{1}{2} & 1 \\ \dfrac{3}{2} & -2 \end{bmatrix}$$

Program 9.5 illustrates the multiplication of a matrix by a scalar number. A sample run of Program 9.5 follows:

```
Enter the number of rows and columns of the matrix: 3 4
Enter the elements of the matrix, row by row:
8 16 9 52
3 15 27 6
14 25 2 10
Enter the scalar multiplier: 10

Display of multiplied matrix elements
 80.000  160.000   90.000  520.000
 30.000  150.000  270.000   60.000
140.000  250.000   20.000  100.000
```

PROGRAM 9.4

```c
#include <stdio.h>
#define ROWS 3
#define COLS 3

void main(void)
{
  int i, j;
  float c[ROWS][COLS] = { 2, 0, 3,
                          4, 7, 5,
                         -1, 2, 6};
  float d[ROWS][COLS] = {-1, 1, 4,
                          0, 2, 4,
                         -1, 0.5, 7};
   float sumcd[ROWS][COLS];

  /* add the corresponding matrix elements */
  for(i = 0; i < ROWS; i++)
    for(j = 0; j < COLS; j++)
      sumcd[i][j] = c[i][j] + d[i][j];

  /* display the resulting array elements */
  printf("\nDisplay of added array elements");
  for(i = 0; i < ROWS; i++)
  {
    printf("\n");
    for(j = 0; j < COLS; j++)
      printf("%6.2f    ", sumcd[i][j]);
  }
  printf("\n");
}
```

PROGRAM 9.5

```c
/* this program performs scalar multiplication of a matrix
   the limit on the maximum number of rows and columns is
   defined by the named constant MAXNUM   */
#include <stdio.h>
#define MAXNUM 20

void main(void)
{
  int rows, cols, i, j;
  float num, matrix[MAXNUM][MAXNUM];

  printf("\nEnter the number of rows and columns of the matrix: ");
  scanf("%d %d", &rows, &cols);

  printf("Enter the elements of the matrix, row by row: ");
  for(i = 0; i < rows; i++)
   for(j = 0; j < cols; j++)
     scanf("%f", &matrix[i][j]);

  printf("Enter the scalar multiplier: ");
  scanf("%f", &num);

  /* multiply each matrix element by the scalar multiplier */
  for(i = 0; i < rows; i++)
   for(j = 0; j < cols; j++)
    matrix[i][j] = num * matrix[i][j];

  /* display the resulting matrix elements */
  printf("\nDisplay of multiplied matrix elements");
  for(i = 0; i < rows; i++)
  {
    printf("\n");
    for(j = 0; j < cols; j++)
      printf("%7.3f  ", matrix[i][j]);
  }
  printf("\n");
}
```

As seen from this output, the final matrix elements are simply the initial matrix elements multiplied by the scalar number.

As the previous examples show, the operations of matrix addition, subtraction, and scalar multiplication are simple extensions of the analogous operations for real numbers. The situation changes drastically, however, when we consider the multiplication of two matrices. No longer is the operation performed on corresponding elements. Additionally, not all matrices of the same order can be multiplied together, and even those that can often have a product with a different order. Other differences, some startling, will become apparent as we proceed.

At first, matrix multiplication appears complicated and unmotivated. It is neither. It is precisely this operation that makes matrices useful as tools in scientific problems. The motivation comes from the applications we investigate in the next section. As a means of uncomplicating the operation itself, we present the multiplication of two matrices as a two-step process: (1) Determine those matrices that can be multiplied, and (2) give the rule for performing the multiplication. The first step simplifies the second.

A simple method for determining whether or not two matrices can be multiplied is first to write their respective orders next to each other. For example, consider the product **AB** if

$$\mathbf{A} = \begin{bmatrix} 0 & 1 & 0 \\ -3 & 4 & 2 \end{bmatrix} \quad \text{and} \quad \mathbf{B} = \begin{bmatrix} 6 \\ 7 \\ 8 \end{bmatrix}$$

Matrix **A** has order 2×3, and **B** has order 3×1. We write

$$(2 \times 3) \; (3 \times 1)$$

Next consider the adjacent numbers, indicated in this expression by the curved arrow. If the adjacent numbers are the same, the multiplication can be performed. If the adjacent numbers are not the same, the multiplication cannot be performed. In this example, the adjacent numbers are both 3, so the product **AB** is defined.

The order of the product (when the multiplication is defined) is obtained by cancelling the adjacent numbers. In the above example, we cancel the adjacent 3's, leaving 2×1 as the order of **A** times **B**. For example, consider the following matrices:

$$\mathbf{C} = \begin{bmatrix} 0 & 1 & 2 \\ 3 & 4 & 5 \end{bmatrix} \quad \mathbf{D} = \begin{bmatrix} 6 & 7 \\ 8 & 9 \\ -1 & -2 \end{bmatrix} \quad \text{and} \quad \mathbf{E} = \begin{bmatrix} 1 & 0 \\ 2 & -1 \\ 3 & -2 \end{bmatrix}$$

The product **CD** is defined because

$$(2 \times 3) \; (3 \times 2) = (2 \times 2)$$

Similarly, for the product **DC** we have

$$(3 \times 2) \; (2 \times 3) = (3 \times 3)$$

For the product **DE**, we write

$$(3 \times 2) \; (3 \times 2)$$

Now, the adjacent numbers are not equal, and the multiplication cannot be performed. Notice that **CD** $\neq$ **DC**; the order of **CD** is 2×2, and the order of **DC** is 3×3. In general, the product of two matrices is not commutative. That is, interchanging the sequence of the matrices being multiplied usually changes the answer. As such, we must be extremely careful to write the orders of matrices in the correct sequence when we use the method given above.

Knowledge of the size of a product is useful in computing the product. For example, for the matrices:

$$\mathbf{C} = \begin{bmatrix} 0 & 1 & 2 \\ 3 & 4 & 5 \end{bmatrix} \quad \text{and} \quad \mathbf{D} = \begin{bmatrix} 6 & 7 \\ 8 & 9 \\ -1 & -2 \end{bmatrix}$$

we know that

$$\mathbf{CD} = \begin{bmatrix} 0 & 1 & 2 \\ 3 & 4 & 5 \end{bmatrix} \begin{bmatrix} 6 & 7 \\ 8 & 9 \\ -1 & -2 \end{bmatrix} = \begin{bmatrix} - & - \\ - & - \end{bmatrix}$$

The product **CD** will have a 1–1 element, a 1–2 element, a 2–1 element, and a 2–2 element. The determination of these elements is defined as follows:

> The i–j element (where i is the row and j is the column) of a product is obtained by multiplying the elements in the ith row of the first matrix by the corresponding elements (the first with the first, the second with the second, and so on) in the jth column of the second matrix and adding the result.

Thus, for the product **CD** the 1–1 element ($i = 1, j = 1$) is obtained by multiplying the elements in the *first row* of **C** by the corresponding elements in the *first column* of **D** and adding the results. This yields:

$$[0 \quad 1 \quad 2] \begin{bmatrix} 6 \\ 8 \\ -1 \end{bmatrix} = (0)(6) + (1)(8) + (2)(-1) = 0 + 8 - 2 = 6$$

The 1–2 element ($i = 1, j = 2$) in **CD** is obtained by multiplying the elements in the first row of **C** by the corresponding elements in the second of **D** and adding the results. It is:

$$[0 \quad 1 \quad 2] \begin{bmatrix} 7 \\ 9 \\ -2 \end{bmatrix} = (0)(7) + (1)(9) + (2)(-2) = 0 + 9 - 4 = 5$$

The 2–1 element ($i = 2, j = 1$) in **CD** is obtained by multiplying the elements in the second row of **C** by the corresponding elements in the first column of **D** and summing the results. It is:

$$[3 \quad 4 \quad 5] \begin{bmatrix} 6 \\ 8 \\ -1 \end{bmatrix} = (3)(6) + (4)(8) + (5)(-1) = 18 + 32 - 5 = 45$$

Finally, the 2–2 element ($i = 2, j = 2$) in **CD** is obtained by multiplying the elements in the second row of **C** by the corresponding elements in the second column of **D** and summing the results. It is:

$$[3 \quad 4 \quad 5] \begin{bmatrix} 7 \\ 9 \\ -2 \end{bmatrix} = (3)(7) + (4)(9) + (5)(-2) = 21 + 36 - 10 = 47$$

Thus, putting the individual elements back into matrix form, we have:

$$\mathbf{CD} = \begin{bmatrix} 6 & 5 \\ 45 & 47 \end{bmatrix}$$

The flowchart for multiplying two matrices is shown in Figure 9.5 (see page 415). Program 9.6 illustrates how this matrix multiplication algorithm can be implemented in C.

PROGRAM 9.6

```
/* this program performs matrix multiplication of two matrices
   the limit on the maximum number of rows and columns is
   defined by the named constant MAXNUM   */
#include <stdio.h>
#define MAXNUM 20

void main(void)
{
  int rows1, cols1, rows2, cols2, i, j, k;
  int sum, matrix1[MAXNUM][MAXNUM], matrix2[MAXNUM][MAXNUM];
  int product[MAXNUM][MAXNUM];

  printf("\nEnter the number of rows and columns of the 1st matrix: ");
  scanf("%d %d", &rows1, &cols1);

  printf("Enter the number of rows and columns of the 2nd matrix: ");
  scanf("%d %d", &rows2, &cols2);

  /* check that the multiplication is defined */
  if (cols1 != rows2)
    printf("\nThe multiplication is not defined for these two matrices");
  else      /* input the matrices and perform the multiplication */
  {
    printf("Enter the elements of the 1st matrix, row by row: ");
    for(i = 0; i < rows1; i++)
      for(j = 0; j < cols1; j++)
        scanf("%d", &matrix1[i][j]);

    printf("Enter the elements of the 2nd matrix, row by row: ");
    for(i = 0; i < rows2; i++)
      for(j = 0; j < cols2; j++)
        scanf("%d", &matrix2[i][j]);

    /* multiply the matrices */
    for(i = 0; i < rows1; i++)
    {
      for(j = 0; j < cols2; j++)
      {
```

(continued on next page)

(continued from previous page)

```
            sum = 0.0;
            for(k = 0; k < cols1; k++)
              sum = sum + matrix1[i][k] * matrix2[k][j];
            product[i][j] = sum;
          }
      }

 printf("\nDisplay of resulting product matrix");
 for(i = 0; i < rows1; i++)
 {
   printf("\n");
   for(j = 0; j < cols2; j++)
     printf("%3d ", product[i][j]);
  }
     printf("\n);
  }      /* end of else */
}
```

Sample runs follow for Program 9.6:

```
Enter the number of rows and columns of the 1st matrix: 2 3
Enter the number of rows and columns of the 2nd matrix: 3 2
Enter the elements of the 1st matrix, row by row:
0 1 2
3 4 5
Enter the elements of the 2nd matrix, row by row:
  6  7
  8  9
-1 -2

Display of resulting product matrix
  6  5
45 47
```

and:

```
Enter the number of rows and columns of the 1st matrix: 3 2
Enter the number of rows and columns of the 2nd matrix: 3 2

The multiplication is not defined for these two matrices
```

The first run of the program is used to multiply the two matrices **C** and **D** that were previously used to illustrate how matrix multiplication is performed. As shown, the output agrees with our hand calculation of the product matrix elements. The second run illustrates that the program correctly detects that a (3 × 2) matrix cannot be multiplied by another (3 × 2) matrix because the columns of the first matrix do not match, in number, the rows of the second matrix.

FIGURE 9.5   Flowchart for Matrix Multiplication

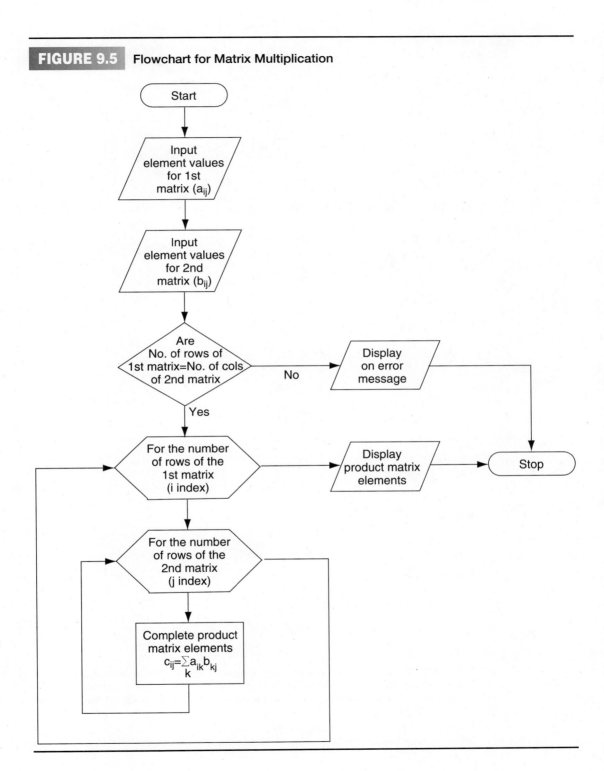

Exercises 9.2

1. Determine the order of the following matrices:

   a. $\mathbf{A} = \begin{bmatrix} 2 & -1 \\ 0 & 3 \end{bmatrix}$

   c. $\mathbf{B} = [1\ 2\ 0\ 0\ 1]$

   b. $\mathbf{C} = \begin{bmatrix} 2 & 1 & 3 \\ -4 & 5 & 6 \end{bmatrix}$

   d. $\mathbf{D} = \begin{bmatrix} 3 & 2 & 1 \\ 4 & 1 & 7 \\ 0 & 0 & 0 \\ 0 & 0 & 0 \end{bmatrix}$

   e. $\mathbf{E} = \begin{bmatrix} -1 \\ 1 \\ -1 \end{bmatrix}$

2. List the 1–1 and 2–2 element, if they exist, for the matrices in Exercises 1a through e.

3. Find $\mathbf{A} + \mathbf{B}$ and $\mathbf{A} - \mathbf{B}$, if they exist, for

   a. $\mathbf{A} = \begin{bmatrix} 1 & 3 \\ 0 & -1 \end{bmatrix}$ $\mathbf{B} = \begin{bmatrix} 1 & -2 \\ 0 & 1 \end{bmatrix}$

   b. $\mathbf{A} = \begin{bmatrix} 1 \\ 2 \\ -1 \end{bmatrix}$ $\mathbf{B} = \begin{bmatrix} 0 \\ 1 \\ 2 \end{bmatrix}$

   c. $\mathbf{A} = \begin{bmatrix} 1 & 0 & 3 \\ 2 & 1 & 1 \end{bmatrix}$ $\mathbf{B} = \begin{bmatrix} 2 & 1 \\ 4 & -1 \end{bmatrix}$

   d. $\mathbf{A} = \begin{bmatrix} 1 & 2 & 3 \\ 4 & 5 & 6 \\ 7 & 8 & 9 \end{bmatrix}$ $\mathbf{B} = \begin{bmatrix} 9 & 8 & 7 \\ 6 & 5 & 4 \\ 3 & 2 & 1 \end{bmatrix}$

   e. $\mathbf{A} = \begin{bmatrix} 1 \\ 3 \\ 5 \\ 7 \end{bmatrix}$ $\mathbf{B} = [2\ 4\ 6\ 8]$

4. Find $5\mathbf{A} + 2\mathbf{B}$ if

$$\mathbf{A} = \begin{bmatrix} 1 & 3 \\ 0 & -1 \end{bmatrix} \qquad \mathbf{B} = \begin{bmatrix} -2 & 3 \\ 7 & 4 \end{bmatrix}$$

5. Find a, b, c, and d if

$$\begin{bmatrix} 1 & a & 3 & b \\ 2 & 1 & 0 & -1 \\ c & 1 & 4 & d \end{bmatrix} = \begin{bmatrix} 1 & 2 & 3 & 4 \\ 2 & 1 & 0 & -1 \\ 4 & 1 & 4 & -5 \end{bmatrix}$$

6. a. Enter and compile Program 9.5 on your computer.

   b. Modify Program 9.5 so that the dimensions entered by the user are checked against the maximum size specified by MAXNUM. If the maximum size is exceeded, display a message informing the user that this condition has occurred and stop program execution.

7. The order of $\mathbf{A}$ is 3×4, the order of $\mathbf{B}$ is 4×1, the order of $\mathbf{C}$ is 1×3, the order of $\mathbf{D}$ is 4×3, and the order of $\mathbf{E}$ is 3×3. Determine the order of:

   a. $\mathbf{AB}$

   b. $\mathbf{BA}$

   c. $\mathbf{CA}$

    d. **AD**

    e. **DA**

    f. **BCE**

    g. **CEA**

    h. **ABCD**

    i. **DABCE**

8. a. Enter and compile Program 9.6 on your computer.

   b. Modify Program 9.6 so that the dimensions entered by the user for each matrix are checked against the maximum size specified by MAXNUM. If the maximum size is exceeded, display a message informing the user that this condition has occurred and stop program execution.

9.3 FOCUS ON PROBLEM SOLVING

In this section we present two problems that can be solved using two-dimensional arrays. The first problem requires storing and manipulating data that conforms readily to a two-dimensional array format. The second problem is a classical method of finding the solution to a system of linear equations using matrices and is called the Gaussian elimination algorithm.

Problem 1: Prepare Sales and Revenue Reports

As part of a program for keeping track of sales and revenues, the owner of two car dealerships has asked you develop a simple demonstration program for review. Each dealership sells the same three sports car models with a minimum price fixed by the dealership at $11,000 for the economy model, $15,000 for the standard model, and $22,000 for the deluxe model. Based on this information the program must permit entry of the number cars of each model that were sold by each dealer. Based on this input data a table of the input data must be displayed along with a second table that displays the total revenue for each model, again by dealership. Finally, a third table should be prepared displaying the total number of all sports cars sold and the total revenue generated by these sales.

Analyze the Problem for Input/Output Requirements   Because this problem requires multiple outputs, it will be helpful to create, on paper, sample output reports. This serves two purposes: First, if the owner agrees with the samples she has already taken the first step in ownership of the result—that is, if the program does in fact produce the output it is something that she has already "signed on to." Secondly, it removes any unpleasant surprises at the end—that is, everyone knows, up front, what the program should produce. To create an actual report, we will have to make up sample input sales for each dealership. For this purpose, we will assume that the first dealership has sold 10, 5, and 3 cars of the economy, standard, and deluxe models, respectively, and that the second dealership's sales numbers were 7, 12, and 1 for the same models (any test numbers can be used here). For these values the three output reports should appear as shown in Figures 9.6, 9.7, and 9.8. To create these reports the data input must consist of how many models of each type were sold, by dealership, which is the data shown in Figure 9.6.

Develop a Solution   The sample reports indicate two natural data structures, both of which are two-dimensional arrays for data storage. The first array can be used to store the input number of each model sold for each dealership. This would make this array a 3 × 2 array having the form shown in Figure 9.6. We will name this array `Sales`.

The second data array, which we will call `Revenues`, will also be a two-dimensional array used to store the data shown in Figure 9.7. The values in each element of the `Revenues` array will be the corresponding value in the `Sales` array times the price of each model.

For convenience, we will store the price of each model in a single-dimensional array named `Prices`. Once these data structures have been defined, the pseudocode describing the program solution becomes:

FIGURE 9.6   Sales Report

```
Summary Report of Models Sold:
Model                 Dealer 1              Dealer 2
--------              ---------             ---------
Economy                  10                    7
Standard                  5                    12
Deluxe                    3                    1
```

FIGURE 9.7   Revenue Report

```
Summary of Revenues:
Model                 Dealer 1              Dealer 2
--------              ---------             ---------
Economy               110000.00             77000.00
Standard               75000.00            180000.00
Deluxe                 66000.00             22000.00
```

FIGURE 9.8   Summary Report

```
Dealer Summary Report:
Dealer                Cars Sold             Tot. Revenue
--------              ---------             ------------
1                        18                  251000.00
2                        20                  279000.00
```

A BIT OF BACKGROUND

To See Things Differently

By 1905, Albert Einstein had developed the *special* theory of relativity, which intimately relates the three dimensions of space with the fourth dimension, time. Although classical mechanics had dealt with both space and time, it took very special insight—the ability to see things differently—to view space–time as a four-dimensional continuum.

By the time Dr. Einstein had formulated the *general* theory of relativity a few years later, mathematical techniques were being developed for expressing space–time in terms of four-dimensional arrays, which were referred to as *tensors*. Seeing the universe in four dimensions led to the postulates that there can be no absolute reference frame; that matter and energy are different manifestations of the same entity; and that the speed of light is constant, regardless of how it is measured. Albert Einstein had reconciled many of the apparent conflicts between the theories of gravitation, mechanics, and electromagnetism. After being forced to flee Nazi Germany in the 1930s because of his religion, he spent much of the rest of his life in Princeton, New Jersey, searching for the elusive insights that would unify all of the forces of nature.

Declare the 3 × 2 array Sales.
Declare the 3 × 2 array Revenues.
Declare and initialize the 3-element Prices array.
Main Module:
    Call input module for entering data.
    Call module to calculate and display Sales and Revenue Reports.
    Call module to calculate and display Dealer Summary Report.

Input Module:
    Use a nested for loop to read data into Sales array in row order.

Sales and Revenue Module:
    Use a nested for loop to generate revenue values for Revenue
      array using the formula:
        *Revenues[row][col] = Sales[row][col] * Prices[row]*
    Display the Sales and Revenues arrays, both in row order.

Dealer Summary Module:
    For each column (which represents a dealer)
      Display dealer number
      Initialize totalCars and totalRevenue to 0
      For each row (which represents a model)
        totalCars = totalCars + Sales[row][col]
        totalRevenue = totalRevenue + Revenues[row][col]
      EndFor
EndFor

Notice that we have chosen to declare the arrays globally. For this program this makes sense for two reasons: First, all of the arrays are used by all of the functions. Secondly, since passing an array is a pass by reference anyway, which provides each function direct access to the array, we can just as easily provide the same access using global arrays to begin with.

Code the Solution   Program 9.7 illustrates C code corresponding to the selected solution.

PROGRAM 9.7

```c
#include <stdio.h>
#define ROWS 3
#define COLS 2
#define ECONOMY 11000.00
#define STANDARD 15000.00
#define DELUXE 22000.00

  /* make the arrays global as they will be shared between functions */
float Prices[] = {ECONOMY, STANDARD, DELUXE};
int Sales[ROWS][COLS];
float Revenues[ROWS][COLS];

void main(void)
{
  void input(void);        /* function prototypes */
  void salesrevs(void);
  void summary(void);

  input();
  salesrevs();
  summary();
}

void input(void)
{
  int i;

  printf("Enter how many of each model were sold, by dealer\n");
  for(i = 1; i <= 2; i++)
  {
    printf(" For dealer %d enter the number of Economy models sold: ",i);
    scanf("%d", &Sales[0][i-1]);
    printf(" For dealer %d enter the number of Standard models sold: ",i);
    scanf("%d", &Sales[1][i-1]);
    printf(" For dealer %d enter the number of Deluxe models sold: ",i);
    scanf("%d", &Sales[2][i-1]);
  }
};

void salesrevs(void)
{
  int i, j;

  printf("\nSummary Report of Models Sold:\n");
  printf("Model        Dealer 1      Dealer 2\n");
  printf("-------      --------      --------\n");
  printf("Economy  %7d %12d\n", Sales[0][0], Sales[0][1]);
```

(continued on next page)

(continued from previous page)
```
  printf("Standard %7d %12d\n", Sales[1][0], Sales[1][1]);
  printf("Deluxe   %7d %12d\n", Sales[2][0], Sales[2][1]);

  /* determine the revenues */
  for(i = 0; i < ROWS; i++)
    for(j = 0; j < COLS; j++)
      Revenues[i][j] = Sales[i][j] * Prices[i];

  printf("\nSummary Report of Revenues:\n");
  printf("Model       Dealer 1     Dealer 2\n");
  printf("-------     ---------     ---------\n");
  printf("Economy %12.02f %12.02f\n", Revenues[0][0], Revenues[0][1]);
  printf("Standard %12.02f %12.02f\n", Revenues[1][0], Revenues[1][1]);
  printf("Deluxe   %12.02f %12.02f\n", Revenues[2][0], Revenues[2][1]);
}

void summary(void)
{
  int i, j, totalCars;
  float totalRevenue;

  printf("\nDealer Summary Report:\n");
  printf("Dealer   Cars Sold   Tot. Revenue\n");
  printf("------   ---------   ------------\n");

  /* do the summary by dealer - note: each dealer data is by column */
  for(i = 0; i < COLS; i++)
  {
    totalCars = 0;      /* set the dealer totals to 0 */
    totalRevenue = 0.0;
    for(j = 0; j < ROWS; j++)
    {
      totalCars += Sales[j][i];
      totalRevenue += Revenues[j][i];
    }
    printf("  %d %10d    %15.02f\n", i+1, totalCars, totalRevenue);
  }
}
```

Program 9.7 is a rather straightforward illustration of two-dimensional array processing techniques. The only real "quirk," so to speak, is in the function summary, where processing is done in column order. Notice in this function that the outer for loop is controlled by the column index and the inner for loop by the row index.

Test and Debug the Program   For debugging purposes it would be useful to insert printf statements into the functions to display the values of the indices and of the results during each iteration. A sample run displays the following:

```
Enter how many of each model were sold, by dealer
For dealer 1 enter the number of Economy models sold: 10
For dealer 1 enter the number of Standard models sold: 5
For dealer 1 enter the number of Deluxe models sold: 3
For dealer 2 enter the number of Economy models sold: 7
For dealer 2 enter the number of Standard models sold: 12
For dealer 2 enter the number of Deluxe models sold: 1

Summary Report of Models Sold:
Model        Dealer 1      Dealer 2
-------      --------      --------
Economy         10            7
Standard         5           12
Deluxe           3            1

Summary Report of Revenues:
Model        Dealer 1      Dealer 2
-------      ---------     ---------
Economy     110000.00      77000.00
Standard     75000.00     180000.00
Deluxe       66000.00      22000.00

Dealer Summary Report:
Dealer   Cars Sold    Tot. Revenue
------   ---------    ------------
  1         18          251000.00
  2         20          279000.00
```

Problem 2: Gaussian Elimination—Using Matrices to Solve a Set of Simultaneous Linear Equations*

A system of simultaneous *linear equations* is a set of equations in two or more variables where each variable is raised only to the first power and multiplied only by a known number. Examples of such systems are:

$$x + 2y = 5$$
$$5x - y = 3$$

and

$$3r + 2s + t = 10$$
$$4r + s + 3t = 15$$

and

$$x + y - 2z = -3$$
$$-x - y + z = 0$$
$$2x + 3y - 2z = 2$$

The first set of equations is a linear system of two equations in the two unknowns, x and y. The second set is a linear system of two equations in three unknowns, r, s, and t, while the last set is an example of a system of three linear

---

*This section requires the material presented in section 9.2.

equations in three unknowns, x, y, and z. An example of a system of equations that is not linear is:

$$x + 3y^2 + 4z = 2$$
$$x - \sqrt{y} + 2z = 1$$
$$3x + 2y + xz = 4$$

In the first equation, y appears squared and, in the second equation, it appears to the one-half power; to be linear each variable must be raised only to the first power. In the third equation, z is multiplied by x; to be linear each variable can be multiplied only by a number. A system is *nonlinear* if any one of its equations is not linear.

Whenever one deals with systems of equations, the primary objective is to find a solution. In general, a *solution* to a system of equations is a set of numbers for the variables that together satisfy *all* of the equations in the system.

Some systems of equations have many different solutions, while other systems have none. In particular a system of simultaneous linear equations has either one, infinitely many, or no solutions. We now develop a straightforward matrix method for determining which systems have solutions and how to obtain the solutions. The first step in this process is to transform the system of linear equations into matrix notation. Let's see how to do this.

Consider this system of linear equations:

$$2x + 4y + 6z = 46$$
$$3x + 12y + 12z = 102$$
$$4x + 5y + z = 28$$

We first collect all the unknowns, here x, y, and z, and place them together in the same vector. We then collect the coefficients of these unknowns and place them together in their own matrix. Similarly we combine the right sides of each equation into one vector. Doing so results in:

$$\begin{bmatrix} 2 & 4 & 6 \\ 3 & 12 & 12 \\ 4 & 5 & 1 \end{bmatrix} \begin{bmatrix} x \\ y \\ z \end{bmatrix} = \begin{bmatrix} 46 \\ 102 \\ 28 \end{bmatrix} \tag{9.1}$$

Multiplying the left two matrices using the matrix multiplication operation defined in Section 9.2 yields the original system of equations. This same procedure can be used to convert any system of simultaneous linear equations into one matrix equation: Collect all the numerical coefficients of the unknown variables into one matrix denoted as **A**. Then collect all the unknown variables into a column vector denoted as **X**. Finally collect all the numbers on the right side of the equations into a column vector denoted by **B**. Then the system of equations will be equivalent to the one matrix equation:

$$\mathbf{AX} = \mathbf{B}$$

In this system, **A** is referred to as the *coefficient matrix*, **X** is referred to as the *unknown vector*, and **B** as the *known vector*.

Solving the matrix equation $\mathbf{AX} = \mathbf{B}$ is accomplished by transforming the equations so that **A** becomes the identity matrix, that is, it has 1's on its diagonal elements and 0's in all other positions. For example, consider the matrix equation:

$$\begin{bmatrix} 1 & 0 & 0 \\ 0 & 1 & 0 \\ 0 & 0 & 1 \end{bmatrix} \begin{bmatrix} x \\ y \\ z \end{bmatrix} = \begin{bmatrix} 2 \\ 3 \\ 5 \end{bmatrix}$$

Multiplying the left side of this equation yields:

$$\begin{bmatrix} x \\ y \\ z \end{bmatrix} = \begin{bmatrix} 2 \\ 3 \\ 5 \end{bmatrix}$$

By the property of matrix equality, this is equivalent to:

$$x = 2$$
$$y = 3$$
$$z = 5$$

One method of transforming a matrix equation so that the coefficient matrix becomes the identity matrix is to use *Gaussian elimination*. To use this method, we must first combine the coefficient matrix **A** and the known vector **B** into an *augmented matrix*. For matrix Equation (9.1) the corresponding augmented matrix is:

$$\begin{bmatrix} 2 & 4 & 6 & | & 46 \\ 3 & 12 & 12 & | & 102 \\ 4 & 5 & 1 & | & 28 \end{bmatrix}$$

We can now proceed to transform the coefficient matrix part of the augmented matrix, which lies to the left of the straight line, into an identity matrix. This, however, must be accomplished in a manner that does not affect the original solution. The operations that are permitted are referred to as *row* operations. There are three such row operations:

1. Any two rows of the augmented matrix can be interchanged.
2. Any row of the augmented matrix can be multiplied or divided by a nonzero number.
3. Any row of the augmented matrix can be multiplied by a constant and added to another row of the matrix.

Let's apply these operations to our example augmented matrix to achieve the desired result. The procedure is to start with the 1–1 element, get it to a 1, and then use this element to obtain zeros below it. We then move to the 2–2 element, get it to a 1, and use this element to get zeros above and below it. We then move to the 3–3 element and do the same, and so on, down the diagonal, until we have transformed the coefficient matrix elements to the desired form.

To transform the 1–1 element in the augmented matrix to the number 1, we divide the complete first row by the value 2 (this is permitted by the second row operation), which yields:

$$\begin{bmatrix} 1 & 2 & 3 & | & 23 \\ 3 & 12 & 12 & | & 102 \\ 4 & 5 & 1 & | & 28 \end{bmatrix}$$

To obtain zeros in both positions below the 1–1 element we apply the third row operation twice; that is, we multiply the first row by -3 and add it to the second row, and then multiply the first row by -4 and add it to the third row. Doing so yields:

$$\begin{bmatrix} 1 & 2 & 3 & | & 23 \\ 0 & 6 & 3 & | & 33 \\ 0 & -3 & -11 & | & -64 \end{bmatrix}$$

Whenever one element is used to transform a second element to zero using a row operation, the first element is called the *pivot element,* or simply the *pivot.* In the previous operations the 1–1 element was the pivot.

Having gotten zeros below the 1–1 element, we now move on to the 2–2 element and make it the pivot. This element is transformed to a 1 by dividing the complete second row by 6. Doing so yields:

$$\begin{bmatrix} 1 & 2 & 3 & | & 23 \\ 0 & 1 & .5 & | & 5.5 \\ 0 & -3 & -11 & | & -64 \end{bmatrix}$$

We now use this element, which is our new pivot, to obtain zeros in the position immediately above it by multiplying the second row by -2 and adding it to the first row, and then multiplying the second row by 3 and adding it to the third row. This yields:

$$\begin{bmatrix} 1 & 0 & 2 & | & 12 \\ 0 & 1 & .5 & | & 5.5 \\ 0 & 0 & -9.5 & | & -47.5 \end{bmatrix}$$

The process is completed by now making the 3–3 element the pivot and using it to obtain zeros above it. The 3–3 element is first set to 1 by dividing the third row by -9.5:

$$\begin{bmatrix} 1 & 0 & 2 & | & 12 \\ 0 & 1 & .5 & | & 5.5 \\ 0 & 0 & 1 & | & 5 \end{bmatrix}$$

To obtain 0's in the positions immediately above the 3–3 element the third row is multiplied by $-.5$ and added to the second row, and then multiplied by -2 and added it to the first row. Doing so results in:

$$\begin{bmatrix} 1 & 0 & 0 & | & 2 \\ 0 & 1 & 0 & | & 3 \\ 0 & 0 & 1 & | & 5 \end{bmatrix}$$

From this transformed augmented matrix the solution vector, **X**, is given as:

$$\mathbf{X} = \begin{bmatrix} 2 \\ 3 \\ 5 \end{bmatrix}$$

From the property of matrix equality this matrix equation can be written as the three single equations:

$$x = 2$$
$$y = 3$$
$$z = 4$$

These, as we have seen, are the solution to the original set of linear equations.

In reviewing the procedure we have used to solve the original system of linear equations, two points should be noted. Mathematically only those systems of linear equations having the same number of equations as unknowns can have a unique solution. This fact implies that the coefficient matrix must have the same number of rows (which corresponds to the number of equations), as columns (which corresponds to the number of unknowns). Secondly, even with the same number of equations as unknowns, a unique solution is not guaranteed. If at any point in the process a nonzero pivot cannot be found, the system does not have a unique solution. In this case the coefficient matrix is said to be singular, and either no solutions exist or an infinity of solutions exists (Exercise 3 at the end of this section explores this point in more depth.)

Having understood both the problem to be solved and the process by which the solution is to be obtained, we can now simply list the top-down development steps summarizing our results.

Analyze the Problem for Input/Output Requirements   The input is the system of equations and the output is a solution to these equations.

Develop a Solution   The solution we will employ is Gaussian elimination using a two-dimensional array. Based on our discussion, the pseudocode for this algorithm is:

Enter the number of equations.
Enter the coefficient matrix.
Enter the known vector.
Form the augmented matrix.
For each row in the augmented matrix
   If the diagonal element (the pivot) for the current row is 0
     Interchange it with a row below it that does not have a 0 in the same column.
     If there is no nonzero element below the pivot that can be interchanged.
      Print that there is no unique solution and stop the program.
    Endif
   Else
     Divide the pivot row by the value of the diagonal element—this sets the pivot to a 1.
   Endif
   For each row in the augmented matrix above and below the pivot row
     Set the variable factor equal to the negative of the element in the current row corresponding to the pivot element in the pivot row.
     Generate a 0 in the columns above and below the pivot by multiplying each element in the pivot row by the factor and adding it to the corresponding element in the current row.
   EndFor
EndFor
Print the values of the solution, which are the values in the last column of the augmented matrix.

Code the Solution   Program 9.8 illustrates how the Gaussian elimination algorithm can be implemented in C.

PROGRAM 9.8

```c
#include <stdio.h>
#define MAXEQS 15

void main(void)
{
  int numeqs, i, j, k, row;
  float augmnt[MAXEQS][MAXEQS + 1];
  float temp, pivot, factor;

  printf("\nEnter the number of linear equations: ");
  scanf("%d", &numeqs);

  printf("Enter the coefficient matrix by rows: ");
  for (i = 0; i < numeqs; i++)
    for (j = 0; j < numeqs; j++)
      scanf("%f", &augmnt[i][j]);

  printf("Enter the known matrix: ");
  for (i = 0; i < numeqs; i++)
    scanf("%f", &augmnt[i][numeqs]);

  /* perform the gaussian elimination */
  for(i = 0; i < numeqs; i++)
  {
      /* get the next pivot */
      pivot = augmnt[i][i];
      row = i + 1;
      /* make sure the pivot is nonzero */
      if ( pivot == 0.0)
      {
        while (pivot == 0.0 && row <= numeqs)
        {
          if (augmnt[row][i] != 0)
            pivot = augmnt[row][i];
          else
            row++;
        }
        /* check that a nonzero pivot was found */
        if (pivot == 0.0)
        {
          printf("A unique solution does not exist for these equations");
          return;
        }
```

(continued on next page)

(continued from previous page)

```
        else    /* interchange this row with the new pivot row */
        {
          for(j = 0; j < numeqs + 1; j++)
          {
            temp = augmnt[i][j];
            augmnt[i][j] = augmnt[row][j];
            augmnt[row][j] = temp;
          }
        }
      } /* end test for nonzero pivot */

      /* at this point we have a nonzero pivot and can */
      /* perform gaussian elimination on the rows above and below the pivot */
      /* first we get the pivot to a 1 */
      pivot = augmnt[i][i];
      for (j = i; j < numeqs + 1; j++)
        augmnt[i][j] = augmnt[i][j] / pivot;

      /* now we get zeros above and below the pivot row */
      for (k = 0; k < numeqs; k++)
      {
        factor = -augmnt[k][i];
        if (k != i)
        {
          for (j = i; j < numeqs + 1; j++)
            augmnt[k][j] = augmnt[k][j] + factor * augmnt[i][j];
        }
      }
   }
   /* print the solutions */
   printf("\nThe solution is: \n");
   for (i = 0; i < numeqs; i++)
     printf("x%d = %f\n", i+1, augmnt[i][numeqs]);
}
```

Test and Debug the Program   The following is a sample run using Program 9.8:

```
Enter the number of linear equations: 3
Enter the coefficient matrix by rows:
2 4 6
3 12 12
4 5 1
Enter the known matrix: 46 102 28

The solution is:
x1 =   2.0000
x2 =   3.0000
x3 =   5.0000
```

This result agrees with the solution of the system of linear equations that we previously calculated by hand. Further tests, which are explored in the exercises, need to be made for the following cases:

1. There are more equations than unknowns (generally no solution).
2. There are fewer equations than unknowns (an infinite number of solutions).
3. The equations are linearly related (this reverts to case 2).

Exercises 9.3

1. a. Compile and run Program 9.8 on a computer. Enter the data necessary to solve the linear equations:

$$2x + 3y = 15.8$$
$$4x + 4y = 24.4$$

   b. Use Program 9.8 to solve the linear equations:

$$2x + 3y + 4z = 11$$
$$5x + 6y = 12$$
$$7x - 8y - 9z = 13$$

2. Modify Program 9.8 to display the intermediate results—that is, the transformed augmented matrix after each pivot has been converted to a 1 and the other elements in the pivot column have been transformed to 0's.

3. a. Determine why the following equations have no solution:

$$2x + y = 7$$
$$2x + y = 14$$

   b. Determine why the following equations have many solutions:

$$2x + y = 10$$
$$6x + 3y = 30$$

4. a. An alternate method of determining the solution of systems of linear equations is provided by Cramer's rule. For two equations of the form:

$$ax + by = c$$
$$dx + ey = f$$

   Cramer's rule provides the solution as:

$$x = \frac{ce - bf}{ae - bd}$$

$$y = \frac{af - cd}{ae - bd}$$

   Notice that when the denominators of these two equations are zero, the equations are singular and no unique solution exists. Using these equations, write a C program that calculates and displays the solution for systems of two linear equations.

   b. Combine the program written for Exercise 4a with Program 9.8 to determine the slope and y intercept of the least-squares straight line directly from the input data points.

5. An extremely common situation is illustrated by Figure 9.9. Here, either experimental or empirical data is obtained and, although a straight line appears to be a reason-

FIGURE 9.9 Experimental Data

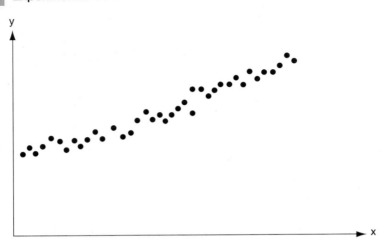

able approximation to the data, no single line of the form $y = mx + b$ contains all of the given data points. Nevertheless, we would like to obtain the equation of the straight line that best fits a set of N data points $(x_1, y_1), (x_2, y_2), (x_3, y_3), \ldots, (x_N, y_N)$.

A commonly used technique for determining the values of m and b is called the *least-squares straight-line* method, where the values of m and b are determined as the solution to the simultaneous equations:

$$Nb + \quad \Sigma x_i m = \Sigma y_i \qquad (9.2)$$
$$\Sigma x_i b + \Sigma(x_i)^2 m = \Sigma x_i y_i \qquad (9.3)$$

Here x_i and y_i denote the values of the ith data point, N is the total number of data points being considered, and Σ is the sigma notation for "the sum of." Thus, once the coefficients of the b and m terms in Equations (9.2) and (9.3) are calculated from the data points, Program 9.7 can be used to solve for the unknowns b and m (m is the slope of the line, and b is the y intercept).

a. Write a C program that prompts the user for the number of data points (N), and then accepts the data points as inputs and calculates the sums indicated in Equations (9.2) and (9.3). As test data use the following points:

(0, 1) (1, 5) (2, 3) (3, 6) (4, 9)

Once you have determined the sums, use Program 9.8 to solve Equations (9.2) and (9.3) to find the values of m and b.

b. Use the program developed in Exercise 5a to determine the equation of the least-squares straight line that best fits the following data points: (1,3), (2,1), (3,2), (4,1), (6,2), (8,5)

6. Experimental results on an unknown resistor produced the following table of voltages and currents:

Voltage (volts)	Current (amps)
1	0.018
2	0.043
3	0.056
4	0.085
5	0.092
6	0.100
7	0.102

The equation relating voltage, V, current, I and resistance, R, is given by Ohm's law, which states that $V = R \times I$. Using this information find the "best" guess at the resistance value, R. (*Hint:* Use a least-squares curve fit. The slope of the line yields R.)

7. Fitting a quadratic curve to a set of N data points, denoted as (x_1,y_1), (x_2,y_2), $x_3,y_3)$,..., (x_n,y_n), requires determining the values of a, b, and c for the equation $y = a + bx + cx^2$ that fits the data in some best manner. One technique for determining the values of a, b, and c is called the *quadratic least-squares fit*. For such a fit, the unknowns a, b, and c are related by the set of equations:

$$Na + b \sum_{i=1}^{N} x_i + c \sum_{i=1}^{N} x_i^2 = \sum_{i=1}^{N} y_i$$

$$a \sum_{i=1}^{N} x_i + b \sum_{i=1}^{N} x_i^2 + c \sum_{i=1}^{N} x_i^3 = \sum_{i=1}^{N} x_i y_i$$

$$a \sum_{i=1}^{N} x_i^2 + b \sum_{i=1}^{N} x_i^3 + c \sum_{i=1}^{N} x_i^4 = \sum_{i=1}^{N} x_i^2 y_i$$

Using Program 9.8 as a starting point, write a C program that accepts the given x and y values as inputs, determines the coefficients of the three equations, and then solves for the values of a, b, and c. (*Hint:* Accept the number of data points as the first input and store the actual data points in two arrays named X and Y, respectively.) Test your program using the data points: (1,0.5), (2,1.5), (3,1), (4,2).

8. a. The official United States population for each census taken since the year 1900 is listed below. The population figures are in millions of people and are rounded off to one fractional digit.

Year	U.S. Population (in millions)
1900	76.2
1910	92.2
1920	106.0
1930	123.2
1940	132.2
1950	151.3
1960	179.3
1970	203.3
1980	226.5

Using the program developed for Exercise 7, determine the equation of the least-squares quadratic curve for this data.

b. Using the equation determined in Exercise 8a, determine an estimate for the population of the United States in the year 2000.

9.4 COMMON PROGRAMMING ERRORS

The common errors associated with multidimensional arrays are almost identical to those for one-dimensional arrays:

1. Forgetting to declare the array. This error results in a compiler error message "Undefined symbol," and is equivalent to omitting the definition of any other variable.

2. Using a scalar variable with subscripts. For example, if `mat` is declared a scalar floating-point variable and subsequently referenced as `mat[1][1]` the compiler will report the error "Invalid indirection." The exact meaning of this error message will become clear in Chapter 10, when the correspondence between arrays and pointers is established.

3. Using a subscript that references a nonexistent array element—For example, declaring the array to be of size 20×25 and using a subscript value of 25 for the row index—results in an error. This error is typically not detected by most C compilers. It will, however, result in a run-time error that will cause either a program crash or a value that has no relation to the intended element being accessed from memory. In either case, it is usually an extremely troublesome error to locate. The only solution to this problem is to make sure, either by specific programming statements or by careful coding, that each subscript references a valid array element.

4. Not using a large enough terminal value in a loop counter to cycle through all the array elements. This error usually occurs when an array is initially declared to be of one size and is later expanded, but the programmer forgets to change the loop parameters used in processing the array. Consistently using named constants ensures that this error will not occur. For example, if the named constants:

```
#define NUMROWS 20
#define NUMCOLS 20
```

are used to define the array, as:

```
int prices[NUMROWS][NUMCOLS]
```

then the same constants can be used in a nested loop used for processing the array elements:

```
for(i = 1; i < NUMROWS; i++)
  for(j = 0; j < NUMCOLS; j++)
```

Changing the values in the named constants ensures that both the size of the array and the parameters used in the processing loop are automatically and correctly adjusted.

5. Forgetting to initialize the array. Although many compilers automatically set all elements of integer and real valued arrays to zero, and all elements of character arrays to blanks, it is up to the programmer to ensure that each array is correctly initialized before processing of array elements begins.

6. Using the same name for both an array and a scalar variable. Once an array name is declared, this same name cannot be used as a scalar variable.

9.5 CHAPTER REVIEW

Key Terms

augmented matrix
coefficient matrix
column vector
Gaussian elimination
identity matrix
known vector
linear equation

main diagonal
matrix
matrix order
row vector
two-dimensional array
unknown vector

Summary

1. A two-dimensional array is declared by listing both a row and a column size with the data type and name of the array. For example, the declaration:

```
int mat[5][7];
```

creates a two-dimensional array consisting of five rows and seven columns of integer values.

2. Two-dimensional arrays can be initialized when they are declared. This is accomplished by listing the initial values, in a row-by row manner, within braces and separating them with commas. For example, the declaration:

```
int vals[3][2] = { {1, 2},
                   {3, 4},
                   {5, 6} };
```

produces the following 3-row by 2-column array:

```
1  2
3  4
5  6
```

Because C uses the convention that initialization proceeds in row-wise order, the inner braces can be omitted. Thus, an equivalent initialization is provided by the statement:

```
int vals[3][2] = { 1, 2, 3, 4, 5, 6};
```

3. A matrix is a rectangular array of elements arranged in horizontal rows and vertical columns enclosed within brackets. For example,

$$\begin{bmatrix} 2 & 1 & \sqrt{5} & 0 \\ -3 & 0 & -2 & 4 \end{bmatrix}$$

4. A matrix with only one row or column is referred to as a *vector*, and is equivalent to a one-dimensional array. All other matrices are equivalent to two-dimensional arrays.

5. The *size* or *order* of a matrix is the number of rows followed by the number of columns in the matrix. For example, the order of the matrix:

$$\begin{bmatrix} 0 & 1 & 2 \\ 3 & 4 & 5 \end{bmatrix}$$

is 2×3 (read "two by three).

6. The main diagonal of a matrix is made up of all the elements whose row position equals their column position.

7. An *identity matrix* is a square matrix having its diagonal elements equal to 1 and all other elements equal to 0. The 3 × 3 identity matrix is:

$$\begin{bmatrix} 1 & 0 & 0 \\ 0 & 1 & 0 \\ 0 & 0 & 1 \end{bmatrix}$$

8. Two matrices are *equal* if they have the same order and if their corresponding elements are equal.

9. The product of a number c with a matrix **A** is obtained by multiplying each element of **A** by c. This is referred to as *scalar multiplication.*

10. The multiplication of two matrices, called *matrix multiplication,* is only defined when the number of columns of the first matrix is equal to the number of rows of the second matrix. The order of the product matrix is the number of rows of the first matrix by the number of columns of the second matrix. The i–j element of the product matrix is obtained by multiplying the elements in the ith row of the first matrix by the corresponding elements in the jth column of the second matrix and adding the results.

Exercises

1. Your professor has asked you to write a C program that can be used to determine grades at the end of the semester. For each student, who is identified by an integer number between 1 and 60, four examination grades must be kept. Additionally, two final grades averages must be computed. The first grade average is simply the average of all four grades. The second grade average is computed by weighting the four grades as follows: the first grade gets a weight of .2, the second grade gets a weight of .3, the third grade a weight of .3, and the fourth grade a weight of .2; that is, the final grade is computed as

```
0.2 * grade-1 + 0.3 * grade-2 + 0.3 * grade-3 + 0.2 * grade-5.
```

Using this information, you are to construct a 60 × 6 two-dimensional array, in which the first column is used for the student number, the next four columns for the grades, and the last two columns for the computed final grades. The output of the program should be a display of the data in the completed array. For test purposes the professor has provided the following data:

Student	Grade 1	Grade 2	Grade 3	Grade 4
1	100	100	100	100
2	100	0	100	0
3	82	94	73	86
4	64	74	84	94
5	94	84	74	64

2. Modify the program written for Exercise 1 by adding an eighth column to the array. The grade in the eighth column should be calculated by computing the average of the top three grades only.

3. a. You are to create a two-dimensional list of integer part numbers and quantities of each part in stock and write a function that displays the data in the array in decreasing quantity order. Assume that no more than 100 different parts are being kept track of, and test your program with the following data:

Part No.	Quantity
1001	62
949	85
1050	33
867	125
346	59
1025	105

   b. Modify the function written in Exercise 3a to display the data in part number order.

4. Assume that the answers to a true–false test are as follows: T T F F T. Given a two-dimensional answer array where each row corresponds to the answers provided on one test, write a function that accepts the two-dimensional array and the number of tests as arguments, and returns a one-dimensional array containing the grades for each test (assume each question is worth 5 points, so that the maximum possible grade is 25). Test your function using the following data:

   Test 1: T F T T T

   Test 2: T T T T T

   Test 3: T T F F T

   Test 4: F T F F F

   Test 5: F F F F F

   Test 6: T T F T F

5. Modify the function that you wrote for Exercise 4 so that each test is stored in column order rather than row order.

6. Write a function that can be used to sort the elements of a 3 × 4 two-dimensional array of integers so that the lowest value is in element position [0][0], the next highest value in element position [0][1], and the highest value in element position [2][3]. [*Hint:* Use the sortnum( ) function in Program 7.12 to swap array elements.]

7. The transpose of a matrix is defined as a new matrix that is obtained from the original matrix by converting all the rows to columns. That is, the first row of the original matrix becomes the first column of the transposed matrix, the second row of the original matrix becomes the second column of the transposed matrix, and so on. Using this information, write a C program that computes and displays the transpose of a user-input matrix.

8. A certain electronic circuit board manufactured by an electronics company is made in three grades: military, commercial, and toy. Each circuit board uses the same number of components: 1 CPU, 4 memory chips, 10 resistors, and 5 capacitors. However, due to the much closer tolerances required for the military version, as compared to both the commercial and toy versions, the manufacturer uses completely different sets of components for the three versions it sells. The cost of individual components used in each version is:

Component	Military	Commercial	Toy
CPU	$300	$180	$60
Memory	$250	$125	$80
Resistors	$5	$2	$1
Capacitors	$8	$3.50	$2

Using this data, write a C program that determines the cost of these components for each version of the circuit board.

9. Write a function that generates a multiplication table and a second function that displays the table. Allow the user to specify the maximum size of the table—so that the table goes from 1×1 to size $\times$ size—and prints only those elements below the diagonal.

10. A magic square is a square of numbers with N rows and N columns in which each of the integer values from 1 to $(N * N)$ appears exactly once, and in which the sum of each column, each row, and each diagonal is the same value. For example, Figure 9.10 shows a magic square in which $N = 3$ and the sum of the rows, columns, and diagonal is 15. Write a program that constructs and displays a magic square for any give odd number N. The algorithm is:

Insert the value 1 in the middle of the first row (element [0] [N%2])
After a value, x, has been placed, move up one row and to the
* right one column. Place the next number, x + 1, there, unless:*
* 1. You move off the top (row = −1) in any column. Then move to*
*   the bottom row and place the next number, x + 1, in the*
*   bottom row of that column.*
* 2. You move off the right end (column = N) of a row. Then*
*   place the next number, x + 1, in the first column of that*
*   row.*
* 3. You move to a position that is already filled or out of the*
*   upper-right corner. Then place the next number, x + 1,*
*   immediately below x.*
Stop when you have placed as many elements as there are in the array.

11. Among other applications Pascal's triangle (see Figure 9.11) provides a means of determining the number of possible combinations of n things taken r at a time. For example, the number of possible combinations of five people (n − 5) taken two at a time ($r = 2$) is 10.

FIGURE 9.10 A Magic Square

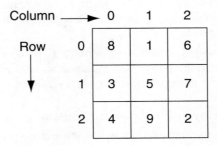

Each row of the triangle begins and ends with 1. Every other in a row is the sum of the element directly above it with the element to the left of the one above it. That is,

```
element[n][r] = element[n - 1][r] + element[n — 1][r — 1]
```

Use this information to write and test a C program to create the first 11 rows of a two-dimensional array representing Pascal's triangle. For any given value of *n* less than 11 and *r* less than or equal to *n*, the program should display the appropriate element. Use your program to determine in how many ways a committee of 8 people can be selected from a group of 10 people.

FIGURE 9.11 Pascal's Triangle

			r				
n	**0**	**1**	**2**	**3**	**4**	**5**	• • •
0	1						
1	1	1					
2	1	2	1				
3	1	3	3	1			
4	1	4	6	4	1		
5	1	5	10	10	5	1	

12. A three-dimensional weather array for the months of July and August 1995 has pages labeled by the month numbers 7 and 8. On each page there are rows, numbered 1 through 31, representing the days, and two columns labeled H and L that represent the day's high and low temperatures, respectively.

Use this information to write a C program that stores this data in a three-dimensional array. The program should either prompt for or assign the high and low temperatures for each element of the array. Then allow the user to request
- Any day's high and low temperature
- Average high and low temperatures for a given month
- Month and day with the highest temperature
- Month and day with the lowest temperature.

Based on the request the appropriate value should be displayed.

CHAPTER

10 | Pointers

Languages such as C, Pascal, Modula-2, and FORTRAN 90 all provide a feature called pointers, which permit the construction of dynamically linked lists (see Section 14.5). One of C's advantages is that it also allows the programmer to access directly the addresses of variables and manipulate them using pointer arithmetic; that is, addresses can be added, subtracted, and compared. This is a feature that is not provided in either Pascal, Modula-2, or FORTRAN 90. Although we have already used the address operator, &, in calling the scanf function, the real power of using addresses is that it allows a programmer to directly enter into the computer's inner workings and access the computer's basic storage structure.

This chapter presents the basics of declaring variables to store addresses. Such variables are referred to as *pointer variables*, or simply pointers. Additionally, methods of using pointer variables to access and use their stored addresses in meaningful ways are presented.

10.1 ADDRESSES AND POINTERS

Every variable has three major items associated with it: its data type, the actual value stored in the variable, and the address of the variable. In C, a variable's data type is declared using a declaration statement. The actual value stored in a variable is referred to as the variable's contents, while the address of the first memory location used for the variable constitutes its address. How many memory locations are actually used by the variable depends on the variable's data type. The relationship between these items is illustrated on Figure 10.1.

439

FIGURE 10.1 A Typical Variable

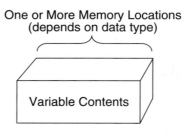

One or More Memory Locations
(depends on data type)

Variable Contents

Variable Address

Programmers are usually concerned only with the value assigned to a variable (its contents) and give little attention to where the value is stored (its address). For example, consider Program 10.1.

PROGRAM 10.1

```
#include <stdio.h>
void main(void)
{
   int num;

   num = 22;
   printf("The value stored in num is %d\n",num);
   printf("The computer uses %d bytes to store this value\n", sizeof(int));
}
```

The output displayed when Program 10.1 is run is:

```
The value stored in num is 22
The computer uses 2 bytes to store this value
```

Program 10.1 displays both the number 22, which is the value stored in the integer variable num (its rvalue), and the amount of storage used for an integer. The information provided by Program 10.1 is illustrated in Figure 10.2. We can go further and obtain the address, corresponding to the variable num. The address that is displayed corresponds to the address of the first byte set aside in the computer's memory for the variable.[1]

To determine the address of num, we must use the *address operator,* &, which means *the address of,* directly in front of the variable name (no space between & and the variable). For example, &num means *the address of* num, &total means

---

[1]Review Section 1.5 if you are unfamiliar with the concept of memory addresses and bytes.

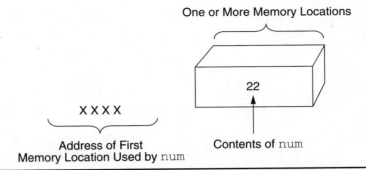

FIGURE 10.2 Somewhere in Memory

One or More Memory Locations

22

X X X X

Address of First
Memory Location Used by num

Contents of num

the address of total, and &price means *the address of* price. Program 10.2 uses the address operator to display the address of the variable num.

PROGRAM 10.2

```c
#include <stdio.h>
void main(void)
{
   int num;

   num = 22;
   printf("num = %d The address of num = %p\n", num, &num);
}
```

The output of Program 10.2 is

```
num = 22 The address of num = FFE0
```

Figure 10.3 illustrates the additional address information provided by the output of Program 10.2. Clearly, the address output by Program 10.2 depends on the computer used to run the program. Every time Program 10.2 is executed, however, it displays the address of the first byte used to store the variable num. Note also that the address is printed using the conversion sequence %p. This conversion sequence is provided in ANSI C to display addresses.[2] As illustrated by the

---

[2] For non-ANSI compilers that do not provide the %p conversion sequence, the unsigned conversion sequence %u may be used in its place. The %u conversion sequence forces the address to be treated as an unsigned integer data type, and what is displayed is printf()'s representation of the address in a decimal format. An address, however, is not an unsigned integer data type—it is a unique data type that may or may not require the same amount of storage as an unsigned integer.

FIGURE 10.3   A More Complete Picture of the Variable num

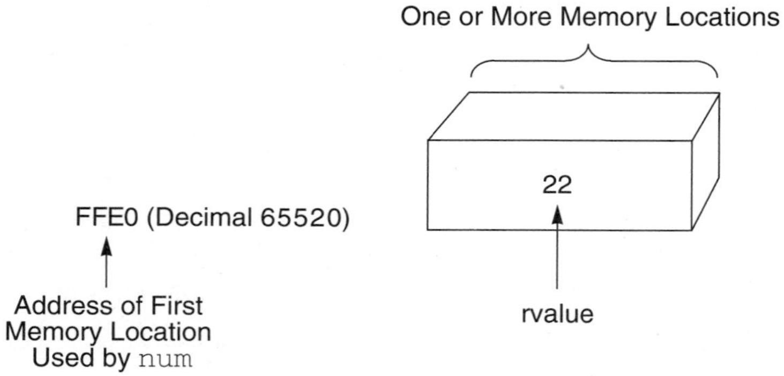

One or More Memory Locations

22

FFE0 (Decimal 65520)

Address of First
Memory Location
Used by num

rvalue

output of Program 10.2, the display is in hexadecimal notation. This display has no impact on how addresses are used internal to the program and merely provides us with a means of displaying addresses that is helpful in understanding them. As we shall see, using addresses as opposed to only displaying them provides the C programmer with an extremely powerful programming tool.

Storing Addresses

Besides displaying the address of a variable, as was done in Program 10.2, we can also store addresses in suitably declared variables. For example, the statement

```
num_addr = &num;
```

stores the address corresponding to the variable num in the variable num_addr, as illustrated in Figure 10.4.

FIGURE 10.4   Storing num's Address into num_addr

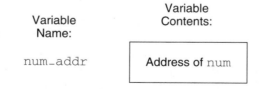

Variable
Name:

Variable
Contents:

num_addr

Address of num

Similarly, the statements

```
d = &m;
tab_point = &list;
chr_point = &ch;
```

store the addresses of the variables m, list, and ch in the variables d, tab_point, and chr_point, respectively, as illustrated in Figure 10.5. The variables num_addr, d, tab_point, and chr_point are formally called *pointer variables,* or pointers, for short. *Pointers* are simply variables that are used to store the addresses of other variables.

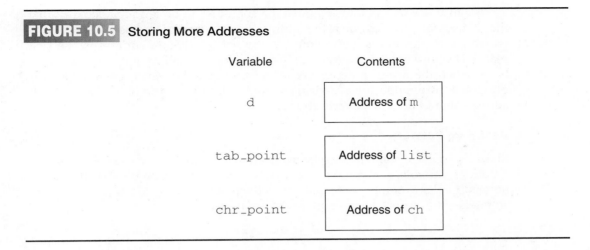

FIGURE 10.5 Storing More Addresses

Variable	Contents
d	Address of m
tab_point	Address of list
chr_point	Address of ch

Using Addresses

To use a stored address, C provides us with an *indirection operator*, *. The * symbol, when followed immediately by a pointer (no space allowed between the * and the pointer), means "the variable whose address is stored in." Thus, if num_addr is a pointer (remember that a pointer is a variable that contains an address), *num_addr means the variable whose address is stored in num_addr. Similarly, *tab_point means the variable whose address is stored in tab_point and *chr_point means the variable whose address is stored in chr_point. Figure 10.6 shows the relationship between the address contained in a pointer variable and the variable ultimately addressed.

Although *d literally means "the variable whose address is stored in d," this is commonly shortened to the statement "the variable pointed to by d." Similarly, referring to Figure 10.6, *y can be read as "the variable pointed to by y." The value ultimately obtained, as shown in Figure 10.6, is qqqq.

When using a pointer variable, the value that is finally obtained is always found by first going to the pointer variable (or pointer, for short) for an address. The address contained in the pointer is then used to get the desired contents. Certainly, this is a rather indirect way of getting to the final value and, not unexpectedly, the term indirect addressing is used to describe this procedure.

FIGURE 10.6 Using a Pointer Variable

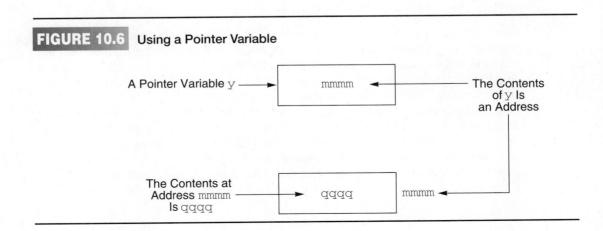

Because use of a pointer requires the computer to do a double lookup (first the address is retrieved, then the address is used to retrieve the actual data), a worthwhile question is, why would you want to store an address in the first place? The answer to this question must be deferred until we get to real applications, when the use of pointers becomes invaluable. However, given what was previously presented for a variable's storage locations, the idea of storing an address should not seem overly strange.

Declaring Pointers

Like all variables, pointers must be declared before they can be used. In declaring a pointer variable, C requires that we also specify the type of variable that is pointed to. For example, if the address in the pointer `num_addr` is the address of an integer, the correct declaration for the pointer is

```
int *num_addr;
```

This declaration is read as "the variable pointed to by `num_addr` (from the `*num_addr` in the declaration) is an integer."

Notice that the declaration int `*num_addr`; specifies two things: first, that the variable pointed to by `num_addr` is an integer; second, that `num_addr` must be a pointer (because it is used with the indirection operator *). Similarly, if the pointer `tab_point` points to (contains the address of) a floating-point number and `chr_point` points to a character variable, the required declarations for these pointers are

```
float *tab_point;
char *chr_point;
```

These two declarations can be read, respectively, as "the variable pointed to by `tab_point` is a `float`" and "the variable pointed to by `chr_point` is a `char`." Notice that in declaring pointers, the data type corresponding to the address being stored must be included in the declaration. Because all addresses appear the same, this additional information is needed by the computer to know how many storage locations to access when it uses the address stored in the pointer. Further examples of pointer declarations are:

```
char *in_addr;
int *num_pt;
float *dst_addr:
double *nm1_addr;
```

To understand pointer declarations, it is helpful to read them "backwards," starting with the indirection operator, the asterisk, *, and translating it either as "the variable whose address is stored in" or "the variable pointed to by." Applying this to pointer declarations, the declaration char `*in_key;`, for example, can be read as either "the variable whose address is stored in `in_key` is a character" or "the variable pointed to by `in_key` is a character." Both of these statements are frequently shortened to the simpler statement that "`in_key` points to a character." Because all three interpretations of the declaration statement are correct, you can select and use whichever description makes a pointer declaration meaningful to you. We now put this together to construct a program using pointers. Consider Program 10.3.

PROGRAM 10.3

```
#include <stdio.h>
void main(void)
{
  int *num_addr;        /* declare a pointer to an int  */
  int miles, dist;      /* declare two integer variables */

  dist = 158;           /* store the number 158 into dist */
  miles = 22;           /* store the number 22 into miles */
  num_addr = &miles;    /* store the 'address of miles' in num_addr */

  printf("The address stored in num_addr is %p\n",num_addr);
  printf("The value pointed to by num_addr is %d\n\n",*num_addr);
  num_addr = &dist; /* now store the address of dist in num_addr */
  printf("The address now stored in num_addr is %p\n",num_addr);
  printf("The value now pointed to by num_addr is %d\n",*num_addr);
}
```

The output of Program 10.3 is:

```
The address stored in num_addr is FFE0
The value pointed to by num_addr is 22

The address now stored in num_addr is FFE2
The value now pointed to by num_addr is 158
```

The only use for Program 10.3 is to help us understand "what gets stored where." Let's review the program to see how the output was produced.

The declaration statement int *num_addr; declares num_addr to be a pointer variable used to store the address of an integer variable. The statement num_addr = &miles; stores the address of the variable miles into the pointer num_addr. The first call to printf causes this address to be displayed. Notice that we have again used the control sequence %p to print the address. The second call to printf in Program 10.3 uses the indirection operator to retrieve and print the value pointed to by num_addr, which is, of course, the value stored in miles.

Because num_addr has been declared as a pointer to an integer variable, we can use this pointer to store the address of any integer variable. The statement num_addr = &dist illustrates this by storing the address of the variable dist in num_addr. The last two printf calls verify the change in num_addr's value and that the new stored address does point to the variable dist. As illustrated in Program 10.3, only addresses should be stored in pointers.

It certainly would have been much simpler if the pointer used in Program 10.3 could have been declared as point num_addr;. Such a declaration, however, conveys no information as to the storage used by the variable whose address is stored in num_addr. This information is essential when the pointer is used with the indirection operator, as it is in the second printf call in Program 10.3.

For example, if the address of an integer is stored in `num_addr`, then only 2 bytes of storage are typically retrieved when the address is used. If the address of a character is stored in `num_addr`, only 1 byte of storage would be retrieved, and a `float` typically requires the retrieval of 4 bytes of storage. The declaration of a pointer must, therefore, include the type of variable being pointed to. Figure 10.7 illustrates this concept.

FIGURE 10.7   Addressing Different Data Types Using Pointers

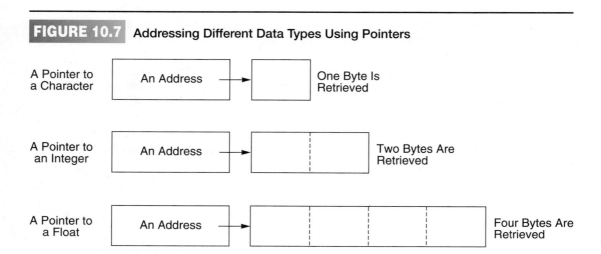

Exercises 10.1

1. If `average` is a variable, what does `&average` mean?

2. For the variables and addresses illustrated in Figure 10.8, determine `&temp`, `&dist`, `&date`, and `&miles`.

3. a. Write a program that includes the following declaration statements. Have the program use the address operator and the `printf` function to display the addresses corresponding to each variable.

   ```
   char key, choice;
   int num, count;
   long date;
   float yield;
   double price;
   ```

   b. After running the program written for Exercise 3a, draw a diagram of how your compiler has set aside storage for the variables in the program. On your diagram, fill in the addresses displayed by the program.

   c. Modify the program written in Exercise 3a to display the amount of storage your computer reserves for each data type (use the `sizeof` operator). With this information and the address information provided in Exercise 3b, determine if your compiler set aside storage for the variables in the order in which they were declared.

4. If a variable is declared as a pointer, what must be stored in the variable?

5. Using the indirection operator, write expressions for the following:

   a. The variable pointed to by x_addr

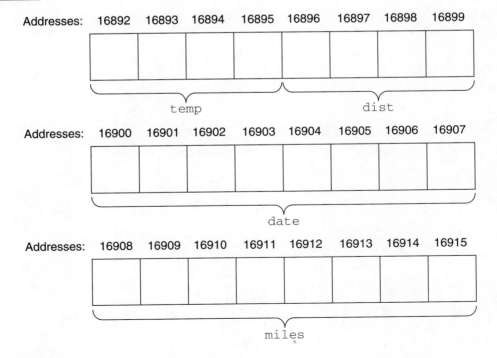

FIGURE 10.8   **Memory Bytes for Exercise 2**

   b. The variable whose address is in `y_addr`

   c. The thing pointed to by `pt_yld`

   d. The variable pointed to by `pt_miles`

   e. The variable pointed to by `mptr`

   f. The variable whose address is in `pdate`

   g. The variable pointed to by `dist_ptr`

   h. The thing pointed to by `tab_pt`

   i. The variable whose address is in `hours_pt`

6. Write declaration statements for the following:

   a. The variable pointed to by `y_addr` is an integer.

   b. The variable pointed to by `ch_addr` is a character.

   c. The variable pointed to by `pt_yr` is a long integer.

   d. The variable pointed to by `amt` is a double-precision variable.

   e. The variable pointed to by `z` is an integer.

   f. The variable pointed to by `qp` is a floating-point variable.

   g. `date_pt` is a pointer to an integer.

   h. `yld_addr` is a pointer to a double-precision variable.

   i. `amt_pt` is a pointer to a floating-point variable.

   j. `pt_chr` is a pointer to a character.

7. a. What are the Exercise 6 variables `y_addr`, `ch_addr`, `pt_yr`, `amt`, `z`, `qp`, `date_ptr`, `yld_addr`, `amt_pt`, and `pt_chr` called?

   b. Why are the variable names `amt`, `z`, and `qp` used in Exercise 6 not good choices for pointer variable names?

8. Write English sentences for the following declarations:

   a. `char *key_addr;`

   b. `int *m;`

   c. `double *yld_addr;`

   d. `long *y_ptr;`

   e. `float *p_cou;`

   f. `int *pt_date;`

9. Which of the following are declarations for pointers?:

   a. `long a;`

   b. `char b;`

   c. `char *c;`

   d. `int x;`

   e. `int *p;`

   f. `double w;`

   g. `float *k;`

   h. `float l;`

   i. `double *z;`

10. For the following declarations,

    `int *x_pt, *y_addr;`

```
long *pt_addr;
double *pt_z;
int a;
long b;
double c;
```

determine which of the following statements is valid:

a. y_addr = &a;

b. y_addr = &b;

c. y_addr = &c;

d. y_addr = a;

e. y_addr = b;

f. y_addr = c;

g. pt_addr = &a;

h. pt_addr = &b;

FIGURE 10.9 **Memory Locations for Exercise 11**

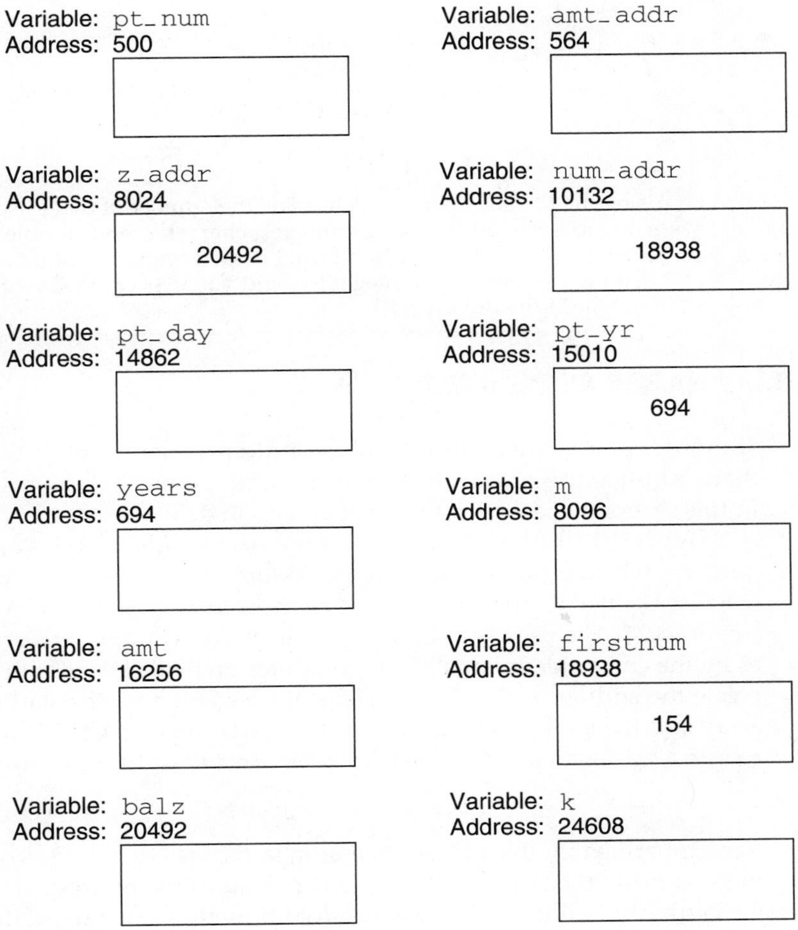

Variable: pt_num	Variable: amt_addr
Address: 500	Address: 564

Variable: z_addr	Variable: num_addr
Address: 8024	Address: 10132
20492	18938

Variable: pt_day	Variable: pt_yr
Address: 14862	Address: 15010
	694

Variable: years	Variable: m
Address: 694	Address: 8096

Variable: amt	Variable: firstnum
Address: 16256	Address: 18938
	154

Variable: balz	Variable: k
Address: 20492	Address: 24608

    i. pt_addr = &c;

    j. pt_addr = a;

    k. pt_addr = b;

    l. pt_addr = c;

    m. pt_z = &a;

    n. pt_addr = &b;

    o. pt_addr = &c;

    p. pt_addr = a;

    q. pt_addr = b;

    r. pt_addr = c;

    s. y_addr = x_pt;

    t. y_addr = dt_addr;

    u. y_addr = pt_addr;

11. For the variables and addresses illustrated in Figure 10.9, fill in the appropriate data as determined by the following statements:

    a. pt_num = &m;

    b. amt_addr = &amt;

    c. *z_addr = 25;

    d. k = *num_addr;

    e. pt_day = z_addr;

    f. *pt_yr = 1987;

    g. *amt_addr = *num_addr;

12. Using the `sizeof` operator, determine the number of bytes used by your computer to store the address of an integer, character, and double-precision number. [*Hint:* `sizeof (*int)` can be used to determine the number of memory bytes used for a pointer to an integer.] Would you expect the size of each address to be the same? Why or why not?

10.2 ARRAY NAMES AS POINTERS

Although pointers are simply, by definition, variables used to store addresses, there is also a direct and intimate relationship between array names and pointers. In this section we describe this relationship in detail.

    Figure 10.10 illustrates the storage of a single-dimensional array named `grades`, which contains five integers. Assume that each integer requires 2 bytes of storage. Using subscripts, the fourth element in the `grades` array is referred to as `grades[3]`. The use of a subscript, however, conceals the extensive use of addresses by the computer. Internally, the computer immediately uses the subscript to calculate the address of the desired element based on both the starting address of the array and the amount of storage used by each element. Calling the fourth element `grades[3]` forces the computer, internally, into the address computation

$$\&grades[3] = \&grades[0] + (3 * 2)$$

Remembering that the address operator, &, means "the address of," this last statement is read "the address of `grades[3]` equals the address of `grades[0]` plus 6." Figure 10.11 illustrates the address computation used to locate `grades[3]`.

FIGURE 10.10   The grades **Array in Storage**

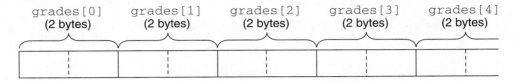

Recall that a pointer is a variable used to store addresses. If we create a pointer to store the address of the first element in the grades array, we can mimic the operation used by the computer to access the array elements. Before we do this, let us first consider Program 10.4.

PROGRAM 10.4

```
#include <stdio.h>
#define NUMS 5

void main(void)
{
  int i, grades[] = {98, 87, 92, 79, 85};

  for (i = 0; i < NUMS; i++)
    printf("Element %d is %d\n", i, grades[i]);
}
```

When Program 10.4 is run, the following display is obtained:

```
Element 0 is 98
Element 1 is 87
Element 2 is 92
Element 3 is 79
Element 4 is 85
```

FIGURE 10.11   **Using a Subscript to Obtain an Address**

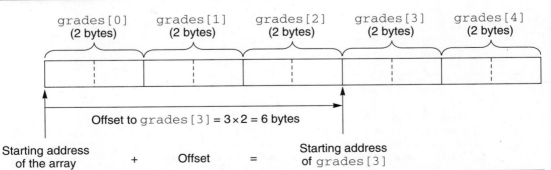

FIGURE 10.12 The Variable Pointed to by *g_ptr Is grades[0]

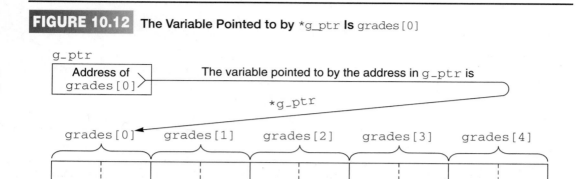

Program 10.4 displays the values of the array grades using standard subscript notation. Now, let us store the address of array element 0 in a pointer. Then, using the indirection operator, *, we can use the address in the pointer to access each array element. For example, if we store the address of grades[0] into a pointer named g_ptr (using the assignment statement g_ptr = &grades[0];), then, as illustrated in Figure 10.12 the expression *g_ptr, which means "the variable pointed to by g_ptr," references grades[0].

One unique feature of pointers is that offsets may be included in expressions using pointers. For example, the 1 in the expression *(g_ptr + 1) is an *offset*. The complete expression references the integer variable that is one beyond the variable pointed to by g_ptr.[3] Similarly, as illustrated in Figure 10.13, the expression *(g_ptr + 3) references the variable that is three integers beyond the variable pointed to by g_ptr. This is the variable grades[3].

Table 10.1 lists the complete correspondence between elements referenced by subscripts and by pointers and offsets. The relationships listed in Table 10.1 are illustrated in Figure 10.14.

FIGURE 10.13 An Offset of 3 from the Address in g_ptr

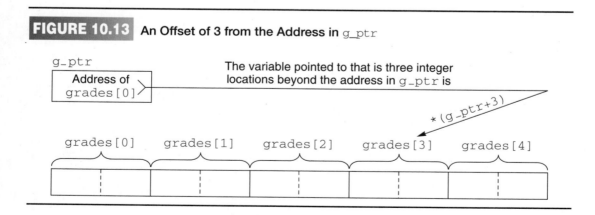

---

[3]The offset indicates the number of elements that are to be skipped over. The correspondence between the number of elements and the number of bytes is handled by the compiler. Thus, the offset is always scaled by the type of data in the array.

TABLE 10.1 Array Elements May Be Referenced in Two Ways

Array Element	Subscript Notation	Pointer Notation
Element 0	grades [0]	*g_ptr
Element 1	grades [1]	*(g_ptr + 1)
Element 2	grades [2]	*(g_ptr + 2)
Element 3	grades [3]	*(g_ptr + 3)
Element 4	grades [4]	*(g_ptr + 4)

FIGURE 10.14 The Relationship Between Array Elements and Pointers

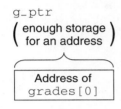
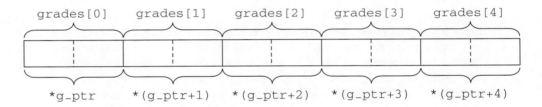

Using the correspondence between pointers and subscripts illustrated in Figure 10.14, the array elements previously accessed in Program 10.4 using subscripts can now be accessed using pointers. This is done in Program 10.5.

PROGRAM 10.5

```c
#include <stdio.h>
#define NUMS 5

void main(void)
{
  int *g_ptr;             /* declare a pointer to an int */
  int i, grades[] = {98, 87, 92, 79, 85};

  g_ptr = &grades[0];     /* store the starting array address */
  for (i = 0; i < NUMS; i++)
    printf("Element %d is %d\n", i, *(g_ptr + i) );
}
```

A   BIT   OF   BACKGROUND

Numerosophy

The ancient Greeks attached great philosophical and religious significance to numbers. They considered the natural (counting) numbers, 1, 2, 3, . . . , to be examples of perfection, and rations of whole numbers (fractions) as somewhat suspect. Diophantus (third century B.C.) called negative numbers "absurd."

According to tradition, Hipparchus (second century B.C.) was drowned when he discussed the scandalous irrational nature of the square root of 2 outside of the Pythagorean Society. The first mention of the square root of a negative number was by Heron of Alexandria (third century A.D.). Such concepts were treated with disbelief and even considered wicked. Today, of course, it is not unusual to use negative, irrational, "artificial," and complex numbers all at once to represent such concepts as vectors and points in a plane. The Greeks of that Golden Age would probably regard our modern mathematics as truly degenerate.

The following display is obtained when Program 10.5 is run:

```
Element 0 is 98
Element 1 is 87
Element 2 is 92
Element 3 is 79
Element 4 is 85
```

Notice that this is the same display produced by Program 10.4. The method used in Program 10.5 to access individual array elements simulates how the computer internally references all array elements. Any subscript used by a programmer is automatically converted to an equivalent pointer expression by the computer. In our case, since the declaration of g_ptr included the information that integers are pointed to, any offset added to the address in g_ptr is automatically scaled by the size of an integer. Thus, *(g_ptr + 3), for example, refers to the address of grades[0] plus an offset of six bytes (3 x 2). This is the address of grades[3] illustrated in Figure 10.12.

The parentheses in the expression *(g_ptr + 3) are necessary to correctly reference the desired array element. Omitting the parentheses results in the expression *g_ptr + 3, which adds 3 to "the variable pointed to by g_ptr." Since g_ptr points to grades[0], this expression adds the value of grades[0] and 3 together. Note also that the expression *(g_ptr + 3) does not change the address stored in g_ptr. Once the computer uses the offset to locate the correct variable from the starting address in g_ptr, the offset is discarded and the address in g_ptr remains unchanged.

Although the pointer g_ptr used in Program 10.5 was specifically created to store the starting address of the grades array, this was, in fact, unnecessary. When an array is created, the compiler automatically creates an internal pointer constant for it and stores the starting address of the array in this pointer. In almost all respects, a pointer constant is identical to a pointer variable created by a programmer, but, as we shall see, there are some differences.

For each array created, the name of the array becomes the name of the pointer constant created by the compiler for the array, and the starting address of the first location reserved for the array is stored in this pointer. Thus, declaring the grades array in both Program 10.4 and Program 10.5 actually reserved enough storage for

FIGURE 10.15   Creating an Array Also Creates a Pointer

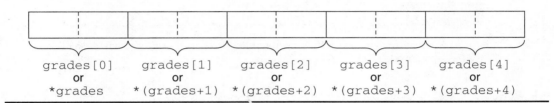

five integers, created an internal pointer named `grades`, and stored the address of `grades[0]` in the pointer. This is illustrated in Figure 10.15. The implication is that every reference to `grades` using a subscript can be replaced by an equivalent reference using `grades` as a pointer. Thus, wherever the expression `grades[i]` is used, the expression `*(grades + i)` can also be used. This is illustrated in Program 10.6, where grades is used as a pointer to reference all of its elements.

PROGRAM 10.6

```
#include <stdio.h>
#define NUMS 5

void main(void)
{
  int i, grades[] = {98, 87, 92, 79, 85};

  for (i = 0; i < NUMS; i++)
    printf("Element %d is %d\n", i, *(grades + i));
}
```

Executing Program 10.6 produces the same output previously produced by Program 10.4 and Program 10.5. However, using `grades` as a pointer made it unnecessary to declare and initialize the pointer `g_ptr` used in Program 10.5.

In most respects an array name and pointer can be used interchangeably. *A true pointer, however, is a variable and the address stored in it can be changed. An array name is a pointer constant and the address stored in the pointer cannot be changed by an assignment statement.* Thus, a statement such as `grades = &grades[2];` is invalid. This should come as no surprise. Since the whole purpose of an array name is to correctly locate the beginning of the array, allowing a programmer to change the address stored in the array name would defeat this purpose and lead to havoc whenever array elements were referenced. Also, expressions taking the address of an array name are invalid because the pointer created by the compiler is internal to the computer, not stored in memory as are pointer variables. Thus, trying to store the address of grades using the expression &grades results in a compiler error.

An interesting sidelight to the observation that elements of an array can be referenced using pointers is that a pointer reference can always be replaced with a subscript reference. For example, if num_ptr is declared as a pointer variable, the expression *(num_ptr + i) can also be written as num_ptr[i]. This is true even though num_ptr is not created as an array. As before, when the compiler encounters the subscript notation, it replaces it internally with the pointer notation.

Exercises 10.2

1. Replace each of the following references to a subscripted variable with a pointer reference.

   a. prices[5]

   b. grades[2]

   c. yield[10]

   d. dist[9]

   e. mile[0]

   f. temp[20]

   g. celsius[16]

   h. num[50]

   i. time[12]

2. Replace each of the following references using a pointer with a subscript reference.

   a. *(message + 6)

   b. *amount

   c. *(yrs + 10)

   d. *(stocks + 2)

   e. *(rates + 15)

   f. *(codes + 19)

3. a. List the three things that the declaration statement double prices[5]; causes the compiler to do.

   b. If each double-precision number uses 4 bytes of storage, how much storage is set aside for the prices array?

   c. Draw a diagram similar to Figure 10.15 for the prices array.

   d. Determine the byte offset relative to the start of the prices array that corresponds to the offset in the expression *(prices + 3).

4. a. Write a declaration to store the string "This is a sample" into an array named samtest. Include the declaration in a program that displays the values in samtest using a for loop and pointer references to each element in the array.

   b. Modify the program written in Exercise 4a to display only array elements 10 through 15 (these are the letters s, a, m, p, l, and e).

5. Write a declaration to store the following values into an array named rates: 12.9, 18.6, 11.4, 13.7, 9.5, 15.2, 17.6. Include the declaration in a program that displays the values in the array using pointer notation.

10.3 POINTER ARITHMETIC

Pointer variables, like all variables, contain values. The value stored in a pointer is, of course, an address. Thus, by adding and subtracting numbers to pointers we can obtain different addresses. Additionally, the addresses in pointers can be compared using any of the relational operators (==, !=, < ,>, etc.) that are valid for comparing other variables. In performing arithmetic on pointers we must be careful to produce addresses that point to something meaningful. In comparing pointers we must also make comparisons that make sense. Consider the declarations:

```
int nums[100];
int *n_pt;
```

To set the address of nums[0] into n_pt, either of the following two assignment statements can be used:

```
n_pt = &nums[0];
n_pt = nums;
```

The two assignment statements produce the same result because nums is a pointer constant that itself contains the address of the first location in the array. This is, of course, the address of nums[0]. Figure 10.16 illustrates the allocation of memory resulting from the previous declaration and assignment statements, assuming that each integer requires 2 bytes of memory and that the location of the beginning of the nums array is at address 18934.

Once n_pt contains a valid address, values can be added and subtracted from the address to produce new addresses. When adding or subtracting numbers to pointers, the compiler automatically adjusts the number to ensure that the result still "points to" a value of the correct type. For example, the statement n_pt = n_pt + 4; forces the compiler to scale the 4 by the correct number to ensure that the resulting address is the address of an integer. Assuming that each integer requires 2 bytes of storage, as illustrated in Figure 10.16, the compiler

---

FIGURE 10.16   The nums **Array in Memory**

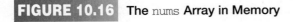
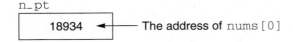
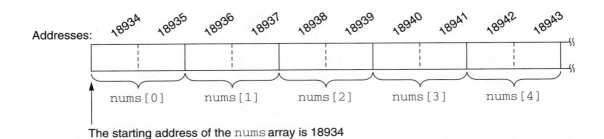

n_pt

| 18934 | ◄─── The address of nums[0]

Addresses: 18934 18935 18936 18937 18938 18939 18940 18941 18942 18943

nums[0]   nums[1]   nums[2]   nums[3]   nums[4]

The starting address of the nums array is 18934

multiplies the 4 by 2 and adds 8 to the address in n_pt. The resulting address is 18942, which is the correct address of nums[4].

This automatic *scaling* by the compiler ensures that the expression n_pt + i, where i is any positive integer, correctly points to the *i*th element beyond the one currently being pointed to by n_pt. Thus, if n_pt initially contains the address of nums[0], n_pt + 4 is the address of nums[4], n_pt + 50 is the address of nums[50], and n_pt + i is the address of nums[i]. Although we have used actual addresses in Figure 10.16 to illustrate the scaling process, the programmer need never know or care about the actual addresses used by the computer. The manipulation of addresses using pointers generally does not require knowledge of the actual address.

Addresses can also be incremented or decremented using both prefix and postfix increment and decrement operators. Adding one to a pointer causes the pointer to point to the next element of the type being pointed to. Decrementing a pointer causes the pointer to point to the previous element. For example, if the pointer variable p is a pointer to an integer, the expression p++ causes the address in the pointer to be incremented to point to the next integer. This is illustrated in Figure 10.17. In reviewing this figure, notice that the increment added to the pointer is correctly scaled to account for the fact that the pointer is used to point to integers. It is, of course, up to the programmer to ensure that the correct type of data is stored in the new address contained in the pointer.

The increment and decrement operators can be applied as both prefix and postfix pointer operators. All of the following combinations using pointers are valid:

```
*pt_num++   /* use the pointer and then increment it */
*++pt_num   /* increment the pointer before using it */
*pt_num--   /* use the pointer and then decrement it */
*--pt_num   /* decrement the pointer before using it */
```

Of the four possible forms, the most commonly used is the form *pt_num++. This is because such an expression allows each element in an array to be accessed as the address is "marched along" from the starting address of the array to the address of the last array element. The use of the increment operator is shown in

---

FIGURE 10.17 Increments Are Scaled When Used with Pointers

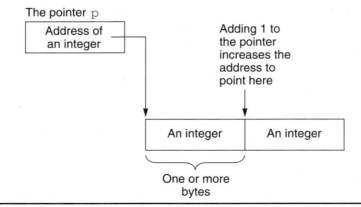

Program 10.7. In this program each element in the nums array is retrieved by successively incrementing the address in n_pt.

PROGRAM 10.7

```c
#include <stdio.h>
#define NUMS 5

void main(void)
{
  int nums[NUMS] = {16, 54, 7, 43, -5};
  int i, total = 0, *n_pt;

  n_pt = nums;    /* store address of nums[0] in n_pt */
  for (i = 0; i < NUMS; i++)
    total = total + *n_pt++;
  printf("The total of the array elements is %d\n", total);
}
```

The output produced by Program 10.7 is:

```
The total of the array elements is 115
```

The expression total = total + *n_pt++ used in Program 10.7 is a standard accumulating expression. Within this expression, the term *n_pt++ first causes the retrieval of the integer pointed to by n_pt. This is done by the *n_pt part of the term. The postfix increment, ++, then adds one to the address in n_pt so that n_pt now contains the address of the next array element. The increment is, of course, scaled so that the actual address in n_pt is the correct address of the next integer element.

Pointers may also be compared. This is particularly useful when dealing with pointers that point to elements in the same array. For example, rather than using a counter in a for loop to access each element in an array correctly, the address in a pointer can be compared to the starting and ending address of the array itself. The expression

$$n\_pt < \&nums[5]$$

is true (nonzero) as long as the address in n_pt is less than the address of nums[5]. Since nums is a pointer constant that contains the address of nums[0], the term &nums[5] can be replaced by the equivalent term nums + 5. Using either of these forms, Program 10.7 can be rewritten as Program 10.8 to continue adding array elements while the address in n_pt is less than or equal to the address of the last array element.

Notice that in Program 10.8 the compact form of the accumulating expression, total += *n_pt++, was used in place of the longer form, total = total + *n_pt++. Also, the expression nums + 5 does not change the address in nums. Since nums is an array name and not a pointer variable, its value cannot be changed. The expression nums + 5 first retrieves the address in nums, adds 5 to this address (appropriately scaled), and uses the result for comparison purposes. Expressions such as *nums++, which attempt to change the address, are invalid. Expressions such as *nums or *(nums + i), which use the address without attempting to alter it, are valid.

PROGRAM 10.8

```c
#include <stdio.h>
#define NUMS 5

void main(void)
{
  int nums[NUMS] = {16, 54, 7, 43, -5};
  int total = 0, *n_pt;
  n_pt = nums;     /* store address of nums[0] in n_pt */
  while (n_pt < nums + NUMS)
    total += *n_pt++;
  printf("The total of the array elements is %d\n", total);
}
```

Pointer Initialization

Like all variables, pointers can be initialized when they are declared. When initializing pointers, however, you must be careful to set an address in the pointer. For example, an initialization such as

```c
int *pt_num = &miles;
```

is only valid if `miles` itself were declared as an integer variable prior to `pt_num`. Here we are creating a pointer to an integer and setting the address in the pointer to the address of an integer variable. Notice that if the variable `miles` is declared subsequently to `pt_num`, as follows,

```c
int *pt_num = &miles;
int miles;
```

an error occurs. This is because the address of `miles` is used before `miles` has even been defined. Since the storage area reserved for `miles` has not been allocated when `pt_num` is declared, the address of `miles` does not yet exist.

Pointers to arrays can be initialized within their declaration statements. For example, if `prices` has been declared an array of floating-point numbers, either of the following two declarations can be used to initialize the pointer named `zing` to the address of the first element in `prices`:

```c
float *zing = &prices[0];
float *zing = prices;
```

The last initialization is correct because `prices` is itself a pointer constant containing an address of the proper type. (The variable name `zing` was selected in this example to reinforce the idea that any variable name can be selected for a pointer.)

Exercises 10.3

1. Replace the `while` statement in Program 10.8 with a `for` statement.

2. a. Write a program that stores the following numbers in the array named `rates`:
   6.25, 6.50, 6.8, 7.2, 7.35, 7.5, 7.65, 7.8, 8.2, 8.4, 8.6, 8.8, 9.0. Display the values in

the array by changing the address in a pointer called `disp_pt`. Use a `for` statement in your program.

    b. Modify the program written in Exercise 2a to use a `while` statement.

3. a. Write a program that stores the string `Hooray for All of Us` into an array named `strng`. Use the declaration `strng[] = "Hooray for All of Us";`, which ensures that the end-of-string escape sequence `\0` is included in the array. Display the characters in the array by changing the address in a pointer called `mess_pt`. Use a `for` statement in your program.

    b. Modify the program written in Exercise 3a to use the `while` statement `while (*mess_pt++ != '\0')`.

    c. Modify the program written in Exercise 3a to start the display with the word `All`.

4. Write a program that stores the following numbers in the array named `miles`: 15, 22, 16, 18, 27, 23, 20. Have your program copy the data stored in `miles` to another array named `dist` and then display the values in the `dist` array.

5. Write a program that stores the following letters in an array named `message`: This is a test. Have your program copy the data stored in `message` to another array named `mess2` and then display the letters in the `mess2` array.

10.4 PASSING AND USING ARRAY ADDRESSES

When an array is passed to a function, its address is the only item actually passed. By this we mean the address of the first location used to store the array, as illustrated in Figure 10.18. Since the first location reserved for an array corresponds to element 0 of the array, the "address of the array" is also the address of element 0.

For a specific example in which an array is passed to a function, let us consider Program 10.9. In this program, the `nums` array is passed to the `find_max` function using conventional array notation.

The output displayed when Program 10.9 is executed is:

```
The maximum value is 27
```

The argument named `vals` in the header line declaration for `find_max` actually receives the address of the array `nums`. As such, `vals` is really a pointer, since pointers are variables (or arguments) used to store addresses. Since the address passed into `find_max` is the address of an integer, another suitable header line for `find_max` is:

FIGURE 10.18 The Address of an Array Is the Address of the First Location Reserved for the Array

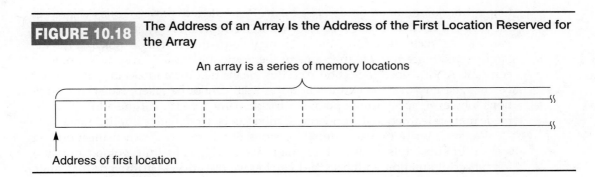

An array is a series of memory locations

Address of first location

PROGRAM 10.9

```c
#include <stdio.h>
#define NUMS 5

void main(void)
{
  int nums[NUMS] = {2, 18, 1, 27, 16};
  int find_max(int [], int);  /* function prototype */

  printf("The maximum value is %d\n", find_max(nums,5));
}

int find_max(int vals[], int num_els)  /* find the maximum value */
{
  int i, max = vals[0];

  for (i = 1; i < num_els; i++)
    if (max < vals[i])
      max = vals[i];
  return(max);
}
```

```c
int find_max(int *vals, int num_els)
/* here vals is declared as a pointer to an integer */
```

The declaration `int *vals;` declares that `vals` is used to store an address of an integer. The address stored is, of course, the location of the beginning of an array. A rewritten version of the `find_max` function follows that uses the new pointer declaration for `vals`, but retains the use of subscripts to refer to individual array elements:

```c
int find_max(int *vals, int num_els)  /* find the maximum value */
{
  int i, max = vals[0];

  for (i = 1; i < num_els; i++)
    if (max < vals[i])
      max = vals[i];
  return(max);
}
```

One further observation needs to be made. Regardless of how `vals` is declared in the function header or how it is used within the function body, it is truly a pointer variable. As such, the address in `vals` may be modified. This is not true for the name `nums`. Since `nums` is the name of the originally created array, it is a pointer constant. As described in Section 10.1, this means that the address in `nums` cannot be changed and that the address of `nums` itself cannot be taken. No such restrictions, however, apply to the pointer variable named `vals`. All the address arithmetic that we learned in the previous section can be legitimately applied to `vals`.

We shall write two additional versions of `find_max`, both using pointers instead of subscripts. In the first version we simply substitute pointer notation for subscript notation. In the second version we use address arithmetic to change the address in the pointer.

As previously stated, a reference to an array element using the subscript notation `array_name[i]` can always be replaced by the pointer notation `*(array_name + i)`. In our first modification to `find_max`, we make use of this correspondence by simply replacing all references to `vals[i]` by the equivalent expression `*(vals + i)`:

```
int find_max(int *vals, int num_els)   /* find the maximum value */
{
  int i, max = *vals;

  for (i = 1; i < num_els; i++)
    if (max < *(vals + i) )
      max = *(vals + i);
  return(max);
}
```

Our second version of `find_max` makes use of the fact that the address stored in `vals` can be changed. After each array element is retrieved using the address in `vals`, the address itself is incremented by one in the altering list of the `for` statement. The expression `*vals++` used initially to set `max` to the value of `vals[0]` also adjusts the address in `vals` to point to the second element in the array. The element obtained from this expression is the array element pointed to by `vals` before `vals` is incremented. The postfix increment, `++`, does not change the address in `vals` until after the address has been used to retrieve the array element.

```
int find_max(int *vals, int num_els)   /* find the maximum value */
{
  int i, max = *vals++;   /* get the first element and increment */

  for (i = 1; i < num_els; i++, vals++)
    if (max < *vals)
      max = *vals;
  return(max);
}
```

Let us review this version of `find_max`. Initially the maximum value is set to "the thing pointed to by `vals`." Since `vals` initially contains the address of the first element in the array passed to `find_max`, the value of this first element is stored in `max`. The address in `vals` is then incremented by one. The one that is added to `vals` is automatically scaled by the number of bytes used to store integers. Thus, after the increment, the address stored in `vals` is the address of the next array element. This is illustrated in Figure 10.19. The value of this next element is compared to the maximum and the address is again incremented, this time from within the altering list of the `for` statement. This process continues until all the array elements have been examined.

The version of `find_max` that you should choose is a matter of personal style and taste. Generally, beginning programmers feel more at ease using subscripts rather than pointers. Also, if the program uses an array as the natural storage structure for the application and data at hand, an array reference using subscripts is more appropriate to clearly indicate the intent of the program. However, as we learn about strings and data structures, the use of pointers becomes an increasingly useful and powerful tool in its own right. In these instances there is no simple or easy equivalence to using subscripts.

FIGURE 10.19 Pointing to Different Elements

Before incrementing: After incrementing:

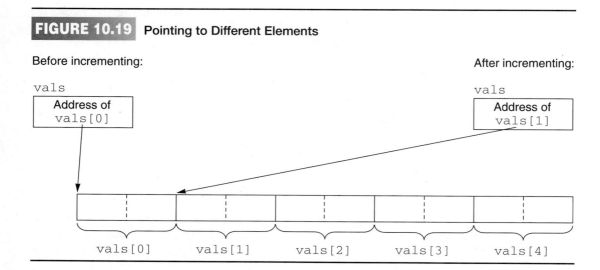

One further "neat trick" can be gleaned from our discussion. Because passing an array to a function really involves passing an address, we can just as well pass any valid address. For example, the function call find_max(&nums[2],3) passes the address of nums[2] to find_max. Within find_max the pointer vals stores the address and the function starts the search for a maximum at the element corresponding to this address. Thus, from find_max's perspective, it has received an address and proceeds appropriately.

Advanced Pointer Notation[4]

Access to multidimensional arrays can also be made using pointer notation, although the notation becomes more and more cryptic as the array dimensions increase. An extremely useful application of this notation occurs with two-dimensional character arrays, one of the topics of the next chapter. Here we consider pointer notation for two-dimensional numeric arrays. For example, consider the declaration

```
int nums[2][3] = { {16,18,20},
                   {25,26,27} };
```

This declaration creates an array of elements and a set of pointer constants named nums, nums[0], and nums[1]. The relationship between these pointer constants and the elements of the nums array is illustrated in Figure 10.20.

The availability of the pointer constants associated with a two-dimensional array allows us to reference array elements in a variety of ways. One way is to consider the two-dimensional array as an array of rows, where each row is itself an array of three elements. Considered in this light, the address of the first element in the first row is provided by nums[0] and the address of the first element in the second row is provided by nums[1]. Thus, the variable pointed to by

---

[4]This topic may be omitted with no loss of subject continuity.

FIGURE 10.20 Storage of the `nums` Array and Associated Pointer Constants

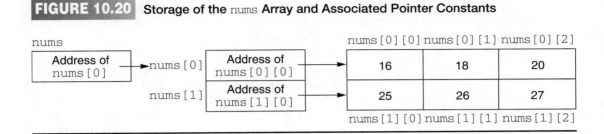

`nums[0]` is `num[0][0]` and the variable pointed to by `nums[1]` is `num[1][0]`. Once the nature of these constants is understood, each element in the array can be accessed by applying an appropriate offset to the appropriate pointer. Thus, the following notations are equivalent:

Pointer Notation	Subscript Notation	Value
`*nums[0]`	`nums[0][0]`	16
`*(nums[0] + 1)`	`nums[0][1]`	18
`*(nums[0] + 2)`	`nums[0][2]`	20
`*nums[1]`	`nums[1][0]`	25
`*(nums[1] + 1)`	`nums[1][1]`	26
`*(nums[1] + 2)`	`nums[1][2]`	27

We can now go even further and replace `nums[0]` and `nums[1]` with their respective pointer notations, using the address of `nums` itself. As illustrated in Figure 10.20, the variable pointed to by `nums` is `nums[0]`. That is, `*nums` is `nums[0]`. Similarly, `*(nums + 1)` is `nums[1]`. Using these relationships leads to the following equivalences:

Pointer Notation	Subscript Notation	Value
`*(*nums)`	`nums[0][0]`	16
`*(*nums + 1)`	`nums[0][1]`	18
`*(*nums + 2)`	`nums[0][2]`	20
`*(*(nums + 1))`	`nums[1][0]`	25
`*(*(nums + 1) + 1)`	`nums[1][1]`	26
`*(*(nums + 1) + 2)`	`nums[1][2]`	27

The same notation applies when a two-dimensional array is passed to a function. For example, assume that the two-dimensional array `nums` is passed to the function `calc` using the call `calc(nums);`. Here, as with all array passes, an address is passed. A suitable function header line for the function `calc` is:

`calc(int pt[2][3])`

As we have already seen, the argument declaration for `pt` can also be

`calc(int pt[][3])`

Using pointer notation, another suitable declaration is

`calc(int (*pt)[3])`

In this last declaration the inner parentheses are required to create a single pointer to objects of three integers. Each object is, of course, equivalent to a single row of the nums array. By suitably offsetting the pointer, each element in the array can be accessed. Notice that without the parentheses the declaration becomes

```
int *pt[3]
```

which creates an array of three pointers, each one pointing to a single integer.

Once the correct declaration for pt is made (any of the three valid declarations can be used), the following notations within the function calc are all equivalent:

Pointer Notation	Subscript Notation	Value
*(*pt)	pt[0][0]	16
*(*pt+1)	pt[0][1]	18
*(*pt+2)	pt[0][2]	20
((pt+1))	pt[1][0]	25
((pt+1)+1)	pt[1][1]	26
((pt+1)+2)	pt[1][2]	27

The last two notations using pointers are encountered in more advanced C programs. The first of these occurs because functions can return any valid C scalar data type, including pointers to any of these data types. If a function returns a pointer, the data type being pointed to must be declared in the function's declaration. For example, the declaration

```
int *calc();
```

declares that calc() returns a pointer to an integer value. This means that an address of an integer variable is returned. Similarly, the declaration

```
float *taxes();
```

declares that taxes() returns a pointer to a floating-point value. This means that an address of a floating-point variable is returned.

In addition to declaring pointers to integers, floating-point numbers, and C's other data types, pointers can also be declared that point to (contain the address of) a function. Pointers to functions are possible because function names, like array names, are themselves pointer constants. For example, the declaration

```
int (*calc)()
```

declares calc to be a pointer to a function that returns an integer. This means that calc will contain the address of a function, and the function whose address is in the variable calc returns an integer value. If, for example, the function sum returns an integer, the assignment calc = sum; is valid.

Exercises 10.4

1. The following declaration was used to create the prices array:

   ```
   double prices[500];
   ```

   Write three different header lines for a function named sort_arr that accepts the prices array as an argument named in_array and returns no value.

2. The following declaration was used to create the keys array:

```
char keys[256];
```

Write three different header lines for a function named find_key that accepts the keys array as an argument named select and returns no value.

3. The following declaration was used to create the rates array:

```
float rates[256];
```

Write three different header lines for a function named prime that accepts the rates array as an argument named rates and returns a float.

4. Modify the find_max function to locate the minimum value of the passed array. Write the function using only pointers.

5. In the last version of find_max presented, vals was incremented inside the altering list of the for statement. Instead, suppose that we do the incrementing within the condition expression of the if statement, as follows:

```
int find_max(int *vals, int num_els)   /* incorrect version
{
  int i, max = *vals++;    /* get the first element and increment */

  for (i = 1; i < num_els; ++i)
    if (max < *vals++)
      max = *vals;
  return(max);
}
```

This version produces an incorrect result. Determine why.

6. a. Write a program that has a declaration in main to store the following numbers into an array named rates: 6.5, 7.2, 7.5, 8.3, 8.6, 9.4, 9.6, 9.8, 10.0. There should be a function call to show that accepts rates in an argument named rates and then displays the numbers using the pointer notation *(rates + i).

   b. Modify the show function written in Exercise 6a to alter the address in rates. Always use the expression *rates rather than *(rates + i) to retrieve the correct element.

10.5 COMMON PROGRAMMING ERRORS

In using the material presented in this chapter, be aware of the following possible errors:

1. Attempting to store an address in a variable that has not been declared as a pointer.

2. Using a pointer to reference nonexistent array elements. For example, if nums is an array of 10 integers, the expression *(nums + 15) points six integer locations beyond the last element of the array. Because C does not do any bounds checking on array references, this type of error is not caught by the compiler. This is the same error that occurs when using a subscript to reference an out-of-bounds array element disguised in its pointer notation form.

3. Incorrectly applying the address and indirection operators. For example, if pt is a pointer variable, the expressions

$$pt = \&45$$
$$pt = \&(miles + 10)$$

are both invalid because they attempt to take the address of a value. Notice that the expression pt = &miles + 10, however, is valid. Here, 10 is added to the address of `miles`. Again, it is the programmer's responsibility to ensure that the final address "points to" a valid data element.

4. Addresses cannot be taken of any register variable. Thus, for the declarations

```
register int total;
int *pt_tot;
```

the assignment

```
pt_tot = &total;
```

is invalid. The reason for this is that register variables are stored in a computer's internal registers, and these storage areas do not have standard memory addresses.

5. Addresses of pointer constants also cannot be taken. For example, given the declarations

```
int nums[25];
int *pt;
```

the assignment

```
pt = &nums;
```

is invalid. `nums` is a pointer constant that is itself equivalent to an address. The correct assignment is `pt = nums`.

6. Another common mistake made by beginning programmers is to initialize pointer variables incorrectly. For example, the initialization:

```
int *pt = 5;
```

is invalid. Since `pt` is a pointer to an integer, it must be initialized with a valid address.

7. A more confusing error results from using the same name as both a pointer and a nonpointer variable. For example, assume that `minutes` is declared as an integer variable in `main` and that main passes the address of `minutes` to the function `time` using the function call `time(&minutes);`. Due to the scope of local variables, the same names used in `main` can also be used in `time` without causing the computer any confusion. Thus, a valid function header for `time` could be:

```
time(int *minutes)
```

With these declarations, the value stored in `minutes` within `main` is accessed using the variable's name, while the same value is accessed in time using the notation `*minutes`. This can be very confusing to a programmer. To avoid this, most programmers usually develop their own systems for naming pointer arguments and variables. For example, prefixing pointer names by `pt_` or suffixing them with the characters `_addr` helps to indicate clearly that the arguments or variables are pointers.

8. The final error that occurs is one common to pointer usage in general. The situation always arises when the beginning C programmer becomes confused about whether a variable contains an address or is an address. Pointer variables and pointer arguments contain addresses. Although a pointer constant is synonymous with an address, it is useful to treat pointer constants as pointer variables with two restrictions:

1. The address of a pointer constant cannot be taken.

2. The address "contained in" the pointer constant cannot be altered.

Except for these two restrictions, pointer constants and variables can be used almost interchangeably. Therefore, when an address is required any of the following can be used:

- A pointer variable name
- A pointer argument name
- A pointer constant name
- A nonpointer variable name preceded by the address operator (e.g., `&variable`)
- A nonpointer argument name preceded by the address operator (e.g., `&argument`).

Some of the confusion surrounding pointers is caused by the cavalier use of the word *pointer*. For example, the phrase "a function requires a pointer argument" is more clearly understood when it is realized that the phrase really means "a function requires an address as an argument." Similarly, the phrase "a function returns a pointer" really means "a function returns an address." Since an address is returned, a suitably declared pointer must be available to store the returned address.

If you are ever in doubt as to what is really contained in a variable, or how it should be treated, use the `printf` function to display the contents of the variable, the "thing pointed to," or "the address of the variable." Seeing what is displayed frequently helps sort out what is really in the variable.

10.6 CHAPTER REVIEW

Key Terms

address	offset
address operator	pointer variable
indirection	scaling
indirection operator	

Summary

1. Every variable has a data type, an address, and a value. In C the address of a variable can be obtained by using the address operator, 8.

2. A pointer is a variable that is used to store the address of another variable. Pointers, like all C variables, must be declared. The indirection operator, *, is used both to declare a pointer variable and to access the variable whose address is stored in a pointer.

3. An array name is a pointer constant. The value of the pointer constant is the address of the first element in the array. Thus, if `val` is the name of an array, `val` and `&val[0]` can be used interchangeably.

4. Any reference to an array element using subscript notation can always be replaced using pointer notation. That is, the notation `a[i]` can always be

replaced by the notation * (a + i). This is true whether a was initially declared explicitly as an array or as a pointer.

5. Arrays are passed to functions by reference. The called function always receives direct access to the originally declared array elements.

6. When a single-dimensional array is passed to a function, the argument declaration for the function can be either an array declaration or a pointer declaration. Thus, the following argument declarations are equivalent:

```
float a[];
float *a;
```

7. Pointers can be incremented, decremented, and compared. Numbers added to or subtracted from a pointer are automatically scaled. The scale factor used is the number of bytes required to store the data type originally pointed to.

Exercises

1. Repeat Exercise 2 in Section 8.2, but use pointer references to access all array elements.

2. Repeat Exercise 3 in Section 8.2, but use pointer references to access all array elements.

3. Write a C program that asks for two lowercase characters. Pass the two entered characters using pointers to a function named capit. The capit function should capitalize the two letters and return the capitalized values to the calling function through its pointer arguments. The calling function should then display all four letters.

4. Write a program that declares three single-dimensional arrays named miles, gallons, and mpg. Each array should be capable of holding 10 elements. In the miles array store the numbers 240.5, 300.0, 189.6, 310.6, 280.7, 216.9, 199.4, 160.3, 177.4, 192.3. In the gallons array store the numbers 10.3, 15.6, 8.7, 14, 16.3, 15.7, 14.9, 10.7, 8.3, 8.4. Each element of the mpg array should be calculated as the corresponding element of the miles array divided by the equivalent element of the gallons array; for example, mpg[0] = miles[0] / gallons[0]. Use pointers when calculating and displaying the elements of the mpg array.

5. a. Write a program that has a declaration in main to store the string Vacation is near into an array named message. There should be a function call to display that accepts message in an argument named strng and then displays the message using the pointer notation * (strng + i).

   b. Modify the display function written in Exercise 5a to alter the address in message. Also, use the expression *strng rather than * (strng + i) to retrieve the correct element.

6. Write a program that declares three single-dimensional arrays named price, quantity, and amount. Each array should be declared in main and be capable of holding 10 double-precision numbers. The numbers to be stored in price are 10.62, 14.89, 13.21, 16.55, 18.62, 9.47, 6.58, 18.32, 12.15, 3.98. The numbers to be stored in quantity are 4, 8.5, 6, 7.35, 9, 15.3, 3, 5.4, 2.9, 4.8. Have your program pass these three arrays to a function called extend, which calculates the elements in the amount array as the product of the equiv-

alent elements in the price and quantity arrays; for example, amount[1] = price[1] * quantity[1].

    After extend has put values into the amount array, display the values in the array from within main. Write the extend function using pointers.

7. a. Determine the output of the following program:

```c
#include <stdio.h>
void main(void)
{
    int nums[2][3] = { {33,16,29},
                       {54,67,99}};
    arr(nums);
}

void arr(int (*val)[3])
{
    printf("\n %d",*(*val) );
    printf("\n %d",*(*val + 1) );
    printf("\n %d",*(*(val + 1) + 2) );
    printf("\n %d",*(*val) + 1 );
}
```

   b. Given the declaration for val in the arr function, would the reference val[1][2] be valid within the function?

8. Define an array of 10 pointers to floating-point numbers. Then read 10 numbers into the individual locations referenced by the pointers. Now add all of the numbers and store the result in a pointer-referenced location. Display the contents of all of the locations.

CHAPTER

11

Working with Character Strings

Each computer language has its own method of handling strings of characters. Some languages, such as C, have an extremely rich set of functions and methods for dealing with such strings. Other languages, such as FORTRAN, which is predominantly used for numerical calculations, added string handling capabilities with later versions of the compiler.

The way strings are stored, accessed, and manipulated is very language dependent. Because of this, the string handling methods presented in this chapter are, of necessity, dependent on C's construction of these units.

On a fundamental level, strings in C are simply arrays of characters that can be manipulated using standard element-by-element array processing techniques. On a higher level, string library functions are available for treating strings as complete entities. This chapter explores the input, manipulation, and output of strings using both approaches. We will also examine the particularly close connection between string handling functions and pointers.

11.1 STRING FUNDAMENTALS

A string constant, informally referred to as a *string*, is any sequence of characters enclosed in double quotes. For example, `"This is a string"`, `"Hello World!"`, and `"xyz 123 *!#@&"` are all strings.

In C a string is stored as an array of characters terminated by a special end-of-string marker called the *null character*. The null character, represented by the escape sequence \0, is the sentinel marking the end of the string. For

FIGURE 11.1   Storing a String in Memory

G	o	o	d		M	o	r	n	i	n	g	!	\0

example, Figure 11.1 illustrates how the string "Good Morning!" is stored in memory. The string uses 14 storage locations, with the last character in the string being the end-of-string marker \0. The double quotes are not stored as part of the string.

Because a string is stored as an array of characters, the individual characters in the array can be input, manipulated, or output using standard array handling techniques utilizing either subscript or pointer notations. The end-of-string null character is useful for detecting the end of the string when handling strings in this fashion.

String Input and Output

Although the programmer has the choice of using either a library or a user-written function for processing a string already in memory, inputting a string from a keyboard or displaying a string always requires some reliance on standard library functions. Table 11.1 lists the commonly available library functions for both character-by-character and complete string input/output. The gets and puts functions deal with strings as complete units. Both are written using the more elemental functions getchar and putchar. The getchar and putchar functions provide for the input and output of individual characters. Programs that access any of these four functions must contain an include instruction of the form #include <stdio.h>. The stdio.h file contains definitions required by the accessed library functions.

Program 11.1 illustrates the use of gets and puts to input and output a string entered at the user's terminal.

PROGRAM 11.1

```c
#include <stdio.h>
#define MAXCHARS 81

void main(void)
{
  char message[MAXCHARS]; /* enough storage for a complete line */

  printf("Enter a string:\n");
  gets(message);
  printf("The string just entered is:\n");
  puts(message);
}
```

TABLE 11.1 Standard String or Character Library
Functions

Input	Output
gets()	puts()
scanf()	printf()
getchar()	putchar()

The following is a sample run of Program 11.1:

```
Enter a string:
This is a test input of a string of characters.
The string just entered is:
This is a test input of a string of characters.
```

The gets function used in Program 11.1 accepts and stores the characters typed
at the terminal into the character array named message until the ENTER key is
pressed. This generates a newline character, \n, which is interpreted by gets as
the end-of-character entry. All the characters encountered by gets, except the
newline character, are stored in the message array. Before returning, the gets
function appends the null character to the stored set of characters, as illustrated
in Figure 11.2(a). The puts function is then used to display the string. As illustrated in Figure 11.2(b), the puts function automatically sends a newline escape
sequence to the display terminal after the string has been printed.

In general, a printf function call can always be used in place of a puts
function call. For example, the statement printf("%s\n",message); is a
direct replacement for the statement puts(message); used in Program 11.1.
The newline escape sequence in the printf function call substitutes for the
automatic newline generated by puts after the string is displayed.

The one-to-one correspondence between the output functions printf and
puts is not duplicated by the input functions scanf and gets. For example,
scanf("%s",message) and gets(message) are not equivalent. The scanf

---

FIGURE 11.2 Inputting and Outputting a String Using the gets and puts Functions

(a)

gets( ) substitutes \0 for the entered \n

(b)

puts( ) substitutes \n when \0 is encountered

function reads a set of characters up to either a blank space or a newline character, whereas `gets` stops accepting characters only when a newline is detected. Trying to enter the characters `This is a string` using the statement `scanf("%s",message);` results in the word `This` being assigned to the `message` array. Entering the complete line using a scanf function call would require a statement such as:

```
scanf("%s %s %s %s", message1, message2, message3, message4);
```

Here, the word `This` would be assigned to the string `message1`, the word `is` is assigned to the string `message2`, and so on. Because a blank is used as a delimiter by `scanf`, this function is not that useful for entering string data.

Note that if the `scanf` function is used for inputting string data, the `&` is not used before the array name. Since an array name is a pointer constant equivalent to the address of the first storage location reserved for the array, `message` is the same as `&message[0]`. Thus, the function call `scanf("%s",&message[0])` can be replaced by `scanf("%s",message)`.

String Processing

Strings can be manipulated using either standard library functions or standard array processing techniques. The library functions typically available for use are presented in the next section. For now we will concentrate on processing a string in a character-by-character fashion. This will allow us to understand how the standard library functions are constructed and to create our own library functions. For a specific example, consider the function `strcopy`, which copies the contents of `string2` to `string1`:

```
void strcopy(char string1[], char string2[]) /* copy string2 to string1 */
{
  int i = 0;                        /* i will be used as a subscript */

  while ( string2[i] != '\0')   /* check for the end-of-string   */
  {
    string1[i] = string2[i];    /* copy the element to string1 */
    i++;
  }
  string1[i] = '\0';            /* terminate the first string */
  return;
}
```

Although this string copy function can be shortened considerably and written more compactly, the function illustrates the main features of string manipulation. The two strings are passed to `strcopy` as arrays. Each element of `string2` is then assigned to the equivalent element of `string1` until the end-of-string marker is encountered. The detection of the null character forces the termination of the `while` loop that controls the copying of elements. Since the null character is not copied from `string2` to `string1`, the last statement in `strcopy` appends an end-of-string character to `string1`. Prior to calling `strcopy`, the programmer must ensure that sufficient space has been allocated for the `string1` array to be able to store the elements of the `string2` array. Program 11.2 includes the `strcopy` function in a complete program.

PROGRAM 11.2

```c
#include <stdio.h>
#define MAXCHARS 81

void main(void)
{
  char message[MAXCHARS];    /* enough storage for a complete line   */
  char new_mess[MAXCHARS];   /* enough storage for a copy of message */
  int i;
  void strcopy(char [], char []); /* function prototype */

  printf("Enter a sentence: ");
  gets(message);
  strcopy(new_mess,message);    /* pass two array addresses */
  puts(new_mess);
}
void strcopy(char string1[], char string2[]) /* copy string2 to string1 */
{
  int i = 0;                      /* i will be used as a subscript */

  while (string2[i] != '\0')   /* check for the end-of-string   */
  {
    string1[i] = string2[i];   /* copy the element to string1 */
    i++;
  }
  string1[i] = '\0';              /* terminate the first string */
  return;
}
```

The following is a sample run of Program 11.2:

```
Enter a sentence: How much wood could a woodchuck chuck.
How much wood could a woodchuck chuck.
```

Character-by-Character Input

Just as strings can be processed using character-by-character techniques, they can be entered and displayed in this manner. For example, consider Program 11.3, which uses the character-input function `getchar` to construct a string one character at a time. The bold portion of Program 11.3 essentially replaces the `gets` function previously used in Program 11.1.

The following is a sample run of Program 11.3:

```
Enter a sentence:
This is a test input of a string of characters.
The sentence just entered is:
This is a test input of a string of characters.
```

The while statement in Program 11.3 causes characters to be read providing the number of characters entered is less than 80 and the character returned by `getchar` is not the newline character. The parentheses around the expression c = getchar are necessary to assign the character returned by `getchar` to the

PROGRAM 11.3

```
#include <stdio.h>
#define MAXCHARS 81

void main(void)
{
  char message[MAXCHARS], c;    /* enough storage for a complete line */
  int i;

  printf("Enter a sentence:\n");
  i = 0;
  while(i < (MAXCHARS - 1) && (c = getchar()) != '\n')
  {
    message[i] = c;        /* store the character entered */
    i++;
  }
  message[i] = '\0';       /* terminate the string */
  printf("The sentence just entered is:\n");
  puts(message);
}
```

variable c prior to comparing it to the newline escape sequence. Otherwise, the comparison operator, !=, which takes precedence over the assignment operator, causes the entire expression to be equivalent to:

$$c = (getchar() != '\n')$$

This has the effect of first comparing the character returned by getchar to '\n'. The value of the relational expression getchar() != '\n' is either 0 or 1, depending on whether or not getchar received the newline character. The value assigned to c then would also be either 0 or 1, as determined by the comparison.

Program 11.3 also illustrates a very useful technique for developing functions. The bold statements constitute a self-contained unit for entering a complete line of characters from a terminal. As such, these statements can be removed from main and placed together as a new function. Program 11.4 illustrates the placement of these statements in a new function called getline.

We can go further with getline and write it more compactly by having the character returned by getchar assigned directly to the strng array. This eliminates the need for the local variable c and results in the following version:

```
void getline(char strng[])
{
  int i = 0;

  while( i < (MAXCHARS - 1) && (strng[i++] = getchar()) != '/n')
    ;
  strng[i] = '\0';        /* terminate the string */
  return;
}
```

PROGRAM 11.4

```c
#include <stdio.h>
#define MAXCHARS 81

void main(void)
{
  char message[MAXCHARS];   /* enough storage for a complete line */
  int i;
  void getline(char []);  /* function prototype */

  printf("Enter a string:\n");
  getline(message);
  printf("The string just entered is:\n");
  puts(message);
}

void getline(char strng[])
{
  int i = 0;
  char c;

  while(i < (MAXCHARS - 1) && (c = getchar()) != '\n')
  {
    strng[i] = c;       /* store the character entered */
    i++;
  }
  strng[i] = '\0';      /* terminate the string */
  return;
}
```

Notice that in addition to assigning the returned character from `getchar` directly to the `strng` array, the assignment statement

$$strng[i++] = getchar()$$

additionally increments the subscript i using the postfix operator, ++. The null statement, ;, then fulfills the requirement that a `while` loop contain at least one statement. Both versions of `getline` are suitable replacements for `gets`, and show the interchangeability between user-written and library functions.

C's enormous flexibility is shown by this ability to replace a library function with a user-written version and its ability to have functions written in various ways. Neither version of `getline` is "more correct" from a programming standpoint. Each version presented (and more versions can be created) has its advantages and disadvantages. While the second version is more compact, the first version is clearer to beginning programmers. In creating your own C programs, select a style that is comfortable and remain with it until your growing programming expertise dictates modifications to your style.

Exercises 11.1

1. The following function can be used to select and display all vowels contained within a user-input string:

```
void vowels(char strng[])
{
  int i = 0;
  char c;

  while ((c = strng[i++]) != '\0')
    switch(c)
    {
      case 'a':
      case 'e':
      case 'i':
      case 'o':
      case 'u':
        putchar(c);
    } /* end of switch */
    putchar('\n');
}
```

   Notice that the switch statement in vowels uses the fact that selected cases "drop through" in the absence of break statements. Thus, all selected cases result in a putchar function call.

   a. Include vowels in a working program that accepts a user-input string and then displays all vowels in the string. In response to the input How much is the little worth worth?, your program should display ouieieoo.

   b. Modify vowels to count and display the total number of vowels contained in the string passed to it.

2. Modify the vowels function given in Exercise 1 to count and display the individual numbers of each vowel contained in the string.

3. a. Write a C function to count the total number of characters, including blanks, contained in a string. Do not include the end-of-string marker in the count.

   b. Include the function written for Exercise 3a in a complete working program.

4. Write a program that accepts a string of characters from a terminal and displays the hexadecimal equivalent of each character.

5. Write a C program that accepts a string of characters from a terminal and displays the string one word per line.

6. Write a function that reverses the characters in a string. (*Hint:* This can be considered as a string copy starting from the back end of the first string.)

7. Write a function called del_char that can be used to delete characters from a string. The function should take three arguments: the string name, the number of characters to delete, and the starting position in the string where characters should be deleted. For example, the function call del_char(strng,13,5), when applied to the string all enthusiastic people, should result in the string all people.

8. Write a function named add_char to insert one string of characters into another string. The function should take three arguments: the string to be inserted, the original string, and the position in the original string where the insertion should begin. For example, the call add_char(" for all",message,6) should insert the characters for all in message starting at message[5].

9. a. Write a C function named to_upper that converts lowercase letters into uppercase letters. The expression c = 'a' + 'A' can be used to make the conversion for any lowercase character stored in c.

b. Add a data input check to the function written in Exercise 9a to verify that a valid lowercase letter is passed to the function. A character is lowercase if it is greater than or equal to a and less than or equal to z. If the character is not a valid lowercase letter, have the function `to_upper` return the passed character unaltered.

c. Write a C program that accepts a string from a terminal and converts all lowercase letters in the string to uppercase letters.

10. Write a C program that accepts a string from a terminal and converts all uppercase letters in the string to lowercase letters.

11. Write a C program that counts the number of words in a string. A word is encountered whenever a transition from a blank space to a nonblank character is encountered. Assume the string contains only words separated by blank spaces.

11.2 FOCUS ON PROBLEM SOLVING

In this section we will focus on constructing two string processing functions. The first function will be used to count the number of characters in a string. The purpose of this problem is to reinforce our concept of a C string and how characters can be accessed one at a time. The second function will be used to count words. Although this seems a simple problem at first glance it is more typical in that it brings up a set of side issues that must be addressed before a final algorithm can be selected. Chief among these issues is coming up with a suitable criteria for defining what constitutes a word. This is necessary so that the function can correctly identify and count a word when it encounters one.

Problem 1: Character Counting

In this problem we want to pass a string to a function and have the function return the number of characters in the string. For our current purposes any character in the string, whether it is a blank, printable, or nonprintable character, is to be counted. The end-of-string null is not to be included in the final count.

Analyze the Problem for Input/Output Requirements This problem is rather straightforward in its I/O requirements: The input to the function is a string and the output returned by the function is the number of characters in the string. Since a string in C is simply an array of characters, we can pass the string to our function simply by passing the character array. Because the function is to return an integer value, the number of characters in the string, it will be defined as returning an `int`.

Develop a Solution Once the function receives the string it must start at the beginning of the string and keep count of each character it encounters as it "marches along" to the end of the string. Since each C string is terminated by a \0 character, we can use this as a sentinel to tell us when the count should stop. As illustrated in Figure 11.3, we examine each character by indexing through the array until the sentinel is reached.

FIGURE 11.3 Counting Characters in a String

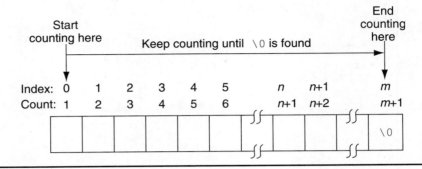

The pseudocode describing our character counting algorithm is:

Accept the string as an array argument.
Initialize a count to 0.
For all the characters in the array
  increment the count.
EndFor
Return the count.

Code the Solution The C code corresponding to our pseudocode solution is:

```
int countchar(char list[])
{
  int i, count = 0;

  for(i = 0; list[i] != '\0'; i++)
    count++;

  return(count);
}
```

Notice that we have used a `for` loop within `countchar`. We could just as easily replace this with a `while loop`.

Test and Debug the Function To test the function, we create a main driver function whose sole purpose is to exercise `countchar`. Program 11.5 includes both the `main` driver and `countchar`.

A sample run using Program 11.5 follows:

```
Type in any number of characters: This is a test of character counts
The number of characters just entered is 34
```

Problem 2: Word Counting

This problem is more complicated than the previous problem, because we must first determine a criteria for identifying a word. At first glance, since each word is followed by a blank space, we might be tempted to simply count spaces. For example, consider the situation pictured in Figure 11.4. The problem with this

PROGRAM 11.5

```c
#include <stdio.h>
#define MAXNUM 1000

void main(void)
{
  char message[MAXNUM];
  int numchar;
  int countchar(char []);   /* function prototype */

  printf("\nType in any number of characters: ");

  gets(message);
  numchar = countchar(message);
  printf("The number of characters just entered is %d\n", numchar);
}

int countchar(char list[])
{
  int i, count = 0;

  for(i = 0; list[i] != '\0'; i++)
    count++;

  return(count);
}
```

approach is that the last word will not have a trailing blank. Even more trouble-some are the cases where more than one blank is used between words and leading blanks are used before the first word. We will have to keep these situations in mind when we develop a solution for counting words.

Analyze the Problem for Input/Output Requirements   From an I/O stand-point this problem is straightforward: The input to the function is a string and the output returned by the function is the number of words in the string. Since a string in C is simply an array of characters, we can pass the string to our function simply by passing the character array. Because the function is to return an integer value, the number of words in the string, it will be defined as returning an int .

Develop a Solution   As we have seen in Figure 11.4, we must come up with a criteria for determining when to increment our word counter; that is, we must

FIGURE 11.4 A Sample Line of Words

| t | h | i | s | | i | s | | t | h | e | | t | y | p | i | c | a | l | | c | a | s | e |

algorithmically define what constitutes a word. Counting spaces will not work without a modification that accounts for extra blanks. An alternative is to increment a counter only when the first character of a word is detected. This approach has the advantages of a positive test for a word and is the approach we will take.

Once this character is found, we can set a flag indicating that we are in a word. This flag can stay on until we come out of a word, which is signified by detecting a blank space. At this point we set the flag to not-in-a-word. The not-in-a-word condition will remain true until a nonblank character is again detected. A pseudocode description of this algorithm is:

Set an inaword flag to NO.
Set the word count to 0.
For all the characters in the array
  If the current character is a blank
    Set inaword to NO
  Else If inaword equals NO
    Set inaword to YES
    Increment the word count.
  EndIf
EndFor
Return the count.

The key to this algorithm is the `if-else` condition. If the current character is a blank, the inaword flag is set to NO, *regardless* of what it was on the previous character. The `else` condition is only executed if the current character is not a blank and checks if we were not in a word. In this case (current character not a blank and we are not in a word) we must be making the transition from a blank to a nonblank character. Since this is the criterion for determining that we have encountered a new word, the word count is incremented and the inaword flag is set to YES.

Code the Solution   The C code corresponding to our solution is:

```
int countword(char list[])
#define YES 1
#define NO 0
{
  int i, inaword, count = 0;

  inaword = NO;
  for(i = 0; list[i] != '\0'; i++)
  {
    if (list[i] == ' ')
      inaword = NO;
    else if (inaword == NO)
    {
      inaword = YES;
      count++;
    }
  }
  return(count);
}
```

Test and Debug the Function   To test the function we create a `main` driver function whose sole purpose is to exercise `countword`. Program 11.6 includes both the `main` driver and `countword`.

PROGRAM 11.6

```c
#include <stdio.h>
#define MAXNUM 1000

void main(void)
{
  char message[MAXNUM];
  int numword;
  int countword(char []);   /* function prototype */

  printf("\nType in any number of words: ");

  gets(message);
  numword = countword(message);
  printf("The number of words just entered is %d\n", numword);
}

int countword(char list[])
#define YES 1
#define NO 0
{
  int i, inaword, count = 0;

  inaword = NO;
  for(i = 0; list[i] != '\0'; i++)
  {
    if (list[i] == ' ')
      inaword = NO;
    else if (inaword == NO)
    {
      inaword = YES;
      count++;
    }
  }
  return(count);
}
```

A sample run using Program 11.6 follows:

```
Type in any number of words: This is a test line with a bunch of words
The number of words just entered is 10
```

Further tests that should be performed using Program 11.6 are as follows:

- Enter words with multiple spaces between them.
- Enter words with leading spaces before the first word.

- Enter words with trailing spaces after the last word.
- Enter a sentence that ends in a period or question mark.

Exercises 11.2

1. Modify the `countchar` function in Program 11.5 to omit blank spaces from the count.

2. Create a function named `cvowels` that counts and returns the number of vowels in a passed string.

3. Modify the `countword` function in Program 11.6 to count both characters and words. (*Hint:* Refer to Section 7.4 on how to return multiple values.)

4. Modify the `countword` function to indirectly return the number of words & characters, excluding spaces and directly return the average number of characters per word.

5. Write a function to count the number of lines entered. (*Hint:* You will not be able to use `gets` to input the lines, since `gets` ends input on receipt of the first newline character.)

6. Write a function to count the number of sentences entered; assume a sentence ends in either a period, question mark, or exclamation point. (*Hint:* You will not be able to use `gets` to input the sentences, since `gets` ends input on receipt of the first newline character.)

7. Modify the function written for Exercise 6 to count the number of words as well as the number of sentences. The function should return the average words per sentence.

8. The fog index is an index used by editors to grade the reading level difficulty of an article, and is described in detail in the following article.[1]

Editors worry about the reading level of their publications. For example, the Wall Street Journal aims for a Fog index of 11, the New York Times about 15, and the New York Daily News 9. The Fog index is a formula generally used to find an approximate reading grade level by measuring the sentence length and the fraction of words with three or more syllables. While reading difficulty is critically dependent on concepts and the presentation, neither factor enters the Fog index.

We looked at one recent issue of NLA News and worked out the Fog index for several articles:

Quantitative methods:	10
Museum staff member:	12
Political scientist:	18
Sociologist:	19

In other words, the last sample is read easily by someone reading at grade 19 level (roughly the doctorate).

To find the Fog index, pick a sample of at least 100 words. Omit all proper names, and then:

1. Count the number of sentences. Clauses separated by colons or semi-colons are treated as separate sentences.

(continued on next page)

---

[1] The *NLA NEWS,* Vol. 7, No. 9, May 1991. Permission to reproduce this article was kindly granted by Dr. John Truxal, Codirector of the New Liberal Arts Program of the Alfred P. Sloan Foundation.

For this exercise obtain samples of at least 10 sentences from any four textbooks you are currently using. For each of these samples manually determine the number of words and big words (these are defined in the preceding article) contained in the sample. Then write a C function to accept the sentences, calculate a fog index, and return it. Check the value returned by your function against your hand calculations.

(continued from previous page)

2. Count the number of "Big Words"—words of three or more syllables. Do not include words that reach three syllables because of "es" or "ed" endings, or because they are compounds of simple words, such as everything or seventeen).

3. Substitute into the formula:

$$\text{Fog index} = 0.4 \left(\frac{\text{Number of words}}{\text{Number of sentences}} + 100 \, \frac{\text{Number of big words}}{\text{Number of words}} \right)$$

As an example, we look at the first three paragraphs of this article. After we leave out numbers and proper names, we have the sample shown below. There are 102 words, 6 sentences, and 19 big words (italicized below).

Editors worry about the reading level of their *publications*. For example, the Wall Street Journal aims for a Fog index of 1, the New York Times about 15, and the New York Daily News 9. The Fog index is a *formula generally* used to find an *approximate* reading grade level by measuring the sentence length and the fraction of words with three or more *syllables*. While reading *difficulty* is *critically dependent* on concepts and the *presentation*, neither factor enters the Fog index.

We looked at one recent issue of NLA News and worked out the Fog index for *several articles:*

Quantitative methods: 10
Museum staff member: 12
Political scientist: 18
Sociologist: 19

In other words, the last sample is read *easily* by someone reading at grade level (roughly the *doctorate*).

For this case the formula gives

$$0.4 * (102/6 + 100 * 19/102) = 14$$

The reading level is grade 14 (college sophomore).

In applying the Fog index to an "I Can Read It All By Myself" book, we find an index of 2—second grade reading level.

11.3 POINTERS AND LIBRARY FUNCTIONS

Pointers are exceptionally useful in constructing string handling functions. When pointer notation is used in place of subscripts to access individual characters in a string, the resulting statements are both more compact and more efficient. In this section we describe the equivalence between subscripts and pointers when accessing individual characters in a string.

A BIT OF BACKGROUND

Anagrams and Palindromes

Some of the most challenging and fascinating word games are played with anagrams and palindromes.

An *anagram* is a rearrangement of the letters in a word or phrase that makes another word or phrase. Although the letters of the word *door* can be rearranged to spell *orod* and *doro,* it is more exciting to discover the words *odor* and *rood.* A word, phrase, or sentence that reads the same forward and backward, such as *top spot* is a *palindrome.*

The origins of most known anagrams and palindromes are lost to anonymity. Here are some collected by Richard Manchester in *The Mammoth Book of Fun and Games* (Hart Publishing Co. Inc., New York City, 1977; pages 229–231);

Apt Anagrams

- The Mona Lisa ➡ No hat, a smile
- The United States of America ➡ Attaineth its cause: freedom!

Interesting Palindromes

- Live not on evil!
- 'Tis Ivan on a visit.
- Yreka Bakery (This is a real place in Yreka, California.)
- Able was I ere I saw Elba. (Might Napoleon have coined this one?)
- Madam, I'm Adam.
- A man, a plan, a canal: Panama!

Computers can be programmed to detect palindromes and find anagrams, but the human brain may be more efficient for doing this.

Consider the `strcopy` function introduced in Section 11.1 This function was used to copy the characters of one string to a second string. For convenience, this function is repeated below:

```
void strcopy(char string1[], char string2[]) /* copy string2 to string1 */
{
  int i = 0;

  while (string2[i] != '\0')    /* check for the end-of-string */
  {
    string1[i] = string2[i];    /* copy the element to string1 */
    i++;
  }
  string1[i] = '\0';            /* terminate the first string */
  return;
}
```

The function `strcopy` is used to copy the characters from one array to another array, one character at a time. As currently written, the subscript `i` in the function is used successively to reference each character in the array named `string2` by "marching along" the string one character at a time. Before we write a pointer version of `strcopy`, we will make two modifications to the function to make it more efficient.

The `while` statement in `strcopy` tests each character to ensure that the end of the string has not been reached. As with all relational expressions, the tested expression, `string2[i] != '\0'`, is either true or false. Using the string `this is a string` illustrated in Figure 11.5 as an example, as long as `string2[i]` does not

FIGURE 11.5   The `while` Test Becomes False at the End of the String

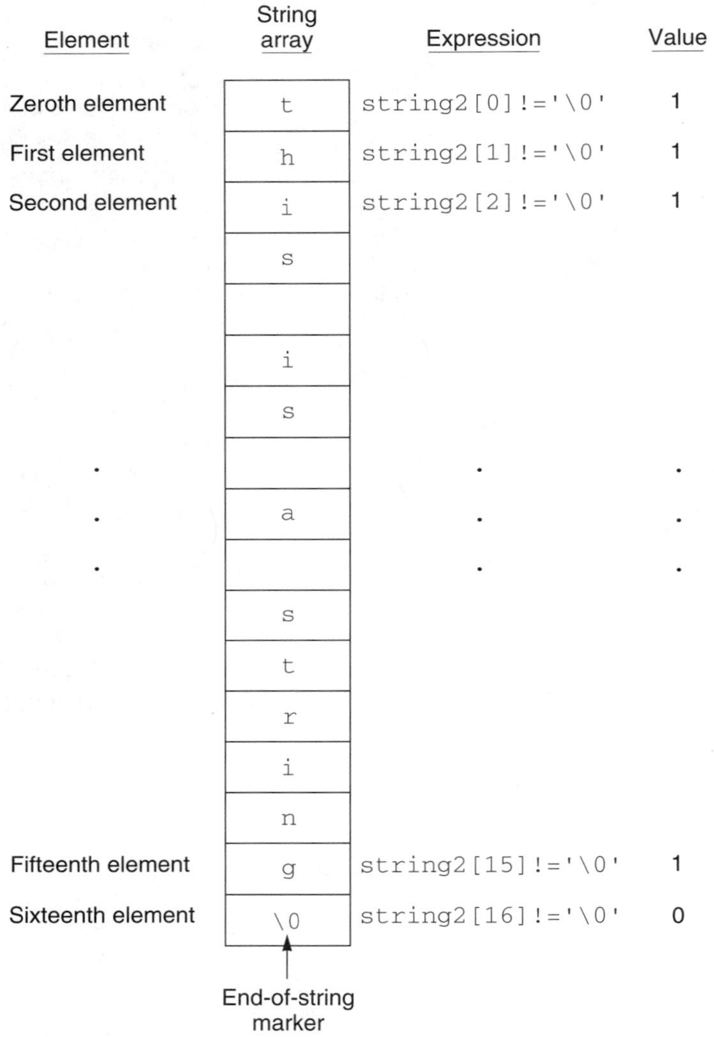

Element	String array	Expression	Value
Zeroth element	t	`string2[0]!='\0'`	1
First element	h	`string2[1]!='\0'`	1
Second element	i	`string2[2]!='\0'`	1
	s		
	i		
	s		
	a		
	s		
	t		
	r		
	i		
	n		
Fifteenth element	g	`string2[15]!='\0'`	1
Sixteenth element	\0	`string2[16]!='\0'`	0

End-of-string
marker

reference the end-of-string character, the value of the expression is nonzero and is considered to be true. The expression is only false when the value of the expression is zero. This occurs when the last element in the string is accessed.

Recall that C defines false as zero and true as anything else. Thus, the expression `string2[i] != '\0'` becomes zero, or false, when the end of the string is reached. It is nonzero, or true, everywhere else. Since the null character has an internal value of zero by itself, the comparison to `'\0'` is not necessary. When `string2[i]` references the end-of-string character, the value of `string2[i]` is zero. When `string2[i]` references any other character, the value of `string[i]` is the value of the code used to store the character and is nonzero. Figure 11.6 lists the ASCII codes for the string `this is a string`. As seen in the figure, each element has a nonzero value except for the null character.

FIGURE 11.6   The ASCII Codes Used to Store `this is a string`

String array	Stored codes	Expression	Value
t	116	string2[0]	116
h	104	string2[1]	104
i	105	string2[2]	105
s	115		
	32		
i	105		
s	115		
	32	.	.
a	97	.	.
	32	.	.
s	115		
t	116		
r	114		
i	105		
n	110		
g	103	string2[15]	103
\0	0	string2[16]	0

Since the expression `string2[i]` is only zero at the end of a string and nonzero for every other character, the expression `while (string2[i] != '0')` can be replaced by the simpler expression `while (strng2[i])`. Although this may appear confusing at first, the revised test expression is certainly more compact than the longer version. Since end-of-string tests are frequently written by advanced C programmers in this shorter form, you should be familiar with this expression. Including this expression in `strcopy` results in the following version:

```
void strcopy(char string1[], char string2[]) /* copy string2 to string1 */
{
  int i = 0;

  while (string2[i])
  {
    string1[i] = string2[i];    /* copy the element to string1 */
    i++;
```

```
    }
    string1[i] = '\0';            /* terminate the first string */
    return;
}
```

The second modification that can be made to this string copy function is to include the assignment inside the test portion of the `while` statement. Our new version of the string copy function is:

```
void strcopy(char string1[], char string2[]) /* copy string2 to string1 */
{
    int i = 0;

    while (string1[i] = string2[i])
        i++;
    return;
}
```

Notice that including the assignment statement within the test part of the `while` statement eliminates the necessity of separately terminating the second string with the null character. The assignment within the parentheses ensures that the null character is copied from the first string to the second string. The value of the assignment expression only becomes zero after the null character is assigned to `string1`, at which point the `while` loop is terminated.

The conversion of `strcopy` from subscript notation to pointer notation is now straightforward. Although each subscript version of `strcopy` can be rewritten using pointer notation, the following is the equivalent of our last subscript version:

```
void strcopy(char *string1, char *string2)    /* copy string2 to string1 */
{
    while (*string1 = *string2)
    {
        string2++;
        string1++;
    }
    return;
}
```

In both subscript and pointer versions of strcopy, the function receives the name of the array being passed. Recall that passing an array name to a function actually passes the address of the first location of the array. In our pointer version of `strcopy` the two passed addresses are stored in the pointer arguments `string1` and `string2`, respectively.

The declarations `char *string1;` and `char *string2;` used in the pointer version of strcopy indicate that `string1` and `string2` are both pointers containing the address of a character, and stress the treatment of the passed addresses as pointer values rather than array names. These declarations are equivalent to the declarations `char string1[]` and `char string2[]`, respectively.

Internal to `strcopy`, the pointer expression `*string2`, which refers to "the element whose address is in `string2`," replaces the equivalent subscript expression `string2[i]`. Similarly, the pointer expression `*string1` replaces the equivalent subscript expression `string1[i]`. The expression `*string1 = *string2` causes the element pointed to by `string2` to be assigned to the element pointed to by `string1`. Since the starting addresses of both strings are passed to `strcopy` and stored in `string1` and `string2`, respectively, the expression `*string1` initially refers to `string1[0]` and the expression `*string2` initially refers to `string2[0]`.

Consecutively incrementing both pointers in `strcopy` with the expressions `string1++` and `string2++` simply causes each pointer to "point to" the next consecutive character in the respective string. As with the subscript version, the pointer version of `strcopy` steps along, copying element by element, until the end of the string is copied.

One final change to the string copy function can be made by including the pointer increments as postfix operators within the test part of the `while` statement. The final form of the string copy function is:

```
void strcopy(char *string1, char *string2)    /* copy string2 to string1 */
{
  while (*string1++ = *string2++)
    ;
  return;
}
```

There is no ambiguity in the expression `*string1++ = *string2++` even though the indirection operator, `*`, and the increment operator, `++`, have the same precedence. Here the character pointed to is accessed before the pointer is incremented. Only after completion of the assignment `*string1 = *string2` are the pointers incremented to correctly point to the next characters in the respective strings.

Most C compilers include a string copy function in their standard library. This library function is typically written exactly like our pointer version of `strcopy`.

Library Functions

Extensive collections of string handling functions and routines are included with most C compilers. The most commonly used of these are listed in Table 11.2.

Library functions and routines are called in the same manner in which all C functions are called. This means that if a library function returns a value the function must be declared within your program before it is called. For example, if a library function named `strngfoo()` returns a pointer to a character, the calling function must be alerted that an address is being returned. Thus, the statement `char *strngfoo();`, which declares that `strngfoo()` returns the address of a character (pointer to `char`), or an include statement for a header file containing the declaration must be used.

Before attempting to use any standard library functions, check that they are included in the C compiler available on your computer system. Be careful to check the type of arguments expected by the function and the data type of any returned value. The header file for the first five functions is `string.h` and the header file for the last four functions is `ctype.h`.

TABLE 11.2 String and Character Library Routines

Name	Description
strcat(string1,string2)	Concatenates string2 to string1.
strchr(string,character)	Locates the position of the first occurrence of the character within the string. Returns the address of the character.
strcmp(string1,string2)	Compares string2 to string1.
	Returns a negative value if string 1 < string 2, a 0 if string1 == string2, and a positive value if string1 > string2.
strcpy(string1,string2)	Copies string2 to string1.
strlen(string)	Returns the length of the string.
isalpha(character)	Returns a nonzero number if the character is a letter; otherwise it returns a zero.
isupper(character)	Returns a nonzero number if the character is uppercase; otherwise it returns a zero.
islower(character)	Returns a nonzero number if the character is lowercase; otherwise it returns a zero.
isdigit(character)	Returns a nonzero number if the character is a digit (0 through 9); otherwise it returns a zero.
toupper(character)	Returns the uppercase equivalent if the character is lowercase; otherwise it returns the character unchanged.
tolower(character)	Returns the lowercase equivalent if the character is uppercase; otherwise it returns the character unchanged.

Exercises 11.3

1. Determine the value of *text, *(text + 3), and *(text + 10), assuming that text is an array of characters and the following has been stored in the array:

   a. now is the time

   b. rocky racoon welcomes you

   c. Happy Holidays

   d. The good ship

2. The following function, convert, "marches along" the string passed to it and sends each character in the string one at a time to the to_upper function until the null character is encountered.

```
char convert(char strng[])    /* convert a string to uppercase letters */
{
  int i = 0;

  while (strng[i] != '\0')
  {
    strng[i] = to_upper(strng[i]);
    i++;
  }
  return;
}
char to_upper(char letter)   /* convert a character to uppercase */
{
  if( letter >= 'a' && letter <= 'z')
    return (letter - 'a' + 'A');
  else
    return (letter);
}
```

The `to_upper` function takes each character passed to it and first examines it to determine if the character is a lowercase letter (a lowercase letter is any character between a and z, inclusive). Assuming that characters are stored using the standard ASCII character codes, the expression `letter = 'a' + 'A'` converts a lowercase letter to its uppercase equivalent.

a. Rewrite the convert function using pointers.

b. Include the `convert` and `to_upper` functions in a working program. The program should prompt the user for a string and echo the string back to the user in uppercase letters. Use `gets` and `puts` for string input and display.

3. Using pointers, repeat Exercise 1 from Section 11.1.

4. Using pointers, repeat Exercise 2 from Section 11.1.

5. Using pointers, repeat Exercise 3 from Section 11.1.

6. Write a function named `remove` that deletes all occurrences of a character from a string. The function should take two arguments: the string name and the character to be removed. For example, if message contains the string `Happy Holidays`, the function call `remove(message,'H')` should place the string `appy olidays` into `message`.

7. Using pointers, repeat Exercise 6 from Section 11.1.

8. Write a program using the `getchar()`, `toupper()`, and `putchar()` library functions that echo back each letter entered in its uppercase form. The program should terminate when the digit 1 key is pressed.

9. Write a function that uses pointers to add a single character at the end of an existing string. The function should replace the existing \0 character with the new character and append a new \0 at the end of the string.

10. Write a function that uses pointers to delete a single character from the end of a string. This is effectively achieved by moving the \0 character one position closer to the start of the string.

11. Determine the string handling functions that are available with your C compiler. For each available function, list the data types of the arguments expected by the function and the data type of any returned value.

11.4 STRING DEFINITIONS AND POINTER ARRAYS

The definition of a string automatically involves a pointer. For example, the definition `char message1[81];` both reserves storage for 81 characters and automatically creates a pointer constant, `message1`, which contains the address of `message1[0]`. As a pointer constant, the address associated with the pointer cannot be changed—it must always "point to" the beginning of the created array.

Instead of initially creating a string as an array, however, it is also possible to create a string using a pointer. This is similar in concept to declaring a passed array as either an array or a pointer argument internal to the receiving function. For example, the definition `char *message2;` creates a pointer to a character. In this case, `message2` is a true pointer variable.

Once a pointer to a character is defined, assignment statements, such as `message2 = "this is a string";`, can be made. In this assignment, `message2` receives the address of the first location used by the computer to store the string.

The main difference in the definitions of `message1` as an array and `message2` as a pointer is the way the pointer is created. Defining `message1` using the declaration `char message1[81]` explicitly calls for a fixed amount of storage for the array. This causes the compiler to create a pointer constant. Defining `message2` using the declaration `char *message2` explicitly creates a pointer variable first. This pointer is then used to hold the address of a string when the string is actually specified. This difference in definitions has both storage and programming consequences.

From a programming perspective, defining `message2` as a pointer to a character allows string assignments, such as `message2 = "this is a string";`, to be made. Similar assignments are not allowed for strings defined as arrays. Thus, the statement `message1 = "this is a string";` is not valid. Both definitions, however, allow initializations to be made using a string assignment. For example, both of the following initializations are valid:

```
char message1[81] = "this is a string";
char *message2 = "this is a string";
```

From a storage perspective, the allocation of space for `message1` and `message2` is different, as illustrated in Figure 11.7. As shown in the figure, both initializations cause the computer to store the same string internally. In the case of `message1`, a specific set of 81 storage locations is reserved and the first 17 locations are initialized. For `message1`, different strings can be stored, but each string will overwrite the previously stored characters. The same is not true for `message2`.

The definition of `message2` reserves enough storage for one pointer. The initialization then causes the string to be stored and the starting storage address of the string to be loaded into the pointer. If a later assignment is made to `message2`, the initial string remains in memory and new storage locations are allocated to the new string. Program 11.7 uses the `message2` character pointer to successively "point to" two different strings.

FIGURE 11.7 String Storage Allocation

| t | h | i | s | | i | s | | a | | s | t | r | i | n | g | \0 |

↑
`message1 = &message[0]` = address of first array location

a. Storage allocation for a string defined as an array

`message2`

Starting
string address

Somewhere in memory:

| t | h | i | s | | i | s | | a | | s | t | r | i | n | g | \0 |

↑
Address of first character location

b. Storage of a string using a pointer

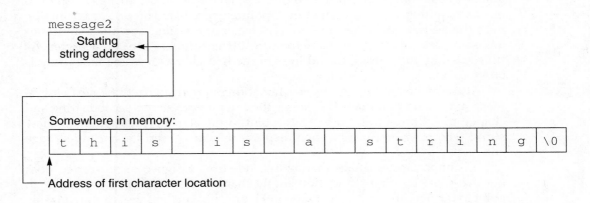

PROGRAM 11.7

```
#include <stdio.h>
void main(void)
{
  char *message2 = "this is a string";

  printf("\nThe string is: %s\n", message2);
  printf(" The first address of this string is %p\n", message2);
  message2 = "A new message";
  printf("The string is now: %s\n", message2);
  printf(" The first address of this string is %p\n", message2);
}
```

A sample output for Program 11.7 is:

```
The string is: this is a string
The first address of this string is 00AA
The string is now: A new message
The first address of this string is 00F8
```

In Program 11.7, the variable message2 is initially created as a pointer variable and loaded with the starting storage address of the first string. The printf function is then used to display this string. When the %s conversion character is encountered by printf, it alerts the function that a string is being referenced. The printf function then expects either a string constant or a pointer containing the address of the first character in the string. This pointer can be either an array name or a pointer variable. The printf function uses the address provided to correctly locate the string, and then continues accessing and displaying characters until it encounters a null character. As illustrated by the output, the address of the first character in the first string is 00AA (hex).

After the first string and its starting address are displayed, the next assignment statement in Program 11.7 causes the computer to store a second string and change the address in message2 to point to the starting location of this new string. The printf function then displays this string and its starting storage address.

It is important to realize that the second string assigned to message2 does not overwrite the first string, but simply changes the address in message2 to point to the new string. As illustrated in Figure 11.8, both strings are stored inside the computer. Any additional string assignment to message2 would result in the additional storage of the new string and a corresponding change in the address stored in message2.

FIGURE 11.8 Storage Allocation for Program 11.7

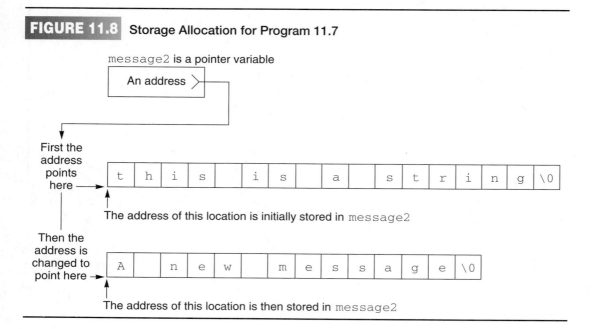

> ## TIPS FROM THE PROS

Pointers, Array Declarations, and lvalues

Although the two declarations

```
char test[5] = "abcd";
```

and

```
char *test = "abcd";
```

both create storage for the characters `'a'`, `'b'`, `'c'`, `'d'`, and `'\0'`, there is a subtle difference between the two declarations and how values can be assigned to `test`.

Except within the declaration, an array declaration, such as `char test[5];` precludes the use of any subsequent assignment expression, such as `test="efgh"`, to assign values to the array. The use of a `strcpy`, such as `strcpy(test, "efgh")`, however, is subsequently valid. The only restriction on the `strcpy` is the size of the array, which in this case is 5 elements. This situation is reversed when a pointer is created.

A pointer declaration, such as `char *test;` precludes the use of a `strcpy` to initialize the memory locations pointed to by the pointer, but it does allow assignments. For example, the following sequence of statements is valid:

```
char *test;
test = "abcd";
test = "here is a longer string";
```

Once a string of characters has been assigned to test, a `strcpy` can be used provided the copy uses no more elements than are currently contained in the string.

The difference in usage is explained by the fact that the compiler automatically allocates sufficient new memory space for any string pointed to by a pointer variable, but does not do so for an array of characters. The array size is fixed by the definition statement.

Formally, any expression that yields a value that can be used on the left side of an assignment expression is said to be an *lvalue*. Thus, a pointer variable can be an lvalue but an array name cannot.

Pointer Arrays

The declaration of an array of character pointers is an extremely useful extension to single string pointer declarations. For example, the declaration:

```
char *seasons[4];
```

creates an array of four elements, where each element is a pointer to a character. As individual pointers, each pointer can be assigned to point to a string using string assignment statements. Thus, the statements:

```
seasons[0] = "Winter";
seasons[1] = "Spring";
seasons[2] = "Summer";
seasons[3] = "Fall";
```

set appropriate addresses into the respective pointers. Figure 11.9 illustrates the addresses loaded into the pointers for these assignments. As shown, the seasons array does not contain the actual strings assigned to the pointers. These strings are stored elsewhere in the computer, in the normal data area allocated to the program. The array of pointers contains only the addresses of the starting location for each string.

FIGURE 11.9   The Addresses Contained in the `seasons[]` Pointers

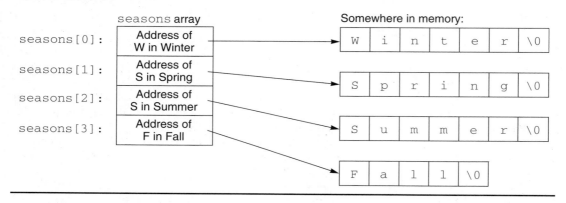

The initializations of the `seasons` array can also be incorporated directly within the definition of the array, as follows:

```
char *seasons[4] = {"Winter",
                    "Spring",
                    "Summer",
                    "Fall"};
```

This declaration both creates an array of pointers and initializes the pointers with appropriate addresses. Once addresses have been assigned to the pointers, each pointer can be used to access its corresponding string. Program 11.8 uses the seasons array to display each season using a `for` loop.

PROGRAM 11.8

```
#include <stdio.h>
#define NUMSEASONS 4

void main(void)
{
  int n;
  char *seasons[] = {"Winter",
                     "Spring",
                     "Summer",
                     "Fall"};
  for( n = 0; n < NUMSEASONS; n++)
    printf("\nThe season is %s.",seasons[n]);
  printf("\n");
}
```

The output obtained for Program 11.8 is:

```
The season is Winter.
The season is Spring.
The season is Summer.
The season is Fall.
```

The advantage of using a list of pointers is that logical groups of data headings can be collected and accessed with one array name. For example, the months in a year can be collectively grouped in one array called `months`, and the days in a week can be collectively grouped in an array called `days`. The grouping of like headings allows the programmer to access and print an appropriate heading by simply specifying the correct position of the heading in the array. Program 11.9 uses the `seasons` array to correctly identify and display the season corresponding to a user-input month.

PROGRAM 11.9

```
#include <stdio.h>
void main(void)
{
  int n;
  char *seasons[] = {"Winter",
                     "Spring",
                     "Summer",
                     "Fall"};

  printf("\nEnter a month (use 1 for Jan., 2 for Feb., etc.): ");
  scanf("%d", &n);
  n = (n % 12) / 3;    /* create the correct subscript */
  printf("The month entered is a %s month.\n", seasons[n]);
}
```

Except for the expression `n = (n % 12) / 3`, Program 11.9 is rather straightforward. The program requests the user to input a month and accepts the number corresponding to the month using a `scanf` function call.

The expression `n = (n % 12) / 3` uses a common program "trick" to scale a set of numbers into a more useful set. Using subscripts, the four elements of the seasons array must be accessed using a subscript from 0 through 3. Thus, the months of the year, which correspond to the numbers 1 through 12, must be adjusted to correspond to the correct season subscript. This is done using the expression `n = (n % 12) / 3`. The expression `n % 12` adjusts the month entered to lie within the range 0 through 11, with 0 corresponding to December, 1 for January, etc. Dividing by 3 then causes the resulting number to range between 0 and 3, corresponding to the possible seasons elements. The result of the division by 3 is assigned to the integer variable `n`. The months 0, 1, and 2, when divided by 3, are set to 0; the months 3, 4, and 5 are set to 1; the months 6, 7, and 8 are set to 2; and the months 9, 10, and 11 are set to 3. This is equivalent to the following assignments:

Months	Season
December, January, February	Winter
March, April, May	Spring
June, July, August	Summer
September, October, November	Fall

The following is sample output for Program 11.9:

```
Enter a month (use 1 for Jan., 2 for Feb., etc.): 12
The month entered is a Winter month.
```

Exercises 11.4

1. Write two declaration statements that can be used in place of the declaration `char text[] = "Hooray!";`.

2. Determine the value of `*text`, `*(text + 3)`, and `*(text + 7)` for each of the following sections of code:

   a. ```
   char *text;
   char message[] = "the check is in the mail";
   text = message;
   ```

   b. ```
   char *text;
   char formal[] = {'t','h','i','s',' ','i','s',' ','a','n','i','n',
                    'v','i','t','a','t','i','o','n','\0'};
   text = &formal[0];
   ```

   c. ```
   char *test;
   char more[] = "Happy Holidays";
   text = &more[4];
   ```

   d. ```
   char *text, *second;
   char blip[] = "The good ship";
   second = blip;
   text = ++second;
   ```

3. Determine the error in the following program:

   ```
   #include <stdio.h>
   void main(void)
   {
     int i = 0;
     char message[] = {'H','e','l','l','o','\0'};

     for( ; i < 5; i++)
         {putchar( *message); message++;}
   }
   ```

4. a. Write a C function that displays the day of the week corresponding to a user-entered input number between 1 and 7. That is, in response to an input of 2, the program displays the name Monday. Use an array of pointers in the function.

   b. Include the function written for Exercise 4a in a complete working program.

5. Modify the function written in Exercise 4a so that the function returns the day of the week, to the calling function.

6. Write a function that will accept 10 lines of user-input text and store the entered lines as 10 individual strings. Use a pointer array in your function.

11.5 FORMATTING STRINGS

Besides the special string handling functions in the standard library provided with your C compiler, both the `printf` and `scanf` functions have string-formatting capabilities. Additionally, two related functions, `sprintf` and `sscanf`, provide further string processing features. In this section we present the additional features that these functions provide when used with strings.

Field width specifiers can be included in a `printf` conversion sequence to control the spacing of integers and decimal numbers. These specifiers can also be used with the `%s` conversion sequence to control the display of a string. For example, the statement

```
printf("|%25s|","Have a Happy Day");
```

displays the message `Have a Happy Day`, right justified, in a field of 25 characters, as follows:

```
|              Have a Happy Day|
```

We have placed a bar (|) at the beginning and end of the string field to delineate clearly the field being printed. Placing a minus sign (−) in front of the field width specifier forces the string to be left justified in the field. For example, the statement

```
printf("|%-25s|","Have a Happy Day");
```

causes the display:

```
|Have a Happy Day              |
```

If the field width specifier is too small for the string, the specifier is ignored and the string is displayed using sufficient space to accommodate the complete string.

The precision specifier used for determining the number of digits displayed to the right of a decimal number can also be used as a string specifier. When used with strings, the precision specifier determines the maximum number of characters that will be displayed. For example, the statement

```
printf("|%25.12s|","Have a Happy Day");
```

causes the first 12 characters in the string to be displayed, right justified, in a field of 25 characters. This produces the display:

```
|              Have a Happy|
```

Similarly, the statement

```
printf("|%-25.12s|","Have a Happy Day");
```

causes 12 characters to be left justified in a field of 25 characters. This produces the display:

```
|Have a Happy              |
```

When a precision specifier is used with no field width specifier, the indicated number of characters is displayed in a field sufficiently large to hold the designated number of characters. Thus, the statement

```
printf("|%.12s|","Have a Happy Day");
```

causes the first 12 characters in the string to be displayed in a field of 12 characters. If the string has less than the number of characters designated by the precision specifier, the display is terminated when the end-of-string marker is encountered.

In-Memory String Conversions

Whereas `printf` displays data to the standard device used by your computer for output and `scanf` scans the standard device used for input, the `sprintf` and `sscanf` functions provide similar capabilities for writing and scanning strings to and from memory variables. For example, the statement

```
sprintf(dis_strn,"%d %d", num1, num2);
```

writes the numerical values of `num1` and `num2` into `dis_strn` rather than displaying the values on the standard output terminal. Here, `dis_strn` is a programmer-selected variable name that must be declared as either an array of characters, sufficiently large to hold the resulting string, or as a pointer to a string.

> ► ► ► **T I P S   F R O M   T H E   P R O S** ◄

Data Type Conversions

Converting from character data to numerical data, in all languages, requires some thought. One neat "trick" that can be applied in C is to use the `sscanf` function to make the conversions for you. For example, assume you need to extract the month, day, and year from the string `07/01/94`, which is stored in a character array named `date`. The simple statement

```
sscanf(date, "%d/%d/%d", &month, &day, &year);
```

extracts the data and converts it into integer form. Such ASCII-to-number conversions really become simple in C! Of course, like other languages, C also provides library functions for simple conversions. The `atoi` function converts a string to a single integer value, and the function `atof` converts a string to a double-precision value. Some compilers provide `itoa` and `ftoa` functions, for converting a single integer and floating-point number, respectively, to their ASCII representations. But if these functions are not available, a call to `sprintf`, as described in the text, can be used for these numeric-to-string conversions.

Typically, the `sprintf` function is used to "assemble" a string from smaller pieces until a complete line of characters is ready to be written, either to the standard output device or to a file (writing data to a file is described in Chapter 13). For example, another string could be concatenated to `dis_strn` using the *strcat* function and the complete string displayed using the *printf* function.

In contrast to `sprintf`, the string scan function `sscanf` may be used to "disassemble" a string into smaller pieces. For example, if the string `"$23.45 10"` were stored in a character array named `data`, the statement

```
sscanf(data,"%c%lf %d",&dol,&price,&units);
```

would scan the string stored in the `data` array and "strip off" three data items. The dollar sign would be stored in the variable named `dol`, the 23.45 would be converted to a double-precision number and stored in the variable named `price`, and the 10 would be converted to an integer value and stored in the variable named `units`. To obtain a useful result, the variables `dol`, `price`, and `units` would have to be declared as the appropriate data types. In this way `sscanf` provides a useful means of converting parts of a string into other data types. Typically, the string being scanned by `sscanf` is used as a working storage area, or buffer, for storing a complete line from either a file or the standard input. Once the string has been filled, `sscanf` disassembles the string into component parts and suitably converts each data item into the designated data type.

Format Strings

When you use any of the four functions `printf`, `scanf`, `sprintf`, or `sscanf`, the control string containing the conversion sequences need not be explicitly contained within the function. For example, the control string `"$%5.2f %d"` contained within the function call

```
printf("$%5.2f %d",num1,num2);
```

can itself be stored as a string and the address of the string used in the call to `printf`. If either of the following declarations for `fmat` is made:

```
char *fmat = "$%5.2f %d";
```

or

```
char fmat[] = "$%5.2f %d";
```

the function call `printf(fmat,num1,num2);` can be made in place of the previous call to `printf`. Here, `fmat` is a pointer that contains the address of the control string used to determine the output display.

The technique of storing and using control strings in this manner is very useful for clearly listing format strings with other variable declarations at the beginning of a function. If a change to a format must be made, it is easy to find the desired control string without the necessity of searching through the complete function to locate the appropriate `printf` or `scanf` function call. Restricting the definition of a control string to one place is also advantageous when the same format control is used in multiple function calls.

Exercises 11.5

1. Determine the display produced by each of the following statements:

   a. `printf("!%10s!","four score and ten");`

   b. `printf("!%15s!","Home!");`

   c. `printf("!%-15s!","Home!");`

   d. `printf("!%15.2s!","Home!");`

   e. `printf("!%-15.2s!",;"Home!");`

2. a. Assuming that the following declaration has been made

   ```
   char *text = "Have a nice day!";
   ```

   determine the display produced by the statements

   ```
   printf("%s", text);

   printf("%c", *text);
   ```

   b. Because both `printf` function calls in Exercise 2a display characters, determine why the indirection operator is required in the second call but not in the first.

3. Write a program that accepts three user-entered integers as one string. Once the string has been accepted, have the program pass the string and the addresses of three floating-point variables to a function called `separate`. The `separate` function should extract the three floating-point values from the passed string and store them using the passed variable addresses.

4. Modify the program written for Exercise 3 to display the input string using the format `"%6.2f %6.2f %6.2f"`.

5. Write a program that accepts a string and two integer numbers from a user. Each of these inputs should be preceded by a prompt and stored using individual variable names. Have your program call a function that assembles the input data into a single string. Display the assembled string using a `puts` call.

11.6 COMMON PROGRAMMING ERRORS

Three errors are frequently made when pointers to strings are used.

The most common error is using the pointer to "point to" a nonexistent data element. When referencing array elements using pointers and moving beyond the last array element. This is, of course, the same error we have already seen using subscripts and results because C does not perform bounds checks on arrays. It is always the programmer's responsibility to ensure that the address in the pointer is the address of a valid data element.

The second common error lies in not providing sufficient space for the end-of-string null character when a string is defined as an array of characters, and not including the \0 character when the array is initialized.

Finally, the last error relates to a misunderstanding of terminology. For example, if message is defined as

```
char *message;
```

the variable message is sometimes referred to as a string. Thus, the terminology "store the characters Hooray for the Hoosiers into the message string" may be encountered. Strictly speaking, calling message a string or a string variable is incorrect. The variable message is a pointer that contains the address of the first character in the string. Nevertheless, referring to a character pointer as a string occurs frequently enough that you should be aware of it.

11.7 CHAPTER REVIEW

Key Terms

getchar	puts
gets	strcat
null character	strcpy
putchar	string

Summary

1. A string is an array of characters that is terminated by the null character.

2. Strings can always be processed using standard array processing techniques. The input and display of a string, however, always require reliance on a standard library function.

3. The gets, scanf, and getchar library functions can be used to input a string. The scanf function tends to be of limited usefulness for string input because it terminates input when a blank is encountered.

4. The puts, printf, and putchar functions can be used to display strings.

5. In place of subscripts, pointer notation and pointer arithmetic are especially useful for manipulating string elements.

6. Many standard library functions exist for processing strings as a complete unit. Internally, these functions manipulate strings in a character-by-character manner, usually using pointers.

7. String storage can be created by declaring an array of characters or a pointer to a character. A pointer to a character can be assigned a string directly. String assignment to a string declared as an array of characters is invalid.

8. Arrays can be initialized using a string assignment of the form

    ```
    char *arr_name[] = "text";
    ```

    This initialization is equivalent to

    ```
    char *arr_name[] = {'t','e','x','t','\0'};
    ```

Exercises

1. Write a function named `trimfrnt()` that deletes all leading blanks from a string. Write the function using pointers.

2. Write a function named `trimrear()` that deletes all trailing blanks from a string. Write the function using pointers.

3. Write a function named `addchar ()` that adds n occurrences of a character to a string. For example the call `addchar(message, 4, '!')` should add !!!! at the end of `message`.

4. Write a function named `extract()` that accepts two strings, s1 and s2, and two integer numbers, n1, and n2, as arguments. The function should extract n2 characters from s2, starting at position n1, and place the extracted characters into s1. For example, if string s1 contains the characters `05/18/95 D169254 Rotech Systems`, the function call `extract(s1, s2, 18, 6)` should place the string `Rotech` in s2. Note that the starting position for counting purposes is in position one. Be sure to close off the returned string with a `'\0'` and make sure that string s1 is defined in the calling function to be large enough to accept the extracted values.

5. Read a sentence with a maximum of 100 characters, one character at a time, from the keyboard into an array of characters. Entry will terminate with a period (.). Search the array to determine how many times a particular character, specified by the user at the keyboard, occurs in the sentence.

6. Given a one-dimensional array of characters, write and test a function that prints the elements in reverse order.

7. Write and test a function that uses an array of characters and returns the position of the first occurrence of a user-specified letter in the array or a −1 if the letter does not occur.

8. A word that reads the same forwards and backwards is a palindrome (see box on page 487). Write a C program that accepts a line of text as input and examines each word entered to determine if it is a palindrome. Each palindrome that is encountered should be displayed following the message `These were the palindromes that were encountered`. If no palindrome was entered, the message `No palindromes were encountered` should be displayed.

9. Write a C program that first initializes a two-dimensional array defined as `list[5][27]` with the following five strings:

    04/12/72 74444 Bill Barnes

    12/28/65 75255 Harriet Smith

    10/17/54 74477 Joan Casey

    02/18/48 74470 Deane Fraser

    06/15/56 75155 Jan Smiley

    Your program should include a function named `printit()` that displays each string in the array. (*Hint:* `&list[i][0]` is the address of the *i*th string in the array.)

10. Write a C program that first initializes a two-dimensional array defined as list[5][51] with the following five strings (do not include headings—they are here to indicate what the data represent:

Shipped Date	Track No.	Part No.	First Name	Last Name	Company
04/12/96	D50625	74444	James	Lehoff	Rotech Sys.
04/12/96	D60752	75255	Janet	Lezar	Rotech Sys.
04/12/96	D40295	74477	Bill	McHenry	Rotech Sys.
04/12/96	D23745	74470	Diane	Kaiser	Rotech Sys.
04/12/96	D50892	75155	Helen	Richardson	NipNap Inc.

The format of each line in the array is identical with fixed length fields defined as follows:

Field Position	Field Name	Starting Col. No.	Ending Col. No.	Field Length
1	Shipped Date	1	8	8
2	Tracking Number	10	15	6
3	Part Number	17	21	5
4	First Name	23	27	5
5	Last Name	29	38	10
6	Company	40	50	11

Using this data your C program should extract the date, part number, first initial, last name, and company name and produce a report listing the extracted data. [*Hint:* Use the extract() function created in Exercise 4.]

11. Write a C program that displays the data given in Exercise 9 so that the displayed lines are in increasing employee number order, where the second field is the employee number. [*Hint:* Use the extract() function developed for Exercise 4 and the selection sort described in Section 8.5.]

12. Some prisoners of war devised a system of communicating with each other through the walls of solitary-confinement cells. This system is based on arranging the letters of the alphabet in five rows as follows:

a	b	c	d	e
f	g	h	i	j
l	m	n	o	p
q	r	s	t	u
v	w	x	y	z

The prisoners spelled messages to each other by tapping the row and column number of the letters on the wall, substituting c for the omitted k. For example, *h* would be 2 taps (row 2), a short pause, and then 3 taps (column 3); and *help* would be "2,3 1,5 3,1 3,5," the digit pairs representing the number of taps for row and column.

Write a program that loads a two-dimensional array with the letters shown in the table. Then write a function to search the array for the letters in a given string and to convert the string to taps, representing the row, column number pairs.

12 | Data Files

The data for the programs we have seen so far has either been assigned internally within the programs or entered interactively during program execution. In this chapter we learn how to store data outside of a program. This external data storage permits a program to use the data without having to recreate it each time the program is run. Additionally, it provides the basis for sharing data between programs, so that the data output by one program can be input directly to another program.

Any collection of data that is stored together under a common name on a storage medium other than the computer's main memory is called a *data file*. Typically data files are stored on floppy diskettes, hard disks, or magnetic tapes. This chapter presents the fundamentals of data files and describes how they are created and maintained in C.

12.1 CREATING AND USING DATA FILES

A data file is physically stored by a computer using a unique filename. Although the maximum number of characters allowed for a filename is operating system dependent, we will use the more restrictive MS-DOS convention that the filename consist of no more than eight characters followed by an optional period and an extension of up to three characters.[1]

---

[1]We use this convention to ensure that our filenames will be compatible with most other operating systems, which typically have less restrictive lengths. For example, on UNIX-based systems, one standard imposes a maximum of 14 characters while another allows up to 255 characters. The maximum in the Windows operating system is 255 characters, while VMX uses the same standard as DOS.

Using the MS-DOS convention, the following are all valid computer data filenames:

```
math.dat      djavg.stk      records
infor.dat     exper1.dat     results.mem
```

Computer data filenames should be chosen to indicate the file's information content. For data files the first eight characters typically are used to describe the data and the three characters after the decimal point are used to describe either the application or are set equal to DAT to indicate a data file. For example, the filename EXPER1.DAT is useful for describing a file of data pertaining to experiment number one. Similarly, the filename DJAVG.STK could be used for the Dow Jones averages required in a stock-related program.

Within a C program a file is always referenced by a variable name that must be declared within the program. The declaration takes the form:

```
FILE *filename;
```

where the filename is selected by the programmer and can be any valid variable name. Examples of valid file declarations are:

```
FILE *in_file;
FILE *factors;
FILE *weights;
FILE *out_file;
```

---

[2]The asterisk in the FILE declaration statement, as described in Sections 10.1, and means that the variable immediately following it is a pointer. In this case it is a pointer to a FILE, where FILE is a predefined structure that is declared in the header file stdio.h.

Within a C program a file is always referenced using the variable (file) name declared in the FILE declaration statement.[2] The correspondence between this "internal" filename and the file's "external" filename (i.e., computer name) is made using a C function named fopen(). In using fopen(), two arguments are required. The first argument is the computer's name for the file; the second argument is the mode in which the file is to be used. The most commonly used modes are "r", "w", and "a", which represent reading, writing, or appending to a file, respectively.[3] For example, the statement:

```
out_file = fopen("exper1.dat","w");
```

opens a file named exper1.dat and assigns this to filename out_file. The name out_file is a programmer-selected name for the file that is declared in the FILE declaration and represents how the file is referenced within the C program that opened the file. A file opened for writing creates a new file and makes the file available for use within the function opening the file or any other function that gets the filename passed as an argument. If a file exists with the same name as a file opened for writing, the old file is overwritten. Thus, the statement

```
out_file = fopen("exper1.dat","w");
```

opens a file named exper1.dat that can now be written to. Once this file has been opened, the program accesses the file using the name out_file, while the computer saves the file under the name exper1.dat.

A file opened for appending makes an existing file available for data to be added to the end of the file. If the file opened for appending does not exist, a new file with the designated name is created and made available to receive output from the program. For example, the statement:

```
out_file = fopen("exper1.dat","a");
```

opens a file named exper1.dat and makes it available for data to be appended to the end of the file.

The only difference between a file opened in write mode and one opened in append mode is where the data is physically placed in the file. In write mode, the data is written starting at the beginning of the file, while in append mode the data is written starting at the end of the file. For a new file, the two modes are identical.

A file opened in read mode retrieves an existing file and makes its data available as input to the program. For example, the open statement:

```
in_file = fopen("test.dat","r");
```

opens the file named test.dat and makes the data in the file available for input. Within the function opening the file, the file is read using the name in_file.

As an executable statement, a call to the fopen() function can be made anywhere within a function after its declaration statements. Because the function prototype for fopen() is contained within the stdio.h header file, any program that will open a file should include the preprocessor command:

```
#include <stdio.h>
```

---

[3]Additional modes are r+, w+, and a+. The r+ mode opens an existing file for reading and writing existing records; the w+ mode erases an existing file and opens a blank file for reading and writing; and the a+ mode allows reading, writing, and appending to a file.

When a call to fopen() is encountered, the computer determines whether the file currently exists on the system. If a file having the indicated filename exists, the file is opened. If the file does not exist, and the file was opened in write or append modes ("w" or "a") a blank file having the indicated name is created. If a file opened for reading does not exist, the fopen() function returns the system named constant NULL. This named constant can be used to test that an existing file has, in fact, been opened.

Program 12.1 illustrates the statements required to open a file in read mode and the use of the returned value from fopen() to check for a successful opening of the file.

PROGRAM 12.1

```
#include <stdio.h>
void main(void)
{
  FILE *in_file;

  in_file = fopen("test.dat","r");   /* request to open the file */

  if (in_file == (FILE *) NULL)  /* check for an unsuccessful open */
  {
    printf("\nFailed to open the data file.\n");
    exit(1);
  }

  printf("\nThe file has been successfully opened for reading.\n");
}
```

When Program 12.1 is run on a system that does have the file named test.dat in the current directory, the message

          The file has been successfully opened for reading.

is displayed. If the file does not exist in the current directory, however, the message

               Failed to open the data file.

is displayed and the execution of the program is halted by the exit statement. The section of code that tests fopen()'s return value is used to ensure that the open was successfully accomplished before any further processing is attempted. The if statement is used to check that the return from fopen(), which is stored in in_file, is a NULL pointer to a FILE. If in_file does contain a NULL, which indicates that the open was not successful, a message is displayed and exit() is called. The exit() function is a request to the operating system that causes termination of the program's execution. The function's integer argument is passed to the operating system for possible further operating system program action. In making open requests it is very important to always check fopen()'s return value—otherwise the program can crash or cause other abnormal behavior when an attempt is made to process a nonexistent file.

TIPS FROM THE PROS

Checking `fopen()`**'s Return Value**

It is important to check the return value when making an `fopen()` call. This is because the call is really a request to the operating system to open a file. For a variety of reasons, the open can fail. (Chief among these reasons is a request to open an existing file for reading that the operating system cannot locate.) If the operating system cannot satisfy the open request you need to know about it and gracefully terminate your program. Failure to do so almost always results in some abnormal program behavior or a subsequent program crash. There are two styles of coding for checking the return value.

The first style is the one coded in Program 12.1. It is used to clearly illustrate the request for the opening as distinct from the return value check, and is repeated below for convenience:

```
in_file = fopen("test.dat","r");   /* request to open the file */

if (in_file) == (FILE *) NULL      /* check for an unsuccessful open */
{
  printf("\nFailed to open the data file.\n");
  exit(1);
}
```

Alternatively, the open request and check can be combined within the `if` statement as:

```
if ((in_file = fopen("test.dat,""r") == (FILE *) NULL)
{
  printf("\nFailed to open the data file.\n");
  exit(1);

}
```

Use whichever style you are initially more comfortable with. As you gain experience in programming be prepared to adopt the second style. It is the one used almost universally by advanced programmers.

Writing to a File

If a file is opened in write mode, data can be written to it using almost identical functions for writing data to a display screen. The functions for writing to a file are listed in Table 12.1. For example, if `out_file` is the file name assigned when the file was opened in either write or append modes, the following statements are valid:

TABLE 12.1 File Writing Functions

Function	Description
`fputc(c,filename)`	Write a single character to the file.
`fputs(string,filename)`	Write a string to the file. (Neither the terminating null nor a newline character is appended.)
`fprintf(filename,"format",args)`	Write the values of the arguments to the file according to the format.

```
fputc('a',out_file);              /* write an a to the file */
fputs("Hello World!",out_file); /* write the string to the file */
fprintf(out_file,"%f %f %f", weight, factor, balance);
```

Notice that the `fprintf` file function is used in the same manner as the equivalent `printf` function, with the addition of the filename as an argument. The filename directs the output to a specific file instead of to the standard display device. Program 12.2 illustrates the use of an `fopen()` function and two subsequent calls to `fprintf()` for writing data to an opened file.

PROGRAM 12.2

```
#include <stdio.h>
void main(void)
{
  FILE *out_file;        /* FILE declaration */
  float weight = 165.0, slope = 7.5, factor = 2.0625;

  out_file = fopen("test.dat","w");  /* request to open file */
  if (out_file == (FILE *) NULL)     /* check if request was satisfied */
  {
    printf("\nFailed to open the file\n");
    exit(1);
  }
  fprintf(out_file,"%f",weight);
  fprintf(out_file,"\n%f %f",slope, factor);
}
```

When Program 12.2 is executed, a file named `test.dat` is created by the computer. After the file is opened, two `fprintf` function call statements are used to write two lines to the `test.dat` file. Formally, each line in a file is referred to as a *record*. Thus, the file produced by Program 12.2 consists of the following two records:

```
165.000000
7.500000   2.062500
```

As illustrated in Program 12.2, writing to a file is essentially the same as writing to the standard output device, except for the explicit designation of the file's name and the use of `fprintf` in place of `printf`. This means that all of the techniques you have learned for creating standard output displays apply to file writes as well. For example, Program 12.3 illustrates storing data from an array into a file opened as `newfile`. Also notice in Program 12.3 that we have placed the name of the file at the top of the program, rather than embed it within the `fopen()` call. The advantages of the filename placement are presented in the Tips from the Pros box located on page 514.

PROGRAM 12.3

```c
#include <stdio.h>
#define NUMS 5
char *exper_file = "exper.dat";   /* put the filename up front */

void main(void)
{
  FILE *newfile;
  int i;
  float result[NUMS] = {16.25, 17.0, 15.75, 18.0, 19.5};

  newfile = fopen(exper_file,"w");   /* open the file */
  if (newfile == (FILE *) NULL)      /* check the return value */
  {
    printf("\nFailed to open the data file named %s\n", exper_file);
    exit(1);
  }

  for (i = 0; i < NUMS; ++i)
    fprintf(newfile,"\n%1d %9.6f", i, result[i]);
  fclose(newfile);
}
```

When Program 12.3 is executed, a file named `exper.dat` is opened by the computer. (If the file does not exist, it is automatically created.) After the file is opened a `for` loop is used to write five lines to the file, with each line containing two items. The file produced by this program consists of the following five lines:

```
0   16.250000
1   17.000000
2   15.750000
3   18.000000
4   19.500000
```

Closing a File

Included in Program 12.3 is a call to the `fclose()` function. This function is used to break the link established by the `fopen()` function call, which releases the internal filename pointer. This filename pointer can then be used for another file. The general form of the call to `fclose()` is

$$fclose(filename);$$

where the filename is the "internal" name of the file used when the file was opened. Because all computers have a limit on the maximum number of files

A Way to Clearly Identify a File's Name and Location

During program development test files are usually placed in the same directory as the program. Therefore, an expression such as `fopen("exper.dat","r")` causes no problems to the operating system. In production systems, however, it is not uncommon for data files to reside in one directory while program files reside in another. For this reason it is always a good idea to include the full path name of any file opened.

For example, if the `exper.dat` file resides in the directory `/test/files`, the `fopen` statement should include the full path name, namely `fopen("test/files/exper.dat", "r")`. Then, no matter where the program is run from, the operating system will know where to locate the file.

Another useful convention is to list all filenames at the top of a program instead of embedding the names deep within the code. This can easily be accomplished by using a pointer to each filename. For example, if a declaration such as:

```
char *in_file = "\test\files\exper.dat";
```

is placed at the top of a program file, it clearly lists both the name of the desired file and its location. Then, if some other file is to be tested, all that is required is a simple one-line change at the top of the program.

Using a pointer to the file's name is also helpful for the return code check. For example, consider the following code:

```
if ((in_ptr = fopen(in_file,"r") == (FILE *) NULL)
{
  printf("\nFailed to open the data file named %s.\n", in_file);
  exit(1);
}
```

Here the correct filename is automatically displayed when the file fails to open.

that can be open at one time, closing files that are no longer needed makes good sense. In the absence of a specific `fclose()` function call, as in Program 12.2, any open files existing at the end of normal program execution are automatically closed by the operating system.

When a file is closed a special end-of-file (EOF) marker is automatically placed by the operating system as the last character in the file. The EOF character has a unique numerical code that has no equivalent representation as a printable character. This special numerical value, which is system dependent, ensures that the EOF character can never be confused with a valid character contained internally within the file. As we will see shortly, this EOF character can be used as a sentinel when reading data from a file.

Reading a File

Reading data from a file is almost identical to reading data from the keyboard. The functions that are used for reading file data are listed in Table 12.2. For example, if `in_file` is the name of a file opened in read mode, the following statements could be used to read data from the file:

TABLE 12.2 File Reading Functions

Function	Description
fgetc(filename)	Read a character from the file.
fgets(stringname,n,filename)	Read from the file until either n-1 characters or a newline character is encountered. Store the characters in the given string name. (If a newline character is read it is stored as the last string character.) A null is appended to the string.
fscanf(filename,"format",&args)	Read values for the listed arguments from the file according to the format.

```
fgetc(in_file);                 /* read the next character in the file */
fgets(message,10,in_file);      /* read the next 9 characters from     */
                                /* the file into message               */
fscanf(in_file,"%f",&factor);   /* read a floating-point number        */
```

All the input functions correctly detect the end-of-file marker. The functions fgetc() and fscanf(), however, return the named constant EOF when the marker is detected. The function fgets() returns a NULL (\0) when it detects the end of a file. Both of these symbolic constants, EOF and NULL, are useful when reading a file to detect when the end of the file has been reached.

PROGRAM 12.4

```c
#include <stdio.h>
char *exper_file = "exper.dat";
#define NUMS 5

void main(void)
{
  FILE *in_file;
  int i, n;
  float val;

  in_file = fopen(exper_file,"r");  /* request an open */
  if (in_file == (FILE *) NULL)     /* check the return value */
  {
    printf("\nFailed to open the file named %s\n", exper_file);
    exit(1);
  }
  for (i = 1; i <= NUMS; ++i)
  {
    fscanf(in_file,"%d  %f", &n, &val);
    printf("\n%d %f",n,val);
  }
  fclose(in_file);
}
```

Reading data from a file requires that the programmer know how the data appears in the file. This is necessary for correct "stripping" of the data from the file into appropriate variables for storage. All files are read sequentially, so that once an item is read the next item in the file becomes available for reading. Program 12.4 uses the fscanf function to read five lines from the exper.dat file written by Program 12.3. Each time the file is read, an integer and a real value are input to the program and displayed.

The display produced by Program 12.4 is:

```
0   16.250000
1   17.000000
2   15.750000
3   18.000000
4   19.500000
```

In addition to using a for loop to read a specific number of lines, as is done in Program 12.4, the EOF marker appended to each file can be used as a sentinel value. When the EOF marker is used in this manner, the following algorithm can be used to read and display each line of the file:

```
while not end-of-file
    read a line
```

Program 12.5 illustrates reading the exper.dat file that was created in Program 12.3 using the EOF marker, which is returned by fscanf when the end of the file is encountered.

PROGRAM 12.5

```c
#include <stdio.h>
char *exper_file = "exper.dat";

void main(void)
{
  FILE *in_file;
  int i, n;
  float val;

  in_file = fopen(exper_file,"r");   /* request an open */
  if (in_file == (FILE *) NULL)      /* check the return value */
  {
    printf("\nFailed to open the file named %s\n", exper_file);
    exit(1);
  }
  while (fscanf(in_file,"%d %f", &n, &val) != EOF)
    printf("\n%d %f",n,val);
  fclose(in_file);
}
```

Program 12.5 continues to read the file until the EOF marker has been detected. Each time the file is read, an integer and floating-point number are input to the program. The display produced by Program 12.5 is the same as that produced by Program 12.4.

In place of the `fscanf()` function used in Program 12.5, an `fgets()` function call can be used. `fgets()` requires three arguments: an address where the first character read will be stored, the maximum number of characters to be read, and the name of the input file. For example, the function call

```
fgets(&line[0],81,in_file);
```

causes a maximum of 80 characters (one less than the specified number) to be read from the file named `in_file` and stored starting at the address of element `line[0]` (recall from Section 10.1 that the ampersand symbol, &, mean "the address of"). `fgets()` continues reading characters until 80 characters have been read or a newline character has been encountered. If a newline character is encountered, it is included with the other entered characters before the string is terminated with the end-of-string marker, `\0`. `fgets()` also detects the EOF marker, but returns the null character when the end of the file is encountered. Program 12.6 illustrates the use of `fgets()` in a working program.

PROGRAM 12.6

```c
#include <stdio.h>
#define MAXCHARS 81
char *exper_file = "exper.dat";

void main(void)
{
  FILE *in_file;
  int i, n;
  float val;
  char line[MAXCHARS];

  in_file = fopen(exper_file,"r"); /* request an open */
  if (in_file == (FILE *) NULL)    /* check the return value */
  {
    printf("\nFailed to open the file named %s\n", exper_file);
    exit(1);
  }
  while (fgets(&line[0], MAXCHARS, in_file) != NULL)
    printf("%s",line);
  fclose(in_file);
}
```

Program 12.6 is really a line-by-line text-copying program, reading a line of text from the file and then displaying it on the terminal. Thus, the output of Program 12.6 is identical to the output of Programs 12.4 and 12.5. If it were necessary to obtain the integer and floating-point numbers as individual variables, either Program 12.4 or Program 12.5 should be used or the string returned by `fgets` in Program 12.6 must be processed further using the string scan function, `sscanf`. For example, the statement

```
sscanf(&line[0],"%d %f", &n, &val);
```

could be used to extract the description and price from the string stored in the line character array (see Section 11.4 for a more complete description of in-memory string formatting).

Standard Device Files

The data filenames we have used have all been logical filenames. A *logical filename* is one that references a file of related data that has been saved under a common name; that is, a data file. In addition to logical filenames, C also supports physical filenames. A *physical filename* refers to a hardware device, such as a keyboard, screen, or printer.

The actual physical device assigned to your program for data entry is formally called the standard input file. Usually this is a keyboard. When a scanf function call is encountered in a C program, the computer automatically goes to this standard input file for the expected input. Similarly, when a printf function call is encountered, the output is automatically displayed or "written to" a device that has been assigned as the standard output file. For most systems this is a CRT screen, although it can be a printer.

When a program is run, the keyboard used for entering data is automatically opened and assigned the internal filename stdin. Similarly, the output device used for display is assigned to the filename stdout. These filenames are always available for programmer use.

The similarities between printf() and fprintf() and between scanf() and fscanf() are not accidental. printf() is a special case of fprintf() that defaults to the standard output file, and scanf() is a special case of fscanf() that defaults to the standard input file. Thus,

```
fprintf(stdout,"Hello World!");
```

causes the same display as the statement

```
printf("Hello World!");
```

and

```
fscanf(stdin,"%d",&num);
```

is equivalent to the statement

```
scanf("%d",&num);
```

In addition to the stdin and stdout filenames, a third file named stderr is assigned to the output device used for system error messages. Although stderr and stdout frequently refer to the same device, the use of stderr provides a means of redirecting any error messages away from the file being used for normal program output.

Just as `scanf` and `printf()` are special cases of `fscanf()` and `fprintf()`, respectively, the `getchar()`, `gets()`, `putchar()`, and `puts()` are also special cases of the more general file functions listed in Table 12.3.[4] The character function pairs listed in Table 12.3 can be used as direct replacements for each other. This is not true for the string handling functions. The difference between the string handling functions is described as follows:

At input, as previously noted, the fgets() function reads data from a file until a newline escape sequence or a specified number of characters has been read. If fgets encounters a newline escape sequence, as we saw in Program 12.6, it is stored with the other characters entered. The gets() function, however, does not store the newline escape sequence in the final string. Both functions terminate the entered characters with an end-of-string null character.

At output, both `puts()` and `fputs()` write all the characters in the string except for the terminating end-of-string null. `puts()`, however, automatically adds a newline escape sequence at the end of the transmitted characters while `fputs()` does not.

Other Devices

The keyboard, display, and error reporting devices are automatically opened and assigned the internal filenames `stdin`, `stdout`, and `stderr`, respectively, whenever a C program begins execution. Additionally, other devices can be used for input or output if the name assigned by the system is known. For example, most IBM or IBM-compatible personal computers assign the name `prn` to the printer connected to the computer. For these computers, the statement `fprintf("prn","Hello World!");` causes the string `Hello World!` to be printed directly at the printer. Here `prn` must be enclosed in quotes because it is not a variable name.

TABLE 12.3 Correspondence Between Selected I/O Functions

Function	General Form
putchar(character)	fputc(character,stdout)
puts(string)	fputs(string,stdout)
getchar(void)	fgetc(stdin)
gets(stringname)	fgets(stringname,n,stdin)

---

[4]All of the routines on the left-hand side of Table 12.3 are defined in the header file `<stdio.h>` using the equivalent functions on the right-hand side of the table. Strictly speaking the functions on the right are true C functions, while those on the left are macros. Macros are more described in detail in Section 15.3.

Exercises 12.1

1. Using the reference manuals provided with your computer's operating system, determine

    a. the maximum number of characters that can be used to name a file for storage by the computer system.

    b. the maximum number of data files that can be open at the same time.

2. Would it be appropriate to call a saved C program a file? Why or why not?

3. Write individual `fopen()` function calls to link the following "external" data file-names to the corresponding "input" filenames. Open each file for writing:

External Name	Internal Name
math.dat	out_file
book.dat	book
resist.dat	resfile
exper2.dat	exfile
prices.dat	pfile
rates.mem	ratefile

4. Write `fclose()` function calls for each of the files opened in Exercise 3.

5. a. Write a C program that stores the following numbers into a file named `result.dat`: 16.25, 18.96, 22.34, 18.94, 17.42, 22.63

    b. Write a C program to read and display the data in the `result.dat` file created in Exercise 5a. Additionally, your program should compute and display the sum and average of the data. Check the sum and average displayed by your program using a hand calculation.

6. a. Write a C program that prompts the user to enter five numbers. As each number is entered, the program should write the number into a file named `user.dat`.

    b. Write a C program that reads the data in the `user.dat` file created in Exercise 6a and displays each individual data item.

7. a. Create a file containing the following car numbers, number of miles driven, and number of gallons of gas used by each car:

Car No.	Miles Driven	Gallons Used
54	250	19
62	525	38
71	123	6
85	1322	86
97	235	14

    b. Write a C program that reads the data in the file created in Exercise 7a and displays the car number, miles driven, gallons used, and the miles per gallon for each car. The output should also display the total miles driven, total gallons used, and average miles per gallon for all the cars. These totals should be displayed at the end of the output report.

8. a. Create a file with the following data containing the part number, opening balance, number of items sold, and minimum stock required:

Part Number	Initial Amount	Quantity Sold	Minimum Amount
310	95	47	50
145	320	162	20
514	34	20	25
212	163	150	160

b. Write a C program to create an inventory report based on the data in the file created in Exercise 8a. The display should consist of the part number, current balance, and the amount that is necessary to bring the inventory to the minimum level.

9. a. Create a file containing the following data:

Identification Number	Rate	Hours
10031	6.00	40
10067	5.00	48
10083	6.50	35
10095	8.00	50

b. Write a C program that uses the information contained in the file created in Exercise 9a to produce the following pay report:

```
ID No.   Rate   Hours   Regular Pay   Overtime Pay   Gross Pay
```

Any hours worked above 40 hours are paid at time and a half. At the end of the individual output for each ID number, the program should display the totals of the regular, overtime, and gross pay columns.

10. a. Store the following data in a file:

```
5  96  87  78  93  21  4  92  82  85  87  6  72  69  85  75  81  73
```

b. Write a C program to calculate and display the average of each group of numbers in the file created in Exercise 10a. The data is arranged in the file so that each group of numbers is preceded by the number of data items in the group. Thus, the first number in the file, 5, indicates that the next five numbers should be grouped together. The number 4 indicates that the following four numbers are a group, and the 6 indicates that the last six numbers are a group. (*Hint:* Use a nested loop. The outer loop should be executed three times.)

11. Rotech Systems is a distributor of high-speed memory devices for specialized computer applications. Each memory device in stock is stored by its tolerance, where lower tolerance devices are sold at a premium and used for more critical applications that require a tighter tolerance. Having just completed an annual check of inventory in stock, Rotech has found it has the following quantities of memory devices in stock:

Device Number	5% Tolerance	2% Tolerance	1% Tolerance
4016	464	612	129
4314	742	1,215	375
4311	517	820	298
4364	684	105	22
4464	771	200	358

Based on this data Rotech wants a report of how many devices should be ordered to ensure that it has at least 800 of each item in stock. Your first task is to create a file containing this inventory data. Each line in the file should consist of a device number and the three inventory levels for that part number. When the file has been created, use it in a program that reads the data into a two-dimensional array, searches the array, and prints a report listing the amount of each that must be ordered.

12. a. Write a C program that uses either the random number generator described in Section 6.3 or one supplied by your computer system to select 1000 random numbers having values between 1 and 100. As each number is selected it should be written to a file called number.

   b. Using the number file created in Exercise 12a, write a C program that reads the data in the file, computes the average of the 1000 data items, and writes a new file consisting of all values that are 10% above or below the calculated average.

13. Instead of using an actual filename in an fopen() function call, a character variable can be used instead. For example, the statement

```
in_file = fopen(fname,"r");
```

equates the internal filename in_file to the filename assigned to the variable fname. Here the variable fname must be declared as a character variable of sufficient length to hold a valid filename. The following code illustrates how this fopen() statement could be used in practice:

```
#include <stdio.h>
#define MAXLEN 14
void main(void)
{
  FILE *in_file, *fopen();
  char fname[MAXLEN];

  printf("Enter a filename: ");
  fgets(fname,MAXLEN,stdin);
  in_file = fopen(fname,"r");
    .
    .
    .
}
```

The variable declaration statement in this code creates a character variable named fname having a length of MAXLEN characters. The code then requests that the filename be entered by the user. The entered name is stored in the character variable fname, which then is used as an argument to the fopen() function. Using this code, rewrite Program 12.3 so that the name of the data file is entered when the program is executed.

12.2 RANDOM FILE ACCESS

File organization refers to the way data is stored in a file. All the files we have used have *sequential organization*. This means that the characters in the file are stored in a sequential manner, one after another. Additionally, we have read the file in a sequential manner. The way data is retrieved from the file is called *file access*. The fact that the characters in the file are stored sequentially, however, does not force us to access the file sequentially.

The standard library functions rewind, fseek(), and ftell() can be used to provide random access to a file. In *random access* any character in the file can be read immediately, without first having to read all the characters stored before it.

The rewind() function resets the current position to the start of the file. rewind requires the pointer name used for the file as its only argument. For example, the statement

```
                          rewind(in_file);
```

resets the file so that the next character accessed will be the first character in the file. A rewind is done automatically when a file is opened in read mode.

The `fseek()` function allows the programmer to move to any position in the file. To understand this function, you must first clearly understand how data is referenced in the file.

Each character in a data file is located by its position in the file. The first character in the file is located at position 0, the next character at position 1, and so on. A character's position is also referred to as its offset from the start of the file. Thus, the first character has a 0 offset, the second character has an offset of 1, and so on for each character in the file.

The `fseek()` function requires three arguments: the name of the file; the offset, as a long integer; and the position from which the offset is to be calculated. The general form of `fseek()` is

```
              fseek(file_name, offset, origin)
```

The values of the origin argument can be either 0, 1, or 2, which are defined in the `stdio.h` header file as the named constants SEEK_SET, SEEK_CUR, and SEEK_END, respectively. An origin of SEEK_SET means the offset is relative to the start of the file. An origin of SEEK_CUR means that the offset is relative to the current position in the file, and an origin of SEEK_END means the offset is relative to the end of the file. A positive offset means move forward in the file and a negative offset means move backward. Examples of `fseek()` are:

```
fseek(in_file,4L,SEEK_SET);    /* go to the fifth character in the file */
fseek(in_file,4L,SEEK_CUR);    /* move ahead five characters */
fseek(in_file,-4L,SEEK_CUR);   /* move back five characters */
fseek(in_file,0L,SEEK_SET);    /* go to start of file - same as rewind() */
fseek(in_file,0L,SEEK_END);    /* go to end of file */
fseek(in-file,-10L,SEEK_END);  /* go to 10 characters before the file's end */
```

In these examples, `in_file` is the name of the file pointer used when the data file was opened. Notice that the offset passed to `fseek()` must be a long integer; the appended `L` tells the compiler to consider the offset as such.

The last function, `ftell`, simply returns the offset value of the next character that will be read or written. For example, if 10 characters have already been read from a file named `in_file`, the function call

```
                          ftell(in_file);
```

returns the long integer 10. This means that the next character to be read is offset 10 byte positions from the start of the file, and is the eleventh character in the file.

Program 12.7 illustrates the use of `fseek()` and `ftell()` to read a file in reverse order, from last character to first. As each character is read it is also displayed.

Assuming the file `temp.dat` contains the following data,

```
                          Bulbs 3.12
```

the output of Program 12.7 is:

```
          EOF : 2 : 1 : . : 3 : : : : s : b : l : u : B :
```

PROGRAM 12.7

```c
#include <stdio.h>
char *file_name = "temp.dat";

void main(void)
{
  int ch, n;
  long offset, last, ftell();
  FILE *in_file;

  in_file = fopen(file_name,"r"); /* request an open */
  if (in_file == (FILE *) NULL)   /* check the return code */
  {
    printf("\nFailed to open the file named %s\n", file_name);
    exit(1);
  }

  fseek(in_file,0L,SEEK_END);      /* move to the end of the file */
  last = ftell(in_file);  /* save the offset of the last character */
  for(offset = 0L; offset  <= last; offset++)
  {
    fseek(in_file, -offset, SEEK_END);     /* move back to the next char-
acter */

    ch = getc(in_file);            /* get the character */
    switch(ch)
    {
      case '\n': printf("LF : ");
            break;
      case EOF : printf("EOF: ");
            break;
      default : printf("%c : ",ch);
            break;
    }
  }
  printf("\n");
  fclose(in_file);
}
```

Program 12.7 initially goes to the last character in the file. The offset of this character, which is the end-of-file character, is saved in the variable last. Since ftell() returns a long integer, both ftell() and last have been declared as long integers.

Starting from the end of the file, fseek() is used to position the next character to be read, referenced from the back of the file. As each character is read, the character is displayed and the offset adjusted in order to access the next character.

Exercises 12.2

1. Determine the value of the offset returned by `ftell()` in Program 12.7. Assume that the file `temp.dat` contains the data

   `Bulbs 3.12`

2. Rewrite Program 12.7 so that the origin for the `fseek()` function used in the `for` loop is the start of the file rather than the end. The program should still print the file in reverse order.

3. The function `fseek()` returns 0 if the position specified has been reached, or a 1 if the position specified was beyond the file's boundaries. Modify Program 12.7 to display an error message if `fseek()` returns 1.

4. Write a program that will read and display every second character in a file named `temp.dat`.

5. Using the `fseek()` and `ftell()` functions, write a function named `f_chars` that returns the total number of characters in a file.

6. a. Write a function named `r_bytes` that reads and displays *n* characters starting from any position in a file. The function should accept three arguments: a file pointer, the offset of the first character to be read, and the number of characters to be read.

   b. Modify the `r_bytes` function written in Exercise 6a to store the characters read into a string or an array. The function should accept the address of the storage area as a fourth argument.

7. Assume that a data file consisting of a group of individual lines has been created. Write a function named `print_line` that will read and display any desired line of the file. For example, the function call `print_line(f_name,5);` should display the fifth line of the filename passed to it.

12.3 FOCUS ON PROBLEM SOLVING

Once a data file has been created, the majority of applications are concerned with updating the file's records to maintain currently accurate data. In this section two such program requirements are presented. The first problem uses a file as a database for storing the 10 most recent pollen counts, which are used in the summer as allergy "irritability" measures. As a new reading is obtained, it is added to the file and the oldest stored reading is deleted.

The second program requirement concerns an expanded file update procedure. In this application a file containing inventory data, consisting of book identification numbers and quantities in stock, is updated by information contained in a second file. This application requires that identification numbers in the two files be matched before a record is updated.

Problem 1: Single File Update

Pollen count readings, which are taken from August through September in the northeastern region of the United States, measure the number of ragweed pollen grains in the air. Pollen counts in the range of 10 to 200 grains per cubic meter of air are typical during this time of year. Typically, pollen counts above 10 begin to affect a small percentage of hay fever sufferers, counts in the range of 30 to 40 will noticeably bother approximately 30% of hay fever sufferers, and counts between 40 and 50 adversely affect more than 60% of all hay fever sufferers.

Program Requirement   A program is to be written that updates a single file containing the 10 most recent pollen counts. As a new count is obtained, it is to be added to the end of the file and the oldest count deleted from the file.[5] Additionally, the averages of the old and new file data are calculated and displayed. The existing file is named `pollen` and contains the data shown in Figure 12.1.

Analyze the Problem   The input data for this problem consists of a file of 10 integer numbers and a user input value of the most recent integer value pollen count. The three required outputs are:

1. A file of the 10 most recent integer values
2. The average of the data values in the existing file
3. The average of the data in the updated file.

Develop a Solution   The algorithm for solving this problem is straightforward and is described by the following pseudocode:

Display a message indicating what the program does.
Request the name of the data file.
Request a new pollen count reading.
Open the data file.
For ten data items
   Read a value into an array
   Add the value to a total
Endfor.
Calculate and display the old 10-day average.
Calculate and display the new 10-day average.
Rewind the data file.
Write the nine most recent pollen counts from the array to the file.
Write the new pollen count to the file.
Close the file.

FIGURE 12.1   Data Currently in the `pollen` File

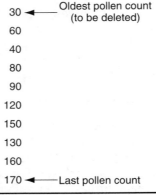

30 ◄——— Oldest pollen count
              (to be deleted)
60
40
80
90
120
150
130
160
170 ◄———Last pollen count

---

[5]This type of data storage is formally referred to as a first-in/first-out (FIFO) list, which is also called a *queue*. If the list is maintained in last-in/first-out (LIFO) order it is called a *stack*.

FIGURE 12.2 **The Update Process**

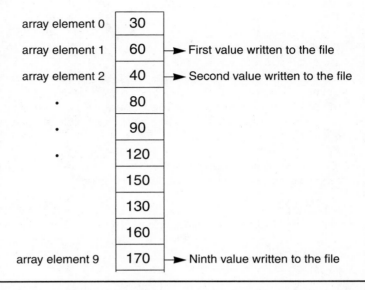

In reviewing this algorithm, notice that an array is used for temporarily storing the contents of the file. Thus, when the file is initially read, the first pollen count in the file is stored in array element zero, the second element in array element one, and so on, as illustrated in Figure 12.2. Once the data is "captured" in the array, the data file can be rewound and written over with the latest 10 counts. As further illustrated in Figure 12.2 the first nine values written to the file are taken from array elements 1 through 9, respectively. Finally, the last count written to the file is the most recent value. Program 12.8 expresses this algorithm in C.

Code the Solution   Program 12.8 presents a C representation of the selected design where the selected algorithm has been coded as the function `pollen_update`.

PROGRAM 12.8

```
#include <stdio.h>
#define POLNUMS 10
#define MAXLEN 13

void main(void)
{
  void pollen_update(void);

  pollen_update();
}
/* the following function reads and updates the pollen file */
void pollen_update(void)
```

(continued on next page)

(continued from previous page)

```c
{
  int newcount, i, a[POLNUMS];
  float sum, average;
  char fname[MAXLEN];
  FILE *pollen;
    /* display a user message */
  printf("\nThis program updates the pollen count file");
  printf("\n and calculates ten count averages");
  printf("\n\nEnter the pollen count filename: ");
    /* get the data filename and most recent pollen count */
  gets(fname);

  pollen = fopen(fname,"r+");    /* request to open the file */
  if (pollen == (FILE *) NULL)   /* check for a successful open */
  {
    printf("\nFailed to open the file named %s", fname);
    printf("\nPlease check that this filename is correct and");
    printf("\nexists in the indicated directory.\n");
    exit(1);
  }

    /* read, sum, and average the existing data */
  sum = 0;
  for(i = 0; i < POLNUMS; i++)
  {
    fscanf(pollen,"%d",&a[i]);
    sum = sum + a[i];
  }

    /* compute and display old average */
  average = sum / (float) POLNUMS;
  printf("\nThe old ten-count average is: %5.2f\n",average);

    /* get the latest pollen count*/
  printf("Enter the latest pollen count reading: ");
  scanf("%d", &newcount);

    /* compute and display the new average */
  sum = sum - a[0] + newcount;  /* update the sum */
  average = sum / (float) POLNUMS;
  printf("The new ten-count average is: %5.2f\n",average);

    /* write updated data to the file */
  rewind(pollen);
  for (i = 0; i < (POLNUMS - 1); i++)
    fprintf(pollen,"%d ",a[i+1]);
  fprintf(pollen,"%d",newcount);
  fclose(pollen);
  printf("\nAn updated data file has been written.\n");
}
```

Test and Debug the Program   Testing Program 12.8 requires that we provide both valid and invalid input data for the program. Invalid data would consist of both a nonexistent filename and a file that contains fewer than 10 items. Valid data consists of a file containing exactly 10 integers. The following is a sample run using Program 12.8 with a valid input file:

```
This program updates the pollen count file
 and calculates ten count averages

Enter the pollen count filename: pollen

The old ten-count average is: 103.00
Enter the latest pollen count reading: 200
The new ten-count average is: 120.00
An updated data file has been written.
```

The updated file created by Program 12.8 is illustrated in Figure 12.3. In reviewing the contents of this file notice that the most current reading has been added to the end of the file and that the other counts are obtained from the original file shown in Figure 12.1, but moved up one position in the file. Also notice that the output of our sample run correctly calculates both the old and new 10-week averages.

Problem 2: Master/Transaction File Update

A common form of file update occurs when the update data is itself contained in a file. Here, the file to be updated is referred to as a master file, and the file containing the update data is referred to as a transactions file. As a specific example of this type of update consider the following scenario:

Program Requirement   Assume that a current master file, named `oldbook.mas`, consists of book identification numbers and quantities in stock as illustrated in Table 12.4. A transactions file, named `book.trn`, contains the quantities of each book

---

FIGURE 12.3   **The Updated** `pollen` **File**

```
60  ◄──── Oldest pollen count
40
80
90
120
150
130
160
170
200  ◄──────── Most recent reading
```

TABLE 12.4 Data Contained in the `oldbook.mas`
File

Book ID No.	Quantity in Stock
125	98
289	222
341	675
467	152
589	34
622	125

TABLE 12.5 Data Contained in the Transaction File Named `book.trn`

ID No.	Date	Sold	Returned	Bought
289	1/10/92	125	34	50
341	1/10/92	300	52	0
467	1/15/92	50	20	200
467	1/20/92	225	0	160
589	1/31/92	75	10	55

bought, sold, or returned to stock each day. This file is sorted by ID number at the end of each month and contains the data illustrated in Table 12.5.

Write a program that uses the data in the transaction file to update the data in the master file so that at the end of the update, the master file contains a correct count of books for each identification number.

Analyze the Problem   Since this application requires more than a simple modification of existing techniques, we present additional background information and perform an exploratory analysis to ensure that we understand the problem.

A standard solution when updating a master file with the data in a transactions file is first to have all the transactions in the same identification number order as the records in the master file. In this case, since the records in the master file, as illustrated in Table 12.4, are in increasing (ascending) identification number order, the transactions must also be kept in ascending order. As illustrated in Table 12.5, this is the case for the `book.trn` file.

Once the two files are in the same ID number order, the standard procedure for creating an updated master file consists of reading a master record from the existing master file and one record from the transaction file. If the ID numbers of the two records match, the transaction record's information is applied to the data in the master record and another transaction record is read. As long as the transaction record's ID number matches the master record's ID number, the update of the master record continues. When the transaction record's ID number does not match the master record's ID number, which indicates that there is no further update data to be applied to the master record, an updated record is written to the new master file. Let's see how this procedure works by doing a hand calculation with the data shown in Tables 12.4 and 12.5.

The first record read from the master file has ID number 125, while the first transaction record has ID number 289. Since the ID numbers do not match, the update of this first master record is complete (in this case there is no update information) and the existing master record is written, without modification, to the new master file. Then the next master record is read, which has an ID number of 289. Since this ID number matches the transaction ID number, the inventory balance for book number 289 is updated, yielding a new balance of 181 books. Because the transaction file can contain multiple update records for the same ID number (notice the two records for ID number 467) the next transaction record is read and checked before writing an updated record to the new master file. Since the ID number of the next transaction record is not 289, the update of this book number is complete and an updated master record is written to the new master file.

This procedure continues, record by record, until the last master record has been updated. Should the end of the transaction file be encountered before the last master record is read from the existing master file, the remaining records in the existing master file are written directly to the new master file with no need to check for update information. The new master file can either be a completely new file, or each updated record can be written back to the old master file. In our update procedure, we will create a new master file so that the original data in the old master file will be left intact. Let's now formalize this algorithm using a pseudocode description.

Develop a Solution   Since we will be using two master files, the old and new masters, a notation must be established to distinguish clearly between them. By convention, the existing master file is always referred to as the old master file, and the updated master file is called the new master file. Using these terms, the pseudocode description of the update procedure found in the analysis step is:

Open the old master file.
Open the transaction file.
Open the new master file (initially blank).
Read the first old master record.
While not at the end of the transaction file
   Read a transaction record
   While the transaction ID does not match the old master ID
      Write an updated master record to the new master file
      Read the next transaction record
   Endwhile.
 If the ID numbers do match
   Calculate a new balance
Endwhile.
*** To get here the last transaction record has just been read.
Write the last updated master to the new master file.
While there are any remaining records in the old master file
      Read an old master record
      Write a new master record
Endwhile.
Close all files.

Code the Solution   In C, the selected design is implemented by Program 12.9.

PROGRAM 12.9

```c
#include <stdio.h>
#define MAXDATE 8
char *old_master = "oldbook.mas";  /* here are the files we will be */
char *new_master = "newbook.mas"; /* working with */
char *transactions = "book.trn";

void main(void)
{
   void do_update(void);

   do_update();
}

void do_update(void)
{
  int idmast, idtrans, balance, sold, returned, bought;
  char date[MAXDATE];
  FILE *oldmast, *newmast, *trans;

     /* open and check the old_master file */
  if ((oldmast = fopen(old_master,"r")) == (FILE *) NULL)
  {
    printf("\nFailed to open the file %s\n", old_master);
    exit(1);
  }
     /* open and check the new_master file */
  if ((newmast = fopen(new_master,"w")) == (FILE *) NULL)
  {
    printf("\nFailed to open the file %s\n", new_master);
    exit(2);
  }
     /* open and check the transactions file */
  if ((trans = fopen(transactions,"r")) == (FILE *) NULL)
  {
    printf("\nFailed to open the file %s\n", trans);
    exit(3);
  }
  fscanf(oldmast,"%d %d", &idmast, &balance);
  while( fscanf(trans,"%d %s %d %d %d",&idtrans,&date,&sold,
         &returned,&bought) != EOF)
  {
      /* if no match keep writing and reading the master file */
    while (idtrans > idmast)
    {
      fprintf(newmast,"%d %d\n",idmast, balance);
      fscanf(oldmast,"%d %d", &idmast, &balance);
    }
    balance = balance + bought - sold + returned;
  }
```

(continued on next page)

(continued from previous page)

```
    /* write the last updated new master file */
  fprintf(newmast,"%d %d\n",idmast, balance);
    /* write any remaining old master records to the new master */
  while (fscanf(oldmast,"%d %d", &idmast, &balance) != EOF)
  {
    fprintf(newmast,"%d %d",idmast, balance);
    fscanf(oldmast,"%d %d", &idmast, &balance);
  }
  fclose(oldmast);
  fclose(newmast);
  fclose(trans);
  printf("\n....File update complete...\n");
}
```

Test and Debug the Program   A sample run using Program 12.9 with an old master file containing the data illustrated in Table 12.4 and a transactions data file containing the data illustrated in Table 12.5 yielded the following data in the file newbook.mas:

```
125   98
289   181
341   427
467   257
589   24
622   125
```

A hand calculation using the data in Tables 12.4 and 12.5 verifies that the data in the second column is the correct new balance for the book identification numbers in the first column. Additional runs should now be made with the transactions file containing data for only the first book in the master file and then with data for only the last book in the master file. These two runs would successfully test the extreme values of the while loops.

Exercises 12.3

1. Write a C program to create the pollen file illustrated in Figure 12.1.

2. An alternate update algorithm to the one used in Program 12.8 is to use two files; the first file is the pollen file illustrated in Figure 12.1 and the second file is the updated file. Using two files the update algorithm becomes:

   Open both files.
   Read and add the first pollen.
   For the next nine pollen records
       Read a pollen count
       Add the count to the total
       Write the count to the new file
   Endfor.
   Request the current pollen count reading.
   Write the current pollen count to the new file.
   Close both files.
   Calculate and display the previous 10-day average.
   Calculate and display the current 10-day average.

Write a C file update program using this algorithm.

3. a. A file named `polar.dat` contains the polar coordinates needed in a graphics program. Currently this file contains the following data:

Distance (inches)	Angle (degrees)
2.0	45.0
6.0	30.0
10.0	45.0
4.0	60.0
12.0	55.0
8.0	15.0

Write a C program to create this file on your computer system.

b. Using the `polar.dat` file created in Exercise 3a, write a C program that accepts distance and angle data from the user and adds the data to the end of the file.

c. Using the `polar.dat` file created in Exercise 3a, write a C program that reads this file and creates a second file named `xycord.dat`. The entries in the new file should contain the rectangular coordinates corresponding to the polar coordinates in the `polar.dat` file. Polar coordinates are converted to rectangular coordinates using the equations

$$x = r\cos\theta$$
$$y = r\sin\theta$$

where r is the distance coordinate and θ is the radian equivalent of the angle coordinate in the `polar.dat` file.

4. a. Write a C program to create both the `oldbook.mas` file, illustrated in Table 12.4, and the `book.trn` file, illustrated in Table 12.5. (*Note:* Do not include the column headings in the file.)

b. Using the files created in Exercise 4a, enter and run Program 12.9 to verify its operation.

c. Modify Program 12.9 to prompt the user for the names of the old master file, the new master file, and the transaction file. The modified program should accept these filenames as input while the program is executing.

d. Using the `book.trn` file created in Exercise 4a, write a C program that reads this file and displays the transaction data in it, including the heading lines shown in Table 12.5.

5. Modify Program 12.9 to use a single master file. Thus, as each record is updated it should be written back to the old master file. Any master file record that does not have to be updated should be left as it currently exists on the master file.

6. a. Write a C program to create a data file containing the following information:

Student ID Number	Student Name	Course Code	Course Credits	Course Grade
2333021	BOKOW, R.	NS201	3	A
2333021	BOKOW, R.	MG342	3	A
2333021	BOKOW, R.	FA302	1	A

Student ID Number	Student Name	Course Code	Course Credits	Course Grade
2574063	FALLIN, D.	MK106	3	C
2574063	FALLIN, D.	MA208	3	B
2574063	FALLIN, D.	CM201	3	C
2574063	FALLIN, D.	CP101	2	B
2663628	KINGSLEY, M.	QA140	3	A
2663628	KINGSLEY, M.	CM245	3	B
2663628	KINGSLEY, M.	EQ521	3	A
2663628	KINGSLEY, M.	MK341	3	A
2663628	KINGSLEY, M.	CP101	2	B

b. Using the file created in Exercise 6a, write a C program that creates student grade reports. The grade report for each student should contain the student's name and identification number, a list of courses taken, the credits and grade for each course, and a semester grade-point average. For example, the grade report for the first student is:

```
Student name: BOKOW, R.
Student ID Number: 2333021

Course        Course         Course
Name          Credits        Grade
------        -------        -----

NS201         3              A
MG342         3              A
FA302         1              A

Total Semester Course Credits Completed: 7
Semester Grade-Point Average: 4.0
```

The semester grade-point average is computed in two steps. First, each course grade is assigned a numerical value (A = 4, B = 3, C = 2, D = 1, F = 0) and the sum of each course's grade value times the credits for each course is computed. This sum is then divided by the total number of credits taken during the semester.

7. a. Write a C program to create a data file containing the following information:

Student ID Number	Student Name	Course Credits	Grade-Point Average (GPA)
2333021	BOKOW, R.	48	4.0
2574063	FALLIN, D.	12	1.8
2663628	KINGSLEY, M.	36	3.5

b. Using the file created in Exercise 7a as a master file and the file created in Exercise 6a as a transactions file, write a file update program to create an updated master file.

12.4 PASSING AND RETURNING FILENAMES

Filenames are passed to a function using the same procedures for passing all function arguments. To pass a filename, the passed argument must be declared as a pointer to a FILE. For example, in Program 12.10 a file named out_file is opened in main and the filename passed to the function in_out, which is then used to write five lines of user-entered text to the file.

PROGRAM 12.10

```c
#include <stdio.h>
#define LINELEN 81    /* longest length of a line of text */
#define NUMLINES 5    /* number of lines of text */
char *file_name = "text.dat";   /* external filename */

void main(void)
{
  FILE *out_file;
  void in_out(FILE *);

  out_file = fopen(file_name,"w");
  if (out_file == (FILE *) NULL)
  {
    printf("\nFailed to open the file %s\n", file_name);
    exit(1);
  }

  in_out(out_file);
  fclose(out_file);
}


void in_out(FILE *fname) /* fname is a pointer to a FILE */
{
  int count;
  char line[LINELEN]; /* enough storage for one line of text */
  printf("Please enter five lines of text:\n");
  for (count = 0; count < NUMLINES; count++)
  {
    gets(line);
    fprintf(fname,"%s\n",line);
  }
  return;
}
```

Within the `main` function of Program 12.10 the file is known as `out_file`. The value in `out_file`, which is an address, is passed to the `in_out()` function. The function `in_out()` stores the address in the argument named `fname` and correctly declares `fname` to be a pointer to a `FILE`.

Returning a filename from a function also requires following the same rules used to return any value from a function. This means including the data type of the returned value in the function header, making sure the correct variable type is actually returned from the function, and alerting the calling function to the returned data type. For example, assume that the function `get_open()` is called with no passed arguments; the purpose of the function is to prompt a user for a filename, open the file for output, and pass the filename back to the calling function. Since `get_open()` returns a filename that is actually a pointer to a `FILE`, the correct function prototype for `get_open()` is:

$$\text{FILE *get\_open(void);}$$

This prototype specifically declares that the function `get_open()` will return a pointer to a `FILE`. It is consistent with the pointer declarations that have been made previously.

Once a function has been declared to return a pointer to a `FILE`, there must be at least one variable or argument in the function consistent with this declaration that can be used for the actual returned value. Consider Program 12.11. In this program, `get_open` returns a filename to `main`.

Program 12.11 is simply a modified version of Program 12.10. It now allows the user to enter a filename from the standard input device. Although the function `get_open()` is in "bare bones" form, it does illustrate the correct function declaration for returning a filename. The `get_open()` function declaration defines the function as returning a pointer to a `FILE`. Within `get_open()`, the returned variable, `fname`, is the correct data type. Finally, since `get_open()` is defined in the program after `main`, `main` is alerted to the returned value by the inclusion of a declaration statement for the `get_open()` function.

`get_open()` is a "bare bones" function in that it does no checking on the file being opened for output. If the name of an existing data file is entered, the file will be destroyed when it is opened in write mode. A useful "trick" to prevent this type of mishap is to open the entered filename in read mode. Then, if the file exists, the `fopen()` function returns a nonzero pointer to indicate that the file is available for input. This can be used to alert the user that a file with the entered name currently exists in the system and to request confirmation that the data in the file can be destroyed and the filename used for the new output file. Before the file can be reopened in write mode, of course, it would have to be closed. The implementation of this algorithm is left as an exercise.

PROGRAM 12.11

```
#include <stdio.h>
#define LINELEN 81    /* longest length of text */
#define NUMLINES 5    /* number of lines of text */
#define MAXNAME 12    /* maximum length of file's external name */

void main(void)
{
  FILE *get_open(void), *out_file;
  void in_out(FILE *);    /* a filename will be passed into in_out */

  out_file = get_open();
  in_out(out_file);
  fclose(out_file);
}
```

(continued on next page)

(continued from previous page)

```
FILE *get_open(void)    /* get_open() returns a pointer to a FILE */
{
  FILE *fname;
  char name[MAXNAME +1]; /* leave room for the \0*/

  printf("\nEnter a filename: ");
  gets(name);
  fname = fopen(name,"w");
  if (fname == (FILE *) NULL)
  {
    printf("\nFailed to open the file %s\n", name);
    exit(1);
  }
  return(fname);
}

void in_out(FILE *fname)  /* fname is a pointer to a FILE */
{
  int count;
  char line[LINELEN];  /* enough storage for one line of text */

  printf("Please enter five lines of text:\n");
  for (count = 0; count < NUMLINES; count++)
  {
    gets(line);
    fprintf(fname,"%s\n",line);
  }
}
```

Exercises 12.4

1. A function named p_file is to receive a filename as an argument. What declarations are required to pass a filename to p_file?

2. a. A function named get_file() is to return a filename. What declarations are required in the function header and internal to the file?

   b. What declaration statement is required in each function that calls get_file() to ensure correct receipt of the filename returned by get_file()? Under what conditions can this declaration be omitted?

3. Write a function named fcheck() that checks whether a file exists. The function should be passed a filename. If the file exists, the function should return a value of 1, otherwise the function should return a value of zero.

4. Rewrite the function get_open() used in Program 12.11 to incorporate the file checking procedures described in the text. Specifically, if the entered filename exists, an appropriate message should be displayed. The user should then be presented with the option of entering a new filename or allowing the program to overwrite the existing file, append to it, or exit.

12.5 TEXT AND BINARY FILES[6]

All of the files created in the previous three sections have been *text files*, which refers to the type of codes used by the computer to store the data in the file. In addition to text files, C permits the construction of *binary files*, which use a different set of codes for storing the data.

In this section the specifics of text and binary data storage are presented, the relative merits of each file type are described, and the mechanics of designating a file's type explicitly when the file is opened are specified.

Text File Storage

Each character in the files that we have been using is stored using a character code, such as the ASCII or EBCDIC codes introduced in Section 2.3. Both of these codes assign a specific code to each letter in the alphabet, to each of the digits 0 through 9, and to special symbols such as the decimal point and dollar sign. The ASCII and EBCDIC uppercase letter codes were previously listed in Table 2.3. Table 12.6 lists the correspondence between the decimal digits 0 through 9 and their ASCII and EBCDIC representations, in both binary and hexadecimal notation. Additionally, the ASCII and EBCDIC codes for a blank space, decimal point, carriage return, and line feed character are included in the table.

Using Table 12.6, we can determine how the decimal number 67432.83, for example, is stored in a data file using the ASCII code. In ASCII, this sequence of digits and decimal point requires eight character storage locations and is stored using the codes illustrated in Figure 12.4.

TABLE 12.6 Selected ASCII Codes

Character	ASCII Binary Value	ASCII Hex. Value	EBCDIC Binary Value	EBCDIC Hex. Value
0	00110000	30	11110000	F0
1	00110001	31	11110001	F1
2	00110010	32	11110010	F2
3	00110011	33	11110011	F3
4	00110100	34	11110100	F4
5	00110101	35	11110101	F5
6	00110110	36	11110110	F6
7	00110111	37	11110111	F7
8	00111000	38	11111000	F8
9	00111001	39	11111001	F9
.	00101110	2E	01001011	B
Blank space	00100000	20	01000000	40
Carriage return	00001101	0D	00001101	0D
Line feed	00001010	0A	00001010	0A

---

[6]This topic may be omitted on the first reading without loss of subject continuity.

FIGURE 12.4 The Number 67432.83 Represented in ASCII CODE

36	37	34	33	32	2E	38	33

The advantage of using ASCII or EBCDIC codes for data files is that the file can be read and displayed by any word processing or editor program that is provided by your computer system. Such editor and word processing programs are called text editors because they are designed to process alphabetical text. The word processing program can read the ASCII or EBCDIC code in the data file and display the letter, symbol, or digit corresponding to the code. This permits a data file created in C to be examined and changed by other than C programs.

A text file is the default file type created in C when a file is opened. An option within the `fopen()` function permits explicit selection of this file type, or selection of the alternative binary form. The explicit selection of a text file is made by adding the letter t after the mode (`"rt"`, `"wt"`, `"at"`, etc.) as the second argument in the `fopen()` function call. As an example employing this option, assume that the following list of experimental results is to be stored in a text file named `exper.dat`.

Experiment Number	Result
1	8
2	12
3	497

Program 12.12 opens a file named `exper.dat` to store this data. Additionally, the `fopen()` function is explicitly instructed to create a text file.

PROGRAM 12.12

```c
#include <stdio.h>
#define NUMS 3
char *file_name = "exper.dat";  /* this is the file we will work with */

void main(void)
{
  int i, result[NUMS] = {8, 12, 497};
  FILE *out_file;

  out_file = fopen(file_name,"wt");
  if (out_file == (FILE *) NULL)
  {
    printf("\nFailed to open the file named %s\n", file_name);
    exit(1);
  }
  for (i = 0; i < NUMS; i++)
    fprintf(out_file,"%2d %3d\n", i+1, result[i]);
  fclose(out_file);
}
```

When Program 12.12 is executed, a file named `exper.dat` is created and saved by the computer. The file is a text file consisting of the following three lines:

```
1    8
2   12
3  497
```

The spacing between data items in the file is due to the formatting used in the fprintf() function call. The stored characters consist of the codes used to store the required digits (one code per digit or letter, which is the hallmark of a text file) plus the blank spaces before each number, a carriage return and newline character at the end of each data line, and a special EOF marker placed as the last item in the file when the file is closed.

Assuming characters are stored using the ASCII code listed in Table 12.6, the exper.dat data file is stored physically as shown in Figure 12.5. For convenience, the character corresponding to each hexadecimal code is listed below the code. Although the actual code used for the EOF marker is system dependent, the hexadecimal codes 00 and 26 (Control Z) are commonly used because they have no equivalent character representation.

Binary Files[7]

An alternative to text files, where each character in the file is represented by a unique code, are binary files. Binary files store numerical values using the computer's internal numerical code. For example, assume that the computer stores numbers internally using 16 bits in the two's complement format described in Section 1.7. Using this format the decimal number 8 is represented as the binary number 0000 0000 0000 1000, the decimal number 12 as 0000 0000 0000 1100, and the decimal number 497 as 0000 0001 1111 1011.

The advantages of using this format are that no intermediary conversions are required for storing or retrieving the data, and the resulting file usually requires less storage space than its text counterpart. The disadvantages are that the file can no longer be visually inspected using a text editing program or transferred between computers that use different internal number representations.

The explicit selection of a binary file is made by adding the letter b after the mode ("rb", "wb", "ab", etc.) as the second argument in the fopen() function call. For example, the function call

```
fopen("exper.bin", "wb")
```

opens the file named exper.bin as an binary file. Binary files require using the fread() and fwrik() functions rather than the formatted fscanf() and fprintf() functions.

If the data previously stored in the text file by Program 12.12 where written to a binary file, the file structure illustrated in Figure 12.6 would be produced. In

---

FIGURE 12.5   The exper.dat **File as Stored by the Computer**

20 31 20 20 20 20 38 0D 0A 20 32 20 20 20 31 32 0D 0A 20 33 20 20 34 39 37 0D 0A 00

    1   8 CR LF   2   1 2 CR LF   3   4 9 7 CR LF EOF

---

[7]This topic assumes that you are familiar with the computer storage concepts presented in Section 1.7.

FIGURE 12.6 The `exper.bin` **File as Stored by the Computer**

Header	1st Val.	2nd Val.	Trailer	
00 00 00 10	00 00 00 01	00 00 00 08	00 00 00 10 ◀	1st Record
00 00 00 10	00 00 00 02	00 00 00 0C	00 00 00 10 ◀	2nd Record
00 00 00 10	00 00 00 03	00 00 01 F1	00 00 00 10 ◀	3rd Record
00 00 00 00 ◀	End of File Marker Record			

---

this figure hexadecimal values are used to indicate the actual binary values that are stored. Although the figure separates the file's records into individual lines to distinguish individual items in each record, the file is actually stored as a consecutive sequence of codes. As shown in the figure, each record in a binary file is preceded by a header value and followed by a trailer value. The values in the header and trailer are always equal and contain the number of bytes in the record (each hexadecimal value is 1 byte in length; review Section 1.7 for a description of a byte). For example, the first record contains 16 bytes, which is indicated by the hexadecimal value 10. Between each header and trailer value are the record's data items. As indicated in Figure 12.6, each record contains two integer values, with each integer stored using 4 bytes (32 bits). The hexadecimal values shown on the first line correspond to the decimal numbers 1 and 8, the values on the second line to the decimal numbers 2 and 12, and the values on the third line to the decimal numbers 3 and 497. These are the same values previously illustrated in Figure 12.4 using the ASCII code. Although the number of bytes used to store an integer is system dependent, the layout of all binary files corresponds to the form shown in Figure 12.6.

The fact that a file uses binary storage codes does not preclude its contents being displayed in text form. The file is simply read in its binary form using the `fread()` function and then displayed using `printf()` function calls.

Exercises 12.5

1. Write individual `fopen()` function calls to explicitly open files having the following characteristics:

   a. A text file named `test.dat` that is to be assigned the internal filename `in_file`. The file is to be opened for reading.

   b. A text file named `descri` that is to be assigned the internal filename `descrip`. The file is to be opened for writing.

   c. A text file named `names` that is to be assigned the internal name `out_file`. The file is to be opened for appending.

   d. A binary file named `types` that is to be assigned the internal filename `disk-type`. The file is to be opened for reading.

   e. A binary file named `codes` that is to be assigned the internal filename `idcodes`. The file is to be opened for writing.

   f. A binary file named `balance.dat` that is to be assigned the internal filename `balances`. The file is to be opened for appending.

2. Redo Exercise 1 but omit all explicit file type designations from the `fopen()` function call when the desired file type is correctly selected by C's default values.

3. Write, compile, and run a C program that writes the four floating points 92.65, 88.72, 77.46, and 82.93 to a text file named `result`. After writing the data to the

file, your program should read the data from the file, determine the average of the four numbers read, and display the average. Verify the output produced by your program by manually calculating the average of the four input numbers.

4. If your system supports binary files, redo Exercise 3 using a binary file.

5. a. Write, compile, and execute a C program that creates a text file named `points` and writes the following numbers to the file:

```
    6.3   8.2 18.25 24.32        ◄───────────────── 1st record
    4.0   4.0 10.0  -5.0         ◄───────────────── 2nd record
   -2.0   5.0  4.0   5.0         ◄───────────────── 3rd record
```

   b. Using the data in the `points` file created in Exercise 5a, write, compile, and run a C program that reads each record and interprets the first and second numbers in each record as the coordinates of one point and the third and fourth numbers as the coordinates of a second point. Using the formulas given in Exercises 1 and 2 of Section 3.5, have your program compute and display the slope and midpoint of the two points entered. Your program should use a `while` statement that uses the EOF marker as a sentinel.

6. If your system supports binary files, redo Exercise 5 using a binary file.

7. a. Write, compile, and run a C program that creates a text file named `grades` and writes the following numbers to the file:

```
100, 100, 100, 100
100,  0, 100,  0
 86, 83,  89, 94
 78, 59,  77, 85
 89, 92,  81, 88
```

   b. Using the data in the `grades` file created in Exercise 7a, write, compile, and run a C program that reads each line in the `grades` file, computes the average for each line, and displays the average.

8. Redo Exercise 3 using a binary file.

12.6 ENRICHMENT STUDY: WRITING CONTROL CODES

In addition to responding to the codes for letters, digits, and special punctuation symbols, which are collectively referred to as printable characters, physical device files such as printers and CRT screens can also respond to a small set of control codes. These codes, which convey control information to the physical device, have no equivalent characters that can be displayed, and are called nonprintable characters.

Two of these codes, which are extremely useful in applications, are the formfeed and bell control codes. When the form-feed control code is sent to a printer, the printer ejects a page of paper and begins printing on the next sheet of paper. If you take care to align the printer to the top of a new page when printing begins, the form-feed control character can be used as an equivalent "top-of-page" command. When the equivalent clear code is sent to a CRT display, the screen is cleared of all text and the cursor is positioned at the left-hand corner of the screen.

Sending control codes to an output device is done in a manner similar to sending a printable character to a file. Recall that sending a printable character to a file requires two pieces of information: the filename and the character being written to the file. For example, the statement `putc('a',out_file);` causes the letter a to be written to the file named `out_file`. Instead of including the actual letter as an argument to `putc()`, we can substitute the numerical storage code for the letter. For computers that use the ASCII code, this amounts to substituting the equivalent ASCII numerical value for the appropriate letter. Referring to Appendix B, we see that in the ASCII code the value for a is 97 as a decimal number, 61 as a hexadecimal number, and 141 as an octal number. Any one of these numerical values can be used in place of the letter a in the previous `putc` function call. Thus, the following four statements are all equivalent.

```
putc('a',out_file);
putc(97, out_file);
putc(0x61 out_file);
putc('\141',out_file);
```

Note that in each of these statements we have adhered to the notation used by C in identifying decimal and hexadecimal numbers. A number with no leading zero is considered a decimal number and a number with a leading 0x is considered a hexadecimal value. Octal character codes must, however, be preceded by a backslash and enclosed in single apostrophes. Since the backslash identifies the number as an octal value, the normal leading zero required of octal values can be omitted. Since most control codes, by convention, are listed as octal values with the traditional leading zero, we will retain this convention in all further examples.

The importance of substituting the numerical code for the letter is only realized when a control code rather than a character code must be sent. Since no equivalent character exists for control codes, the actual code for the command must be used. Although each computer can have its own code for clearing the CRT screen, the bell code and the printer form-feed code are fairly universal. To activate the bell, the octal code 07 is used. The octal form-feed code for most printers is 014. Thus, if `out_file` has been opened as the printer in write mode, the statement

```
putc('\014',out_file);
```

causes the printer to eject the current page. Similarly, if `scrn` has been opened as the CRT screen in write mode, the statement

```
putc('\07',scrn);
```

causes the bell to be activated for a short "beep."

For personal computers and compatible machines, the clear code for the CRT screen is a coded value. For your computer, check the manual for the CRT screen to obtain the proper clear-screen control code. You must also check the name by which your computer "knows" the printer and CRT screen. For IBM personal computers the printer has the name `prn` and the CRT screen the name `con` (short for console). Program 12.13 illustrates the use of control codes to eject a page of paper from the printer and alert the user with a "beep" if the printer is not turned on. Using `#define` commands, the appropriate codes have been equated to more readable symbolic names.

The `if-else` statement in Program 12.13 is used to ensure that the printer has been opened and is ready for output. The named constants BELL and TOPOFPAGE can be used freely within the program because they have been properly defined (see Section 3.5). Each of these constants is sent to the printer using a `putc` function call. Since the CRT screen is the standard output device

PROGRAM 12.13

```c
#include <stdio.h>
#define BELL '\07'
#define TOPOFPAGE '\014' /* page eject code */
char *printer = "prn";

void main(void)
{
  FILE *print;

  print = fopen(printer, "w");
  if(print == (FILE *) NULL)   /* check that the file has been opened */
  {
    putc(BELL,stdout);
    printf("The printer cannot be opened for output.\n");
    printf("Please check that the printer is on and ready for use.\n");
  }
  else
    putc(TOPOFPAGE,print);
}
```

for the computer used to run Program 12.13, the CRT did not have to be opened as a new file. Instead, the filename stdout was used to send the BELL constant to the screen.

In addition to the BELL code, all CRT screens have control codes to position the cursor directly at different screen locations. This enables the programmer to place messages anywhere on the screen. Since these codes differ for various CRT models, you should check the manual for your computer to determine the proper codes. Additionally, many C compilers for personal computers include standard library functions that provide the same cursor-positioning capabilities.

12.7 COMMON PROGRAMMING ERRORS

Four programming errors are common when using files. An extremely common error is to use the file's external name in place of the internal filename when accessing the file. The only standard library function that uses the data file's external name is the fopen() function. All the other standard functions presented in this chapter require the variable name assigned to the file when it was initially opened.

The next error is to omit the filename altogether. Programmers used to the scanf() and printf() functions that access the standard input and output devices, where a filename is not required, sometimes forget to include a file pointer when accessing data files.

A third error occurs when using the EOF marker to detect the end of a file. Any variable used to accept the EOF must be declared as an integer variable, not a character variable. For example, if ch has been declared as a character variable the expression

```c
while ( (c = getc(in_file)) != EOF)
```

produces an infinite loop. This occurs because a character variable can never take on an EOF code. EOF is an integer value that has no character representation. This ensures that the EOF code can never be confused with any legitimate character encountered as normal data in the file. To terminate the above expression, the variable ch must be declared as an integer variable.

The last error concerns the offset argument sent to the function fseek(). This offset must be a long integer constant or variable. Any other value passed to fseek() can result in an unpredictable effect.

12.8 CHAPTER REVIEW

Key Terms

binary file	ftell()
data file	internal filename
external filename	logical filename
fclose()	physical filename
file access	random access
file organization	sequential organization
fopen()	text file
fseek()	

Summary

1. A data file is any collection of data stored together in an external storage medium under a common name.

2. Data files are opened using the fopen() library function. This function connects a file's external name with an internal filename. After the file is opened, all subsequent accesses to the file require the internal filename.

3. A file can be opened for reading, writing, or appending. A file opened for writing creates a new file or erases any existing file having the same name as the opened file. A file opened for appending makes an existing file available for data to be added to the end of the file. If the file does not exist, it is created. A file opened for reading makes an existing file's data available for input.

4. An internal filename must be declared as a FILE. This means that a declaration of the type

```
FILE *file-name;
```

must be included with the declarations in which the file is opened. file-name can be replaced with any user-selected variable name. Additionally, the header file stdio.h must be included within a program that uses files.

5. In addition to any files opened within a function, the standard files stdin, stdout, and stderr are automatically opened when a program is run. stdin is the name of the physical file used for data entry by scanf(); stdout is the name of the physical file device used for data display by printf(); and stderr is the name of the physical file device used for displaying system error messages.

6. Data files can be accessed randomly using the rewind(), fseek(), and ftell() functions.

7. Table 12.7 lists the standard file library functions.

TABLE 12.7 Standard File Library Functions

Function Name	Purpose
fopen	Open or create a file
fclose	Close a file
fgetc and getc	Character input
getchar	Character input from stdin
fgets	String input
gets	String input from stdin
fscanf	Formatted input
scanf	Formatted input from stdin
fputc and putc	Character output
putchar	Character output to stdout
fputs	String output
puts	String output to stdout
fprintf	Formatted output
printf	Formatted output to stdout
fseek	File positioning
rewind	File positioning
ftell	Position reporting

Exercises

1. You are to write a C program that allows the user to enter the following information from the keyboard for each of up to 20 students in a class:

   Name   Exam 1 Grade   Exam 2 Grade   Homework Average   Final Exam Score

   For each student your program should first calculate a final grade, using the formula:

   Final Grade = 0.20 * Exam 1 + 0.20 * Exam 2 + 0.35 * Homework
                 + 0.25 * Final Exam

   and assigns a letter grade on the basis of 90—100 = A, 80—89 = B, 70—79 = C, 60—69 = D, less than 60 = F. All of the information, including the final grade and the letter grade, should then be displayed and written to a file.

2. Write a C program that permits a user to enter the following information about your small company's 10 employees, sorts the information in decreasing value by years with the company, and writes the sorted information to a file.

   ID No.   Sex (M/F)   Hourly Wage   Years with the Company

3. Write a C program that allows you to read the file created in Exercise 2, change the hourly wage or years for any employee, and create a new, updated file.

4. Write a C program that reads the file created in Exercise 2, one record at a time, asks for the number of hours worked by that employee each month, and calculates and displays each employee's total pay for the month.

5. a. You have collected information about cities in your state. You decide to store each city's name, population, and the name of its mayor in a file.

Write a C program to accept the data for a number of cities from the keyboard and store the data in a file in the order in which they are entered.

b. Read the file created in Exercise 5a, sort the data alphabetically by city name, and display the data.

6. A bank's customer records are to be stored in a file and read into a set of arrays so that an individual's records can be accessed randomly by account number. Either create the file by entering five customer records, with each record consisting of an integer account number (starting with account number 1000), a first name having a maximum of 10 characters, a last name having a maximum of 15 characters, and a floating-point balance.

Once the file is created, write a C program that reads the records into 4 separate arrays. The starting address of any element in the account array can then be calculated as the address of the first record in the array plus (account number - 1000) * sizeof(sint). Using this information, your program should request a user input account number and display the corresponding name and account balance.

7. Write and test a function named extract() that extracts m characters of string s2, starting at location n, and places the characters in string s2. The header line for the function should be extract(char *s1, char *s2, int n, int m). For example, if string s2 is "Life is a bowl of cherries", the call extract(s1, s2, 11, 16) should place the characters "bowl of cherries" into string s1. Note that the starting position for counting purposes is that the first character is in position one. Be sure to close off the returned string with a '\0' and make sure that the string is defined in the calling function to be large enough to accept the extracted values.

8. Either create an ASCII a file with the following data or use the file named shipped.dat on the diskette provided with this text: The headings are not part of the file but indicate what the data represents.

Shipped Date	Tracking Number	Part Number	First Name	Last Name	Company
04/12/96	D50625	74444	James	Lehoff	Rotech Systems
04/12/96	D60752	75255	Janet	Lezar	Rotech Systems
04/12/96	D40295	74477	Bill	McHenry	Rotech Systems
04/12/96	D23745	74470	Diane	Kaiser	Rotech Systems
04/12/96	D50892	75155	Helen	Richardson	NipNap Inc.

The format of each line in the file is identical with fixed length fields defined as follows:

Field Position	Field Name	Starting Col. No.	Ending Col. No.	Field Length
1	Shipped Date	1	8	8
2	Tracking Number	12	17	6
3	Part Number	22	26	5
4	First Name	31	35	5
5	Last Name	39	38	10
6	Company	51	64	14

Using this data file you are to write a C program that reads the file; extracts the date, part number, first initial, last name, and company name; and produces a report listing the extracted data. (*Hint:* Use the `extract` function created in Exercise 7.)

9. Modify the program written for Exercise 8 so that the report is in increasing part number order. Do this by either using the `extract` function developed in Exercise 7 and using string comparisons or convert the part number to an integer using in-memory string conversion and compare integer values. For sorting purposes use the selection sort presented in Section 8.5.

13 | Records as Data Structures

An array allows access to a list or table of data of the same data type using a single variable name. At times, however, we may want to store information of varying types—such as a string name, an integer part number, and a real price together in one structure. A structure that stores different types of data under a single variable name is called a *data record*, or simply a *record*.

To make the discussion more tangible, consider the data items typically used in preparing mailing labels, as illustrated in Figure 13.1. Each of the individual data items listed in the figure is an entity by itself, which is called a *data field*. Taken together, all the data fields form a single unit, a record, representing a natural organization of the data for a mailing label. In C, a record is referred to as a *structure*.

Although there could be thousands of names and addresses in a complete mailing list, the form of each mailing label, or its structure, is identical. In dealing

---

FIGURE 13.1 **Typical Mailing List Components**

          Name:
          Street Address:
          City:
          State:
          Zip Code:

FIGURE 13.2   The Contents of a Structure

Rhona Bronson-Karp
614 Freeman Street
Orange
NJ
07052

---

with structures it is important to distinguish between the form of the structure and the data content of the structure.

The form of a structure consists of the symbolic names, data types, and arrangement of individual data fields in the structure. The content of a structure refers to the actual data stored in the symbolic names. Figure 13.2 shows acceptable contents for the structure illustrated in Figure 13.1.

In this chapter, we describe the C statements required to create, fill, use, and pass records between functions.

13.1 SINGLE RECORDS

Using a record structure requires the same two steps needed for using any variable. First the record structure must be declared. Then specific values can be assigned to the individual record elements. Declaring a record requires listing the data types, data names, and arrangement of data items. For example, the definition

```
struct
{
  int month;
  int day;
  int year;
} birth;
```

gives the form of a record structure called `birth` and reserves storage for the individual data items listed in the structure. The `birth` structure consists of three data items or fields, which are called *members* of the structure.

Assigning actual data values to the data items of a structure is called populating the structure, and is a relatively straightforward procedure. Each member of a structure is accessed by giving both the structure name and individual data item name, separated by a period. Thus, `birth.month` refers to the first member of the birth structure, `birth.day` refers to the second member of the structure, and `birth.year` refers to the third member. Program 13.1 illustrates assigning values to the individual members of the `birth` structure (observe that the `printf()` statement call has been continued across two lines).

PROGRAM 13.1   Defining and Populating a Structure

```c
#include <stdio.h>
void main(void)
{
  struct
  {
    int month;
    int day;
    int year;
  } birth;

  birth.month = 12;
  birth.day = 28;
  birth.year = 72;

  printf("My birth date is %d/%d/%d\n",
          birth.month, birth.day, birth.year);
}
```

The output produced by Program 13.1 is:

```
My birth date is 12/28/72
```

The spacing of the structure definition used in Program 13.1 is not rigid. For example, the birth structure could just as well have been defined

```
struct {int month; int day; int year} birth;
```

Also, as with all C definition statements, multiple variables can be defined in the same statement. For example, the definition statement

```
struct {int month; int day; int year} birth, current;
```

creates two structures having the same form. The members of the first structure are referenced by the individual names `birth.month`, `birth.day`, and `birth.year`, while the members of the second structure are referenced by the names `current.month`, `current.day`, and `current.year`. Notice that the form of this particular structure definition statement is identical to the form used in defining any program variable: The data type is followed by a list of variable names.

A commonly used modification when defining structures is listing the form of the structure with no following variable names. In this case, however, the list of structure members must be preceded by a *tag name*. For example, in the declaration

```
struct Date
{
  int month;
  int day;
  int year;
};
```

the term `Date` is a tag name. By increasingly common usage, tag names are identified using an initial capital letter, as in the name `Date`. Although the initial capital letter is not required, we will adhere to this convention.

The declaration for the Date structure provides a *template* for the structure without actually reserving any storage locations. As such it is not a definition statement. The template presents the form of a structure called Date by describing how individual data items are arranged within the structure. Actual storage for the members of the structure is reserved only when specific variable names are assigned. For example, the definition statement

```
struct Date birth, current;
```

reserves storage for two structures named birth and current, respectively. Each of these individual structures has the form previously declared for the Date structure. In effect, the declaration for Date creates a structure type named Date. The variables birth and current are then defined to be of this structure type.

Like all variable declarations, a structure may be declared globally or locally. Program 13.2 illustrates the global declaration of a Date structure. Internal to main(), the variable birth is defined to use the global template.

PROGRAM 13.2

```
#include <stdio.h>
struct Date
{
   int month;
   int day;
   int year;
};

void main(void)
{
   struct Date birth;

   birth.month = 12;
   birth.day = 28;
   birth.year = 72;

   printf("My birth date is %d/%d/%d\n",
          birth.month, birth.day, birth.year);
}
```

The output produced by Program 13.2 is identical to the output produced by Program 13.1.

The initialization of structures follows the same rules as for the initialization of arrays: External and local structures may be initialized by following the definition with a list of initializers.[1] For example, the definition statement

```
struct Date birth = {12, 28, 72};
```

---

[1] This is true for ANSI C compilers. For non-ANSI C compilers the reserved word static must be placed before the reserved word struct for initialization within the declaration statement.

can be used to replace the first four statements internal to `main()` in Program 13.2. Notice that the initializers are separated by commas, not semicolons, and are used to separate member names in the declaration of the structure.

The individual members of a structure are not restricted to integer data types, as illustrated by the `Date` structure. Any valid C data type can be used. For example, consider an employee record consisting of the following data items:

Name:

Identification Number:

Regular Pay Rate:

Overtime Pay Rate:

A suitable declaration for these data items is:

```
struct Pay_rec
{
  char name[20];
  int id_num;
  float reg_rate;
  float ot_rate;
};
```

Once the template for `Pay_rec` is declared, a specific structure using the `Pay_rec` template can be defined and initialized. For example, the definition

```
struct Pay_rec employee = {"H. Price",12387,15.89,25.50};
```

creates a structure named `employee` using the `Pay_rec` template. The individual members of `employee` are initialized with the respective data listed between braces in the definition statement.

Notice that a single structure is simply a convenient method for combining and storing related items under a common name. Although a single structure is useful in explicitly identifying the relationship among its members, the individual members could be defined as separate variables. The real advantage to using structures is only realized when the same template is used in a list many times over. Creating lists with the same structure template is the topic of the next section.

Before leaving single structures, it is worth noting that the individual members of a structure can be any valid data type, including both arrays and structures. An array of characters was used as a member of the employee structure defined previously. Accessing an element of a member array requires giving the structure's name, followed by a period, followed by the array designation. For example, `employee.name[4]` refers to the fifth character in the `employee.name` array.

Including a structure within a structure follows the same rules for including any data type in a structure. For example, assume that a structure is to consist of a name and a date of birth, where a `Date` structure has been declared as:

```
struct Date
{
  int month;
  int day;
  int year;
};
```

A suitable definition of a structure that includes a name and a `Date` structure is:

```
                              struct
                              {
                                char name[20];
                                struct Date birth;
                              } person;
```

Notice that in declaring the `Date` structure, the term `Date` is a structure tag name. A tag name always appears before the braces in the declaration statement and identifies a structure template. In defining the `person` structure, `person` is the name of a specific structure, not a structure tag name. The same is true of the variable named `birth`. This is the name of a specific structure having the form of `Date`. Individual members in the `person` structure are accessed by preceding the desired member with the structure name followed by a period. For example, `person.birth.month` refers to the `month` variable in the `birth` structure contained in the `person` structure.

Exercises 13.1

1. Declare a structure template named `s_temp` for each of the following records:

    a. A student record consisting of a student identification number, number of credits completed, and cumulative grade-point average

    b. A student record consisting of a student's name, date of birth, number of credits completed, and cumulative grade-point average

    c. A mailing list consisting of the items previously illustrated in Figure 13.1

    d. A stock record consisting of the stock's name, the price of the stock, and the date of purchase

    e. An inventory record consisting of an integer part number, part description, number of parts in inventory, and an integer reorder number

2. For the individual structure templates declared in Exercise 1, define a suitable structure variable name, and initialize each structure with the appropriate following data:

    a. `Identification Number: 4672`
       `Number of Credits Completed: 68`
       `Grade-Point Average: 3.01`

    b. `Name: Rhona Karp`
       `Date of Birth: 8/4/60`
       `Number of Credits Completed: 96`
       `Grade-Point Average: 3.89`

    c. `Name: Kay Kingsley`
       `Street Address: 614 Freeman`
       `Street`
       `City: Indianapolis`
       `State: IN`
       `Zip Code: 07030`

    d. `Stock: IBM`
       `Price Purchased: 134.5`
       `Date Purchased: 10/1/86`

    e. `Part Number: 16879`
       `Description: Battery`
       `Number in Stock: 10`
       `Reorder Number: 3`

◆ **A C L O S E R   L O O K** ◆

Homogeneous and Heterogeneous Data Structures
Both arrays and records are structured data types. The difference between these two data structures is the types of elements they contain. An array is a *homogeneous* data structure, which means that each of its components must be of the same type. A record is a *heterogeneous* data structure, which means that each of its components can be of different data types. Thus, an array of records would be a homogeneous data structure whose elements are of the same heterogenous type.

3. a. Write a C program that prompts a user to input the current month, day, and year. Store the data entered in a suitably defined record and display the date in an appropriate manner.

   b. Modify the program written in Exercise 3a to use a record that accepts the current time in hours, minutes, and seconds.

4. Write a C program that uses a structure for storing the name of a stock, its estimated earnings per share, and its estimated price-to-earnings ratio. Have the program prompt the user to enter these items for five different stocks, each time using the same structure to store the entered data. When the data has been entered for a particular stock, have the program compute and display the anticipated stock price based on the entered earnings and price-per-earnings values. For example, if a user entered the data XYZ 1.56 12, the anticipated price for a share of XYZ stock is (1.56)*(12) = $18.72.

5. Write a C program that accepts a user-entered time in hours and minutes. Have the program calculate and display the time one minute later.

6 a. Write a C program that accepts a user-entered date. Have the program calculate and display the date of the next day. For purposes of this exercise, assume that all months consist of 30 days.

   b. Modify the program written in Exercise 6a to account for the actual number of days in each month.

13.2 ARRAYS OF RECORDS

The real power of record structures is realized when the same structure is used for lists of data. For example, assume that the data shown in Figure 13.3 must be processed. Clearly, the employee numbers can be stored together in three separate, parallel arrays. In using such arrays the first array would store the employee numbers as a list of integers, the second array would store the names as a list of characters, and the third array would store the pay rates as either floating-point or double-precision numbers. In organizing the data in this fashion, each column in Figure 13.3 is considered as a separate list, which is stored in its own array. Using arrays, the correspondence between items for each individual employee is maintained by storing an employee's data in the same array position in each array.

The separation of the complete list into three individual arrays is unfortunate, since all of the items relating to a single employee constitute a natural organization of data into records, as illustrated in Figure 13.4.

FIGURE 13.3 A List of Employee Data

Employee Number	Employee Name	Employee Pay Rate
32479	Abrams, B.	6.72
33623	Bohm, P.	7.54
34145	Donaldson, S.	5.56
35987	Ernst, T.	5.43
36203	Gwodz,K.	8.72
36417	Hanson, H.	7.64
37634	Monroe, G.	5.29
38321	Price, S.	9.67
39435	Robbins, L.	8.50
39567	Williams, B.	7.20

Using a data structure, the integrity of the data organization as a record can be maintained and reflected in any program using the data structure. Under this approach, the list illustrated in Figure 13.4 is processed as a single array of 10 structures.

FIGURE 13.4 A List of Records

	Employee Number	Employee Name	Employee Pay Rate
1st record ⟶	32479	Abrams, B.	6.72
2nd record ⟶	33623	Bohm, P.	7.54
3rd record ⟶	34145	Donaldson, S.	5.56
4th record ⟶	35987	Ernst, T.	5.43
5th record ⟶	36203	Gwodz, K.	8.72
6th record ⟶	36417	Hanson, H.	7.64
7th record ⟶	37634	Monroe, G.	5.29
8th record ⟶	38321	Price, S.	9.67
9th record ⟶	39435	Robbins, L.	8.50
10th record ⟶	39567	Williams, B.	7.20

```
  ┌─────────────────────────────────────────────────────────────┐
  ◄►        T I P S   F R O M   T H E   P R O S               ◄►
  └─────────────────────────────────────────────────────────────┘
```

Using a `typedef` Statement

A commonly used programming technique when dealing with structure declarations is to use a `typedef` statement. This provides a simple method for creating a new and typically shorter name for an existing structure type (*see section 15.1 for a complete description of* `typedef`). For example, assuming the following global structure declaration has been made

```
struct Date
{
  int month;
  int day;
  int year;
};
```

then the `typedef` statement

```
typedef struct Date DATE
```

makes the name `DATE` a synonym for the terms `struct Date`. Now, whenever a variable is to be declared as a `struct Date`, the term `DATE` can be used instead. Thus, for example, the declaration

```
struct Date a, b, c;
```

can be replaced by the statement

```
DATE a, b, c;
```

Similarly, if a record structure named `Pay_rec` had been declared and the statement

```
typedef struct Pay_rec PAYRECS
```

had been made, the declaration

```
PAYRECS employee[5];
```

could be used in place of the longer declaration

```
struct Pay-rec employee[5];
```

By convention all `typedef` names are written in uppercase but this is not mandatory. The names used in a `typedef` statement can be any name that conforms to C's identifier naming rules.

Declaring an array of structures is the same as declaring an array of any other variable type. For example, if the template `Pay_rec` is declared as

```
struct Pay_rec
{
  long idnum;
  char name[20];
  float rate;
};
```

then an array of 10 such structures can be defined as

```
struct Pay_rec employee[10];
```

This definition statement constructs an array of 10 elements, each of which is a structure of the type `Pay_rec`. Notice that the creation of an array of 10 structures has the same form as the creation of any other array. For example, creating an array of 10 integers named employee requires the declaration

```
int employee[10];
```

In this declaration the data type is integer, while in the former declaration for employee the data type is a structure using the `Pay_rec` template.

Once an array of structures is declared, a particular data item is referenced by giving the position of the desired structure in the array followed by a period and the appropriate structure member. For example, the variable employee[0].rate references the `rate` member of the first employee structure in the employee array. Including structures as elements of an array permits a list of records to be processed using standard array programming techniques. Program 13.3 displays the first five employee records illustrated in Figure 13.4.

PROGRAM 13.3

```c
#include <stdio.h>
#define NUMRECS 5
struct Pay_rec
{
  long id;
  char name[20];
  float rate;
};           /* construct a global template */

void main(void)
{
  int i;
  struct Pay_rec employee[NUMRECS] =
  {
    { 32479, "Abrams, B.", 6.72 },
    { 33623, "Bohm, P.", 7.54},
    { 34145, "Donaldson, S.", 5.56},
    { 35987, "Ernst, T.", 5.43 },
    { 36203, "Gwodz, K.", 8.72 }
  };

  for ( i = 0; i < NUMRECS; i++)
    printf("%ld %-20s %4.2f\n",employee[i].id,
                    employee[i].name,employee[i].rate);
}
```

The output displayed by Program 13.3 is:

```
32479 Abrams,    B. 6.72
33623 Bohm,      P. 7.54
34145 Donaldson, S. 5.56
35987 Ernst,     T. 5.43
36203 Gwodz,     K. 8.72
```

In reviewing Program 13.3, notice the initialization of the array of structures. Although the initializers for each structure have been enclosed in inner braces, these are not strictly necessary because all members have been initialized. The `%-20s` format included in the `printf()` function call forces each name to be displayed left justified in a field of 20 spaces.

Exercises 13.2

1. Define arrays of 100 structures for each of the structures described in Exercise 1 of the previous section.

2. a. Using the template:

   ```
   struct Mon_days
   {
     char name[10];
     int days;
   };
   ```

   define an array of 12 structures of type `Mon_days`. Name the array `convert[]`, and initialize the array with the names of the 12 months in a year and the number of days in each month.

   b. Include the array created in Exercise 2a in a program that displays the names and number of days in each month.

3. Using the structure defined in Exercise 2a, write a C program that accepts a month from a user in numerical form and displays the name of the month and the number of days in the month. Thus, in response to an input of 3, the program would display `March has 31 days`.

4. a. Declare a single structure template suitable for an employee record of the type illustrated below:

Number	Name	Rate	Hours
3462	Jones	4.62	40
6793	Robbins	5.83	38
6985	Smith	5.22	45
7834	Swain	6.89	40
8867	Timmins	6.43	35
9002	Williams	4.75	42

   b. Using the template declared in Exercise 4a, write a C program that interactively accepts the above data into an array of six structures. Once the data has been entered, the program should create a payroll report listing each employee's name, number, and gross pay. Include the total gross pay of all employees at the end of the report. Assume that all hours over 40 are paid at a rate of time and a half.

5. a. Declare a single structure template suitable for a car record of the type illustrated:

Car Number	Miles Driven	Gallons Used
25	1450	62
36	3240	136
44	1792	76
52	2360	105
68	2114	67

   b. Using the template declared for Exercise 5a, write a C program that interactively accepts the above data into an array of five structures. Once the data has been entered, the program should create a report listing each car number and the miles per gallon achieved by the car. At the end of the report include the average miles per gallon achieved by the complete fleet of cars.

13.3 RECORD STRUCTURES AS FUNCTION ARGUMENTS

Individual record structure members may be passed to a function in the same manner as any scalar variable. For example, given the structure definition

```
struct
{
    int id_num;
    double pay_rate;
    double hours;
} emp;
```

the statement:

```
display(emp.id_num);
```

passes a copy of the structure member `emp.id_num` to a function named `display()`. Similarly, the statement:

```
calc_pay(emp.pay_rate,emp.hours);
```

passes copies of the values stored in structure members `emp.pay_rate` and `emp.hours` to the function `calc_pay()`. Both functions, `display()` and `calc_pay`, must declare the correct data types of their respective arguments. Assuming `display()` returns no value and `calc_pay` returns a double, the following are suitable prototypes for these two functions:

```
void display(int);
double calc_pay(double, double);
```

Complete copies of all members of a structure can also be passed to a function by including the name of the structure as an argument to the called function. For example, the function call

```
calc_net(emp);
```

passes a copy of the complete `emp` structure to `calc_net()`. Internal to `calc_net()`, an appropriate declaration must be made to receive the structure. Program 13.4 declares a global template for an `Employee` record. This template is then used by both the `main()` and `calc_net()` functions to define specific structures with the names `emp` and `temp`, respectively.

The output produced by Program 13.4 is:

```
The net pay for employee 6782 is $361.66
```

In reviewing Program 13.4, observe that both `main()` and `calc_net()` use the same global template to define their individual structures. The structure defined in `main()` and the structure defined in `calc_net()` are two completely different structures. Any changes made to the local `temp` structure in `calc_net()` are not reflected in the `emp` structure of `main()`. In fact, since both structures are local to their respective functions, the same structure name could have been used in both functions with no ambiguity.

PROGRAM 13.4

```c
#include <stdio.h>
struct Employee      /* declare a global template */
{
  int id_num;
  double pay_rate;
  double hours;
};

void main(void)
{
  struct Employee emp = {6782, 8.93, 40.5};
  double net_pay;
  double calc_net(struct Employee);    /* function prototype */

  net_pay = calc_net(emp);       /* pass copies of the values in emp */

  printf("The net pay for employee %d is $%6.2f\n",emp.id_num,net_pay);
}

double calc_net(struct Employee temp) /* temp is of data type struct Employee */
{
  return(temp.pay_rate * temp.hours);
}
```

When `calc_net()` is called by `main()`, copies of `emp`'s structure values are passed to the `temp` structure. `calc_net()` then uses two of the passed member values to calculate a number, which is returned to `main()`.

Although the structures in both `main()` and `calc_net()` use the same globally defined template, this is not strictly necessary. For example, the structure in `main()` could have been defined directly as:

```c
struct
{
  int id_num;
  double pay_rate;
  double hours;
}  emp = {46782, 8.93, 40.5};
```

Similarly, the structure in `calc_net()` could have been defined as:

```c
struct
{
  int id_num;
  double pay_rate;
  double hours;
} temp;
```

The global declaration of the `Employee` template provided in Program 13.4 is highly preferable to these latter two individual structure specifications because the global template centralizes the declaration of the structure's organization. Any change that must subsequently be made to the structure need only be made once to the global template. Making changes to individual structure definitions requires that all occurrences of the structure definition be located, in every function defining the structure. For larger programs this usually results in an error when a change to one of the structure definitions is inadvertently omitted.

An alternative to passing a copy of a structure is to pass the address of the structure. This, of course, allows the called function to make changes directly to the original structure. For example, referring to Program 13.4, the call to `calc_net()` can be modified to

calc_net(&emp);

In this call, an address is passed. To correctly store this address, `calc_net()` must declare the argument as a pointer. A suitable function definition for `calc_net()` is

calc_net(struct Employee *pt)

Here, the declaration for `pt` declares this argument as a pointer to a structure of type `Employee`. The pointer variable, `pt`, receives the starting address of a structure whenever `calc_net()` is called. Within `calc_net()`, this pointer is used to directly reference any member in the structure. For example, `(*pt).id_num` refers to the `id_num` member of the structure, `(*pt).pay_rate` refers to the `pay_rate` member of the structure, and `(*pt).hours` refers to the `hours` member of the structure. These relationships are illustrated in Figure 13.5.

The parentheses around the expression `*pt` in Figure 13.5 are necessary to initially access "the structure whose address is in `pt`." This is followed by a reference to access the desired member within the structure. In the absence of the parentheses, the structure member operator (.) takes precedence over the indirection operator. Thus, the expression `*pt.hours` is another way of writing `*(pt.hours)`, which would refer to "the variable whose address is in the `pt.hours` variable." This last expression clearly makes no sense because there is no structure named `pt` and `hours` does not contain an address.

FIGURE 13.5   A Pointer Can Be Used to Access Structure Members

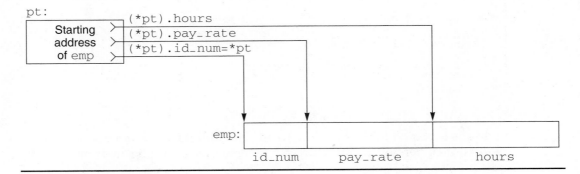

As illustrated in Figure 13.5, the starting address of the emp structure is also the address of the first member of the structure. Thus, the expressions *pt and (*pt).id_num both refer to the id_num member of the emp structure.

The use of pointers is so common with structures that a special notation exists for them. The general expression (*pointer).member can always be replaced with the notation pointer->member, where the -> operator is constructed using a minus sign followed by a right-facing arrow (greater-than symbol). Either expression can be used to locate the desired member. For example, the following expressions are equivalent:

>   (*pt).id_num can be replaced by pt->id_num
>
>   (*pt).pay_rate can be replaced by pt->pay_rate
>
>   (*pt).hours can be replaced by pt->hours

Program 13.5 illustrates passing a structure's address and using a pointer with the new notation to directly reference the structure.

The name of the pointer argument declared in Program 13.5 is, of course, selected by the programmer. When calc_net() is called, emp's starting

PROGRAM 13.5

```
#include <stdio.h>
struct Employee      /* declare a global template */
{
  int id_num;
  double pay_rate;
  double hours;
};

void main(void)
{
  struct Employee emp = {6782, 8.93, 40.5};
  double net_pay;
  double calc_net(struct Employee *);    /* function prototype */

  net_pay = calc_net(&emp);       /* pass copies of the values in emp */

  printf("The net pay for employee %d is $%6.2f\n",emp.id_num,net_pay);
}

double calc_net(struct Employee *pt) /* pt is a pointer to a structure of Employee type */
{
  return(pt->pay_rate * pt->hours);
}
```

address is passed to the function. Using this address as a reference point, individual members of the structure are accessed by including their names with the pointer.

FIGURE 13.6 Changing Pointer Addresses

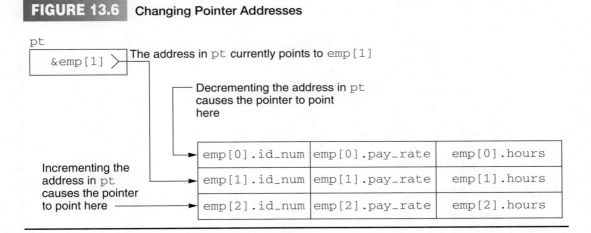

As with all C expressions that reference a variable, the increment and decrement operators can also be applied to structure references. For example, the expression

++pt->hours

adds one to the hours member of the emp structure. Since the -> operator has a higher priority than the increment operator, the hours member is accessed first and then the increment is applied.

Alternatively, the expression (++pt)>hours uses the prefix increment operator to increment the address in pt before the hours member is accessed. Similarly, the expression (pt++)->hours uses the postfix increment operator to increment the address in pt after the hours member is accessed. In both of these cases, however, there must be sufficient defined structures to ensure that the incremented pointers actually point to legitimate structures.

As an example, Figure 13.6 illustrates an array of three structures of type Employee. Assuming that the address of emp[1] is stored in the pointer variable pt, the expression ++pt changes the address in pt to the starting address of emp[2], while the expression --pt changes the address to point to emp[0].

Returning Structures

In practice, most structure handling functions receive direct access to a structure by passing the address of the structure to the function. Then any changes can be made directly by the function using pointer references. If you want to have a function return a separate structure, however, and your compiler supports this option, you must follow the same procedures for returning complete structures as for returning scalar values. These include both declaring the function appropriately and alerting any calling function to the type of structure being returned. For example, the function get_vals() in Program 13.6 returns a complete structure to main().

PROGRAM 13.6

```c
#include <stdio.h>
struct Employee         /* declare a global template */
{
  int id_num;
  double pay_rate;
  double hours;
};

void main(void)
{
  struct Employee emp;
  struct Employee get_vals(void);        /* function prototype */

  emp = get_vals();

  printf("The employee id number is %d\n", emp.id_num);
  printf("The employee pay rate is $%5.2f\n", emp.pay_rate);
  printf("The employee hours are %5.2f\n", emp.hours);
}

struct Employee get_vals(void)
{
  struct Employee starting;

  starting.id_num = 6789;
  starting.pay_rate = 16.25;
  starting.hours = 38.0;

  return(starting);
}
```

The following output is displayed when Program 13.6 is run:

```
The employee id number is 56789
The employee pay rate is $16.25
The employee hours are 38.00
```

Since the `get_vals()` function returns a structure, the function header for `get_vals()` must contain the type of structure being returned. Because `get_vals()` does not receive any arguments, the function header has no argument declarations and consists of the single line

```
struct Employee get_vals(void)
```

Within `get_vals()`, the variable `starting` is defined as a structure of the type to be returned. After values have been assigned to the `starting` structure, the structure values are returned by including the structure name within the parentheses of the return statement.

On the receiving side, `main()` must be alerted that the function `get_vals()` will be returning a structure. This is handled by including a function declaration for `get_vals()` in `main()`. Notice that these steps for returning a structure from a function are identical to the normal procedures for returning scalar data types previously described in Chapter 6. Structures, of course, can always be passed and directly altered using pointers.

Exercises 13.3

1. Write a C function named `days()` that determines the number of days from the turn of the century for any date passed as a structure. The `Date` structure should use the template

```
struct Date
{
  int month;
  int day;
  int year;
};
```

In writing the `days()` function, use the convention that all years have 360 days and each month consists of 30 days. The function should return the number of days for any `Date` structure passed to it. Make sure you declare the returned variable a long integer to reserve sufficient room for dates such as 12/19/89.

2. Write a function named `dif_days()` that calculates and returns the difference between two dates. Each date is passed to the function as a structure using the following global template:

```
struct Date
{
  int month;
  int day;
  int year;
};
```

The `dif_days()` function should make two calls to the `days()` function written for Exercise 1.

3. Rewrite the `days()` function written for Exercise 1 to receive a pointer to a `Date` structure, rather than a copy of the complete structure.

4. a. Write a C function named `larger()` that returns the later date of any two dates passed to it. For example, if the dates 10/9/62 and 11/3/62 are passed to `larger()`, the second date would be returned.

   b. Include the `larger()` function that was written for Exercise 4a in a complete program. Store the `Date` structure returned by `larger()` in a separate `Date` structure and display the member values of the returned `Date`.

5. a. Modify the function `days()` written for Exercise 1 to account for the actual number of days in each month. Assume, however, that each year contains 365 days (that is, do not account for leap years).

   b. Modify the function written for Exercise 5a to account for leap years.

6. a. Define an array of records for up to 10 factory employees, in which each record contains fields for name, age, social security number, hourly wage, and years with the company.

b. Write a C function that prompts a user for data for each field in the array of records defined in Exercise 6a and populates the array correctly.

c. Write a C function that accepts the array of records populated by the function written for Exercise 6b and displays each record in the array.

7. Rewrite Program 13.3 in Section 13.2 so that the display of structures in the array is accomplished by a function named `display`. (*Hint:* The function's argument is an array of type `struct Pay_rec`.)

13.4 FOCUS ON PROBLEM SOLVING

In this section we will focus on two problems that use and manipulate data structures. The first problem is concerned with obtaining data for a single record that is to be used in preparing a set of shipping instructions. The second problem addresses the processing of an array of records.

Problem 1: Populating and Processing a Data Structure

In this problem a customer will call in an order for bicycles, giving his or her name, and address, number of bicycles desired, and the kind of bicycle. For now, all bicycles on one order must be the same kind (a restriction removed in Exercise 3 at the end of this section). Mountain bikes cost $269.95 each and street bikes, $149.50. The total bill is to be calculated for the order. Additionally, based on the user's knowledge of the customer, the customer will be classified as either a good or bad credit risk. Based on the input data, the computer is to prepare shipping instructions listing the customer's name, address, number and type of bikes, and the total amount due. Based on the credit worthiness of the customer, the computer must indicate on the shipping instructions if this is a C.O.D. (cash on delivery) shipment or whether the customer will be billed separately.

Analyze the Problem for Input/Output Requirements   The input and output requirements of this problem are relatively simple. On the input side the items that must be obtained are:

1. Customer's name
2. Customer's address
3. Number of bicycles ordered
4. Type of bicycle (mountain or street)
5. Credit worthiness of the customer (good or bad).

For output a set of shipping instructions is to be generated. The instructions must contain the first four input items, the total cost of the order, and the type of billing. The total cost is obtained as the number of bicycles ordered (input item number 2) times the appropriate cost per bicycle, while the type of billing is determined by the credit worthiness of the customer (input item number 3). If the customer is credit worthy a bill will be sent; otherwise, the order requires cash payment on delivery.

Develop a Solution   The input data can be considered to be a record, with the five input items as fields within the record. Additionally, we will add a sixth field

---

FIGURE 13.7   Customer Record Layout

Field No.	Field Contents	Field Type
1	Customer name	character[50]
2	Customer address	character[50]
3	Bicycles ordered	integer
4	Bicycle type	character—M or S
5	Credit worthy	character—Y or N
6	Dollar value of order	float

---

to contain the total dollar value of the order. Figure 13.7 illustrates the data types that we will use for this customer record.

A suitable data structure for the record layout of Figure 13.7 is:

```
#define MAXSTRLEN 500
struct Customer
{
  char name[MAXSTRLEN];
  char address[MAXSTRLEN];
  int numbikes;
  char biketype;
  char goodrisk;
  float amount;
};
```

Having developed a suitable layout for the data, the design of the program is rather straightforward. The program will have to request the input data, determine the total dollar value of the order, and then print the shipping instructions. For this problem we will use one function to populate the structure and a second function to print the shipping instructions. Figure 13.8 presents a structure chart for this solution. In pseudocode the solution is:

Define the data structure.

Function main
  Populate the data using the function recvorder.
  Print the shipping instructions using the function shipslip.

Function recvorder
  Input data for name, address, number of bicycles, and type of bicycle.
  Calculate dollar value of order.

Function shipslip
  Print name, address, number of bicycles, and type of bicycle.
  Determine if this is a C.O.D. or separate billable order.
  Print the order type and the dollar value of the order.

FIGURE 13.8   Structure Chart

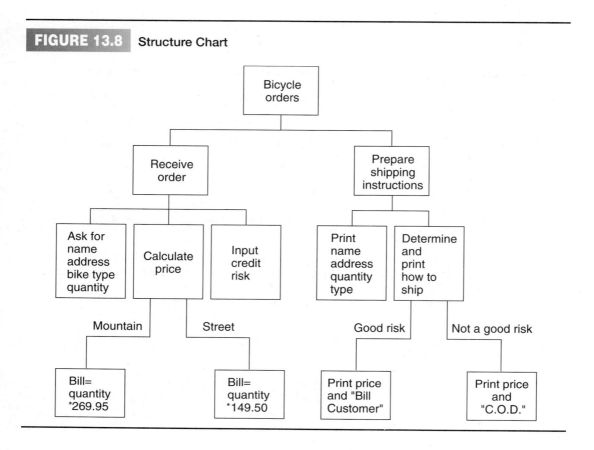

Code the Solution   The C code corresponding to our solution is contained in Program 13.7. Notice that the code uses named constants for the maximum string length and the prices of the bicycles. This is in keeping with good programming practice that "magic" numbers are not buried deep within the code where they will be hard to locate. Also notice that the function recvorder validates the data entered for bike and credit risk type before storing values in the appropriate data fields.

Notice in Program 13.7 that the function recvorder returns a single data structure to main, while shipslip receives a single data structure as its argument. Also notice that within each function, assignments and displayed values are performed for individual values in the fields, not for the entire record.

Test and Debug the Program   The errors most likely to be encountered in a program that uses records are those related to undefined or incompatible variables. Such errors occur when the user attempts to use a field name alone (such as numbikes), without specifying the record to which it belongs (record.numbikes). Also, it is a common mistake to attempt to use a record name without specifying the field (such as writing record instead of record.name).

Testing should include valid data as well as illegal values for record.biketype and record.goodrisk, and perhaps addresses that exceed

50 characters. Check some results to make sure that the final dollar amount of the bill is calculated correctly. Here is a sample run:

```
Enter customer information:
  Name: Jim Watson
  Address: 2 Hopper Lane, Rye NH 86662

How many Bicycles are ordered: 6
Type of Bicycle ordered:
   M Mountain
   S Street
Choose one (M or S): s

Is this customer a good risk (Y or N): y


       Shipping Instructions:
To: Jim Watson
    2 Hopper Lane, Rye NH 86662
Ship: 6 Street Bikes
by freight, and bill the customer $897.00
```

PROGRAM 13.7

```c
#include <stdio.h>
#include <ctype.h>
#define MAXSTRLEN 500
#define TRUE 1
#define FALSE 0
#define MPRICE 269.95      /* price of a mountain bike */
#define SPRICE 149.50      /* price of a street bike */
struct Customer
{
  char name[MAXSTRLEN];
  char address[MAXSTRLEN];
  char numbikes;
  char biketype;
  int goodrisk;
  float amount;
};

void main(void)
{
  struct Customer client;
  struct Customer recvorder(void);     /* function prototypes */
  void shipslip(struct Customer);
  client = recvorder();  /* enter the order */
  shipslip(client);        /* prepare shipping instructions */
}

struct Customer recvorder(void) /* return a structure of type Customer */
{
  struct Customer record; /* record is local to this function */
  char btype = 'N';
```

(continued on next page)

(continued from previous page)

```
  char risk = 'U';
  float price;
  printf("\nEnter customer information: ");
  printf("\n Name: ");
  gets(record.name);
  printf(" Address: ");
  gets(record.address);
  printf("\nHow many Bicycles are ordered: ");
  scanf("%d", &record.numbikes);
  printf("Type of Bicycle ordered:");
  while( !(btype == 'M' || btype == 'S') )
  {
    printf("\n M Mountain");
    printf("\n S Street");
    printf("\nChoose one (M or S): ");
    scanf("\n%c", &btype);
    btype = toupper(btype);    /* make sure its in uppercase */
  }
     /* determine the price of the bike */
  if (btype == 'M')
    price = MPRICE;
  else if (btype == 'S')
    price = SPRICE;

  record.amount = record.numbikes * price;
  record.biketype = btype;

  while( !(risk == 'Y' || risk == 'N') )
  {
    printf("\nIs this customer a good risk (Y or N): ");
    scanf("\n%c", &risk);
    risk = toupper(risk);
  }
  record.goodrisk = risk;

  return(record);
}

void shipslip(struct Customer record)
{
  printf("\n        Shipping Instructions:");
  printf("\nTo: %s",record.name);
  printf("\n    %s", record.address);
  printf("\nShip %d", record.numbikes);
  if (record.biketype == 'M')
    printf(" Mountain Bikes");
  else if (record.biketype == 'S')
    printf(" Street Bikes");
  if (record.goodrisk == 'Y')
    printf("\nby freight, and bill the customer $%.2f", record.amount);
  else
    printf("\nC.O.D.  Amount due on delivery = $%.2f", record.amount);
}
```

Problem 2: Sorting and Searching an Array of Records

Arrays of records can be sorted and searched just like an array of any other type of data. An entire record can be assigned, as a single unit, to another record variable of the same type, and when that is done all of the fields within it are individually assigned. This is a distinct advantage of records over parallel arrays, where each field must be moved individually.

Usually, when sorting or searching a database consisting of an array of records, you are interested in a particular field in each record. For example, you may want to sort in order of increasing age or alphabetically by last name. The field sorted on is referred to as the *key field*, and sorting and searching are said to be performed "by record key."

Different fields can be designated as keys at different times for different purposes. Searching is facilitated when the key is unique in each record; that is, when no two records have the same key value. Therefore, it is common for unique values, such as social security number, employee number, or account number, to be designated as the primary key of a record. If a primary key (such as a last name) is not unique, then another field is often designated as a secondary key, and the sorting and searching occur first in order by the primary key, and then by the secondary key.

In this problem we are going to sort an array of Employee records by name, and then search for all employees making less than a user-entered hourly rate. For this problem assume that our database consists of the records shown in Figure 13.9.

Analyze the Problem for Input/Output Requirements   The inputs to this problem consist of the records contained within the database, which are listed in Figure 13.9, and a user input hourly rate.

The required outputs are the list of Employee records, sorted by name, and a listing of all employees having an hourly rate less than the input value.

Develop a Solution   The data shown in Figure 13.9 will be stored in an array of data structures. We will use a selection sort (see Section 8.5) to sort the array into alphabetical order by name; thus the name field is our primary key field. The sorted array will then be displayed to the screen.

FIGURE 13.9 An Unsorted Array of Employee Records

Employee Number	Employee Name	Hourly Rate
34145	Donaldson, S.	5.56
33623	Bohm, P.	7.54
36203	Gwodz, K.	8.72
32479	Abrams, B.	6.72
35987	Ernst, T.	5.43

A linear search through the sorted array of records is performed, using the rate field as the key field, to find and display all employees having a lower hourly rate than a user-input value. Thus, our program will do the following:

- Define the array of Employee records.
- Sort the array by the name field and display the sorted array.
- Prompt the user for an hourly rate and accept the input data.
- Search the sorted array and display all employees making less than the input hourly rate.

Refining this initial algorithm, the following pseudocode expands on how the program will input and process the data.

Function Main
    Define an array of data structures and populate it.
    Sort the array of data structures using the function selsort.
    Display the sorted array using the function display.
    Prompt the user for an hourly rate and accept the data.
    Perform a linear search for records having a lower hourly rate and display
        the employee number and name for all records found using the function
        linsearch.

Function selsort
    Perform a selection sort on the array based on the name field.

Function display
    For each record in the array
        Display the record's contents.

Function linsearch
    Search each record and examine its rate field.
    If the rate value is less than the input value
        Display the record's number and name fields.

Code the Solution   Program 13.8 illustrates C code that performs the steps indicated by our program solution. In examining the code, notice that we have used a named constant for the array size and that we have made all functions general purpose—in that they are not restricted for sorting and searching only five records; they can be used for any size of database. If you are unfamiliar with the code used in the selsort function, you should review Section 8.5.

Test and Debug the Program   The sort and search procedures are modifications of those in Section 8.5. Compare these to see what changes have been made to accommodate record arrays.

This is clearly a lengthy program, but debugging can be straightforward if you begin with the main function and then follow through each called function. Substituting stub functions (or just inserting printf commands to indicate when you enter and exit each function) will help you trace the program's flow and locate errors.

PROGRAM 13.8

```c
#include <stdio.h>
#include <string.h>
#define ARRAYSIZE 5    /* size of the array */
#define MAXNAME 30     /* maximum length of a name */

struct Pay_rec
{
  long id;
  char name[MAXNAME];
  float rate;
};          /* construct a global template */

void main(void)
{
  struct Pay_rec employee[ARRAYSIZE] =
          {
              { 34145, "Donaldson, S.", 5.56},
              { 33623, "Bohm, P.", 7.54},
              { 36203, "Gwodz, K.", 8.72 },
              { 32479, "Abrams, B.", 6.72 },
              { 35987, "Ernst, T.", 5.43 }
          };
  float cutrate;
  void selsort(struct Pay_rec [], int); /* 1st arg is an array of records */
  void display(struct Pay_rec [], int);
  void linsearch(struct Pay_rec [], int, float);

  selsort(employee, ARRAYSIZE);
  display(employee, ARRAYSIZE);
  printf("\n\nEnter the cutoff pay rate: ");
  scanf("%f", &cutrate);
  linsearch(employee, ARRAYSIZE, cutrate);
}

void selsort(struct Pay_rec array[], int numel)
{
  int i, j, minidx;
  char minstrng[MAXNAME];
  struct Pay_rec temp;

  for(i = 0; i < (numel -1); i++)
  {
    strcpy(minstrng, array[i].name); /*assume minimum is first name in list*/
    minidx = i;
    for(j = i + 1; j < numel; j++)
    {
      if ( strcmp(array[j].name, minstrng) < 0 ) /* if we've located a */
      {                                          /* lower name, */
```

(continued on next page)

(continued from previous page)

```
capture it */
      strcpy(minstrng, array[j].name);
      minidx = j;
       }
     }
    if ( strcmp(minstrng, array[i].name) < 0 )  /* check for a new minimum */
    {
      temp = array[i];
      array[i] = array[minidx];
      array[minidx] = temp;
    }
  }
}


void linsearch(struct Pay_rec array[], int numel, float minrate)
{
  int i;

  printf("\nThe employees making less than this rate are:");
  for (i = 0; i < numel; i++)
    if (array[i].rate < minrate)
      printf("\n %ld   %-20s",array[i].id, array[i].name);
  printf("\n");
}


void display(struct Pay_rec array[], int numel)
{
    int i;

    printf("\nThe sorted array of structures is:");
    for (i = 0; i < numel; i++)
    printf("\n %ld   %-20s %4.2f",array[i].id, array[i].name, array[i].rate);
}
```

Here is a sample run.

```
            The sorted array of structures is:
               32479 Abrams, B.        6.72
               33623 Bohm, P.          7.54
               34145 Donaldson, S.     5.56
               35987 Ernst, T.         5.43
               36203 Gwodz, K.         8.72


            Enter the cutoff pay rate: 7.00


            The employees making less than this rate are:
              32479 Abrams, B.
              34145 Donaldson, S.
              35987 Ernst, T.
```

Exercises 13.4

1. Write a C program that defines a record for a single item inventory in a store. The record should contain fields for the description, inventory number, storage bin location, quantity-on-hand, and wholesale cost of the item. A function should request a new wholesale cost and quantity-on-hand and change the data in the record appropriately. If the quantity drops below 10, display a warning message that the stock is low.

2. Develop a program that handles a single record describing the produce in your store. Each record should have fields for the produce name, quantity-on-hand, and retail price. As you order or sell each type, the quantity-on-hand will change. If the amount-on-hand of any type drops to less than 30, print a message suggesting that more be ordered. If the amount on hand is more than 200, print a message that advertises them for sale at 25% off the regular retail price.

3. Modify Program 13.7 so that a customer may order a variety of types of bicycles. (*Hint:* Change the record so that there is a number field for each bicycle type containing how many of that type were ordered. Name these fields nummtnbikes and numstbikes, and eliminate the biketype field.)

4. Construct a data structure that contains all of the short biographical information about yourself that you might think is important, such as name, age, height, hair color, eye color, monthly salary, address, and so on. Write a C program that will allow you to enter data into the record and to change the contents of the fields when necessary.

5. Expand the inventory problem of Exercise 1 to handle an array of up to five item records. Load the inventory array with five records. Have the program give you a report of all of the inventory items and make up order forms for those whose quantity is less than 10 items on hand.

6. Modify Program 13.7 to handle an array of records so that you can take up to five orders for bicycles during the day and prepare shipping orders for all of them at once at the end of the day.

7. a. Representative information about a group of medical patients is shown in Figure 13.10. Define a data structure that will record this information for five patients.

FIGURE 13.10

Name	Address	Age	Amount owed	Days of care
First	Street		Hospital	Inpatient
Last	City		Doctor	Outpatient
	State		Pharmacy	
	Zip code			
Robert	1182 25th Street	61	$217.90	2
Sorenson	Remington		84.25	6
	OR		63.44	
	98762			

b. Using the data structure defined in Exercise 7a, write a C program that displays the patient's name, address, total days of care (inpatient + outpatient), and total charges (hospital + doctor + pharmacy). Print bills for all patients 65 or older, with their name, address, and a listing of their hospital, doctor, and pharmacy charges. Then calculate and print on the bill a display of the total charges less a 20% senior citizen discount.

To test your program use the following data:

```
Robert Sorensen
1182 25th Street
Remington OR 98762
61     217.90      84.25      63.44      2        6

Rita Martinez
815 Buchanan Ave
Williams AZ 82173
27     582.96     479.63      84.90     29        0

Francine Appleton
513 Perington Blvd
St. Francis MN 21394-3005
68    2123.23     654.00     228.21     32        5

George Thomas
10865 Doughboy St
Los Angeles CA 90413-8273
53     105.49     486.88     241.56      2       45

Gary Allred
226 Mountain Road
Hoover NB 70014-1275
78     409.54     441.32     142.09     31        0
```

13.5 UNIONS[2]

A *union* is a data type that reserves the same area in memory for two or more variables, each of which can be a different data type. A variable that is declared as a union data type can be used to hold a character variable, an integer variable, a double-precision variable, or any other valid C++ data type. Each of these types, but only one at a time, can actually be assigned to the union variable.

The definition of a union has the same form as a structure definition, with the keyword union used in place of the keyword structure. For example, the declaration

```
union
{
  char key;
  int num;
  double price;
} val;
```

---

[2] This topic may be omitted on first reading with no loss of subject continuity.

creates a union variable named `val`. If val were a structure it would consist of three individual members. As a union, however, `val` contains a single member that can be either a character variable named `key`, an integer variable named `num`, or a double-precision variable named `price`. In effect, a union reserves sufficient memory locations to accommodate its largest member's data type. This same set of locations is then referenced by different variable names depending on the data type of the value currently residing in the reserved locations. Each value stored overwrites the previous value, using as many bytes of the reserved memory area as necessary.

Individual union members are referenced using the same notation as structure members. For example, if the `val` union is currently being used to store a character, the correct variable name to access the stored character is `val.key`. Similarly, if the union is used to store an integer, the value is accessed by the name `val.num`, and a double-precision value is accessed by the name `val.price`. In using union members, it is the programmer's responsibility to ensure that the correct member name is used for the data type currently residing in the union.

Typically a second variable is used to keep track of the current data type stored in the union. For example, the following code could be used to select the appropriate member of `val` for display. Here the value in the variable `u_type` determines the currently stored data type in the `val` union.

```
switch(u_type)
{
  case 'c': printf ("%c", val.key);
            break;
  case 'i': printf ("%d", val.num);
            break;
  case 'd': printf ("%f", val.price);
            break;
  default : printf ("Invalid type in u_type : %c", u_type);
}
```

As they are in structures, a tag names can be associated with a union. For example, the declaration

```
union Date_time
{
    long int days;
    double time;
};
```

provides a template for a union without actually reserving any storage locations. This template can then be used to define any number of variables. For example, the definition

```
Date_time first, second, *pt;
```

creates a union variable named `first`, a union variable named `second`, and a pointer that can be used to store the address of any union having the form of `Date_time`. Once a pointer to a union has been declared, the same notation used to access structure members can be used to access union members. For example, if the assignment `pt = &first;` is made, then `pt->date` references the date member of the union named `first`.

Unions may themselves be members of structures or arrays, or structures, arrays, and pointers may be members of unions. In each case, the notation used to access a member must be consistent with the nesting employed. For example, in the structure defined by

```
struct
{
  char u_type;
  union
  {
    char *text;
    float rate;
  } u_tax;
}  flag;
```

the variable rate is referenced as

```
flag.u_tax.rate
```

Similarly, the first character of the string whose address is stored in the pointer text is referenced as

```
*flag.u_type.text
```

Exercises 13.5

1. Assume the following definition:

```
union
{
  float rate;
  double taxes;
  int num;
} flag;
```

For this union write an appropriate printf() call stream to display the various members of the union.

2. Define a union variable named car that contains an integer named year, an array of 10 characters named name, and an array of 10 characters named model.

3. Define a union variable named yield that would allow a floating-point number to be referenced by both the variable names interest and rate.

4. Declare a union data type named Amt that contains an integer variable named int_amt, a double precision variable named dbl_amt, and a pointer to a character named pt_key.

5. a. What do you think will be displayed by the following section of code?:

```
union
{
  char ch;
  float btype;
} alt;
alt.ch = 'y';
cout << alt.btype;
```

   b. Include the code presented in Exercise 5a in a program and run the program to verify your answer to Exercise 5a.

13.6 COMMON PROGRAMMING ERRORS

Three common errors are often made when using structures or unions. The first error occurs because structures and unions, as complete entities, cannot be used in relational expressions. For example, even if `tel_typ` and `phon_type` are two structures of the same type, the expression `tel_typ  == phon_typ` is invalid. Individual members of a structure or union can, of course, be compared using any of C's relational operators.

The second common error is really an extension of a pointer error as it relates to structures and unions. Whenever a pointer is used to "point to" either of these data types, or whenever a pointer is itself a member of a structure or a union, care must be taken to use the address in the pointer to access the appropriate data type. Should you be confused about just what is being pointed to, remember, "If in doubt, print it out."

The final error relates specifically to unions. Since a union can store only one of its members at a time, you must be careful to keep track of the currently stored variable. Storing one data type in a union and accessing it by the wrong variable name can result in an error that is particularly troublesome to locate.

13.7 CHAPTER REVIEW

Key Terms

data field	structure member
data record	tag name
key field	template
structure	union

Summary

1. A data structure allows individual variables to be grouped under a common variable name. Each variable in a structure is referenced by its structure name, followed by a period, followed by its individual variable name. Another term for a structure is a record. The general form for declaring a structure is:

```
struct Structure.name;
{
    individual member declarations;
    structure variables;
}
```

2. A structure tag name can be used to create a generalized structure template describing the form and arrangement of elements in a structure. This name can then be used to define specific structure variables.

3. Structures are particularly useful as elements of arrays. Used in this manner, each structure becomes one record in a list of records.

4. Individual members of a structure are passed to a function in the manner appropriate to the data type of the member being passed. Complete structures can also be passed, in which case the called function receives a copy of each

element in the structure. The address of a structure may also be passed, which provides the called function with direct access to the structure.

5. Structure members can be any valid C data type, including structures, unions, arrays, and pointers.

6. Unions are declared in the same manner as structures. The definition of a union creates a memory overlay area, with each union member using the same memory storage locations. Thus, only one member of a union may be active at a time.

Exercises

1. Define a record data type and member variables for a business, including fields for the business name, description of the product or services, address, number of employees, and annual revenue.

2. Define a record data type and member variables for a single kind of screw in your parts inventory, with fields for inventory number, screw length, diameter, kind of head (Phillips or standard slot), material (steel, brass, other), and cost.

3. A record type is defined as:

```
struct Inventory
{
   char description[50];
   int prodnum;
   int quantity;
   float price;
};
```

Write the following:

a. A declaration for an array of 100 records of type Inventory

b. An assignment of inventory number 4355 to the 83rd Inventory item

c. A statement that reads the price of the 15th Inventory item

4. Define an array of records for up to 50 factory employees, in which each record contains fields for name, age, social security number, hourly wage, and years with the company. Write the following:

a. Statements that display the name and number of years with the company for the 25th employee in the array

b. A loop that, for every employee, adds 1 to the number of years with the company and that adds 50 cents to the hourly wage

5. a. In two dimensions a vector is a pair of numbers that represent directed arrows in a plane, as shown by the vectors $v1$ and $v2$ in Figure 13.11.

Two-dimensional vectors can be written in the form (a,b), where a and b are called the x and y components of the vector. For example, for the vectors illustrated in Figure 13.11, $v1 = (9,4)$ and $v2 = (3,5)$. For vectors, the following operations apply:

$$\text{If } v1 = (a,b) \text{ and } v2 = (c,d)$$
$$v1 + v2 = (a,b) + (c,d) = (a + c, b + d)$$
$$v1 - v2 = (a,b) - (c,d) = (a - c, b - d)$$

FIGURE 13.11   The grades **Array in Storage**

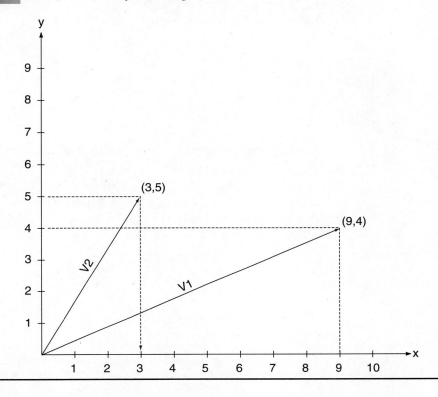

Using this information write a C program that defines an array of two vector records, where each record consists of two floating-point components a and b. Your program should permit a user to enter two vectors, call two functions that return the sum and difference of the entered vectors, and display the results calculated by these functions.

b. In addition the operations defined in Exercise 5a, two additional vector operations are negation and absolute value. For a vector $v1$ with components (a,b) these operations are defined as follows:

$$\text{negation: } -v1 = -(a,b) = (-a,-b)$$
$$\text{absolute value: } |v1| = \text{sqrt}(a * a + b * b)$$

Using this information modify the program that you wrote for Exercise 5a to display the negation and absolute values of both vectors input by a user as well as the negation and absolute value of the sum of the two input vectors.

14 | Dynamic Data Structures

The scalar, array, and structure variables that we have used so far have all had memory space reserved at compile time. Thus, in defining an array we have always had to declare its maximum size, which is used by the compiler in determining how much memory to allocate for the array. Once set, the array's size could only be extended by redefining its size and recompiling the program.

An alternative to this fixed memory allocation is to use a dynamic memory allocation in which memory space grows or diminishes under program control at run time. Under a dynamic allocation scheme, it is not necessary to reserve a fixed amount of memory for a scalar variable, array, or structure in advance. Rather, requests are made for allocation and release of memory space while the program is running. In this chapter we will see how this is accomplished. We will also investigate three types of data structures that commonly use dynamic memory allocation in their construction: stacks, queues, and linked lists.

14.1 DYNAMIC MEMORY ALLOCATION

As each variable is defined in a program, sufficient storage for it is assigned from a pool of available computer memory. Once specific memory locations have been reserved for a variable, these locations are fixed for the life of that variable, whether they are used or not. For example, if a definition statement requests storage for an array of 500 integers, the storage for the array is allocated and fixed from the point of the array's definition. If the application requires less than 500 integers, the unused allocated storage is not released back to the system until the array goes out of existence. If, on the other hand, the application requires more than 500 integers, the size of the integer array must be increased and the function defining the array recompiled.

An alternative to this fixed or static allocation of memory storage locations is the dynamic allocation of memory. Under *dynamic memory allocation*, the amount of storage allocated is determined and adjusted as a program is run, rather than being fixed at compile time.

Dynamic allocation of memory is extremely useful when dealing with lists, because it allows the list to expand as new items are added and contract as items are deleted. For example, in constructing a list of grades, the exact number of grades ultimately needed may not be known. Rather than creating a fixed array to store the grades, it is extremely useful to have a mechanism whereby the array can be enlarged and shrunk as necessary. Four C functions, `malloc()`, `calloc()`, `realloc()`, and `free()` provide a sophisticated memory allocation package. They are described in Table 14.1. The function prototypes for these functions are contained in the `stdlib.h` header file.

Although, in practice, the `malloc()` and `calloc()` functions can frequently be used interchangeably, we will use the `malloc()` function exclusively because it is the more general purpose of the two functions. In requesting a new allocation of storage space using `malloc()`, the user must provide the function with an indication of the amount of storage needed. This may be done by either requesting a specific number of bytes or, more commonly, by requesting enough space for a particular type of data. For example, the function call `malloc(10 * sizeof(char))` requests enough memory to store 10 characters, while the function call `malloc(sizeof(int))` requests enough storage to store an integer number.

In a similar manner and of more usefulness is the dynamic allocation of arrays and structures. For example, the expression

$$malloc(200 * sizeof(int))$$

reserves a sufficient number of bytes to store 200 integers.[1] Although we have used the constant 200 in this example declaration, a variable, as we will soon show, can also be used. The space allocated by `malloc()` comes from the com-

TABLE 14.1 C Functions for Memory Allocation

Function Name	Description
`malloc()`	Reserves the number of bytes requested by the argument passed to the function. Returns the address of the first reserved location or NULL if sufficient memory is not available.
`calloc()`	Reserves space for an array of *n* elements of the specified size. Returns the address of the first reserved location and initializes all reserved bytes to zeros, or returns a NULL if sufficient memory is not available.
`realloc()`	Changes the size of previously allocated memory to a new size. If the new size is larger than the old size, the additional memory space is uninitialized and the contents of the original allocated memory remain unchanged; otherwise, the new allocated memory remains unchanged up to the limits of the new size.
`free()`	Releases a block of bytes previously reserved. The address of the first reserved location is passed as an argument to the function.

[1] The equivalent `calloc()` call is `calloc(200,sizeof(int))`.

puter's free storage area, which is formally referred to as the *heap*. The heap consists of unallocated memory that can be allocated to a program, as requested, while the program is executing. All such allocated memory is returned to the heap, either explicitly using the `free()` function or automatically when the program requesting additional memory is finished executing.[2]

In allocating storage dynamically, we do not know in advance where the computer system will physically reserve the requested number of bytes, and we have no explicit name to access the newly created storage locations. To provide access to these locations, `malloc()` returns the address of the first location that has been reserved. This address must, of course, be assigned to a pointer. The return of a pointer by `malloc()` is especially useful for creating either arrays or a set of data structures. Before illustrating the actual dynamic allocation of an array or data structure, we need to consider one logistic problem created by `malloc()`.

The `malloc()` function always returns the address of the first byte of storage reserved, where the returned address is declared as a pointer to a void. Any function that calls `malloc()` must either include a function prototype declaring this return type or use the `stdlib.h` header file.

Since the returned address is always a pointer to a void, regardless of the data type requested, the returned address must always be reinterpreted as pointing to the desired type. To use this address to reference the correct data type, it must be reinterpreted as pointing to the correct type using a cast. In this case, then, we need to cast (or force) the returned pointer into a pointer to the desired data type. For example, if the variable `grades` is a pointer to an integer and `key` is a pointer to a void, the statement:

```
grades = (int *) key
```

redefines the address key as the address of an integer. The address is not changed physically, but any subsequent reference to the address in `grades` will now cause the correct number of bytes to be accessed for an integer value. For example, consider the following section of code, which can be used to create an array of integers whose size is determined by the user at run time as an input value:

```
int *grades;      /* define a pointer to an integer */

printf("\nEnter the number of grades to be processed: ");
scanf("%d", &numgrades);

 /* here is where the request for memory is made */
grades = (int *) malloc(numgrades * sizeof(int));
```

In this sequence of instructions the actual size of the array that is created depends on the number input by the user. Because pointer and array names are related, each value in the newly created storage area can be accessed using standard array notation, such as `grades[i]`, rather than the equivalent pointer notation `*(grades + i)`. Program 14.1 illustrates this sequence of code in the context of a complete program.

---

[2] In a similar fashion the compiler automatically provides the same type of dynamic allocation and deallocation of memory for all auto variables and function arguments. In these cases, however, the allocation and deallocation is made from the stack storage area.

PROGRAM 14.1

```c
#include <stdio.h>
#include <stdlib.h>

void main(void)
{
  int numgrades, i;
  int *grades;

  printf("\nEnter the number of grades to be processed: ");
  scanf("%d", &numgrades);

  grades = (int *) malloc(numgrades * sizeof(int));
    /* here we check that the allocation was satisfied*/
  if (grades == (int *) NULL)
  {
    printf("\nFailed to allocate grades array\n");
    exit(1);
  }
  for(i = 0; i < numgrades; i++)
  {
    printf(" Enter a grade: ");
    scanf("%d", &grades[i]);
  }
  printf("\nAn array was created for %d integers", numgrades);
  printf("\nThe values stored in the array are:\n");
  for (i = 0; i < numgrades; i++)
    printf(" %d\n", grades[i]);

  free(grades);

}
```

A sample run of Program 14.1 follows:

```
Enter the number of grades to be processed: 4
  Enter a grade: 85
  Enter a grade: 96
  Enter a grade: 77
  Enter a grade: 92

An array was created for 4 integers
The values stored in the array are:
 85
 96
 77
 92
```

As seen by this output, dynamic storage allocation is used to successfully create storage for four integer values as the program is running.

Although the call to `malloc()` in Program 14.1 is rather simple, two important concepts related to the call should be noted. First, notice the code immediately after the call to `malloc()`, which is repeated below:

```
/* here we check that the allocation was satisfied */
if (grades == (int *) NULL)
{
  printf("\nFailed to allocate grades array\n");
  exit(1);
}
```

This section of code tests `malloc`'s return value to ensure that the memory request was successfully satisfied. If `malloc()` cannot obtain the desired memory space it returns a `NULL`, which in Program 14.1 would be cast into a pointer to an integer by the statement making the `malloc()` call. Thus `grades` must subsequently be compared to `(int *) NULL` in the `if` statement. In making requests for dynamic memory allocation, it is extremely important to check the return value—otherwise the program will crash when a subsequent access to nonexisting memory is made.

Next, notice that Program 14-1 uses the `free()` function to restore the allocated block of storage back to the operating system at the end of the program.[3] The only address required by `free` is the starting address of the block of storage that was dynamically allocated. Thus, any address returned by `malloc()` can subsequently be used by `free()` to restore reserved memory to the computer. The `free()` function does not alter the address passed to it, but simply makes the storage pointed to available for future memory allocation calls.

In addition to requesting data space for arrays, as is done in Program 14.1, `malloc()` is more typically used for dynamically allocating memory for data structures. For example, consider the declaration of a data structure named `Office_info`:

```
struct Office_info
{
  any number of data members declared in here;
};
```

Regardless of the number and type of data members declared in `Office_info`, the call `malloc(sizeof(struct Office_info))` requests enough storage for one structure of the `Office_info` type. To use the return pointer value provided by `malloc()` once again requires us to cast the return address into a pointer of the correct structure type. Typically this is done using a sequence of statements similar to the following:

---

[3] The allocated storage would automatically be returned to the heap when the program has completed execution. It is, however, good practice to restore the allocated storage formally to the heap using `free` when the memory is no longer needed. This is especially true for larger, longer running programs that make numerous requests for additional storage areas.

```
if ((Off = (struct office_info *) malloc(sizeof(struct office_info)))==(struct office_info) *NULL)
{
  printf("\nAllocation of office info record failed\n");
  exit(1);
}
```

```
struct Office_info *Off;  /* create a pointer to store the allocated address */

  /* request space for one record */
Off = (struct Office_info *) malloc(sizeof(struct Office_info));

  /* check that space was allocated */
if ((Off == (struct Office_info) char *NULL)
{
  printf("\nAllocation of office info record failed\n");
  exit(1);
}
```

This type of dynamic allocation is extremely useful in a variety of advanced programming situations. One of these is in the reading of records from a data file. Rather than allocating a fixed amount of space for a file's data, record space is dynamically allocated as the data file is being read. As a specific example of this type of application, consider the following program requirement.

Program Requirement

A software distribution company is constantly opening and closing offices throughout the United States, Europe, and Asia. In its New York office it maintains a file that contains an up-to-date listing of offices and their time zones. Currently the company's file contains the following data:

Paris	+1
London	0
NewYork	−5
Chicago	−6
Dallas	−7
SanFrancisco	−8
Honolulu	−10
Tokyo	+9

The information in this file must be read each morning. It is then used by a program that automatically sends faxes to each office with the time adjusted to local time. For example, New York time is five hours behind London time and Tokyo is nine hours ahead of London time. Thus, when it is 12 noon in London it is 7 A.M. in New York and 9 P.M. in Tokyo.

Due to the nature of the software company's business, offices are frequently opened and closed. Management has asked you to write a function that reads in the file's data regardless of how many office records are currently contained in the file.

Analyze the Program   This is an ideal problem for using dynamic allocation. Since the size of the file can change daily, we will let the program allocate space for each record as needed. As a practical matter, we will initially allocate enough space for five records (the number is arbitrary) and then reallocate space in chunks of five records whenever the current allocation is about to be exceeded. For this problem we have the following considerations:

Input Data: Each record in the file consists of a string and an integer. This can be defined using the data structure:

```
#define MAXSIZE 20

struct Office_info
{
  char offname[MAXSIZE];
  int timezone;
};
```

Output Data: An array of data structures that contains the information provided by the file. Additionally, in keeping with good programming practice, we will provide an error message if the file has not been successfully input, either because the file could not be successfully opened or the dynamic allocation call fails.

Processing Algorithm: The initial request for record space will be made by the call

```
Off = (struct Office_info *) malloc(TAB_INC * sizeof(struct Office_info));
```

where `TAB_INC` is defined as five. After each group of five records has been read, a reallocation will be made by the call

```
Off = (struct Office_info *) realloc(Off, (Size + TAB_INC) * sizeof(struct Office_info));
```

where `Size` is used to contain the current allocation size and `Size + TAB_INC` is the requested new size. In both of these calls the return addresses provided by `malloc()` and `realloc()` are cast into pointers to a structure and stored in a pointer named `Off`.

Notice that we are not concerned with how the data that we read will be used. Although the program statement gives us information on using `time-zone`, for our purposes this is irrelevant. Our task is to ensure that the data is correctly read and stored.

Develop a Solution   The final design can be described in pseudocode as follows:

Define the data structure for an office record.
Open the file, with a suitable error message on failure.
Allocate a chunk of memory (enough space for five records), with
  a suitable error message on failure.
Initialize the memory space allocated.
While not End-of-File
  Read a record
  Store the record into memory
  If (records exceed allocated memory)
    reallocate memory in additional chunks of five, with a
    suitable error message on failure.
Endwhile
Close the file

Code the Solution   The required header information and a function that performs our selected design follows:

```c
#include <stdio.h>
#include <stdlib.h>
#define MAXSIZE 20
#define NOZONE -20
#define TAB_INC 5      /* increase the table by this amount */
static int Size = 0;  /* actual size of the table */
char *offices = "offices.dat";    /* the name of the data file */

struct Office_info
{
  char offname[MAXSIZE];
  int timezone;
};

static struct Office_info *Off;  /* a pointer to the Office_info struct */

/* read and store the office data into a dynamically allocated and
   maintained structure */
#define LINESIZE 81
void read_offices(void)
{
  char line[LINESIZE];
  FILE * in_file;
  int i, j;

  if (Size == 0)  /* if no space has been allocated previously */
  {
    Off = (struct Office_info *) malloc(TAB_INC * sizeof(struct Office_info));
    if (Off == (struct Office_info *) NULL)
    {
      printf("\nFailed to initially allocate memory for office data\n");
      exit(1);
    }
    Size += TAB_INC;
  }

  /* initialize the newly allocated memory */
  for (i = 0; i < Size; i++)
  {
    Off[i].offname[0] = '\0';
    Off[i].timezone = NOZONE;
  }

  in_file = fopen(offices,"r");
  if (in_file == (FILE *) NULL)
  {
    printf("\nFailed to open the office file\n");
    exit(2);
  }
  i = 0;
  while(fgets(line,LINESIZE,in_file) != NULL)
  {
```

(continued on next page)

(continued from previous page)

```
        sscanf(line, "%s %d", Off[i].offname, &(Off[i].timezone));
        i++;

          /* reallocate space in chunks of TAB_INC, as necessary */
        if (i == Size) /* if no more room in the allocated space */
        {
          Off = (struct Office_info *) realloc(Off,
                (Size + TAB_INC) * sizeof(struct Office_info));
          if (Off == (struct Office_info *) NULL)
          {
              printf("\nFailed to reallocate memory for office data\n");
              exit(3);
          }
          Size += TAB_INC;

          /* initialize the additionally allocated space */
          for (j = Size - TAB_INC; j < Size; j++)
          {
            Off[j].offname[0] = '\0';
            Off[j].timezone = NOZONE;
          }
        }  /* end of reallocation section */

      } /* end of while */
      fclose(in_file);
    }
```

Test and Debug the Program   The testing of our function requires a driver program
and a display of the memory space allocated and used. Program 14.2 provides a complete program for this purpose.

PROGRAM 14.2

```
#include <stdio.h>
#include <stdlib.h>
#define MAXSIZE 20
#define NOZONE -20
#define TAB_INC 5        /* increase the table by this amount */
int Size = 0;            /* actual size of the table */
char *offices = "offices.dat";    /* the name of the data file */

struct Office_info
{
  char offname[MAXSIZE];
  int timezone;
};

static struct Office_info *Off;  /* a pointer to the Office_info struct */
void main(void)
{
  void read_offices();  /* read the file and store the data into a */
```
(continued on next page)

(continued from previous page)

```
                              /* dynamically created and maintained list of structures */
  void display_table(); /* display the data stored in the dynamic list of structures */

  read_offices();
  display_table();
}

/* read and store the office data into a dynamically allocated and
   maintained structure */
#define LINESIZE 81
void read_offices(void)
{
  char line[LINESIZE];
  FILE * in_file;
  int i, j;

  if (Size == 0) /* if no space has been allocated previously */
  {

    Off = (struct Office_info *) malloc(TAB_INC * sizeof(struct Office_info));
    if (Off == (struct Office_info *) NULL)
    {
      printf("\nFailed to initially allocate memory for office data\n");
      exit(1);
    }
    Size += TAB_INC;
  }

  /* initialize the newly allocated memory */
  for (i = 0; i < Size; i++)
  {
    Off[i].offname[0] = '\0';
    Off[i].timezone = NOZONE;
  }

  in_file = fopen(offices,"r");
  if (in_file == (FILE *) NULL)
  {
    printf("\nFailed to open the office file\n");
    exit(2);
  }
  i = 0;
  while(fgets(line,LINESIZE,in_file) != NULL)
  {
    sscanf(line, "%s %d", Off[i].offname, &(Off[i].timezone));
    i++;
      /* reallocate space in chunks of TAB_INC, as necessary */
    if (i == Size) /* if no more room in the allocated space */
    {
```

(continued on next page)

(continued from previous page)

```
    Off = (struct Office_info *) realloc(Off,
          (Size + TAB_INC) * sizeof(struct Office_info));
    if (Off == (struct Office_info *) NULL)
    {
        printf("\nFailed to reallocate memory for office data\n");
        exit(3);
    }
    Size += TAB_INC;

    /* initialize the additionally allocated space */
    for (j = Size - TAB_INC; j < Size; j++)
    {
        Off[j].offname[0] = '\0';
        Off[j].timezone = NOZONE;
    }
    } /* end of reallocation section */
  } /* end of while */
  fclose(in_file);
}


void display_table(void)
{
  int i;

  printf("\nOffice Location   Time Zone");
  printf("\n--------------   ---------\n");

  for(i = 0; Off[i].timezone != NOZONE; i++)
    printf("%-20s %3d\n", Off[i].offname, Off[i].timezone);
}
```

A sample run using Program 14.2 provides the following output:

```
      Office Location    Time Zone
      ---------------    ---------
      Paris                  1
      London                 0
      NewYork               -5
      Chicago               -6
      Dallas                -7
      SanFrancisco          -8
      Honolulu             -10
      Tokyo                  9
```

In addition to using dynamically allocated memory to store information from a file, another advanced set of applications is the construction and maintenance of software stacks, queues, and dynamically linked lists. All of these applications are specific cases of linked lists that require each data structure in the list to contain at least one pointer data member. Thus, before we investigate these three applications, we need to understand what a linked list is and how pointers can be incorporated within data structures as data members. This is the topic of the next section.

TIPS FROM THE PROS

Checking `malloc()`'s Return Value

It is really important to check return values when making `malloc` (and `realloc`) function calls. If the operating system cannot satisfy the allocation request, you need to know about it and gracefully terminate your program. Failure to do so almost always results in a program crash if the memory was not allocated and a subsequent program statement attempts to use the memory. There are two styles of coding for checking the return value.

The first style is the one coded in Program 14.1, which is repeated below for convenience. Notice that it clearly separates the request for memory from the subsequent check of the returned value.

```
    /* here is where the request for memory is made */
  grades = (int *) malloc(numgrades * sizeof(int));
    /* here we check that the allocation was satisfied */
  if (grades == (int *) NULL)
  {
    printf("\nFailed to allocate grades array\n");
    exit(1);
  }
```

Alternatively, the request and check can be combined together within the `if` statement as:

```
  if ( (grades = (int *) malloc(numgrades * sizeof(int))) == (int *) NULL)
  {
    printf("\nFailed to allocate grades array\n");
    exit(1);
  }
```

Exercises 14.1

1. Describe what the `malloc()`, `calloc()`, `realloc()`, and `free()` functions do?

2. Why does the `malloc()` function returns an address? What does this address represent? Why is a cast typically used on the returned address?

3. Write `malloc()` function calls to do the following:

   a. Reserve space for an integer variable

   b. Reserve space for an array of 50 integer variables

   c. Reserve space for a floating-point variable

   d. Reserve space for an array of 100 floating-point variables

   e. Reserve space for a structure of type `Name_rec`

   f. Reserve space for an array of 150 structures of type `Name_rec`

4. Write `calloc()` function calls for Exercises 3b, 3d, and 3f.

5. Rewrite Program 14.1 using a `calloc()` call in place of `malloc()`.

6. Using the data read by Program 14.2, write a function named `time_dif` that returns the time difference between any two offices. An office is identified by its first two letters. Thus, the call `time_dif(NE,TO)` is a request for the time difference between New York and Tokyo, and should result in a return value of 14.

Similarly, the call `time_dif(TO,NE)` should result in a return value of –14. (*Hint:* Use the `toupper` intrinsic function call.)

7. Rewrite Program 14.2 to dynamically allocate memory, under user control, to store one record of the following data structure:

```
struct Tel_typ
{
  char name[25];
  char phon_no[15];
}
```

Your program should ask the user whether a record is to be entered. If the user responds with a 'y', the program should dynamically allocate sufficient room for one record and then ask for a name and telephone number to be stored in the newly allocated memory area.

14.2 INTRODUCTION TO LINKED LISTS

To understand the concept of a linked list, consider the alphabetical telephone list shown in Figure 14.1. Starting with this initial set of names and telephone numbers, assume that we are required to add new records to the list in the proper alphabetical sequence, and to delete existing records in such a way that the storage for deleted records is eliminated. Although the insertion or deletion of ordered records could be accomplished using an array of structures, these arrays are not efficient representations for adding or deleting records internal to the array. Deleting a record from an array creates an empty slot that requires either special marking or shifting up all elements below the deleted record to close the empty slot. Similarly, adding a record to the body of an array of structures requires that all elements below the addition be shifted down to make room for the new entry; or the new element could be added to the bottom of the existing array and the array then resorted to restore the proper order of the records. Thus, either adding or deleting records to such a list generally requires restructuring and rewriting the list—a cumbersome, time-consuming, and inefficient practice.

A linked list provides a convenient method for maintaining a constantly changing list, without the need to continually reorder and restructure the complete list. A *linked list* is simply a set of structures in which each structure contains

---

FIGURE 14.1   A Telephone List in Alphabetical Order

Acme, Sam
(201) 898–2392

Dolan, Edith
(213) 682–3104

Lanfrank, John
(415) 718–4581

Mening, Stephen
(914) 382–7070

Zemann, Harold
(718) 219–9912

FIGURE 14.2 Using Pointers to Link Structures

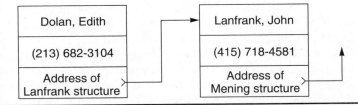

at least one member whose value is the address of the next logically ordered structure in the list. Rather than requiring each record to be physically stored in the proper order, each new record is physically added either to the end of the existing list or wherever the computer has free space in its storage area. The records are "linked" by including the address of the next record in the record immediately preceding it. From a programming standpoint, the current record being processed contains the address of the next record, regardless of where the next record is actually stored.

The concept of a linked list is illustrated in Figure 14.2. Although the actual data for the Lanfrank structure illustrated in the figure may be physically stored anywhere in the computer, the additional member included at the end of the Dolan structure maintains the proper alphabetical order. This member provides the starting address of the location where the Lanfrank record is stored. As you might expect, this member is a pointer.

The usefulness of the pointer in the Dolan record is illustrated by adding a telephone number for June Hagar into the alphabetical list shown in Figure 14.1. The data for June Hagar is stored in a data structure using the same template as that used for the existing records. To ensure that the telephone number for Hagar is correctly displayed after the Dolan telephone number, the address in the Dolan record must be altered to point to the Hagar record, and the address in the Hagar record must be set to point to the Lanfrank record. This is illustrated in Figure 14.3. Notice that the pointer in each structure simply

FIGURE 14.3 Adjusting Addresses to Point to Appropriate Records

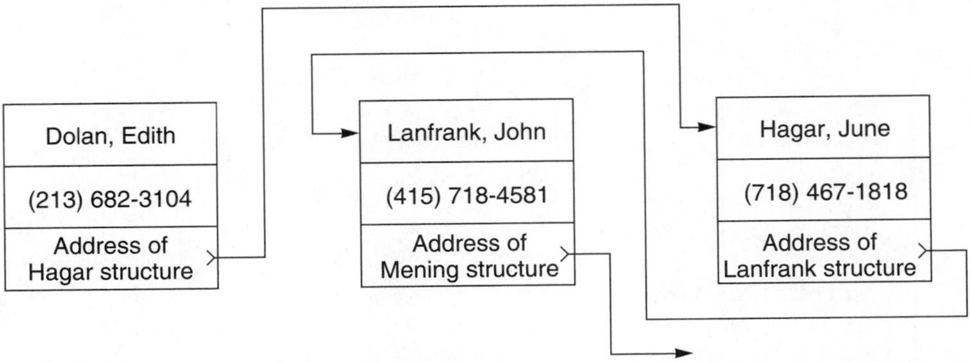

Dolan, Edith	Lanfrank, John	Hagar, June
(213) 682-3104	(415) 718-4581	(718) 467-1818
Address of Hagar structure	Address of Mening structure	Address of Lanfrank structure

points to the location of the next ordered structure, even if that structure is not physically located in the correct order. Removal of a structure from the ordered list is the reverse process of adding a record. The actual record is logically removed from the list by simply changing the address in the structure preceding it to point to the structure immediately following the deleted record and freeing the storage area of the deleted record.

Each structure in a linked list has the same format; however, it is clear that the last record cannot have a valid pointer value that points to another record, since there is none. To accommodate this situation, all programming languages that support pointers provide a special pointer value, usually called NULL or NIL, that acts as a sentinel or flag to indicate when the last record has been processed. In C, this special pointer value is a NULL pointer value that, like its end-of-string counterpart, has a numerical value of zero. Besides an end-of-list sentinel value, a special pointer must also be provided for storing the address of the first structure in the list. Figure 14.4 illustrates the complete set of pointers and structures for a list consisting of three names.

The inclusion of a pointer in a structure should not seem surprising. As we discovered in Section 12.1, a structure can contain any C data type. For example, the structure declaration

```
struct Test
{
  int id_num;
  double *pt_pay
};
```

declares a structure template consisting of two members. The first member is an integer variable named id_num, and the second variable is a pointer named pt_pay, which is a pointer to a double-precision number. Program 14.3 illustrates that the pointer member of a structure is used like any other pointer variable.

PROGRAM 14.3

```
#include <stdio.h>
struct Test
{
  int id_num;
  double *pt_pay;
};

void main(void)
{
  struct Test emp;
  double pay = 456.20;

  emp.id_num = 12345;
  emp.pt_pay = &pay;

  printf("Employee number %d was paid $%6.2f\n",
          emp.id_num, *emp.pt_pay);
}
```

FIGURE 14.4 Use of the Initial and Final Pointer Values

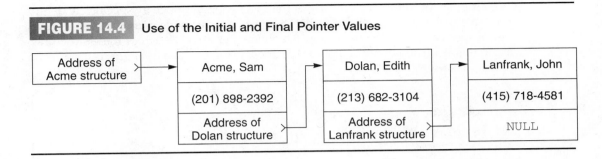

The output produced by executing Program 14.3 is:

```
Employee number 12345 was paid $456.20
```

Figure 14.5 illustrates the relationship between the members of the emp structure defined in Program 14.3 and the variable named pay. The value assigned to emp.id_num is the number 12345 and the value assigned to pay is 456.20. The address of the pay variable is assigned to the structure member emp.pt_pay. Since this member has been defined as a pointer to a double-precision number, placing the address of the double-precision variable pay in it is a correct use of this member.

Finally, since the member operator . has a higher precedence than the indirection operator *, the expression used in the printf call in Program 14.3 is correct. The expression *emp.pt_pay is equivalent to the expression *(emp.pt_pay), which is translated as "the variable whose address is contained in the member emp.pt_pay."

Although the pointer defined in Program 14.3 has been used in a rather trivial fashion, the program does illustrate the concept of including a pointer in a structure. This concept can be easily extended to create a linked list of structures suitable for storing the names and telephone numbers previously listed in Figure 14.1. The following declaration creates a template for such a structure:

```
struct Tele_typ
{
  char name[30];
  char phone_no[15];
  struct Tele_typ *nextaddr;
};
```

The Tele_typ template consists of three members. The first member is an array of 30 characters, suitable for storing names with a maximum of 29 letters and an end-of-string NULL marker. The next member is an array of 15 characters, suitable for storing telephone numbers with their respective area codes. The last member is a pointer suitable for storing the address of a structure of the Tele_typ type.

FIGURE 14.5 Storing an Address in a Structure Member

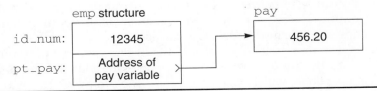

Program 14.4 illustrates the use of the `Tele_typ` template by specifically defining three structures having this form. The three structures are named `t1`, `t2`, and `t3`, respectively, and the name and telephone members of each of these structures are initialized when the structures are defined, using the data of Figure 14.1.

PROGRAM 14.4

```c
#include <stdio.h>
#define MAXNAME 30
#define MAXPHONE 15
struct Tele_typ
{
  char name[MAXNAME];
  char phone_no[MAXPHONE];
  struct Tele_typ *nextaddr;
};

void main(void)
{
  struct Tele_typ t1 = {"Acme, Sam","(201) 898-2392"};
  struct Tele_typ t2 = {"Dolan, Edith","(213) 682-3104"};
  struct Tele_typ t3 = {"Lanfrank, John","(415) 718-4581"};
  struct Tele_typ *first;    /* create a pointer to a structure */

  first = &t1;            /* store t1's address in first */
  t1.nextaddr = &t2;     /* store t2's address in t1.nextaddr */
  t2.nextaddr = &t3;     /* store t3's address in t2.nextaddr */
  t3.nextaddr = NULL;    /* store the NULL address in t3.nextaddr */

  printf("\n%s \n%s \n%s\n",first->name,t1.nextaddr->name,t2.nextaddr->name);
}
```

The output produced by executing Program 14.4 is:

```
Acme, Sam
Dolan, Edith
Lanfrank, John
```

Program 14.4 demonstrates the use of pointers to access successive structure members. As illustrated in Figure 14.6, each structure contains the address of the next structure in the list. The initialization of the names and telephone numbers for each of the structures defined in Program 14.4 is straightforward. Although each structure consists of three members, only the first two members of each structure are initialized. Because both of these members are arrays of characters, they can be initialized with strings. The remaining member of each structure is a pointer. To create a linked list, each structure pointer must be assigned the address of the next structure in the list.

The four assignment statements in Program 14.4 perform the correct assignments. The expression `first` = `&t1` stores the address of the first structure in the list in the pointer variable named `first`. The expression `t1.nextaddr` = `&t2` stores

FIGURE 14.6   The Relationship Between Structures in Program 14.4

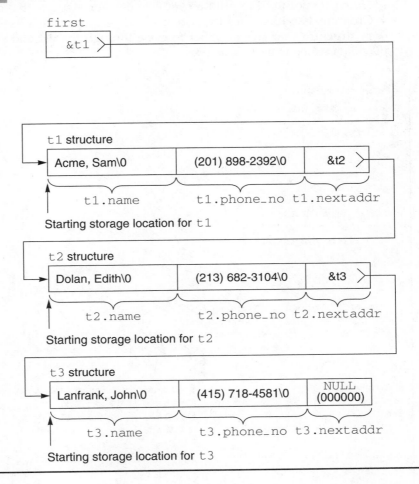

the starting address of the t2 structure into the pointer member of the t1 structure. Similarly, the expression t2.nextaddr = &t3 stores the starting address of the t3 structure into the pointer member of the t2 structure. To end the list, the value of the NULL pointer, which is zero, is stored into the pointer member of the t3 structure.

Once values have been assigned to each structure member and correct addresses have been stored in the appropriate pointers, the addresses in the pointers are used to access each structure's name member. For example, the expression t1.nextaddr->name refers to the name member of the structure whose address is in the nextaddr member of the t1 structure. The precedence of the member operator . and the structure pointer operator –> are equal, and are evaluated from left to right. Thus, the expression t1.nextaddr->name is evaluated as (t1.nextaddr)->name. Since t1.nextaddr contains the address of the t2 structure, the proper name is accessed.

The expression t1.nextaddr->name can, of course, be replaced by the equivalent expression (*t1.nextaddr).name, which explicitly uses the indirection operator. This expression also refers to "the name member of the variable whose address is in t1.nextaddr."

The addresses in a linked list of structures can be used to loop through the complete list. As each structure is accessed it can be either examined to select a specific value or used to print a complete list. For example, the display function in Program 14.5 illustrates the use of a `while` loop, which uses the address in each structure's pointer m.ember to cycle through the list and successively display data stored in each structure.

PROGRAM 14.5

```c
#include <stdio.h>
#define MAXNAME 30
#define MAXPHONE 15

struct Tele_typ
{
  char name[MAXNAME];
  char phone_no[MAXPHONE];
  struct Tele_typ *nextaddr;
};

void main(void)
{
  struct Tele_typ t1 = {"Acme, Sam","(201) 898-2392"};
  struct Tele_typ t2 = {"Dolan, Edith","(213) 682-3104"};
  struct Tele_typ t3 = {"Lanfrank, John","(415) 718-4581"};
  struct Tele_typ *first;   /* create a pointer to a structure */
  void display(struct Tele_typ *);       /* function prototype */

  first = &t1;         /* store t1's address in first */
  t1.nextaddr = &t2;   /* store t2's address in t1.nextaddr */
  t2.nextaddr = &t3;   /* store t3's address in t2.nextaddr */
  t3.nextaddr = NULL;  /* store the NULL address in t3.nextaddr */

  display(first);      /* send the address of the first structure */
}

void display(struct Tele_typ *contents) /* contents is a pointer to a structure */
{                                        /* of type Tele_typ */
  while (contents != NULL)               /* display till end of linked list */
  {
    printf("%-30s %-20s\n",contents->name, contents->phone_no);
    contents = contents->nextaddr;       /* get next address */
  }
  return;
}
```

The output produced by Program 14.5 is:

```
        Acme, Sam              (201) 898-2392
        Dolan, Edith           (213) 682-3104
        Lanfrank, John         (415) 718-4581
```

The important concept illustrated by Program 14.5 is the use of the address in one structure to access members of the next structure in the list. When the `display()` function is called, it is passed the value stored in the variable named first. Since first is a pointer variable, the actual value passed is an address (the address of the t1 structure). display() accepts the passed value in the argument named contents. To store the passed address correctly, contents is declared as a pointer to a structure of the Tele_typ type. Within display,() a while loop is used to cycle through the linked structures, starting with the structure whose address is in contents. The condition tested in the while statement compares the value in contents, which is an address, to the NULL value. For each valid address, the name and phone number members of the addressed structure are displayed. The address in contents is then updated with the address in the pointer member of the current structure. The address in contents is then retested, and the process continues while the address in contents is not equal to the NULL value. display() "knows" nothing about the names of the structures declared in main or even how many structures exist. It simply cycles through the linked list, structure by structure, until it encounters the end-of-list NULL address. Since the value of NULL is zero, the tested condition can be replaced by the equivalent expression !contents.

A disadvantage of Program 14.5 is that exactly three structures are defined in main() by name, and storage for them is reserved at compile time. Should a fourth structure be required, the additional structure would have to be declared and the program recompiled. In the next three sections we show how to combine data structures containing pointer members with dynamic memory allocation to create three different types of dynamically expanding and contracting lists: stacks, queues, and dynamically linked lists.

Exercises 14.2

1. Modify Program 14.5 to prompt the user for a name. Have the program search the existing list for the entered name. If the name is in the list, display the corresponding phone number; otherwise display the message "The name is not in the current phone directory."

2. Write a program containing a linked list of 10 integer numbers. Have the program display the numbers in the list.

3. Using the linked list of structures illustrated in Figure 14.6, write the sequence of steps necessary to delete the record for Edith Dolan from the list.

4. Generalize the description obtained in Exercise 3 to describe the sequence of steps necessary to remove the nth structure from a list of linked structures. The nth structure is preceded by the $(n-1)$st structure and followed by the $(n+1)$st structure. Make sure you store all pointer values correctly.

5. a. A doubly linked list is a list in which each structure contains a pointer to both the following and previous structures in the list. Define an appropriate template for a doubly linked list of names and telephone numbers.

   b. Using the template defined in Exercise 5a, modify Program 14.5 to list the names and phone numbers in reverse order.

14.3 STACKS

A *stack* is a special type of linked list in which records can only be added and removed from the top of the list. As such it is a *last-in/first-out (LIFO)* data structure—a structure in which the last item added to the list is the first item that can be removed. An example of this type of operation is a stack of dishes in a cafeteria, where the last dish placed on top of the stack is the first dish removed. Another example is the in-basket on a desk, where the last paper placed in the basket is typically the first one removed. Stacks provide this simple reversal capability.

Push and Pop

The operation of placing a new item on the top of a stack is called a *push* and removing an item from a stack is called a *pop*. Let's see how these operations are implemented in practice.

Figure 14.7 illustrates a stack consisting of three records. As shown, each record consists of a name member and a pointer member containing the address of the previous record stored on the stack. In addition, there is a separate stack pointer, which we will call the top-of-stack pointer (tosp), that contains the address of the last record added to the stack.

Pushing a new record on a stack, such as that shown in Figure 14.7 involves the following algorithm:

Push (add a new record to the stack)
  Dynamically create a new a record.
  Put the address in the top-of-stack pointer into
    the address field of the new record.
  Fill in the remaining fields of the new record.
  Put the address of the new record into the top-of-stack pointer.

For example, if we were to push a new record onto the stack illustrated in Figure 14.7, the resulting stack would appear as shown in Figure 14.8.

The only record that can be removed from a stack is always the topmost record. Thus, for the stack shown in Figure 14.8, the next record that can be removed is

FIGURE 14.7 A Stack Consisting of Three Records

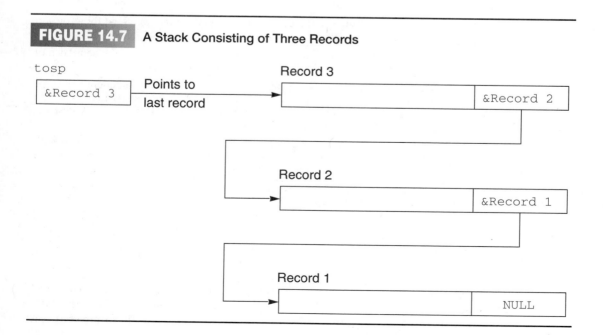

FIGURE 14.8   The Stack after a PUSH

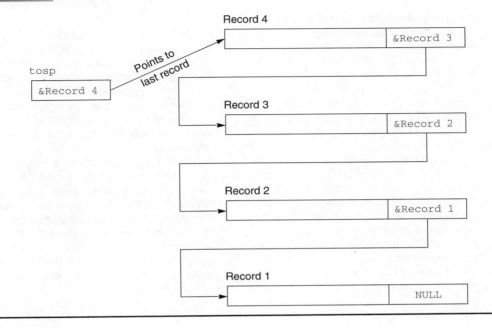

record 4. After this record is removed ("popped") record three can be removed, and so on. The operation of popping a record off the stack is defined by the algorithm:

Pop (remove a record from the top of the stack)
   Move the record contents pointed to by the top-of-stack pointer
      into a work area.
   Free the record pointed to by the top-of-stack pointer.
   Move the address in the work area address field into the
      top-of-stack pointer.

If these operations are carried out on the stack illustrated in Figure 14.8, the stack would revert to that shown in Figure 14.7.

As a specific demonstration of a dynamically allocated stack, assume that the record type of data to be stored on the stack is declared as:

```
#define MAXCHARS 30
struct Name_rec
{
  char name[MAXCHARS];
  struct Name_rec *prior_addr;
};
```

This is simply a record consisting of a name and a pointer member of the type illustrated in Figures 14.7 and 14.8. The push and pop stack operations for this particular record type can now be described[5]:

_____
[5] A function named isempty(), which returns a 1 if the stack is empty and a 0 if the stack in nonempty, is also typically defined. This function is then used to determine when pops should terminate.

A   B I T   O F   B A C K G R O U N D

Dr. Lukasiewicz and RPN

Dr. Jan Lukasiewicz, born in 1878, studied and taught mathematics at the University of Lvov, in Poland, before becoming a respected professor at the University of Warsaw. He received an appointment in 1919 to the post of Minister of Education in Poland and, with Stanislaw Lesniewski, founded the Warsaw School of Logic.

After World War II, Dr. Lukasiewicz and his wife, Regina, found themselves exiled in Belgium. When he was offered a professorship at the Royal Academy in Dublin, they moved to Ireland, where they remained until his death in 1956.

In 1951 Dr. Lukasiewicz developed a new set of postfix algebraic notation, which was critical in the design of early microprocessors in the 1960s and 1970s.

The actual implementation of postfix algebra was done using stack arithmetic, in which data were pushed on a stack and popped off when an operation needed to be performed. Such stack handling instructions require no address operands and make it possible for very small computers to handle large tasks effectively.

Stack arithmetic, which is based on Dr. Lukasiewicz's work, reverses the more commonly known prefix algebra and became known as Reverse Polish Notation (RPN). Pocket calculators developed by the Hewlett-Packard Corporation are especially notable for their use of RPN and have made stack arithmetic the favorite of many scientists and engineers.

Function PUSH(a name)

   Allocate a new record space.

   Assign a value to the name field.

   Assign the address value from the tosp to the pointer field (thus, each
     record contains a pointer that points to the previous record location).

   Assign the address of the new record space to tosp.

Function POP(a name)

   If tosp is not a NULL

     Assign field values referenced by tosp to a temporary record.

     Deallocate the record space on the top of the stack.

     Assign the pointer member of the temporary record to the tosp (thus, the
     tosp now points to the record previous to the record just popped).

The two functions, `push()` and `pop()`, described by this pseudocode are included within Program 14.6.

In general, Program 14.6 is straightforward: the function `read_push()` allows the user to enter names and pushes the names on the stack by calling `push()`. Similarly, the function `pop_show()` pops the names from the stack by calling `pop` and then displays them. Notice that the address of a name is used as an argument in both `push()` and `pop()`. This was done for convenience and to keep the example simple. More generally, the name of a record containing the data to be pushed onto the stack would be passed to `push` and a pointer to the record that will be popped from the stack would be passed to `pop()`. A sample run using Program 14.6 produced the following:

Enter as many names as you wish, one per line
To stop entering names, enter a single x
Enter a name: Jane Jones
Enter a name: Bill Smith
Enter a name: Jim Robinson
Enter a name: x

The names popped from the stack are:
Jim Robinson
Bill Smith
Jane Jones

PROGRAM 14.6

```c
#include <stdio.h>
#include <stdlib.h>
#define MAXCHARS 30
#define DEBUG 0

/* here is the declaration of a stack record */
struct Name_rec
{
  char name[MAXCHARS];
  struct Name_rec *prior_addr;
};

/* here is the definition of the top-of-stack pointer */
struct Name_rec *tosp;

void main(void)
{
  void read_push(void); /* function prototypes */
  void pop_show(void);

  tosp = NULL;      /* initialize the top-of-stack pointer */
  read_push();
  pop_show();
}

/* get a name and push it onto the stack */
void read_push(void)
{
  char name[MAXCHARS];
  void push(char []);

  printf("\nEnter as many names as you wish, one per line");
  printf("\nTo stop entering names, enter a single x\n");
  while (1)
  {
    printf("Enter a name: ");
```

(continued on next page)

(continued from previous page)

```
      gets(name);
      if (strcmp(name,"x") == 0)
        break;
      push(name);
  }
}

/* pop and display names from the stack */
void pop_show(void)
{
  char name[MAXCHARS];
  void pop(char []);

  printf("\nThe names popped from the stack are:\n");
  while (tosp != NULL) /* display till end of stack */
  {
    pop(name);
    printf("%s\n",name);
  }
  return;
}

void push(char *name)
{
  struct Name_rec *newaddr; /* pointer to structure of type Name_rec */

  if (DEBUG)
    printf("Before the push the address in tosp is %p", tosp);

  newaddr = (struct Name_rec *) malloc(sizeof(struct Name_rec));
  if (newaddr == (struct Name_rec *) NULL)
  {
    printf("\nFailed to allocate memory for this record\n");
    exit(1);
  }
  strcpy(newaddr->name,name); /* store the name */
  newaddr->prior_addr = tosp; /* store address of prior record */
  tosp = newaddr;             /* update the top-of-stack pointer */

  if (DEBUG)
    printf("\n After the push the address in tosp is %p\n", tosp);
}

void pop(char *name)
{
  struct Name_rec *temp_addr;

  if (DEBUG)
    printf("Before the pop the address in tosp is %p\n", tosp);
```

(continued on next page)

(continued from previous page)

```
    strcpy(name,tosp->name); /* retrieve the name from the top-of-stack */
    temp_addr = tosp->prior_addr;  /* retrieve the prior address */
    free(tosp);                      /* release the record's memory space */
    tosp = temp_addr;              /* update the top-of-stack pointer */

    if (DEBUG)
      printf(" After the pop the address in tosp is %p\n", tosp);
}

void push(char *name)
{
  struct Name_rec *newaddr; /* pointer to structure of type Name_rec */

  if (DEBUG)
    printf("Before the push the address in tosp is %p", tosp);

  newaddr = (struct Name_rec *) malloc(sizeof(struct Name_rec));
  strcpy(newaddr->name,name); /* store the name */
  newaddr->prior_addr = tosp; /* store address of prior record */
  tosp = newaddr;              /* update the top-of-stack pointer */

  if (DEBUG)
    printf("\n After the push the address in tosp is %p\n", tosp);
}

void pop(char *name)
{
  struct Name_rec *temp_addr;

  if (DEBUG)
    printf("Before the pop the address in tosp is %p\n", tosp);

  strcpy(name,tosp->name);  /* retrieve the name from the top-of-stack */
  temp_addr = tosp->prior_addr; /* retrieve the prior address */
  free(tosp);                      /* release the record's memory space */
  tosp = temp_addr;              /* update the top-of-stack pointer */

  if (DEBUG)
    printf(" After the pop the address in tosp is %p\n", tosp);
}
```

Exercises 14.3

1. a. Describe the steps necessary to perform a push operation on a stack.

   b. Describe the steps necessary to perform a pop operation on a stack.

   c. What value should the top-of-stack pointer contain when the stack is empty?

2. Assume that the first record allocated by Program 14.6 is allocated at memory location 100, the second at memory location 150, and the third at memory location 200.

Using this information, construct a figure similar to Figure 14.7 that shows the values in the `tosp` and each record after the third name has been pushed onto the stack.

3. State whether a stack structure would be appropriate for each of the following tasks. Indicate why or why not.

    a. A character storage program that must remember a line of up to 80 characters. Pressing the Backspace key deletes the previous character, and pressing CTR/Backspace deletes the entire line. Users must be able to undo deletion operations.

    b. Customers must wait one to three months for delivery of their new automobiles. The dealer creates a list that will determine the "fair" order in which customers should get their cars; the list is to be prepared in the order in which customers placed their requests for a new car.

    c. You are required to search downward in a pile of magazines to locate the issue for last January. Each magazine was placed on the pile as soon as it was received.

    d. A programming team accepts jobs and prioritizes them on the basis of urgency.

    e. A line formed at a bus stop.

4. Modify Program 14.6 so that the argument to `push` is a record and the argument to `pop` is a pointer to a record rather than both being a single field variable.

5. Write a stack program that accepts a record consisting of an integer identification number and a floating-point hourly pay rate.

6. Add a menu function to Program 14.6 that gives the user a choice of adding a name to the stack, removing a name from the stack, or listing the contents of the stack without removing any records from it.

14.4 QUEUES

A second important data structure that relies on linked records is called a *queue*. Items are removed from a queue in the order in which they were entered. Thus a queue is a *first-in/first-out (FIFO)* structure.

As an example of a queue, consider a waiting list of people that want to purchase season tickets to a professional football team. The first person on the list is to be called for the first set of tickets that become available, the second person should be called for the second available set, and so on. For purposes of illustration assume that the names of the people currently on the list are shown in Figure 14.9. As illustrated in this figure, the names have been added in the same fashion as on a stack; that is, as new names are added to the list they have been stacked on top of the existing names. The difference in a queue is in how the names are popped off the list. Clearly the people on this list expect to be serviced in the order in which they were placed on the list—that is, first-in/first-out. Thus, unlike a stack, the most recently added name to the list *is not* the first name removed. Rather, the oldest name still on the list is always the next name removed.

FIGURE 14.9   A Queue with Its Pointers

Harriet Wright ◄———	**last name on the queue** (queue_in)
Jim Robinson	
Bill Smith	
Jane Jones ◄———	**first name on the queue** (queue_out)

A BIT OF BACKGROUND

Stacking the Deque

Stacks and queues (pronounced "cues") are two special forms of a more general data structure called a *dequeue* or *deque* (pronounced "deck"). Dequeue stands for *double-ended queue*.

In a deque structure, data can be handled in one of four ways:

1. Insert at the end and remove from the end. This is the last-in/first-out (LIFO) stack structure.
2. Insert at the end and remove from the beginning. This is the first-in/first-out (FIFO) queue structure.
3. Insert at the beginning and remove from the end, which represents a type of inverted FIFO queue.

4. Insert at the beginning and remove from the beginning, which also a LIFO technique.

Implementation 1 (stack structure) was presented in Section 14.3 and implementation 2 (queue structure) is presented in Section 14.4. Implementations 3 and 4 are sometimes used for keeping track of memory addresses—such as when programming is done in machine language or when records are handled in a file. When a high-level language, such as C, manages the data area automatically, users may not be aware of where the data are being stored or of which type of deque is being applied.

To keep the list in proper order, where new names are added to one end of the list and old names are removed from the other end, it is convenient to use two pointers: One points to the front of the list for the next person to be serviced, and the other points to the end of the list where new people will be added. The pointer that points to the front of the list here the next name is to be removed, will be referred to as the `queue_out` pointer. The second pointer, which points to the last person in line and indicates where the next person entering the list is to be placed, will be called the `queue_in` pointer. Thus, for the list shown in Figure 14.9, `queue_out` points to Jane Jones and `queue_in` to Harriet Wright. If Jane Jones were now removed from the list and Lou Hazlet and Teresa Filer were added, the queue and its associated pointers would appear as shown in Figure 14.10.

Enqueue and Serve

The operation of placing a new item on top of the queue is formally referred to as *enqueueing* and the operation of removing an item from a queue is formally

FIGURE 14.10 The Updated Queue Pointers

```
Teresa Filer      ◄────── queue_in

Lou Hazlet

Harriet Wright

Jim Robinson

Bill Smith        ◄────── queue_out
```

referred to as *serving*. Except for the pointers used in each operation, enqueueing on a queue is similar to the operation of pushing on one end of a stack, and serving from a queue is similar to the operation of popping from the other end of a stack. Let's see how these operations are implemented for a queue.

Figure 14.11 illustrates a queue consisting of three records. As shown, each record consists of a name member and a pointer member. Unlike a stack, where the pointer member points to the previous record in the list, in a queue each pointer member points to the next list record. In addition, there are two separate queue pointers: the `queue_in` pointer, which contains the address of the last record added to the queue, and the `queue_out` pointer, which contains the address of the first record stored on the queue.

Enqueueing (pushing) a new record onto an existing queue, such as that shown in Figure 14.11, involves the following algorithm:

Enqueue (add a new record to an existing queue)
  Dynamically create a new a record.
  Set the address field of the new record to a NULL.
  Fill in the remaining fields of the new record.
  Set the address field of the prior record (which is pointed to by the queue_in pointer) to the address of the newly created record.
  Update the address in the queue_in pointer with the address of the newly created record.

For example, if we were to add a new record onto the queue illustrated in Figure 14.11, the resulting queue would appear as shown in Figure 14.12.

The only record that can be removed from a queue is always the earliest record put on the queue. Thus, for the queue shown in Figure 14.12, the next record that can be removed is record 1. After this record is removed ("served") record two can

FIGURE 14.11 A Queue Consisting of Three Records

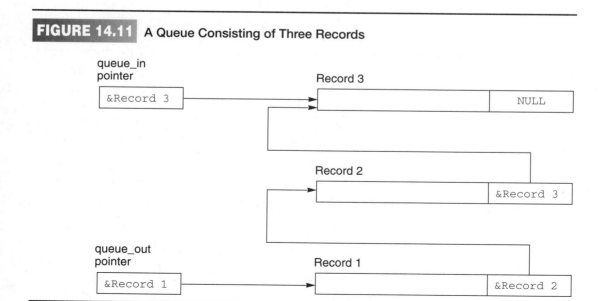

FIGURE 14.12 The Queue After an Enqueue Operation (PUSH)

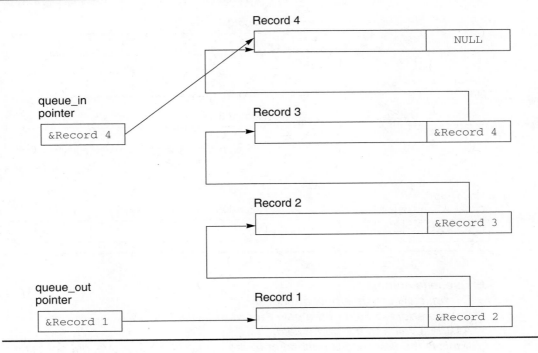

be removed, and so on. The operation of serving (popping) a record from an existing queue is defined by the algorithm:

Serve (remove a record an existing queue)
Move the contents of the record pointed to by the queue_out pointer into a work area.
Free the record pointed to by the queue_out pointer.
Move the address in the work area address field into the queue_out pointer.

If these operations are carried out on the queue illustrated in Figure 14.12, the queue would consist of the records and pointers shown in Figure 14.13.

As a specific demonstration of a dynamically allocated queue, assume that the record type of data to be stored on the queue is declared as:

```
#define MAXCHARS 30
struct Name_rec
{
  char name[MAXCHARS];
  struct Name_rec *next_addr;
};
```

This is simply a record consisting of a name and a pointer member of the type illustrated in Figures 14.11, 14.2, and 14.13. The enqueue and serve queue operations for this particular record type can now be described.

FIGURE 14.13 The Queue After a Serve (POP)

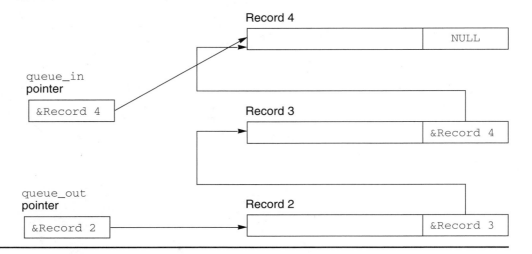

Enqueue (a name)
Dynamically create a new a record.
Set the address field of the new record to a NULL.
Assign a value to the name field.
If this is the first record pushed onto the queue (that is, queue_out contains
a NULL) then update the address in the queue_out pointer with the address
of the newly created record.
If the queue is not empty (that is, queue_in does not contain a NULL) then
set the address field of the prior record (which is pointed to by the queue_in
pointer) to the address of the newly created record (thus, each record con-
tains a pointer that points to the next record in the queue).
Update the address in the queue_in pointer with the address of the newly
created record.

Serve (a name)
If queue_out is not a NULL
Move the contents of the record pointed to by the queue_out pointer into
a work area.
Free the record pointed to by the queue_out pointer.
Move the address in the work area address field into the queue_out pointer.

These are essentially the same algorithms as described previously, with the addition of the proper procedure to account for the special case where the queue is empty.[6] For this case, both `queue_in` and `queue_out` pointers will contain `NULL`s. The two functions, `enque()` and `serve()`, described by this pseudocode are included within Program 14.7.

---

[6] In practice functions named `isempty()` and `isfull()` would also be defined to simplify the code for servicing and enqueueing, respectively.

```
PROGRAM 14.7

#include <stdio.h>
#include <stdlib.h>
#define MAXCHARS 30
#define DEBUG 0

/* here is the declaration of a queue record */
struct Name_rec
{
  char name[MAXCHARS];
  struct Name_rec *next_addr;
};

/* here is the definition of the top and bottom queue pointers */
struct Name_rec *queue_in, *queue_out;

void main(void)
{
  void read_enque(void); /* function prototypes */
  void serve_show(void);

  queue_in = NULL; /* initialize queue pointers */
  queue_out = NULL;
  read_enque();
  serve_show();
}

/* get a name and enque it onto the queue */
void read_enque(void)
{
  char name[MAXCHARS];
  void enque(char []);

  printf("\nEnter as many names as you wish, one per line");
  printf("\nTo stop entering names, enter a single x\n");
  while (1)
  {
    printf("Enter a name: ");
    gets(name);
    if (strcmp(name,"x") == 0)
      break;
    enque(name);
  }
}

/* serve and display names from the queue */
void serve_show(void)
{
  char name[MAXCHARS];
  void serve(char []);
```

(continued on next page)

(continued from previous page)

```c
  printf("\nThe names served from the queue are:\n");
  while (queue_out != NULL) /* display till end of queue */
  {
    serve(name);
    printf("%s\n",name);
  }
  return;
}

void enque(char *name)
{
  struct Name_rec *newaddr; /* pointer to structure of type Name_rec */

  if (DEBUG)
  {
    printf("Before the enqueue the address in queue_in is %p", queue_in);
    printf("\nand the address in queue_out is %p", queue_out);
  }

  newaddr = (struct Name_rec *) malloc(sizeof(struct Name_rec));
  if (newaddr == (struct Name_rec *) NULL)
  {
    printf("\nFailed to allocate memory for this record\n");
    exit(1);
  }

  /* these next two if statements handle the empty queue initialization */
  if (queue_out == NULL)
    queue_out = newaddr;
  if (queue_in != NULL)
    queue_in->next_addr = newaddr; /* fill in prior record's address field */

  strcpy(newaddr->name,name); /* store the name */
  newaddr->next_addr = NULL; /* set address field to NULL */
  queue_in = newaddr; /* update the top-of-queue pointer */

  if (DEBUG)
  {
    printf("\n After the enqueue the address in queue_in is %p\n", queue_in);
    printf(" and the address in queue_out is %p\n", queue_out);
  }
}

void serve(char *name)
{
  struct Name_rec *next_addr;

  if (DEBUG)
    printf("Before the serve the address in queue_out is %p\n", queue_out);
```

(continued on next page)

(continued from previous page)

```
strcpy(name,queue_out->name); /* retrieve the name from the bottom-of-queue */
next_addr = queue_out->next_addr; /* capture the next address field */
free(queue_out);
queue_out = next_addr; /* update the bottom-of-queue pointer */

if (DEBUG)
    printf(" After the serve the address in queue_out is %p\n", queue_out);
}
```

In general, Program 14.7 is straightforward: The function `read_enque()` allows the user to enter names and pushes the names on the queue by calling `enque()`. Similarly, the function `serve_show()` pops the names from the queue by calling `serve()` and then displays them. Notice that the address of a name is used as an argument in both `push` and `pop`. This was done for convenience and to keep the example simple. More generally, the name of a record containing the data to be pushed onto the queue would be passed to `enque()` and a pointer to the record that will be popped from the queue would be passed to `serve()`. A sample run using Program 14.7 produced the following:

```
Enter as many names as you wish, one per line
To stop entering names, enter a single x
Enter a name: Jane Jones
Enter a name: Bill Smith
Enter a name: Jim Robinson
Enter a name: x

The names popped from the queue are:
Jane Jones
Bill Smith
Jim Robinson
```

Exercises 14.4

1. a. Describe the steps necessary to add a record to an existing queue.

   b. Describe the steps necessary to remove a record from an existing queue.

   c. What value should the `queue_in` and `queue_out` pointers contain when a queue is empty?

2. Assume that the first record allocated by Program 14.7 is allocated at memory location 100, the second at memory location 150, and the third at memory location 200. Using this information, construct a figure similar to Figure 14.11 showing the values in the `tosp` and each record after the third name has been pushed onto the stack.

3. State whether a queue, a stack, or neither structure would be appropriate for each of the following tasks. Indicate why or why not.

   a. A waiting list of customers to be seated in a restaurant.

   b. A group of student tests waiting to be graded.

   c. An address book listing names and telephone numbers in alphabetical order.

   d. A line at a bus stop.

4. Modify Program 14.7 so that the argument to `enque()` is a record and pop the argument to `serve()` is a pointer to a record rather than both being a single field variable.

5. Write a queue program that accepts a record consisting of an integer identification number and a floating-point hourly pay rate.

6. Add a menu function to Program 14.7 that gives the user a choice of adding a name to the queue, removing a name from the queue, or listing the contents of the queue without removing any records from it.

14.5 DYNAMICALLY LINKED LISTS

Both stacks and queues are examples of linked lists in which elements can only be added to and removed from the ends of the list. In a dynamically linked list, this capability is extended to permit addition or deletion of a record from anywhere in the list. Such a capability is extremely useful when records must be kept within a specified order, such as alphabetically, and the list must expand as new records are added and contract as records are removed from the list.

In Section 14.2 we saw how to construct a fixed set of linked lists. In this section we show how to dynamically allocate and free records from such a list. For example, in constructing a list of names and phone numbers the exact number of structures ultimately needed may not be known. Nevertheless, we may want the to maintain the list in alphabetical last name order regardless of how many names are added or removed from the list. A dynamically allocated list that can expand and contract is ideally suited for this type of list maintenance.

Insert and Delete

The operation of adding a new record to a dynamically linked list is called an *insert* and removing a record from such a list is called a *delete*. Let's see how these operations are implemented in practice.

Figure 14.14 illustrates a linked list consisting of three records. As shown, each record consists of a name member and a pointer member containing the address of the next record in the list. Several observations can be made for this list that apply to all dynamically maintained linked lists.

First, notice that each record shown in Figure 14.4 contains one pointer member, which is the address of the next record in the list. Also notice that the start-of-list pointer contains the address of the first record in the list and that the pointer member of the last record is a NULL address. This configuration is required of all dynamically linked lists regardless of any other data members present in each record.

Next notice that the records illustrated in Figure 14.4 are in alphabetical order. In general, every dynamically linked list is maintained based on the value of a particular field in each record. The field on which the list is ordered is referred to as the *key field*, and insertions and deletions are always made to preserve the ordering of this field.

Now assume that we want to insert the name Carter into the list. After dynamically allocating new memory space for the Carter record, the record addresses would have to be adjusted as shown in Figure 14.15 to maintain the proper alphabetical ordering.

FIGURE 14.14 The Initial Linked List

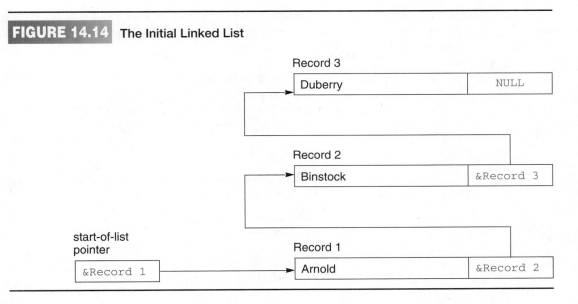

The algorithm for performing an insertion into a linked list is as follows:

INSERT (add a new record into a linked list)
  Dynamically allocate space for a new record.
  If no records exist in the list
    Set the address field of the new record to a NULL.
    Set the address in the first record pointer to the address of the newly
      created record.
  Else / we are working with an existing list */*
    Locate where this new record should be placed.
    If this record should be the new first record in the list
      Copy the current contents of the first record pointer into the address
        field of the newly created record.
      Set the address in the first record pointer to the address of the newly
        created record.
    Else
      Copy the address in the prior record's address member into the address
        field of the newly created record.
      Set the address field of the prior record's address member to the
        address of the newly created record.
    EndIf
  EndIf

This algorithm provides the steps for correctly updating the pointer members of each record in a list such as that shown in Figure 14.15, including the first record pointer when necessary. The algorithm does not, however, indicate how to locate the exact position in the list where the insertion should be made. The location of the insertion point can be made by a linear search (see Section 8.5) of the existing list. The pseudocode for a linear search to determine the correct insertion point is:

LINEAR LOCATION of a NEW RECORD
  If the key field of the new record is less than the first record's key field the
    new record should be the new first record.
  Else
    While there are still more records in the list
      Compare the new record's key value to each record key.
      Stop the comparison when the new record key either falls between two
        existing records or belongs at the end of the existing list.
    EndWhile
  EndIf

As a specific demonstration of insertions into a linked list, assume that the record type of data stored in the list is declared as:

```
#define MAXCHARS 30
struct Name_rec
{
  char name[MAXCHARS];
  struct Name_rec *next_addr;
};
```

This is simply a record consisting of a name and pointer member of the type illustrated in Figures 14.14 and 14.15. The insert and linear locate algorithms are included within Program 14.8.

FIGURE 14.15 Adding a New Name to the List

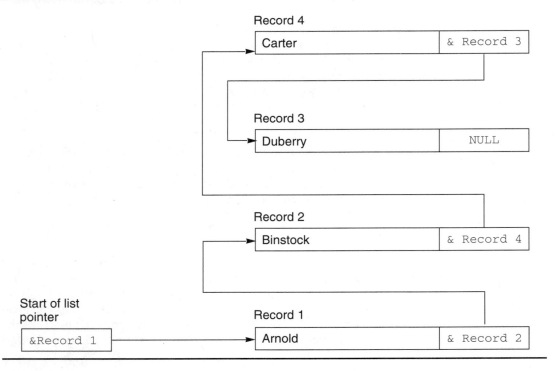

A BIT OF BACKGROUND

Artificial Intelligence

One of the major steps toward creating dynamic machines that "learn" as they work was the development of dynamic data structures.

In 1950, Alan Turing proposed a test in which an expert enters questions at an isolated terminal. Presumably, artificial intelligence (AI) is achieved when the expert cannot discern whether the answers returned to the screen have been produced by a human or by a machine. Although there are problems with the Turing test, its concepts have spawned numerous research efforts.

By the mid 1960s, many AI researchers believed the efforts to create "thinking machines" were futile. Today, however, much lively research and development is focused on such topics as dynamic problem solving, computer vision, parallel processing, natural language processing, and speech and pattern recognition—all of which are encompassed within the field of artificial intelligence.

Development of techniques that allow machines to emulate humans have proliferated in recent years with the development of computers that are small, fast, powerful, and inexpensive. Most people agree that computers could never replace all human decision making. There is also general agreement that society must remain alert and remain in control of important decisions that require human compassion, ethics, and understanding.

PROGRAM 14.8

```c
#include <stdio.h>
#include <stdlib.h>
#define MAXCHARS 30
#define DEBUG 0

/* here is the declaration of a linked list record */
struct Name_rec
{
  char name[MAXCHARS];
  struct Name_rec *next_addr;
};

/* here is the definition of the first record pointer */
struct Name_rec *first_rec;

void main(void)
{
  void read_insert(void); /* function prototypes */
  void display(void);

  first_rec = NULL; /* initialize list pointer */
  read_insert();
  display();
```

(continued on next page)

(continued from previous page)

```c
}

/* get a name and insert it into the linked list */
void read_insert(void)
{
  char name[MAXCHARS];
  void insert(char []);

  printf("\nEnter as many names as you wish, one per line");
  printf("\nTo stop entering names, enter a single x\n");
  while (1)
  {
    printf("Enter a name: ");
    gets(name);
    if (strcmp(name,"x") == 0)
      break;
    insert(name);
  }
}

void insert(char *name)
{
  struct Name_rec *locate(char *); /* function prototype */
  struct Name_rec *newaddr, *here; /* pointers to structure of type Name_rec */

  newaddr = (struct Name_rec *) malloc(sizeof(struct Name_rec));
  if (newaddr == (struct Name_rec *) NULL) /* check the address */
  {
    printf("\nCould not allocate the requested space\n");
    exit;
  }

    /* locate where the new record should be placed and */
    /* update all pointer members */
  if (first_rec == NULL) /* no list currently exists */
  {
    newaddr->next_addr = NULL;
    first_rec = newaddr;
  }
  else if (strcmp(name, first_rec->name) < 0) /* a new first record */
  {
    newaddr->next_addr = first_rec;
    first_rec = newaddr;
  }
  else /* record is not the first record of the list */
  {
    here = locate(name);
    newaddr->next_addr = here->next_addr;
    here->next_addr = newaddr;
```

(continued on next page)

(continued from previous page)

```
  }

  strcpy(newaddr->name,name); /* store the name */
}

/* locate the address of where a new record should be inserted */
/* within an existing list */
struct Name_rec *locate(char *name)
{
  struct Name_rec *one, *two;

  one = first_rec;
  two = one->next_addr;

  if (two == NULL)
    return(one); /* new record goes after the existing single record */
  while(1)
  {
    if(strcmp(name,two->name) < 0) /* we've located its position within the List */
    {
      break;
    }
    else if(two->next_addr == NULL) /* it goes after the last record */
    {
      one = two;
      break;
    }
    else /* more records to search against */
    {
      one = two;
      two = one->next_addr;
    }
  } /* the break takes us here */
  return(one);
}

/* display names from the linked list */
void display(void)
{
  struct Name_rec *contents;

  contents = first_rec;
  printf("\nThe names currently on the list are:\n");
  while (contents != NULL) /* display till end of list */
  {
    printf("%s\n",contents->name);
    contents = contents->next_addr;
  }
  return;
}
```

To test Program 14.8 adequately, we need to enter names on a new list and then add names that should be inserted before the first name, after the last name, and between two existing names. The following sample run performs these tests.

```
Enter as many names as you wish, one per line
To stop entering names, enter a single x
Enter a name: Binstock
Enter a name: Arnold
Enter a name: Duberry
Enter a name: Carter
Enter a name: x

The names currently on the list are:
Arnold
Binstock
Carter
Duberry
```

Notice that the first name entered forces `insert()` to construct the list, while the second name forces `insert()` to place this new name at the beginning of the list. The third name, Duberry, forces `locate()` to correctly determine that this name should be placed at the end of the list, while the last name, Carter, forces `locate()` to correctly position the name between two existing names.

Deleting a record in a linked list is essentially the reverse process of inserting a record. That is, a deletion requires us to determine where the selected record currently resides—at the beginning, at the end, or within the list—and then adjust all pointer values accordingly and deallocate record space. We leave the detailed construction of the deletion algorithm as an exercise.

Exercises 14.5

1. Draw a diagram that illustrates how the linked list created by Program 14.8 looks as each name is inserted into the list. Make sure to include the first record pointer in your diagram.

2. a. Write the pseudocode for deleting an existing structure from the linked list of structures created by Program 14.8. The algorithm for deleting a linked structure should follow the sequence developed for deleting a structure developed in Exercise 4 in Section 14.2.

   b. Write C code for the algorithm developed in Exercise 2a.

3. Write a function named `modify` that can be used to modify the name member of the structures created in Program 14.8. The argument passed to `modify` should be the address of the structure to be modified. The `modify` function should first display the existing name and phone number in the selected structure and then request new data for these members.

4. Write a C program that initially presents a menu of choices for the user. The menu should consist of the following choices:

```
A. Create an initial linked list of names and phone numbers.
B. Insert a new structure into the linked list.
C. Modify an existing structure in the linked list.
D. Delete an existing structure from the list.
E. Exit from the program.
```

   Upon selection by the user, the program should execute the appropriate functions to satisfy the request.

14.6 COMMON PROGRAMMING ERRORS

The most common programming errors in using dynamically allocated storage areas are as follows:

1. Not checking the return codes provided by `malloc()`, `calloc()`, and `realloc()`. If any of these functions returns a `NULL` pointer, the user should be notified that the allocation did not take place and the normal program operation must be altered in an appropriate way. You simply cannot assume that all calls to `malloc()`, `calloc()`, and `realloc()` will result in the requested allocation of memory space.

2. Not correctly updating all relevant pointer addresses when adding or removing records from dynamically created stacks, queues, and linked lists. Unless extreme care is taken when updating addresses, each of these dynamic data structures can quickly become corrupted.

3. Forgetting to free previously allocated memory space when the space is no longer needed. This is typically only a problem in a large application program that is expected to run continuously and can make many requests for allocated space based on user demand.

4. Not preserving the integrity of the addressed contained in the top-of-stack pointer, queue-in, queue-out, and other list pointers when dealing with a stack, queue, and dynamically linked list, respectively. Because each of these pointers locates a starting position in their respective data structures, the complete list will be lost if the starting addresses are incorrect.

5. Related to the previous error is the equally disastrous one of not correctly updating internal record pointers when inserting and removing records from a stack, queue, or dynamically linked list. Once an internal pointer within a singly linked list contains an incorrect address, it is almost impossible to locate and reestablish the missing set of records.

14.7 CHAPTER REVIEW

Key Terms

dynamic memory allocation	linked list
enqueue	pop
first-in/first-out (FIFO)	push
heap	queue
key field	serve
last-in/first-out (LIFO)	stack

Summary

An alternative to fixed memory allocation for variables at compile time is the dynamic allocation of memory at run time. Such a scheme allocates and deallocates memory storage under program control and is extremely useful when dealing with a list of data that can expand and contract as items are added and deleted from the list. In C, the functions used for dynamic memory allocation are `malloc()`, `calloc()`, `realloc()`, and `free`.

The `malloc()` function reserves a requested number of bytes and returns a pointer to the first reserved byte. For example, the expression `malloc(50 * sizeof(int))` reserves a sufficient number of bytes to store 50 integers. The `malloc()` function will either return a pointer to the first byte of reserved storage or return a `NULL` pointer if the request cannot be satisfied. Since the returned pointer always "points to" a character, it must always be cast into a pointer of the desired type. Thus, this specific request for storage would be made using the expression

```
pointer_to_int = (int *) malloc(50 * sizeof(int))
```

where `pointer_to_int` has been declared as a pointer to an integer.

In using `malloc()` you should always check its return value to ensure that a `NULL` pointer was not returned, which would indicate that the request for memory space was not satisfied. Continuing with our example, this check would take the form

```
if (pointer_to_int == (int *)NULL))
{
  do an error procedure in here
  typically an exit
}
```

The `calloc()` functions operaters in the same manner as `malloc()` but reserves space for an array of elements.

The `realloc()` function also operates in a fashion similar to that of the `malloc()` function except is used to expand or contract an existing allocated space. If the new size is larger than the previously allocated space, only the additional space remains uninitialized and the previously allocated space retains its contents; otherwise, the new space retains its prior contents up to its new limits. As with `malloc()`, the return address provided by `realloc()` should always be checked.

The `free()` function is used to deallocate previously allocated memory space.

Once of the most important uses of dynamic allocation is for creating adjustable size data structures, such as stacks, queues, and linked lists. All of these data structures, when created dynamically, require a pointer member to store the address of either the next or previous record in the list.

A *stack* is a list consisting of records that can only be added and removed from the top of the list. Such a structure is a LIFO list in which the last record added to the list is the first record removed. The pointer member of each record in a stack always points to the prior record in the list. Additionally, one pointer variable is always required to contain the address of the current top-of-stack record.

A *queue* is a list consisting of records that are added to the top of the list and removed from the bottom of the list. Such a structure is a FIFO list in which records are removed in the order in which they were added. The pointer member of each record in a queue always points to the next record in the list. Additionally, one pointer is always required to contain the address of the current top-of-queue record and one pointer is required to contain the current bottom-of-queue record.

A *dynamically linked list* consists of records that can be added or removed from any position in the list. Such lists are used to keep records in a specified order, such as alphabetically. The pointer member of each record in a dynamically linked list always points to the next record in the list. Additionally, one pointer is always required to contain the address of the first record in the list.

Exercises

1. Write a C program that simulates a stack of integer numbers using an array. Include `push()` and `pop()` functions that add and remove a number from the

array, respectively. (*Hint:* Let the `top_of_stack` indicator be the index of the item placed in the array last. `top_of_stack` = –1 when the array is empty.

2. Implement a stack that represents an in-box on your desk. Each record in the stack should consist of a character field of up to 50 characters and an integer field. The character field is used to describe the task to be done and the integer contains a time stamp of when the job arrived; for example 950 and 1426 would represent 9:50 A.M. and 2:26 P.M., respectively. Your secretary fills the box with a number of tasks when the mail arrives in the morning and adds work periodically. You work continuously, all day long, to pop the tasks from the stack and take care of them. All tasks must be completed by the end of the day.

3. A group of people have arrived at a bus stop and are lined up in the order indicated:

1. Chaplin	4. Laurel	7. Oliver	10. Garland
2. West	5. Smith	8. Hardy	11. Wayne
3. Taylor	6. Grisby	9. Burton	12. Stewart

   a. Read the names from an input file into a stack and display the order in which they board the bus. (*Hint:* Use two stacks.)

   b. Read the names from an input file into a queue and display the order in which they board the bus.

4. Write a single-line word processor. As characters are typed they are to be `pushed` onto a stack. Some characters have special meanings:

#	Erase the previous character (`pop` it from the stack).
@	Kill the entire line (empty the stack).
?, !, ., or Enter	Terminate line entry. Move the characters to an array and write the contents of the array to the screen.

5. In recursive functions, the parameters are usually stored on a stack. For example, when the function

```
factorial(int n)
{
    int fact;

    if (n = 0)
       fact = 1;
    else
       fact = n * Factorial(n - 1);
    return (fact);
}
```

is called, the successive values of the parameter *n* are stored on a stack. For example, if the initial call where `value` = `factorial(5)`, then 5 would be pushed on to the stack for *n*. The next call to factorial would push 4, then 3, and so on, until the last parameter value of 0. Then the values would be popped one at a time and multiplied by the previous product until the stack is empty.

   Using this information, write a C program that performs the same operation as the factorial procedure for a given value of *n*, entered by the user. After each push, the contents of the stack should be displayed. After each pop, the contents of the stack and the value of `factorial()` should be displayed. Once the display indicates proper operation of your function, stop the display and simply have the function return the proper factorial value.

6. Write a queue-handling program that asks each customer for their names as they place orders at a fast food restaurant. Each record in the queue should consist of a name field with a maximum of 20 characters and an integer field, which keeps track of the total number of customers served. The value in the integer field should be automatically provided by the program each time a name is entered. Orders are processed in the sequence in which they are placed. The order-taker examines the queue and calls the names when the order is ready. When the queue is empty, print a message telling the staff to take a break.

7. Descriptions of jobs waiting in a computer for the printer are generally kept in a queue. Write a C program that keeps track of printing jobs, recorded by user name and anticipated printer time (in seconds) for the job. Add jobs to the queue as printouts are requested, and remove them from the queue as they are serviced. When a user adds a job to the queue, display a message giving an estimate of how long it will be before the job is printed. The estimate is to consist of the sum of all the prior jobs in the queue (*Hint:* Store the accumulated times in a separate variable.)

8. a. On your electronic mail terminal you receive notes to call people. Each message contains the name and phone number of the caller as well as a date in the form month/day/year and a 24-hour integer clock in the form hours:minutes that records when the message was received. A latest_attempt field is initially set to 0, indicating that no attempt has yet been made to return the call. For example, a particular record may appear as:

   ```
   Jan Williamson (215)666-7777 8/14/96 17:05 0
   ```

   Write a C program to store these records in a queue as they arrive and to feed them to you, one at a time, on request. If you cannot reach a person when you try to call, place that record at the end of the queue and fill the latest_attempt field with the time you tried to return the call, in the form days_later/hours:min. Thus, if your last unsuccessful attempt to return Jan Williamson's call was on 8/16/96 at 4:20, the new enqueued record would be

   ```
   Jan Williamson (215)666-7777 8/14/96 17:05 2/16:20
   ```

   b. Modify the program written for Exercise 8a so that the time and date fields are automatically filled in using system calls to time and date functions provided by your compiler.

Additional Capabilities

Previous chapters have presented C's basic capabilities, statements, and structure. The variations on each of these, which are almost endless, are a source of delight to many programmers who continuously find new possibilities of expression using variations of the basic language building blocks. This chapter presents additional capabilities that you will find useful as you progress in your understanding and use of C. For completeness we also include one statement that is part of the C language but is almost never used by knowledgeable C programmers.

15.1 ADDITIONAL STATEMENTS

In this section four statements are presented. Of these only the `typedef` declaration is used extensively.

The `typedef` Declaration Statement

The `typedef` declaration statement permits programmers to construct alternate names for an existing C data type name. For example, the statement:

```
typedef float REAL;
```

makes the name REAL a synonym for `float`. The name REAL can now be used in place of the term `float` anywhere in the program after the synonym has been declared. For example, using this `typedef` declaration makes the definition:

```
REAL val;
```

equivalent to the definition:

```
float val;
```

The `typedef` statement does not create a new data type; it creates a new name for an existing data type. Using uppercase names in `typedef` statements is not mandatory. It is done simply to alert the programmer to a user-specified name, as is done with uppercase names in `#define` statements. In fact, the equivalence produced by a `typedef` statement can frequently be produced equally well by a `#define` statement. The difference between the two, however, is that `typedef` statements are processed directly by the compiler while `#define` statements are processed by the preprocessor.

Compiler processing of `typedef` statements allow for text replacements that are not possible with the preprocessor. For example, the statement:

```
typedef float REAL;
```

actually specifies that `REAL` is a placeholder that will be replaced with another variable name. A subsequent declaration such as:

```
REAL val;
```

has the effect of substituting the variable named `val` for the placeholder named `REAL` in the terms following the word `typedef`. Substituting `val` for `REAL` in the `typedef` statement and retaining all terms after the reserved word `typedef` results in the equivalent declaration `float val;`.

Once the mechanics of the replacement are understood, more useful equivalences can be constructed. Consider the statement

```
typedef int ARRAY[100];
```

Here, the name `ARRAY` is actually a placeholder for any subsequently defined variables. Thus, a statement such as `ARRAY first, second;` is equivalent to the two definitions

```
int first[100];
int second[100];
```

Each of these definitions is obtained by replacing the name `ARRAY` with the variable names `first` and `second` in the terms following the reserved word `typedef`.

As another example, consider the following statement:

```
typedef struct
{
  char name[20];
  int id_num;
} EMP_REC;
```

Here `EMP_REC` is a convenient placeholder for any subsequent variable. For example, the declaration `EMP_REC employee[75];` is equivalent to the declaration

```
struct
{
  char name[20];
  int id_num;
} employee[75];
```

This last declaration is obtained by directly substituting the term `employee[75]` in place of the word `EMP_REC` in the terms following the word `typedef` in the original `typedef` statement. More typically a `typedef` is used in place of a structure tag name using the method illustrated in the *Tips from the Pros* box on page 558.

The enum Specifier

The *enum* specifier creates an enumerated data type, which is simply a user-defined list of values that is given its own data type name. Such data types are identified by the reserved word enum followed by an optional, user-selected name for the data type and a listing of acceptable values for the date type. Consider the following user-specified data types:

```
enum flag {true, false};
enum time {am, pm};
enum day {mon, tue, wed, thr, fri, sat, sun};
enum color {red, green, yellow};
```

The first user-specified data type is a type named flag. Any variable subsequently declared to be of this type can take on only a value of true or false. The second statement creates a data type named time. Any variable subsequently declared to be of type time can take on only a value of am or pm. Similarly, the third and fourth statements create the data types day and color, respectively, and list the valid values for variables of these two types. For example, the statement

```
enum day a,b,c;
```

declares the variables a, b, and c to be of type day, and is consistent with the declaration of variables using standard C data types such as char, int, float, or double. Once variables have been declared as enumerated types, they may be assigned values or compared to variables or values appropriate to their type. This again is consistent with standard variable operations. For example, for the variables a, b, and c declared above, the following statements are valid:

```
a = red;
b = a;
if (c == yellow) printf("\nThe color is yellow");
```

Internally, the acceptable values for each enumerated data type are ordered and assigned sequential integer values beginning with 0. For example, for the values of the user-defined type color, the correspondences created by the C compiler are that red is equivalent to 0, green is equivalent to 1, and yellow is equivalent to 2. The equivalent numbers are required when inputting values using scanf() or printing values using printf().

Program 15.1 illustrates a user-defined data type.

A sample run of Program 15.1 produced the following output:

```
The color is 0
Enter a value: 2
The crayon is yellow.
```

As illustrated in Program 15.1, expressions containing variables declared as user-defined data types must be consistent with the values specifically listed for the type. Although a switch statement would be more appropriate in Program 15.1, the expressions in the if-else statement better highlight the use of enumerated values. Program 15.1 also shows that the initialization of a user-specified data type variable is identical to the initialization of standard data type variables. For input and output purposes, however, the equivalent integer value assigned by the C compiler to each enumerated value must be used in place of the actual data type value. This is also seen in the program.

PROGRAM 15.1

```
#include <stdio.h>
void main(void)
{
  enum color {red, green, yellow};
  enum color crayon = red;     /* crayon is declared to be of type */
                               /* color and initialized to red */
  printf("\nThe color is %d\n", crayon);
  printf("Enter a value: ");
  scanf("%d", &crayon);
  if (crayon == red)
    printf("The crayon is red.\n");
  else if (crayon == green)
    printf("The crayon is green.\n");
  else if (crayon == yellow)
    printf("The crayon is yellow.\n");
  else
    printf("The color is not defined.\n");
}
```

To assign equivalent integers to each user-specified value, the C compiler retains the order of the values as they are listed in the enumeration. A side effect of this ordering is that expressions can be constructed using relational and logical operators. For example, for the data type `color` created in Program 15.1, expressions such as `crayon < yellow` and `red < green` are both valid.

The numerical value assigned by the compiler to enumerated values can be altered by direct assignment when a data type is created. For example, the definition

```
enum color (red, green= 7, yellow);
```

causes the compiler to associate the value `red` with the integer 0 and the value `green` with the integer 7. Altering the integer associated with the value `green` causes all subsequent integer assignments to be altered too; thus, the value `yellow` is associated with the integer 8. If any other values were listed after `yellow`, they would be associated with the integers 9, 10, 11, etc., unless another alteration was made.

Naming a user-defined data type is similar to naming a template for structures. Just as a tag name can be omitted when defining a structure by declaring the structure directly, the same can be done with user-defined data types. For example, the declaration `enum {red,green,yellow} crayon;` defines `crayon` to be a variable of an unnamed data type with the valid values of `red`, `green`, and `yellow`.

Scope rules applicable to the standard C data types also apply to enumerated data types. For example, placing the statement `enum color {red, green, yellow};` before the `main()` function in Program 15.1 would make the data type named `color` global and available for any other function in the file.

Finally, because there is a one-to-one correspondence between integers and user-defined data types, the cast operator can either coerce integers into a user-specified data value or coerce a user-specified value into its equivalent integer.

Assuming that `val` is an integer variable with a value of 1, and `color` has been declared as in Program 15.1, the expression `(enum color) val` has a value of `green` and the expression `(int) yellow` has a value of 2. The compiler will not warn you, however, if a cast to a nonexistent value is attempted.

Conditional Expressions

In addition to expressions formed with the arithmetic, relational, logical, and bit operators, C provides a conditional expression. A *conditional expression* uses the conditional operator, `? :`, and provides an alternate way of expressing a simple `if-else` statement.

The general form of a conditional expression is:

```
expression1 ? expression2 : expression3
```

If the value of `expression1` is nonzero (true), `expression2` is evaluated; otherwise `expression3` is evaluated. The value for the complete conditional expression is the value of either `expression2` or `expression3`, depending on which expression was evaluated. As always, the value of the expression may be assigned to a variable.

Conditional expressions are most useful in replacing simple `if-else` statements. For example, the `if-else` statement:

```
if ( hours > 40)
    rate = 0.045;
else
    rate = 0.02;
```

can be replaced with the one-line conditional statement

```
rate = (hours > 40) ? 0.045 : 0.02;
```

Here, the complete conditional expression

```
(hours > 40) ? 0.045 : 0.02
```

is evaluated before any assignment is made to rate, because the conditional operator, `? :`, has a higher precedence than the assignment operator. Within the conditional expression, the expression `hours > 40` is evaluated first. If this expression has a nonzero value, which is equivalent to a logical true value, the value of the complete conditional expression is set to .045; otherwise the conditional expression has a value of .02. Finally, the value of the conditional expression, either .045 or .02, is assigned to the variable rate.

The conditional operator, `? :`, is unique in C in that it is a ternary operator. This means that the operator connects three operands. The first operand is always evaluated first. It is usually a conditional expression that uses the logical operators. The next two operands are any other valid expressions, which can be single constants, variables, or more general expressions. The complete conditional expression consists of all three operands connected by the condition operator symbols `?` and `:`.

Conditional expressions are only useful in replacing `if-else` statements when the expressions in the equivalent `if-else` statement are not long or complicated. For example, the statement:

```
max_val = a > b ? a : b;
```

is a one-line statement that assigns the maximum value of the variables a and b to max_val. A longer, equivalent form of this statement is:

```
if (a > b)
    max_val = a;
else
    max_val = b;
```

Because of the length of the expressions involved, a conditional expression would not be useful in replacing the following if-else statement:

```
if (amount > 20000)
    taxes = 0.025(amount - 20000) + 400;
else
    taxes = 0.02 * amount;
```

The goto Statement

The *goto* statement provides an unconditional transfer of control to some other statement in a program. The general form of a goto statement is:

```
goto label;
```

where label is any unique name chosen according to the rules for creating variable names. The label name must appear, followed by a colon, in front of any other statement in the function that contains the goto statement. For example, the following section of code transfers control to the label named err if division by zero is attempted:

```
if (denom == 0.0)
    goto err;
else
    result = num /denom;
        .
        .
        .
err: printf("Error - Attempted Division by Zero");
```

The astute reader will realize that in this case goto provides a cumbersome solution to the problem. It would require a second goto above the printf() statement to stop this statement from always being executed. Generally it is much easier either to call an error routine for unusual conditions or to use a break statement if this is necessary.

Theoretically, a goto statement is never required because C's normal structures provide sufficient flexibility to handle all possible flow control requirements. Also, gotos tend to complicate programs. For example, consider the following code:

```
if (a == 100)
    goto first;
else
    x = 20;
goto sec;
first: x = 50;
sec: y = 10;
```

Written without a `goto` this code is:

```
if (a == 100)
   x = 50;
else
   x = 20;
y = 10;
```

Both sections of code produce the same result; however, the second version is clearly easier to read. It is worthwhile to convince yourself that the two sections of code do, in fact, produce the same result by running the code on your computer. This will let you experience the sense of frustration when working with `goto`-invaded code.

Using even one `goto` statement in a program is almost always a sign of bad programming structure. Possibly the only case that conceivably might use a `goto` is that of a nested loop where some error condition requires escape from both the inner and outer loop structure (a break will only exit from the inner loop). If such an escape were ever used in developing a program, the code should ultimately be rewritten as a function where the escape is replaced by an exit from the function.

15.2 BITWISE OPERATIONS

C operates with complete data entities that are stored as one or more bytes, such as character, integer, and double-precision constants and variables. In addition, C provides for the manipulation of individual bits of character and integer constants and variables. These manipulations are termed *bitwise* operations.

The operators that are used to perform bit manipulations are called bit operators. They are listed in Table 15.1. The operators listed in Table 15.1 are binary operators, requiring two operands. In using the bit operators, each operand is treated as a binary number consisting of a series of individual 1's and 0's. The respective bits in each operand are then compared on a bit-by-bit basis and the result is determined based on the selected operation.

The AND Operator

The AND operator causes a bit-by-bit AND comparison between its two operands. *The result of each bit-by-bit AND comparison is a 1 only when both bits being compared are 1's, otherwise the result of the AND operation is a 0.*

TABLE 15.1 Bit Operators

Operator	Description
&	Bitwise AND
|	Bitwise inclusive OR
^	Bitwise exclusive OR
~	Bitwise one's complement
<<	Left shift
>>	Right shift

FIGURE 15.1 A Sample AND Operation

$$10110011$$
$$\&\,11010101$$
$$\overline{10010001}$$

To perform an AND operation, each bit in one operand is compared to the bit occupying the same position in the other operand. Figure 15.1 illustrates the correspondence between bits for these two operands. As shown in the figure, when both bits being compared are 1's, the result is a 1, otherwise the result is a 0. The result of each comparison is, of course, independent of any other bit comparison.

Program 15.2 illustrates the use of an AND operation. In this program, the variable op1 is initialized to the octal value 325, which is the octal equivalent of the binary number 1 1 0 1 0 1 0 1, and the variable op2 is initialized to the octal value 263, which is the octal representation of the binary number 1 0 1 1 0 0 1 1. These are the same two binary numbers illustrated in Figure 15.1.

PROGRAM 15.2

```c
#include <stdio.h>
void main(void)
{
  int op1 = 0325, op2 = 0263;

  printf("%o ANDed with %o is %o\n", op1, op2, op1 & op2);
}
```

Program 15.2 produces the following output:

```
325 ANDed with 263 is 221
```

The result of ANDing the octal numbers 325 and 263 is the octal number 221. The binary equivalent of 221 is the binary number 1 0 0 1 0 0 0 1, which is the result of the AND operation illustrated in Figure 15.1.

AND operations are extremely useful in masking, or eliminating, selected bits from an operand. This is a direct result of the fact that ANDing any bit (1 or 0) with a 0 forces the resulting bit to be a 0, while ANDing any bit (1 or 0) with a 1 leaves the original bit unchanged. For example, assume that the variable op1 has the arbitrary bit pattern x x x x x x x x, where each x can be either 1 or 0, independent of any other x in the number. The result of ANDing this binary number with the binary number 0 0 0 0 1 1 1 1 is:

$$op1 = x\,x\,x\,x\,x\,x\,x\,x$$
$$op2 = 0\,0\,0\,0\,1\,1\,1\,1$$
$$\overline{Result = 0\,0\,0\,0\,x\,x\,x\,x}$$

As can be seen from this example, the zeros in op2 effectively mask, or eliminate, the respective bits in op1, while the ones in op2 filter, or pass, the respective bits in op1 through with no change in their values. In this example, the variable op2 is called a mask. By choosing the mask appropriately, any individual bit in an operand can be selected, or filtered, out of an operand for inspection. For example, ANDing the variable op1 with the mask 0 0 0 0 0 1 0 0 forces all the bits of the result to be zero, except for the third bit. The third bit of the result will be a copy of the third bit of op1. Thus, if the result of the AND is zero, the third bit of op1 must have been zero, and if the result of the AND is a nonzero number, the third bit must have been a 1.

The Inclusive OR Operator

The inclusive OR operator, |, performs a bit-by-bit comparison of its two operands in a fashion similar to that of the bit-by-bit AND. The result of the OR comparison, however, is determined by the following rule: *The result of the comparison is 1 if either bit being compared is a 1, otherwise the result is a 0.*

Figure 15.2 illustrates an OR operation. As shown in the figure, when either of the two bits being compared is a 1, the result is a 1, otherwise the result is a 0. As with all bit operations, the result of each comparison is, of course, independent of any other comparison.

Program 15.3 illustrates an OR operation, using the octal values of the operands illustrated in Figure 15.2.

PROGRAM 15.3

```c
#include <stdio.h>
void main(void)
{
   int op1 = 0325, op2 = 0263;

   printf("%o ORed with %o is %o\n",op1, op2, op1 | op2);
}
```

Program 15.3 produces the following output:

```
325 ORed with 263 is 367
```

The result of ORing the octal numbers 325 and 263 is the octal number 367. The binary equivalent of 367 is 1 1 1 1 0 1 1 1, which is the result of the OR operation illustrated in Figure 15.2.

FIGURE 15.2 A Sample OR Operation

$$1\ 0\ 1\ 1\ 0\ 0\ 1\ 1$$

$$|\ 1\ 1\ 0\ 1\ 0\ 1\ 0\ 1$$

$$1\ 1\ 1\ 1\ 0\ 1\ 1\ 1$$

Inclusive OR operations are extremely useful in forcing selected bits to take on a 1 value or for passing through other bit values unchanged. This is a direct result of the fact that ORing any bit (1 or 0) with a 1 forces the resulting bit to be a 1, while ORing any bit (1 or 0) with a 0 leaves the original bit unchanged. For example, assume that the variable op1 has the arbitrary bit pattern x x x x x x x x, where each x can be either 1 or 0, independent of any other x in the number. The result of ORing this binary number with the binary number 1 1 1 1 0 0 0 0 is:

$$op1 = x\,x\,x\,x\,x\,x\,x\,x$$
$$op2 = \underline{1\,1\,1\,1\,0\,0\,0\,0}$$
$$Result = 1\,1\,1\,1\,x\,x\,x\,x$$

As can be seen from this example, the 1's in op2 force the resulting bits to 1, while the 0's in op2 filter, or pass, the respective bits in op1 through with no change in their values. Thus, an OR operation produces a masking operation that is similar to that of an AND operation, except the masked bits are set to 1's rather than cleared to 0's. Another way of looking at this is to say that ORing with a 0 has the same effect as ANDing with a 1.

The Exclusive OR Operator

The exclusive OR operator, ^, performs a bit-by-bit comparison of its two operands. The result of the comparison is determined by the following rule: *The result of the comparison is 1 if one and only one of the bits being compared is a 1, otherwise the result is 0.*

Figure 15.3 illustrates an exclusive OR operation. As shown in the figure, when both bits being compared are the same value (both 1 or both 0), the result is a 0. Only when both bits have different values (one bit a 1 and the other a 0) is the result a 1. Again, each pair or bit comparison is independent of any other bit comparison.

An exclusive OR operation can be used to create the opposite value, or complement, of any individual bit in a variable. This is a direct result of the fact that exclusive ORing any bit (1 or 0) with a 1 forces the resulting bit's value to be of the opposite of its original state, while exclusive ORing any bit (1 or 0) with a 0 leaves the original bit unchanged. For example, assume that the variable op1 has the arbitrary bit pattern x x x x x x x x, where each x can be either 1 or 0, independent of any other x in the number. Using the notation that $\bar{x}$ is the complement (opposite) value of x, the result of exclusive ORing this binary number with the binary number 0 1 0 1 0 1 0 1 is:

$$op1 = x\,x\,x\,x\,x\,x\,x\,x$$
$$op2 = \underline{0\,1\,0\,1\,0\,1\,0\,1}$$
$$Result = x\,\bar{x}\,x\,\bar{x}\,x\,\bar{x}\,x\,\bar{x}$$

FIGURE 15.3   A Sample Exclusive OR Operation

$$1\,0\,1\,1\,0\,0\,1\,1$$
$$\char`\^\,1\,1\,0\,1\,0\,1\,0\,1$$
$$\overline{}$$
$$0\,1\,1\,0\,0\,1\,1\,0$$

As can be seen from this example, the 1's in `op2` force the resulting bits to be the complement of their original bit values, while the 0's in `op2` filter, or pass, the respective bits in `op1` through with no change in their values.

The Complement Operator

The complement operator, `~`, is a unary operator that changes each 1 bit in its operand to 0 and each 0 bit to 1. For example, if the variable `op1` contains the binary number 1 1 0 0 1 0 1 0, `~op1` replaces this binary number with the number 0 0 1 1 0 1 0 1. The complement operator is used to force any bit in an operand to 0, independent of the actual number of bits used to store the number. For example, the statement

$$op1 = op1 \ \& \ \sim 07;$$

or its shorter form

$$op1 \ \&= \ \sim 07;$$

both set the last three bits of `op1` to 0, regardless of how `op1` is stored within the computer. Either of these two statements can, of course, be replaced by ANDing the last three bits of `op1` with 0's, if the number of bits used to store `op1` is known. In a computer that uses 16 bits to store integers, the appropriate AND operation is

$$op1 = op1 \ \& \ 0177770;$$

For a computer that uses 32 bits to store integers, the above AND sets the leftmost or higher order 16 bits to 0 also, which is an unintended result. The correct statement for 32 bits is:

$$op1 = op1 \ \& \ 027777777770;$$

Using the complement operator in this situation frees the programmer from having to determine the storage size of the operand and, more importantly, makes the program portable between machines using different integer storage sizes.

Different-Size Data Items

When the bit operators `&`, `|`, and `^` are used with operands of different sizes, the shorter operand is always increased in bit size to match the size of the larger operand. Figure 15.4 illustrates the extension of a 16-bit unsigned integer into a 32-bit number. As the figure shows, the additional bits are added to the left of the original number and filled with 0's. This is the equivalent of adding leading 0's to the number, which has no effect on the number's value.

When extending signed numbers, the original leftmost bit is reproduced in the additional bits that are added to the number. As illustrated in Figure 15.5, if the original leftmost bit is 0, corresponding to a positive number, 0 is placed in each of the additional bit positions. If the leftmost bit is 1, which corresponds to a negative number, 1 is placed in the additional bit positions. In either case, the resulting binary number has the same sign and magnitude of the original number.

FIGURE 15.4   Extending 16-Bit Unsigned Data to 32 Bits

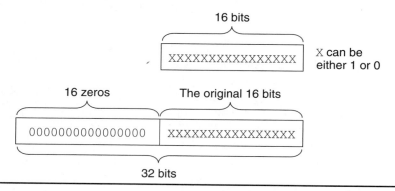

The Shift Operators

The left shift operator, $<<$, causes the bits in an operand to be shifted to the left by a given amount. For example, the statement

```
op1 = op1 << 4;
```

causes the bits in `op1` to be shifted 4 bits to the left, filling any vacated bits with a 0. Figure 15.6 illustrates the effect of shifting the binary number 1111100010101011 to the left by 4 bit positions.

FIGURE 15.5   Extending 16-Bit Signed Data to 32 Bits

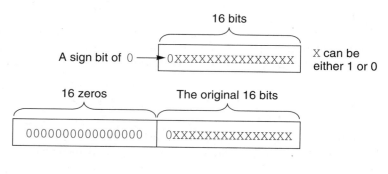

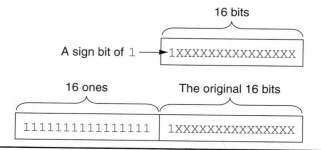

FIGURE 15.6 An Example of a Left Shift

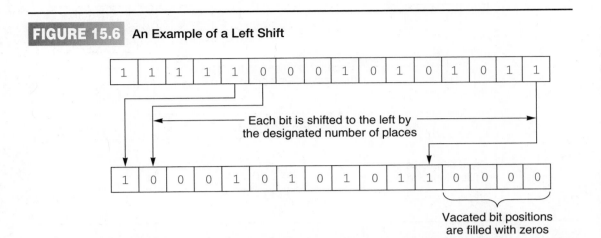

For unsigned integers, each left shift corresponds to multiplication by two. This is also true for signed numbers using two's complement representation, as long as the leftmost bit does not switch values. Since a change in the leftmost bit of a two's complement number represents a change in both the sign and magnitude represented by the bit, such a shift does not represent a simple multiplication by two.

The right shift operator, >>, causes the bits in an operand to be shifted to the right by a given amount. For example, the statement

```
op1 = op1 >> 3;
```

causes the bits in op1 to be shifted to the right by 3 bit positions. Figure 15.7(a) illustrates the right shift of the unsigned binary number 1111100010101011 by 3 bit positions. As illustrated, the three rightmost bits are shifted "off the end" and are lost.

For unsigned numbers, the leftmost bit is not used as a sign bit. For this type of number, the vacated leftmost bits are always filled with zeros. This case is illustrated in Figure 15.7(a).

For signed numbers, what is filled in the vacated bits depends on the computer. Most computers reproduce the original sign bit of the number. Figure 15.7(b) illustrates the right shift of a negative binary number by 4 bit positions, where the sign bit is reproduced in the vacated bits. Figure 15.7(c) illustrates the equivalent right shift of a positive signed binary number. The type of fill illustrated in Figures 15.7(b) and (c), where the sign bit is reproduced in vacated bit positions, is called an arithmetic right shift. In an arithmetic right shift, each single shift to the right corresponds to a division by two.

Instead of reproducing the sign bit in right-shifted signed numbers, some computers automatically fill the vacated bits with zeros. This type of shift is called a *logical shift*. For positive signed numbers, where the leftmost bit is zero, both arithmetic and logical right shifts produce the same result. The results of these two shifts are only different when negative numbers are involved.

FIGURE 15.7a An Unsigned Arithmetic Right Shift

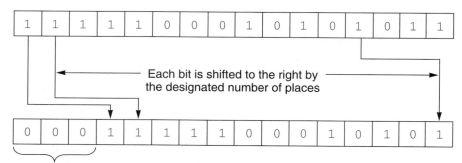

Each bit is shifted to the right by the designated number of places

Vacated bit positions are filled with zeros

FIGURE 15.7b The Right Shift of a Negative Binary Number

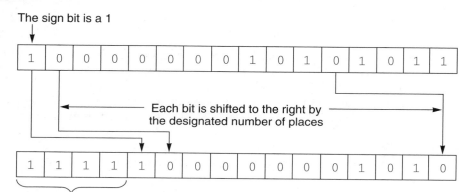

The sign bit is a 1

Each bit is shifted to the right by the designated number of places

Vacated bit positions are filled with 1s

FIGURE 15.7c The Right Shift of a Positive Binary Number

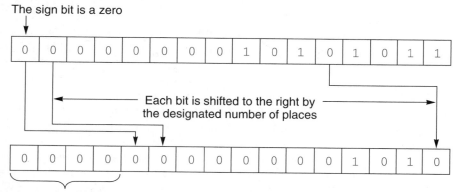

The sign bit is a zero

Each bit is shifted to the right by the designated number of places

Vacated bit positions are filled with 0s

15.3 MACROS

In its simplest form, the #define preprocessor is used to equate constants and operators to symbolic names. For example, the statement:

```
#define SALESTAX 0.05
```

equates the symbolic name SALESTAX to the number 0.05. When SALESTAX is used in any subsequent statement or expression, the equivalent value of 0.05 is substituted for the symbolic name. The substitutions are made by the C preprocessor just prior to program compilation.

C places no restrictions on the equivalences that can be established with the #define statement. Thus, in addition to using #define preprocessor statements for simple equivalences, these statements can also be used to equate symbolic names to text, a partial or complete expression, and may even include arguments. When the equivalence consists of more than a single value, operator, or variable, the symbolic name is referred to as a *macro*, and the substitution of the text in place of the symbolic name is called a *macro expansion* or *macro substitution*. The word *macro* refers to the direct, in-line expansion of one word into many words. For example, the equivalence established by the statement:

```
#define FORMAT "The answer is %f\n"
```

enables us to write the statement:

```
printf(FORMAT, 15.2);
```

When this statement is encountered by the preprocessor, the symbolic name FORMAT is replaced by the equivalent text "The answer is %f\n". The compiler always receives the expanded version after the text has been inserted in place of the symbolic name by the preprocessor.

In addition to using #define statements for straight text substitutions, these statements can also be used to define equivalences that use arguments. For example, in the statement:

```
#define SQUARE(x)x * x
```

x is an argument. Here, SQUARE(x) is a true macro that is expanded into the expression x * x, where x is itself replaced by the variable or constant used when the macro is utilized. For example, the statement:

```
y = SQUARE(num);
```

is expanded into the statement:

```
y = num * num;
```

The advantage of using a macro such as SQUARE(x) is that since the data type of the argument is not specified, the macro can be used with any data type argument. If num, for example, is an integer variable, the expression num * num produces an integer value. Similarly, if num is a double-precision variable, the SQUARE(x) macro produces a double-precision value. This is a direct result of the text substitution procedure used in expanding the macro and is an advantage of making SQUARE(x) a macro rather than a function.

Care must be taken when defining macros with arguments. For example, in the definition of SQUARE(x), there must be no space between the symbolic name `SQUARE` and the left parenthesis used to enclose the argument. There can, however, be spaces within the parentheses if more than one argument is used.

Additionally, because the expansion of a macro involves direct text substitution, unintended results may occur if you do not use macros carefully. For example, the assignment statement:

```
val = SQUARE(num1 + num1);
```

does not assign the value of `(num1 + num2) * (num1 + num2)` to `val`. Rather, the expansion of `SQUARE(num1 + num2)` results in the equivalent statement:

```
val = num1 + num2 * num1 + num2;
```

This statement results from the direct text substitution of the term `num1 + num2` for the argument `x` in the expression `x * x` that is produced by the preprocessor.

To avoid unintended results, always place parentheses around all macro arguments wherever they appear in the macro. For example, the definition

```
#define SQUARE(x) (x) * (x)
```

ensures that a correct result is produced whenever the macro is invoked. Now the statement

```
val = SQUARE(num1 + num2);
```

is expanded to produce the desired assignment

```
val = (num1 + num2) * (num1 + num2);
```

Macros are extremely useful when the calculations or expressions they contain are relatively simple and can be kept to one or at most two lines. Larger macro definitions tend to become cumbersome and confusing and are better written as functions. If necessary, a macro definition can be continued on a new line by typing a backslash character, \, before the RETURN or ENTER key is pressed. The backslash acts as an escape character that causes the preprocessor to treat the RETURN literally and not include it in any subsequent text substitutions.

The advantage of using a macro instead of a function is an increase in execution speed. Because the macro is directly expanded and included in every expression or statement using it, there is no execution time loss due to the call and return procedures required by a function. The disadvantage is the increase in required program memory space when a macro is used repeatedly. Each time a macro is used, the complete macro text is reproduced and stored as an integral part of the program. Thus, if the same macro is used in ten places, the final code includes ten copies of the expanded text version of the macro. A function, however, is stored in memory only once. No matter how many times the function is called, the same code is used. The memory space required for one copy of a function used extensively throughout a program can be considerably less than the memory required for storing multiple copies of the same code defined as a macro.

15.4 COMMAND LINE ARGUMENTS

Arguments can be passed to any function in a program, including the `main()` function. In this section we describe the procedures for passing arguments to main() when a program is initially invoked and having main() correctly receive and store the arguments passed to it. Both the sending and receiving sides of the transaction must be considered. Fortunately, the interface for transmitting arguments to a main() function has been standardized in C, so both sending and receiving arguments can be done almost mechanically.

All the programs that have been run so far have been invoked by typing the name of the executable version of the program after the operating system prompt is displayed. The command line for these programs consists of a single word, which is the name of the program. For computers that use the UNIX operating system the prompt is usually the $ symbol and the executable name of the program is a.out. For these systems, the simple command line

$a.out

begins program execution of the last compiled source program currently residing in a.out.

If you are using a C compiler on an IBM PC, the equivalent operating system prompt is either A> or C>, and the name of the executable program is typically the same name as the source program with a .exe extension rather than a .c extension. Assuming that you are using an IBM PC with the C> operating system prompt, the complete command line for running an executable program named showad.exe is C>showad. As illustrated in Figure 15.8, this command line causes the showad program to begin execution with its main() function, but no arguments are passed to main().

Now assume that we want to pass the three separate string arguments three blind mice directly into showad's main function. Sending arguments into a main() function is extremely easy. It is accomplished by including the arguments on the command line used to begin program execution. Because the arguments are typed on the command line, they are, naturally, called *command line arguments*. To pass the arguments three blind mice directly into the main() function of the showad program, we need only add the desired words after the program name on the command line:

C> showad three blind mice

Upon encountering this command line, the operating system stores it as a sequence of four strings. Figure 15.9 illustrates the storage of this command line, assuming that each character uses 1 byte of storage. As shown in the figure, each

---

FIGURE 15.8 Invoking the showad **Program**

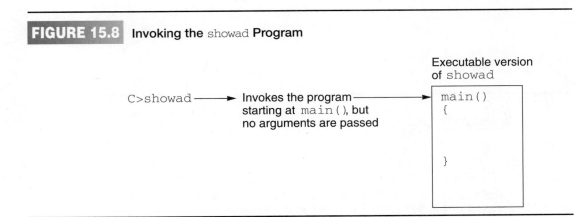

FIGURE 15.9 The Command Line Stored in Memory

| s | h | o | w | a | d | \0 | t | h | r | e | e | \0 | b | l | i | n | d | \0 | m | i | c | e | \0 |

---

string terminates with the standard C null character \0. Sending command line arguments to main() is always this simple. The arguments are typed on the command line and the operating system nicely stores them as a sequence of separate strings. We must now handle the receiving side of the transaction and let main() know that arguments are being passed to it.

Arguments passed to main(), like all function arguments, must be declared as part of the function's definition. To standardize argument passing to a main() function, only two items are allowed: a number and an array. The number is an integer variable, which must be named argc (short for argument counter), and the array is a one-dimensional list, which must be named argv (short for argument values). Figure 15.10 illustrates these two arguments.

The integer passed to main() is the total number of items on the command line. In our example, the value of argc passed to main() is four, which includes the name of the program plus the three command line arguments. The one-dimensional list passed to main() is a list of pointers containing the starting storage address of each string typed on the command line, as illustrated in Figure 15.11.

We can now write the complete function definition for main() to receive arguments by declaring their names and data types. For main's two arguments C requires that they be named argc and argv, respectively. Because argc is an integer, its declaration will be int argc. Because argv is the name of an array whose elements are addresses that point to where the actual command line arguments are stored, its proper declaration is char *argv[]. This is nothing more than the declaration of an array of pointers. It is read "argv is an array whose elements are pointers to characters." Putting all this together, the full function header for a main() function that will receive command line arguments is[1]:

FIGURE 15.10 An Integer and an Array Are Passed to main()

argc | Integer |

argv | Table of addresses |

---

[1]In non-ANSI C, this header is written as:

```
void main(argc,argv)
int argc;
char *argv[];
```

In both ANSI and non-ANSI C if main() is to return a value, which is typically an integer, the void declaration in the header line must be changed to int.

FIGURE 15.11 Addresses Are Stored in the `argv` Array

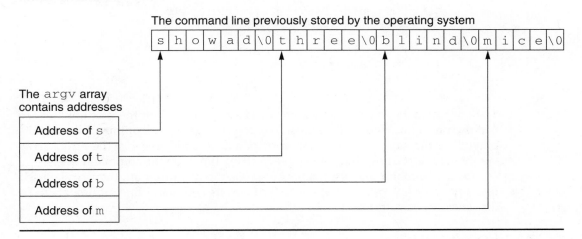

```
void main(int argc, char *argv[])   /* complete main() header line */
```

No matter how many arguments are typed on the command line, `main()` only needs the two standard pieces of information provided by `argc` and `argv`: the number of items on the command line and the list of starting addresses indicating where each argument is actually stored.

Program 15.4 verifies our description by printing the data actually passed to `main()`. The variable `argv[i]` used in Program 15.4 contains an address. The notation `*argv[i]` refers to "the character pointed to" by the address in `argv[i]`.

PROGRAM 15.4

```c
#include <stdio.h>
void main(int argc, char *argv[])
{
  int i;

  printf("\nThe number of items on the command line is %d\n\n",argc);
  for (i = 0; i < argc; i++)
  {
    printf("The address stored in argv[%d] is %p\n", i, argv[i]);
    printf("The character pointed to is %c\n", *argv[i]);
  }
}
```

Assuming that the executable version of Program 15.4 is named `showad.exe`, a sample output for the command line `showad three blind mice` is[2]:

---

[2]Some compilers store the full path name of the program in `argv[0]`.

```
The number of items on the command line is 4

The address stored in argv[0] is FFDA
The character pointed to is s
The address stored in argv[1] is FFEB
The character pointed to is t
The address stored in argv[2] is FFF1
The character pointed to is b
The address stored in argv[3] is FFF7
The character pointed to is m
```

The addresses displayed by Program 15.4 clearly depend on the machine used to run the program. Figure 15.12 illustrates the storage of the command line as displayed by the sample output. As anticipated, the addresses in the argv array "point" to the starting characters of each string typed on the command line.

Once command line arguments are passed to a C program, they can be used like any other C strings. Program 15.5 causes its command line arguments to be displayed from within main().

PROGRAM 15.5

```c
/* A program that displays command line arguments */
#include <stdio.h>
void main(int argc, char *argv[])
{
  int i;

  printf("\nThe following arguments were passed to main(): ");
  for (i = 1; i < argc; i++)
    printf("%s ", argv[i]);
  printf("\n");
}
```

FIGURE 15.12 The Command Line Stored in Memory

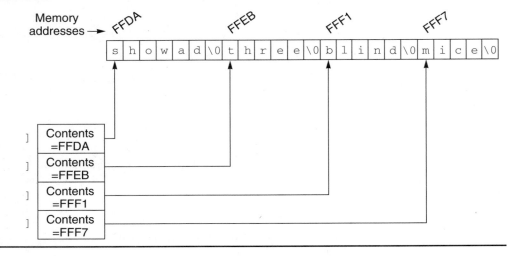

Assuming that the name of the executable version of Program 15.5 is `a.out`, the output of this program for the command line `a.out three blind mice` is:

```
The following arguments were passed to main(): three blind mice
```

Notice that when the addresses in `argv[]` are passed to the `printf()` function in Program 15.5, the strings pointed to by these addresses are displayed. When these same addresses were passed to the `printf()` function in Program 15.4, the actual values of the addresses were printed. The difference in displays is caused by the `printf()` function. When a `%s` control sequence is used in `printf()`, as it is in Program 15.5, it alerts the function that a string will be accessed. `printf()` then expects the address of the first character in the string which is exactly what each element in `argv[]` supplies. Once `printf()` receives the address, the function performs the required indirection to locate the actual string, that is displayed. The `%p` control sequence used in Program 15.4 displays the value of the address stored in `argv[i]`. As we have noted before, since pointers are a unique data type, C provides the specific control sequence, `%p`, for the output of the addresses stored in pointer variables.

One final comment about command line arguments is in order. Any argument typed on a command line is considered to be a string. If you want numerical data passed to `main()`, it is up to you to convert the passed string into its numerical counterpart. This is seldom an issue, however, since most command line arguments are used as flags to pass appropriate processing control signals to an invoked program.

15.5 CHAPTER REVIEW

Key Terms

bitwise
command line argument
conditional expression
enum

`goto`
macro
`typedef`

Summary

1. A `typedef` statement creates synonym names for any C data type name. For example, the statement:

   ```
   typedef int WHOLE_NUM;
   ```

   makes `WHOLE_NUM` a synonym for `int`.

2. An enumerated data type is a user-defined scalar data type. The user must select a name and list the acceptable values for the data type. For example, the enumeration:

   ```
   enum color {red, green, yellow}
   ```

   creates a `color` data type. Any variable may be subsequently declared with this data type and may store one of the acceptable values listed. An enumerated data type may also be `typedef`ed.

3. A conditional expression provides an alternate way of expressing a simple `if-else` statement. The general form of a conditional expression is:

```
       expression1 ? expression2 : expression3
```
The equivalent if-else statement for this is:
```
           if (expression1)
              expression2;
           else
              expression3;
```

4. C also provides a goto statement. In theory this statement need never be used. In practice it produces confusing and unstructured code, and should be used only in a very limited and controlled manner, if at all.

5. Individual bits of character and integer variables and constants can be manipulated using C's bit operators. These are the AND, inclusive OR, exclusive OR, one's complement, left shift, and right shift operators.

6. The AND and inclusive OR operators are useful in creating masks. These masks can be used to pass or eliminate individual bits from the selected operand. The exclusive OR operator is useful in complementing an operand's bits.

7. When the AND and OR operators are used with operands of different sizes, the shorter operand is always increased in bit size to match the size of the larger operand.

8. The shift operators produce different results depending on whether the operand is a signed or an unsigned value.

9. Using the #define command, complete expressions can be equated to symbolic names. When these expressions include arguments they are referred to as *macros*.

10. Arguments passed to main() are termed command line arguments. C provides a standard argument-passing procedure in which main() can accept any number of arguments passed to it. Each argument passed to main() is considered a string and is stored using a pointer array named argv. The total number of arguments on the command line is stored in an integer variable named argc.

Exercises

1. Rewrite each of the following if-else statements using a conditional expression:

   a. ```
   if (a < b);
       min_val = a;
   else
       min_val = b;
   ```

   b. ```
   if (num < 0)
       sign = -1;
   else
       sign = 1;
   ```

   c. ```
   if (flag == 1)
       val = num;
   else
       val = num * num;
   ```

   d. ```
   if (credit == plus)
       rate = prime;
   else
       rate = prime + delta;
   ```

    e. `if (!bond)`
       `cou = .075;`
     `else`
       `cou = 1.1;`

2. Determine the results of the following operations:

   a.   11001010   b.   11001010   c.   11001010
      & 10100101 | 10100101   ^ 10100101

3. Write the octal representations of the binary numbers given in Exercise 2.

4. Determine the octal results of the following operations, assuming unsigned numbers:

   a. the octal number 0157 shifted left by 1 bit position

   b. the octal number 0701 shifted left by 2 bit positions

   c. the octal number 0673 shifted right by 2 bit positions

   d. the octal number 067 shifted right by 3 bit positions

5. Repeat Exercise 4 assuming that the numbers are treated as signed values.

6. a. Assume that the arbitrary bit pattern xxxxxxxx, where each x can represent either 1 or 0, is stored in the integer variable `flag`. Determine the octal value of a mask that can be ANDed with the bit pattern to reproduce the third and fourth bits of `flag` and set all other bits to zero. The rightmost bit in `flag` is considered bit 0.

   b. Determine the octal value of a mask that can be inclusively ORed with the bit pattern in `flag` to reproduce the third and fourth bits of flag and set all other bits to 1. Again, consider the rightmost bit in `flag` to be bit 0.

   c. Determine the octal value of a mask that can be used to complement the values of the third and fourth bits of `flag` and leave all other bits unchanged. Determine the bit operation that should be used with the mask value to produce the desired result.

7. a. Write the two's complement form of the decimal number −1, using 8 bits. (*Hint:* Refer to Section 1.8 for a review of two's complement numbers.)

   b. Repeat Exercise 7a using 16 bits to represent the decimal number −1 and compare your answer to your previous answer. Could the 16-bit version have been obtained by sign-extending the 8-bit version?

8. Write a C program that displays the first 8 bits of each character value input into a variable named `ch`. (*Hint:* Assuming each character is stored using 8 bits, start by using the hexadecimal mask 80, which corresponds to the binary number 10000000. If the result of the masking operation is a 0, display a 0; else display a 1. Then shift the mask one place to the right to examine the next bit, and so on until all bits in the variable `ch` have been processed.)

9. Write a C program that reverses the bits in an integer variable named `okay` and stores the reversed bits in the variable named `rev_okay`. For example, if the bit pattern 11100101, corresponding to the octal number 0345, is assigned to okay, the bit pattern 10100111, corresponding to the octal number 0247, should be produced and stored in `rev_okay`.

10. a. Define a macro named `NEGATE(x)` that produces the negative of its argument.

   b. Include the `NEGATE(x)` macro defined in Exercise 10a in a complete C program and run the program to confirm proper operation of the macro for various cases.

11. a. Define a macro named `ABS_VAL(x)` that produces the absolute value of its argument.

    b. Include the `ABS_VAL(x)` macro defined in Exercise 11a in a complete C program and run the program to confirm proper operation of the macro for various cases.

12. a. Define a macro named `CIRCUM(r)` that determines the circumference of a circle of radius r. The circumference is determined from the relationship `circumference = 2.0 * PI * radius`, where `PI` equals 3.1416.

    b. Include the `CIRCUM(r)` macro defined in Exercise 12a in a complete C program and run the program to confirm proper operation of the macro for various cases.

13. a. Define a macro named `MIN(x,y)` that determines the minimum value of its two arguments.

    b. Include the `MIN(x,y)` macro defined in Exercise 13a in a complete C program and run the program to confirm proper operation of the macro for various cases.

14. a. Define a macro named `MAX(x,y)` that determines the maximum value of its two arguments.

    b. Include the `MAX(x,y)` macro defined in Exercise 14a in a complete C program and run the program to confirm proper operation of the macro for various cases.

15. a. Write a program that accepts the name of a data file as a command line argument. Have your program open the data file and display its contents, line by line, on the CRT screen.

    b. Would the program written for Exercise 15a work correctly for a program file?

16. a. Modify the program written for Exercise 15a so that each line displayed is preceded by a line number.

    b. Modify the program written for Exercise 16a so that the command line argument -p will cause the program to list the contents of the file on the printer attached to your system.

17. Write a program that accepts a command line argument as the name of a data file. Given the name, your program should display the number of characters in the file. (*Hint:* Use the `fseek()` and `ftell()` library functions discussed in Section 12.2.)

18. Write a program that accepts two integer values as command line arguments. The program should multiply the two values entered and display the result. (*Hint:* The command line must be accepted as string data and converted to numerical values before multiplication.)

APPENDIX

A Operator Precedence Table

Table A.1 presents the symbols, precedence, descriptions, and associativity of C's operators. Operators toward the top of the table have a higher precedence than those toward the bottom. Operators within each box have the same precedence and associativity.

TABLE A.1 Summary of C Operators

Operator	Description	Associativity
()	Function call	Left to right
[]	Array element	
->	Structure member pointer reference	
.	Structure member reference	
++	Increment	Right to Left
--	Decrement	
-	Unary minus	
!	Logical negation	
~	One's complement	
(type)	Type conversion (cast)	
sizeof	Storage size	
&	Address of	
*	Indirection	
*	Multiplication	Left to right
/	Division	
%	Modulus (remainder)	
+	Addition	Left to right
-	Subtraction	
<<	Left shift	Left to right
>>	Right shift	
<	Less than	Left to right
<=	Less than or equal to	
>	Greater than	
>=	Greater than or equal to	
==	Equal to	Left to right
!=	Not equal to	
&	Bitwise AND	Left to right
^	Bitwise exclusive OR	Left to right
|	Bitwise inclusive OR	Left to right
&&	Logical AND	Left to right
||	Logical OR	Left to right
?:	Conditional expression	Left to right
=	Assignment	Left to right
+= -= *=	Assignment	
/= %= &=	Assignment	
^= |=	Assignment	
<<= >>=	Assignment	
,	Comma	Left to right

B ASCII Character Codes

Key(s)	Dec	Oct	Hex	Key	Dec	Oct	Hex	Key	Dec	Oct	Hex
Ctrl 1	0	0	0	+	43	53	2B	V	86	126	56
Ctrl	1	1	1	'	44	54	2C	W	87	127	57
Ctrl B	2	2	2	−	45	55	2D	X	88	130	58
Ctrl C	3	3	3	.	46	56	2E	Y	89	131	59
Ctrl D	4	4	4	/	47	57	2F	Z	90	132	5A
Ctrl E	5	5	5	0	48	60	30	[	91	133	5B
Ctrl F	6	6	6	1	49	61	31	\	92	134	5C
Ctrl G	7	7	7	2	50	62	32	]	93	135	5D
Ctrl H	8	10	8	3	51	63	33	^	94	136	5E
Ctrl I	9	11	9	4	52	64	34	−	95	137	5F
\n	10	12	A	5	53	65	35	`	96	140	60
Ctrl K	11	13	B	6	54	66	36	a	97	141	61
Ctrl L	12	14	C	7	55	67	37	b	98	142	62
RETURN	13	15	D	8	56	70	38	c	99	143	63
Ctrl N	14	16	E	9	57	71	39	d	100	144	64
Ctrl O	15	17	F	:	58	72	3A	e	101	145	65
Ctrl P	16	20	10	;	59	73	3B	f	102	146	66
Ctrl Q	17	21	11	<	60	74	3C	g	103	147	67
Ctrl R	18	22	12	=	61	75	3D	h	104	150	68
Ctrl S	19	23	13	>	62	76	3E	i	105	151	69
Ctrl T	20	24	14	?	63	77	3F	j	106	152	6A
Ctrl U	21	25	15	@	64	100	40	k	107	153	6B
Ctrl V	22	26	16	A	65	101	41	l	108	154	6C
Ctrl W	23	27	17	B	66	102	42	m	109	155	6D
Ctrl X	24	30	18	C	67	103	43	n	110	156	6E
Ctrl Y	25	31	19	D	68	104	44	o	111	157	6F
Ctrl Z	26	32	1A	E	69	105	45	p	112	160	70
Esc	27	33	1B	F	70	106	46	q	113	161	71
Ctrl <	28	34	1C	G	71	107	47	r	114	162	72
Ctrl /	29	35	1D	H	72	110	48	s	115	163	73
Ctrl =	30	36	1E	I	73	111	49	t	116	164	74
Ctrl −	31	37	1F	J	74	112	4A	u	117	165	75
Space	32	40	20	K	75	113	4B	v	118	166	76
!	33	41	21	L	76	114	4C	w	119	167	77
"	34	42	22	M	77	115	4D	x	120	170	78
#	35	43	23	N	78	116	4E	y	121	171	79
$	36	44	24	O	79	117	4F	z	122	172	7A
%	37	45	25	P	80	120	50	{	123	173	7B
&	38	46	26	Q	81	121	51	|	124	174	7C
'	39	47	27	R	82	122	52	}	125	175	7D
(	40	50	28	S	83	123	53	~	126	176	7E
)	41	51	29	T	84	124	54	del	127	177	7F
*	42	52	2A	U	85	125	55				

C   Program Entry, Compilation, and Execution

In this appendix we first examine the steps required to enter, compile, and execute compiled versions of C programs. These steps are:

1. Logging into (and eventually out of) the computer
2. Creating and Editing the program
3. Compiling and Linking the program
4. Loading and executing the program

Logging Into and Out Of the Computer

As illustrated in Figure C.1, a computer can be thought of as a self contained world that is entered by a special set of steps called a *login procedure*. For computers such as IBM personal computers (PCs), and other desk-top computers, the login procedure is as simple as turning the computer's power switch on. Larger multi-user

---

FIGURE C.1   Viewing a Computer as a Self-Contained World

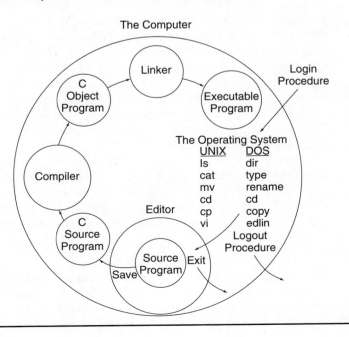

TABLE C.1 Operating System Commands (Fill In for Your System)

Task	Command	Example
Log-in procedure		
Log-out procedure		
List a program		
Copy a program		
Delete a program		
Rename a program		

systems, such as DEC VAX computers, typically require a login procedure consisting of turning a terminal on and supplying an account number and password.

Once you have successfully logged in to your computer system you are automatically under the control of a computer program called the operating system (unless the computer is programmed to switch you into a specific application program). The *operating system* is the program that effectively runs the computer. It is used to gain access to the services provided by the computer, which include the programs needed for entering, compiling, and executing a C program.

Communicating with the operating system is accomplished either by using a specific set of commands that are recognized by the operating system or by selecting graphical icons presented in a window. Although each computer system type (IBM, APPLE, DEC, etc.) has one or more available operating systems, all operating systems provide commands that permit logging on to the system, exiting from the system, creating programs and a means of quickly listing, deleting, copying, and renaming programs.

The specific operating system commands and any additional steps used for exiting from a computer, such as turning the power off, are collectively referred to as the *logout procedure.* Make sure you know the logout procedure for your computer at the time you login to ensure that you can effectively "escape" when you are ready to leave the system. The operating system command for listing a program typically has a name such as LIST, TYPE, cat, or PRINT; the command for deleting a program typically has a name such as DELETE, DEL, ERASE, UNSAVE, REMOVE, or rm; the command for copying a program typically has a name such as COPY, COP, or cp; and the operating system command for renaming a program typically has a name such as RENAME, REN, RN, or mv. Use Table C.1 to list the specific operating system command names used by your system to perform these tasks.

The commands to list, copy, delete, or rename a program are all concerned with manipulating existing programs. Let us now turn our attention to creating, compiling, and executing a new C program. The procedures for doing these tasks are illustrated in Figure C.2. As shown in this figure, the procedure for creating an executable C program consists of three distinct operations: editing, compiling, and linking.

Editing

Both the creation of a new C program and the modification of an existing C program requires the use of an editor program. The function of such a program is to allow a user to type statements at a keyboard and to save the typed statements together under a common name, called a *source program file name.*

FIGURE C.2   Creating an Executable C Program

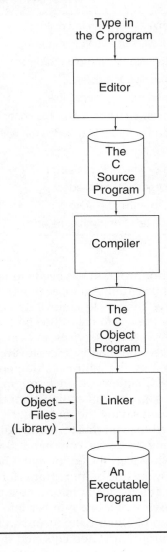

As illustrated in Figure C.1, an editor program is contained within the environment controlled by the operating system, either as a separate program or as part of the services provided with a C compiler. This means that the editor program can only be accessed using an operating system command, which either starts up the editor program directly or the C compiler that provides its own editor.

Some editors handle one line at a time; to add, change, or delete text, you refer to a specific line by number and edit that line. Line editors are sometimes inconvenient to use, but they make efficient use of memory and CPU time. Full-screen editors permit you to move the cursor to insert, delete, or change text at any point on the screen. Many C compilers for small computers are packaged with an editor; on larger machines you will have to use the general editor for that machine.

TABLE C.2 Editor Commands (Fill In for Your System)

Task	Command(s)	Example
Save the program and exit from the editor		
Save the program without exiting from the editor		
Exit from the editor without saving the program		
Switch to text mode (if applicable)		
Switch to command mode (if applicable)		
List the complete program from within the editor		
Delete the complete program from within the editor		
Delete a set of lines from within the editor		
Delete a single line from within the editor		
Name a program from within the editor		
Search for text from within the editor		
Search and replace text from within the editor		

Once the editor program has been requested the operating system relinquishes control to this program. Again, as illustrated in Figure C.1, this means that you temporarily leave the world controlled by the operating system and its commands and enter the world controlled by the editor. The editor, like the operating system, has its own set of services and commands and you will need to become familiar with these commands to create and modify your source programs. The services provided by the editor include entering C statements, modifying and deleting existing C statements in a program, listing a program, naming a program, saving a program, and exiting from the editor back into the operating system with or without saving the program.

In using an editor you must carefully distinguish between entering a C statement and entering an editor command. Some editors make this distinction by using special keys to alert the editor that what is being typed is a command to the editor rather than the line of a program (for example, in older versions of BASIC the line number automatically informs the editor that the entered line is a statement and the absence of a line number informs the editor that the entered line is an editor command). Other editors contain two modes: a text mode for entering and modifying program statements and a command mode for entering editor commands. For this latter type of editor there is always a means of switching from text to command mode and back from command to text mode. In both cases the commands recognized by the editor depend on the editor being used. After filling in the operating system command needed to enter the editor, use Table C.2 to list the specific editor command names or procedures provided by your editor.

```
            Operating system command
            to enter the editor:_____
```

Compiling and Linking

The translation of a C source program into a form that can be executed by the computer is accomplished using a program called a compiler. The compiler, like the editor, is accessed using an operating system command. Each operating system uses a different command for calling the compiler into action and giving the compiler the name of the source file that is to be translated. Determine and then list the command used by your computer for performing this operation:

```
Command to compile a program:_____
```

The output produced by the compiler is called an object program. An *object program* is simply a translated version of the source program that can be executed by the computer system with one more processing step. Let us see why this is so.

Most C programs contain statements that use preprogrammed routines, for input and output and for finding such quantities as square roots, absolute values, and other commonly encountered mathematical calculations. Additionally, a large C program may be stored in two separate program files. In such a case, each file can be compiled separately. However, both files must ultimately be combined to form a single program before the program can be executed. In both of these cases it is the task of the linker to combine all of the preprogrammed routines and individual object files into a single program ready for execution. This final program is called an *executable program.* Determine and then list the command used by your compiler for performing this operation.

```
Command to compile and link a program:_____
```

A Word of Caution

You will want to print the source code files to the screen or printer using operating system commands, such as TYPE, PRINT, or something similar—so that you can see and work with these files. This can be done because the source program is actually text consisting of a sequence of character codes. Do NOT, however, try to print the object or executable files in the same manner, because these are files consist of binary numbers, not text. If you attempt to print these files, at best, you will see unrecognizable characters on the screen or printer as the binary code comprising these files are displayed as text. Even worse, you may lock-up the keyboard or print a ream of paper with one character on each page when some of the binary codes perform terminal control functions.

Executing

Finally, once a C source program has been compiled and linked, it must be executed. To execute (or run) the program you simply type the name of the executable file in response to the operating system prompt. Determine and then list the command for performing this operation:

```
Command to execute a
compiled and linked program:_____
```

D Input and Output Redirection

The display produced by the `printf()` function is normally sent to the terminal where you are working. This terminal is called the standard output device because it is where the display is automatically directed, in a standard fashion, by the interface between your C program and your computer's operating system. On most systems it is possible to redirect the output produced by `printf()` to some other device, or to a file, using the output redirection symbol, >, at the time the program is invoked. In addition to the symbol, you must specify where you want the displayed results to be sent.

For purposes of illustration, assume that the command to execute a compiled program named `salestax`, without redirection, is

```
salestax
```

This command is entered after your computer's system prompt is displayed on your terminal. When the salestax program is run, any `printf()` function calls within it automatically cause the appropriate display to be sent to your terminal. Suppose we would like to have the display produced by the program sent to a file named `results`. To do this, we use the command

```
salestax > results
```

The redirection symbol, >, tells the operating system to send any display produced by `printf()` directly to a file named `results` rather than to the standard output device used by the system. The display sent to `results` can then be examined by using either an editor program or by issuing another operating system command. For example, under the UNIX® operating system the command

```
cat results
```

causes the contents of the file `results` to be displayed on your terminal. The equivalent command under the IBM PC disk operating system (DOS) is

```
type results
```

In redirecting an output display to a file, the following rules apply:

1. If the file does not exist, it will be created.
2. If the file exists, it will be overwritten with the new display.

In addition to the output redirection symbol, the output append symbol, >>, can also be used. The append symbol is used in the same manner as the redirection symbol, but it causes any new output to be added to the end of a file. For example, the command

```
salestax >> results
```

causes any output produced by `salestax` to be added to the end of the `results` file. If the `results` file does not exist, it will be created.

Besides having the display produced by `printf()` redirected to a file, using either the `>` or `>>` symbols, the display can also be sent to a physical device connected to your computer, such as a printer. You must, however, know the name used by your computer for accessing the desired device. For example, on an IBM PC or compatible computer, the name of the printer connected to the terminal is designated as `prn:`. Thus, if you are working on an IBM or compatible machine, the command

```
salestax > prn:
```

causes the display produced in the `salestax` program to be sent directly to the printer connected to the terminal. In addition to `printf()`, output redirection also affects the placement of displays produced by the `puts()` and `putchar()` functions, and any other function that uses the standard output device for display.

Corresponding to output redirection, it is also possible to redesignate the standard input device for an individual program run using the input redirection symbol, `<`. Again, the new source for input must be specified immediately after the input redirection symbol.

Input redirection works in a similar fashion as output redirection, but it affects the source of input for the `scanf()`, `gets()`, and `getchar()` functions. For example, the command

```
salestax < dat_in
```

causes any input functions within `salestax` that normally receive their input from the keyboard to receive it from the `dat_in` file instead. This input redirection, like its output counterpart, is only in effect for the current execution of the program. As you might expect, the same run can have both an input and output redirection. For example, the command

```
salestax < dat_in > results
```

causes an input redirection from the file `dat_in` and an output redirection to the file results.

In addition to standard input and output redirection, the device to which all error messages are sent can also be redirected. On many systems this file is given an operating system designation as device file 2. Thus, the redirection

```
2> err
```

causes any error messages that would normally be displayed on the standard error device, which is usually your terminal, to be redirected to a file named `err`. As with standard input and output redirection, standard error redirection can be included on the same command line used to invoke a program. For example, the command

```
salestax < dat_in > show 2> err
```

causes the compiled program named `salestax` to receive its standard input from a file named `dat_in`, write its results to a file named `show`, and send any error messages to a file named `err`.

Because the redirection of input, output, and error messages is generally a feature of the operating system used by your computer and not typically part of your C compiler, you must check the manuals for your particular operating system to ensure these features are available.

Floating-Point Number Storage

The two's compliment binary code used to store integer values was presented in Section 1.5. In this appendix we present the binary storage format typically used to store single-precision and double-precision numbers, which are stored as floats and doubles, respectively, in C. Collectively, both single- and double-precision values are commonly referred to as floating-point values.

Like their decimal number counterparts, which use a decimal point to separate the integer and fractional parts of a number, floating-point numbers are represented in a conventional binary format with a binary point. For example, consider the binary number 1011.11. The digits to the left of the binary point (1011) represent the integer part of the number and the digits to the right of the binary point (11) represent the fractional part.

To store a floating-point binary number, a code similar to decimal scientific notation is used. To obtain this code, the conventional binary number format is separated into a mantissa and exponent. The following examples illustrate floating-point numbers expressed in this exponential notation:

Conventional Binary Notation	Binary Exponential Notation
1010.0	1.01 exp 011
-10001.0	-1.0001 exp 100
0.001101	1.101 exp -011
-0.000101	-1.01 exp -100

In binary exponential notation, the term exp stands for exponent. The binary number in front of the exp term is the mantissa and the binary number following the exp term is the exponent value. Except for the number zero, the mantissa always has a single leading 1 followed immediately by a binary point. The exponent represents a power of 2 and indicates the number of places the binary point should be moved in the mantissa to obtain the conventional binary notation. If the exponent is positive, the binary point is moved to the right. If the exponent is negative, the binary point is moved to the left. For example, the exponent 011 in the number

1.01 exp 011

means move the binary point three places to the right, so that the number becomes 1010. The - 011 exponent in the number

1.101 exp - 011

means move the binary point three places to the left, so that the number becomes .001101.

TABLE E.1 IEEE Standard 754-1985 Floating-Point Specification

Data Format	Sign Bits	Mantissa Bits	Exponent Bits
Single-precision	1	23	8
Double-precision	1	52	11
Extended-precision	1	64	15

In storing floating-point numbers, the sign, mantissa, and exponent are stored individually within separate fields. The number of bits used for each field determines the precision of the number. Single-precision (32-bit), double-precision (62-bit), and extended-precision (80-bit) real data formats are defined by the Institute of Electrical and Electronics Engineers (IEEE) Standard 754-1985 to have the characteristics given in Table E.1. The format for a single-precision real number is illustrated in Figure E.1.

FIGURE E.1 Single-Precision Real Number Storage Format

Bit	31	30 ←→ 23	22 ←————→ 0
	Sign	Exponent	Mantissa

The sign bit shown in Figure E.1 refers to the sign of the mantissa. A sign bit of 1 represents a negative number and a zero sign bit represents a positive value. Because all mantissas, except for the number zero, have a leading 1 followed by their binary points, these two items are never stored explicitly. The binary point implicitly resides immediately to the left of mantissa bit 22, and a leading 1 is always assumed. The binary number zero is specified by setting all mantissa and exponent bits to zero. For this case only, the implied leading mantissa bit is also zero.

The exponent field contains an exponent that is biased by 127. For example, an exponent of 5 would be stored using the binary equivalent of the number 132 (127 + 5). Using eight exponent bits, this is coded as 100000100. The addition of 127 to each exponent allows negative exponents to be coded within the exponent field without the need for an explicit sign bit. For example, the exponent -011, which corresponds to -3, would be stored using the binary equivalent of +124 (127 − 3).

FIGURE E.2 The Encoding and Storage of the Decimal Number 59.75

1	10000100	11011110000000000000000

Figure E.2 illustrates the encoding and storage of the decimal number 59.75 as a 64-bit, single-precision binary number. The sign, exponent, and mantissa are determined as follows:

The conventional binary equivalent of

$$-59.75$$

is

$$-111011.11$$

Expressed in binary exponential notation this becomes

$$-1.110111 \text{ exp } 101$$

The minus sign is signified by setting the sign bit to 1. The mantissa's leading 1 and binary point are omitted and the 23-bit mantissa field is encoded as

$$11011110000000000000000$$

The exponent field encoding is obtained by adding the exponent value of 101 to 1111111, which is the binary equivalent of the 127_{10} bias value.

$$
\begin{array}{rcl}
1\,1\,1\,1\,1\,1\,1 & = & 127_{10} \\
+\,1\,0\,1 & = & +\,5_{10} \\
\hline
1\,0\,0\,0\,0\,1\,0\,0 & = & 132_{10}
\end{array}
$$

A Brief C Reference

This appendix is meant to serve as a quick summary of the data types, statements, program forms, and routines described in the text. Both general forms and specific examples are included.

KEYWORDS

auto	default	float	register	switch
break	do	for	return	typedef
case	double	goto	short	union
char	else	if	signed	unsigned
const	enum	int	sizeof	void
continue	extern	long	static	volatile
			struct	while

OPERATORS

The following table lists C's operators from highest to lowest priority. Operators on the same row have the same priority and are evaluated according to the order of evaluation listed.

Type	Symbols	Order of Evaluation
Primary	() [] . ->	Left to right
Unary	++ -- & * - ! ~ sizeof	Right to left
Arithmetic	* / %	Left to right
Arithmetic	+ -	Left to right
Shift	<< >>	Left to right
Relational	< <= > >=	Left to right
Relational	== !=	Left to right
Bitwise	& (AND)	Left to right
Bitwise	^ (NOT)	Left to right
Bitwise	| (OR	Left to right
Logical	&&	Left to right
Logical	||	Left to right
Conditional	?:	Right to left
Assignment	= += -= /= %= etc.	Right to left
Comma	,	Left to right

SCALER DATA TYPES

Type		Sample Declaration
char		char key;
int		int num;
short	(or short int)	short count;
long	(or long int)	long int date;
unsigned	(or unsigned int)	unsigned val;
float		float rate;
double	(or long float)	double taxes;

ARRAYS

An *array* is a list of elements of the same data type. The first element in an array is referred to as the zeroth element. Examples of array declarations are:

```
int prices[5];
char name[20];
float rates [4][15];
```

STRUCTURES

A structure is a data type whose elements need not be of the same data type. For example,

```
struct TelRecord
{
  char name[20]
  int id;
  double rate;
}
```

COMMENTS

Comments are enclosed within a /* and */.

```
/* this is a sample of a comment */
```

STATEMENTS

A *null statement* consists of a semicolon only:

```
;        /* the null statement */
```

For example,

```
double a                   /* declaration statement */
taxes = rate * income;     /* and expression statement */
printf("Hello World!");    /* function statement */
```

A *compound statement* consists of one or more statements enclosed within braces. For example,

```
{                 /* start of compound statement */
  taxes = rate * income;
  count++
}                 /* end of compound statement /
```

A *simple statement* is a null, declaration, expression, or a function statement. *Flow control statements* are structured statements consisting of a keyword (if, while, for, do, switch) followed by an expression within parentheses followed by a simple or compound statement.

Statement	Example
if (expression) *statement;*	```if (age == 13)``` ``` printf("Welcome Teenager!");```

if (expression)
  statement1;
else
  statement2;
	```if (num == 5)```
	``` printf("Bingo!");```
	```else```
	``` printf("You Lose!");```

if (expression)
  statement1;
else if (expression)
  statement2;
    ⋮
else
  statement3;
	```if (grade <= 90)```
	``` printf("You got an A");```
	```else if (grade <= 80)```
	``` printf("You got a B"):```
	```else if (grade <= 70);```
	``` printf("You got a C");```
	```else```
	``` printf("You got a D");```

switch (expression)
{
  case value_1:
    statement1;
  case value_2:
    statement2;
      ⋮
  default:
    statementn;
}
	```switch (marcode)```
	```{```
	``` case 1:```
	``` printf("Good Morning\n");```
	``` break;```
	``` case 2:```
	``` printf("Good Afternoon\n");```
	``` break;```
	``` default:```
	``` printf("Good Night\n");```
	```}```

for (init; expression; alter) *statement;*	```for (i = 0; i < 10; ++i)``` ``` printf("%d %d", i, i*i);```

while (expression)
  statement;
	```while (num < 10)```
	```{```
	``` printf("number i %d",num);```
	``` num++```
	```}```

do
  statement;
while (expression);
	```do```
	```{```
	``` printf("Hello");```
	``` count++;```
	```}```
	```while (count < 10);```

PROGRAMS AND FUNCTIONS

A program must have one and only one `main()` function. Statements within `main()` are enclosed within an opening and closing brace pair.

```
void main(void)                 /* function name */
{                               /* opening brace */
  variable declarations;
  other C statements;

}                               /* closing brace */
```

Typically a program consists of preprocessor commands, a `main()` function, and other user-created functions. Preprocessor commands always begin with a # symbol in the first column and are placed outside of any function. Program execution always starts with the `main()` function regardless of where this function is located in the program. Other user-written functions follow one another and cannot be nested. The general form of a function definition is:

```
function_return_type  function_name(formal argument declarations)
{
   variable declarations;
   other C statements (including return statements);
}
```

FUNCTION PROTOTYPES

A function prototype declares the return type and arguments expected by the function. The most commonly used form of a function prototype is

```
function_return_type   function_name(List of argument data types);
```

VARIABLE SCOPE

A variable can have either a *local* or *global* scope. *Local variables* are defined within a function and are only meaningful when used in expressions or statements inside of the function. *Global variables* are defined outside of a function and can be used in any function following the definition.

VARIABLE STORAGE CLASS

Each variable has a storage class associated with it. The storage classes are:

```
auto
register
extern
static
```

`auto` and `register` variables are always local variables that are created when the function is invoked and destroyed when the function ends.

extern declares a global variable that resides in another file.

static variables are local to the scope in which they are declared. They cannot be externed. Thus, global static variables can only be used in the file in which they are declared (and are effectively private within the file). Except for static variables, all other variables get initialized each time they come into scope.

VARIABLE DECLARATIONS AND DEFINITIONS

A variable declaration declares the storage class and data type of a variable. The general form of a declaration statement is

```
storage-class data-type list of variable names;
```

For example,

```
auto int num;   /* can be written as int num; */
static int  num1, num2, num3;
extern float price;
```

A declaration statement that also forces the compiler to reserve storage areas for the variable is a *definition statement*. Except for explicitly declared extern variables, all declaration statements are also definition statements.

VARIABLE INITIALIZATIONS

Variables can be initialized when they are defined.

Scaler variables are explicitly initialized when they are declared by following the variable name with an equal sign and an expression consisting of one or more constants, including previously defined variables or arguments. For example,

```
double rate = .05;
```

Arrays can be explicitly initialized by enclosing a list of initializers within braces. For example,

```
int prices[3] = {1.25, 3.69, 8.32};
```

If an array is explicitly initialized, the size of the array can be omitted and will be determined by the compiler by counting the number of initializers.

Character arrays can be explicitly initialized as a list of characters or as a string. For example,

```
char name[] = "Howard Karp";
```

External and static variables are initialized once at compile time. External and static variables that are not explicitly initialized are set to zero or blanks, as appropriate, by default.

An explicitly initialized automatic or register variable is initialized each time the function declaring them is invoked. Uninitialized automatic and register variables are not set to zero and contain "garbage" values.

G Solutions to Selected Odd-Numbered Exercises

EXERCISES 1.1

1.a. A computer program is a structured combination of data and instructions that is used to operate a computer.

b. Programming is the process of using a programming language to produce a computer program.

c. A programming language is the set of instructions, data, and rules that can be used to construct a program.

d. A high-level language is a programming language that uses instructions that resemble a written language, such as English, and can be translated to run on a variety of computer types.

e. A low-level language is a programming language that uses instructions that are directly tied to one type of computer. They consist of machine-level and assembly languages.

f. A machine language contains the binary codes that can be executed by a computer. Such languages are frequently referred to as executables.

g. An assembly language permits symbolic names to be used for mathematical operations and memory addresses. Assembly languages are low level.

h. A procedure-oriented language has instructions that are used to create procedures. A procedure is a logically consistent set of instructions that produces a specific result.

i. An object-oriented language permits the construction of objects, which can be manipulated and displayed. Such languages are gaining increasing use in graphically oriented programs.

j. A source program consists of the program statements comprising a C or other programming language program.

k. A compiler is a program that is used to translate a high-level source program as a complete unit before any one statement is actually executed.

l. An interpreter is a program that translates individual source program statements, one at a time, into executable statements. Each statement is executed immediately after translation.

3.a. Analytical engine, England. The first recorded attempt at creating a machine that would respond to precoded and changeable instructions.

b. ABC, Iowa State University. The first successful computer to manipulate binary numbers under program control. The program consisted of external wiring.

c. ENIAC, University of Pennsylvania. The first successful large-scale computer. It used external wiring to control its operation and could perform 5000 additions or 360 multiplications per second.

d. Mark I, Harvard University. An early large-scale computer built at Harvard University that used mechanical relay switches to store numbers.

e. EDSAC, Cambridge University, England. The first successful large-scale computer that used a stored program in its memory to control its operation.

5.a. Low-level languages use instructions that are directly tied to one computer and generally execute at the fastest level possible. High-level languages are portable, but must be compiled into a low-level language before it can be executed.

b. A procedure-oriented language uses instructions to create procedures, which are self-contained units that manipulate input values to produce resulting outputs. An object-oriented language permits the construction of objects, such as rectangles, that can be manipulated and displayed. Typically, object-oriented languages are used for producing programs that have a graphical component.

7.a.   Add the data in memory location 1 to the data in memory location 2.

Multiply the data in memory location 3 by the data in memory location 2.

Subtract the data in memory location 4 from the data in memory location 3.

Divide the data in memory location 3 by the data in memory location 5.

b. $3 + 5 = 8$
$6 * 3 = 18$
$14 - 6 = 8$
$6 / 4 = 1.5$

EXERCISES 1.3

1.a.   *Clearly define the problem:* To ensure that the problem is clearly understood, including what inputs will be given and what outputs are required.

Develop a solution: Define an appropriate set of steps, called an algorithm, to solve the problem.

Code the solution: Write the program by translating the solution into a source program.
Test and correct the program: Test the completed computer program to ensure that it does provide a solution to the problem.

b.   *Documentation:* Provide adequate user documentation for people who will use the program and programmer documentation for people who will maintain the program.

Maintenance: Keep the solution up to date by making modifications required whether due to changes in requirements or because errors are found during program execution.

EXERCISES 1.4

1.   One possible solution:
a.   *Make sure the car is parked, the engine is off, and the key is out*
 of the ignition switch.
Go to the trunk.
Put the correct key into the trunk.
Open the trunk.
Remove the spare tire and the jack.
Put the jack under the car . . . and so on.
b.   *Go to a phone.*
Remove the handset from the phone.
Wait for the dial tone.
Take out the correct change for the call.
Put the correct change into the phone.
Dial the number.
c.   *Arrive at the store.*
Walk through the door.
Go to the bread aisle.
Select the desired bread.
Go to the cashier.
Pay for the bread and leave.
d.   *Prepare the turkey.*
Preheat the oven.
Open the oven door.
Put the turkey in the oven.
Close the oven door.
Wait the appropriate time for the turkey to cook.

3.   Step 1: Pour the contents of the first cup into the third cup.

Step 2: Rinse the first cup.

Step 3: Pour the contents of the second cup into the first cup.

Step 4: Rinse the second cup.

Step 5: Pour the contents of the third cup into the second cup.

5.	Step 1: Compare the first number with the second number and use the smallest of these numbers for the next step.

Step 2: Compare the smallest number found in step 1 with the third number. The smallest of these two numbers is the smallest of all three numbers.

7.a.	Step 1: Compare the first name in the list with the name WESTBY. If the names match, stop the search; else go to step 2.

Step 2: Compare the next name in the list with the name WESTBY. If the names match, stop the search; else repeat this step.

8.	Step 1: Look at the first letter.
If it is an 'e' then set COUNT to 1;
else set COUNT to 0.

Step 2: Look at the next letter.
If it is 'e' then add one to COUNT.

Step 3: Continue to repeat step 2 until a period '.' is encountered.

EXERCISES 2.1

1.	
m1234()	Valid. Not a mnemonic.
new_bal()	Valid. A mnemonic.
abcd()	Valid. Not a mnemonic.
A12345()	Valid. Not a mnemonic.
1A2345()	Invalid. Violates rule 1; starts with a number.
power()	Valid. A mnemonic.
abs_val()	Valid. A mnemonic.
mass()	Valid. A mnemonic.
do()	Invalid. Violates rule 3; is a reserved word.
while()	Invalid. Violates rule 3; is a reserved word.
add_5()	Valid. Could be a mnemonic.
taxes()	Valid. A mnemonic.
net_pay()	Valid. A mnemonic.
12345()	Invalid. Violates rule 1; starts with a number.
int()	Invalid. Violates rule 3; a reserved word.
new_balance()	Valid. A mnemonic.
a2b3c4d5()	Valid. Not a mnemonic.
salestax()	Valid. A mnemonic.
amount()	Valid. A mnemonic.
$sine()	Invalid. Violates rule 1; starts with a special character.

3.a.	These functions, as indicated by their names, most likely would be in a billing program for the following purposes:

```
input_bill();       /* input the items purchased */
calc_salestax();    /* compute required sales tax */
calc_balance();     /* determine balance owed */
```

b.
```
void main(void)
{
    input_bill();
    calc_salestax();
    calc_balance();
}
```

5.a. `int main(void)`
b. `char main(void)`
c. `float main(void)`
d. `double main(void)`

7.a.
```
#include <stdio.h>
void main(void)
{
    printf("Computers, computers everywhere\n");
    printf("   as far as I can see\n");
    printf("I really, really like these things,\n");
    printf("   Oh joy, Oh joy for me!\n");
}
```

9.   The two operations are a line feed to bring the cursor down one line, and a carriage return to bring the cursor to the first column of the current line.

Note: Many solutions are possible for Exercises 11 through 15. The following are possible answers.

11.   Determine the placement of the light fixtures.
      If you are capable and allowed to do so
        Purchase the necessary materials including the fixtures and wire the lights in accordance with local ordinances.
      Else hire a licensed electrician.

13.   Determine the courses needed for law school.
      Take the right courses.
      Maintain an appropriate grade average.
      Prepare for the LSATs.
      Contact law schools for admission interview requirements.
      Determine what area of law you want to practice.
      Get letters of recommendation.

15.   Select and reserve a camp site.
      Prepare list of items to take along.
      Purchase needed supplies.
      Reserve a camper at the rental agency (optional).
      Arrange for someone to feed plants and watch house.
      Make arrangements for care of pets (optional).
      Check and service automobile.

EXERCISES 2.2

1. a. Yes.
   b. It is not in standard form. To make programs more readable and easier to debug, the standard form presented in Section 2.2 of the text should be used.
3. a. Two backslashes in a row cause one backslash to be displayed.
   b. `printf("\\ is a backslash.\n");`

EXERCISES 2.3

1. a. float or double
   b. integer
   c. float or double
   d. integer
   e. float or double
   f. character
3.   1.26e2   6.5623e2   3.42695e3   4.8932e3   3.21e-1   1.23e-2   6.789e-3
5. a. $3 + 4 * 6 = 3 + 24 = 27$
   b. $3 * 4 / 6 + 6 = 12 / 6 + 6 = 2 + 6 = 8$
   c. $2 * 3 / 12 * 8 / 4 = 6 / 12 * 8 / 4 = 0 * 8 / 4 = 0$
   d. $10 * (1 + 7 * 3) = 10 * (1 + 21) = 10 * 22 = 220$
   e. $20 - 2 / 6 + 3 = 20 - 0 + 3 = 23$
   f. $20 - 2 / (6 + 3) = 20 - 2 / 9 = 20 - 0 = 20$
   g. $(20 - 2) / 6 + 3 = 18 / 6 + 3 = 3 + 3 = 6$
   h. $(20 - 2) / (6 + 3) = 18 / 9 = 2$
   i. $50 \% 20 = 10$
   j. $(10 + 3) \% 4 = 13 \% 4 = 1$
7.   Since all of the operands given are integers, the result of each expression is an integer value.
   a. $10 / 5 + 3 = 2 + 3 = 5$
   b. $50 / 5 + 10 - 10 * 1 = 10 + 10 - 10 = 10$
   c. $50 - 3 * 10 + 4 * 1 = 50 - 30 + 4 = 24$
   d. $1 / 5 = 0$ (truncation)
   e. $18 / 5 = 3$
   f. $-5 * 10 = -50$
   g. $-50 / 20 = -2$

h. (50 + 10) / (5 + 1) = 60 / 6 = 10
i. 50 + 10 / 5 + 1 = 50 + 2 + 1 = 53
9.   answer1 is the integer 2
     answer2 is the integer 5
11.

```
#include<stdio.h>
void main(void)
{
  printf("%f * %f = %f\n", 3.0, 5.0, 3.0*5.0);
  printf("%f * %f - %f = %f\n", 7.1, 8.3, 2.2, 7.1*8.3-2.2);
  printf("%f / (%f * %d) = %f\n", 3.2, 6.1, 5, 3.2/(6.1*5));
}
```

13.

	K	I	N	G	S	L	E	Y
a.	01001011	01001001	01001110	01000111	01010011	01001100	01000101	01011001
b.	11010010	11001001	11010101	11000111	11100010	11010011	11000101	11101000

17.a. 'm' − 5 = 'h'
  b. 'm' + 5 = 'r'
  c. 'G' + 6 = 'M'
  d. 'G' − 6 = 'A'
  e. 'b' − 'a' = 1
  f. 'g' − 'a' + 1 = 6 + 1 = 7
  g. 'G' − 'A' + 1 = 6 + 1 = 7

EXERCISES 2.4

1.   The following are not valid:
     12345   Does not begin with either a letter or underscore
     while   Reserved word
     $total   Does not begin with either a letter or underscore
     new bal   Cannot contain a space
     9ab6   Does not begin with either a letter or underscore
     sum.of   Contains a special character
3.a. int count;
  b. float grade;
  c. double yield;
  d. char initial;
5.a. int firstnum, secnum;
  b. float price, yield, coupon;
  c. double maturity;
7.a.

```
#include <stdio.h>
void main(void)
{
  int num1, num2, total;   /* declare the integer variables num1,
                               num2 & total */


  num1 = 25;     /* assign the integer 25 to num1 */
  num2 = 30;     /* assign the integer 30 to num2 */
  total = num1 + num2;  /* assign the sum of num1 and num2 to total */
  printf("The total of %d and %d is %d.\n",num1,num2,total);
                          /* prints: The total of 25 and 30 is 55. */

}
```

  b. The total of 25 and 30 is 55.

9.
```
#include <stdio.h>
void main(void)
{
     int length, width, perimeter;

     length = 16;
     width = 18;
     perimeter = length + length + width + width;
     printf("The perimeter is %d.\n",perimeter);
}
```

11. The average is 16.5, but the program will store 16 in the variable average. To ensure that the correct answer will be printed, the variable average must be declared as a float value, and the printf() statement must contain the conversion control sequence %f.

13.
```
#include <stdio.h>
void main(void)
{
  printf("Bytes for an integer = %d\n", sizeof(int));
  printf("Bytes for a long integer = %d\n", sizeof(long));
  printf("Bytes for a float = %d\n", sizeof(float));
  printf("Bytes for a double = %d\n", sizeof(double));
  printf("Bytes for a char = %d\n", sizeof(char));
}
```

15.a. All definitions are declarations but not all declarations are definitions.

b. Definition statements reserve storage areas in memory for the variables. In this sense variables are created (come into existence) by definition statements. Before a variable is used it must exist. Thus definition statements must precede any statement that uses the variables. They need not, however, always precede all other statements. For example, in the following code the variable b is defined within the second block of code.
```
#include <stdio.h>
void main(void)
{
     { /* first block of code */
         int a;
         a = 5;
         printf(" a = %d\n",a);
     }
     { /* second block of code */
         int b;
         b = 5;
         printf(" b = %d\n",b);
     }
}
```

17.a.

Address:	159	160	161	162	163	164	165	166
	| a |		| b |	u |	n |	c	| h |	| \ |
	cn1	cn2	cn3	cn4	cn5	cn6	cn7	key

Address:	167	168	169	170	171	172	173	174
	| ' |	o |	f |		|	|	|	|
	sch	inc	inc1					

b. cn1=01100001
    cn2=00100000
    cn3=01100010
    cn4=01110101

```
cn5=01101110
cn6=01100011
cn7=01101000
key=01011100
sch=00101101
inc=01101111
inc1=01100110
```

EXERCISES 2.5

1.a.   One output: the dollar amount
 b.   Five inputs: half dollars, quarters, dimes, nickels, pennies
 c.   Dollar amount = 0.50 * halfs + 0.25 * quarters + 0.10 * dimes + 0.05 * nickels + 0.01 * pennies
 d.   Dollar amount = 0.50 * 0 + 0.25 * 17 + 0.10 * 24 + 0.05 * 16 + 0.01 * 12 = 7.57

3.a.   One output : the amount of Ergies
 b.   Two inputs: Fergies, Lergies
 c.   Ergies = Fergies * sqrt(Lergies)
 d.   Ergies = 14.65 * sqrt(Lergies) = 29.3

5.a.   One output: distance
 b.   Three inputs: s, d, and t
 c.   distance = s - 0.5 * d * t * t

7.a.   4 outputs: gross pay and net pay for both individuals
 b.   6 inputs: the two hourly rates, tax rate, medical benefit rate, number of hours worked for each individual
 c.   Gross1 = rate1 * hours1
      Gross2 = rate2 * hours2
      Net1 = gross1 - gross1 * taxrate - gross1 * medrate
      Net2 = gross2 - gross2 * taxrate - gross2 * medrate
 d.   Gross1 = 8.43 * 40 = 337.20
      Gross2 = 5.67 * 35 = 198.45
      Net1 = 337.20 - 337.20 * 0.20 - 337.20 * 0.02 = 263.02
      Net2 = 198.45 - 198.45 * 0.20 - 198.45 * 0.02 = 154.79

9.a.   One output: y
 b.   Two inputs: e and x
 c.   y = pow(e , x)
 d.   y = pow(2.718 , 10) = 22003.64

EXERCISES 2.6

1.a.
```
#include<stdio.h>
void main(void)
{
     float time, length, pi;

     pi = 3.1416;
     time = 2.0;
     length = 12.0 * 32.2 * time / (2.0*pi) * time / (2.0*pi);
     printf(" The length is %4.2f inches.\n", length);
}
```
3.a.
```
#include<stdio.h>
void main(void)
{
     unsigned long numin, lines;

     numin = 1000;
     lines = numin * (numin - 1) / 2;
     printf("The number of lines needed is %ld\n", lines);
}
```

5.a.

```c
#include <stdio.h>
void main(void)
{
    float fahr, cel;

    fahr = 98.6;
    cel = (5.0 / 9.0) * (fahr - 32.0);
    printf("For a fahrenheit temperature of %4.1f degrees, \n", fahr);
    printf("the equivalent\n");
    printf("celsius temperature is %4.1f degrees\n", cel);
}
```

7.a.

```c
#include <stdio.h>
void main(void)
{
    float speed = 58.0, dist = 183.67, time;
    time = dist / speed;
    printf("The elapsed time for the trip is %f hours",time);
}
```

9.a.

```c
#include <stdio.h>
#include <math.h>
void main(void)
{
    int Tinit = 150, A = 60, t = 20;
    float e = 2.71828, k = 0.0367, Tfin;

    Tfin = (Tinit - A) * pow(e, -k * t) + A;
    printf("The final temperature is %f\n", Tfin);
}
```

11.a.

```c
#include <stdio.h>
#include <math.h>
void main(void)
{
    int a = 5000, n = 10, m = 4;
    float i = 0.06, amount;

    amount = a * pow((1 + i / m), m * n);
    printf("The amount of money available is $%5.2f\n", amount);
}
```

EXERCISES 2.9

1.a.   valid
   b.   not valid since the variable distyance is not declared
   c.   valid
   d.   valid
   e.   valid but nonsensical since average is a float that will be converted to an integer by assignment; casting a float to a float makes no sense
   f.   valid since the numerical value of letter is used
   g.   valid
   h.   not valid since the modulus operator is not defined for floats
   i.   valid
   j.   valid
   k.   valid
   l.   valid
   m.   valid
   n.   valid but dangerous since the result of the subtraction will be truncated to an integer
   o.   valid

3. Since all of the operands given are floating-point numbers, the result of each valid expression is a floating-point number.
    a. 5.
    b. 10.
    c. 24.
    d. 0.2
    e. 3.6
    f. −50.
    g. −2.5
    h. 10.
    i. 53.
5. The algorithm does not solve the problem because it fails when both numbers have the same value. According to the algorithm this case will result in an indication that the second number is larger than the first.
7.a. 'A' + 32 = 'a'
    'Z' + 32 = 'z'
    b. 'a' − 'A' = 32
    c. uppercase letter + 'a' − 'A' = lowercase letter

EXERCISES 3.1

1. `c = 2 * 3.1416 * r;`
3. `celsius = 5.0 / 9.0 * (fahrenheit - 32.0);`
5. `elapsed_time = (total_dist / avg_speed) * 60.0;`
7. The first integer displayed is 4.
    The second integer displayed is 4.
9. The sum is 0.000000.
    The sum is 26.270000.
    The final sum is 28.238000.
11.a.
```
#include <stdio.h>
void main(void)
{
        ←— missing declaration for all variables
      width = 15 ←— missing semicolon
      area = length * width; ←— no value assigned to length
      printf("The area is %d\n",area ←— missing );
}
```

The corrected program is:

```
#include <stdio.h>
void main(void)
{
      int length, width, area;

      width = 15;
      length = 20;      /* must be assigned some value */
      area = length * width;
      printf("The area is %d\n", area);
}
```
b.
```
#include <stdio.h>
void main(void)
{
      int length, width, area;

      area = length * width; ←—This should come after the
                                assignment of values
      length = 20;            to length and width.
      width = 15;
      printf("The area is %d\n", area);
}
```

The corrected program is:

```c
#include <stdio.h>
void main(void)
{
        int length, width, area;

        length = 20;
        width = 15;
        area = length * width;
        printf("The area is %d\n", area);
}
```

c.
```c
#include <stdio.h>
void main(void)
{
        int length = 20, width = 15, area;

        length * width = area;  ◄── incorrect assignment
                                      statement
        printf("The area is %d\n", area);
}
```

The corrected program is:

```c
#include <stdio.h>
void main(void)
{
        int length = 20, width = 15, area;
        area = length * width;
        printf("The area is %d\n", area);
}
```

13.
Radius	Height	Volume
1.62	6.23	51.365200
2.86	7.52	193.241669
4.26	8.95	510.261932
8.52	10.86	2476.623291
12.29	15.35	7283.884277

EXERCISES 3.2

1. answer1 is the integer 2.
    answer2 is the integer 5.

3.
```c
#include<stdio.h>
void main(void)
{
        printf("3.0 * 5.0 = %f\n", 3.0 * 5.0);
        printf("7.1 * 8.3 - 2.2 = %f\n", 7.1 * 8.3 - 2.2);
        printf("3.2 / (6.1 * 5) = %f\n", 3.2 / (6.1 * 5));
}
```

5.a. The comma is within the control string and the statement is not terminated with a semicolon. This statement will generate a compiler error, even if the semicolon is appended to the statement.

b. The statement uses a floating-point control sequence with an integer argument. It will compile and print an unpredictable result.

c. The statement uses an integer control sequence with a floating-point constant. It will compile and print an unpredictable result.

d. The statement has no control sequences for the numerical arguments. It will compile and print the letters a b c. The constants are ignored.

e. The statement uses a floating-point control sequence with an integer argument. It will compile and print an unpredictable result.

f. The f conversion character has been omitted from the control string. The statement will compile and print %3.6. The constants have no effect.

g. The formatting string must come before the arguments. The statement will compile and produce no output.

7.a. The number is 26.27.
The number is 682.30.
The number is 1.97.

b. $ 26.27
682.30
1.97
─────
$710.54

c. $ 26.27
682.30
1.97
─────
$710.54

d. 34.16
10.00
─────
44.17

9. The value of 14 in octal is 16.
The value of 14 in hexadecimal is E.
The value of 0xA in decimal is 10.
The value of 0xA in octal is 12.

EXERCISES 3.3

1.a. `sqrt(6.37)`
 b. `sqrt(x - y)`
 c. `sin(30 * 3.1416 / 180)`
 d. `sin(60 * 3.1416 / 180)`
 e. `abs(pow(a,2) - pow(b,2))`
 f. `exp(3)`

3.a. `b = sin(x) - cos(x);`
 b. `b = pow(sin(x),2) - pow(cos(x),2);`
 c. `area = (c * b * sin(a)) / 2;`
 d. `c = sqrt(pow(a,2) + pow(b,2));`
 e. `p = sqrt(abs(m - n));`
 f. `sum = (a * (pow(r,n) - 1)) / (r - 1);`

5.
```
#include<stdio.h>
#include<math.h>
void main(void)
{
    float distance, x1, x2, y1, y2;

    x1 = 7;
    x2 = 3;
    y1 = 12;
    y2 = 9;

    distance = sqrt(pow((x1 - x2),2) + pow((y1 - y2),2));
    printf("The distance is %f\n", distance);
}
```

7.
```
#include<stdio.h>
#include<math.h>
void main(void)
{
    float population, year = 1995;
    population = 5.5 * (1 + exp(.02 * (year - 1990)));
    printf("The population will be %f\n", population);
}
```

EXERCISES 3.4

1.a. `scanf("%d", &firstnum);`
  b. `scanf("%f", &grade);`
  c. `scanf("%lf", &secnum);    /* note - the lf is required */`
  d. `scanf("%c", &keyval);`
  e. `scanf("%d %d %f", &month, &years, &average);`
  f. `scanf("%c %d %d %lf %lf",&ch, &num1, &num2, &grade1, &grade2);`
  g. `scanf("%f %f %f %lf %lf",&interest,&principal,&capital,&price,&yield);`
  h. `scanf("%c %c %c %d %d %d",&ch,&letter1,&letter2,&num1,&*num2,&num3);`
  i. `scanf("%f %f %f %lf %lf %lf",&temp1, &temp2, &temp3, &volts1, &volts2);`

3.a. Missing & operator in front of `num1`. The correct form is:
      `scanf("%d", &num1);`
  b. Missing & operator in front of `firstnum` and wrong control sequence for price. The correct form is:
      `scanf("%d %f %lf", &num1, &firstnum, &price);`
  c. The wrong control sequence for `num1, secnum,` and `price`. The correct form is:
      `scanf("%d %f %lf", &num1, &secnum, &price);`
  d. Missing & operators in front of all the variables. The correct form is:
      `scanf("%d %d %lf", &num1, &num2, &yield);`
  e. Missing control string entirely. The correct form is:
      `scanf("%d %d", &num1, &num2);`
  f. Reversed address and control string. The correct form is:
      `scanf("%d", &num1);`

5.  ```
    #include <stdio.h>
    void main(void)
    {
         float radius, area;

         printf("Enter the radius of a circle: ");
         scanf("%f", &radius);
         area = 3.1416 * radius * radius;
         printf("The area is %f\n", area);
    }
    ```

Radius	Area
1.0	3.141600
1.5	7.068600
2.0	12.566400
2.5	19.635000
3.0	28.274400
3.5	38.484600

7.a.
```
#include<stdio.h>
void main(void)
{
     float num1, num2, num3, num4, avg;

     printf("Enter a number: ");
     scanf("%f", &num1);
     printf("Enter a second number: ");
     scanf("%f", &num2);
     printf("Enter a third number: ");
     scanf("%f", &num3);
     printf("Enter a fourth number: ");
     scanf("%f", &num4);
     avg = (num1 + num2 + num3 + num4) / 4.0;
     printf("The average of the four numbers is %f\n", avg);
}
```

Numbers	Answer
100, 100, 100, 100	100.000000
100, 0, 100, 0	50.000000
92, 98, 79, 85	88.500000
86, 84, 75, 86	82.750000
63, 85, 74, 82	76.000000
```

b.
```c
#include<stdio.h>
void main(void)
{
      float number, avg, sum = 0;

      printf("Enter a number: ");
      scanf("%f", &number);
      sum = sum + number;
      printf("Enter a second number: ");
      scanf("%f", &number);
      sum = sum + number;
      printf("\Enter a third number: ");
      scanf("%f", &number);
      sum = sum + number;
      printf("Enter a fourth number: ");
      scanf("%f", &number);
      sum = sum + number;
      avg = sum / 4.0;
      printf("The average of the four numbers is %f\n", avg);
}
```

9.
```c
#include<stdio.h>
#include<math.h>
void main(void)
{
      float b, t;

      printf("Enter the time in hours: ");
      scanf("%f", &t);
      b = 300000 * exp(-.032 * t);
      printf("The number of bacteria would be %f\n", b);
}
```

11.
```c
#include <stdio.h>
void main(void)
{
   float num1, num2, temp;

   printf("Please type in a number: ");
   scanf("%f", &num1);
   printf("Please type in another number: ");
   scanf("%f", &num2);
   printf("Before the swap num1 is %f and num2 is %f\n", num1, num2);
   temp = num1;    /* store num1 in temp */
   num1 = num2;    /* copy num2 to num1  */
   num2 = temp;    /* copy temp to num2  */
   printf("After the swap num1 is %f and num2 is %f\n", num1, num2);
}
```

13.
```c
#include <stdio.h>
void main(void)
{
      float num;

      printf("Please type in a number: ");
      scanf("%f", &num);
      printf("The number is %f\n", num);
}
```
Entering an integer value displays the result of an integer with a decimal point and six trailing zeros.

Entering a float value with less than six decimal places displays the result with the empty decimal places padded with zeros.

Entering a float value with more than six decimal places displays the result only up to the sixth decimal place.

Entering a character value displays a -0.000000.

15.a. It is quite easy for a user to enter incorrect data. If wrong or unexpected data is given by the user, either incorrect results will be obtained or the program will crash. A crash is an unexpected and premature program termination.

b. In a data type check the input is checked to ensure that the values entered are of the correct type for the declared variables. This includes checking that integer values are entered for integer variables, and so on. A data reasonableness check determines that the value entered is reasonable for the particular program. Such a check would determine if a large number was entered when a very small number was expected, if a small number was entered when a large number was expected, or if a zero (which could cause problems if the number was the denominator in a division) or a negative number was entered when a positive number was expected, and so on.

c. A reasonable check on the velocity is that it should be a positive number that is also less than some value, say, 100 miles per hour (more if the car is a race car) and that the acceleration lies within the limits of acceleration and deceleration speeds acceptable for cars.

EXERCISES 3.5

1.
```
#define GRAV 32.2
#include<math.h>
#include<stdio.h>
void main(void)
{
    double time, height;
    height = 800.0;
    time = sqrt(2.0 * height / GRAV);
    printf("It will take %4.2lf seconds\n", time);
    printf("to fall %7.3lf feet.\n", height);
}
```

3.
```
#define PRIME 0.08
#include<stdio.h>
#include<math.h>
void main(void)
{
    float prime, amount, interest;

    printf("Enter the amount: ");
    scanf("%f", &amount);
    interest = PRIME * amount;
    printf("The interest earned is %f dollars\n", interest);
}
```

EXERCISES 3.6

3. The problem with the program is that the scanf() request for data comes between the heading and data lines produced by the program. For example, a typical output is:

```
e to the x        Approximation      Difference
-------------     -------------      -------------
Enter a value of x: 2
   7.389056            1.000000         6.389056
   7.389056            3.000000         4.389056
   7.389056            5.000000         2.389056
   7.389056            6.333333         1.055723
```

5.a.

The computed standard normal deviate for the data is 1.325.

b.

```c
#include <stdio.h>
void main(void)
{
  float x, mu, sigma, deviate;

  printf("Enter a value of x: ");
  scanf("%f", &x);
  printf("Enter the mean: ");
  scanf("%f", &mu);
  printf("Enter the standard deviation: ");
  scanf("%f", &sigma);
  deviate = (x - mu) / sigma;
  printf("The standard normal deviate is %f\n", deviate);
}
```

EXERCISES 3.9

1.a.
```c
#include<stdio.h>
void main(void)
{
      float slope, x1, x2, y1, y2;

      x1 = 3;
      x2 = 8;
      y1 = 7;
      y2 = 12;

      slope = (y2 - y1) / (x2 - x1);
      printf("The slope of the line is %f\n", slope);
}
```
b.   At least one hand calculation to verify the result needs to be made.
d.   This is clearly a valid case and corresponds to a boundary condition. In this case the line is parallel to the y axis and has an infinite slope. Some check will have to be added to the program to isolate this case so the program provides the correct result, in a way that the user understands, to the input data.

3.
```c
#include<stdio.h>
void main(void)
{
      float slope, x1, x2, y1, y2;

      x1 = 3;
      x2 = 8;
      y1 = 7;
      y2 = 12;

      slope = (y2 - y1) / (x2 - x1);
      printf("The slope of the line is %6.2f\n", slope);
}
```

5.a.
```c
#include<stdio.h>
void main(void)
{
        int change, dollars, quarters, dimes, nickels, pennies;
        float paid = 10.00, check = 6.07;

        change = (paid - check) * 100;
        dollars = change / 100;
        quarters = (change - dollars * 100) / 25;
        dimes = (change - dollars * 100 - quarters * 25) / 10;
        nickels = (change - dollars * 100 - quarters * 25 - dimes * 10) / 5;
        pennies = (change - dollars * 100 - quarters * 25 - dimes * 10 -
         nickels * 5);
        printf("%d dollars\n", dollars);
        printf("%d quarters\n", quarters);
        printf("%d dimes\n", dimes);
        printf("%d nickels\n", nickels);
        printf("%d pennies\n", pennies);
}
```

7.
```c
#include<stdio.h>
#include<math.h>
void main(void)
{
        float num;

        printf("Enter the number to find the fourth root of: ");
        scanf("%f", &num);
        printf("The fourth root is %f\n", pow(num, 1.0/4.0));
}
```

9.
```c
#include<stdio.h>
#include<math.h>
void main(void)
{
        float a, x, r, n;

        printf("Enter amount of the initial deposit: ");
        scanf("%f", &x);
        printf("Enter the interest rate as a percent (ie. 8.3): ");
        scanf("%f", &r);
        printf("Enter the time period in years: ");
        scanf("%f", &n);
        a = x * pow((1.0 + r / 100), n);
        printf("The amount of money available would be $%7.2f\n", a);
}
```

EXERCISES 4.1

1.a. The relational expression is true. Therefore, its value is 1.
  b. The relational expression is true. Therefore, its value is 1.
  c. The final relational expression is true. Therefore, its value is 1.
  d. The final relational expression is true. Therefore, its value is 1.
  e. The final relational expression is true. Therefore, its value is 1.
  f. The arithmetic expression has a value of 10.
  g. The arithmetic expression has a value of 4.
  h. The arithmetic expression has a value of 0.
  i. The arithmetic expression has a value of 10.
3.a. age == 30
  b. temp > 98.6
  c. ht < 6.00
  d. month == 12

e. let_in == 'm'
f. age == 30 && ht > 6.00
g. day == 15 && month == 1
h. age > 50 || employ >= 5
i. id < 500 && age > 55
j. len > 2.00 && len < 3.00

EXERCISES 4.2

1.a.
```
if (angle == 90)
   printf("The angle is a right angle");
else
   printf("The angle is not a right angle");
```
b.
```
if (temperature > 100)
   printf("above the boiling point of water");
else
   printf("below the boiling point of water");
```
c.
```
if (number > 0)
   number = number + possum;
else
   number = number - possum;
```
d.
```
if (slope < .5)
   flag = 0;
else
   flag = 1;
```
e.
```
if ((num1 - num2) < .001)
   approx = 0;
else
   approx = (num1 - num2) / 2.0;
```
f.
```
if ((temp1 - temp2) > 2.3)
   error = (temp1 - temp2) * factor;
```
g.
```
if ((x > y) && (z < 20))
   scanf("%d",&p);
```
h.
```
if ((distance > 20) && (distance < 35))
   scanf("%d", &time);
```
3.
```
#define LIMIT 20000
#define REGRATE .02
#define HIGHRATE .025
#define FIXED 400
#include <stdio.h>
void main(void)
{
     float taxable, taxes;

     printf("Please type in the taxable income: \n");
     scanf("%f", &taxable);
     if (taxable <= LIMIT)
          taxes = REGRATE * taxable;
     else
          taxes = HIGHRATE * (taxable - LIMIT) + FIXED;
     printf("Taxes are $%7.2f\n", taxes);
}
```

5.a.
```
#include <stdio.h>
  void main(void)
  {
     float nyrs, rate;

     printf("Enter the time, in years, money was left in the account: ");
     scanf("%f", &nyrs);
        if (nyrs > 2.000)
           rate = 8.50;
        else
           rate = 7.00;
      printf("The interest rate is %f\n", rate);
  }
```
b. At least three runs should be made: one input under 2.000, one at 2.000, and one over 2.000. Another run, if necessary, might be made for some unexpected input, such as "six."

EXERCISES 4.3

1.
```
#include<stdio.h>
main()
{
     char marcode;
     printf("Enter a marital code: \n");
     scanf("%c",&marcode);

     if (marcode == 'M' || marcode == 'm')
         printf("Individual is married.\n");
     else if (marcode == 'S' || marcode == 's')
         printf("Individual is single.\n");
     else if (marcode == 'D' || marcode == 'd')
         printf("Individual is divorced.\n");
     else if (marcode == 'W' || marcode == 'w')
         printf("Individual is widowed.\n");
     else
         printf("An invalid code was entered.\n");

     printf("Thanks for participating in the survey\n");
}
```

3.
```
#include <stdio.h>
void main(void)
{
     float angle;

     printf("Enter the angle: ");
     scanf("%f", &angle);
     if (angle < 90.0)
         printf("The angle is acute.\n");
     else if (angle == 90.0)
         printf("The angle is a right angle.\n");
     else if (angle > 90.0)
         printf("The angle is obtuse.\n");
}
```

5.
```c
#include <stdio.h>
void main(void)
{
      float grade;
      char letter;

      printf("Enter the student's numerical grade: ");
      scanf("%f", &grade);
      if (grade >= 90.0) letter = 'A';
      else if (grade >= 80.0) letter = 'B';
      else if (grade >= 70.0) letter = 'C';
      else if (grade >= 60.0) letter = 'D';
      else letter = 'F';
      printf("The student receives a grade of %c\n", letter);
}
```
Notice that an `if-else` chain is used. If simple `if` statements were used, a grade entered as 75.5, for example, would be assigned a "C" because it was greater than 60.0. But the grade would then be reassigned to "D" because it is also greater than 60.0.

7.
```c
#include <stdio.h>
void main(void)
{
      float fahr,cels,in_temp;
      char letter;

      printf("Enter a temperature followed by");
      printf(" one space and the temperature's type\n");
      printf(" (an f designates a fahrenheit temperature");
      printf("  and a c designates a celsius temperature): ");
      scanf("%f %c", &in_temp, &letter);
      if (letter == 'f' || letter == 'F')
      {
          cels = (5.0/9.0)*(in_temp - 32.0);
          printf("%6.2f deg Fahrenheit = %6.2f deg Celsius\n",
              in_temp, cels);
      }
      else if (letter == 'c' || letter == 'C')
      {
          fahr = (9.0/5.0)*in_temp + 32.0;
          printf("%6.2f deg Celsius = %6.2f deg Fahrenheit\n",
              in_temp, fahr);
      }
      else printf("The data entered is invalid.\n");
}
```

9.a. This program will run. It will not, however, produce the correct result.

b. & c. This program evaluates correct incomes for mon_sales less than 20000.00 only. If 20000.00 or more were entered, the first else-if statement would be executed and all others would be ignored. That is, for 20000.00 or more, the income for >= 10000.00 would be calculated and displayed.

Had if statements been used in place of the else-if statements, the program would have worked correctly, but inefficiently (see comments for Exercise 4b).

EXERCISES 4.4

1.
```
switch (let_grad)
{
    case 'A':
      printf("The numerical grade is between 90 and 100\n");
      break;
    case 'B':
      printf("The numerical grade is between 80 and 89.9\n");
      break;
    case 'C':
      printf("The numerical grade is between 70 and 79.9\n");
      break;
    case 'D':
      printf("How are you going to explain this one\n");
      break;
    default:
      printf("Of course I had nothing to do with the grade.\n");
      printf("It must have been the professor's fault.\n");
}
```

3.
```
switch (code)
{
    case 1:
      printf("360 Kilobyte Drive (5 1/2 inch)\n");
      break;
    case 2:
      printf("1.2 Megabyte Drive (5 1/2 inch)\n");
      break;
    case 3:
      printf("722 Kilobyte Drive (3 1/4 inch)\n");
      break;
    case 4:
      printf("1.4 Megabyte Drive (3 1/4 inch)\n");
      break;
}
```

5. The expression in the switch statement must evaluate to an integer quantity and be tested for equality. The if-else chain in Program 4.6 uses floating-point values and inequalities, violating both requirements of the switch statement's requirements.

EXERCISES 4.5

1.a.
```
#include <stdio.h>
void main(void)
{
  char ret_key;
  int opselect;
  double fnum, snum;
  printf("Please type in two numbers: ");
  scanf("%lf %lf%c", &fnum, &snum, &ret_key);
  printf("Enter a select code: ");
  printf("      a 1 for addition\n");
  printf("      a 2 for multiplication\n");
  printf("      or a 3 for division: \n");
  scanf("%d", &opselect);
  switch (opselect)
  {
    case 1:
      printf("The sum of the numbers entered is %6.3lf\n", fnum+snum);
      break;
    case 2:
      printf("The product of the numbers entered is %6.3lf\n", fnum*snum);
      break;
    case 3:
      printf("The first number divided by the second is %6.3lf\n", fnum/snum);
      break;
  }      /* end of switch */
}
```

b.   Floating-point error: Divide by 0.
      Abnormal program termination

c.

```c
#include <stdio.h>
void main(void)
{
  char ret_key;
  int opselect;
  double fnum, snum;
  printf("Please type in two numbers: ");
  scanf("%lf %lf%c", &fnum, &snum, &ret_key);
  printf("Enter a select code: \n");
  printf("     a 1 for addition\n");
  printf("     a 2 for multiplication\n");
  printf("     or a 3 for division: ");
  scanf("%d", &opselect);
  switch (opselect)
  {
    case 1:
      printf("The sum of the numbers entered is %6.3lf\n", fnum+snum);
      break;
    case 2:
      printf("The product of the numbers entered is %6.3lf\n", fnum*snum);
      break;
    case 3:
      if (snum == 0)
        printf("Division by zero is not permitted!\n");
      else
        printf("The first number divided by the second is %6.3lf\n",  fnum/snum);
              break;
  }   /* end of switch */
}
```

3.a.
```c
#include <stdio.h>
void main(void)
{
  float angle;

  printf("Enter an angle: ");
  scanf("%f", &angle);

  if (angle < 0 || angle > 360)
      printf("An incorrect angle was entered.\n");
  else if (angle > 0 && angle < 90)
      printf("The angle is in quadrant I.\n");
  else if (angle > 90 && angle < 180)
      printf("The angle is in quadrant II.\n");
  else if (angle > 180 && angle < 270)
      printf("The angle is in quadrant III.\n");
  else if (angle > 270 && angle < 360)
      printf("The angle is in quadrant IV.\n");
}
```

b.
```c
#include <stdio.h>
void main(void)
{
  float angle;

  printf("Enter an angle: ");
  scanf("%f", &angle);

  if (angle < 0 || angle > 360)
      printf("An incorrect angle was entered.\n");
  else if (angle > 0 && angle < 90)
      printf("The angle is in quadrant I.\n");
  else if (angle > 90 && angle < 180)
      printf("The angle is in quadrant II.\n");
  else if (angle > 180 && angle < 270)
      printf("The angle is in quadrant III.\n");
  else if (angle > 270 && angle < 360)
      printf("The angle is in quadrant IV.\n");
  else if (angle == 0)
      printf("The angle is on the positive X axis.\n");
  else if (angle == 90)
      printf("The angle is on the positive Y axis.\n");
  else if (angle == 180)
      printf("The angle is on the negative X axis.\n");
  else if (angle == 270)
      printf("The angle is on the negative Y axis.\n");
}
```

5a.
```c
#include <stdio.h>
void main(void)
{
  int year, weight, wclass;
  float fee;

  printf("Enter a model year: ");
  scanf("%d", &year);
  printf("Enter a weight in pounds: ");
  scanf("%d", &weight);

  if (year <= 1970)
  {
    if (weight < 2700)
    {
      wclass = 1;
      fee = 16.50;
    }
    else if (weight >= 2700 && weight <= 3800)
    {
      wclass = 2;
      fee = 25.50;
    }
    else if (weight > 3800)
    {
      wclass = 3;
      fee = 46.50;
    }
  }
  else if (year >= 1971 && year <= 1979)
  {
    if (weight < 2700)
```

(continued on next page)

(continued from previous page)

```
            {
                wclass = 4;
                fee = 27.00;
            }
            else if (weight >= 2700 && weight <= 3800)
            {
                wclass = 5;
                fee = 30.50;
            }
            else if (weight > 3800)
            {
                wclass = 6;
                fee = 52.50;
            }
        }
        else if (year >= 1980)
        {
            if (weight < 3500)
            {
                wclass = 7;
                fee = 19.50;
            }
            else if (weight >= 3500)
            {
                wclass = 8;
                fee = 52.50;
            }
        }
        printf("The weight class is %d, and the registration \n", wclass);
        printf("fee is $%5.2f.\n", fee);
    }
```

7.
```
    #include <stdio.h>
    void main(void)
    {
        int card1, card2, card3, total;

        printf("Enter three cards. (Enter an ace as 1 and picture ");
        printf("cards as 10.");
        scanf("%d %d %d", &card1, &card2, &card3);

        total = card1 + card2 + card3;
        if (total < 21 && (card1 == 1 || card2 == 1 || card3 == 1))
            if (total - 1 + 11 <= 21)
                total = total - 1 + 11;
        printf("The total is %d\n", total);
    }
```

Note: The only useful possibility of counting the ace as an 11 rather than as a 1 occurs when the total is less than 21 and one of the cards is an ace.

EXERCISES 4.8

1.a.
```
    printf("Enter two temperatures: ");
    scanf("%d %d", &temp_one, &temp_two);
    if (temp_one == temp_two)
        printf("%d\n", temp_one);
```

b.
```c
printf("Enter two capital letters: ");
scanf("%c %c", &letter1, &letter2);
  /* the following two statements can be used to ensure capital
   letters - if you use them you must #include<ctype.h>
   */
letter1 = toupper(letter1);  /* ensure a capital letter */
letter2 = toupper(letter2);  /* ensure a capital letter */
if (letter1 <= letter2)
  printf("%c   %c\n", letter1, letter2);
else
  printf("%c   %c\n", letter2, letter1);
```

c.
```c
printf("Enter three integer values: ");
scanf("%d %d %d", &num1, &num2, &num3);
if (num1 < num2 && num1 < num3)        /* num1 is the smallest */
  if (num2 < num3)
    printf("%d %d %d\n", num1, num2, num3);
  else
    printf("%d  %d  %d\n", num1, num3, num2);
else if (num2 < num1 && num2 < num3)   /* num2 is the smallest */
  if (num1 < num3)
    printf("%d  %d  %d\n", num2, num1, num3);
  else
    printf("%d  %d  %d\n", num2, num3, num1);
else                                   /* num3 is the smallest */
  if (num1 < num2)
    printf("%d  %d  %d\n", num3, num1, num2);
  else
    printf("%d  %d  %d\n", num3, num2, num1);
}
```

3.a.
```c
#include <stdio.h>
void main(void)
{
    char in_key;

    printf("Type a u if you feel great today: ");
    scanf("%c",&in_key);
    if (in_key == 'u' || in_key == 'U')
        printf("I feel great today!\n");
    else
        printf("I feel down today #$*!\n");
}
```

b. At least three runs should be made: one input alphabetically less than "u", one with "u", and one alphabetically greater than "u". Another run, if necessary, might be made for capital letters or numeric values.

5.a.
```c
#include <stdio.h>
void main(void)
{
  char in_key;

  printf("Enter a letter: \n");
  scanf("%c", &in_key);
  if (in_key >= 'A' && in_key <= 'Z')
    printf("The character just entered is an uppercase letter\n");
  else
    printf("The character just entered is not an uppercase letter\n");
}
```

7. The error is that the intended relational expression `letter == 'm'` has been written as the assignment expression `letter = 'm'`. When the expression is evaluated
the character `m` is assigned to the variable `letter` and the value of the expression
itself is the value of `'m'`. Since this is a nonzero value, it is taken as true and the
message is displayed.

Realize that, as written in the program, the `if` statement is equivalent to the following two statements:

```
letter = 'm';
if(letter) printf("Hello there!\n");
```

A correct version of the program is:

```
#include <stdio.h>
void main(void)
{
      char letter;

       printf("Enter a letter: \n");
      scanf("%c", &letter);
      if (letter == 'm') printf("Hello there!\n");
}
```

EXERCISES 5.1

1.
```
#include <stdio.h>
void main(void)
{
      int count = 2;

      while (count <= 10)
      {
            printf("%d  ",count);
            count = count + 2;
      }
}
```

3.a. Twenty-one items are displayed, which are the integers from 1 to 21.
  c. Twenty-one items are displayed, which are the integers from 0 to 20.

5.
```
#include <stdio.h>
void main(void)
{
      int pcount, count = 0;

      while (count <= 9)
      {
            pcount = count;
            while (pcount > 0)
            {
                  printf(" ");
                  pcount--;
            }
            printf("%d\n",count);
            count++;
      }
}
```

7.
```c
#include <stdio.h>
void main(void)
{
    int feet;
    float meters;
    printf("FEET    METERS\n");
    printf("----    ------\n");
    feet = 3;

    while (feet <= 30)
    {
        meters = feet / 3.28;
        printf("%3d%11.2f\n", feet, meters);
        feet = feet + 3;
    }
}
```

9.
```c
#include <stdio.h>
void main(void)
{
    float time, miles;
    printf("TIME    MILES\n");
    printf("----    -----\n");
    time = .5;

    while (time <= 4)
    {
        miles = 55 * time;
        printf("%4.1f%10.2f\n", time, miles);
        time = time + .5;
    }
}
```

EXERCISES 5.2

1.
```c
#include <stdio.h>
void main(void)
{
  int count, reps;
  float num, total;

  count = 1;     /* These initializations can be */
  total = 0;     /* included within the declarations */
  reps = 8;

  while (count <= reps)
  {
    printf("Enter a number: ");
    scanf("%f", &num);
    total = total + num;
    printf("The total is now %f\n", total);
    ++count;
  }
  printf("\nThe final total is %f\n", total);
}
```

3.a.
```c
#include <stdio.h>
void main(void)
{
      float cels, fahr, incr;
      int num, count = 0;

      printf("Enter the starting temperature ");
      printf("in degrees Celsius: ");
      scanf("%f", &cels);
      printf("Enter the number of conversions to be made: ");
      scanf("%d", &num);
      printf("Now enter the increment between conversions ");
      printf("in degrees Celsius: ");
      scanf("%f", &incr);
      printf("Celsius     Fahrenheit\n");
      printf("---------------------\n");
      while (count <= num)
      {
         fahr = (9.0/5.0)*cels + 32.0;
         printf("%7.2f%15.2f\n", cels, fahr);
         cels = cels + incr;
         count++;
      }
}
```

5.
```c
#include <stdio.h>
#define MAXNUMS 10  /* could define this as a variable instead */
void main(void)
{
  int count;
  float num, total, average;

  printf("This program will ask you to enter some numbers.\n");
  count = 1;
  total = 0;
  while (count <= MAXNUMS)
  {
    printf("Enter a number: ");
    scanf("%f", &num);
    total = total + num;
    count = count + 1;
  }
  count = count - 1;
  average = total / count;
  printf("The average of the numbers is %f\n", average);
}
```

7. This program still calculates the correct values, but the average is now calculated four times. Since only the final average is desired, it is better to calculate the average once outside of the while loop.

9.
```c
#include <stdio.h>
#include <math.h>
#define MAXTERM 100  /* could define this as a variable instead */
void main(void)
{
  int n = 1;
  float a = 1, r = .5, term, total = 0.0;

  printf("Term No.  Term Value\n");
  printf("--------  ----------\n");
  while (n <= MAXTERM)
  {
    term = a * pow(r, n-1);
    total = total + term;
    printf("%5d%15.6f\n", n, term);
    n++;
  }
  printf("The total of the series is %6.6f\n", total);
}
```

15.
```
#include <stdio.h>
void main(void)
{
  int id, inven, income, outgo, bal;
  int sentval = 999;   /* sentinel value */

  printf("Enter a book ID or 999 to exit: ");
  scanf("%d", &id);
  while (id != sentval)
  {
    printf("Enter inventory at the beginning of the month: ");
    scanf("%d", &inven);
    printf("Enter the number of copies received during the month: ");
     scanf("%d", &income);
       printf("Now enter the number of copies sold during the month: ");
    scanf("%d", &outgo);
    bal = inven + income - outgo;
    printf("\nBook #%d new balance is %d\n\n", id, bal);
    printf("\nEnter a book ID or 999 to exit: ");
    scanf("%d", &id);
  }
}
```
Notice that the lines for entering the book ID are repeated. This is a characteristic of
the while statement used in this way. If these lines were only included inside the
while loop, the user would not be able to exit without creating an inventory for
book number 999 and the program would calculate and print a new balance for the
"phantom" book with ID number 999.

EXERCISES 5.3

1.a. `for(i=1; i<=20; i++)`
  b. `for(icount=1; icount<=20; icount=icount+2)`
  c. `for(j=1; j<=100; j=j+5)`
  d. `for(icount=20; icount>=1; icount--)`
  e. `for(icount=20; icount>=1; icount=icount-2)`
  f. `for(count=1.0; count<=16.2; count=count+0.2)`
  g. `for(xcnt=20.0; xcnt>=10.0; xcnt=xcnt-0.5)`
3.a. 10
  b. 1024
  c. 75
  d. −5
  e. 40320
  f. 0.031250
5.
```
#include <stdio.h>
void main(void)
{
    int num;

    printf("NUMBER    SQUARE    CUBE\n");
    printf("------    ------    ----\n");
    for (num = 0; num <= 20; num += 2)
      printf("%3d       %3d       %4d\n", num, num*num, num*num*num);
}
```

7.
```c
#include <stdio.h>
void main(void)
{
      int count;
      float f, c;
      printf("Fahrenheit      Celsius\n");
      printf("----------      -------\n");
      for (f = 20.0, count = 1; count <= 20; ++count)
      {
        c = (f - 32.0)*(5.0/9.0);
        printf("%4.1f              %5.2f\n", f, c);
        f += 4.0;
      }
}
```

9.a.
```c
#include <stdio.h>
void main(void)
{
    long salary;
    int year;

    printf("Year       Salary\n");
    printf("----       ------\n");
    for (salary = 25000,  year = 1; year <= 10; year++)
    {
      printf("%2d           %5ld\n", year, salary);
      salary += 1500;
    }
}
```

  b.
```c
#include <stdio.h>
void main(void)
{
    float salary;
    int year;

    printf("Year       Salary\n");
    printf("----       ------\n");
    for (salary = 25000,  year = 1; year <= 10; year++)
    {
      printf("%2d        %7.2f\n", year, salary);
      salary = salary + salary*.05;
    }
}
```

11.
```c
#include <stdio.h>
#include <math.h>
void main(void)
{
    float prob, ex;
    int lamda = 3;   /* average no. of arrivals per minute */
    long factorial = 1;  /* denominator of the probability expression */
    int customer;

    printf(" No. of\n");
    printf("Arriving      Probability\n");
    printf("Customers      (as a %)\n");
    printf("---------      ----------\n");

    ex = exp(-lamda);    /* only need to do this calculation once */
    for (customer = 1; customer <= 10; customer++)
    {
       factorial = factorial * customer;
       prob = (pow(customer, lamda) * ex / factorial) * 100;
       printf("  %2d          %8.4f\n", customer, prob);
    }
}
```

13.
```c
#include <stdio.h>
void main(void)
{
  int n, preceed1, preceed2, term;
  long fib;

  printf("Enter the desired term: ");
  scanf("%d", &n);
  if (n < 2)
    fib = n;
  else
  {
    preceed2 = 0;
    preceed1 = 1;
    for (term = 3; term <= n; term++)
    {
      fib = preceed1 + preceed2;
     /* now adjust the preceding terms for the next calculation */
      preceed2 = preceed1;
      preceed1 = fib;
    }
  }
  printf("The fibonacci number for term %d is %ld\n", n, fib);
}
```

15.
```c
#include <stdio.h>
void main(void)
{
  int yr;
  double sales, profit, tot_sales=0.0, tot_profit=0.0;

  printf("SALES AND PROFIT PROJECTION\n");
  printf("--------------------------\n\n");
  printf("YEAR      EXPECTED SALES   PROJECTED PROFIT\n");
  printf("----      -------------    ---------------\n");
  for (yr = 1, sales = 10000000.00; yr <= 10; ++yr)
  {
    profit = 0.10*sales;
    printf("%3d        $%11.2f        $%10.2f\n",
    yr, sales, profit);
    tot_sales = tot_sales + sales;
    tot_profit = tot_profit + profit;
    sales = 0.96*sales;
  }
  printf("-------------------------------------------\n");
  printf("Totals:    $%10.2f       $%9.2f\n",
    tot_sales, tot_profit);
}
```

EXERCISES 5.4

1.
```c
#include <stdio.h>
void main(void)
{
  int count;
  float fahren, celsius;

  for(count = 1; count <= 6; count+)
  {
    printf("Enter a fahrenheit temperature: ");
    scanf("%f", &fahren);
    celsius = (5.0/9.0)*(fahren - 32.0);
    printf(" The corresponding celsius temperature is %5.2f\n",celsius);
  }
}
```

3.
```c
#include <stdio.h>
void main(void)
{
  int count, reps;
  float gallons, liters;

  printf("Please type in the total number of data values ");
  printf("to be added: ");
  scanf("%d", &reps);
  for(count = 1; count <= reps; count++)
  {
    printf("Enter an amount in gallons : ");
    scanf("%f", &gallons);
    liters = 3.785 * gallons;
    printf(" The corresponding amount in liters is %5.2f\n",liters);
  }
}
```

5.
```c
#include <stdio.h>
void main(void)
{
  int i, poscnt, negcnt, reps;
  float usenum, postot, negtot, posavg, negavg;
  postot = 0;
  negtot = 0;
  poscnt = 0;
  negcnt = 0;

  printf("Please type in the total number of data values ");
  printf("to be added: ");
  scanf("%d", &reps);
  for(i = 1; i <= reps; i++)
  {
    printf("Enter an number (positive or negative) : ");
    scanf("%f", &usenum);
    if (usenum > 0)
    {
       poscnt++;
       postot = postot + usenum;
    }
    else if (usenum < 0)
    {
     negcnt++;
     negtot = negtot + usenum;
    }
  }
  posavg = postot / poscnt;
  negavg = negtot / negcnt;
  printf("The positive total is %f\n", posavg);
  printf("The negative total is %f\n", negavg);
}
```

7.
```c
#include <stdio.h>
void main(void)
{
    int count = 0, i = 0, num;
    printf("The first 20 whole numbers divisible by 3 are:\n");
    while (count < 20)
    {
        i++;
        if(i%3 == 0)  /* can be replaced by if(!(i%3)) */
        {
            count++;
            printf("%d ",i);
        }
    }
}
```

9.a.
```c
#include <stdio.h>
#include <math.h>
void main(void)
{
  double x, y;

  printf("x value      y value\n");
  printf("--------     ----------\n");
  for (x = 5.0; x <= 10.0; x = x + 0.2)
  {
      y = 3*pow(x,5) - 2*pow(x,3) + x;
      printf("%8.6f    %10.6f\n", x, y);
  }
}
```

b.
```c
#include <stdio.h>
#include <math.h>
void main(void)
{
  double x, y;

  printf("x value      y value\n");
  printf("--------     ----------\n");
  for (x = 1.0; x< = 3.0; x = x + 0.1)
  {
      y = 1 + x + (pow(x,2)/2) + (pow(x,3)/6) + (pow(x,4)/24);
      printf("%8.6f    %10.6f\n", x, y);
  }
}
```

c.
```c
#include <stdio.h>
#include <math.h>
void main(void)
{
  double t, y;

  printf("t value      y value\n");
  printf("--------     ----------\n");
  for (t = 4.0; t <= 10.0; t = t+0.2)
  {
      y = 2*exp(.8*t);
      printf("%8.6f    %10.6f\n", t, y);
  }
}
```

11.
```c
#include <stdio.h>
#include <math.h>
#define GRAV 32.2
void main(void)
{
  float v = 500;    /* initial velocity */
  float height, t;

  printf(" Time     Height\n");
  printf("(sec)     (feet)\n");
  printf("-----     --------\n");
  for (t = 0; t <= 10; t = t + 0.5)
  {
    height = v * t - 0.5 * GRAV * pow(t,2);
    printf("%5.2f    %8.2f\n", t, height);
  }
}
```

13.
```c
#include <stdio.h>
void main(void)
{
  float fahr, cels;
  int i, calcs, incr = 5;

  printf("Enter the starting Fahrenheit temperature: ");
  scanf("%f", &fahr);
  printf("Enter the number of conversions to be made: ");
  scanf("%d", &calcs);

  printf("Fahrenheit   Celsius\n");
  printf("----------   -------\n");
  for (i = 0; i < calcs; i++)
  {
    cels = (5.0/9.0) *(fahr - 32.0);
    printf(" %6.2f       %6.2f\n", fahr, cels);
    fahr += incr;
  }
}
```

EXERCISES 5.5

1.
```c
#include <stdio.h>
void main(void)
{
  int i, j;
  float total, avg, data;

  for (i = 1; i <= 4; ++i)
  {
    printf("Enter 6 results for experiment #%d: ",i);
    for (j = 1, total = 0.0; j <= 6; ++j)
    {
      scanf("%f", &data);
      total += data;
    }
    avg = total/6;
    printf("   The average for experiment #%d is %.2f\n\n", i, avg);
  }
}
```
Note: When entering data for each experiment, the six individual results may be
entered on one line with a space between each entry, on six individual lines, or any
combination of these.

3.a.
```c
#include <stdio.h>
void main(void)
{
  int bowler, game;
  float score, plyr_tot, plyr_avg;

  for(bowler = 1; bowler <= 5; ++bowler)
  {
    for(game = 1, plyr_tot = 0; game <= 3; ++game)
    {
      printf("Enter the score for bowler %d game %d: ",bowler,game);
      scanf("%f",&score);
      plyr_tot = plyr_tot + score;
    }
    plyr_avg = plyr_tot/3.0;
    printf("   The average for bowler %d is %5.2f\n",bowler,plyr_avg);
  }
}
```

b.
```c
#include <stdio.h>
void main(void)
{
  int bowler, game;
  float score, plyr_tot, plyr_avg, team_tot, team_avg;

  for(bowler = 1, team_tot = 0; bowler <= 5; ++bowler)
  {
    for(game = 1, plyr_tot = 0; game <= 3; ++game)
    {
      printf("Enter the score for bowler %d game %d: ",bowler,game);
      scanf("%f",&score);
      plyr_tot = plyr_tot + score;
    }
    team_tot = team_tot + plyr_tot;
    plyr_avg = plyr_tot/3.0;
    printf("   The average for bowler %d is %5.2f\n",bowler,plyr_avg);
  }
  team_avg = team_tot / 15.0;
  printf("The average for the whole team is %5.2f",team_avg);
}
```

5.
```c
#include <stdio.h>
#include <math.h>
#define SMALLDIF 0.00001

void main(void)
{
  float x, y, z;

  printf("   x        y        z  \n");
  printf("-------  -------   -------\n");
  for (x = 1.0; x <= 5.0; x += 0.2)
    for (z = 2.0; z <= 6.0; z += 0.5)
      if (fabs(x - z) > SMALLDIF)
      {
   y = x * z / (x - z);
   printf("%6.2f   %6.2f    %6.2f\n", x, z, y);
      }
      else
      printf("%6.2f    %6.2f   FUNCTION UNDEFINED\n", x, z);
}
```

7.
```c
#include <stdio.h>
void main(void)
{
  long sal;
  int dep;
  float deduct;

  printf("                |<---------------------- Deducti");
  printf("ons ----------------------->|\n");
  printf(" Salary  |  0          1          2      ");
  printf("   3          4          5   |\n");
  printf("-------   -------   -------   -------   ------- ");
  printf("-------   -------   --------\n");
  for(sal = 10000L; sal <= 50000L; sal += 10000L)
  {
    printf("% ld     ", sal);
    for(dep = 0; dep <= 5; dep++)
    {
      deduct =  dep * 500 + 0.05 * (50000L - sal);
      printf("%8.2f   ", deduct);
    }
    printf("\n");
  }
}
```

EXERCISES 5.6

1.a.
```c
#include <stdio.h>
#define LOWGRADE 0
#define HIGHGRADE 100
void main(void)
{
  int grade;

  do
  {
      printf("Enter a grade: ");
      scanf("%d", &grade);
  } while (grade < LOWGRADE || grade > HIGHGRADE);
  printf("\nThe grade entered is %d\n", grade);
}
```

3.a.
```c
#include <stdio.h>
void main(void)
{
  int num, digit;

  printf("Enter an integer: ");
  scanf("%d", &num);
  printf("The number reversed is: ");
  do
  {
    digit = num % 10;
    num /= 10;
    printf("%d", digit);
  } while (num > 0);
}
```

5.
```c
#include <stdio.h>
#include <math.h>
#define OKDIF 0.00001
void main(void)
{
  float num, root, approx;

  printf("Enter a number for which you want the square root: ");
  scanf("%f", &num);
  printf("Enter your best guess for this number's square root: ");
  scanf("%f", &approx);
  do
  {
    root = approx;    /* save the approx */
    approx = (num/root + root)/2.0;     /* calculate a new approx */
  }
  while ( fabs(approx - root) > OKDIF);
  printf("The square root is %.4f\n", root);
}
```

EXERCISES 5.8

1.
```c
#include<stdio.h>
void main(void)
{
  int num;
  char letter;

  for(num = 33; num >= 3; num -= 3)
    printf("%d   ", num);
  for(letter = 'Z'; letter >= 'A'; letter--)
    printf("%c ", letter);
}
```

3.
```c
#include <stdio.h>
#include <math.h>
#define OKDIF 1.0e-6

void main(void)
{
  double next_approx = 1.0; /* first approximation */
  double old_approx;
  int i = 1;
  double factor = 1;

  old_approx = 0;   /* make sure the loop starts */

  while(fabs(next_approx - old_approx) > OKDIF)
  {
    old_approx = next_approx;
    factor = factor * i;
    next_approx = old_approx + 1/factor;
    i++;
  }
  printf("Euler's number, accurate to %lf, is %lf\n", OKDIF,
next_approx);
}
```

5.
```c
#include <stdio.h>
void main(void)
{
  float balance = 8000.0;
  float rate = 0.10/12;
  float payment = 300;
  float interest, principal;

  printf("  Beginning    Interest    Principal   Ending Loan\n");
  printf("   Balance     Payment     Payment     Balance  \n");
  printf("------------------------------------------------------\n");

  while(balance > 0.05)
  {
    printf("%11.6f  ", balance);
    interest = rate * balance;
    principal = payment - interest;
    balance = balance - principal;
    printf("%10.6f  %10.6f  %11.6f\n",interest, principal, balance);
  }
}
```

Note: The last balance will always be a penny or two off due to fractional amounts. Therefore, the while loop stops when a balance of 5 cents or less is achieved. It is instructive to run this program and alter the 0.05 in the while statement to 0.0. In practice, the last payment would be altered to achieve a zero balance.

7.
```c
#include <stdio.h>
#include <math.h>
#define MINRATE 1.0
#define MAXRATE 25.0
void main(void)
{
    float balance, rate, years;
    float payment;  /* monthly payment, in dollars */
    float mrate;     /* monthly interest rate */
    float interest, principal;
    float cumint = 0.0, cumpay = 0.0;
    int pmtnum = 0;

    printf("What is the amount of the loan? $ ");
    scanf("%f", &balance);

    do
    {
      printf("What is the annual percentage rate? ");
      scanf("%f", &rate);
    }
    while (rate < MINRATE || rate > MAXRATE);

    printf("How many years will you take to pay back the loan? ");
    scanf("%f", &years);

    mrate = rate/(12.0 * 100.0);  /* monthly rate as a decimal */
    payment =  balance * mrate/(1.0 - pow((1.0+mrate),-(years*12.0)));
    payment = (int)(payment * 100 + 0.5)/100.0;  /* round to cents */
    printf("Amount %8.2f  Annual %% Interest %5.2f",balance, rate);
    printf("  Years %4.2f  Monthly Payment %8.2f\n\n", years, payment);
    printf("Payment  Interest   Principal   Cumulative   Total Paid   New Balance\n");
    printf(" Number    Paid       Paid       Interest     to Date       Due   \n");
    printf("-----------------------------------------------------------------------\n");

    while(balance > 0.05)
    {
      pmtnum++;
      interest = balance * mrate;
      principal = payment - interest;
      cumint += interest;
      cumpay += payment;
      balance = balance - principal;
      printf(" %3d     %5.2f    %8.2f     %8.2f      %8.2f     %8.2f\n",
      pmtnum, interest, principal, cumint, cumpay, balance);
    }
}
```

Note: The rounding of the payment to a whole number of cents means that the last balance will not exactly reach zero. It is for this reason that the while statement stops the loop when the remaining balance is less than or equal to a nickel. In practice, the last payment would be altered to achieve a zero balance.

9.
```
#include <stdio.h>
#include <math.h>
void main(void)
{
  int n = 0;
  long Max = 30000L;
  long PowerOfThree = 1L;

  while(PowerOfThree <= Max)
  {
    PowerOfThree = 3 * PowerOfThree;
    n++;
  }
  printf("The value of n is %d\n", n);
  printf("3 raised to the %d power is %f\n", n, pow(3,n));
}
```
Note: Long integers are used here because of the possibility that the next power of three value will exceed 32,000, which it does. As a check, we have used the power function to ensure that our calculation of PowerOfThree is correct.

EXERCISES 6.1

1.a. factorial() expects to receive one integer value.
  b. price() expects to receive one integer and two double precision values, in that order.
  c. An int and two double precision values, in that order, must be passed to yield().
  d. A character and two floating-point values, in that order, must be passed to inter-est().
  e. Two floating-point values, in that order, must be passed to total().
  f. Two integers, two characters, and two floating-point values, in that order, must be passed to roi().
  g. Two integers and two character values, in that order, are expected by get_val().
3.a. The find_abs() function is included within the larger program written for Exercise 3b.
  b.
```
#include <stdio.h>
void main(void)
{
  double num;
  void find_abs(double); /* function prototype */

  printf("Enter a double-precision number: ");
  scanf("%lf", &num);   /* the %lf is required for doubles */
  find_abs(num);
}

void find_abs(double funct_num)
{
if (funct_num >= 0)
  printf("The double precision number is  %lf\n\n",
funct_num);
else
  printf("The double precision number is  %lf\n\n",
-funct_num);
}
```

5.a. The sqr_it() function is included in the larger program written for Exercise 5b.

  b.
```c
#include <stdio.h>
void main(void)
{
    void sqr_it(double);    /* function prototype */
    double first;

    printf("Please enter a number: ");
    scanf("%lf",&first); /* the %lf must be used for a double */
    sqr_it(first);
}

void sqr_it(double num)
{
    printf("The square of %f is %f\n", num, num*num);
}
```

7.a. The function for producing the required table is included in the larger program written for Exercise 7b.

  b.
```c
#include <stdio.h>
void main(void)
{
    void table(void);    /* function prototype */
    table();        /* call the table() function */
}

void table(void)
{
    int num;

    printf("NUMBER    SQUARE    CUBE\n");
    printf("------    ------    ----\n");

    for (num = 1; num <= 10; ++num)
        printf("%3d      %3d       %4d\n", num, num*num, num*num*num);
}
```

EXERCISES 6.2

1.
```c
#include <stdio.h>
void main(void)
{
    float firstnum, secnum, max;
    float find_max(float, float);  /* function prototype */
    printf("\nEnter a number: ");
    scanf("%f", &firstnum);
    printf("Great! Please enter a second number: ");
    scanf("%f", &secnum);
    max = find_max(firstnum, secnum);
    printf("\nThe maximum of the two numbers is %f.\n", max);
}

float find_max(float x, float y)
{
    float maxnum;

    if (x >= y)
        maxnum = x;
    else
        maxnum = y;

    return(maxnum);
}
```

3.a. `void check(int x, float y, double z)`
 b. `double find_abs(double x)`
 c. `float mult(float x, float y)`
 d. `float sqr_it(int x)`
 e. `int powfun(int base, int power)`
 f. `void table(void)`
5.a. The `mult()` function is included in the program written for Exercise 5b.
 b.
```
#include <stdio.h>
#include <iostream.h>
void main(void)
{
  double mult(double, double);    /* function prototype */
  double first,second;

  printf("Please enter a number: ");
  scanf("%lf",&first);
  printf("Please enter another number: ");
  scanf("%lf", &second);
  printf("The product of these numbers is %f\n",
          mult(first,second);
}

double mult(double num1, double num2)
{
  return (num1*num2);
}
```
7. The polynomial function is included in the following working program:
```
#include <stdio.h>
void main(void)
{
    float a, b, c, x, result;
    float poly_two(float, float, float, float); /* prototype */

    printf("Enter the coefficient for x^2 : ");
    scanf("%f", &a);
    printf("Enter the coefficient for x : ");
    scanf("%f", &b);
    printf("Enter the constant: ");
    scanf("%f", &c);
    printf("Enter the value for x: ");
    scanf("%f", &x);
    result = poly_two(a, b, c, x);
    printf("\n\nThe result is  %f\n", result);
}

float poly_two(float c1, float c2, float c3, float x)
{
    return (c1*x*x + c2*x + c3);
}
```
9.a.
```
#include <stdio.h>
#include <math.h>
void main(void)
{
    double amount, rate = .08675, total = 0;
    double round(double);  /* function prototype */

    printf("Enter an amount: ");
    scanf("%lf", &amount);
    total = amount + amount * rate;
    printf("The total is %lf\n", round(total));
}

double round(double num)
{
  num = num * pow(10,2);
  num = num + .5;
  return((int)num / pow(10,2));
}
```

11.a. The `fracpart()` function is included in the program written for Exercise 11b.

b.
```
#include <stdio.h>
#include <iostream.h>
void main(void)
{
  double num;
  double fracpart(double);  /* function prototype */

  printf("Enter a number: ");
  scanf("%lf", &num);
  printf("The fraction part of %f is %f\n", num, fracpart(num);
}

double fracpart(double x)
{
  int whole(double);    /* function prototype */
  return (x - whole(x));
}

int whole(double n)
{
  int a;

  a = n;   /* a = (int) n is preferred - see Section 3.1 */
  return(a);
}
```

EXERCISES 6.3

1.
```
#include <stdio.h>
void main(void)
{
    int heads, tails, i, tosses;
    float seed, x, flip, perheads, pertails;
    float rand(float);

    printf("Enter an odd 6 digit number not ending in 5: ");
    scanf("%f", &seed);
    heads = 0;
    tails = 0;
    printf("Enter the number of tosses: ");
    scanf("%d", &tosses);

for (i = 1; i <= tosses; ++i)
{
    seed = rand(seed);
    flip = seed / 1.e6;
    if (flip > 0.5)
        heads = heads + 1;
    else
        tails = tails + 1;
    }
    perheads = (heads / (float)tosses) * 100.0;
    pertails = (tails / (float)tosses) * 100.0;
    printf("Heads came up %f percent of the time\n", perheads);
    printf("Tails came up %f percent of the time\n", pertails);
}
float rand(float x)
{
    int i;
    i = 997.0 * x / 1.e6;
    x = 997.0 * x - i * 1.e6;
    return(x);
}
```

```
3.    #include <stdio.h>
      #define DEBUG 0
      void main(void)
      {
        char choice, retkey;
        int guess, count, val;
        float seed;
        float rand(float);
        do
        {
            printf("Enter an odd 6 digit number not ending in 5: ");
            scanf("%f", &seed);

            seed = rand(seed);
            val = (int) ((seed/1.e6)*100);
            if (DEBUG)
                printf("\nseed = %f  val = %d\n", seed, val);
            count = 0;

            do
            {
                printf("Enter your guess: ");
                scanf("%d", &guess);
                count++;
                if (guess < val)
                    printf("Your guess was too low - guess again!\n");
                else if (guess > val)
                    printf("Your guess was too high - guess again!\n");
            } while (guess != val);

            printf("Congratulations!  You did it in %d guesses\n", count);
            printf("\nWOULD YOU LIKE TO PLAY AGAIN - 'Y'/'N'?: \n");
            scanf("%c%c", &retkey, &choice);

        } while (choice == 'Y' || choice == 'y');
      }

      float rand(float x)
      {
        int i;
        i = 997.0 * x / 1.e6;
        x = 997.0 * x - i * 1.e6;
        return(x);
      }
5.    #include <stdio.h>
      #include <stdlib.h>
      #define NUMSELS 1000   /* number of random no. selections */

      void main(void)
      {
        int i, seed;
        float factor;
        int zerocount, onecount, twocount, threecount;
        int fourcount, fivecount, sixcount, sevencount;
        int eightcount, ninecount, val;

        zerocount = onecount = twocount = threecount = fourcount = 0;
        fivecount = sixcount = sevencount = eightcount = ninecount = 0;
        srand(seed);      /* set the seed for rand() */
```

(continued on next page)

(continued from previous page)

```c
        for (i = 1; i <= NUMSELS; i++)
        {
          seed = rand();
          val = ((float)seed/RAND_MAX)*10; /* RAND_MAX is the maximum no */
          switch (val)  /* returned by rand() and is defined in stdlib.h */
          {
            case 0:
              zerocount++;
              break;
            case 1:
              onecount++;
              break;
            case 2:
              twocount++;
              break;
            case 3:
              threecount++;
              break;
            case 4:
              fourcount++;
              break;
            case 5:
              fivecount++;
              break;
            case 6:
              sixcount++;
              break;
            case 7:
              sevencount++;
              break;
            case 8:
              eightcount++;
              break;
            case 9:
              ninecount++;
          }
        }
        factor = 100.0 / NUMSELS;
        printf(" Zeros:  %7.4f%%\n", zerocount * factor);
        printf(" Ones:   %7.4f%%\n", onecount * factor);
        printf(" Twos:   %7.4f%%\n", twocount * factor);
        printf(" Threes: %7.4f%%\n", threecount * factor);
        printf(" Fours:  %7.4f%%\n", fourcount * factor);
        printf(" Fives:  %7.4f%%\n", fivecount * factor);
        printf(" Sixes:  %7.4f%%\n", sixcount * factor);
        printf(" Sevens: %7.4f%%\n", sevencount * factor);
        printf(" Eights: %7.4f%%\n", eightcount * factor);
        printf(" Nines:  %7.4f%%\n", ninecount * factor);
    }
7.  int quadrant(float angle)
    {
      int val;

      if (angle < 0 || angle > 360)
        val = -1;
      else if (angle > 0 && angle < 90)
        val = 1;
      else if (angle > 90 && angle < 180)
        val = 2;
      else if (angle > 180 && angle < 270)
        val = 3;
      else if (angle > 270 && angle < 360)
        val = 4;
      else
        val = 0;
      return (val);
    }
```

9.
```c
float regfee(int year, int weight)
{
  float fee;

  if (year <= 1970)
  {
    if (weight < 2700)
      fee = 16.50;
    else if (weight >= 2700 && weight <= 3800)
      fee = 25.50;
    else if (weight > 3800)
      fee = 46.50;
  }
  else if (year >= 1971 && year <= 1979)
  {
    if (weight < 2700)
      fee = 27.00;
    else if (weight >= 2700 && weight <= 3800)
      fee = 30.50;
    else if (weight > 3800)
      fee = 52.50;
  }
  else if (year >= 1980)
  {
    if (weight < 3500)
      fee = 19.50;
    else if (weight >= 3500)
      fee = 52.50;
  }
  return (fee);
}
```

EXERCISES 6.6

1.
```c
#include <stdio.h>
void main(void)
{
  int i;
  float num, den;
  float FractionToDecimal(float, float);

  for(i = 0; i < 3; i++)
  {
    printf("Enter a numerator and denominator: ");
    scanf("%f %f", &num, &den);
    printf("The return value is %f\n", FractionToDecimal(num,
den));
  }
}

float FractionToDecimal(float numerator, float denominator)
{
  return(numerator/denominator);
}
```
Note: Whenever a function is created, a driver function must be constructed to test the function. In this case it is easy to let the driver function request three sets of values. In this case the first test data should be within the normal range of data for the function, while the second and third data sets test the boundary points. Thus, a useful set of test data might be 1 and 2; 0 and 1; 2 and 0.

3.a.

```c
#include <stdio.h>
void main(void)
{
  float n1, n2, d1, d2;
  char choice;
  float result;
  float addfrac(float, float, float, float);
  float FractionToDecimal(float, float);
  float multfrac(float, float, float, float);

  printf("A. Add two fractions\n");
  printf("B. Convert a fraction to a decimal\n");
  printf("C. Multiply two fractions\n");
  printf("D. Quit\n");
  printf("   Enter your choice (A, B, C, or D): ");
  scanf("%c", &choice);
  switch(choice)
  {
    case 'a': case'A':
      printf("Enter the first fraction as a/b (Ex. 4/7): ");
      scanf("%f/%f", &n1, &d1);
      printf("Enter the second fraction as a/b (Ex. 1/2): ");
      scanf("%f/%f", &n2, &d2);
      result = addfrac(n1, d1, n2, d2);
      break;
    case 'b': case 'B':
      printf("Enter the fraction as a/b (Ex. 5/6): ");
      scanf("%f/%f", &n1, &d1);
      result = FractionToDecimal(n1, d1);
      break;
    case 'c': case 'C':
      printf("Enter the first fraction as a/b (Ex. 4/7): ");
      scanf("%f/%f", &n1, &d1);
      printf("Enter the second fraction as a/b (Ex. 1/2): ");
      scanf("%f/%f", &n2, &d2);
      result = multfrac(n1, d1, n2, d2);
      break;
    default:
      break;
  }
}

/* here are the stub functions */
float addfrac(float num1, float den1, float num2, float den2)
{
  printf("Into addfrac()\n");
  printf("The passed values are %f  %f  %f  %f\n", num1, den1, num2, den2);
  return;
}

float FractionToDecimal(float num1, float den1)
{
  printf("Into FractionToDecimal()\n");
  printf("The passed values are %f  %f\n", num1, den1);
  return;
}

float multfrac(float num1, float den1, float num2, float den2)
{
  printf("Into multfrac()\n");
  printf("The passed values are %f  %f  %f  %f\n", num1, den1, num2, den2);
  return;
}
```

Notice the use of the control string "%f/%f" used in the scanf() function. This string defines the delimiter between input values as a /, and effectively permits the user to enter the data as fractions.

5.
```c
#include <stdio.h>
void main(void)
{
  int num1, num2, result;
  int gcd(int, int);

  printf("Enter two integer values: ");
  scanf("%d %d", &num1, &num2);
  result = gcd(num1, num2);
  printf("return value from gcd() is %d\n", result);
}


/* here is the stub */
int gcd(int n1, int n2)
{
  return(n1 + n2);
}
```

Returning n1*n2 is not a good idea, because if one of the test values was 0, a zero would be returned. This gives no indication that the second value was correctly received.

7.a. The tax() function is included in the program written for Exercise 7b.

b.
```c
#include <stdio.h>
void main(void)
{
   float amount, rate;
   float tax(float, float);   /* function prototype */

   printf("Enter the dollar amount and tax rate: ");
   scanf("%f %f", &amount, &rate);
   printf("The tax due is $%4.2f\n", tax(amount, rate));
}

float tax(float a, float r)
{
   return(a * r);
}
```

9.a. The convertdays() function is included in the program written for Exercise 9b.

b.
```c
#include <stdio.h>
void main(void)
{
  int month, day, year;
  long convertdays(int, int, int);   /* function prototype */

  printf("Enter the month, day, and year: ");
  scanf("%d %d %d", &month, &day, &year);
  printf("The integer code is %ld\n", convertdays(month, day, year));
}

long convertdays(int m, int d, int y)
{
   return(y*10000L + m*100L + d);
}
```

10.   The code causes no problems for the compiler. Each function operates on its own arguments and variables.

EXERCISES 7.1

1.a.

```
Variable name   Data type          Scope
-----------------------------------------------------------------------
  price         integer            global to main(), roi(), and step()
  years         long integer       global to main(), roi(), and step()
  yield         double-precision   global to main(), roi(), and step()
  bondtype      integer            local to main() only
  interest      double-precision   local to main() only
  coupon        double-precision   local to main() only
  count         integer            local to roi() only
  eff_int       double-precision   local to roi() only
  numofyrs      integer            local to step() only
  fracpart      float              local to step() only
```

Note: Although arguments of each function assume a value that is dependent on the calling function, these arguments can change values within their respective functions. This makes them behave as if they were local variables within the called function.

   c. roi() expects two integer values and will return a double-precision value.

      step() expects two float values and will return an integer value.

3. Arguments also have a scope and are local to the function where they are declared.

5. The following is displayed:

   20

   10

   Even though the global and local variables have the same name, main() cannot access the global variable firstnum because the declaration in main() has precedence over the global declaration.

EXERCISES 7.2

1.a. Local variables can be automatic, static, or register. It is important to realize that not all variables declared inside of functions are necessarily local. An example of this is an external variable.

   b. Global variables can be static. A nonstatic global variable can be extended into another file or function by being declared extern. Static global variables are private to the file they are declared in and may not be externed into another file.

3. The first function declares yrs to be a static variable and assigns a value of one to it only once when the function is compiled. Each time the function is called thereafter, the value in yrs is increased by two. The second function also declares yrs to be static, but assigns it the value one every time it is called, and the value of yrs after the function is finished will always be 3. By resetting the value of yrs to 1 each time it is called, the second function defeats the purpose of declaring the variable to be static.

5. The scope of a variable tells where the variable is recognized in the program and can be used within an expression. If, for example, the variable years is declared inside a function, it is local and its scope is inside that function only. If the variable is declared outside of any function, it is global and its scope is anywhere below the declaration but within that file, unless another file of the same program declares that same variable to be external.

EXERCISES 7.3

1.a. float *amount;

   b. double *price;

   c. int *minutes;

   d. char *key;

   e. double *yield;

3.a. void time(int *sec, int *min, int *hrs)

   b. time(&seconds, &minutes, &hours);

5.   The function is included with a driver function for testing purposes.

```c
#include <stdio.h>
void main(void)
{
    float amount;
    int quarters, dimes, nickels, pennies;
    void change(float, int *, int *, int *, int *);  /* function prototype */

    printf("\nEnter a dollar value: ");
    scanf("%f", &amount);

    change(amount, &quarters, &dimes, &nickels, &pennies);

    printf("quarters = %d\nnickels = %d\ndimes = %d\npennies = %d\n",
        quarters, dimes, nickels, pennies);
}

void change(float amt, int *q, int *d, int *n, int *p)
{
    *q = *d = *n = *p = 0; /* initialize all counts */

    while(amt >= 0.25)
    {
        amt -= 0.25;
        *q = *q + 1;
    }
    while (amt > 0.10)
    {
        amt -= 0.10;
        *d = *d + 1;
    }
    while (amt > 0.05)
    {
        amt -= 0.05;
        *n = *n + 1;
    }
    *p = (int)(amt * 100);
}
```

In place of the while loops, for loops could be used. For example, the following
for loop could be used to replace the first while loop:

```c
                for( ; amt > 0.25; ++*q, money -= 0.25)
                    ;    /* The Null statement is necessary */
```

One of C's advantages is its ability to be written in many forms. Although harder to
understand, the following program is much more compact and would produce less
machine code because of the elimination of the four loops.

```c
void change(float amount, int *q, int *d, int *n, int *p)
{
    *q = amt/0.25;          /* q is the number of times .25 goes into */
                            /*    the total amount evenly */
    amt -= *pt_q * 0.25;    /* adjust the amount to the amount remaining */
    *d = amt/0.10;
    amt -= *d * 0.10;
    *n = amt/0.05;
    amt -= *n * 0.05;
    *p = amt * 100;         /* pennies = what's left over */
                            /*    but each 0.01 left in money is 1 */
                            /*    for the integer p */
}
```

This last function makes use of the fact that integer assignment yields an integer. For example if amt = 0.49, the statement

$$*q = amt/0.25$$

results in the variable pointed to by q being one. Then,

$$amt\ -=\ (*q\ *\ 0.25)$$

yields 0.24 as the remaining amount.

7. In main(), the variables min and hour refer to integer quantities; in time() the variables min and hours are pointers to integers. Thus, there are four distinct variables in all, two of which are known in main() and two of which are known in time(). The computer (actually, the compiler) keeps track of each variable with no confusion. The effect on a programmer, however, may be quite different.

When in main(), the programmer must remember to use the names min and hour as integer variables. When in time(), the programmer must "switch" viewpoints and use the same names as pointer variables. Debugging such a program can be quite frustrating because the same names are used in two different contexts. It is, therefore, more advisable to avoid this type of situation by adopting different names for pointers than those used for other variables. A useful "trick" is to either prepend (prefix) each pointer name with a pt_ notation or append (suffix) each pointer name with _addr.

EXERCISES 7.4

1.
```
#include <stdio.h>
void main(void)
{
  int n, result;
  int fibon(int);

  printf("Enter the desired term: ");
  scanf("%d", &n);
  result = fibon(n);
  printf("Term %d of the fibonacci sequence is %d\n", n, result);
}

int fibon(int n)
{
  if(n < 2)
    return(n);
  else
    return(fibon(n-1) + fibon(n - 2));
}
```

3.
```
#include <stdio.h>
void main(void)
{
  int x, n, result;
  int XToTheN(int, int);

  printf("Enter the value of x and n: ");
  scanf("%d %d", &x, &n);
  result = XToTheN(x, n);
  printf("%d raised to the power %d is %d\n", x, n, result);
}

int XToTheN(int x, int n)
{
  if(n == 0)
    return(1);
  else
    return(x * XToTheN(x, n-1));
}
```

5.
```
#include <stdio.h>
void main(void)
{
  int n, a, d, result;
  int arithseq(int, int, int);

  printf("Enter the desired term: ");
  scanf("%d", &n);
  printf("Enter the first term and common difference: ");
  scanf("%d  %d", &a, &d);
  result = arithseq(a, d, n);
  printf("Term %d of the sequence is %d\n", n, result);
}

int arithseq(int a, int d, int n)
{
  if(n == 1)
    return(a);
  else
    return(d + arithseq(a, d, n-1));
}
```

EXERCISES 7.5

3. The required function is included with a driver function.
```
#include <stdio.h>
void main(void)
{
  double pi(void);

  printf("The value of pi is %lf\n", pi());
}

double pi(void)
{
#include <math.h>
  return (2 * asin(1.0));
}
```
5. The required function is included with a driver function.
```
#include <stdio.h>
void main(void)
{
  float x1, y1, x2, y2;
  float result;
  float distance(float, float, float, float);

  printf("Enter the coordinates of the first point: ");
  scanf("%f %f", &x1, &y1);
  printf("Enter the coordinates of the second point: ");
  scanf("%f %f", &x2, &y2);

  result = distance(x1, y1, x2, y2);
  printf("The distance between points is %f\n", result);
}

#include <math.h>
float distance(float x1, float y1, float x2, float y2)
{
  float dist;

  dist = sqrt( pow((x2 - x1),2) + pow((y2 - y1),2) );
  return (dist);
}
```

9. The required functions are included with a driver function.

```
#include <stdio.h>
void main(void)
{
  float a, b, c, d, e, f, g, h, i;
  float determinant;
  float det3(float, float, float, float, float, float, float, float, float);

  printf("Enter the first row's coefficients: ");
  scanf("%f %f %f", &a, &b, &c);
  printf("Enter the second row's coefficients: ");
  scanf("%f %f %f", &d, &e, &f);
  printf("Enter the third row's coefficients: ");
  scanf("%f %f %f", &g, &h, &i);

  determinant = det3(a, b, c, d, e, f, g, h, i);
  printf("The determinant is %f\n", determinant);
}

float det3(float a,float b,float c,float d,float e,float f,float g,float
h,float i)
{
  float det2(float, float, float, float);

  return(a*det2(e, f, h, i) - d*det2(b, c, h, i) + g*det2(b,c,e,f));
}

float det2(float a11, float a12, float a21, float a22)
{
  return (a11 * a22 - a21 * a12);
}
```

EXERCISES 7.7

1.
```
void time(int tot_sec, int *hr_addr, int *min_addr, int *sec_addr)
{
  *hr_addr = tot_sec/3600;       /* 3600 seconds = 1 hour */
    /*  Integer division yields the whole */
    /*  number of times 3600 goes into tot_sec */
  tot_sec -= *hours * 3600;
  *min_addr = tot_sec/60;
  tot_sec -= *min * 60;
  *sec_addr = tot_sec;
}
```

3. The required function is included with a driver function.

```
#include <stdio.h>
void main(void)
{
  double num;
  double dabsr(double);

  printf("Enter a number: ");
  scanf("%lf", &num);

  printf("The absolute value of %lf is %lf\n", num, dabsr(num));
}

double dabsr(double num)
{
  if(num > 0.0)
    return (num);
  else
    return(-num);
}
```

EXERCISES 8.1

1.a. `float grades[100];`
  b. `float temp[50];`
  c. `char code[30];`
  d. `int year[100];`
  e. `float velocity[32];`
  f. `float dist[1000];`
  g. `int code[6];`

3.a.
```
scanf("%d",&grades[0]);
scanf("%d",&grades[2]);
scanf("%d",&grades[6]);

scanf("%f",&grades[0]);
scanf("%f",&grades[2]);
scanf("%f",&grades[6]);

scanf("%f",&amps[0]);
scanf("%f",&amps[2]);
scanf("%f",&amps[6]);

scanf("%d",&dist[0]);
scanf("%d",&dist[2]);
scanf("%d",&dist[6]);

scanf("%f",&velocity[0]);
scanf("%f",&velocity[2]);
scanf("%f",&velocity[6]);

scanf("%f",&time[0]);
scanf("%f",&time[2]);
scanf("%f",&time[6]);
```
  b.
```
for(i = 0; i < 20; i++)
    scanf("%d", &grades[i]);

for(i = 0; i < 10; i++)
    scanf("%f", &grades[i]);

for(i = 0; i < 16; i++)
    scanf("%f", &amps[i]);

for(i = 0; i < 15; i++)
    scanf("%d", &dist[i]);

for(i = 0; i < 25; i++)
    scanf("%f", &velocity[i]);

for(i = 0; i < 100; i++)
    scanf("%f", &time[i]);
```

5.a. elements: 3, 4, 5, 6
  b. elements: 2, 4, 6
  c. elements: 5, 6, 7, 8, 9, 10, 11
  d. elements: 4, 7, 10, 13
  e. elements: 3, 5, 7, 9, 11

7.
```
#include <stdio.h>
void main(void)
{
    int temp[8], total = 0, count;
    float avg;
```

(continued on next page)

(continued from previous page)

```c
        for(count = 0; count < 8; ++count)
        {
            printf("Enter number %d: ", count + 1);
            scanf("%d", &temp[count]);
            total += temp[count];
        }
        avg = total/8.0;
        for(count = 0; count < 8; ++count)
            printf("Element #%d = %d\n", count, temp[count]);
        printf("\n   The average is %f\n\n", avg);
    }
```

9.a.
```c
#include <stdio.h>
void main(void)
{
  int grades[14], total, i;
  float avg, deviation[14];

  total = 0;
  for(i = 0; i <= 13; ++i)
  {
      printf("Enter grade #%d: ", i + 1);
      scanf("%d", &grades[i]);
      total += grades[i];
  }
  avg = total/14.0;
  printf("\n The average of the grades is %5.2f\n",avg);
  printf("Element      Element       Deviation\n");
  printf("Number       Value        from Avg.\n");
  printf("-------      -------       ----------\n");
  for(i = 0; i <= 13; ++i)
  {
    deviation[i] = grades[i] - avg;
    printf("%5d       %10d     %10.2f\n",i, grades[i],
    deviation[i]);
  }
}
```

11.
```c
#include <stdio.h>
void main(void)
{
    double raw[10], sorted[10], min = 1.e5;
    int i, j, index;

    for(i = 0; i <= 9; ++i)
    {
        printf("Enter value #%d: ", i+1);
        scanf("%lf", &raw[i]);
    }
    for(i = 0; i <= 9; ++i)
    {
      for(j = 0; j <= 9; ++j) /* find the minimum for this pass */
      {
        if(raw[j] < min) /* look for next min */
        {
            min = raw[j];
            index = j;
        }
      }
    sorted[i] = min;      /* put min in next sorted element */
    min = 1.e5;           /* reset min for start of search */
    raw[index] = 1.e7;    /* don't select this element again */
    }
    printf("The elements in sorted order are:\n");
    for( i = 0; i <= 9; ++i)
    printf("%f  ",sorted[i]);
    }
```

b. To locate each minimum, make a complete pass through the array and find the first minimum. Now only nine numbers need be searched since one has been used. After the second lowest element has been selected, only the remaining eight need be searched. Instead of 10 squared passes through the loop, only 10 factorial passes are needed. The number of passes can be reduced using a shell sort rather than a bubble sort.

EXERCISES 8.2

1.a. `int grades[10] = {89, 75, 82, 93, 78, 95, 81, 88, 77, 82};`
  b. `double amount[5] = {10.62, 13.98, 18.45, 12.68, 14.76};`
  c. `double rates[100] = {6.29, 6.95, 7.25, 7.35, 7.40, 7.42};`
  d. `float temp[64] = {78.2, 69.6, 68.5, 83.9, 55.4, 67.0, 49.8, 58.3, 62.5, 71.6};`
  e. `char code[15] = {'f', 'j', 'm', 'q', 't', 'w', 'z'};`

3.
```
#include <stdio.h>
void main(void)
{
      int i, index_max, index_min;
      float max, min;
      float slopes[9] = {17.24, 25.63, 5.94, 33.92, 3.71, 32.84,
            35.93, 18.24, 6.92};

      max = slopes[0];
      min = slopes[0];
      for (i=0; i<9; i++)
      {
            if(slopes[i] > max)
            {
                  max = slopes[i];
                  index_max = i + 1;
            }
            if(slopes[i] < min)
            {
                  min = slopes[i];
                  index_min = i + 1;
            }
            printf("%5.2f\n", slopes[i]);
      }
      printf("The maximum is %5.2f and occurs at element %d\n",
            max, index_max);
      printf("The minimum is %5.2f and occurs at element %d\n",
            min, index_min);
}
```

5.
```
char goodstr1[13] = {'G', 'o', 'o', 'd', ' ',
      'M', 'o', 'r', 'n', 'i', 'n', 'g'};

char goodstr1[] = {'G', 'o', 'o', 'd', ' ',
      'M', 'o', 'r', 'n','i', 'n', 'g'};

char goodstr1[] = "Good Morning";
```
Note: This last declaration creates an array having one more character than the first two. The extra character is the null character.

7.a.
```
#include <stdio.h>
void main(void)
{
   int i;
   char strtest[] = "This is a test";

   for (i=0; i<=14; i++)
        printf("%c", strtest[i]);
}
```

b.
```c
#include <stdio.h>
void main(void)
{
    int i;
    char strtest[] = "This is a test";

    for (i=10; i<=14; i++)
        printf("%c", strtest[i]);
}
```

c.
```c
#include <stdio.h>
void main(void)
{
    char strtest[] = "This is a test";

    printf("%s\n",strtest);
}
```

d.
```c
#include <stdio.h>
void main(void)
{
    int i=0;
    char strtest[] = "This is a test";
    do
    {
        printf("%c", strtest[i++]);
    }
    while (strtest[i] != '\0');
}
```

EXERCISES 8.3

1.
```c
void sort_arr(double in_array[500])
        or
void sort_arr(double in_array[])
```

3.
```c
void prime(char rates[256])
        or
void prime(char rates[])
```

5.
```c
#include <stdio.h>
void main(void)
{
    float rates[9] = {6.5, 7.2, 7.5, 8.3, 8.6,
                      9.4, 9.6, 9.8, 10.0};
    void show(float []);   /* function prototype */

    show(rates);
}

void show(float rates[])
{
    int i;

    printf("The elements stored in the array are:\n");
    for(i = 0; i <= 8; ++i)
        printf("\n %4.1f", rates[i]);
}
```

7.

```c
#include <stdio.h>
void main(void)
{
   double price[10] = {10.62, 14.89, 13.21, 16.55, 18.62, 9.47, 6.58,
                       18.32, 12.15, 3.98};
   double quantity[10] = {4.0, 8.5, 6.0, 7.35, 9.0, 15.3, 3.0, 5.4,
                          2.9, 4.8};
   double amount[10];
   int i;
   void extend(double [[], double [], double []); /* prototype */

   extend(price, quantity, amount);
   printf("The elements in the amount array are:\n");
   for(i = 0; i <= 9; ++i)
      printf(" %7.3lf\n", amount[i]);
}

void extend(double prc[], double qnty[], double amt[])
{
   int i;

   for(i = 0; i <= 9; ++i)
     amt[i] = prc[i]*qnty[i];
}
```

EXERCISES 8.4

1.

```c
#include <stdio.h>
#include <math.h>
#define NUM_ELS 10

void main(void)
{
   int values[NUM_ELS];
   float average, stddev;
   float find_avg(int[], int);
   float std_dev(int[], int, float);
   void entvals(int []);

   entvals(values);
   average = find_avg(values, NUM_ELS);
   stddev = std_dev(values, NUM_ELS, average);
   printf("The average of the numbers is %5.2f\n", average);
   printf("The standard deviation of the numbers is %5.2f\n",
          stddev);
}

float find_avg(int nums[], int numel)
{
   int i;
   float sumnums = 0.0;

   for (i=0; i<numel; i++)
     sumnums = sumnums + nums[i];
   return(sumnums/numel);
}

float std_dev(int nums[], int numel, float av)
{
   int i;
   float sumdevs = 0.0;
```

(continued on next page)

(continued from previous page)

```
        for (i=0; i<numel; i++)
            sumdevs = sumdevs + pow((nums[i] - av),2);
            return(sqrt(sumdevs/numel));
    }

    void entvals(int vals[])
    {
      int i;

      for (i = 0; i < NUM_ELS; i++)
      {
        printf("Enter value %d: ", i + 1);
        scanf("%d", &vals[i]);
      }
    }
```

3.
```
#include <stdio.h>
#include <math.h>

void main(void)
{
    int values[10] = {98, 82, 67, 54, 78, 83, 95, 76, 68, 63};
    int highest;
    float average, stddev;
    float find_avg(int[], int);
    float std_dev(int[], int, float);
    int high(int[], int);

    average = find_avg(values, 10);
    stddev = std_dev(values, 10, average);
    highest = high(values, 10);

    printf("The average of the numbers is %5.2f\n", average);
    printf("The standard deviation of the numbers is %5.2f\n", stddev);
    printf("The highest of the numbers is %d\n", highest);
}
float find_avg(int nums[], int numel)
{
    int i;
    float sumnums = 0.0;
    for (i=0; i<numel; i++)
        sumnums = sumnums + nums[i];
    return(sumnums/numel);
}
float std_dev(int nums[], int numel, float av)
{
    int i;
    float sumdevs = 0.0;

    for (i=0; i<numel; i++)
        sumdevs = sumdevs + pow((nums[i] - av),2);
    return(sqrt(sumdevs/numel));
}

int high(int nums[], int numel)
{
    int i;
    int max = nums[0];
    for (i=0; i<numel; i++)
        if(nums[i] > max)
            max = nums[i];
    return(max);
}
```

7.
```c
#include <stdio.h>

void main(void)
{
    char alphabet[] = {'B', 'J', 'K', 'M', 'S', 'Z'};
    char newlet;
    void adlet(char[], char);

    printf("Enter a new letter to add: ");
    scanf("%c", &newlet);
    adlet(alphabet, newlet);
}
void adlet(char alpharray[], char addlet)
{
    int i=0, endpos, newpos;
    while(alpharray[i] < addlet)
        i++;
    newpos = i;

    while(alpharray[i] != 'Z')
        i++;
    endpos = i;
    for (i=endpos; i>=newpos; —i)
        alpharray[i+1] = alpharray[i];
    alpharray[newpos] = addlet;
    for (i=0; i<=6; i++)
        printf("%c", alpharray[i]);
}
```

EXERCISES 8.5

1.
```c
#include <stdio.h>
#include <math.h>
#define NUMEL 100
void main(void)
{
    int nums[NUMEL];
    int i, moves;
    float seed;
    int selection_sort(int [], int);

    srand(1);   /* seed the random number generator */
    printf("The original array values are:\n");
    for(i = 0; i < NUMEL; ++i)
    {
        nums[i] = (int) (rand());
        printf("%d  ", nums[i]);
    }

    moves = selection_sort(nums, NUMEL);

    printf("\nThe sorted list, in ascending order, is:\n");
    for (i = 0; i < NUMEL; ++i)
        printf("%d  ",nums[i]);
    printf("\n %d moves were made to sort this list\n", moves);
}
```

(continued on next page)

(continued from previous page)

```
int selection_sort(int num[], int numel)
{
  int i, j, min, minidx, temp, moves = 0;
  void swap(int *, int *);  /* function prototype */

  for ( i = 0; i < (numel - 1); i++)
  {
    min = num[i];  /* assume minimum is the first array element */
    minidx = i;      /* index of minimum element */
    for(j = i + 1; j < numel; j++)
    {
      if (num[j] < min)  /* if we've located a lower value */
      {                        /* capture it */
     min = num[j];
     minidx = j;
      }
    }
    if (min < num[i])  /* check if we have a new minimum */
    {                    /* and if we do, swap values */
      temp = num[i];
      num[i] = min;
      num[minidx] = temp;
      moves++;
    }
  }
  return (moves);
}
```

3. The swap() function, as it would be used in Program 8.10, is:

```
#include <stdio.h>
#include <math.h>
#define NUMEL 10
void main(void)
{
  int nums[NUMEL] = {22,5,67,98,45,32,101,99,73,10};
  int i, moves;
  float seed;
  int selection_sort(int [], int);

  moves = selection_sort(nums, NUMEL);

  printf("\nThe sorted list, in ascending order, is:\n");
  for (i = 0; i < NUMEL; ++i)
    printf("%d  ",nums[i]);
  printf("\n %d moves where made to sort this list\n", moves);
}

int selection_sort(int num[], int numel)
{
  int i, j, min, minidx, temp, moves = 0;
  void swap(int *, int *);  /* function prototype */

  for ( i = 0; i < (numel - 1); i++)
  {
    min = num[i];  /* assume minimum is the first array element */
    minidx = i;      /* index of minimum element */
    for(j = i + 1; j < numel; j++)
    {
      if (num[j] < min)    /* if we've located a lower value */
      {                        /* capture it */
```

(continued on next page)

(continued from previous page)

```
              min = num[j];
              minidx = j;
                }
            }
          if (min < num[i])  /* check if we have a new minimum */
          {                       /* and if we do, swap values */
            swap(&num[i], &num[minidx]);
            moves++;
          }
        }
      return (moves);
    }
    void swap(int *first, int *second)
    {
      int temp;

      temp = *first;
      *first = *second;
      *second = temp;
    }
```

5.a.
```
    #include <stdio.h>
    #define NUMEL 20
    void main(void)
    {
      int nums[NUMEL] = {4, 7, 5, 9, 1, 3, 8, 34, 68, 74, 52, 63, 67,
                      32, 45, 73, 98, 101, 99, 29};
      int i;
      void quicksort(int[], int, int);

      quicksort(nums, 0, NUMEL-1);

      printf("\nThe sorted list, in ascending order, is:\n");
      for (i=0; i<NUMEL; ++i)
          printf("%d ", nums[i]);
    }

    void quicksort(int num[], int lower, int upper)
    {
      int i, j, pivot;
      int partition(int[], int, int);

      pivot = partition(num, lower, upper);

      if (lower<pivot)
          quicksort(num, lower, pivot-1);
      if (upper>pivot)
          quicksort(num, pivot+1, upper);
    }

    int partition(int num[], int left, int right)
    {
      int pivot, temp;

      pivot = num[left];
      while (left<right)
      {
          while(num[right]>=pivot && left<right)
              right--;
          if (right!=left)
```

(continued on next page)

(continued from previous page)

```
        {
              num[left]=num[right];
              left++;
        }
        while(num[left]<=pivot && left<right)
              left++;
        if (right!=left)
        {
              num[right] = num[left];
              right--;
        }
      }
      num[left] = pivot;
      return(left);
    }
```

EXERCISES 8.7

1. a.
```
#include <stdio.h>
#include <math.h>
#define MAXGRADES 200   /* a suitably large number */
void main(void)
{
  int i = 0;
  float grades[MAXGRADES];
  float average, stddev;
  float find_avg(float [], int);           /* function prototype */
  float std_dev(float [], int, float);   /* function prototype */

  printf("Enter a grade or -1 to terminate data entry: ");
  scanf("%f", &grades[i]);
  while (grades[i] >= 0.0 && i < MAXGRADES)
  {
    i++;
    printf("Enter a grade or -1 to terminate data entry: ");
    scanf("%f", &grades[i]);
  }

  if (i > 0)
  {
    average = find_avg(grades, i); /* call the function */
    stddev = std_dev(grades, i, average); /* call the function */

    printf("The average of the grades is %5.2f\n", average);
    printf("The standard deviation of the grades is %5.2f\n",
        stddev);
  }
  else
    printf("No grades were entered\n");
}

float find_avg(float nums[], int numel)
{
  int i;
  float sumnums = 0.0;

  for (i = 0; i < numel; i++) /* calculate the sum of the grades */
    sumnums = sumnums + nums[i];
```

(continued on next page)

(continued from previous page)

```
        return (sumnums / numel);      /* calculate and return the average */
      }

      float std_dev(float nums[], int numel, float av)
      {
        int i;
        float sumdevs = 0.0;

        for (i = 0; i < numel; i++)
          sumdevs = sumdevs + pow((nums[i] - av),2);

        return(sqrt(sumdevs/numel));
      }
```

3. The function is included with a driver function.

```
      #include <stdio.h>
      #define MAXNUMS 10
      void main(void)
      {
        int vals[MAXNUMS] = {0, 1, 2, 3, 4, 5, 6, 7, 8, 9};
        void printrev(int [], int);

        printrev(vals, MAXNUMS); /* call the function */
      }

      void printrev(int num[], int numel)
      {
        int i;

        for (i = (numel -1); i >= 0; i—)
          printf("%d  ", num[i]);
        return;
      }
```

5.

```
      #include <stdio.h>
      #include <math.h>
      #define MAXGRADES 50
      void main(void)
      {
        int i = 0, j;
        float grades[MAXGRADES];
        void descend_sort(float [], int);

        printf("Enter a grade or -1 to terminate data entry: ");
        scanf("%f", &grades[i]);
        while (grades[i] >= 0.0 && i < MAXGRADES)
        {
          i++;
          printf("Enter a grade or -1 to terminate data entry: ");
          scanf("%f", &grades[i]);
        }

        if (i > 0)
        {
          descend_sort(grades, i); /* call the function */
          printf("The grades, in descending order, are:\n");
          for(j = 0; j < i; j++)
            printf("%f  ", grades[j]);
          printf("\n");
        }
        else
          printf("No grades were entered\n");
      }
```

(continued on next page)

(continued from previous page)

```c
void descend_sort(float num[], int numel)
{
  int i, j, max, maxidx;
  float temp;

  for ( i = 0; i < (numel-1); i++)
  {
    max = num[i];   /* assume maximum is the first array element */
    maxidx = i;      /* index of maximum element */
    for(j = i + 1; j < numel; j++)
    {
      if (num[j] > max)    /* if we've located a higher value */
      {                    /* capture it */
        max = num[j];
        maxidx = j;
      }
    }
    if (max > num[i])   /* check if we have a new maximum */
    {                   /* and if we do, swap values */
      temp = num[i];
      num[i] = max;
      num[maxidx] = temp;
    }
  }
  return;
}
```

EXERCISES 9.1

1.a.   `int array[6][10];`
  b.   `int array[2][5];`
  c.   `char array[7][12];`
  d.   `char array[15][7];`
  e.   `float array[10][25];`
  f.   `float array[16][8];`

3.a.
```c
#include <stdio.h>
void main(void)
{
  int total=0, i, j;
  int val[3][4] = {8,16,9,52,3,15,27,6,14,25,2,10};

  for (i = 0; i < 3; i++)
    for (j = 0; j < 4; j++)
    {
      total += val[i][j];
      printf("%2d  ", val[i][j]);
    }
  printf("The total is: %d\n", total);
}
```

  b.
```c
#include <stdio.h>
void main(void)
{
  int rowtotal, i, j;
  int val[3][4] = {8,16,9,52,3,15,27,6,14,25,2,10};

  for (i = 0; i < 3; i++)
  {
    rowtotal = 0;
    for (j = 0; j < 4; j++)
    {
      rowtotal += val[i][j];
      printf("%2d  ", val[i][j]);
    }
    printf("The total of row %d is: %d\n", i, rowtotal);
  }
}
```

5.a.
```c
#include <stdio.h>
void main(void)
{
    int i, j, max;
    int array[4][5] = 16,22,99,4,18,-258,4,101,5,98,
                       105,6,15,2,45,33,88,72,16,3};

    max=array[0][0];
    for (i = 0; i < 4; i++)
      for (j = 0; j < 5; j++)
        if (max < array[i][j])
           max = array[i][j];
    printf("\nThe maximum value is: %d\n", max);
}
```

b.
```c
#include <stdio.h>
void main(void)
{
    int i, j, max, mrow = 0, mcol = 0;
    int array[4][5] = {16,22,99,4,18,-258,4,101,5,98,
                       105,6,15,2,45,33,88,72,16,3};

    max = array[0][0];
    for (i = 0; i < 4; i++)
      for (j = 0; j < 5; j++)
        if (max < array[i][j])
        {
            max = array[i][j];
            mrow = i;
            mcol = j;
        }
    printf("\nThe maximum value is: %d\n", max);
    printf("It occurs at row %d and column %d.\n", mrow, mcol);
}
```

7.a.
```c
#include <stdio.h>
void main(void)
{
    int i, j, a = 0, b = 0, c = 0, d = 0, e = 0;
    float grade[3][5];

    for (i = 0; i < 3; i++)
      for (j = 0; j < 5; j++)
      {
          printf("Enter grade: ");
          scanf("%f", &grade[i][j]);
          if (grade[i][j] >= 90) a++;
          else if (grade[i][j] >= 80) b++;
          else if (grade[i][j] >= 70) c++;
          else if (grade[i][j] >= 60) d++;
          else e++;
      }
    printf("\nTotals:\n");
    printf("          Grades < 60: %d\n", e);
    printf("Grades => 60 and < 70: %d\n", d);
    printf("Grades => 70 and < 80: %d\n", c);
    printf("Grades => 80 and < 90: %d\n", b);
    printf("          Grades >= 90: %d\n", a);
}
```

EXERCISES 9.2

1.a. 2×2
   b. 1×5
   c. 2×3
   d. 4×3
   e. 3×1

3.a. $\mathbf{A} + \mathbf{B} = \begin{vmatrix} 2 & 1 \\ 0 & 0 \end{vmatrix}$ $\mathbf{A} - \mathbf{B} = \begin{vmatrix} 0 & 5 \\ 0 & -2 \end{vmatrix}$

   b. $\mathbf{A} + \mathbf{B} = \begin{vmatrix} 1 \\ 3 \\ 1 \end{vmatrix}$ $\mathbf{A} - \mathbf{B} = \begin{vmatrix} 1 \\ 1 \\ -3 \end{vmatrix}$

   c. The sum is not defined because the matrices are of different orders.
   d. $\mathbf{A} + \mathbf{B} = \begin{vmatrix} 10 & 10 & 10 \\ 10 & 10 & 10 \\ 10 & 10 & 10 \end{vmatrix}$ $\mathbf{A} - \mathbf{B} = \begin{vmatrix} -8 & -6 & -4 \\ -2 & 0 & 2 \\ 4 & 6 & 8 \end{vmatrix}$
   e. The sum is not defined because the matrices are of different orders.

5. $a = 2$
   $b = 4$
   $c = 4$
   $d = -5$

7.a. 3×1
   b. Multiplication cannot be performed.
   c. 1×4
   d. 3×3
   e. 4×4
   f. 4×3
   g. 1×4
   h. Multiplication cannot be performed.
   i. 4×3

EXERCISES 9.3

1.a. The solution is $x = 2.5$ and $y = 3.6$.
   b. The solution is $x = 3.209$, $y = -0.6744$, and $z = 1.6512$.
3.a. The equations are inconsistent. In the first equation the sum of $2x + y$ is given as 7 and in the next equation the same sum is given as 14.
   b. The second equation is obtained by multiplying the first equation by 2. As such, it adds no new information. (Such equations are said to be linearly dependent.) Thus, we really have one equation in two unknowns, for which there are an infinite number of solutions. For example, $x = 0$, $y = 10$; $x = 5$, $y = 0$;, $x = 1$, $y = 8$; etc.

5.

```c
#include <stdio.h>
void main(void)
{
   int numpts, i;
   float x, y;
   float sumx, sumy, sumsqrx, sumxy;

   sumx = sumy = sumsqrx = sumxy = 0.0;

   printf("Enter the number of data points: ");
   scanf("%d", &numpts);
   for(i = 1; i <= numpts; i++)
   {
      printf("Enter the x and y values for point %d: ", i);
      scanf("%f %f", &x, &y);
      sumx += x;
      sumy =+ y;
      sumsqrx += (x*x);   /* parentheses are necessary here */
      sumxy += (x*y);
   }
```

(continued on next page)

(continued from previous page)

```
       printf("The required coefficients are:\n");
       printf("                    N:  %d\n", numpts);
       printf("         sum of x: %f\n", sumx);
       printf("         sum of y: %f\n", sumy);
       printf("sum of x squared: %f\n", sumsqrx);
       printf("sum of x times y: %f\n", sumxy);
   }
```

EXERCISES 9.5

1.

```
   #include <stdio.h>
   #define STUDENTS 60
   #define INFO 7
   #define NUMGRADES 4
   void main(void)
   {
     float grades[STUDENTS][INFO];
     int i, j, num;
     float sum;

     printf("Enter the number of students: ");
     scanf("%d", &num);

     for(i = 0; i < num; i++)
     {
       printf("Enter the grades for student %d\n", i+1);
       for(j = 1; j <= NUMGRADES; j++)
       {
         printf("  Grade %d: ", j);
         scanf("%f", &grades[i][j]);
         sum += grades[i][j];
       }
       grades[i][0] = (float) i+1;
       grades[i][NUMGRADES+1] = sum / NUMGRADES;
       grades[i][NUMGRADES+2] =  0.2 * grades[i][1]
                       + 0.3 * grades[i][2]
                       + 0.3 * grades[i][3]
                       + 0.2 * grades[i][4];
     }
     printf("\nThe final grades array is:\n");
     for(i = 0; i < num; i++)
     {
       printf("\n");
       for(j = 0; j < INFO; j++)
         printf("%f   ", grades[i][j]);
     }
   }
```

3.

```
#include <stdio.h>
#define ROWS 100
#define COLS 2
void main(void)
{
  int track[ROWS][COLS], i, j;
  int numparts;
  void sort(int [ROWS][COLS], int);

  printf("Enter how many parts: ");
  scanf("%d", &numparts);

  for(i = 0; i < numparts; i++)
  {
    printf("Enter a part no. and quantity: ");
    scanf("%d  %d", &track[i][0], &track[i][1]);
  }
  printf("\nThe entered data is:\n");
  for(i = 0; i < numparts; i++)
    printf("%d  %d\n", track[i][0], track[i][1]);

  sort(track, numparts);

  printf("\nThe sorted data is:\n");
  for(i = 0; i < numparts; i++)
    printf("%d  %d\n", track[i][0], track[i][1]);

}

void sort(int num[ROWS][COLS], int numel)
{
  int i, j, max, maxidx, temp, part;

  for ( i = 0; i < (numel - 1); i++)
  {
    max = num[i][1];  /* assume maximum is first quantity */
    part = num[i][0]; /* save the corresponding part no. */
    maxidx = i;       /* index of maximum element */
    for(j = i + 1; j < numel; j++)
    {
      if (num[j][1] > max)   /* if we've located a higher value */
      {                      /* capture it */
       max = num[j][1];
       maxidx = j;
       part = num[j][0];
      }
    }
    if (max > num[i][1])  /* check if we have a new minimum */
    {                     /* and if we do, swap values */
      temp = num[i][1];    /* swap quantities */
      num[i][1] = max;
      num[maxidx][1] = temp;
      temp = num[i][0];   /* swap part no.s */
      num[i][0] = part;
      num[maxidx][0] = temp;
    }
  }
  return;
}
```

EXERCISES 10.1

1. &average **means "the address of the variable named** average."

3.a.

```
#include <stdio.h>
void main(void)
{
   char key, choice;
   int num, count;
   long date;
   float yield;
   double price;

   printf("The address of the variable key is %p\n",&key);
   printf("The address of the variable choice is %p\n",&choice);
   printf("The address of the variable num is %p\n",&num);
   printf("The address of the variable count is %p\n",&count);
   printf("The address of the variable date is %p\n",&date);
   printf("The address of the variable yield is %p\n",&yield);
   printf("The address of the variable price is %p\n",&price);
}
```

c.

```
#include <stdio.h>
void main(void)
{
   printf("\nNo. of bytes for a char: %d\n", sizeof(char));
   printf("No. of bytes for an int: %d\n", sizeof(int));
printf("No. of bytes for a long: %d\n", sizeof(long));
   printf("No. of bytes for a float: %d\n", sizeof(float));
printf("No. of bytes for a double: %d\n", sizeof(double));
}
```

5.a. *x_addr
  b. *y_addr
  c. *pt_yld
  d. *pt_miles
  e. *mptr
  f. *pdate
  g. *dist_ptr
  h. *tab_pt
  i. *hours_pt

7.a. Each of these variables is pointers. This means that addresses will be stored in each of these variables.

  b. They are not very descriptive names and do not give an indication that they are pointers.

9. All pointer variable declarations must have an asterisk. Therefore, c, e, g, and i are pointer declarations.

11. Variable: pt_num   Variable: amt_addr
      Address: 500   Address: 564

8096		16256

      Variable: z_addr   Variable: num_addr
      Address: 8024   Address: 10132

20492		18938

      Variable: pt_day   Variable: pt_yr
      Address: 14862   Address: 15010

20492		694

(continued on next page)

Variable: years   Variable: m
Address: 694   Address: 8096

1987		

Variable: amt   Variable: firstnum
Address: 16256   Address: 18938

154	154

Variable: balz   Variable: k
Address: 20492   Address: 24608

25	154

EXERCISES 10.2

1.a. `*(prices + 5)`
  b. `*(grades + 2)`
  c. `*(yield + 10)`
  d. `*(dist + 9)`
  e. `*mile`
  f. `*(temp + 20)`
  g. `*(celsius + 16)`
  h. `*(num + 50)`
  i. `*(time + 12)`

3.a. The declaration `double prices [5];` causes storage space for five double-precision numbers, creates a pointer constant named `prices`, and equates the pointer constant to the address of the first element (`&prices[0]`).

  b. Each element in `prices` contains 4 bytes, and there are five elements for a total of 20 bytes.

  c.

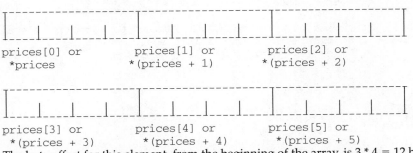

  d. The byte offset for this element, from the beginning of the array, is 3 * 4 = 12 bytes.

EXERCISES 10.3

1.
```
#include <stdio.h>
void main(void)
{
      int nums[5] = {16, 54, 7, 43, -5};
      int total = 0, *n_pt;

      for (n_pt=nums; n_pt<=nums+4; *n_pt++)
            total += *n_pt;
      printf("The total of the array elements is %d\n", total);
}
```

3.a.
```
#include <stdio.h>
void main(void)
{
   char strng[] = "Hooray for all of us";
   char *mess_pt;

   mess_pt = &strng[0];    /* mess_pt = strng; is equivalent */
   printf("The elements in the array are: ");
   for(   ; *mess_pt != '\0'; ++mess_pt)
   printf("%c", *mess_pt);
}
```

b.
```
#include <stdio.h>
void main(void)
{
   char strng[] = "Hooray for all of us";
   char *mess_pt;

   mess_pt = &strng[0];    /* mess_pt = strng; is equivalent */
   printf("The elements in the array are: ");
   while (*mess_pt != '\0')   /* search for the null character */
         printf("%c", *mess_pt++);
}
```

c.
```
#include <stdio.h>
void main(void)
{
   char strng[] = "Hooray for all of us";
   char *mess_pt;

   mess_pt = &strng[11];    /* mess_pt = strng; is equivalent */
   printf("The elements in the array are: ");
   for(   ; *mess_pt != '\0'; ++mess_pt)
         printf("%c", *mess_pt);
}
```

EXERCISES 10.4

1.
```
void sort_arr(double in_array[500])
void sort_arr(double in_array[])
void sort_arr(double *in_array)
```
3.
```
void prime(float rates[256])
void prime(float rates[])
void prime(float *rates)
```
5. The problem to this method of finding the maximum value lies in the line

```
if(max < *vals++)   max = *vals;
```

This statement compares the correct value to max, but then increments the address in the pointer before any assignment is made. Thus, the element assigned to max by the expression max = *vals is one element beyond the element pointed to within the parentheses.

EXERCISES 10.6

1.
```c
#include <stdio.h>
void main(void)
{
   char *messag1 = "Input the following data";
   char *messag2 = "-----------------------";
   char *messag3 = "Enter the date:";
   char *messag4 = "Enter the Account Number:";

   printf("\n%s\n",messag1);
   printf("%s\n",messag2);
   printf("%s\n",messag3);
   printf("%s\n",messag4);
}
```

3.   The `capit()` function is included within a complete program.
```c
#include <stdio.h>
void main(void)
{
   char ch1, ch2;
   void capit(char *, char *);

   printf("Enter two lowercase letters: ");
   scanf("%c %c", &ch1, &ch2);

   printf("\nThe letters entered are %c and %c\n", ch1, ch2);
   capit(&ch1, &ch2);
   printf("The letters, capitalized, are %c and %c\n", ch1, ch2);
}

void capit(char *let1, char *let2)
{
   *let1 = 'A' + (*let1 - 'a');
   *let2 = 'A' + (*let2 - 'a');
}
```

5.a.
```c
#include <stdio.h>
void main(void)
{
   char *message = "Vacation is near";
   void display(char *);

   display(message);
}

void display(char *strng)
{
   int i = 0;
   while(*(strng + i) != '\0')
   {
     printf("%c", *(strng + i));
     i++;
   }
}
```

b.

```
#include <stdio.h>
void main(void)
{
  char *message = "Vacation is near";
  void display(char *);

  display(message);
}

void display(char *strng)
{
  while(*strng != '\0')
  {
    printf("%c", *strng);
    strng++;          /* alter the address in string by one */
  }
}
```

7.a. The following output is obtained:

33
16
99
34

This is why:

```
*(*val) = *(val[0]) = val[0][0] = 33;
*(*val + 1) = *(val[1]) = val[1][0] = 16;
*(*val + 1) + 2) = *(*(val[1]) + 2) = *(val[1][2]) = 99;
*(*val) + 1 = *(val[0]) + 1 = val[0][0] + 1 = 33 + 1 = 34.
```

In other words, for any two-dimensional array, arr[x][y], what we really have is two levels of pointers. What is meant by *(arr + x) is that there are x number of pointers, each successively pointing to arr[1][0], arr[2][0], arr[3][0], ... , arr[x][0]. So an expression such as *(*(arr + x) + y) translates to arr[x][y].

EXERCISES 11.1

1.b.

```
#include <stdio.h>
void main(void)
{
  char line[81];
  void vowels(char []); /* function prototype */

  printf("Enter a string.\n");
  gets(line);
  vowels(line);
}

void vowels(char strng[])
{
  int i = 0, v = 0; /* Array element number and vowel counter */
  char c;

  while((c = strng[i++]) != '\0')
      switch(c)
      {
          case 'a':
          case 'e':
          case 'i':
          case 'o':
          case 'u':
              putchar(c);
              ++v;
      }
  putchar('\n');
  printf("There were %d vowels.", v);
}
```

3.a.   The function is included in the program written for Exercise 3b.

b.
```c
#include <stdio.h>
void main(void)
{
  char strng[81];
  void count_str(char []);  /* function prototype */

  printf("Enter a line of text\n");
  gets(strng);
  count_str(strng);
}

void count_str(char message[])
{
  int i;
  for(i = 0; message[i] != '\0'; ++i);  /* The semicolon at */
                                         /* the end of this  */
                                         /* statement is the */
                                         /* null statement   */
  printf("\nThe number of total characters, including blanks,");
  printf(" in the line just entered is %d.", i);
}
```

5.
```c
#include <stdio.h>
void main(void)
{
    char strng[81];
    char c;
    int i = 0;

    printf("Enter a string: ");
    gets(strng);
    while((c = strng[i++]) != '\0')
        if (c==' ')
            printf("\n");
        else
            printf("%c", c);

}
```

7.
```c
#include <stdio.h>
void main(void)
{
  char word[81];
  void del_char(char [], int, int);   /* function prototype */

  printf("Enter a string\n");
  gets(word);
  printf("\n%s\n",word);
  del_char(word, 13, 5);
  puts(word);
}

void del_char(char strng[], int x, int pos)
{
  int i, j;

  i = pos-1; /* first element to be deleted (actually, overwritten) */
  j = i + x;   /* first element beyond delete range */
  while (strng[j] != '\0')
    strng[i++] = strng[j++];  /* copy over an element */
  strng[i] = '\0';   /* close off the edited string */
  return;
}
```

This program assumes the number of characters to be deleted actually exists. Otherwise the `while` loop would not terminate (unless it just happened to encounter another null character somewhere in memory beyond the original string).

9.a. The `to_upper()` function is included in the program for Exercise 9c.

c.
```c
#include <stdio.h>
#define MAXCHARS 81
void main(void)
{
    char strng[MAXCHARS];
    int i = 0;
    char to_upper(char ch);    /* function prototype */

    printf("Enter a line of text\n");
    gets(strng);
    while (strng[i] != '\0')   /* get the character */
    {
        strng[i] = to_upper(strng[i]); /* send it to the function*/
        i++;        /* move to next character */
    }
    printf("The string, with all lowercase letters converted is:\n");
    puts(strng);
}
char to_upper(char ch)
{
    if ( ch >= 'a' && ch <= 'z')    /* test it */
        return(ch - 'a' + 'A');     /* change it, if necessary*/
    else
        return(ch);
}
```

11.
```c
#include <stdio.h>
#define MAXCHARS 81
void main(void)
{
    char strng[MAXCHARS];
    int i = 0, count = 1;

    printf("Enter a line of text\n");
    gets(strng);
    if(strng[i] == ' ' || strng[i] == '\0')
        count-;
    while(strng[i] != '\0')
    {
        if(strng[i] == ' ' && (strng[i + 1] != ' ' &&
           strng[i + 1] != '\0'))
            count++;        /* encountered a new word */
        i++;                /* move to the next character */
    }
    printf("\nThe number of words in the line just entered is %d",
           count);
}
```

The program increases the word count whenever a transition from a blank to a nonblank character occurs. Thus, even if words are separated by more than one space the word count will be incremented correctly. Initially the program assumes the text starts with a word (count = 1). If the first character is either a blank or an end-of-string Null, this assumption is incorrect and the count is decremented to zero.

EXERCISES 11.2

1.
```c
#include <stdio.h>
#define MAXCHARS 81
void main(void)
{
    char message[MAXCHARS];
    int i;
    void getline(char[]);

    printf("Enter a string:\n");
    getline(message);
    printf("The string just entered is:\n");
    puts(message);
}
void getline(char strng[])
{
    int i=0;
    char c;

    while(i < (MAXCHARS -1) && (c = getchr()) != '\n')
    {
        strng[i] = c;
        i++;
    }
    strng[i] = '\0';
    return;
}
```

3. The function is included within a complete program:
```c
#include <stdio.h>
#define MAXNUM 1000

void main(void)
{
  char message[MAXNUM];
  int numword, numchar;
  void countword(char [], int *, int *);  /* function prototype */

  printf("\nType in any number of words: ");

  gets(message);
  countword(message, &numword, &numchar);
  printf("The number of words just entered is %d\n", numword);
  printf("The number of characters just entered is %d\n", numchar);
 }

int countword(char list[], int *countword, int *countchar)
#define YES 1
#define NO 0
{
  int i, inaword, cword = 0;

  inaword = NO;
  for(i = 0; list[i] != '\0'; i++)
  {
    if (list[i] == ' ')
      inaword = NO;
    else if (inaword == NO)
    {
      inaword = YES;
      cword++;
    }
  }
  *countword = cword;   /* pass the word count back */
  *countchar = i;   /* pass the character count back */
  return;
}
```

5.   The function is included within a complete program:

```c
#include <stdio.h>
#define MAXNUM 1000

void main(void)
{
  char message[MAXNUM];
  int i, c, numlines, numchar;
  int countlines(char [], int);   /* function prototype */

  printf("\nType in any number of lines of text: ");

  i = 0;
  while (c = getchar())
  {
    if (c == EOF || i == MAXNUM)
      break;
    else
    {
      message[i] = c;   /* store the entry */
      i++;
    }
  }
  numlines = countlines(message, i);
  printf("The number of lines just entered is %d\n", numlines);
}

int countlines(char list[], int numvals)
{
  int i, cline = 0;

  for(i = 0; i < numvals; i++)
  {
    if (list[i] == '\n')
      cline++;
  }
  cline++;  /* last line is terminated with an EOF, not a \n */
   return(cline);
}
```

EXERCISES 11.3

1.a.   `*text = 'n'`
       `*(text + 3) = ' '`
       `*(text + 10) = ' '`
  b.   `*text = 'r'`
       `*(text + 3) = 'k'`
       `*(text + 10) = 'o'`
  c.   `*text = 'H'`
       `*(text + 3) = 'p'`
       `*(text + 10) = 'd'`
  d.   `*text = 'T'`
       `*(text + 3) = ' '`
       `*(text + 10) = 'h'`

3.
```c
#include <stdio.h>
#define MAXCHARS 81
void main(void)
{
 char line[MAXCHARS];
 void vowels(char *);   /* function prototype */

 printf("Enter a string.\n");
 gets(line);
 vowels(line);
}

void vowels(char *strng)  /* strng treated as a pointer variable */
{
 int v = 0;   /* v = vowel counter */
 char c;

 while((c = *strng++) != '\0')  /* an address is incremented */
 switch(c)
 {
   case 'a':
   case 'e':
   case 'i':
   case 'o':
   case 'u':
     putchar(c);
     ++v;
 }
 putchar('\n');
 printf("There were %d vowels.", v);
}
```

5.
```c
#include <stdio.h>
#define MAXCHARS 81
void main(void)
{
  char strng[MAXCHARS];
  void count_str(char *);   /* function prototype */

  printf("Enter a line of text\n");
  gets(strng);
  count_str(strng);
}

void count_str(char *message)    /* message as a pointer variable */
{
  int count;

  for(count = 0; *message++ != '\0'; ++count)
           ;       /* A null (do-nothing) statement */
  printf("\nThe number of total characters, including blanks, in");
  printf(" the line just entered is %d.", count);
}
```

7.
```
#include <stdio.h>
#define MAXCHARS 81
void main(void)
{
      char forward[MAXCHARS], rever[MAXCHARS];
      void reverse(char *, char *); /* function prototype */

      printf("Enter a line of text:\n");
      gets(forward);
      reverse(forward,rever);
      printf("\n\nThe text: %s \n",forward);
      printf("spelled backwards is: %s \n",rever);
}
void reverse(char *forw, char *rev)
{
      int i = 0;

      while(*(forw + i) != '\0')          /* count the elements */
            ++i;                   /* in the string        */
      for(-i; i >= 0; -i)
            *rev++ = *(forw + i);
      *rev = '\0';/* close off reverse string */
      return;
}
```

9.   The function is included within a complete program:
```
#include <stdio.h>
#define MAXCHARS 81
void main(void)
{
   char ch, line[MAXCHARS];
   void append_c(char, char *);   /* function prototype */

   printf("Enter a line of text: ");
   gets(line);
   printf("Enter a single character: ");
   ch = getchar();
   append_c(ch, line);
   printf("The new line of text with the appended last character is:\n");
   puts(line);
}
void append_c(char c, char *strng)
{
   while(*strng++ != '\0')    /* this advances the pointer */
            ;                  /* one character beyond '\0 '*/
   strng-;      /* point to the '\0') */
   *strng++ = c;                 /* replace it with the new char*/
   *strng = '\0';               /* close the new string       */
}
```

EXERCISES 11.4

1.   `char *text = "Hooray!";`
       `char text[] = {'H','o','o','r','a','y','\0'};`

3.   message is a pointer constant. Therefore, the statement message++, which is an attempt to alter its address, is invalid. A correct statement is:

$$putchar(*(message + i));$$

Here the address in message is unaltered and the character pointed to is the character offset i bytes from the address corresponding to message.

5.

```
#include <stdio.h>
#define MAXCHAR 10
void main(void)     /* Driver function to test week() */
{
  int num;
  char day[MAXCHAR];
  void day_of_wk(int choice, char *); /* function prototype */

  printf("Enter a number from one to seven: ");
  scanf("%d", &num);
  day_of_wk(num, &day);
  printf("\nThis is a %s.", day);
}

#include <string.h>
void day_of_wk(int choice, char *whichday)
{
  int i;
  char *day[7] = {"Sunday", "Monday", "Tuesday",
           "Wednesday", "Thursday", "Friday", "Saturday"};

  choice--;  /* Sunday now corresponds to 0  */
  strcpy(whichday, day[choice]);
  return;
}
```

EXERCISES 11.5

1.a. !four score and ten! /* field width specifier is ignored */
  b.   !   Home!!
  c.   !Home!
  d.   !Ho   !
  e.   !   Ho!
3.
```
#include <stdio.h>
void main(void)
{
  char strn[30];
  float num1, num2, num3;
  void separate(char *, float *, float *, float *);/* function prototype */

  printf("Enter three numbers on the same line,");
  printf("\n separating the numbers with one or more spaces:");
  gets(strn);     /* read the numbers in as a string */
  separate(strn, &num1, &num2, &num3);
  printf("The three numbers are %f %f %f",num1, num2, num3);
}

void separate(char *st_addr, float *n1_addr, float *n2_addr,float *n3_addr)
{
  sscanf(st_addr,"%f %f %f",n1_addr, n2_addr, n3_addr);
  return;
}
```

Functions like separate() are useful when reading data from a file. Rather than read individual items sequentially, a complete line of the file is read in as a string and then dissembled internally within the program. This isolates any line that does not have the required number and types of data items.

5.     ```c
       #include <stdio.h>
       #define MAXS1 80
       #define MAXS2 100
       void main(void)
       {
         char strng1[MAXS1], strng2[MAXS2];
         int num1, num2;
         void combine(char *, char *, int, int);  /* function prototype */

         printf("Enter a string: ");
         gets(strng1);
         printf("Enter an integer number: ");
         scanf("%d",&num1);
         printf("Enter a second integer number: ");
         scanf("%d",&num2);
         combine(strng1, strng2, num1, num2);
         printf("A string containing all inputs is: ");
         puts(strng2);
       }
       void combine(char *source, char *dest, int n1, int n2)
       {
         sprintf(dest,"%s %d %d",source, n1, n2);
         return;
       }
       ```

Functions like combine() are useful in assembling separate data items into a single line for output to a file. The file will then contain identically formatted lines, each line containing the same number and types of data items. Additionally, the file will be in ASCII, which can easily be read by any word processing program, for easy inspection external to the program that created it.

EXERCISES 11.7

1.   The function, within the context of a complete program is:
       ```c
       #include <stdio.h>
       #include <string.h>
       void main(void)
       {
         char *message = "     this is the string";
         void trimfrnt(char *);

         printf("|%s|\n", message);
         printf("string length is %d\n", strlen(message));

         trimfrnt(message);

         printf("|%s|\n", message);
         printf("string length is %d\n", strlen(message));

       }

       void trimfrnt(char *strng1) /* trim leading blanks */
       {
         char *strng2;

         strng2 = strng1;         /* save the string's starting address */
         while (*strng2 == ' ')   /* move along to the first non-blank */
           ++strng2;
         while (*strng1++ = *strng2++) /* copy over the rest of the string */
           ;
         return;
       }
       ```
       ```

3.   The function, within the context of a complete program is:

```c
#include <stdio.h>
#include <string.h>
void main(void)
{
  char *message = "this is the string";
  void addchars(char *, int, char);

  printf("|%s|\n", message);
  printf("string length is %d\n", strlen(message));

  addchars(message, 5, '!');

  printf("|%s|\n", message);
  printf("string length is %d\n", strlen(message));
}

void addchars(char *strng, int n, char ch)
{
  if (n <= 0) return;
  while (*strng != '\0')    /* move to the end of the string */
    ++strng;
  while(n- != 0)            /* add n occurrences of the character */
    *strng++ = ch;
  *strng = '\0';           /* terminate the string */
  return;
}
```

5.

```c
#include <stdio.h>
#define MAXNUM 1000

void main(void)
{
  char message[MAXNUM], keychar;
  int i, c, occur;
  int searchchar(char [], char);  /* function prototype */

  printf("\nType in a sentence: ");

  i = 0;
  while (c = getchar())
  {
    if (c == '.' || i == MAXNUM)
      break;
    else
    {
      message[i] = c;  /* store the entry */
      i++;
    }
    message[i] = '\0';  /* close off the string */
  }
  fflush(stdin);  /* clear the buffer of any characters */
  printf("\nEnter the search character: ");
  scanf("%c", &keychar);
  occur = searchchar(message, keychar);
  printf("The number of times the character %c was typed is %d\n",
         keychar, occur);
}

int searchchar(char list[], char key)
```

(continued on next page)

(continued from previous page)

```
{
  int count = 0;

  while (*list != '\0')
  {
    printf("%c", *list);
    if (*list == key)
        count++;
    list++;
  }

  return(count);
}
```

EXERCISES 12.1

1.a. The maximum number of characters permitted for a filename depends on the operating system. For MS-DOS, a filename may have up to eight characters, and optionally a decimal point followed by three more characters. If a string is used to hold the
filename, an extra character should be provided for the NULL, for a total of 13 characters within a C program. For MS-Windows 3.0 and 3.1 the maximum file name can
be 255 characters. For Windows 95 the maximum file name is also 255 characters.
Earlier versions of UNIX impose a maximum name length of 14 characters, while in
later versions of UNIX the maximum is 256.

  b. This is also operating system dependent and usually can be changed. In MS-DOS
the number of files that can be open at once can be set by the FILES command.

3.
```
out_file = fopen("math.dat", "w");
book = fopen("book.dat", "w");
resfile = fopen("resist.dat", "w");
exfile = fopen("exper2.dat", "w");
pfile = fopen("prices.dat", "w");
ratefile = fopen("rates.dat", "w");
```

5.a.
```
#include <stdio.h>
#include <stdlib.h>
#define NUMS 6
void main(void)
{
  FILE *in_file;
  int i;
  float data[NUMS] = {16.25, 18.96, 22.34, 18.94, 17.42,  22.63};

  in_file = fopen("result.dat","w");

  if (in_file == (FILE *) NULL)
  {
    printf("\nFailed to open the data file.\n");
    exit(1);
  }
  for (i = 0; i < NUMS; i++)
     fprintf(in_file,"%5.2f\n", data[i]);
  fclose(in_file);
}
```

b.
```c
#include <stdio.h>
#include <stdlib.h>
#define NUMS 6
void main(void)
{
  FILE *in_file;
  int i;
  float data, sum, average;

  in_file = fopen("result.dat","r");

  if (in_file == (FILE *) NULL)
  {
      printf("\nFailed to open the data file.\n");
      exit(1);
  }
  for (i = 0; i < NUMS; i++)
  {
    fscanf(in_file,"%f", &data);
    sum += data;
  }
  average = sum / NUMS;
  printf("\nThe sum is %6.2f", sum);
  printf(", and the average is %5.2f\n", average);
  fclose(in_file);
}
```

7.a.
```c
#include <stdio.h>
#define MAXCHARS 81
#define MAXLINES 5
void main(void)
{
  FILE *out;
  int i, car_no;
  float miles, gallons;
  char strng[MAXCHARS];

  out = fopen("travel.dat", "w");
  for (i = 1; i <= MAXLINES; i++)
  {
    printf("\nEnter the car number: ");
    scanf("%d", &car_no);
    printf("Enter the miles traveled: ");
    scanf("%f",&miles);
    printf("Enter the gallons used: ");
    scanf("%f",&gallons);

    sprintf(strng, "%d %f %f",car_no,miles,gallons);
    fputs(strng,out);        /* write the string out */
    putc('\n',out);     /* append a newline character */
  }
  fclose(out);
  printf("End of data input.\n");
  printf("The file has been written.\n");
}
```

b.

```c
#include <stdio.h>
#define MAXCHARS 81
void main(void)
{
  FILE *in;
  char line[MAXCHARS];
  int car_no;
  float miles, gallons;
  float tot_miles = 0, tot_gallons = 0;
  float mpg, avg_mpg;

  in = fopen("travel.dat", "r");
  printf("\nCar No.  Miles Driven   Gallons Used   Miles per Gallon");
  printf("\n-------  -----------    -----------    ----------------");

  while(fgets(line,( MAXCHARS - 1), in) != NULL)
  {
    sscanf(line, "%d %f %f", &car_no, &miles, &gallons);
    mpg = miles / gallons;
    tot_miles += miles;
    tot_gallons += gallons;
    printf("\n%5d %13.2f  %12.2f  %16.2f", car_no, miles, gallons,
               mpg);
  }
  avg_mpg = tot_miles / tot_gallons;
  printf("\n-------------------------------------------------------");
  printf("\n      %13.2f  %12.2f  %16.2f", tot_miles, tot_gallons,
           avg_mpg);
  printf("  average mpg");
  fclose(in);
}
```

9.a.

```c
#include <stdio.h>
#define MAXCHARS 81
#define MAXLINES 4
void main(void)
{
  FILE *out;
  char strng[MAXCHARS];
  int i, id, hours;
  float rate;

  out = fopen("employ.dat", "w");
  for (i = 1; i <= MAXLINES; i++)
  {
    printf("\nEnter the ID No: ");
    scanf("%d", &id);
    printf("Enter the rate: ");
    scanf("%f",&rate);
    printf("Enter the hours: ");
    scanf("%d",&hours);

    /* now the line to be written is assembled in memory */
    sprintf(strng, "%5d %6.2f%5d",id,rate,hours);
    fputs(strng,out);      /* write the string out */
    putc('\n',out);        /* append a newline character  */
    getchar();             /* clear out the input buffer  */
  }
    fclose(out);
    printf("\nEnd of data input.");
    printf("\nThe file has been written.");
  }
```

EXERCISES 12.2

1. The fseek() function call moves the character pointer to the last character in the file, which is the EOF character at offset position 12. The ftell() function reports the offset of the character currently pointed to. This is the EOF character. Thus, a 12 is returned by ftell().

3.

```c
#include <stdio.h>
#include <stdlib.h>
char *file_name = "temp.dat";

void main(void)
{
  int ch, n;
  long offset, last;
  FILE *in_file;


  in_file = fopen(file_name, "r");
  if (in_file == (FILE *) NULL)
  {
  printf("\nFailed to open the file named %s\n",
    file_name);
  exit(1);
  }

  fseek(in_file, 0 , SEEK_END);
  last = ftell(in_file);
  for(offset = 0; offset <= last; offset++)
  {
  if(fseek(in_file, -offset, SEEK_END) != 0)
  {
    printf("\nExceeded file boundaries!");
    exit(1);
  }
  ch = getc(in_file);
  switch(ch)
  {
      case '\n': printf("LF : ");
        break;
      case EOF : printf("EOF: ");
        break;
      default  : printf("%c : ", ch);
        break;
  }
  }
  printf("\n");
  fclose(in_file);
}
```

5.   The f_chars() function is included in the following program:

```
#include <stdio.h>
#define MAXNAME 12
void main(void)
{
  FILE *fopen(), *in;
  char f_name[MAXNAME + 1]; /* leave room for the \0 */
  int numchar;
  int f_chars(FILE *);

  printf("\nEnter a file name: ");
  scanf("%s", f_name);
  in = fopen(f_name, "r");
  numchar = f_chars(in);
  printf("\nThere are %d characters in the file %s\n", numchar, f_name);
  fclose(in);
}

int f_chars(fname)    /* this is the required function */
FILE *fname;          /* a pointer to a FILE is passed */
{
  fseek(fname,0L,SEEK_END);  /* move to the end of the file */
  return(ftell(fname));
}
```

EXERCISES 12.3

1.

```
#include <stdio.h>
#define NUMPOLS 10
void main(void)
{
  FILE *out_file;
  int i, data;

  out_file = fopen("pollen","w");

  if (out_file == (FILE *) NULL)
  {
printf("\nFailed to open the data file.\n");
exit(1);
  }
  printf("\nEnter the last %d pollen counts: ", NUMPOLS);
  for (i = 1; i <= NUMPOLS; i++)
  {
scanf("%d", &data);
fprintf(out_file,"%d  ", data);
  }
  fclose(out_file);
}
```

3.a.

```
#include <stdio.h>
#include <stdlib.h>
char *file_name = "temp.dat";

void main(void)
{
  int ch, n;
  long offset, last;
  FILE *in_file;


  in_file = fopen(file_name, "r");
  if (in_file == (FILE *) NULL)
  {
  printf("\nFailed to open the file named %s\n",
      file_name);
  exit(1);
  }

  fseek(in_file, 0 , SEEK_END);
  last = ftell(in_file);
  for(offset = 0; offset <= last; offset++)
  {
  if(fseek(in_file, -offset, SEEK_END) != 0)
  {
    printf("\nExceeded file boundaries!");
    exit(1);
  }
  ch = getc(in_file);
  switch(ch)
  {
      case '\n': printf("LF : ");
        break;
      case EOF : printf("EOF: ");
        break;
      default  : printf("%c : ", ch);
        break;
  }
  }
  printf("\n");
  fclose(in_file);
}
```

EXERCISES 12.4

1. The filename referred to in the exercise is an internal pointer name. The definition of p_file() is:

$$p\_file(FILE *fname)$$

3.   The `fcheck()` function is included in the following program with a driver function used to test it:

```
#include <stdio.h>
#define MAXNAME 12
void main(void)      /* driver function to test fcheck() */
{
  int fcheck(char *);    /* function prototype */
  char name[MAXNAME + 1]; /* leave room for the \0 */

  printf("\nEnter a file name: ");
  scanf("%s", name);
  if(fcheck(name) == 1)
    printf("The file exists and can be opened.\n");
  else
    printf("The file cannot be opened - check that it exists.\n");
}

int fcheck(char *fname)
{
  if(fopen(fname, "r") == 0)
    return(0);
  else
    return(1);
}
```

EXERCISES 12.5

1.a.   `in_file = fopen("test.dat","rt");`
 b.   `descrip = fopen("descri","wt");`
 c.   `out_file = fopen("names","at");`
 d.   `disktype = fopen("types","rb");`
 e.   `idcodes = fopen("codes","wb");`
 f.   `balances = fopen("balance.dat","ab");`
3.

```
#include <stdio.h>
#define NUMLINES 4
void main(void)
{
  int i;
  float number, total, average;
  float nums[NUMLINES] = {92.65, 88.72, 77.46, 82.93};
  FILE *test;

  test = fopen("result","wt");
  for (i = 0; i < NUMLINES; i++)
  fprintf(test,"%f\n", nums[i]);
  printf("The file has been written.\n");
  fclose(test);
  test = fopen("result", "rt");  /* open for reading */
  total = 0.0;  /* this can be moved to the declaration */
  for (i = 0; i < NUMLINES; i++)  /* now read the file */
  {
    fscanf(test,"%f", &number);
    total = total + number;
  }
  average = total / NUMLINES;
  printf("The total of the numbers in the file is %.2f\n",
            total);
  printf("The average of these numbers is %.2f\n", average);
  fclose(test);
}
```

5.
```
#include <stdio.h>
#define ROWS 3
#define COLS 4
void main(void)
{
  int i, j;
  float x1, y1, x2, y2;
  float slope, midxpt, midypt;
  float nums[ROWS][COLS] = { 6.3, 8.2, 18.25, 24.32,
                 4.0, 4.0, 10.0, -5.0,
                  -2.0, 5.0, 4.0, 5.0 };

  FILE *coord;

  coord = fopen("points","wt");
  for (i = 0; i < ROWS; i++)
  {
    for (j = 0; j < COLS; j++)
   fprintf(coord,"%f  ", nums[i][j]);
    printf("\n");      /* start a new line in the file */
  }
  printf("The file has been written.\n");
  fclose(coord);
  coord = fopen("points", "rt");  /* open for reading */
  i = 1;
  while(fscanf(coord,"%f %f %f %f",&x1,&y1,&x2,&y2)!=EOF)
  {
    slope = (y2 - y1) / (x2 - x1);
    midxpt = (x1 + x2) / 2.0;
    midypt = (y1 + y2) / 2.0;
    printf("Slope %d = %.3f\n", i, slope);
    printf("Midpoint coordinates %d = (%.3f,%.3f)\n",i,midxpt,midypt);
    i++;
  }
  fclose(coord);
}
```

EXERCISES 12.8

1.
```
#include <stdio.h>
#define MAXSTUDENTS 20
#define MAXNAME 20
char *fname = "grade.dat";
void main(void)
{
  int i;
  char lname[MAXNAME], lgrade;
  float g1, g2, h1, f1, fingrade;
  FILE *out_file;

  out_file = fopen(fname,"a");
  if (out_file == (FILE *) NULL)
  {
    printf("\nFailed to open the file named %s\n", fname);
    exit(1);
  }

  for (i = 1; i <= MAXSTUDENTS; i++)
```

(continued on next page)

(continued from previous page)

```
      {
    printf("\nEnter student's last name (xx 0 0 0 0 to exit) & four scores: ");
        scanf("%s %f %f %f %f", lname, &g1, &g2, &h1, &f1);
        if (toupper(lname[0]) == 'X' && toupper(lname[1]) == 'X')
          break;
        else
        {
          fingrade = 0.20*g1 + 0.20*g2 + 0.35*h1 + 0.25*f1;
          if(fingrade >= 90) lgrade = 'A';
          else if (fingrade >= 80) lgrade = 'B';
          else if (fingrade >= 70) lgrade = 'C';
          else if (fingrade >= 60) lgrade = 'D';
          else fingrade = 'F';

          printf("For this data the following data has been saved to the
                  file:\n");
          printf("    %20s %6.2f %6.2f %6.2f %6.2f %6.2f  %c\n",
               lname, g1, g2, h1, f1, fingrade, lgrade);
          fprintf(out_file,"%20s %6.2f %6.2f %6.2f %6.2f %6.2f  %c\n",
               lname, g1, g2, h1, f1, fingrade, lgrade);
        }
      }
    }
  }
```

3.
```
    #include <stdio.h>
    #include <ctype.h>
    #define EMPLOYEES 10
    #define TRUE 1;
    #define FALSE 0;
    void main(void)

    {
      int i, found;
      int id[EMPLOYEES], tid;
      char sex[EMPLOYEES];
      float wage[EMPLOYEES], twage;
      int years[EMPLOYEES], tyears;
      char *fname = "EMPLOY.DAT";
      FILE *out_file;
      void sort(int [], char [], float [], int [], int);

      out_file = fopen(fname,"r");
      if (out_file == (FILE *) NULL)
      {
        printf("\nFailed to open the file named %s\n", fname);
        exit(1);
      }

      printf("\nThe stored data is currently:\n");
      printf("ID NO. S    WAGE     YR\n");
      printf("------ -    ----     --\n");
      for(i = 0; i < EMPLOYEES; i++)
      {
        fscanf(out_file,"%d %c %f %d", &id[i], &sex[i], &wage[i], &years[i]);
        printf("%6d  %c   %7.2f  %2d\n", id[i], sex[i], wage[i], years[i]);
      }
```

(continued on next page)

(continued from previous page)

```
while (1)
{
  printf("Enter Employee ID  Wage  Years (-99 0 0 to stop): ");
  scanf("%d %f %d", &tid, &twage, &tyears);
  if(tid == -99)
    break;
  found = FALSE;
  for(i = 0; i < EMPLOYEES; i++)
  {
    if(id[i] == tid)
    {
    found = TRUE;
    wage[i] = twage;
    years[i] = tyears;
    break;
    }
  }
  if (!found)
    printf("This ID No. is not in the list\n");
  else
  {
    sort(id, sex, wage, years, EMPLOYEES);
    printf("\nThe data is currently:\n");
    printf("ID NO. S   WAGE  YR\n");
    printf("------ -    ----  --\n");
    for(i = 0; i < EMPLOYEES; i++)
     printf("%6d  %c  %7.2f  %2d\n", id[i], sex[i], wage[i], years[i]);
  }
  fclose(out_file);
  out_file = fopen(fname,"w");
  for(i = 0; i < EMPLOYEES; i++)
    fprintf(out_file, "%6d  %c  %7.2f  %2d\n", id[i], sex[i], wage[i], years[i]);
  printf("This data has been written to the %s file.\n", fname);
}
void sort(int id[], char sex[], float wage[], int years[], int numel)
{
  int i, j, max, maxidx, temp;
  int tid;
  char tsex;
  float twage;

  for ( i = 0; i < (numel - 1); i++)
  {
    max = years[i];   /* assume maximum is first quantity */
    tid = id[i];      /* save the corresponding id */
    tsex = sex[i];    /* save the corresponding sex */
    twage = wage[i];  /* save the corresponding wage */
    maxidx = i;       /* index of maximum element */
    for(j = i + 1; j < numel; j++)
    {
      if (years[j] > max) /* if we've located a higher value */
      {                   /* capture it */
      max = years[j];
      maxidx = j;
      }
    }
    if (max > years[i])  /* check if we have a new maximum */
    {                            /* and if we do, swap values */
```
(continued on next page)

(continued from previous page)

```
                temp = years[i];      /* swap quantities */
                years[i] = max;
                years[maxidx] = temp;
                tid = id[i];
                id[i] = id[maxidx];
                id[maxidx] = tid;
                tsex = sex[i];
                sex[i] = sex[maxidx];
                sex[maxidx] = tsex;
                twage = wage[i];
                wage[i] = wage[maxidx];
                wage[maxidx] = twage;


            }
        }
        return;
    }
```

EXERCISES 13.1

1.a.
```
    struct S_temp
    {
      int id_num;
      int credits;
      float avg;
    };
```
  b.
```
    struct S_temp
    {
      char name[40];
      int month;
      int day;
      int year;
      int credits;
      float avg;
    };
```
  c.
```
    struct S_temp
    {
      char name[40];
      char street[80];
      char city[40];
      char state[2];
      int zip;            /* or char zip[5];  */
    };
```
  d.
```
    struct S_temp
    {
      char name[40];
      float price;
      char date[8];   /* Assumes a date in the form XX/XX/XX */
    };
```
  e.
```
    struct S_temp
    {
      int part_no;
      char desc[100];
      int quant;
      int reorder;
    };
```

3.a.
```
#include <stdio.h>
void main(void)
{
    struct Date
    {
        int month;
        int day;
        int year;
    };

    struct Date curdate;     /* define a structure variable named curdate */

    printf("Enter the current month: ");
    scanf("%d", &curdate.month);
    printf("Enter the current day: ");
    scanf("%d", &curdate.day);
    printf("Enter the current year: ");
    scanf("%d", &curdate.year);
    printf("\nThe date entered is %d/%d/%d.\n",
            curdate.month, curdate.day, curdate.year);
}
```

b.
```
#include <stdio.h>
void main(void)
{
    struct Clock
    {
        int hours;
         int minutes;
         int seconds;
    };

    struct Clock time;     /* define a structure variable named time */

    printf("Enter the current hour: ");
    scanf("%d", &time.hours);
    printf("Enter the current minute: ");
    scanf("%d", &time.minutes);
    printf("Enter the current second: ");
    scanf("%d", &time.seconds);
    printf("\nThe time entered is %02d:%02d:%02d\n",
            time.hours, time.minutes, time.seconds);
}
```
Note the use of the conversion sequence %02d. The 0 forces the field of 2 to be filled with leading zeros.

5.
```
#include <stdio.h>
void main(void)
{
    struct Time
    {
        int hours;
        int minutes;
    };

    struct Time clock;  /* define a structure variable named clock */
    printf("Enter the current hour: ");
    scanf("%d", &clock.hours);
```

(continued on next page)

(continued from previous page)

```
        printf("Enter the current minute: ");
        scanf("%d", &clock.minutes);
        if(clock.minutes != 59)
           clock.minutes += 1;
        else
        {
           clock.minutes = 0;
           if(clock.hours != 12)
              clock.hours += 1;
           else
              clock.hours = 1;
        }
        printf("\nThe time in one minute will be %02d:%02d\n",
                 clock.hours, clock.minutes);
}
```

Note the use of the conversion sequence %02d. The 0 forces the field of 2 to be filled with leading zeros.

EXERCISES 13.2

1.a.
```
struct S_temp
{
  int id_num;
  int credits;
  float avg;
};

#include <stdio.h>
void main(void)
{
  struct S_temp student[100];
```

b.
```
struct S_temp
{
  char name[40];
  int month;
  int day;
  int year;
  int credits;
  float avg;
};

#include <stdio.h>
void main(void)
{
  struct S_temp student[100];
```

c.
```
struct S_temp
{
  char name[40];
  char street[80];
  char city[40];
  char state[2];
  int zip;              /* or char zip[5];   */
};

#include <stdio.h>
void main(void)
{
  struct S_temp address[100];
```

(continued on next page)

```
d.    struct S_temp
      {
        char name[40];
        float price;
        char date[8];   /* Assumes a date in the form XX/XX/XX  */
      };

      #include <stdio.h>
      void main(void)
      {
        struct S_temp stock[100];
  e.  struct S_temp
      {
        int part_no;
        char desc[100];
        int quant;
        int reorder;
      };

      #include <stdio.h>
      void main(void)
      {
        struct S_temp inven[100];
3.    struct Mon_days
      {
        char name[10];
        int days;
      };

      #include <stdio.h>
      void main(void)
      {
        struct Mon_days convert[12] = { "January", 31,"February", 28,
          "March", 31, "April", 30, "May", 31, "June", 30, "July", 31,
          "August", 31, "September", 30, "October", 31, "November", 30,
          "December", 31};
        int i;
        printf("\nEnter the number of a month: ");
        scanf("%d", &i);
        printf("%s has %d days.\n", convert[i-1].name, convert[i-1].days);
      }
```

5.a.   The declaration for the structure is included in the program written for Exercise 5b.
  b.

```
struct Car_rec
{
  int num;
  int miles;
  int gallons;
}
#define NUMCARS 5

#include <stdio.h>
void main(void)
{
  struct Car_rec cars[NUMCARS];
  int i;
  float mpg, totmiles = 0, totgals = 0, avg_mpg;

  for(i = 0; i < NUMCARS; i++)
      {
```

(continued on next page)

(continued from previous page)

```
        printf("\nEnter car number: ");
        scanf("%d", &cars[i].num);
        printf("Enter miles driven: ");
        scanf("%d", &cars[i].miles);
        printf("Enter gallons used: ");
        scanf("%d", &cars[i].gallons);
    }
    printf("\nCar Number  Miles Driven  Gallons Used  MPG\n");
    printf("-------------------------------------------\n");
    for( i = 0; i < NUMCARS; i++)
    {
      mpg = (float) cars[i].miles / cars[i].gallons;
      printf("%6d %13d %11d  %10.2f\n", cars[i].num, cars[i].miles,
                cars[i].gallons, mpg);
      totmiles += cars[i].miles;
      totgals += cars[i].gallons;
    }
    avg_mpg = totmiles/totgals;
    printf("\nThe average miles per gallon is %5.2f\n", avg_mpg);
}
```

EXERCISES 13.3

1.

```
struct Date
{
  int month;
  int day;
  int year;
};

#include <stdio.h>
void main(void)
{
  struct Date present;
  long num;
  long days(struct Date);   /* function prototype */

  printf("Enter the month: ");
  scanf("%d", &present.month);
  printf("Enter the day: ");
  scanf("%d",&present.day);
  printf("Enter the year: ");
  scanf("%d", &present.year);
  num = days(present);
  printf("The number of days since the turn of the century is %ld\n",
          num);
}

long days(struct Date temp)
{
  return(temp.day + 30*(temp.month - 1) + 360*temp.year);
}
```

Note: The pointer version of the function `long days()` is written for Exercise 3.

3. The function is included within a complete program. Notice the use of the delimiter within the `scanf()` call in `main()` to accept the date in the form mm/dd/yy.

```c
struct Date
{
  int month;
  int day;
  int year;
};

#include <stdio.h>
void main(void)
{
  struct Date present;
  long num;
  long days(struct Date *);

  printf("Enter the first date as mm/dd/yy: ");
  scanf("%d/%d/%d", &present.month, &present.day, &present.year);
  num = days(&present);
  printf("\nThe number of days since the turn of the century is %ld\n",
              num);
}

long days(struct Date *temp)
{
  return(temp->day + 30*(temp->month - 1) + 360*temp->year);
}
```

5.a.

```c
struct Date
{
  int month;
  int day;
  int year;
};

#include <stdio.h>
void main(void)
{
  struct Date present;
  long num;
  long days(struct Date);   /* function prototype */

  printf("Enter the date as mm/dd/yy: ");
  scanf("%d/%d/%d", &present.month, &present.day, &present.year);
  num = days(present);
  printf("\nThe number of days since the turn of the century is %ld\n",
              num);
}

long days(struct Date temp)
{
  long act_days;
  int daycount[12] = { 0, 31, 59, 90, 120, 151, 181, 212, 243, 273,
                       304, 334};

  act_days = temp.day + daycount[temp.month-1] + 365*temp.year;
  return(act_days);
}
```

EXERCISES 13.4

1.

```c
#include <stdio.h>
#define MAXDES 40
struct Item
{
  char des[MAXDES];
  int number;
  int bin;
  int quantity;
  float cost;
};

void main(void)
{
  struct Item inventory;
  void update(struct Item *);   /* prototype */

  strcpy(inventory.des, "Test Item");
  inventory.number = 22;
  inventory.bin = 56;
  inventory.quantity = 34;
  inventory.cost = 9.35;
  update(&inventory);
  printf("\nThe data for this item is now:\n");
  printf("  Description: %s\n",inventory.des);
  printf("  Number: %d   Bin: %d   Quantity: %d   Cost: %6.2f\n",
     inventory.number, inventory.bin, inventory.quantity, inventory.cost);
}

#define LOWQUANTITY 10
void update(struct Item *thisitem)
{
  printf("\n\nThe data for this item is currently:\n");
  printf("  Description: %s\n",thisitem->des);
  printf("  Number: %d   Bin: %d   Quantity: %d   Cost: %6.2f\n",
     thisitem->number, thisitem->bin, thisitem->quantity, thisitem->cost);
  printf("\nEnter the new quantity and cost: ");
  scanf("%d %d", &thisitem->quantity, &thisitem->quantity);
  if (thisitem->quantity < LOWQUANTITY)
    printf("The stock on this item is low.\n");
}
```

3.   The required structure for this program is:

```c
struct Customer
{
  char name[MAXSTRLEN];
  char address[MAXSTRLEN];
  int nummtnbikes;
  int numstbikes;
  int goodrisk;
  float amount;
};
```

5.

```
#include <stdio.h>
#define MAXDES 40
#define MAXITEMS 5
struct Item
{
  char des[MAXDES];
  int number;
  int bin;
  int quantity;
  float cost;
};

void main(void)
{
  struct Item inventory[MAXITEMS] = {{"Item 1", 122, 1, 55, 1.65},
                     {"Item 2", 123, 2, 88, 2.95},
                     {"Item 3", 124, 3,  9, 5.49},
                     {"Item 4", 125, 4, 37, 6.53},
                     {"Item 5", 126, 5,  7, 8.42}
                    };
  void report(struct Item [], int);
  void order(struct Item *, int);

  report(inventory, MAXITEMS);
  order(inventory, MAXITEMS);
}

void report(struct Item inventory[], int numitems)
{
  int i;

  printf("\n\nThe data in inventory is currently:\n");
  for (i = 0; i < numitems; i++)
  {
    printf("  Description: %s\n",inventory[i].des);
    printf("    Number: %d  Bin: %d  Quantity: %d   Cost: %6.2f\n",
     inventory[i].number, inventory[i].bin, inventory[i].quantity,
     inventory[i].cost);
  }
}

#define LOWSTOCK 10
void order(struct Item inventory[], int numitems)
{
  int i;

  printf("\n\nThe following are below normal stock quantities:\n");
  for (i = 0; i < numitems; i++)
  {
    if (inventory[i].quantity < LOWSTOCK)
    {
      printf("  Description: %s\n",inventory[i].des);
      printf("    Number: %d  Bin: %d  Quantity: %d   Cost: %6.2f\n",
       inventory[i].number, inventory[i].bin, inventory[i].quantity,
       inventory[i].cost);
    }
  }
}
```

EXERCISES 13.5

1. `printf()` function calls, with the correct control sequences, are contained within the following program:

```
union
{
    float rate;
    double taxes;
    int num;
} flag;

#include <stdio.h>
void main(void)
{
    flag.rate = 22.5;
    printf("\nThe rate is %f",flag.rate);
    flag.taxes = 44.7;
    printf("\ntaxes are %f",flag.taxes);
    flag.num = 6;
    printf("\nnum is %d",flag.num);
}
```

3. ```
   union
   {
     float interest;
     float rate;
   } yield;
   ```

5. Since a value has not been assigned to `alt.btype`, the display produced is unpredictable (the code for a `'y'` resides in the storage locations overlapped by the variables `alt.ch` and `alt.btype`). Thus, either a garbage value will be displayed or the program could even crash.

EXERCISES 13.7

1.
```
#define MAXNAME 30
#define MAXADD1 30
#define MAXADD2 30
#define MAXDESC 40
struct Business
{
  char name[MAXNAME]
  char address[MAXADD1]
  char ctystzip[MAXADD2]
  char descrip[MAXDESC]
  int employees;
  float annualrev;
};
```

3.a. `struct Inventory item[100];`

b. `inventory[83].prodnum = 4355;`

c. `scanf("%f", &inventory[15].price);`
```

5.
```c
#include <stdio.h>
#define MAXVECTS 2
struct VectorType
{
  int xcomp;
  int ycomp;
};

void main(void)
{
  struct VectorType vector[MAXVECTS], sumvect, difvect;

  void input(struct VectorType [], int);
  struct VectorType sum(struct VectorType, struct VectorType);
  struct VectorType diff(struct VectorType, struct VectorType);

  input(vector, MAXVECTS);
  sumvect = sum(vector[0], vector[1]);
  difvect = diff(vector[0], vector[1]);
  printf("\n(%d, %d) + (%d, %d) = (%d, %d)\n", vector[0].xcomp,
         vector[0].ycomp, vector[1].xcomp, vector[1].ycomp,
         sumvect.xcomp, sumvect.ycomp);
  printf("\n(%d, %d) - (%d, %d) = (%d, %d)\n", vector[0].xcomp,
         vector[0].ycomp, vector[1].xcomp, vector[1].ycomp,
         difvect.xcomp, difvect.ycomp);
}

void input(struct VectorType vector[], int numvects)
{
  int i;

  for (i = 0; i < numvects; i++)
  {
    printf("Enter the x component for vector %d: ", i+1);
    scanf("%d", &vector[i].xcomp);
    printf("Enter the y component for vector %d: ", i+1);
    scanf("%d", &vector[i].ycomp);
  }
}

struct VectorType sum(struct VectorType vector1, struct VectorType vector2)
{
  int i;
  struct VectorType temp;

  temp.xcomp = vector1.xcomp + vector2.xcomp;
  temp.ycomp = vector1.ycomp + vector2.ycomp;

  return (temp);
}

struct VectorType diff(struct VectorType vector1, struct VectorType vector2)
{
  int i;
  struct VectorType temp;

  temp.xcomp = vector1.xcomp - vector2.xcomp;
  temp.ycomp = vector1.ycomp - vector2.ycomp;
  return (temp);
}
```

Notice that the input routine can be used for any number of vectors, while the sum and difference routines only work on the two specific vectors passed as arguments.

EXERCISES 14.1

1. `malloc()` reserves the number of bytes requested by the argument passed to the function. It returns the address of the first reserved location or NULL if sufficient memory is not available.

    `calloc()` reserves space for an array of n elements of the specified size. It returns the address of the first reserved location and initializes all reserved bytes to zeros, or returns a NULL if sufficient memory is not available.

    `realloc()` changes the size of previously allocated memory to a new size. If the new size is larger than the old size, the additional memory space is uninitialized and the contents of the original allocated memory remain unchanged; otherwise, the new allocated memory remains unchanged up to the limits of the new size.

    `free()` releases a block of bytes previously reserved. The address of the first reserved location is passed as an argument to the function.

3.a. `malloc(sizeof(int));`
 b. `malloc(50 * sizeof(int));`
 c. `malloc(sizeof(float));`
 d. `malloc(100 * sizeof(float));`
 e. `malloc(sizeof(struct Name_rec));`
 f. `malloc(150 * sizeof(struct Name_rec));`

5. The only change that needs to be made is to change the statement:

    `grades = (int *) malloc(numgrades * sizeof(int));`

    to

    `grades = (int *) calloc(numgrades, sizeof(int));`

EXERCISES 14.2

1.
```
#include <stdio.h>
struct Tele_typ
{
  char name[30];
  char phone_no[15];
  struct Tele_typ *nextaddr;
};

#include <stdio.h>
void main(void)
{
  struct Tele_typ t1 = {"Acme, Sam", "(201) 898-2392"};
  struct Tele_typ t2 = {"Dolan, Edith", "(213) 682-3104"};
  struct Tele_typ t3 = {"Lanfrank, John", "(415) 718-4518"};
  struct Tele_typ *first;
  char strng[30];
  void search(struct Tele_typ *, char *); /* function prototype */

  first = &t1;
  t1.nextaddr = &t2;
  t2.nextaddr = &t3;
  t3.nextaddr = NULL;
  printf("Enter a name: ");
  gets(strng);
  search(first, strng);
}

void search(struct Tele_typ *contents, char *strng)
```

(continued on next page)

(continued from previous page)

```
    {
        printf("\n%s",strng);
        while(contents != NULL)
        {
            if(strcmp(contents->name,strng) == 0)
            {
                printf("\nFound. The number is %s.", contents->phone_no);
                return;
            }
            else
            {
                contents = contents->nextaddr;
            }
        }
        printf("\nThe name is not in the current phone directory.");
    }
```

3. To delete the second record, the pointer in the first record must be changed to point to the third record.

5.a.
```
struct Phone_bk
{
    char name[30];
    char phone_no[15];
    struct Phone_bk *previous;
    struct Phone_bk *next;
};
```

EXERCISES 14.3

1.a. *Dynamically create a new record.*
Put the address contained in the top-of-stack pointer into the address field of the newly created record.
Populate the new record's remaining fields.
Put the address of the new record into the top-of-stack pointer.

b. *Move the record contents pointed to by the top-of-stack pointer into a work area.*
Free the record pointed to by the top-of-stack pointer.
Move the address in the work area address field into the top-of-stack pointer.

c. a `NULL` *address*

3.a. As the problem is stated this is ideal for a stack, because the last characters typed in are the first out when deletions are made. Also, the deletions can be stored in a stack for the undo operation.

b. No, because in stack order the last person on the list would be the first to receive a car.

c. Yes, because the search is from the most recent to the least recent.

d. No, in a stack the priority is last in, first out.

e. No, because the first on line is the first on the bus, which is not the last-in/first-out order used in a stack.

5.

```
#include <stdio.h>
#include <stdlib.h>
#define DEBUG 0

/* here is the declaration of a stack record */
struct Id_rec
{
  int idnum;
  float hrlypay;
  struct Id_rec *prior_addr;
};

/* here is the definition of the top-of-stack pointer */
struct Id_rec *tosp;

void main(void)
{
  void read_push(void);   /* function prototypes */
  void pop_show(void);

  tosp = NULL;       /* initialize the top-of-stack pointer */
  read_push();
  pop_show();
}

/* get a record and push it onto the stack */
void read_push(void)
{
  struct Id_rec temp;
  void push(struct Id_rec temp); /* function prototype */

  printf("\nEnter data for each record as requested");
  printf("\nTo stop entering data, enter 999\n");
  while (1)
  {
    printf("Enter an ID number: ");
    scanf("%d", &temp.idnum);
    if (temp.idnum == 999)
      break;
    printf("Enter the hourly rate: ");
    scanf("%f", &temp.hrlypay);
    if (temp.hrlypay == 999)
      break;
    push(temp);    /* send a record into push */
  }
}

/* pop and display the record data from the stack */
void pop_show(void)
{
  struct Id_rec temp;
  void pop(struct Id_rec *);  /* function prototype */

  printf("\nThe data popped from the stack is:\n");
  while (tosp != NULL)  /* display till end of stack */
  {
    pop(&temp);    /* use temp to indirectly receive the popped record */
    printf("Id = %d   Hourly Pay = %6.2f\n", temp.idnum, temp.hrlypay);
  }
return;
}
```

(continued on next page)

(continued from previous page)

```
void push(struct Id_rec record)
{
   struct Id_rec *newaddr;   /* pointer to structure of type Id_rec */

   if (DEBUG)
     printf("Before the push the address in tosp is %p", tosp);

   newaddr = (struct Id_rec *) malloc(sizeof(struct Id_rec));
   if (newaddr == (struct Id_rec *) NULL)
   {
     printf("\nFailed to allocate memory for this record\n");
     exit(1);
   }
   newaddr->idnum = record.idnum;      /* store the id number */
   newaddr->hrlypay = record.hrlypay;  /* store the hourly wage */
   newaddr->prior_addr = tosp;  /* store address of prior record */
   tosp = newaddr;              /* update the top-of-stack pointer */

   if (DEBUG)
     printf("\n After the push the address in tosp is %p\n", tosp);
}

void pop(struct Id_rec *record)
{
   struct Id_rec *temp_addr;

   if (DEBUG)
     printf("Before the pop the address in tosp is %p\n", tosp);
   record->idnum = tosp->idnum;      /* retrieve the ID number from the
                                                        top-of-stack */

   record->hrlypay = tosp->hrlypay; /* retrieve the hourly pay from the
                                                        top-of-stack */

   temp_addr = tosp->prior_addr;     /* retrieve the prior address */
   free(tosp);                       /* release the record's memory space */
   tosp = temp_addr;                 /* update the top-of-stack pointer */

   if (DEBUG)
     printf(" After the pop the address in tosp is %p\n", tosp);
}
```

EXERCISES 14.4

1.a. *Dynamically create a new a record.*
       Set the address field of the new record to a NULL.
       Fill in the remaining fields of the new record.
       *Set the address field of the prior record (which is pointed to
          by the queue_in pointer) to the address of the newly created
          record.*
       *Update the address in the queue_in pointer with the address of the newly
          created record.*

  b.   *Move the contents of the record pointed to by the queue_out
          pointer into a work area.*
       Free the record pointed to by the queue_out pointer.
       *Move the address in the work area address field into the
          queue_out pointer.*

  c. Both pointers should contain a NULL address.

3.a.   Yes, because this represents a first-in/first-out situation.
  b.   Yes, because this is also a first-in/first-out situation.
  c.   No, because the order of retrieval is not first in, first out.
  d.   Yes, because this is also a first-in/first-out situation.

5.

```c
#include <stdio.h>
#include <stdlib.h>
#define DEBUG 0

/* here is the declaration of a queue record */
struct Id_rec
{
  int idnum;
  float hrlypay;
  struct Id_rec *next_addr;
};

/* here is the definition of the top and bottom queue pointers */
struct Id_rec *queue_in, *queue_out;

void main(void)
{
  void read_enque(void);  /* function prototypes */
  void serve_show(void);

  queue_in = NULL;        /* initialize queue pointers */
  queue_out = NULL;
  read_enque();
  serve_show();
}

/* get a record and enque it onto the queue */
void read_enque(void)
{
  struct Id_rec temp;
  void enque(struct Id_rec temp); /* function prototype */

  printf("\nEnter data for each record as requested");
  printf("\nTo stop entering names, enter 999\n");
  while (1)
  {
    printf("Enter an ID number: ");
    scanf("%d", &temp.idnum);
    if (temp.idnum == 999)
      break;
    printf("Enter the hourly rate: ");
    scanf("%f", &temp.hrlypay);
    if (temp.hrlypay == 999)
      break;
    enque(temp);    /* send a record into enque() */
  }
}

/* serve and display the records from the queue */
void serve_show(void)
{
  struct Id_rec temp;
  void serve(struct Id_rec *); /* function prototype */

  printf("\nThe records served from the queue are:\n");
  while (queue_out != NULL)  /* display till end of queue */
  {
    serve(&temp);   /* use temp to indirectly receive the served record */
    printf("ID = %d   Hourly Pay = %6.2f\n", temp.idnum, temp.hrlypay);
  }
  return;
}
```

(continued on next page)

(continued from previous page)

```c
void enque(struct Id_rec record)
{
  struct Id_rec *newaddr;  /* pointer to structure of type Id_rec */

  if (DEBUG)
  {
    printf("Before the enque the address in queue_in is %p", queue_in);
    printf("\nand the address in queue_out is %p", queue_out);
  }

  newaddr = (struct Id_rec *) malloc(sizeof(struct Id_rec));
  if (newaddr == (struct Id_rec *) NULL)
  {
    printf("\nFailed to allocate memory for this record\n");
    exit(1);
  }

  /* these next two if statements handle the empty queue initialization */
  if (queue_out == NULL)
    queue_out = newaddr;
  if (queue_in != NULL)
    queue_in->next_addr = newaddr;/* fill in prior record's address field*/

  newaddr->idnum = record.idnum;       /* store the ID number */
  newaddr->hrlypay = record.hrlypay; /* store the hourly wage */
  newaddr->next_addr = NULL;    /* set address field to NULL */
  queue_in = newaddr;              /* update the top-of-queue pointer */

  if (DEBUG)
  {
    printf("\n  After the enque the address in queue_in is %p\n"
               queue_in);
    printf("  and the address in queue_out is %p\n", queue_out);
  }
}

void serve(struct Id_rec *record)
{
  struct Id_rec *next_addr;

  if (DEBUG)
    printf("Before the serve the address in queue_out is %p\n", queue_out);

  record->idnum = queue_out->idnum;       /* retrieve the id number from the
                                               bottom-of-queue */
  record->hrlypay = queue_out->hrlypay; /* retrieve the hourly pay from the
                                               bottom-of-queue */
  next_addr = queue_out->next_addr;   /* capture the next address field */
  free(queue_out);
  queue_out = next_addr;              /* update the bottom-of-queue pointer */

  if (DEBUG)
    printf("  After the serve the address in queue_out is %p\n",
    queue_out);
}
```

EXERCISES 14.5

3. The modify() function in the complete program below is used to verify that modify() works correctly. The driver function creates a single structure, populates it, and then calls modify(). modify() itself calls the function repop(). An interesting extension is to write repop() such that an ENTER key response retains the original structure member value.

```c
#include <stdio.h>
#define MAXCHARS 30
struct Name_rec
{
  char name[MAXCHARS];
  struct Name_rec *nextaddr;
};

void main(void)
{
  int i;
  struct Name_rec *list;
  void populate(struct Name_rec *);  /* function prototype */
  void modify(struct Name_rec *);    /* function prototype */

  list = (struct Name_rec *) malloc(sizeof(struct Name_rec));
  populate(list); /* populate the first structure */
  list->nextaddr = NULL;
  modify(list);   /* modify the structure members */
}

void modify(struct Name_rec *addr)
{
  void display(struct Name_rec *);  /* function prototype */
  void repop(struct Name_rec *);  /* function prototype */

  printf("\nThe current structure members are:");
  display(addr);
  repop(addr);
  printf("\nThe structure members are now:");
  display(addr);
  return;
}

void populate(struct Name_rec *record)
{
  printf("\nEnter a name: ");
  gets(record->name);
  return;
}

void repop(struct Name_rec *record)
{
  printf("\n\nEnter a new name: ");
  gets(record->name);
  return;
}

void display(struct Name_rec *contents)
{
  while(contents != NULL)
  {
    printf("\n%-30s", contents->name);
    contents = contents->nextaddr;
  }
  return;
}
```

EXERCISES 15.5

1.a. `min_val = (a < b) ? a : b;`
  b. `sign = (num < 0) ? -1 : 1;`
  c. `val = (flag == 1) ? num : num*num;`
  d. `rate = (credit == plus) ? prime : prime + delta;`
  e. `cou = (!bond) ? .75 : 1.1;`
3.a. 0200
  b. 0357
  c. 0157
5.a. 0336
  b. 0701
  c. If the octal number was valid in the exercise, the right shift would replicate the sign bit rather than fill it with zeros, as it does in a logical right shift.
  d. See the note for part c.
7.a. By either using an 8-bit value box, as described in Section 2.8, or using the more conventional one's complement plus one algorithm, the 8-bit two's complement representation of the decimal number -1 is 1111 1111.
  b. By either using a 16-bit value box, as described in Section 2.8, or using the more conventional one's complement plus one algorithm, the 16-bit two's complement representation of the decimal number -1 is 1111 1111 1111 1111. This representation could also have been obtained by sign extending the 8-bit version.
9. The algorithm for this exercise is as follows:
    For all bits in the variable okay:
       Mask the LSB of the variable okay.
       Shift the bits of the variable rev_okay to the left.
       Add the masked bit to the variable rev_okay.
       Shift the bits of the variable okay one bit to the right.
    A program for this follows:

```
#include <stdio.h>
void main(void)
{
    int i, temp, okay, rev_okay = 0;
    int mask = 001;    /* bit mask to isolate LSB */

    printf("Enter an octal number: ");
    scanf("%o",&okay);
    for (i = 1; i <= 8; ++i)
    {
       temp = okay & mask;       /* strip off LSB */
       rev_okay = rev_okay <1;   /* shift left one position */
       rev_okay += temp;         /* add LSB to rev_okay */
       okay = okay >> 1;          /* shift next bit to LSB */
    }
    printf("\nThe reversed pattern, in octal, is %o",rev_okay);
}
```

11.a. `#define ABS_VAL(x) - (x)`
   b.

```
#define ABS_VAL(x) - (x)
#include <stdio.h>
void main(void)
{
    float num, fudge;

    printf("Enter a number: ");
    scanf("%f", &num);
    fudge = -2.0 * num;
    printf("\nThe absolute value of -2 times %f is %f.",
            num, ABS_VAL(fudge));
}
```

13.a. `#define MIN(x,y) ( (y) <= (x) ) ? (y) : (x)`
   b.

```
#define MIN(x,y) ( (y) <= (x) ) ? (y) : (x)
#include <stdio.h>
void main(void)
{
  float num1, num2;

  printf("Enter two numbers, separated by at least a space: ");
  scanf("%f %f", &num1, &num2);
  printf("\nThe smallest number entered is %f", MIN(num1,num2));
}
```

15.a. The following program opens the file, reads each character, and displays it.

```
#include <stdio.h>
main(int argc, char *argv[])   /* standard argument declarations */
/* for command line arguments      */
{
  FILE *fopen(), *in_file;
  char cc;

  in_file = fopen(argv[1],"r");
  while( (cc = getc(in_file)) != EOF)
    putchar(cc);
  fclose(in_file);
}
```

Note: Instead of reading each character until the end-of-file character is reached, the `fgets()` function could have been used to read in a line at a time. Since `fgets()` returns a NULL when it encounters the end-of-file sentinel, the appropriate statement would be

```
              while (fgets(line, 81, in_file) != NULL);
```
If this statement is used, `line` would have to be declared as
```
              char line[81];
```
To output a line at a time either the `puts()` or `fputs()` functions can be used. The `puts()` function adds its own newline escape sequence at the end of each line; the `fputs()` function does not.

   b. The program will open and display the contents of any file. The file can, therefore, be either a data or a program file.

Index

CROSS AND TAPPER ON EVIDENCE